TOWERS & BELLS OF DEVON

TOWERS & BELLS OF DEVON

by

John G. M. Scott
Prebendary Emeritus of Exeter Cathedral
M.A. Oxon
Life Member & Past President of the Central Council of Church Bell Ringers
former Bell Consultant to the Diocese of Exeter
Librarian & Past Master of the Guild of Devonshire Ringers

with

the late
Frank D. Mack
B.Sc Bristol, M.I.Biol.
former Member of the Central Council of Church Bell Ringers
Past Master of the Guild of Devonshire Ringers

and

James M. Clarke
M.C.I.O.B., M.I.M.B.M.
Member of the Central Council of Church Bell Ringers
Bell Consultant to the Diocese of Exeter

Part 1

First published in Great Britain by The Mint Press, 2007

© John Scott 2007

The right of John Scott to be identified as editor of this work has been asserted by him in accordance with the Copyright, Designs & Patents Act 1988.

All rights reserved. No part of this publication may be reproduced in any form or by any means without the prior permission of the copyright holders

ISBN 9781903356449

Cataloguing in Publication Data
CIP record for this title is available from the British Library

The Mint Press
76 Longbrook Street
Exeter, Devon
England EX4 6AP

Cover design by Delphine Jones

Typeset by Kestrel Data, Exeter.

Printed and bound in Great Britain by
Short Run Press Ltd, Exeter.

CONTENTS

Foreword   vii

Preface   ix

1. Church Towers in Devon   1
2. Bells in Devon: the Historical Picture   30
3. Casting Bells   42
4. The Bellfounders: before the Reformation   66
5. The Bellfounders: after the Reformation   86
6. The Pennington Family   128
7. Bellhanging and Bellhangers   153
8. Bell Ringing and Bellringers   167
9. The Church Clocks   188

Appendix
   I. Pennington Documents   201
   II. Bellfounding Documents   205
   III. Bellhanging   230
   IV. Bell Ringing   235

Bibliography   241

Index   245

Subscribers   265

Plates   267

FOREWORD

The Right Reverend Michael Langrish, Lord Bishop of Exeter

It's hard to think of almost any English village without at the same time calling to mind its church, its tower, spire or belfry and its bells. From time immemorial the towers and bells of Devon have played a prominent part in people's lives. Their architecture often mirrors the story of the local community, at various times, the priest might have actually lived in the tower or belfry, which also served as a watch tower and a fortified place for parishioners to resort to in time of unrest. And then there are the bells which have rung out to call people to worship, to mark the passing of the hours, to signal births and death and marriages, to warn people of impending danger and to celebrate important events in local and national life. We can so easily take the sound of church bells for granted until, as happened during the Second World War recently, for a time they were not rung at all.

I am therefore delighted to welcome this book *Towers & Bells of Devon* which in a fascinating way tells us so much about this feature of our county's life. The last history on the church bells in Devon was published in 1867 so a new one is long overdue. I am most grateful to the three authors for their valuable work as Bell Consultants to the Diocese of Exeter. It was while gathering details of the towers and bells they visited on behalf of the Diocese that they realised just how much more there was to be discovered about the bell-founders who cast the bells and how little had ever been published on the design of Devon towers. It is wonderful to see such a comprehensive work now in print.

+ Michael Exon

PREFACE

John Scott

This all began when Fred Wreford, one of the ringers at St Thomas's, Exeter, gave the newly-ordained curate a copy of H.T. Ellacombe's *Church Bells of Devon*. As I was a ringer and a history graduate with a penchant for buildings, it was not long before I started exploring some nearby towers to look at bells which looked interesting, and soon I began to find that Ellacombe's book was so long out of date, as well as containing many mistakes and misprints, that I began to make my own record, in the hope that at least I could unravel some of the bellfounding history which Ellacombe had barely begun to study.

Let nobody denigrate Ellacombe's work. In four years he visited the towers of Devon (with one exception – the majority of them in two years) and recorded the details of nearly 3,000 bells, a task which I, with much help, have managed to complete in 54; I and my colleagues have had the benefit of motor transport, photography and electric torches; he had to use the railways, the "station fly", and a bulls-eye lantern, yet more than once he recorded six towers in a day – at the age of over 70. Since his day, the development of bell shape and casting techniques have been extensively studied, so that uninscribed bells can be dated with much more confidence. I have also had the advantage of the public record offices, where I can consult the records of hundreds of parishes under one roof instead of having to search them out in parish chests. In addition, he has provided us with details of a great many bells, some of them historically very important, which have been recast or scrapped since his day.

It was the encouragement and energy of the late Frank Mack, who joined me as Bell Consultant in the 1980s, that opened the possibility of making and perhaps publishing a complete new survey of Devon's bells and towers, including the clocks, and setting down as much of the history of Westcountry bellfounding as we have been able to discover; the development of the computer has also made an enormous difference. Sadly, Frank died before the work could be completed, and I have had the invaluable help of James Clarke in finishing the field-work and also in checking the text.

The first volume of this work describes the towers of the county and their architecture, the history of the bells, their founders, hangers and ringers, and of the clocks which exist in many of the towers. All this is mine, and any errors or omissions will be mine; there will surely be such; in addition it is almost inevitable that even as this book is being published there will be some augmentations, recastings or rehangings, and I hope that readers may let me know when they find any errors, because in these days this kind of information can be kept up to date and corrected as a permanent running source of information. Mine, too are the histories of the bellfounders, and the guesswork which has sometimes been necessary to make sense of scanty and perplexing material.

The second volume contains a list of the Anglican churches in Devon, along with some of the secular buildings which contain bells and clocks. It is as complete as we could make it; we have not been able to examine all the bells in Roman Catholic churches, though we have been able to include some of the most notable. As far as secular buildings are concerned, we have included as many as we could – and they are often well worth inclusion. Although I have visited all but a handful of the church towers in the county myself, it was often with the help of Frank Mack or James Clark, and I have relied on them and the records of the late George Elphick for the rest; in some cases we have been glad to use the records of bellfounders, bellhangers and clockmakers to fill the gaps for secular buildings and provide weights and other details.

Bell historians are generous people, and I have been helped and encouraged over the years by many of them. The late Fred Sharpe set me on my way, and Ranald Clouston and George Elphick helped me along it; all three were men to whom I could turn for advice and information, knowing that any part of their enormous knowledge and expertise would be freely passed on to me. I have also had invaluable help from bell historians George Dawson, Christopher Pickford, Christopher Dalton, Mary Bliss, Alan Buswell, Trevor Jennings, David Bryant, the Rev. David Cawley.and Squadron-Leader George Massey who was specially helpful in checking lists of bells by the Bilbies and the Wroths. Access to the list of Cornish bells made for the Council for the Care of Churches by George Elphick and revised by Christopher Dalton and others has been extremely valuable.

The bellfounders and bellhangers have been immensely co-operative: Albert A. Hughes, Donald Hughes, Bill Hughes and Alan Hughes of the Whitechapel Foundry, the staff of the Loughborough Foundry particularly Andrew Higson, Andrew Nicholson, Arthur Fidler and Matthew Higby must all the mentioned with gratitude.

In Exeter John Allan, Stuart Blaylock, the late Chris Henderson and others at the Museum and the Archaeological Field Unit have been generous with their expertise and information, and Stephen Minnitt at the Taunton County Museum likewise; the staff of the Department of Coins & Medals at the British Museum also helped to identify a number of coin impressions for me. Dr Andre Lehr of the Bell Museum at Asten in the Netherlands helped with some of the continental bells which we have found. In the realm of archaeology I have also had much help and encouragement from R.F. Tylecote, Martin Biddle, Philip Rahtz, Tom Blagg, Alan Graham and Rosemary Robinson.

The documentary research could not have been done without the unfailing cooperation of the staff of the Devon county record offices in Exeter, Barnstaple and Plymouth (the last now under Plymouth City Council), the Cornwall County Record Office in Truro and the Westcountry Studies Library in Exeter, the first Librarian (and largely the originator) of which, the late Geoffrey Paley, first set me on my way in researching the archives and later became a dear friend. The archives of Exeter Cathedral are among the most interesting and complete in the country, and there too I was given wonderful help and advice.

I got into the study of clocks more or less by chance, but once engaged in it I was helped and encouraged by David Nettell, T.R. Robinson, Gideon Berman, James Bellchambers and his father Jack, and Chris McKay. Here in Devon I owe a great debt to Clive Ponsford, who passed on to me not only the results of his researches into clocks and their makers, but also extracts from documents which mentioned bells. Ken Woodley of Newton Poppleford and David Jones of Cornwall, turret clock specialists, have also been a great help.

Roderick Butler, a leading authority on domestic brassware, and his wife Valentine, David Cook who studies monumental brasses, Dr Joanna Mattingley one of Cornwall's leading historians, Richard Larn who researches shipwrecks, Bilbie enthusiasts Roy Rice and A.J. Moore (who also passed on material about the Wroths), Robert Sherlock, John David of Guernsey, the late Richard Bass of Chulmleigh, and the late Theo Brown with her incomparable knowledge of Devon folklore, have all helped to relate my study of Devon bells and clocks to other allied fields.

Dr Theresa Goatham gave me some very useful information about the family of Willliam Hambling from which she is descended; the late Cdr. Walter Raleigh Gilbert, the late Michael Kelly of Kelly House, Josephine James of Modbury, D.J.B. Coulter of Yarnscombe, Philip Tremaine of St Columb Major, Tony Beard of Widecombe-in-the-Moor, Jonathan Bint of Chagford, Dr Ronald Homer and Arthur Mennell of Ottery St Mary, John Bax of Tavistock, John Birkle a descendant of the Penningtons and Richard Bowden who has made a study of the Ellacombe family, all helped with valuable material.

And then there are the hundreds of people – incumbents, churchwardens and other church officers, tower captains and house-owners who have made it possible for us to examine their bells. Because at the beginning of our researches this book was hardly contemplated we did not keep a complete record of all their names, but without their cooperation it would not have been possible. I have also had the pleasure of being accompanied on many expeditions by a number of companions and assistants – including my wife Claire and children Rebecca, John and Joe, Derrick Collier, Don Roberts and Tim King, and, of course, my fellow-authors Frank Mack and James Clarke.

Both the field-work and the research for this book have been fascinating. We have climbed towers in city centres and in remote country places, and explored the roof-spaces of country houses and public buildings; in church vestries and in county record offices the study of parish records, particularly churchwardens' accounts, was a task which never failed to provide delightful surprises; the problem has always been to resist being led into curious backwaters (particularly the organization and administration of mediaeval country parishes) which have nothing directly to do with the matter in hand: it was hard, for instance, to leave someone else to discover what lay behind the note in the Cullompton accounts for 1721, agreeing to pay for the prosecution of "*all such persons as were in any wise concern'd in pulling down the Bogg house . . .*" An added pleasure and excitement has been to be involved with the archaeological investigation of bellfoundry sites, and to visit bellfoundries in the Netherlands and in France where the technology has changed far less since the Middle Ages than it has in Britain.

Devon has more bells than any administrative county in Britain, and few counties are richer in parish churches. It was also, for over four centuries, home to a major bellfounding industry, which is still not fully chronicled. We aspire in this book to offer an account of its towers and bells which can bring their history up to the beginning of the twenty-first century.

1

CHURCH TOWERS IN DEVON

The Mediaeval Towers: Their Building and Use

THE EARLIEST CHRISTIAN CHURCHES appear to have been of two types: the *basilican* plan consisted of a hall, with arcaded aisles if it was a large one, and frequently with an apse at one end, and is the one most familiar to people in Western Europe, but in the East the commonest type was, and in many areas still is, built on a centralized plan, consisting of a central area with its upper stage carried on arches, and flanked on all four sides with transepts or apses forming a Greek cross on plan. In the East churches of this type usually have domes covering their central areas – Hagia Sofia in Istanbul is the classic example – but in the West it is more usual to find low-pitched pyramidal roofs. In France the earliest church still largely in its original form, at Germigny-des-Prés near Orleans, was built on this plan (it later had its western arm replaced by a longer nave), and there are examples in Britain, including three probable ones in Devon, though all of these have been much changed.

In churches of this type, then, the tower was the essential core of the building and needed to serve no other function, but the evidence of many of the early basilican churches in Britain, which are the great majority, suggests that their towers were added to them. There must, then, have been a particular reason for building towers, and in fact there were probably several reasons.

It is often claimed that our mediaeval church towers were designed to serve as defensive refuges for the community against invaders or raiders, but in most cases the evidence is unconvincing. The great majority of our towers, in Devon at any rate, were built with large doorways at ground level and open arches to the rest of the church; about a quarter of them have spiral stairs which run anti-clockwise and would therefore be difficult to defend against an intruder; and although the great majority of their parapets are crenellated the battlements are often quite useless defensively, as for example on top of *Newton St Cyres*'s stair-turret [12] where the battlements are less than a foot high and only inches above the level of the roof. In fact in most cases the parapets on church towers are not high enough to protect anyone standing behind them; during the 14th and 15th centuries crenellation became an architectural convention, used to give a dramatic finish to the parapet of almost any kind of building. In any case, with the exception of a very few which have stone vaulting above the first stage, anyone resorting to a church tower as a refuge from an enemy would be in grave danger of being burnt alive, with timber floors at all levels and only one way out.

Undoubtedly a strong motive for tower building was simply to attract the eye and emphasise the importance and grandeur of a building which was created to provide simple people with an experience of heaven as far as earth could provide it; the place where Christ lived sacramentally among his people. It was necessary then to give it as much prominence as the community's resources could afford, and a tall tower was one way of achieving this. There were certainly less spiritual motives, and local patriotism could be a strong one; the rivalry which led the people of Beauvais to build a spire higher than Strasbourg's – and led inevitably to the collapse of their cathedral – was echoed in a great many humbler but no less competitive communities up and down Europe. In Devon, for instance, it is clear that the tower at *Pyworthy* had a stage added to its top at some time in the late-14th or 15th century, giving it an attenuated and not very graceful outline, and the same may have been done at *Ashprington*: perhaps one needs look no further for an explanation than to their neighbours, *Bridgerule* and *Holsworthy* towers in the one case and *Cornworthy*'s in the other, all of them newly-built in just the same period.

Some of our towers were evidently designed to be inhabited, as fireplaces and sometimes provision for disposing of waste water were included in the building, but whether they were intended to be occupied permanently is not clear. Curiously, the Devon towers with these features are almost all in one corner of the county, around Torbay – *Cockington, Kingskerswell, Broadhempston, Dittisham, Churston Ferrers* and *East Ogwell*; *Bere Ferrers* is an outlier. In the case of *Cockington* which belonged to Torre Abbey, the accommodation may have been provided for a visiting priest from the Abbey, but there is no evidence that the other churches belonged to monastic houses except Broadhempston which belonged to a community in the Midlands. In all except Bere Ferrers the accommodation is in the middle stage of the tower.

Especially when they are near the sea, church towers can serve as navigation marks, and there is a strong suggestion that the top of the stair-turret at *Charleton* was designed to carry a fire-beacon. In fact, however, where the village was accessible from seaward to pirates or raiders, mediaeval builders tended to place their churches out of sight from the sea,[1] but *Stoke Fleming, Torquay St Marychurch, Bigbury, Wembury* and *Stoke (Hartland)*, most of them on cliff-tops, all stand out very boldly, and the 19th-century tower of *Plymouth St Peter* is still used as a transit mark for vessels entering the Sound, while *Wembury* is used in the same way for clearing Warren Point at the entrance to the Yealm. *Whitestone* and *St Marychurch* towers were at one time limewashed on their seaward-facing sides as aids to navigation, and it is recorded that when the comparatively modest 15th-century tower at *St Marychurch* was replaced by Hugall's 100-footer, the fishermen of Torbay demanded that the vicar have it limewashed like the old one: the vicar said that he had no objection, provided they were prepared to limewash it themselves!

Nevertheless, the most familiar purpose of a tower in our own day is for hanging bells, and this has been the case from very early times indeed. A tower can accommodate a whole ring of bells rather than one or two; it keeps them under cover; and it provides a proper space from which to ring them: it also enables them to speak out over a wider area than a bell hung in a bellcote. It is plain that bells had a great importance in the life of any mediaeval community, not only from a purely religious point of view but as part of the daily life of the neighbourhood, so one may not need to look for any other motive in tower-building in many of our churches.

Less commendable but very widespread is the use of church towers as repositories for unwanted lumber. Church people are reluctant to throw away church property however unlikely may be its future usefulness, and the writers have often been astonished at the pains that past parishioners have taken to hoist into towers large and awkward articles which are quite difficult of access: pews, lecterns, old hymn-books and bibles, scouts' camping equipment, framed pictures, rotting hassocks have been laboriously carried up worn and winding stairs or even up ladders: we remember climbing a long vertical ladder and wriggling through a trap-door to find that someone had with much effort and no small hazard stored up there two orange-boxes full of old jam-pots. This is no new thing; we find in the *Dartington* Churchwardens' Accounts for 1566, "*pd to Harry Wendyatt & his men for having up the tember & other troshe of the church up in to the towere*". The tower's ground floor, if it is not used as a ringing-room (and alas sometimes when it is) is also sometimes used as a church glory-hole – unwise and perilous when the churchyard mower and its petrol cans are stored there.

Church towers are not occupied only by human beings. They can provide homes for a wide variety of wildlife, some of it harmless – small birds, hibernating butterflies and moths; some potentially a nuisance – bats, bees,

---

1. One could cite *Littleham (Exmouth), Seaton, Branscombe, Dawlish, Brixham St Mary, Plymouth St Andrew, Clovelly, Mortehoe, Lynton* and *Combe Martin* as churches which seem to have been deliberately hidden from seaward.

barn-owls,[2] cluster-flies; and some an unmitigated menace – jackdaws, feral pigeons, death-watch beetles and furniture-beetles, the last two probably introduced by jackdaws with their nesting material. Jackdaws, if they are allowed access, will bring in anything up to a cubic yard of sticks in one season, and fill the whole of a tower stair with rubbish; roosting pigeons will coat every horizontal or nearly horizontal surface in a tower with six inches of noisome guano, and birds' nests and droppings can be a real danger to the health of anyone working in a belfry without protection. It is a curious fact that one species of moth, the Herald, *Scoliopteryx libatrix,* has a particular liking for hibernating inside bells, and during the winter as many as a dozen or more can be found in one bell, apparently untroubled by ringing.

It is clear, as one travels around the county, that towers were very important symbols to the people of Devon. Few areas in England can have such a high proportion of parish churches with towers, and one is repeatedly struck by the care and expense that was lavished on them by very small communities. Tiny parishes such as *Bradstone*, *Dunterton* [31], *Clyst St Lawrence*, *Huish* and *Sheepstor*, some of them in Devon's poorest areas and none of them with a population of over 200 at any time in history, have towers which must have represented a huge proportion of the community's wealth and cost as much as the whole of the rest of the church or even more, leaving one admiring the motivation and sacrifice involved in their building, and embarrassed to know that our far more affluent generation sometimes finds them a burden to keep in repair. There may have been various motives for building them, but the glory of God was surely the most important one, and we do their builders an injustice if we allow our 21st-century cynicism to doubt it.

Devon is not rich in early towers, and this is because between 1400 and the early 16th century Devon reached a peak in economic prosperity accompanied by a great in surge in church building and rebuilding. As one travels round the county, one can sometimes imagine with amazement the sight which would have met one's eyes in, say, 1450, with new towers under construction every few miles in village after village. Something similar must have been the case in the late 19th century, the time of the widespread Victorian restorations, but in many cases at that time it was the naves and chancels that were being rebuilt and the mediaeval towers allowed to remain. There are all too few reliable records by which our towers can be dated, but we have fairly good authority for *Ashcombe* 1259, *Denbury* 1291, *Broadhempston* c1300, *Modbury* 1328, *Ottery St Mary* 1337, *Buckland Brewer* (since largely rebuilt) 1399, *Moretonhampstead* 1418, *Highweek* 1428, *Plympton St Maurice* 1446, *Totnes* 1451, *Ashburton, Tavistock* and *Buckland Monachorum* just before that date, *Plymouth St Andrews* 1460 and *Chulmleigh* 1524. *Cullompton* tower was apparently still being built when the Reformation was in progress.

Tower Design

The great majority of our mediaeval country churches in England were the work of local teams of builders who designed and built them, moving around in a fairly limited area – unlike the builders of the great churches and cathedrals, who might travel over half of Europe in the course of their working lives. So we can expect to see in different parts of a county such as Devon groups of churches which share an identifiable common style or common features: we will also see in a few particularly important churches (such as *Cullompton, Chittlehampton* [29] and *Tiverton St Peter*) the influence of more sophisticated workmen from outside the county.

The Tower Plan. Most people, if asked to draw a church, would draw a building with a tower at one end; certainly over 90 per cent of our Devon churches have western towers, but as we have seen there is a very ancient

---

2. Bats and barn-owls need to be protected, and one is always glad to see them, but one must admit that their droppings can make belfry maintenance hazardous and unpleasant, though Churchwardens should resist the temptation to emulate the *Braunton* wardens who in 1701 spent 4 pence on *powder & shott to kill the Batts*.

Fig. 1. South Brent, formerly the central tower of a cruciform church.

tradition for central towers, either in cruciform or in aisleless three-cell churches. Devon has very few mediaeval central towers (*Crediton* [19], *Shute*, *Aveton Gifford*, *Axminster*, *Colyton*, *Kingsbridge*, *Tawstock* in cruciform churches and *Branscombe* in a three-cell church),[3] but three others (*Hemyock*, *South Brent* and *Bratton Clovelly*) evidently once belonged to cruciform churches where the body of the church was later demolished and replaced by a new church to the east of the old tower. These central-towered churches, notably *South Brent*, *Hemyock* and *Tawstock*,

Fig. 2. Braunton, one of the North Devon transeptal towers, with a timber spire.

strongly support the theory that in early times the centralized plan was more prevalent – i.e. a central tower with four arms of more or less equal projection built against it. At *Tawstock* the crossing itself is larger on plan than the tower, which is carried on a double set of squinch arches, and recent research suggests that there was originally a short, apsidal chancel. It is probably significant that several of the churches with surviving central towers are ancient foundations.

There is a distinct group of fifteen churches in the northern half of the county which have their towers placed transeptally, north or south; south transeptal at *Barnstaple St Peter*, *Braunton* and *Shirwell*, and north transeptal at *Bishops Tawton*, *East Down*, *Pilton*, *Mortehoe*, *Fremington*, *Yarnscombe*, *Beaford*, *Ashreigney*, *Burrington*, *Ashford*, *Abbotsham* and *Ilfracombe*

---

3. Two other very early (some claim Saxon) axial towers in three-cell churches were demolished in the 19th century at *Bishopsteignton* and *Teignmouth St Michael*.

Fig. 3. High Bickington, where the 12th-century transeptal tower has been replaced by one at the west end.

Holy Trinity. There were formerly others at *High Bickington* and *Goodleigh*, both replaced by 15th-century western towers, giving clear evidence that these transeptal towers are ancient; another, at *(Great) Torrington*, was replaced in a 19th-century rebuilding though the base of the tower remains as a transept like that at High Bickington, and there was also one in the priory church at *Frithelstock*. These towers generally have massive walls and are very simple. What connection, if any, there is between the layout of these and the twin transeptal towers of the Cathedral in Exeter (and of *Ottery St Mary* which is a model of it) is not clear, nor is there any obvious reason why (apart from *Ringmore* which has a tower over its south porch, and *Topsham* where the tower was apparently incorporated into a south aisle) there are no mediaeval transeptal towers in South Devon.

Two other towers are oddly sited, but came to be so only when the rest of the building was altered – *Otterton* which was over the chancel prior to a 19th-century rebuilding, and *East Buckland* where the nave and chancel were demolished leaving the north aisle with the tower almost detached. However, as we have seen, the great majority of our towers are placed at the west end of the nave, with an arch opening into the body of the church and usually with a door and a window in the west wall; the evidence of some very ancient towers such as *Sidbury* and the former *Exeter St Mary Major* in our own diocese and Saxon towers elsewhere in England suggests that this practice derives from the porch-towers of very early basilican churches.

Typically, a western tower is an extension or addition to the nave or occasionally to an aisle, but there are exceptions: at *Churston Ferrers* the tower is built halfway into the nave, and at *Cookbury* there is a kind of narthex at the west end of the church with an internal stone wall some 8 feet east of the main west wall; these are extended upwards to form the east and west walls of the tower, the north and south walls being carried on beams which span between the walls; *Clyst St Mary* is similar though the church was turned through 90° in a 19th-century rebuilding and enlargement.

Circular towers, common in East Anglia, some of them dating from

Fig. 4. Loxbeare, the "basic box" of masonry, probably of the 13th-century.

Saxon times, do not feature in Devon, though one is intrigued by the recorded finding of circular moorstone foundations under the base of *Bridestowe* tower when it was being rebuilt in 1828. All our towers are either square on plan or rectangular, the rectangular towers usually being designed with their longer axis running N-S. In some cases this gives the tower quite different aspects from different directions: *Stoke Canon*, for instance, presents itself as a slender building as one approaches the village from Exeter or from Tiverton, but looks much sturdier as one passes its west face.

Measurement of a number of Devon towers suggests that the mediaeval builders often worked to a rough rule allowing a wall thickness at ground level of approximately half the width of the space inside. The walls were reduced in thickness by offsets internally (to carry the floors and bellframe) and externally, and by batter in the outer walls, so that a typical tower may have walls six feet (2m) thick at ground level and no more than 2ft 6ins (300mm) thick at the level of the belfry – a principle of good engineering which was not always followed in the 19th-century.

A church tower is basically a box – in Devon a box of masonry, for we have no timber towers. There is no Devon tower more primitive, and probably not many more ancient, than *Loxbeare*, which consists simply of four walls with a few plain and rather randomly placed openings, an arched opening into the church on the east side, and a newel stair in one corner. The roof is of lead, and there is a plain parapet without battlements, not very far above the ridge of the nave roof. Such a tower has so few notable details that it is almost impossible to date it, but it is probably not later than 1300. Nevertheless, every church tower, up to and including the tallest and finest like *Chittlehampton* and *Hartland*, is really a stone box, albeit with a number of added features.

Building a stone box strong enough to stand 60 or 70 feet and take the thrust of swinging bells demanded a great deal of stone, and it was not long before the mediaeval masons realized that they could save material by concentrating mass at the points where it was most needed. The vertical projecting pilasters which had a purely decorative function in Norman towers like *Exeter Cathedral* and *Sidbury* grew into **buttresses** which gave strength and weight to the walls at the corners of the tower while allowing the walls themselves to be less massive. It seems likely that the first buttresses were later additions to strengthen an ailing tower, but by the 14th century they had become an important element in tower design, and their builders probably valued them more for their visual effect than for their structural importance; the walls of towers with buttresses are not normally much slighter than those without. Buttresses which are set at right-angles to the walls are known as **clamp buttresses,** and from about 1370 the Westcountry tower-builders were conspicuously clever in their use of these, soon realizing that buttresses which are set back, so that the quoins project between them, give a much livelier visual effect than buttresses placed right on the corner of the tower so that they meet in a re-entrant angle: this seems to have become the fashion around 1400, just at the beginning of our greatest tower-building era: at *Ottery St Mary*, built in 1337, the very prominent buttresses are not set back, (the fact that

Fig. 5. Ottery St Mary. The 14th-century transeptal towers have buttresses meeting at the quoins.

Fig. 6. Merton. A typical 15th-century west Devon tower, with the buttresses set back.

Fig. 7. Drewsteignton, the granite ashlar tower with diagonal buttresses running up into pinnacles set at 45°.

Buckfastleigh's buttresses are not set back, coupled with a corbel-table, suggests that this is one of the earliest towers with a central stair-turret) but by 1399 *Buckland Brewer*'s were set back, and from then on buttresses of this kind, like *Merton*'s, became almost universal in Devon and Cornwall: incidentally, anyone travelling in Cornwall can see how Isambard Kingdom Brunel clearly noticed and appreciated this feature, and copied it in designing the piers of his railway viaducts. The suggestion that buttresses on mediaeval towers were largely cosmetic is supported by the fact that on several towers, *Halwell* and *Chivelstone* for instance, the set-back buttresses on the east face are terminated with corbels at roof level so as not to intrude into the interior of the nave. **Diagonal buttresses** set at 135° on the corners provide less structural support, but can give a more graceful though less robust visual impact, as they do at *Drewsteignton*; in Devon towers they are less common than clamp buttresses, and in many of our simpler towers they only appear on the NW and SW angles, with right-angled buttresses, or one right-angled buttress and a stair-turret, on the other two corners. Clasping buttresses which cover the quoin and in effect form square turrets at the corners occur on only three Devon towers, *Littleham* (North Devon), *Langtree* and *Brendon*, and may belong to 19th-century rebuildings. Skilful placing of the offsets in the buttresses can very much enhance the outline of a tower; there are good examples at *Alwington*, *South Tawton* and *Chulmleigh*. Some towers, especially those which show Somerset influence, have the offsets of the buttresses ornamented with hunkapunks (*Combe Martin*,

Fig. 8. Littleham (N. Devon), with corner buttresses.

Fig. 9. Alwington; the design of the set-offs on the buttresses and of the string-courses is remarkably subtle for an out-of-the-way church.

Berrynarbor) or small free-standing pinnacles (*Broadclyst, Cullompton*), while several of the south-west Dartmoor group have small pinnacles on the offsets which, being built in granite, needed to be engaged rather than free-standing (*Plymouth St Andrew, Widecombe-in-the-Moor, Sampford Courtenay, Chulmleigh*).

Much of the art of architecture lies in using a practical element in the design to serve an aesthetic purpose, as we have seen with buttressing. The same is true of the projecting **string-courses** which serve to take rainwater clear of the walls but form another important visual feature in tower design. At its most primitive a string-course, as at *Martinhoe*, can take the form of projecting slates set at a slightly sloping angle between the courses of the masonry, but very soon the tower builders evidently saw the visual benefit of dividing the tower horizontally into stages – which might or might not be related to the internal divisions; string-courses were also used to disguise the external offsets in the walls. As the design of mediaeval towers evolved, one can see how string-courses came to be used with increasing subtlety to enhance a tower's proportions, and how they could be designed either to coincide with the offsets in the buttresses, or to complement them by being set at different levels: at *Alwington* the builders added intermediate string-courses round the quoins and the buttresses with a most elegant effect. The typical Devon tower is divided into three stages by two string-courses between the parapet and the ground, but some (e.g. *Ipplepen*) gain a special elegance from being only two-staged. Very few mediaeval towers are without string-courses; one such, at *Bampton*, is impressively massive but not particularly graceful.

Access to the upper stages of a tower can be achieved in various ways; **ladders** were often used in early towers, and are still found in many; *Cheriton Fitzpaine* has a ladder in the middle stage which is probably contemporary with the tower, and consists of two oak beams set parallel to each other with blocks of oak, triangular in section, spiked to them to form the treads: *Widworthy* formerly had a similar one, and *Kingsnympton* has a good example of an ancient ladder of the more normal type which may be equally ancient. Access by ladders is never very satisfactory especially if it involves negotiating a heavy trap-door at the top, and more particularly if the ladder is

Fig. 10. Bampton; the tower's massive proportions and the absence of string-courses make it impressive rather than elegant.

Fig. 11. Cheriton Fitzpane. A very early internal timber stair, probably contemporary with the building.

vertical; unfortunately some 20th-century architects have resorted to vertical ladders in new towers – often now with prominent hoops intended to make them safer – or even to cleats in the walls which make access extremely hazardous and inevitably make for poor maintenance for anything above ground level.

There is evidence in some towers (*Newton St Cyres* is one) that at some point a stone newel **stair** was added to the tower to replace ladders, but many of our most ancient towers included a stair as part of the design from the outset. At *Exeter Cathedral* the 12th-century towers have internal stairs in the corners, and at *Aveton Gifford*, *Branscombe* and the former *Exeter St Mary Major*, 11th- or 12th-century towers of the same period have round external stair-turrets,[4] at *Aveton Gifford* and *St Mary Major* with conical stone tops. Less ambitious country churches often had their towers built with stair-turrets rectangular on plan, projecting from the wall to about half

---

4. The Reverend John Swete whose charming water-colours are printed in Todd Gray (ed), *Travels in Georgian Devon (Tiverton, 1997-2000)*, shows ancient towers (which he believed to be Saxon and were certainly Norman) at *East Teignmouth* and *Bishopsteignton*, both with circular stair-turrets.

Fig. 12. Newton St Cyres, the stair-turret added to the tower in the 15th-century.

Fig. 13. Uplyme. The face of the stair-turret is flush with the face of the tower, throwing the east elevation out of symmetry.

the diameter of the stair; others have polygonal turrets. Analysis of these shows that rectangular turrets were usually set on the face least often seen from the village, and it seems clear that at first the stair-turret was regarded as a necessary excrescence which should not be allowed to mar the facade of the building and so was put if possible on the less visible face as it was at *Uplyme*, until later builders came to understand that a stair-turret, especially a more elegant polygonal one, could be an important feature in the design, and placed it on the face from which the tower was most seen as at *Seaton*. It could then be carried up above the tower parapet, topped with battlements or a weather-vane, decorated with stone panelling (e.g. *Branscombe*, where the top of the 12th-century turret was extended in the 15th) or a course of carved decoration (*Plymtree*), topped with a spirelet (*Broadhembury*) or a little dome (*Newton Poppleford*), or given a crown of little pinnacles (*Broadwoodwidger*, *Ashwater* and *Dawlish*). Stair-turrets placed right on the corner of a tower are less rare (*Pilton*, *Burlescombe* and *Lapford* are examples): more often turrets are placed at or near the end of a face; when the face of the turret is flush with that of the tower this gives an unbalanced appearance to the tower (*Dunsford*, *Bratton Clovelly*), so many stair-turrets are set a little way back, allowing the quoin to define the corner of the tower itself; even a few inches of set-back is enough to define the line between tower and turret.

A group of towers in the south-west of the county are built with a stair at one corner which partly projects but is clasped and partly disguised by clamp-buttresses; at *Bickleigh, Buckland Monachorum, Petertavy* and *Walkhampton* this feature is combined with big octagonal pinnacles, but not at *Tamerton Foliot:* as we shall see, Bickleigh, Buckland and Tamerton also shared granite waggon-roofs on their towers. At *Alwington*, an astonishingly subtle tower for so small a community, a low rectangular projection for the stair at the E end of the N

Fig. 14. Seaton. The polygonal stair-turret is set slightly back from the E corner. The tower, built of flint with Beer stone dressings, has external putlog-holes.

Fig. 15. Buckland-in-the-Moor, an unbuttressed tower with a "South Hams" central stair-turret.

face is cleverly disguised by a buttress in the same way, and the pinnacle in that corner is set in to match the other three.

In the South Hams the tower-builders evolved a distinctive way of handling stair-turrets, placing them centrally in the facade of the tower: as we have seen, *Buckfastleigh* may well be an early example of this. In some of their simpler towers, such as *Woodland* and *Buckland-in-the-Moor*, the effect is a little stark, but when a central stair-turret is combined with bold buttressing the effect can be most dramatic, especially if set-back clamp buttresses are used. As the light strikes across the planes of buttresses, quoins, walls and turret, it creates an appearance almost like folded drapery, while the austere vertical lines of the tower contrast with the complex angularity of the horizontal string-courses. *Ipplepen* and *Torbryan* are particularly successful examples of this type, and in their case the vertical emphasis is enhanced by the roughcast which covers the horizontal courses of the masonry. The builder of *Totnes* tower, Roger Growdon, copied the stair and buttresses from *Ashburton* which he had been instructed to use as one of his models, and in 1890 E. H. Harbottle incorporated a central stair in his very impressive tower at *St Michael's, Heavitree*. When a central stair is combined with diagonal buttresses, as at *Blackawton* and *Sherford*, the effect is less striking. In several of these South Hams towers – *Totnes*, *Torbryan*,

Fig. 16. Torbryan, the fully-developed South Hams tower with set-back buttresses, figure niches in the façade, and retaining its roughcast.

Ipplepen and others – the stair emerges at belfry level not directly into the belfry but into the reveal of one of the flanking window-openings. This may have been designed to remedy the inherent weakness of this design, viz; a series of openings one above another in the middle of the wall face.

Another unusual feature found in some other towers in the South Hams is that a stair in the NE or SE corner is entered by a doorway set in the West wall of the nave; there are examples at *Malborough, Diptford, Broadhempston, Staverton* and *Dartington* old church.

Although this plan reached its full development in the South Hams, there are four towers in North Devon with central stair-turrets, *Clawton, Langtree, Westleigh* and *Yarnscombe*, and a cluster in West Somerset, including *Wellington, West Buckland* and *Bradford-on-Tone*. These may be simply an independent development unconnected with the South Hams, but one suspects a link in that *Langtree* has the South Hams feature of the stair emerging into a window embrasure at belfry level. Although we have seen internal stairs in the 12th-century towers of the Cathedral, the majority of towers with internal stairs seem to belong to the great tower-building boom of the 15th century, and particularly to the West Devon and East Cornwall style. Where towers are small, space is found for a stair by placing an angled wall across the internal corner, or sometimes by partly filling in the angles between buttresses outside. Not all internal stairs extend further than the belfry, but when they do reach the tower roof a pinnacle may be made slightly larger to accommodate the stair and doorway, as at *Buckland Monachorum*. The great majority of internal stairs in Devon are placed in the north-west corner – why is not clear; perhaps it was just customary.

Inevitably there are some tower stairs which fit into no neat category; at *Hartland* and at *Kenton*, the stair from the ground to the second stage is in one corner, and to the upper stage in another: at *Butterleigh* there is an external stair on the S face to the second stage and an internal stair in the NW corner to the belfry: at *Abbotsham* there is a ladder to the second stage, from which an internal stair goes up the SE corner to the belfry and another separate stair, entered by another doorway, runs in the same corner from the belfry to the roof: at *Broadhempston* there is a short internal stair to the roof reached by a ladder from the belfry stage.

Most tower stairs are entered from inside the church, but a few have external access, and some have both. Many 19th-century incumbents did not want their ringers to be able to enter or leave the ringing-room without passing through the church, and for that reason some external access doorways have been closed up. For the same reason many upstairs ringing-rooms or closed galleries were replaced by ground-floor ringing-rooms where the ringers would be under the eyes of the clergy, but some 18th-century ringing galleries survive (*Newton St Cyres, Dartmouth St Saviour*): both were associated with west galleries, and in a number of towers a blocked doorway will reveal an access to a vanished gallery. At *Bigbury* and *Buckerell*, the ringing-room door is reached by a short flight of steps

Fig. 17. Bridgerule: type B octagonal pinnacles, built up on an octagonal barrel.

outside. Towards the end of the 20th century ringing-galleries again became popular, especially as they allow the ground-floor to accommodate choir vestries, catering and washing-up facilities or toilets.

Access to central towers involves special problems. In a simple cruciform church, it is possible to have a stair-turret in the angle between one of the transepts and the nave, as at *Aveton Gifford,* but where there are side-aisles this is not possible. In big buildings such as *Crediton* or *Axminster*, a stair can be contained in one of the piers, but in smaller churches, *Tawstock* and *Colyton* for example, there may be a stair in the corner of the transept and a wooden gallery or catwalk close beneath the roof to the central tower. At *Shute*, where the ringers stand in the crossing and access is needed only for maintenance, we had to climb over the church boiler to a stair in the transept and then walk across the roof to a door on the W face of the tower, and at *Crediton,* since the stair in the pier ceased to be used, one walks across the side-aisle roof to a stair in the tower's NW corner.

Buttresses, string-courses and stair-turrets all serve practical purposes. **Pinnacles** likewise were not entirely for show. Masonry is not glued together; the mortar between the stones serves mainly to provide a continuous bedding between one stone and the next, and a wall needs weight to be really firm. A pinnacle at the corner of a building provides the masonry with a super-incumbent weight at the point where its integrity is most vital; for the same reason pinnacles cap the flying buttresses of most Gothic cathedrals. This is particularly important for a tower containing swinging bells, the oscillation of which will tend to loosen any masonry which is not well anchored down. The pinnacles of *Exeter Cathedral*'s towers are substantial little buildings in their own right, and elsewhere large pinnacles are built up from courses of stone, but small pinnacles generally are made from a single stone placed on a short plinth built up from the parapet.

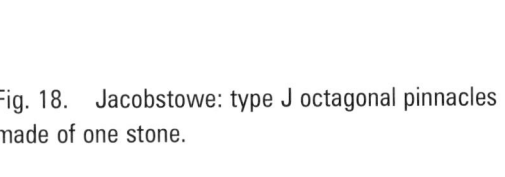

Fig. 18. Jacobstowe: type J octagonal pinnacles made of one stone.

Fig. 19. Crediton: type C octagonal pinnacles with the chamfer at the base of the parapet.

Fig. 20. Plympton St Mary: type P octagonal pinnacles the chamfer is level with the tops of the buttresses, and like them is decorated with a small engaged pinnacle.

Over England in general, the most familiar type of pinnacle is square on plan and decorated with projecting crockets. This type is found in most parts of Devon, but sparingly: it is especially elegant when set at 45° on top of a diagonal buttress (*Drewsteignton* [7], *Cheriton Bishop*). Devon pinnacles, notably in the west of the county (and in E Cornwall), are more often octagonal, consisting of crocketted tapering tops, often standing on octagonal drums with collars of rudimentary battlements. These fall into a number of types, according to the way in which the octagon is developed from the square corner of the tower, but the evidence, such as it is, points to their having been built between 1430 and the Reformation and being associated with the areas where granite was the chief building stone – though not all of them are built of granite. We can group them into five categories:

Type B (*Bridgerule, Bradworthy*) has a built-up pinnacle on an octagonal barrel which starts at the level of the parapet top.

Type J (*Jacobstowe, Black Torrington*) also commences at the parapet top, but consists of a single stone, usually of granite, with rudimentary crockets, resting on a square base. These two types are almost entirely restricted to the NW quarter of the county.

Fig. 21. Walkhampton: big type S pinnacles with the chamfer at the belfry stage

Type C (*Crediton*) has a built-up pinnacle on an octagonal drum, where the octagonal begins with a stop-chamfer at the base of the parapet.

Type P (*Plymouth St Andrew, Dunterton, Widecombe-in-the-Moor, Plympton St Mary* has the octagon beginning with a stop-chamfer a little below the parapet string-course, and usually level with the tops of clamp buttresses. The effect of this is very satisfying, especially where the stop-chamfers and the tops of the buttresses are decorated with small engaged pinnacles in clusters of three at each corner.

Type S (*Shaugh Prior, Walkhampton* has the stop-chamfer at the base of the belfry stage. These last two types are found mainly in the SW corner of Devon, with outliers at *Holsworthy* and *Chulmleigh*. They usually have the top of the octagonal drum decorated with a collar of miniature crenellations.

Ugborough and *Bickleigh* are the only examples in Devon of the *St Austell* type, where the octagonal turrets are corbelled out at a point half-way up the belfry stage or level with the parapet string. Although big octagonal pinnacles are typical of South-west Devon and East Cornwall and particularly associated with granite, the tower at *Crediton* has very similar pinnacles built of local stone with Beer stone dressings, as does *Totnes St Mary* (the pinnacles apparently based by Roger Growdon on *Buckland Monachorum*'s) with red sandstone and Beer stone. At *South Milton, Totnes, South Pool* and *Shaugh Prior* big octagonal pinnacles are combined with a South Hams stair-turret; *Thurlestone, Littlehempston* and *Chivelstone* were similar but have apparently had their pinnacles removed, like the towers at *Newton Ferrers* and *Wembury* which also once had big octagonal pinnacles.

An element of competition seems to have broken out over pinnacles in the south-west corner of the county and in Cornwall, each parish seeking to have pinnacles bigger than it neighboour's; the towers at *Buckland Monachorum, Bickleigh* and *Walkhampton* have actually been endangered by the swaying weight of their pinnacles which caused severe cracks through the belfry openings; and at *Petertavy* it appears that the builders began to build equally big pinnacles and then, probably wisely, curbed their ambition, as the corner turrets are reduced in girth just above the level of the parapet.

From a distance the pinnacles at *Stowford* [32], *Lydford* and *Sampford Spiney* look as though they belong to this group, but they are in fact square in section, though their proportions are similar to the octagonal ones. *Bridestowe*'s are the same, and may have been so before the tower was rebuilt in the early 19th century.

The simplest type of pinnacle is the plain obelisk, often a later replacement for a mediaeval type, and these are found all over the county, some of them dating from the 18th century.

Pinnacles are not difficult to add to a tower, and are all too easy to remove. *Tawstock*'s and *North Molton*'s have disappeared in recent years; in the former case they were taken down as insecure and subsequently broken up; in the latter, one pinnacle was struck by lightning and damaged the church roof, and the others were removed for

Fig. 22. Tamerton Foliot: the tower's remarkable wagon roof made of granite.

Fig. 23. Combpyne: a rare Devon example of a mediaeval saddleback roof.

safety. At *Bishopsnympton*, tall octagonal pinnacles of the *Bradworthy* type were taken down and replaced without their turrets, much to the detriment of the fine tower's proportions, and *Wembury*, *Thurlestone* and *Littlehempston* all lost big octagonal pinnacles at some point in their history.

Tower roofs are usually concealed behind the parapet. The commonest roofing materials in Devon towers are lead – usually laid on a low-pitched ridge or inward-sloping roof – and slate, which in North Devon especially was often used with steep pitches sloping inwards to a lead valley. Later, less conventional materials were used including corrugated iron, which roofed *Clawton* tower until the 1960s. After the Second World War there was a fashion among architects to replace tower roofs in reinforced concrete; this has almost always proved a mistake; it is liable to crack and admit water, the reinforcement tends to rust and break away the concrete, and it makes for very poor acoustics in a tower with bells.

One very remarkable type of tower roof can be seen at *Tamerton Foliot*, where a slated roof is supported on a West-country type waggon-roof constructed of *granite*. Four arched braces are connected by purlins and a ridge, all tenon-and-mortised together; the abutments of similar braces can also be found at *Buckland Monachorum* and *Bickleigh*, though there the rest of the stonework has been replaced by timber.

A very early pattern of tower roof was the saddleback, which is common in Normandy and Britanny but much less so on this side of the Channel. Two such mediaeval roofs remain in Devon, at *Combpyne* and (probably) *Hollacombe* (near Holsworthy); a saddleback roof at *Morebath* was part of a 1885 restoration by Butterfield who claimed without any known authority that he was "putting the tower back into its original form"; it previously had a battlemented parapet. In England most ancient saddleback roofs, some of which survive not far away in

Somerset, have their ridges aligned on the same axis as the church's main roofs, but *Morebath*'s and *Hollacombe*'s have their ridges running north-south, which is very impractical as it makes the guttering on the east face difficult and expensive to keep in proper order.

Although tower roofs are generally little seen, they become very conspicuous when they are drawn up to form a **spire**. Although a spire might seem to be much more costly than a low-pitched roof, it has to be remembered that before the 18th-century many churches were roofed with oak shingles which require a fairly steep pitch, and a small shingled spire might well be little more expensive than a roof of imported slate or lead. Here again we

Fig. 24. Swimbridge: a short, plain tower with the belfry housed within the base of a timber spire.

Fig. 25. Brushford: a timber belfry stage topped with a spirelet, formerly covered in shingles.

find in Devon a conspicuous north/south divide; all except one of the mediaeval spires in North Devon are timber-framed; all except possibly one in South Devon are of stone: *Ottery St Mary* and *Exeter Cathedral* (formerly) with timber spires may be counted as being in no-man's-land. Spires are divided between *parapet spires* which spring from within the tower parapet, and *broach spires* which extend over the tops of the walls with *broaches* to square the octagon: Devon has both types, both in timber and in stone.

Several of the North Devon towers with timber broach spires have their belfries contained within the base of the spire with the belfry sound-openings in the spire (*Barnstaple St Peter*, *Swimbridge* and *Kingsnympton*), while *Brushford* and *Washford Pyne* have square timber belfries above their tower walls, *Brushford*'s with a spirelet on top. There is documentary evidence that *Cruwys Morchard*, *Cheldon* and *Torrington* formerly had spires of timber belfies of this type. Timber spires above the belfry stage, such as *Hatherleigh*, are usually of the parapet type: Hatherleigh's is notable in having been blown off bodily on

Fig. 26. Hatherleigh: the shingled timber spire was lifted off by a gale in January, 1990.

Fig. 27. Modbury: a broach spire in South Devon slate-stone. The belfry lights are slits, and the buttresses are not set back.

January 25th 1992, to fall through the roof of the church; it has since been rebuilt. A number of these timber-framed spires were formerly covered with shingles; *Brushford*'s was until the 1970s when it was slated (a questionable move), and *Hatherleigh*'s is so still; others have been clad with lead (*Braunton, St Peter's Barnstaple, Swimbridge*), copper shingles (*Kingsnympton*) or slates (*West Worlington*). Some very simple churches have pyramidal roofs which almost form spires (*Cookbury, Bittadon, Beaworthy*). The timber-work in these mediaeval timber spires is very impressive, but *Kingsnympton*'s was replaced in the early 20th century by a steel framework which has created serious problems. *Sidbury* has had at least three spires of various types including a very ugly tall four-sided one which can be seen in old prints.

Bishops Tawton has the only mediaeval stone spire in North Devon; in the south there is a group in the South Hams which includes broach spires at *Modbury, Malborough, Diptford* and *Slapton*, and parapet spires at *Holbeton, Kingsbridge, North Huish, Ermington, Buckfastleigh, Ringmore, Rattery* and *Ashburton St Lawrence*. The contrast between north and south in this respect is much easier to explain than some other differences; much of north Devon was covered by the great forest which gave its name to the *Nymets* and *Morchards*, so that it would have been natural there to build in timber rather than the intractable stone of the Culm Measures: Buckfastleigh's spire is now built of brick and it is not clear what preceded it. Most of the stone spires, by reason of their material, are austere, not to say stark in their outline: they include the celebrated twisted spire at *Ermington*, which evidently became distorted in the distant past, but was deliberately rebuilt with a kink during the 19th century. There is

Fig. 28. Rattery: an early tower with corbel-table and a short stone parapet spire.

Fig. 29. Colyton: a local supply of fine freestone enabled the people to create their splendid lantern.

evidence, in the buildings or in records, for a number of spires which have now disappeared. There are squinches in the middle stage of *Pyworthy* tower which suggest that there was a spire here before the tower was raised in height, and former spires are recorded at *Culmstock*, *Dodbrooke* (fell in 1785), *Sampford Peverell*, *Dartmouth St Petrox* and *South Brent*: *Uffculme* had a spire prior to the building of the present one, and *Beer*'s 19th-century tower had a tall pyramidal spire until the 1920s.

Devon has only two octagon-topped towers; the major one is at *Colyton*, where the close availability of high-quality freestone encouraged the masons to build a magnificent lantern on the church's central tower: the other is at *St Petrock's, Exeter*, where the octagonal top stage is capped by a lantern roof built of wood, simply, perhaps, in order to house six bells in a very small belfry.

Getting rid of rain-water from a tower roof was formerly a simple matter of using a gargoyle or a long spout to throw it well clear of the walls, but this can cause problems with damp (especially where roughcast has been stripped away), and since the mid-19th century many towers have been fitted with downpipes, sometimes in lead but more often in cast-iron. These have the disadvantage of easily getting blocked, and when this happens they often remain blocked for some time during which they cause far more damage than a spout. Even worse is the

Fig. 30. Chittlehampton: built from the proceeds of a local saint's shrine, the tower, richly decorated with pinnacles and with its twin belfry openings with stone screens instead of louvres, must be the work of Somerset masons.

practice of bringing the rainwater services down inside the tower, sometimes using open troughs, where a blockage can have very serious consequences, especially if the switchboard and fuseboxes are in the base of the tower, as they often are.

Openings in towers consist, typically, of a west door with a window of 3 or 4 lights above it, a small window in the middle stage, and belfry openings in the top stage. The simplest belfry openings in the oldest and most basic towers are nothing more than slits in the stonework, perhaps no more than six inches wide on the outer face but splayed inside (*Dolton, Branscombe, Morebath, Combpyne, Slapton*); later and more ambitious towers have two- or three-light arched openings with simple tracery in the heads (*Alwington*); square-headed openings with two lights are very common in Devon and probably date from the 15th century and later, and in the area round Torbay there is a group of towers with square-headed belfry openings of three or four lights, suggesting that there was a school of tower building in that area with its own individual fashions (*Brixham St Mary, Berry Pomeroy, Marldon*). Paired belfry lights, which are common enough in Somerset, appear in Devon only in towers with Somerset influence, notably *Chittlehampton*, and the 13th-century towers at *Crediton* [19] and *Clyst Honiton*. It seems likely that many early towers had their belfry lights filled with pierced wooden shutters such as still survive at *Ashcombe*, but louvres, made of wood or in Devon more commonly slate, became the norm; the existence of a rebate in the jambs of louvred openings suggests that in some cases the louvres replaced wooden shutters. In a few towers in the west of the county such as *Bradstone*, the belfry openings are filled with pierced slate shutters. Louvres, though they look traditional, are in practice less satisfactory than shutters, in that they admit more rain and snow, they allow birds to enter the tower (or if there is netting to nest and roost between the louvres and the netting) and they throw the sound down on to the people who, being closest to the bells, are least in need of it. In the last hundred years a few towers have been provided with sound-lanterns in the roof which provide the best means of propagating bell music; *Buckfast Abbey, Kingsteignton, Exeter St Thomas, Newton Abbot* and most recently *Tavistock* all benefit in this way, and have the openings in their belfry walls partly or entirely blocked.

Decoration is generally scarce on towers in Devon, where, except in the south-east, the most readily available building materials do not submit to delicate carving. Simple moulding on string-courses, parapets and pinnacles is often found in granite towers, and in East Devon the freestone from Beer and Salcombe Regis allowed some more ambitious decoration (*Sidmouth, Sidbury, Colyton*), but in the south the shilletty limestone constrained most builders to go for elegance of form rather than decoration. In the north there was a modest supply of workable

Fig. 31. Kenton: new red sandstone and white Beer stone, with image-niches on the façade and at each corner of the parapet.

stone, which allowed the builders of *Berrynarbor, Hartland, High Bray* and *Combe Martin* among others to indulge in gargoyles and hunkapunks. The exceptions are in the major parish churches which belonged to prosperous communities in the 15th and 16th centuries which not only could afford imported fine-quality freestone but could employ master-builders of exceptional quality. *Chittlehampton* is often described as the finest tower in Devon, but perhaps more accurately as the finest Somerset tower in Devon, for there can be no doubt that it was built by a Somerset team; likewise the towers built by the wealthy wool communities of *Tiverton (St Peter), Cullompton* and probably also *Broadclyst* show very strong Somerset influence. These towers exult in composite pinnacles, gargoyles, niches and openwork parapets.

Niches and statues adorn many mediaeval towers – again generally in the more prosperous centres: some of them still retain the saints and angels which were too inaccessible for the 16th-century iconoclasts, so St Nectan still stands on the east face of *Stoke* church facing Hartland Town, *Totnes* has some very weathered figures on its south face, and even little *Cadeleigh* has a number of niches with figures including a delightful St Antony with his pig and bell. *Cadeleigh, Upton Pyne, Talaton* and *Kenton* all have small figures in canopied niches in each corner of their parapets, as well as larger ones lower down, and probably were the work of the same team of builders.

Putlog holes are a feature of most mediaeval towers – almost always open to the inner faces, but at *Seaton* [14] very evident on the outside. Their purpose was to carry the beams of the scaffolding used in the building of a tower – most mediaeval towers seem to have been built from the inside – and they were left open to encourage water in the masonry to dry out. In many belfries they can contain an interesting array of old bottles, used over the ages to bring oil for the bearings.

Rendering was used to cover almost all mediaeval towers unless they were built of ashlar. Evidence of this is sometimes quite conclusive, as at *Newton St Cyres* where the upper part of the stair-turret, added perhaps a century or two after the tower's first building, still has a layer of limewashed rendering between it and the tower walls. Later church accounts often contain entries for rendering or "rough-scatting" the tower, and it remained for the 19th-century to strip off the tower's protective coat and expose "the beautiful old stonework" to view – and to the ravages of rain and frost. One has only to compare the elegant lines of roughcast *Torbryan* and *Ipplepen* with the gloomy bare stone of *Halwell* and *Churchstow* to appreciate the difference but such was the zeal of Victorian architects and experts to remove it that at one time a list was published of the towers in North Devon which had been so backward and dilatory as still to be rendered – including *Atherington*, where the roughcast was duly removed and the tower has suffered grievous problems from water ingress ever since.

Fig. 32.   Dunterton: granite ashlar, type P buttresses and pinnacles. Even tiny communities managed to afford quite elaborate towers.

Fig. 33.   Stowford: bands of local stone and granite.

Materials, as we have already seen, have strongly affected the design of our towers, and to a great extent their performance. The slaty rocks of the South Hams and the Culm Measures of North Devon gave the mediaeval masons no opportunity for decoration and tend to allow damp to penetrate in the absence of rendering, but their strong horizontal bonding made for durable towers and often tall ones. In the east of the county, the freestones from the Beer area are often mixed with flint and chert, and here we find more ambitious decoration; but flint and chert especially do not bond well, and many East Devon towers are stocky and may have a history of structural trouble; the freestone from that area was exported as far as Cornwall, but mainly for internal work. In the Dartmoor area granite is supreme, and was exported to some distance, for dressings, window tracery and mouldings at least; the granite quarries probably turned out ecclesiastical stonework to be sold virtually "off the shelf"; there used to be a scratching-post in a field in Tetcott which had obviously started as a crocketted pinnacle, but it had evidently been broken when the crockets were only roughed out and was sold off to a farmer. Around the edge of Dartmoor, granite is used for dressings, with walling in the local limestone (*Plymouth St Andrew*, *Egg Buckland*) but some quite humble communities (*Dunterton*, *Sheepstor*, *Gidleigh*) as well as more prosperous ones (*Widecombe-in-the-Moor*, *Plympton St Mary* [20], *Holsworthy*) built their towers in granite ashlar: *Stowford* and

Tetcott have bands of granite alternating with local stone. In the Tavistock area the Hurdwick stone, a kind of trap, supplied *Tavistock*, *Bradstone* and *Milton Abbot*, while the traps to the north of Exeter appear at *Thorverton*, *Newton St Cyres*, *Crediton* and other churches up the Exe and Creedy valleys. In Exeter itself and its neighbourhood, red sandstone conglomerate was used at *Alphington* and has proved very weak, but *Kenn*, *Kenton* [30], *Exminster* and *Powderham* employed a stronger red sandstone. The old red sandstone gives *Totnes* its beautiful colour, and was used in a number of towers around Torbay.

Post-mediaeval Towers

The traditions of mediaeval tower-building did not disappear immediately after the Reformation; most of the towers which came to be built or rebuilt between 1550 and 1830s show that Devon masons were following the old style. *Christow* tower is dated 1630, but virtually indistinguishable from towers a century older, and the tower of *Dartmouth St Petrox* was rebuilt, or more likely built new, in 1641 (there is nothing which obviously survives from an earlier one) and is a typical South Hams tower, unbuttressed but with a strong batter and a central stair-turret,

Fig. 34. Plymouth, Charles Church, completed in 1708, but the proportions and style are still mediaeval. Only the window-tracery and the pineapples betray its late date.

Fig. 35. Georgenympton: here the builders in 1673 used locally-burnt brick, but followed the traditional style of two centuries earlier.

only the wide single-light belfry openings with segmental arches suggesting its 17th-century date. *Charles Church* in *Plymouth* (1658) is distinguishable from a pre-Reformation tower only through its cusp-less window-tracery and the pineapples which adorn its parapet, and the men who built *Georgenympton* in 1673 made their bricks in the parish but built a tower which otherwise shows its date only in the window openings, the outline and proportions still mediaeval: at *Cheldon* too only the single-light square-headed belfry lights betray the 18th-century rebuilding of the upper stage. *West Down* (1712) and *Luffincott* (1790) could at first glance be mistaken for 16th or 15th century towers; during the 18th and early 19th centuries it was only in the urban churches, designed by architects rather than local masons, that the new fashions were adopted. *St Aubyn's, Devonport* (1772) has a west facade consisting of a big pediment with a short tower and octagonal spire embedded in it: James Green in 1816 gave the second *Exeter St David* a "pepper-pot" on a classical pediment. The turret of *Tiverton St George* (1733) is classical in design and *Exeter Holy Trinity* (1820) is "Gothick", but John Foulston at *St Paul's Stonehouse* in Plymouth paid at least some respect to pre-reformation style, as did the builder of *Totnes St John's* in 1832.

These Devon towers which were built in mediaeval style were survivals, not imitations, of the old tradition, but by the early 19th-century the vernacular tradition was lost, and in 1837 Charles Fowler designed *Honiton St Paul* in a conscious (and very inaccurate) imitation of the "Norman" style, with round-headed windows, pilasters, blind arcading and zig-zag mouldings. Structurally too this tower owes little to traditional tower-building, as it is built

Fig. 36. Tiverton St George: Georgian classicism has at last taken over in 1714.

Fig. 37. Brooking: a charming country church of the 1850s Gothic Revival, by an architect unknown.

Fig. 38. Exmouth, Holy Trinity. Fellowes Prynne, some f whose planned towers were never built, completed this very fine one in 1907.

with the walls almost the same thickness from top to bottom; as a result it suffers from severe movement when the bells are rung: in this Fowler was not alone among 19th-century architects. The following year *Blackborough* was built by J. T. Knowles, vaguely gothic is style but very poorly constructed. Of eighteen Devon churches dating between 1835 and 1843, only two others have towers; *Chardstock*'s (1840) and *Salcombe*'s (1843) belonging to the early gothic revival. The other eleven all have bellcotes or nothing at all.

The first towers from the true academic Gothic Revival in Devon came in 1845, with *Barnstaple Holy Trinity*, a tall, Somerset-inspired (but perhaps a little top-heavy) tower by Mackintosh & Abbot, and *Sowton*, which was designed by John Hayward with big West Devon-style pinnacles. Of the many new or rebuilt towers which followed during the 19th century, one might specially cite *Uffculme* (John Hayward, 1846), *Landscove* (J. L.Pearson, 1849), the delightful *Brooking St Barnabas* (1855 by an unknown architect) and *Torquay, St Mary Magdalene, Upton,* (1849, Salvin); all these with spires. J. W. Hugall's impressive tower at *St Marychurch* (1861) dominates its hill above Torquay, in company with the rather ungainly outline of William Butterfield's *All Saints, Babbacombe*. Designs from Edward Ashworth include the former *Exeter St Mary Major*, now happily no longer competing with the Cathedral,[5] and a workmanlike tower at *Exmouth St John's, Withycombe Raleigh*, both 1864. One of the best of all Devon's Victorian towers is arguably *Exeter St Michael, Mount Dinham*, by Rohde Hawkins (1865), with its fine spire flanked by pinnacles; in Plymouth, the skyline is graced by *St Matthias*, very much in the Somerset style with its complex pinnacles and pierced stone belfry openings, by Hine & Odgers, 1887. In the same way, Exmouth has *Holy Trinity* (G. H. Fellowes Prynne, 1905) dominating its skyline and visible from many miles away, and Teignmouth has *St Michael* (Robert Medley Fulford, 1889) enhancing its seafront however much one may regret the destruction of the former 12th-century tower there.

One of the oddest 19th-century towers is *East Worlington* (Clark & Holland, 1879), a late and unsuccessful attempt at "Norman" architecture with grotesquely over-sized round-headed windows. Clarke's other Devon church, at *Filleigh*, probably incorporates part of the previous tower, and is rather less idiosyncratic.

A remarkable number of new 19th- and early 20th-century churches were left uncompleted, and in most cases it

---

5. There is a charming watecolour, which used to be in the vestry of St Petrock's, Exeter, now in the Westcountry Studies Library, of old St Mary Major, painted by Ashworth; it is astonishing that after painting it with such evident affection, he was party to its destruction.

Fig. 39. Exeter, Emmanuel. The raw brickwork at the SW corner shows where the ambitiously-planned tower should have been.

Fig. 40. Plymouth, St Mary's Laira. This tower reached its second stage, but was then finished off with a timber spire.

was the tower which never materialized. In Exeter, *Emmanuel*'s design by Harold Brakspear included an impressively tall tower with a convex-sided rectangular spire which was never begun; *St Matthew*'s, which Fulford & Harvey designed to have a West tower on an oblong plan with pinnacles and a four-sided parapet spire covered in polychrome tiles, was stopped at the first stage. In Plymouth, *St Thomas's, Keyham*'s tower was never started and *St Philip's Weston Mill* and *St Mary's Laira* never got beyond the first or second stage, while *Emmanuel*'s tower was very unsatisfactorily finished off with a flat roof instead of the spire planned by T.C. Rogers. In Ilfracombe, *St Peter*'s, a good church by Fellowes Prynne, stopped at the tower's first stage, and another good tower design by the same architect at *Budleigh Salterton* is represented only by an extraordinarily massive baptistry and the architect's drawing for a fine tower and spire still to be seen inside the church. We can regret particularly the loss of Fellowes Prynne's towers, as those which were completed by him, at *Plymouth St Peter*'s and *Exmouth Holy Trinity*, are very fine: his father, incidentally, was the founder and first incumbent of St Peter's, Plymouth. Other Devon churches with absent or unfinished towers are *Paignton, St Andrew* by Fulford, Tait & Harvey, 1892, and *St Mary's, Abbotsbury*, Newton Abbot, by E.H. Sedding, 1904. *Torquay St John*, which stands sentinel over the harbour, was designed by G.E. Street as early as 1861; his design included the tower but it was only completed in 1885, by his son.

One thing that is striking about the designers of almost all our 19th- and early 20th-century towers is the scant recognition which they show to Devon's vernacular tradition. W. D. Caroe gave *St David's, Exeter* a tower which combines great originality with a definite but almost subliminal Devon feel, and *Yelverton* (Nicholson & Corlette, 1915) looks like a Devon tower: but until the end of the 19th century even local architects such as Ashworth, Fulford and Hayward, and Prynne, a Devonian by birth but practising in London, were designing towers in what

Fig. 41. Torquay, St John. Designed by G.E. Street and completed by his son, the French-style tower stands sentinel over the harbour.

Fig. 42. Exeter, St David. W.D. Carö's unusual and very effective design replaced a "pepper-pot" on a classical building of the early 19th-centuiry.

was supposed to be the "English" gothic style, regardless of the striking regional variations that existed in gothic England. So we find at *Exeter St Michael*, *Plymouth St Jude*, *Uffculme* and *Torquay Holy Trinity* towers and spires which if they were mediaeval could belong only in the East Midlands, and at *Torquay St Marychurch*, *Exmouth Holy Trinity* and *Teignmouth St Michael* towers with no particular regional character; Pearson built the tower for *Dartington*'s new church to the dimensions of the former (which still stands) but in an unmistakably Somerset style; so did Harbottle with *Exeter St Michael*, *Heavitree* and Hine & Odgers with *Plymouth St Matthias*. Other towers of this period seem to have no mediaeval pattern though their detailing may belong to the Gothic revival; *Ilfracombe SS Philip & James* (Hayward, 1856) with its curious pyramidal spire, and *Torquay All Saints, Babbacombe* (Butterfield, 1872) with its quirky, inelegant silhouette, show no clear ancestry in pre-Reformation England. And however impressive the tall tower of *Torquay St John* may be, its design must surely derive from the 16th-century "flamboyant" style of Northern France.

After the First World War we have a different concept in tower design, and little harking back to any earlier styles. *Exeter St Mark* (E.F. Hooper, 1934) is a good traditional clamp-buttressed tower in brick, as is *Paignton St Paul, Preston* (N.F. Cachemaille Day, 1939), but *Paignton St George, Goodrington* (E. Maufe, 1939) has a central tower which is entirely mid-20th century. *Exeter St James* (Gordon Jackson 1955) with its jolly little cupola and gold ball finials recalls the spirit of the 1951 Festival of Britain, but *Plymouth St Bartholomew* (Luxton 1958), *The Ascension, Crownhill* (Potter & Hare, 1956) with its butterfly roof and limestone cladding, *Exeter St Boniface, Whipton* (Charles Ware & Partners, 1953) and the stark concrete chimney of *Plymouth St Paul, Efford* (Pearn & Proctor, 1963) are all uncompromisingly "contemporary" (and all, we might add from personal experience, have extremely difficult and hazardous access to their upper stages). Several 20th-century churches have towers but little or no provision for putting anything in them: *Paignton St George, Goodrington*, and *Plymouth St Chad, Whitleigh* with large central towers have bells hung on brackets outside, and *Paignton St Paul, Preston* with a massive and very fine brick tower has no bell at all. Other new churches of this period were given neither towers nor bells – *Exeter St Paul, Burnthouse Lane* and *St Andrew, Alphington Road*, and *Tiverton St Andrew* for example – despite the requirement of Canon Law that every church should have one bell at least.

Over the county as a whole, Devon has more mediaeval towers than mediaeval churches, for a number of churches were entirely rebuilt during the 19th-century apart from the tower – *Bideford, Brampford Speke, Goodleigh, Hockworthy, Huish, Huntsham, Kilmington, Kingswear, Lympstone, Monkokehampton, Oakford, Otterton, Plymouth Stoke Damarel, Romansleigh, Stoke Canon, Teignmouth St James, Topsham*, and *West Buckland* are examples; there are many more where the church itself was largely but not entirely rebuilt and the tower was allowed to remain virtually unchanged.

Fig. 43. Crownhill, The Ascension. The porch-tower of 1956 with its butterfly roof was designed with a foundation for a bellframe, but so far has only one small bell.

Churches without Towers

Although the majority of tower-less Devon churches now have stone bellcotes, this may not always have been the case. *Satterleigh*, with its weatherboarded box turret on the west gable-end, is now unique in the county though the charming lead-covered bell-hutch at *Landcross*, reputed to date from the 1820s, may well have replaced one of the same type, but old prints, drawings and written descriptions (particularly Davidson's notes of the 1840s) make it clear that many similar turrets were replaced by bellcotes in Victorian rebuildings. *Cove* and *Petton* almost certainly had timber belfries, and *Creacombe, Bulkworthy* (described by Ellacombe as a "box turret") and *East Putford*, were probably similar. Among the post-Reformation town churches, *Exeter Holy Trinity* and *Plymouth St Catherine* were built with timber bell-turrets and *Tiverton St George*'s is in brick. Most of our bellcotes are placed over the west gable-end, but *Cowley* and *Westward Ho!* have theirs over the chancel arch, where they are almost completely inaccessible and could involve serious damage if a bell were to fall. *Gunn* chapel and *Plymouth, St Francis, Honicknowle* have bellcotes which are combined with chimney-stacks.

A particularly interesting case is at *Trusham*, where the church originally had a two-light bellcote on the west

Fig. 44. Satterleigh: several small Devon churches had timber "bell-hutches" like this, but many of them were replaced by stone bell-cotes in the 19th-century.

gable. During the early 15th century the south, west and north sides of a tower were built against the church's west wall, and the bellcote was incorporated into its east face; the two bell openings remain with the projecting stones which carried the bell bearings, there is a string-course across what is now the inner face of the tower, there are straight joints in the NE and SE corners, and the opening into the church at ground level is not an arch but a rather crude hole broken through the wall.

Although Devon can never vie with the glories of Somerset in tower design and decoration, it probably has more church towers than any other county in Britain, and one of the delights of travelling through its countryside is to see the towers standing boldly on hilltops like sentinels, nestling among trees and sometimes from a distance the only sign of a community, or looking over the rooftops like shepherds over their flocks; still better if one can hear the music which they give out – which brings us to Devon's bells.

Fig. 45. Landcross: here the timber bell-turret is slate-hung, with a lead roof.

2

BELLS IN DEVON: THE HISTORICAL PICTURE

The Historical Picture

BELLS WERE USED BY the church from the 4th century in Italy and other parts of Europe, and in Britain certainly from the 6th century onwards, and although some of the bells mentioned in history and legend may have been handbells like the surviving ancient examples in Ireland, there is no doubt that bells big enough to be hung in buildings were widely used during the Anglo-Saxon period; indeed, it was laid down by Canute that one of the qualifications for a *ceorl* to be "*thegn-right*" was possession of "church and kitchen, bell-house and burh-gate". By the time Devon's see was moved to Exeter in 1050 the new Cathedral had seven bells hung it its tower, and Bishop Leofric augmented them to thirteen. At this time it seems likely that most parish churches had their bells hung in gables or bell-cotes; Devon has no Saxon towers surviving, but in so well forested a county there may have been timber "bell-houses" which were replaced by stone towers when people could afford them.

The earliest bells in Devon were probably cast by founders from outside the county; for instance, the identity of the founders who cast the seven bells recorded as hanging in Leofric's cathedral in 1050 is a complete mystery, and there is no surviving bell known to have been cast by a Devon founder which can be dated earlier than the end of the 14th century; before that time any surviving bells can be attributed to founders from "up the country", or have no inscriptions to link them with known makers. Very early bells have a distinctive "long-waisted" shape; it was during the 14th century that bellfounders, seeking partial tones which produced a harmonious sound, developed a profile very like the one which we use today. However, from that time, when the Exeter foundry was established, until the beginning of the 19th century, the majority

Fig. 46. One of the two bells, c1300, at Petton. The absence of a parting line in the head shows that it was wax moulded. The cannons are decorated.

of the bells in our churches were cast in Devon or, latterly, not far across the Cornish border in Lezant or Stoke Climsland.

Most parish churches probably had only one or two bells until the great surge in tower-building and bellfounding in the 15th century, when the vast majority of our mediaeval towers were built or rebuilt, and when about 80 per cent of our surviving pre-Reformation bells were cast; after 1500 the evidence points to a decline in augmentations and a less thriving bellfounding industry. In 1552 the **Inventory of Church Goods** ordered by Edward VI's council gives us our first accurate list of Devon bells; the 480 churches and chapels listed possessed a total of 1725 bells, with another 13 in the Cathedral; 225 churches had four bells, the most usual number, 182 had rings of three, and 36 had rings of five. Two parishes are credited with eight bells each, but they (*Wolborough* and *Highweek*) each had their bells distributed between the parish church and a chapel-of-ease. Only three parishes are given as having no bells, but as one of them is Plymouth it is clear that some special circumstances must have prevailed in that case at least. Of the bells listed in the Inventory, at least 178 remain today.

There were also the bells of the **religious houses**, of course, the fate of which for the most part is obscure. A survey was made during the reign of Mary I, which gives us the number and value of the bells in each house, and from that we can guess as to their weight. The small community of St Nicholas Priory, Exeter, rather surprisingly led the way with 6 bells weighing about 73 cwt in total; the great Bemedictine abbey of Tavistock followed with six of 67 cwt, Barnstaple (5, 60 cwt), Newnham (5, 62 cwt), Plympton and Torre (5, 58 cwt), Ford (5, 51cwt), and Buckfast (5, 46 cwt): then rings of four at St John's Hospital, Exeter (46 cwt), Buckland (44 cwt), Dunkeswell (43 cwt), Canonsleigh (42 cwt), Hartland (39 cwt), Frithelstock (24 cwt), and Totnes (20 cwt). The Canonesses of Cornworthy had three (9 cwt), and Polsloe had two (9 cwt): the four Friaries, two in Exeter and two in Plymouth, had two bells apiece, bringing the total of bells in Devon to over 1800. In two cases, Ford (now in Somerset) and Buckfast, the bells were bought by the parishioners, but what then happened to them is not clear though there is a very beautiful mediaeval bell (cast by one of the Brasiers of Norwich) still hanging at Ford Abbey. Buckfastleigh parish church had only four bells in 1553, and there must have been some bells there before the Dissolution, so the five Abbey bells cannot simply have been rehung in the parish church as is often stated; perhaps they or the parish's existing bells were sold on. No doubt more of these bells were acquired by local parish churches, and this may account for some London-cast bells which appear in unlikely places; but the information, such as it is, suggests that most of the monastic bells were scrapped and converted into cash as soon as possible, to help pay for Henry VIII's French wars as Joyce Youings[6] suggests in her essay on the subject; the Polsloe Priory bells were acquired by Thomas Arundell, who sold them to Sir George Carew for £6 13s 4d, and the six bells of Tavistock Abbey, weighng 6,800lb, were bought by John Servington, a member of a local family, for £50 10s 6d. One example has been found of a small bell with monastic origins which can be established with some certainty; the Benedictine "alien" Priory at Modbury, a cell of the French Abbey of Dives, founded a chapel to serve a group of farms which it owned in neighbouring Ermington parish; the chapel has vanished, but one farm has a Chapel Field, and on the wall of its farmhouse hangs a small bell which is clearly of Continental origin and 15th or 16th-century date.

Prior to the Reformation, many English bells, and the majority of bells in Devon, bore nothing to identify their founder or date; the London founders often used marks to identify their work, like the shield and lozenge used by Joanna Hille at *Manaton* and the shields identifying William Chamberlain at *Marldon* and *Dartmouth St Clement*; William Dawe used a mark bearing the words *William Foundor me fecit*, and Thomas Geffries of Bristol used his initials. In Devon Robert Norton used a mark with his initials, as did the founder whose initials were I.T., but it is far from certain that they always used these marks on their bells, and until the end of the 16th century no other Exeter founder identified himself. Nor do we have any English bells which are dated until the very end of the 16th

---

6. Joyce Youings, *Devon Monastic Bells*, in "Devon Documents", ed Todd Gray, D & C Notes & Queries, 1996.

century. Founders have to be identified, if they can be, by their style of workmanship and the very scanty documentary clues in church accounts and legal documents. But after 1600 it became almost universally the custom for bellfounders to date their bells, and most of them placed at least their initials in their inscriptions; most of the bells which bear no founder'name or initials can be attributed to a known founder by their lettering, though we still have a few whose names elude us.

The Reformation naturally brought about an enormous change in bell ringing and in the bellfounding business; much of the ringing, which had punctuated and regulated the life of every parish, came to an end or was assigned a different purpose – the morrow-mass bell for instance being still rung in many places to mark the beginning of the secular working day.

The biggest threat to our bells came with the **Prayer Book Rebellion** which had simmered in Cornwall and finally came to the boil in Sampford Courtenay on Whit-monday 1549; the rebel host, summoned by the bells of the churches rung backwards, marched towards Exeter under the Banner of the Five Wounds, fought a battle at Crediton Barns, camped on St David's Down and laid siege to the City. Inside the walls the city bosses supported the new Prayer Book, the King and the Protector (or perhaps recognized theirs as the side on which their bread was buttered) but among the rank and file of the citizens the majority supported the rebels: what happened next is graphically described by John Hoker (who was a strong Protestant):

> *On a sonedaie beinge but two daies before the deliverie of the Citie aboute eighte of the clocke in the forenoone a companye of theime in everie quarter of the Citie havinge their consortes in a readynes to ioyne and serve wth theim if neede so requyred geyt up in the streetes walkinge wth theire weapons and in theire armure as to fight wth theire enemyes and crie oute: 'Come oute theis Heretiques and two penye booke men where be theye by Godds wondes and blood we will not be pynned in to serve theire turne: we will go oute and have in oure Neighbours they be honest good & godlie men', their pretence and meaninge being then that it if anye of the contraries syde had come out they would have quarrelled wth theim & so have taken occasion to sett upon hym and so raise a newe tumulte: but by the providence and goodnes of God it so fell oute that some beinge in theire howses and some at theire churches the Mayer and Maiestrates were first advertised hereof before the others heard anye thinge of the matter: And theye accordinge to theire wisdomes pacified the matter: and sent John Vincent, John Sharke and others the bell-wethers of this flok unto theire howses: Howbe it in the Southgate strete and at the Southegate there was a lytle sturre,wch being sone stopped there ensewed no hurte thereof other then a broken pate or two.*

A mainly mercenary army under Sir John Russell was sent to deal with the rising, and a major battle was fought at Fenny Bridges, about four miles west of Honiton, where, in the word of John Hoker:

> *The Lorde Russells companye folowed the chase neere three myles and himselffe then throughlie mynded and bente to have passed through the Cities: but one Joll his foole who was then in haste com from honyton and where he had herde as also by the waye as he came bells ringinge in sundrie pishe churches and supposinge the same to be a larome* (alarm) *came wth a foule mouthe to my Lorde and cryed that all the countrie behynde hym were up and commynge upon hym: . . . Whereupon they all retyred and retorned againe to Honyton.*

So the rebels lived to fight again – and be defeated – at Clyst St Mary, but it was a false alarm; everyone had forgotten that it was a Sunday and the bells were ringing for service: two of the bells which Joll would have heard are still ringing at *Buckerell*, one at Awliscombe and one, formerly at Awliscombe, is at Bishops Lydeard in Somerset. After the rising had been put down in a final battle, at Sampford Courtenay where it had all begun, the

Privy Council ordained that the parishes of Devon and Cornwall, as a punishment for their supposed involvement, should have their bells confiscated except for one in each church; the order is quoted as follows in Raven's *Church Bells of Dorset*:

> *From my Lord Protector & the counsell to my Lord Previe seall.*
>
> *After our right hartie commendacons to your lordshipp where the rebells of the country of Devonshyre and Cornwall have used the belles in every parishe as an instrument to sturr the multytude and call them together. Thinkyng good to have this occasyon of attempting the lyke hereafter to be taken frome them, and remebrying with all the lyke that by taking downe of them the Kyngs Matie maie have some commoditie towards his great charges that waye, we have thought good to pray yor good lordshipp to geve order for taken down the sayd bells in all the churches within these two counties, levying in every churche one bell, the lest of the ryng that nowe is in the same, which maie serve to call the paryshoners to the sermone and devyne servis; in the doyng hereof we require yor lordshipp to cause such moderacion to be used as the same may be done with as moche quietnes and as lytill force of the common people as maie be*
>
> *And thus we bid your lordshipp most hartely farewell*
>
> *From Westm^r this xijth of September 1549.*
>
> | | |
> |---|---|
> | A. Somerset | W. Sanct John |
> | T. Cant | W. Petre sy. |
> | A. North | |
> | B. Wotton | R. Sadler |

Commissioners were appointed to carry this out (in the process giving us the valuable Inventory), but in fact they seem to have used a great deal more "moderacion" than the Lord Protector may have expected, for the confiscation appears to have been effected in very few places outside Exeter – and even there the situation is unclear. In Exeter in many places the Inventory, taken three years after the defeat of the rising, lists two, three of four bells and then says that one is "left"; in the case of *St Mary Major*, *"left: one to serve the citie - xiiij^c the o^{y}r to the p^{y}she use"*. However, although at *St Mary Arches* the Commissioners' draft listed *"one warning bell which remaineth in the tower"*, two 15th-century bells still remain to this day, and in the rest of the county today rings containing two, three or even four pre-Reformation bells make it clear that the confiscation was never carried out, even with as much quietness and as little force as possible.[7] Perhaps the authorities realized that taking away their bells from the people of Devon could cause another insurrection. An entry in the Morebath accounts makes it clear what in fact happened: the clappers were in theory "confiscated", and had to be bought back by the parish.

> *The contentis of ye byll for byeing of ye clappers.*
>
> *Thys byll madyn ye xxvij day of June in ye v ere of our Soverant lord Edward ye vj by ye grace of God of Igland fransse & erland kyng defender of ye fayth & of ye churche of Igland and erland (in erthe) ye supreme hedd. Wytnyssyd y^t we John Courtnay esquyre & Edward Ford gentylman have resseuyd of John Norman & Thomas Myll & Edward Rumbelow xxvj^s & viij^d for ye bell clappers of Morebath w^t ye hole furneture apptaynyng un to ye said bellis to ye use of Sir Arture Chapman knyzth & John Chechester*

---

7 An exception may be St Thomas, Exeter, where the Inventory lists only one bell, and where the Vicar, Robert Walsh, a former Prior of Tavistock Abbey and a supporter of the rebels, had been hanged from the tower by Sir John Russell.

Esquyre to them gevyn by ye kyngis mageste hys letter patent. In wytnysse where of we have subscribid our name ye day & ye ere above wrytyn.
   By me John Courtnay
   By me Edward Ford
(and the Vicar adds)
   We gave Rumbelow x^s in ye byeng of them for hys fader in law ys sake.

The effect of the symbolic confiscation was to levy a fine – quite a heavy one – on the parishes of the area in which the rebellion had broken out and, incidentally, to reward some of the local gentry for their loyalty to the new regime, but there was a temporary limitation of ringing, as we learn from the *Woodbury* churchwardens' accounts, where there is a memorandum, *that the Comocyon was at Clyst at Lammas tyde thys same yere and then after the pishoners were comandyd to ring but one bell.* In 1552 they spent 12d *for mending off the bawders for the bellys to ryng againe when my Lady Mary was proclaymed Quene whych was the xxiii day off Julii*.

The century between the Reformation and the Civil War was a disturbed and insecure time for any religious institution, and the parish churches went through changes which must at the time have been almost unimaginable to Devon village people. The bells cast in the years immediately following the Reformation suggest that the trade was in some turmoil; there are bells by unknown and unidentifiable founders using patterns which occur nowhere else or patterns which must have been old and disused for many years; inscriptions which are deliberately meaningless or apparently coded; and only a very slow growth in business between the accession of Elizabeth I and that of Charles I, when the arrival of Thomas Pennington II in Exeter signals the beginning of a real revival as well as a major change in technique, as we shall see.

The Civil War saw a drop in bellfounding activity; it must have been a grim time of almost unimaginable insecurity and fear, but one bell at Trusham recalls a happy story from that time. John Stooke, a young lad who lived in Trusham, was walking home from work in Bovey Tracey on the evening when a troop of Parliamentarian cavalry surprised some Royalist officers in a house in Bovey. John Stooke heard the sound of a furiously galloping horse approaching behind him, and prudently hid in the ditch; as the horseman dashed past,

Fig. 47. Puddington tenor, an "alphabet" bell probably from the time of the Reformation.

Fig. 48. Eggesford 2nd: in 1652 John Pennington may have thought the seals of the local squire less risky than coins of Charles I.

he threw something away, and when he and his pursuers had gone John searched in the ditch and found it to be a bag of gold. He bought some land, and by hard work and good management died a rich man. His monument records his gifts to the poor in all the six parishes in which he had property, and he gave the 3rd bell to Trusham church: it is there still, and bears his name.[8]

The Commonwealth regime is often credited with more influence on everyday life than seems to have been the reality – some of the iconoclasm and desecration popularly attributed to "Oliver Cromwell" should be attributed to the time and agency of Thomas Cromwell a century earlier. Long before the inauguration of the Commonwealth the rood-lofts and most of the stained glass, all the images and most wall-paintings had been destroyed or defaced, and despite the fact that the Presbyterian and Independent religious leaders disapproved of bells, Devon people seem to have taken remarkably little notice of their disapproval; when the supporters of the Parliament gained the ascendancy in Exeter in December 1642, we are told that "Parliament, (. . . presumably acting at the request of its local adherents) authorized the mayor and deputy lieutenants to seize the cathedral bells and melt them down for ammunition",[9] but this certainly never happened: on the contrary, one of the cathedral bells was recast in 1658, at a time when the Commonwealth was still in power and the cathedral was divided by a brick wall, the Presbyterians having "East Peter's" and the Independents "West Peter's": who paid for the recasting seems to be a mystery. Several parish church guide-books make special mention of a bell which was cast during the Commonwealth, but in fact Commonwealth bells are not very uncommon; at least 27 in Devon are either existing or documented, and one of our earliest surviving complete rings of four, at *St Mary Steps, Exeter*, was cast during that time: John Pennington of Exeter who often used coin-impression to decorate his bells substituted seal-impressions on his bells at

---

8. There are other versions of this story; one may be found in *Some traditions concerning the brief visit of Cromwell & Fairfax to BoveyTracey & its neighbourhood in 1646, Devonshire Association Transactions,* Vol. 39, 1907, by the Rev. W.H. Thornton.

9. Mark Stoyle, *From Deliverance to Destruction,* University of Exeter, 1996, p.71.

Eggesford and *Holcombe Burnell*, but *Spreyton* 5/6 (1650) and *Thurlestone* tenor (1654) bear impressions of coins of Charles I. Nevertheless, there was a great decline in bellfounding (and probably in bellringing, though the evidence is lacking through the scarcity of parish accounts), and the cathedral records suggests that seventeen years after the restoration of the King to his throne and the Dean & Chapter to their cathedral the bells were still in dire need of restoration.

The 18th century saw bellfounding's second boom, this time through a great surge of enthusiasm for bell ringing. The boom in the 15th century had been stimulated by a rise in economic prosperity and probably of religious zeal which expressed itself in the building and furnishing of church towers: the second was doubtless also linked with economic prosperity – particularly in the wool and cloth trade – but probably less with religious zeal, although the 18th century church was no doubt less stagnant that later writers liked to portray it, and the Church's decline was probably worse in the early 19th century than in the 18th.[10] Improvements in bellhanging also encouraged the boom: bells could now be controlled at either end of their swing thanks to the invention of "sally-way" hanging, and the bellfounders were casting shorter bells which were easier to control. It was the popularity of ringing as a recreation and as an expression of community life in the Georgian period which led to the augmentation and recasting of so many of our rings of bells in Devon. The wardens and vestries in villages and small towns, and corporations of the cities, were willing to pay for more ringing days in the year, and technical developments in bell hanging made it possible to change the order of the bells and strike them accurately, so encouraging bands of ringers to compete against one another. Towards the end of the 18th century, however, churchwardens began to regret their generosity to their ringers and sought to cut down paid ringing.

The first thirty years of the 19th century were some of the worst in the Church of England's history; Rural Deans reported badly-maintained and even ruinous churches, and the wars against France had caused a sharp decline in bellfounding activity, but as the 19th century went on, the Evangelical and Tractarian movements created a great burst of activity in the Church, aided by the arrival in the parishes of a generation of clergymen who were better connected, better educated, better off, and more professionally zealous than the church had seen for a long time – perhaps ever. The Victorian era saw scores of new churches built in Devon and hundreds restored – often it is true in a style which is unpopular today – and in many cases saved from complete collapse. The motivation for ringing was often too "secular" to suit the new-style clergy, but it continued to be a communal activity and a popular one, and as a result the augmentations and recastings continued almost unabated, though by the middle of the century the day of the local foundries was over and the railways were carrying bells cheaply and easily to and fro between Devon parishes and London, Oxford, Loughborough or Bristol, where the foundries, fewer in number but larger than ever before, were taking advantage of new technical developments in both casting and hanging.

The era between the two World Wars saw another boom in activity while the number of foundries dwindled even further; since World War II the British foundries have been reduced to two, but at the same time there has been a marked and welcome increase in the number of small bellhanging enterprises and also of do-it-yourself restoration by local groups of ringers. The most recent development has been the arrival of foreign foundries in the market, led by Eisbouts of Asten in the Netherlands.

Bell Inscriptions

With the lost wax technique, placing an inscription or decoration on a bell was a simple matter, and most of the earliest known bells are inscribed, normally with raised letters, though we have seen some early Italian bells which

---

10. A strong argument for revising the popular view of the 18th-century church is made in Arthur Warne, *Church and Society in Eighteenth century Devon,* David & Charles, 1969.

were inscribed by incising a wax or tallow pattern. The technique of placing these inscriptions and decorations on a bell will be dealt with when we come to casting techniques, but the content of inscriptions is more a historical subject than a technological one.

Fig. 49. Tresmere treble. The word "bothe" is spelt with the letter *thorn*.

Throughout western Europe Latin was the language of literacy in general before about 1400, and of the Church until the Reformation; even after the Reformation it was still the language of scholarship: so before the Reformation bell inscriptions in English are rare, and indeed Latin remained quite common until the end of the 19th century – in later years particularly, perhaps, when a Vicar felt like showing off his classical erudition. Devon churches have no examples of English inscriptions on pre-Reformation bells, but there is one very fine Exeter foundry bell in Somerset at Brompton Ralph [59], with the inscription: GABRIEL IS MI NAME IN ME IE SHOLLE FINDE NO BLAME and we may here take the opportunity to mention the two remarkable 14th-century bells belonging to Tresmere in Cornwall but now in Devon at the *Okehampton Museum of Dartmoor Life*. They are inscribed WE BEUT IMAKID BOYE FOR TO WAKIE ELEANORE FOR TO KACHE GAME and HAC DO BI MINE REDE YENK ON HVVS SOVLE AND SO WAS HIS NAME, (*We were both made to wake Eleanor to catch game: but do by my advice think on Hugh's soul, and so was his name*) using a Lombardic alphabet which (perhaps uniquely) included the Saxon letter *thorn*, (represented above by a Y), and so apparently was designed for inscriptions in English, and which has been found on only one other bell, in Somerset (by contrast, one may note that the Exeter Lombardic founder used an "I" in "MI", so evidently his alphabet was designed specifically for Latin). Devon's earliest inscribed bells, at *Petersmarland* and *Combpyne* and formerly at *Brentor St Michael de Rupe*, carry the rhyming hexameters known as "Leonines"; both these bells are probably by London founders, and the earliest Exeter inscriptions are simple invocations of God or the saints, with the exceptions of the Brompton Ralph bell and Dorchester Abbey, Oxon, 7/8, which has PETRE TVIS APERI DA PAVLE TVIS MISERERI, probably composed by a member of the community there. Under Robert Norton in about 1430, the Exeter foundry adopted a set of "stock" Leonine inscriptions, as we shall see, but quite a high proportion of its bells still carried invocations of the "... *ora pro nobis*" type. In some cases these pre-Reformation inscriptions assigned a name to a bell, as at *Exeter, St Petrock,* "Iohannes est nomen eius", (*His name is John*) and the favourite stock inscription, "Est michi collatum ihc istud nomen amatum", (*To me is given that beloved name, Jesus*). A bell by William Dawe of London at *Abbotsham* has "IN MVLTIS ANNIS RESONAT CAMPANA IOHANNIS (*For many years may John's bell sound*); at *Dartmouth St Clement* William Chamberlain named one of his bells for St Augustine, and London bells at *Brushford* and *Wolborough* bear a well-known Leonine naming them after St Katherine, who was a popular saint in bell invocations because of her association with dispelling thunder and lightning. The former bell at *Brentor*, too was named "the cock", with its inscription, GALLVS VOCO EGO SUPER OMNIA SONO (*I am named the cock; I sound above all*).

Latin did not entirely disappear at the Reformation, but with very few exceptions inscriptions whether Latin or English become notably Reformed in style. Early bells by the Birdalls often have meaningless inscriptions as we have mentioned; some simply record the names of donors or churchwardens, and others have Puritan-inspired mottoes such as PRAYSE NOT THY SELF and PRAYSE GOD. This theme was taken up by the Penningtons with their favourite, SOLI DEO DETVR GLORIA (*Be glory given to God alone*). However, pre-Reformation inscriptions which were deemed to the doctrinally innocuous were still sometimes used, as at Yeovil in 1626, when Thomas Pennington II reproduced the mediaeval inscription on the 9th, IN MVLTIS ANNIS RESONET

Fig. 50. Widecombe 5th, for which young John Hamlyn collected money from the "young men and mayds" in 1632.

CAMPANA IOHANNIS, and at *Iddesleigh* and *Cheldon* where he (rather inaccurately) used FILI DEI MISERERE MEI (*Son of God have mercy on me*). More remarkable is *Molland* 5/6 by Thomas Wroth, which is inscribed SANTIE SANCTE NICHOLIA ORA PRO NOBIS, together with the names of the Vicar and one churchwarden, and the arms of the Courtenay family, the Molland branch of which were Roman Catholic recusants. Increasingly, though, inscriptions in the 17th and 18th centuries consist of the names of the Churchwardens, donors, and sometimes the incumbent, with the founder's name or initials. The long and elaborate Latin inscriptions on *Payhembury* 1/6 and 2/6, 1635 and 1621, are exceptional and seem to imply that the bells in question were the property of the local gentry, and the inscription on *Widecombe-in-the-Moor* 5/8 records that it was subscribed to by the young people of the parish in 1632. After the Reformation we get, for the first time, the date of casting recorded on bells; this became almost invariable, and has remained so to the present day, along with the name or initials of the founder.

Most of our 18th-century bells continue the style of the previous century, with the names of the churchwardens and, less often, the incumbent who at this period was far less concerned with the material affairs of the church than were the wardens. However, a number of mottoes also became fashionable – variants on I CALL THE QUICK TO CHURCH, THE DEAD TO GRAVE, RELIGION DEATH AND PLEASURE MAKE ME RING, (or the Latin version, NOS RESONARE IUBENT PIETAS MORS ATQUE VOLUPTAS) or I TO THE CHURCH THE LIVING CALL AND TO THE GRAVE I SUMMON ALL, on a tenor, and I CALL YE TO FOLLOW ME or WHEN I CALL FOLLOW ME ALL on a treble. COME LET US RING FOR CHURCH AND KING, PEACE AND GOOD NEIGHBOURHOOD, GOD BLESS THE CHURCH and PROSPERITY TO THIS PARISH were popular, the latter sometimes given a parochial slant as in GOD PRESERVE THE KING AND PROSPER THE TRADE OF NORTHAM or FLOREAT BISHOPS MORCHARD. Some founders adopted sets of inscriptions for their bells, and there is reason to believe that the Rudhalls of Gloucester sometimes cast bells to be sold "off the shelf", leaving one – usually the 5th of a six or the 4th of a five – to be cast with the names of the churchwardens on it; *Brixton* may be an example. John Stadler at *Chivelstone* apparently used a rhyming set of inscriptions, though we only have one surviving and Ellacombe's record of two others may be incomplete; they were, MUSIC IS NOT WORTH A GROAT (and probably another line not recorded) on the treble, BUT YET THE MUSIC WONT AGREE UNLESS TIS SECONDED BY ME on the 2nd, and ending with YET ALL IS A CONFUSED NOISE WITHOUT MY LAST COMMANDING VOICE on the tenor. There do not seem to be any other examples of this set, and it is a pity that the complete text has been lost. The Whitechapel Foundry had a favourite set of this kind, which Pack & Chapman used at *Newton Abbot* –

1	ALTHO I AM BUT LIGHT AND SMALL I WILL BE HEARD ABOVE YOU ALL
2	IF YOU HAVE A IUDICIOUS EAR YOULL OWN MY VOICE IS SWEET & CLEAR
3	YE PEOPLE ALL WHO HER ME RING BE FAITHFUL TO YOUR GOD & KING
4	WHILE THUS WE IOIN IN CHEARFUL SOUND MAY LOVE & LOYALTY ABOUND
5	OUR VOICES SHALL WITH IOYFUL SOUND MAKE HILLS & VALLEYS ECHO ROUND
6	YE RINGERS ALL THAT PRIZE YOUR HEALTH & HAPPINESS BE SOBER MERRY WISE AND YOULL THE SAME POSSESS.

Founders would sometimes give themselves a "puff" in their inscriptions, even as early as the Exeter foundry's "Me melior vere non est campana sub ere" (*Truly beneath the sky there is no better bell than I*). Pack & Chapman did this in the second motto of their set; WHEN YOU ME RING I'LL SWEETLY SING, and I MEAN TO MAKE IT UNDERSTOOD THAT THO' I'M LITTLE YET I'M GOOD, versions of which were used by several founders; Thomas Wroth II at *Goodleigh* claimed I AM LITTLE SMART AND SMALL, LUCK MADE ME CONCORD TO ALL – which anyone familiar with Wroth's work will recognize as being uncharacteristically honest. By the time the Bilbies arrived in Devon they had largely given up their habit of "knocking" the opposition in their bell inscriptions, but Thomas I still gave us, on *Cullompton* tenor, BILBIE THE FOUNDER, BUSH THE HANGER, HEATHFIELD'S THE MAN WHO RINGS THE TENOR, and on *Kenton* 5th, BILBIE THE FOUNDER, RUGG THE HANGER, CARTER THE SMITH & TREBLE RINGER. *Hemyock* 5th of 1821, by Pannell, has the rather curious motto TRUE HEARTS AND SOUND BOTTOMS.

As we have seen, a number of bells, and several whole rings of bells, were from the earliest times given by

Fig. 51. Kenton 5th by Thomas Bilbie I, 1747, commemorating "Carter the smith & treble ringer".

wealthy individuals or bodies; the Cathedral perpetuates the names of Bishops Grandison, Peter Courtenay, Stafford, Fox and Oldham, and Deans Cobthrone and Earle in its bells, and several of them bear the legend RENOVAT EX IMPENSIS DECANI ET CAPITOLI (recast at the expense of the Dean and Chapter). The majority of the inscriptions recording these benefactors belong to the 18th and 19th centuries, but *Plympton St Mary* Tenor, 1614, calls "Mr Marie Strode" the "founder of this bell", though whether the title should have been "Mrs", or "Marie" should have been "Maire" (Mayor) is not clear: the gift in 1684 of *Trusham* 3/6 by John Stooke was part of a wonderfully romantic story as we have seen. The names of donors on Devon bells reads like a *Burke's Landed Gentry* of the county; Yonge and Harris at *Ashburton*, Ilbert at *West Alvington*, Chichester in several North Devon towers, Rolle, Fortescue, Davie, Bampfylde, Woolcombe, Drake, Courtenay – and we have the arms of Ferrers, Fortescue, Yarde, Harris, Yonge, Chichester, Drake, Crymes, Aishford and Huyshe as well. These benefactors were usually the local landowners, but at *Ashburton* it was the borough's Members of Parliament who gave the bells. One of the most recent examples is at *Marldon*, where the new treble was donated by Commander Walter Raleigh Gilbert and members of the Gilbert family all over the world, and decorated with the family crest and motto. At *Chittlehampton* Samuel Rolle, Esq. is described simply as A GOOD BENEFACTOR, but at *Bradstone* the inscription on the 3rd proclaims, SQUIRE ARUNDELL THE GREAT OUR WHOLE EXPENSE DID RAISE, NOR SHALL OUR TONGUES ABATE TO CELEBRATE HIS PRAISE. John Taylor of Buckland Brewer did rather overestimate his poetical talent; at *Hartland*, 1826, he gave us:

> THE NAMES OF DENNIS HEARD CHOPE & ROWE: WITH US WILL NEVER DIE
> THEY SAVED OUR LIVES NOT ONLY SO: BUT BADE US MULTIPLY.

And at *Halwill*, 1829:

> HAMS DURRENT AND SOBY URGD OUR PLEA
> AND TOWNSMEN JOIND THEIR GENEROUS FEE
> OR READER WE HAD CHIMED OUR LAST
> BUT THANKS TO THEM WE WERE RECAST

but surely the worst example of Taylor versification is at *Pilton*:

RECAST BY JOHN TAYLOR & SON
WHO THE BEST PRIZE FOR CHURCH BELLS WON
AT THE GREAT EX-HI-BI-TI-ON
IN LONDON 1 8 5 AND 1

Latin never disappeared entirely from bell inscriptions; it was still the language of scholarship until the 19th century, and perhaps gave educated gentry and clergy the chance of showing off their erudition. Indeed some bellfounders may have had some Latin; the 17-year-old Thomas Pennington III scribbled some Latin in the register of St Paul's Exeter when his father was churchwarden, and the Evanses used sets of Latin mottoes on the bells of *Chulmleigh* and *Cruwys Morchard*. During the 19th century Latin inscriptions increase noticeably, due partly to the influx of clergy who were better educated (and possibly more aloof from their parishioners) than their predecessors, and partly to a diminishing suspicion of all things Roman: *Arlington, Torquay, All Saints' Babbacombe* and *Sowton* have good examples of sets of Latin mottoes. During this period the inscriptions also become notably more "religious" in tone, and there is a fashion in some quarters for lettering in mediaeval style, using Lombardic as at *Revelstoke* or black-letter as at *Sowton*. There is also a tendency for the inscriptions of recast bells to be reproduced, sometimes in facsimile towards the end of the century and more often in the 20th.

The commemoration of members of the Ilbert family at *West Alvington* is touching because it is so unusual in the late 18th century – but towards the end of the 19th century it became much commoner for bells to be given in memory of the dead, and commemorative inscriptions are very frequent today. It also becomes more popular for the ringers' names to be inscribed on a bell, especially if they gave it; this can be seen at *Newton St Cyres* and *Gittisham*.

3
CASTING BELLS

Bellfounding Techniques

THE EARLIEST CHURCH BELLS were cast by the *cire perdu* technique, one of the oldest methods of casting metal. It involves making a model of the required object in wax, covering it in a mixture of clay and other materials, and baking it so that the wax melts and runs out to leave a void into which the metal can be poured. It is still the method used for most bronze castings, and can produce very fine detail indeed in the final product. The earliest bells in the county, at *Haccombe, Bulkworthy* and *Petton*, are all comparatively small and all were moulded in wax or tallow; the evidence for this is the absence of a parting-line between the cope and the head. All of them are uninscribed. The technique is the one described by Theophilus in the 10th century and is illustrated in the Bellfounders' Window at York Minster; it involved mounting a wooden core so that it could be turned, probably horizontally as in a lathe for a small bell, laying over it strips of wax rolled out to the required thickness of the bell, and shaping it with a tool while the core was revolved. This would be satisfactory enough for small bells, but when large bells had to be cast the quantities of wax or tallow would have been extravagant and there would be no easy way of controlling the thickness of the wax model, which is of course critical in determining the pitch of the bell. (Theophilus gives a formula for casting an octave set of bells by weighing out the wax in proportion for each bell; this leads me to agree with the late Douglas Hughes of the Whitechapel Foundry, who was convinced that Theophilus had indeed himself cast a bell, but equally had never cast a ring of eight.) The solution to both these problems was found in the use of a clay model which was shaped with a template or *strickle* mounted on a spindle passing through the centre of the core which was set upright and made of sand, brick or stone: this made it possible to control the thickness of the bell at every part of its profile.

The Archaeological Record

Archaeological work on foundry sites has cast some useful light on early bell-founding technology. Probably the earliest site so far discovered in Devon, and the first to be excavated, was in the base of the tower of the former 12th-century church of *St Mary Major, Exeter*, the first of several sites excavated and written up in great detail by the Exeter Archaeological Field Unit. Here the pit had been dug through Roman remains including a street surface. Many fragments of the mould were recovered from the back-filling of the pit, but none showed any signs of inscription or moulding-wires; there were also fragments of a more friable mixture which appeared to have been from the clay model, and rough, heavily burnt loam which probably came from the lining of the furnace. Unlike later examples the closing stop between the core and the cope was made by making an annular trough at the base of the core into which the base of the cope fitted, and the mould was built over a trench in which a fire had been lit to bake it.

The site of the mediaeval Exeter foundry in Guinea Street produced very little of interest; the ground had been worked over so many times that it consisted simply of a mass of broken loam, but the Birdall foundry in Albany Street and the Pennington site in Paul Street disclosed mould-bases built on brick and stone footings, the soil inside

Fig. 52. The bell-casting pit under the tower of St Mary Major, Exeter, probably 12th century.

Fig. 53. The furnace of the Paul St foundry site, used by the Exeter Penningtons.

the footings coloured a deep red and showing a central hole for the peg which carried the bottom pivot of the strickle. None of these sites produced any pieces of bell inscriptions, but the Birdall site, to our delight, produced part of the mould for a skillet-handle inscribed "..N BIRDALL". The Paul Street excavation also uncovered the fire-box of a furnace which had evidently been in use for a number of years as its brick lining had been renewed more than once. There must be a great many similar remains in churchyards and elsewhere around the county where bells have been cast, some of which may not have been destroyed for grave-digging; the spot still known as "Bell-pit" in *Buckerell* parish, where one assumes the old ring of three was cast in the 15th century, has since been used successively as a marl-pit and a rubbish-dump, and its name is probably its main interest.

The cathedral accounts of 1372 describe the casting of a new bell and the recasting of another by Thomas Karoun, who was paid for his labour only, so that all the materials and other labour (including a man to *turn the forma of the bell*) is itemized in the account. The process is described in "*Casting a Bell for Exeter Cathedral, 1372*" in the *Transactions of the Devonshire Association*, 1967, and clearly involved the use of a clay model. Church-wardens' accounts in a number of Devon parishes combine to fill out the picture which is outlined there, and the foundries at Villedieu-les-Pöeles and at Orleans still use very similar methods today.

Casting a Bell

When a bell was cast on site, as was very often the case before the 18th century, much of the detail of the process can be discovered from church accounts. First of all, a building had to be erected or borrowed for the temporary foundry. The *bell house*, or *shade* as the *Buckfastleigh* wardens called it, was most often built of posts and thatched with reed or furze: at *Ashwater* for instance in 1671 the bell house was thatched and the walls were planked or weatherboarded with *rige*, which were softwood planks imported from Riga in the Baltic [App.II:9]; at *South Milton*, however, the churchwardens in 1725 undertook to allow Christopher Pennington the use of a house *already built in the churchyard* [App.II:14]; at *Braunton* the Evanses in 1717 rented the Church House, now the Museum, and at *Cullompton* in 1749 Thomas Bilbie used part of the almshouse [App.II:16]: a bell was cast in the workhouse garden at *Plymouth* in 1731, and Bilbie used the same site in 1748. As we have seen, at *St Mary Major, Exeter*, a bell was cast inside the tower, possibly before the latter was completed.

Bells were cast in pits, so that the metal could flow into the mould by gravity and so that the mould could be surrounded by rammed earth, so the digging of the pit was the next task; it was the usual practice for the mould to be made in the pit, in which case a beam was fastened across it for the top bearing of the strickle and for hoisting the outer mould or *cope*. The *core* (inner mould) and cope were formed from *loam*, a mixture of clay and horse-dung, the same material which is used today; at *Buckfastleigh*, 1743, Ambrose Gooding the bellfounder and a Mr Wade went to Ranscombs *to View the Clay* and *expenc'd* ninepence, while 3 shillings was paid, perhaps to children, *for gathering of horse dung*: often a fibrous material was mixed in with the loam; this was certainly very often hemp which is mentioned in the 1372 cathedral account and is used today at the Bollée foundry in Orleans. The core was usually built on a stone footing with a hollow centring of brick or stone which was covered with successive layers of loam, each air-dried. The final shape was formed with the *strickle*, a board mounted on a spindle to rotate around the core, its inner edge shaped to the inside profile of the bell; this is described as *formam campane* in the Exeter 1372 account, and *a bord for ye Moulds* at Goodleigh 1684 [App.II:8]. At St Mary Major, probably in the 12th century, the mould was built over a stone-lined trench, and the excavation showed that the loam had probably been laid over a cone of sand, which had been removed once the loam had dried; the trench was then lined with clay – finger-marks showing clearly that this had been applied after the mould was completed – and then a charcoal fire lit in the trench to bake the mould. In the Birdall and Pennington foundries the moulds were built on circular footings of stones or bricks with gaps to allow air to pass through.

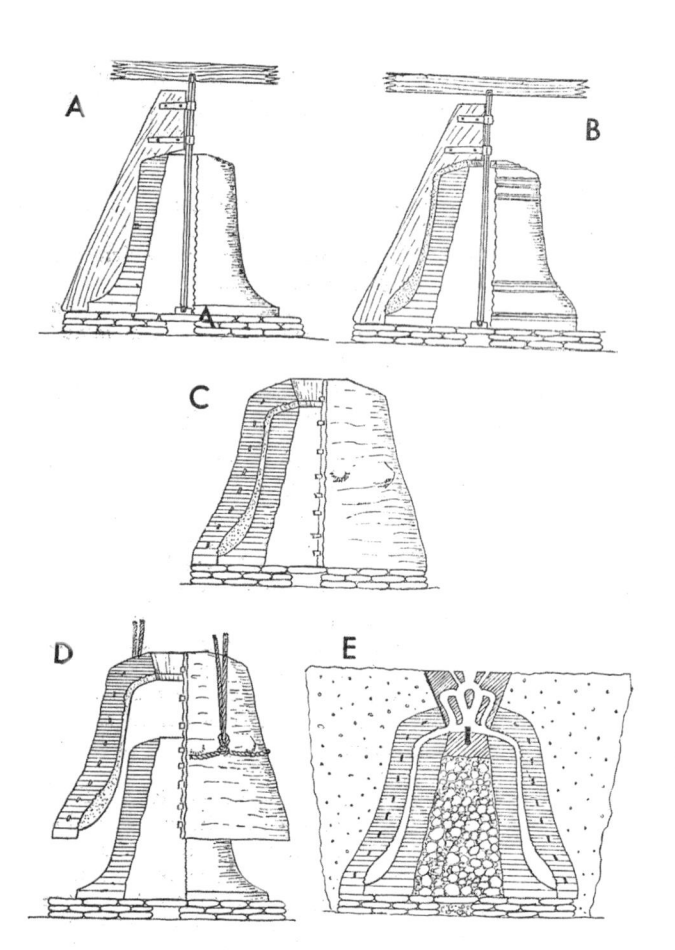

FIG. 1. A, *Strickling the Core*. B, *Strickling the Model*. C, *Putting on the Cope*. D, *Lifting off the Cope and Model*. E, *Ready for Pouring*

Fig. 54. Moulding a bell, using a false clay pattern.

Once the core had been made and dried, it was covered with grease or tallow and then a pattern bell was laid over it made from a more friable clay mixture: the strickle was cut back to the outer profile of the bell, and notches made in it for the *moulding-wires* on the head, above and below the inscription-band, and above and below the soundbow. The earliest Exeter bells show the raised flat band above the inscription-band (and occasionally also below it) which is characteristic of 14th and early 15th-century bells from the London foundries; later the standard wire-patterns sometimes have a concave band between wires, but the flat raised band disappears in the middle of the 15th century (to be revived briefly at the end of the 16th). During the 15th century, after Robert Norton and up to the death of Robert Russell in 1502, the bells from the Exeter foundry show a number of standard patterns of moulding-wires which must have been made using a tool of some kind; as bells with the same pattern of wires can be of different sizes, they cannot simply have been moulded with the same strickle, and it seems probable that the founders had a set of swages with which the notches in the strickle were made. Many bells of the mid-16th century have moulding-wires which were obviously not strickled but formed by hand, sometimes very crudely.

One entry in the Exeter 1372 account is for *wax for the letters of the bell*, and wax often figures in other accounts; at this time virtually all inscriptions and decorations on bells were applied in the form of wax paterae which were cast in a "negative" pattern and stuck on to the clay model: the technique is still used today by the Continental foundries, and produces extremely fine detail in the final casting. When the Plymouth bells were recast by Lawrence Wright in 1585, one pound and three quarters of wax was used *to make the townes armes in the bells*; the arms on the bells at *Totnes* and *Ashburton* were no doubt made in this way.

The pattern was then covered, first with a thin slurry of loam – at the Orleans foundry this is applied with a goose's wing – then with successive layers to make the cope, with iron or wooden hoops to strengthen it. The clay and horse dung were usually obtainable nearby, but transport was involved, and quantities could be considerable; Christopher Pennington, casting one bell for *South Milton*, required six *seams* (pack-horse pannier-loads) each of clay and horse dung, a hundredweight of hay, a truss of straw and three knitches of reed for his mould and pattern. [App.II:11] He also demanded four gallons of beer lees – *dregs* are included in the items at *Braunton* [App.II:4], 1594, and *Goodleigh*, 1684 – but their purpose is a mystery. Other materials used in the moulds were flock (*Buckfastleigh* 1743), hair, hay, hemp and rope.

When the cope was completed, the whole assembly was baked by lighting a charcoal fire inside it for some days; the loam had to be dried very carefully, but not fired, so the heat was carefully controlled. The wax was melted out by the heat and left the lettering and decoration imprinted in the surface of the cope. Once completely dried the cope was lifted off and the pattern broken out: the original purpose of the moulding-wires was to key the pattern into the cope and reduce the risk of its breaking up and damaging the mould as the cope was lifted, but moulding-wires became such a familiar feature of a bell's appearance that they are still used today even though the method used by British foundries has no practical need for them.

Before about 1300 the patterns for small bells were moulded in tallow or wax, and the bell and its head and cannons were all moulded together, so these bells, for example the two at *Petton*, show no parting-line between the cope and the head. On all later bells until the late 19th-century the head of the bell was moulded separately. The *argent* and *cannons* were cast individually in wax in piece-moulds – the parting-line is usually visible on the sides of the cannons – and assembled on a board, with rods of wax fitted to the top of the argent to form the "runner" through which the metal would be poured and the "risers" for the gas to escape. This pattern was invested with loam and baked separately; the wax could be recovered, so does not appear in the accounts. The same technique can be seen in use today at Villedieu and Orleans, where some of the cannon patterns are highly decorative.

Before the cope was replaced on the core the iron crown-staple for the clapper was prepared – one for *Woolfardisworthy East* in 1728 was made by Lewis Pridham the Sandford clockmaker; the middle of the core was filled with well-rammed earth, and the staple fitted into the top of it with the roots projecting. Then the cope could be lowered into place and the head was fitted into the top of it. There were bulges at the base of the argent to cover the roots of the crown-staple, so it was vital to fit it at the right alignment, and the cross scratched in the head-mould of many 15th-century Exeter bells may have been for this purpose.

The whole mould was then buried in its pit and the earth rammed well around it – *pd laborers to rame earth about the mooles* (*Plymouth*, 1595, App.II:5) – until only the runner and risers were visible in the ground. A clay-lined gutter was made from the plug-hole of the furnace to the runner.

The furnace might be inside the bell-house or adjoining it; thatching the furnace is sometimes a separate item. It was a reverberatory furnace (in which the heat from the fire was directed by the flue downwards over the bowl containing the metal) with a fire-box of brick and stone and iron bars for the grate which usually had to be hired and which were wasted by the heat; *Plymouth* 1595 had *morestones for the bottom and mouth of the furnice*. The Pennington furnace in Paul Street, Exeter had stone around the opening and had been lined, and later relined, with brick. The bowl of the furnace was lined with clay or loam, and the plug-hole closed with a clay plug, inserted from inside the bowl.

The metal was more often than not obtained from the old bells, but when a new bell had to be cast the metal would have to be bought in. Breaking up the old bells is sometimes mentioned in the accounts, and at *Braunton*, 1593 and at *Goodleigh*, 1684, a broken sledge-hammer had to be paid for [App.II:8]. At *Buckfastleigh* the metal was *inclos'd in a room* in the church, which may have been necessary because Holne bells were being recast there at the same time. Additional tin was needed to replace the tin which would vaporize when the scrap bell-metal was melted. In some cases extra metal was given; at *Braunton*, 1591, a *great crock* was bought at Annery for 21 shillings; a boat was hired for 3d to bring it to Vilata (Vellator), and a man and two horses brought it the rest of the way for 4d: *Crediton* also acquired a *great brasse crock weying six score pound* from Mr John Northcott for recasting their third bell. When *Plymouth* bells were recast in 1595, Sir Francis Drake and Sir John Hawkins gave a broken piece of ordnance; it must have been in the hold of a ship as ballast, or possibly even on the bed of the harbour, because *rommagenge & bringing it to shoare* cost 6s 8d. The Plymouth metal also included small bells given or sold to the parish, some brass *bases* which included some iron, and *shruff*, which was scrap brass.

There are several items in these accounts which are hard to account for or even to identify – we have already noticed beer lees at *South Milton* and elsewhere. Ashes, sometimes lime ashes or *comers ashes*, appear in several places and may have been used with grease to make a parting agent on the moulds; *rasome* is presumably resin or rosin; *drawsens for the bellfounder* (*Braunton*) might be material or refreshment; but what were *collens* (*Braunton*) and *bolmet* (*Ashwater*), and what was the purpose of turpentine and frankincense at *Braunton*? One frequently mentioned item was *tin glass* (bismuth) which was presumably added to the metal, but very often was paid for separately by the parish. It was used in foundry work to enable finer detail in the casting to be obtained, and may have been an "optional extra".

The furnaces were wood-fired, and *hard wood* is often specified, and needed cleaving; at *Ashwater* and *Buckfastleigh* it was stored in the church to keep it dry; at Buckfastleigh they used furze to light the furnace. It is seldom possible to calculate just how much wood was needed, as doubtless much if not all of it was often given; it is not mentioned in the *South Milton* [App.II:14] contract, and sometimes only the transport of wood is included. Furnaces seem to have relied on natural draught, though in the 1372 Exeter casting it was necessary to borrow bellows to finish melting the metal; the entry *in follibus conductis ad [fusione campane] complendam* (for bellows brought to complete the casting of the bell) may hide the record of a stressful half-hour for the founder.

There is a tradition in many places, certainly all over Europe and possibly all over the world, that certain bells sound exceptionally good because precious metal was added to them in the casting – a tradition which persists despite modern bellfounders' assertion that gold or silver, if present in enough quantity to make any difference, would spoil a bell's tone, not improve it. I have no doubt that early bellfounders knew by experiment that this was true, so why is the story still circulating – and is it connected with the impressions of coins and medals which so often were used to embellish bells from the 15th century onwards?

There is a story told about *Belstone* bells, that when they were being recast – presumably in 1761 by Fitzantony Pennington – the founder put the word about that silver would give the bells a specially fine tone. The villagers accordingly collected coins, spoons and shoe-buckles to add to the metal, but when the day for the casting came round, and Fitzantony announced that no outsiders were to be allowed to witness it, the Belstone people became suspicious: when the bells had been cast they came in a body, turned out Fitzantony's pockets, and found their silverware still there. Could the bellfounders have had their own reasons for perpetuating the myth of the *silver-toned bells*, could the coin-impressions have been partly intended (in the words of Poo-Bah) "to add verisimilitude to an otherwise bald and unconvincing narrative"?

The traditional method of testing the heat of the metal was to thrust an ash pole into it; if the temperature was correct, the pole would squeal: at the Bollée foundry at Orleans they claim also that gas from the burning wood helps to mix the metal. At the right moment the stopper of the bowl was driven in with an iron bar, and the metal would run down clay-lined gutters to the runners of the moulds, the metal being diverted with iron paddles to fill each mould in turn, and the dross skimmed off as it ran.

This moment had an important effect on a completely different industry, and one which was to change the landscape of the South West for ever. In the 1730s, so his memoirs recall, the Plymouth apothecary William Cookworthy visited a bellfounder working in Fowey with medicines for "bellfounder's ague". There he saw being used in preparing the moulds a whitish material which when fired looked like porcelain. The bellfounder, who was probably Christopher Pennington of Lezant, said that the powder was *"but the pot growan that comes from up yonder somewhere in the hills; 'tis what we always use, and our fathers before us"*. Cookworthy made a mental note of it, and later, when he became involved in the search for the secret of making porcelain, identified *"pot growan"* as kaolin, the mysterious material which for centuries had given the Chinese a monopoly in porcelain-making. The "Cornish Alps" around St Austell and the vast remodelling of South-west Dartmoor are all, if you like, the result of what an observant young chemist saw in a Cornish bellfounder's casting shed.

The actual casting of the bell was usually watched by the Churchwardens at least, who if necessary would travel a long way for the purpose, and they would probably stay until the bells could be taken out of the casting pit and weighed. The bells would need a day or two to cool down before they could be dug out of the casting-pit, and a night-watchman might be hired to guard them during that time.

Casting a bell was always a risky and uncertain business, and failures were not uncommon. William Evans had to cast the "Old Nine-o'Clock" (now the 10th) at *Exeter Cathedral* twice before he got a good bell; according to his letter to the Dean this was because he was *"stinted to an impossibility as to weight"*. Thomas Purdue in casting "Cobthorne" ran out of metal for the cannons and argent; he had to hang the bell with four bolts through the crown and sign an undertaking to recast the bell if it failed: many bells from all periods turn out to have poor and drossy metal in the cannons. A bell, now recast, cast by John Pennington senior and junior of Tavistock in 1702 for *St Marychurch* and later acquired by the Roman Catholic church there, had a huge distortion inside the waist where the core had evidently broken before or during the casting; *Hennock* treble evidently suffered from a broken cope, and the metal which ran through the resulting crack had to be chipped off, leaving a long scar.

Although, before the advent of the tuning machine, bellfounders did their best to cast "maiden bells" which were perfectly in tune, the bells might be found to need tuning. This was sometimes done by the founder, but might be done later by one of the specialist bell-tuners whose names appear in church accounts. Mordecai Cockey in 1682 *"cheeped"* the little bell which he had cast for *Chivelstone*, and paid 4 shillings to the churchwardens for the metal which he had removed, while at *Buckfastleigh* in 1743 when Ambrose Gooding recast the bells, there is an entry for putting the *"chippings"* in safe keeping. Richard Beavis is often mentioned in connection with bell tuning during the late 17th century; at *Tedburn St Mary* in 1689, after John Pennington had cast the Treble, two men rode *"on be half of the whole parish to gitt an Artis to tune o[u]r bells"*, and Mr Beavis incurred £1 6s in charges *"to tune our bells"*, but a payment of 5s to *Mr Beavis's man* may reveal who actually did the work. Other bell-tuners seem to have been itinerant specialists, like William Mitchell who tuned *Halberton* bells in 1619 and *St Peter's, Tiverton* in 1620 (at the cost of no less than 40 shillings), and the bell-tuner who appears most often in the Devon records, Ferdinando Combe, who tuned *Cheriton Fitzpaine* bells in 1710, *Cullompton* in 1718, *Broadhembury* in 1719, *Woodbury* in 1720, *Talaton* in 1732 and *Cullompton* again in 1732. At *Coldridge* the bells were tuned by a Mr Lusey or Lussey after they had been recast by John Pennington II of Lezant. Anyone whose calling involved spending hours with his head inside a bell, knocking chips out of it with a hammer and chisel arouses our admiration and sympathy but not our envy. Some 18th-century founders and tuners used what has been called "scratch tuning", probably done with a rasp, which leaves fine grooves in the metal. Of course until the late 19th-century no one in Britain knew how to tune anything more than the strike-note of a bell, and when tuners attempted to raise the pitch of a strike-note by "skirting" the lip the result was usually a ruined bell.

During the 19th-century, many small bells were cast in sand from wooden patterns. They are identifiable by having no moulding-wires (which would have prevented the pattern from being withdrawn from the mould), and having "peg argents" instead of cannons. They are usually described as "brass-foundry bells", and are either blank or have engraved inscriptions: many school bells are of this type.

Making Inscriptions & Decorations

From the introduction of the clay model in the 13th or 14th century to the invention of the iron bell-case in the 19th, bellfounding technique changed little in Britain, with one notable exception. We have seen how the pre-Reformation founders applied their inscriptions and decoration to the clay model in the form of wax paterae moulded in wooden or clay matrices, and this method is still preferred by the French and Dutch for the sake of the elaborate three-dimensional detail and the beautiful sharpness of the castings made in this way. In Britain, however, as Latin came to be largely replaced by English for inscriptions, and Roman lettering replaced Gothic black-letter and Lombardic capitals, the bellfounders experimented with new ways of inscribing their bells. The first was to use letters cut out of a sheet of thick parchment, sheet metal or even perhaps leather and stuck to the clay model; this was used by Robert Pennington of Bodmin, Thomas Pennington I of Barnstaple (*Eggesford* tenor is a good example), sometimes in conjunction with wax as on *Yarnscombe* 5/6, and by the early Purdues in Somerset, but this cut-out (sometimes called "sheet-metal") lettering was inevitably clumsy and its relief very shallow; Thomas Pennington II was the first Devon founder – George Elphick believed perhaps the first in Britain – to adopt the much more versatile and satisfactory technique of impressing the lettering using carved wooden stamps. To make this possible the area for the inscription was left on the clay model as a raised band, so that it formed a recessed groove round the inside of the cope. After the cope had been dried and lifted, this was then filled with fresh loam and the inscription and decorations stamped into it; examination of stamped inscriptions show a depressed area round the edges of the letters which was created as the loam was displaced by the stamp, and on some bells, particularly John Stadler's, one can see the square edges of the stamps where they were pressed in too deeply. Proof of this technique exists in *Thurlestone* 2/6, where provision was made for a second line of inscription but not used, and the

Fig. 55. Eggesford tenor, by Thomas Pennington I, 1618, has "cut-out" lettering.

Fig. 56. Thurlestone 2nd: the raised lower inscription-band shows that a groove was left in the cope, to be filled with loam after the mould had been baked, so that the inscription could be impressed; it was in fact never used.

lower groove was not filled in, so that it appears on the bell as a raised band. (It may be significant that at the Loughborough foundry, which often uses a different terminology from the other foundries, the inscription-band is known as the "mulley groove". "Mulley" may well be a corruption of the French "mouillé", meaning moist).

As well as lettering, coins and other decorations could be impressed; medals and trade tokens, pieces of decorative metalwork, even buttons perhaps, can be identified, and seals appear quite often; *Eggesford* 2/3, 1652, has a large oval seal bearing the Chichester arms [Pl 36h] and a small signet of the Warwick bear-and-ragged-staff [Pl 36i], and *Holcombe Burnell* 6/6, also cast during the Commonwealth, a signet of the Yarde arms [Pl 36j]. All these are "negatives" made by impressing the seal itself which must have been lent for the purpose or even impressed by the owner, but the big Beauchamp seal [Pl 36k] on *Talaton* tenor was a wax impression, so one assumes that Roger Semson the founder must have had the original seal, as the impression also appears at Bradford-on-Tone, Somerset. How he acquired it is a mystery; perhaps it came into his possession as scrap metal. For large decorations such as the big coats-of-arms [Pl 36b,c] on the waists of the *Ashburton* bells of 1740 lost wax was still used well into the 18th century.

Both this and the lost-wax technique make it quite easy for a founder to reproduce marks from another bell or elsewhere by taking a squeeze in clay; a wheel-shaped decoration used on *Abbotsham* 5/6 by William Dawe also appears on a Robert Norton bell at *Broadwindsor*, Dorset, and *Denbury* 4/5 has rather crudely-cast copies of the "I.T." mark and Robert Norton's black-letter "a" and "p" on a bell of 1634: the founder of *Molland* 3/6, William Preston, took a wax impression from a monumental brass, and the single word "lemosinary" repeated on *Abbotsham* tenor and on the clock bell at *Torre Abbey* was probably made in the same way. Where the founder had no suitable stamps he might simply scratch something into the cope, as on *Washford Pyne* 5/6.

John Warner of London patented the cast-iron bell-case in 1853 and it was soon adopted by the other major British foundries at Whitechapel, Croydon and Loughborough, though it has never been taken up by the Continental foundries. The case is lined with loam and dispenses with the clay model altogether, the core and cope being strickled separately; it is also much more suited to bells cast without cannons, and was probably one of the factors which caused the end of itinerant bellfounding, the last recorded Devon example of which was Pannell's recasting of *Plympton St Maurice* tenor in 1833; until then a bellfounder's essential equipment could probably have been made by the founder himself and transported on a couple of packhorses.

One bell in Devon bears witness to a 19th-century return to old techniques; in 1897 the Taylor foundry at Loughborough, with an eye to the Dutch market, cast an experimental bell using a clay model and *cire perdu* decoration; subsequently they cast a few more bells using this method, including some in Loughborough Parish Church. The experimental bell, which proved to be a very beautiful one, was to have been sold off to a Mr William Torrance in Edinburgh, but he countermanded the order, and it found its final home at *St Helen's, Bucks Mills* [88].

Lettering and Decoration

The earliest bells had their inscriptions made, apparently, by simply scratching letters or figures into the moulds, or by shaping thin rolls of wax into letters and applying them to the model; these letters show characteristic curls at the ends of the strokes. No such bells survive in Devon, and our earliest inscribed bells, at *Petersmarland, Combpyne* and the two in Okehampton Museum, have Lombardic lettering moulded from wooden or clay patterns. William Dawe of London in about 1380 cast *Abbotsham* 5/6 which, alone of his surviving bells, is all in Lombardic capitals; it is presumably the earliest known by him: the ring of three which he cast for *Brushford* has Lombardic initials and black-letter lower-case letters, as have all the other inscribed mediaeval London bells in the county, by Johanna Hille, John Bird and William Chamberlain.

The Exeter founders began with a set of Lombardic capitals [Pl 2a] and a cross [Pl 1a] which goes with them; both letters and cross so closely resemble a set from Gloucester that it needs close scrutiny to tell them apart; one must surely be derived from the other – but which is the earlier? We shall see. This is the well-known set with the cracked "M" and "N"; the only example so far discovered without the crack is at *Chilthorne Domer* in Somerset.

Robert Norton inherited this lettering when he took over the foundry, and probably with it a small Lombardic set of which only one example survives, at *Clyst St Mary*. However, he very soon brought Exeter into the new fashion by creating a black-letter alphabet, and went on to pioneer a remarkably advanced labour-saving system for inscribing most of his bells. Having adopted a number of "stock" inscriptions, all of them in the form of "Leonine" verses (a dactylic hexameter with a rhyme at the caesura and the end, to be precise), such as "*Me melior vere non est campana sub (a)ere*", he had patterns made for these with a whole word, or even two short words – "*sub ere*" in this case – on a single patera. So instead of having to make, trim and apply (in the above example) thirty-one very small paterae of wax to his clay pattern, he could do the job with eight much more manageable ones. This system also probably meant that he could leave the application of the inscription to an illiterate journeyman who needed only to put the paterae in the right order and the right way up – though he might not always be successful, as some examples show. Where a bell had to be cast to order with a special inscription such as an invocation to a saint, the black-letter alphabet was used, but even so short-cuts could be made: a bell by Robert Norton at *St Erney* in Cornwall bears the longest and most unusual inscription of any Exeter bell. This bell's unique inscription, the only one from the Exeter foundry occupying two lines, must have been ordered by the parish priest; it will be described in more detail when we come to the Exeter foundry. Most of the single letters are from the black-letter alphabet, but groups of two or more letters are "lifted" from stock inscriptions. Similar tricks can be found on other bells with non-stock inscriptions. Bells by Robert Norton seldom have corrupt inscriptions, but bells by later founders sometimes have words inverted or even words from two different inscriptions jumbled together. During and after the Reformation, bells – apparently by the Birdalls – are found with odd words or bits of words along with a

Fig. 57. St Erney, Cornwall: the treble by Robert Norton, with its inscription partly made up from lettering from "stock" inscriptions.

meaningless string of letters from different alphabets as on *Honeychurch* treble which seems to be from 1572. Most "alphabet" bells, bearing just the alphabet in part or whole, probably date from this time, though the *Hennock* treble bears Robert Norton's mark.

The period from 1549 to the beginning of the 17th century seems to have been one of great confusion in the industry, and presents many puzzles. A number of unknown founders were apparently working, albeit sporadically, casting bells like those at *Highampton* [Pl 14a], *Torbryan* [Pl 14b] and *Frithelstock* with large, crude letters and mis-spelt inscriptions still more or less pre-Reformation in character; Roger Semson of Ash Priors cast some of his bells – presumably during the reign of Mary I – with invocations of saints in big bold decorated capitals, as at *Talaton*, and others with meaningless (or could they be coded?) inscriptions in crude Roman letters. Another founder, William Preston of Crediton, seems to have used wax impressions from monumental brasses for his inscriptions, as we have seen – *Molland* 3rd has "Here lies Master John Cooke", backwards, upside down and in Latin – and the Birdalls in Exeter, as well as using lettering and crosses inherited from Robert Norton and his successors, must have acquired at least one other set of Lombardic capitals for an "alphabet" bell at *Combeinteignhead*, and another set of very large capitals which they used at *Whimple* and *Aylesbeare* [Pl 5d]. Thomas and John Birdall must have come by an incomplete set of letters decorated with foliage, and with great ingenuity cut and assembled pieces of them to make up letters which were missing [Pl 6d-h]. John's initials I.B. on the Cathedral 4th are complete, but some of those at *Berry Pomeroy* have been pieced together.

Two of the very earliest Pennington bells, at *Minehead* and *Yarnscombe*, inscribed "TP" and "R P" and dated 1607 and 1608, have wax-moulded lettering in small black-letter with Lombardic initials; they are apparently by Robert of Bodmin and Thomas I of Barnstaple. By 1616, however, Thomas I was using cut-out type lettering at *Templeton*, and Robert of Bodmin was still using it in 1633 at *E Ogwell* and *Denbury*, but by this time Thomas II had developed stamped inscriptions, though his earliest alphabet seems to have consisted of thicker cut-out letters, possibly of lead, so that they were capable of being put in back to front.

The moulds and stamps used by the founders often had a long life-span; the Lombardic lettering used by the earliest Exeter founders at the end of the 14th century came back into use, apparently, during the Reformation period; some of the crosses and lettering introduced by Robert Norton were evidently still in the foundry when the Birdalls moved to St Thomas's, and the "I.T." mark, dating from the mid-1400s, was used by John Birdall II until his death in 1624. The Exeter Penningtons' lettering also had a long life, and the small bell mark introduced by Thomas Bilbie II when he set up the Cullompton foundry in 1754 lived on to the end of the Pannell foundry in 1855, just as one can see 200-year-old patterns in the Villedieu foundry in use today.

Decoration on English bells has always been restrained in comparison with the exuberance of many Continental founders; the most elaborately decorated bell in Devon is probably the 1539 Albert Hachman bell at *Walrond's Almshouses, Tiverton*, which was cast in Cleve in Germany. Westcountry mediaeval founders confined themselves to a simple cross, which was almost invariably used on bells before the Reformation, a founder's mark perhaps, and one or two simple motifs such as fleurs-de-lys, crowns or roundels, though a bell at *Payhembury* bears a fine dragon with a knot in its tail, and one at *Zennor* in Cornwall has two strange winged beasts with human faces.

After 1600 Thomas Pennington II introduced two sizes of fleur-de-lys frieze which he used above the inscription-band, as filling in an empty space in an inscription-band, or in short sections between words. At least two larger fleur-de-lys friezes appear on Exeter Pennington bells later, but they are rare. Thomas Purdue's bells are sometimes quite handsomely decorated with a variety of friezes, the commonest being a vine-trail which was used by other members of his family and also by Mordecai Cockey. He used a large rose frieze on "Peter" and "Stafford" at *Exeter Cathedral*, and on *Awliscombe* tenor he used a set of decorative capitals with crowns above them; here and on "Peter" he also used his little "sprigs" around and between the letters of his inscriptions. The Gloucester foundry of the Rudhall family also used some handsome friezes, two of which appear at *Brixton*.

The use of **coins** [Pll 38, 39] and other objects to decorate bells has already been mentioned; curiously, although it was by no means confined to the West Country, this subject has not been given much attention in other bell literature, so it may be useful to deal with it in some detail. There may have been various motives for using coins in this way, apart from the rather dubious one mentioned above: a coin would confirm the date, or at least the reign, when the bell was cast, though as we shall see there are notable exceptions: if it was specially unusual or of high denomination it might record a notable donation to the casting: or it might be making a statement about the political stance of the bell's owner or founder, which would explain the coins of Charles I which appear on Commonwealth bells at *Exeter Cathedral* and *Thurlestone,* and possibly coins of Charles I and II and James II on bells cast after 1688. The Exeter founders used coin-impressions in the heads of their bells at two periods, under Robert Russell in the later 15th century and during the Reformation period; dating of the coins confirms this [Pl 38 a,b,c,]. Two London mediaeval founders, John Sturdy and his widow Johanna, also used groats on their bells, as did the Wokingham foundry, always in the inscriptions. After 1600 coins always seem to be found in the inscription-band or on the waist: Thomas Pennington I used 1577 and 1591 groats on a bell of 1616 at *Templeton*, and his son Thomas II adopted the custom of using coins as stops along with his characteristic 5-dot stop; most of these are shillings of James I or Charles I [Pl 38f], but occasionally more unusual coins appear, such as the daalder of 60 groot from the Spanish Netherlands at *Iddesleigh*, 1620 [Pl 39c], and the half-écu of Henri IV of Navarre & Béarn at *Holcombe Rogus*, 1626 [Pl 39a,b]. John and Thomas III of Exeter continued the practice; once again shillings are the most common, but we find a Portuguese cruzado of 500 reis at *Spreyton*, 1650 [39e], and a Charles I half-crown at *Horwood*, 1662. *Thurlestone* tenor, 1654, which seems to have been a combined effort by Thomas of Tavistock and John of Exeter, bears an equestrian half-crown of Charles I and a thaler of Queen Christina of Sweden [Pl 39d]. The Cornish Penningtons also used coins right up to the 19th century; most of them are silver, but gold sovereigns or guineas appear at *Rattery*, 1754 [Pl 39i], *North Tawton*, 1765 and *St Budeaux*, 1775; *Rattery* tenor, 1763, in addition has a splendid gold dobra of 8 escudos of John V of Portugal [Pl 39i], worth about £5 in its day; a good number of these Portuguese gold coins of John V, popularly known as "Joes" and "half-Joes", circulated in Britain during the 18th century. Foreign silver coins used by the Cornish Penningtons include a Spanish dollar of Ferdinand II at *North Tawton*, 1765 [Pl 39f], and one of Charles III at *Drewsteignton*, 1784 [Pl 39h], and there is one copper foreign coin, a 10-ore of Francis II of Sweden at *Lydford*, 1789 [Pl 39g]. This last is singular as a great many foreign silver and gold coins were in circulation when the value of the coinage went by weight and most merchants had their scales to weigh them, but copper foreign coins must have been far less common. Mordecai Cockey, John Stadler and Ambrose Gooding also used coin-impressions, as did the unidentified founders of the disused bell at *Cockington*, 1653, two *Georgenympton* bells, 1680, *Fremington* tenor, 1709, and "W.K." on the clock bell at *Great Torrington*, 1732. The Wroths of Wellington have a Portuguese coin of 400 reis on bells at *Lympstone*, 1746, as well as English coins at *Feniton* and *Holcombe Rogus*; the Bridgwater founders used them frequently in their beautiful castings, and we have occasional coin-impressions on bells by the Evanses of Chepstow. Thomas Bilbie I used a George II shilling at *Kenton* in 1747, but the Cullompton Bilbies seem to have used coin-impressions seldom if at all, though the Pannells used them in 1854 at *Colebrooke* and in 1855 at *Upton, Torquay*: William Hambling used coins at *Halwell* and *Denbury* in the 1820s. The custom still continues, in the same spirit as the placing of current coins under foundation-stones; pennies of Edward VII were placed on the *Bovey Tracey* bells by Gillett & Johnston in 1902, and the *Kingston* trebles, by the Whitechapel foundry, 1979, have 50p piece impressions. In addition to coins of the realm, we also find **tokens** of the kind that were much used to supplement the coinage during the 17th, 18th and early 19th centuries. The earliest identifiable is a small token of Abisha Brocas, an Exeter bookseller [Pl 38g], on a bell at *Sidbury* by John Pennington of Exeter, 1662; a similar-looking one, but unidentifiable, appears at *St Petrock's, Exeter*, on a 1693 bell by Stadler. At *Thrushelton*, 1718, on a bell by John Pennington II of Lezant, there is a token, so far unidentified, with a two-headed eagle and the initials S F [Pl 18k], and Christopher and John have an Exeter Penny, obverse and reverse, at *Lapford*, 1797 [Pl 38m]. During the latter part of the Napoleonic Wars through a shortage of silver coinage, the banks were permitted to issue tokens provided they were of different denominations from coins of the realm; one of these, a 3-shilling bank token [Pl 38l], is on a bell by John Pennington IV of Stoke Climsland, 1815, at *Kingskerswell*. Perhaps the oddest Westcountry example of a trade token appears at *Broadway* in Somerset, where George Davis of Bridgwater used a token bearing the words "EXETER CHANGE, STRAND, LONDON" and a cow with two heads: it was issued by Pidcock's Menagerie.

Medals were issued for a variety of reasons from 1600 onwards, and some of these too came to be used for bell decoration; Fitzantony Pennington I used a large religious medal depicting the sacrifice of Isaac [Pl 17e] at *Frithelstock*, 1656 and *Mortehoe* (recast in not very clear facsimile) 1657; at *Ottery St Mary*, 1671, and *St Martin's, Exeter* [96], 1673, Thomas Pennington III used satirical medals showing either a cardinal's or a bishop's head and a pope's or a king's [Pl 16g], depending which way up they are. One is surprised to find Thomas, whose father had been so staunchly for church and king during the Commonwealth, using anything so anti-monarchical and anti-church, especially some years after the Restoration; perhaps he was acting under orders. Stadler used a medal of Charles II [Pl 25j] at *Exeter St Petrock's*, 1693, and Evans used one of Archbishop Laud – the original is reputedly in the Cathedral Library – on "Grandison" in 1729. *Ermington*, 1747, has a medal commemorating Admiral Vernon's capture of Portobello the previous year [Pl 38h]; around the figure of the Admiral (nicknamed "Old Grog", and after whom the Navy's "grog" or watered rum was named) is the inscription "*The British Glory restor'd by Admiral Vernon*". *Jacobstowe* has a Diamond Jubilee medal of Queen Victoria [Pl 33g] on a bell which celebrated the event but which was cast two years after the Queen's death, and *Bradford* a Coronation medal of George V and Queen Mary [Pl 33h], both cast by Taylor.

In addition to the Beauchamp, Chichester, Warwick and Yarde **seals** already mentioned, there are a number of impressions of what seems to be a seal [Pl 21l], on bells by the Penningtons between 1790 and 1802. The impression is a "negative", so it must have been made with the seal itself, and bears two scallop-shells with sprigs of foliage above and below; it presumably belonged to the Penningtons, and may have been John's own personal seal.

Coats-of arms appear on a good many bells in Devon. The large blazons of Sir William Yonge and John Harris at *Ashburton* have already been mentioned, and the Exeter founder "I.T." put two large coats of arms used by the Luttrell family on the waist of a bell at *East Quantoxhead* in Somerset (unfortunately he seems to have become confused by the need to make his pattern in "negative", so one of the coats shows a bend sinister; perhaps the Luttrells never spotted it). Also from the Exeter founders are the arms of Ferrers [Pl 36b] at *Churston Ferrers* and Dinham [Pl 36c] at *Coffinswell*; another unidentified coat-of-arms [Pl 36d] – HTE attributed it to the Guille family – a lion rampant on a field fretty, must have come to be used simply for decoration as it appears at *Dunchideock, East Portlemouth, Yeovilton, St Michael Caerhayes* and *Colaton Raleigh*. The Exeter Penningtons decorated *Burlescombe* tenor with the Ayshford arms [Pl 37a] on a splendid cartouche, John and Christopher Pennington of Lezant in the early 1700s cast bells at *Buckland Monachorum* [Pl 36l,m], *Dean Prior, Stowford* [Pl 36g] and *East Allington* [Pl 36o,p] with beautifully clean small coats-of arms of the local squires in small roundels, while Thomas Wroth used the Huyshe arms [Pl 36q] at *Sidbury* and the Courtenay arms [Pl 36f] at *Molland*, the latter being of particular interest as the Courtenays of Molland were recusant Roman Catholics at the time. Abraham Rudhall decorated the *Totnes* bells with the arms of the town [Pl 36p], Sir William Yonge and John Harris had theirs on the bells they gave to *Ashburton*, and in our own time Commander W.R.Gilbert had his family's arms cast on the new treble at *Marldon*, to commemorate their giving the bell, while the new (2004) *Crediton* bells have a shield bearing the symbol of St Boniface and the seal of the Governors of Crediton Church

The **fleur-de-lys** was of course one of the most widespread decorative motifs throughout the Middle Ages thanks to its association with the Blessed Virgin Mary; many of the cross designs on pre-Reformation bells include or are made up of fleurs-de-lys. It continued to be used by bellfounders after the Reformation, often as a stop between words, and the Exeter, Tavistock and Cornish Penningtons all had their own versions, as did Roger Semson, John Stadler, Thomas Purdue and the Wroths. There does not seem to be any obvious reason why a **scallop-shell** should be so popular a decoration for bellfounders in the 18th century, but the fact is that the Penningtons in Cornwall [Pl 21f,m] and the Bilbies in Cullompton [Pl 30f] used very similar shell decorations on a great many bells, and a smaller shell stamp [Pl 29f] was used by the Bridgwater founders, often four shells arranged in a cross; James Smith and Thomas Roskelly of Closworth used a similar arrangement [Pl 24k,l]. A stamp used by Christopher Pennington II between 1686 and 1702 consists of a roundel containing a **rose and crown** [Pl 17h]; it appears at *Frithelstock*, *Monkokehampton* and *Dunterton*. This is almost certainly an impression of one of the lead cloth seals which were used to certify bolts of cloth; the Royal Albert Memorial Museum in Exeter has an example very similar but not identical.

Ambrose Gooding had a number of **decorations**, some of them very attractive, including a king's head [Pl 26o], a dove [Pl 26l], a crown [Pl 26p] and what seems to be the impression of a fine intaglio gem [PL 26q] depicting a cockerel; also a small round pattern [Pl 26m] which could be the impression of a button. Of all the Westcountry bellfounders, the Bridgwater firm during the 18th century produced the most consistently clean castings, and many of the most decorative. Many of their bells have a mask flanked by trails of foliage [Pl 29a], and some, for example *Honiton St Paul's* tenor, have the founders' names in a cartouche formed by foliage patterns [Pl 29g]. Close examination of these reveals that they were made by adapting spandrel-mounts made for the dials of domestic clocks; no doubt the Bridgwater foundry, which made a wide variety of domestic metalware including clocks, had plenty of these handy for use in the moulding shop. Another small swag decoration used by these founders may have been made from the pattern for the drop-handle of a drawer. In addition, these founders, particularly Bayley & Street, sometimes inscribed their names in a splendid high-relief cartouche, as at *Sidbury* [Pl. 29j].

Cannons & Crown-staples

Before the late 19th century a bell was hung from one or more loops cast on the head of the bell, by which it can be hung. The central and largest loop is called the *argent,* and the *cannons*[11] are smaller loops running from the head of the bell to the argent. From very early times the cannons seem often to have been decorated: the bell of 1081 in Verona had its single loop moulded from a 3-strand cable of wax, and a 12th-century bell with a flat head and convex profile at Citta di Castello also has cabled cannons. The *Haccombe* bell has cannons whose upper surface has a fine cabled pattern, the pair of 13th-century bells at *Petton* and another of similar date at *Bulkworthy* have a plaited moulding, and *Petersmarland* tenor by Richard de Wymbis has a cable. On all of these British examples, unlike the Italian bells mentioned, it is clear that the patterns for the cannons were cast in wax using piece-moulds, and this technique continued virtually unchanged until the development, at Whitechapel in the 19th-century, of ingenious wooden patterns which could be removed piecemeal. The parting-lines which can be seen on the sides of most cannons represent the parting of the moulds in which the wax patterns were cast.

The mediaeval Exeter founders normally made cannons with a simple raised band moulding, with just occasionally a more elaborate decoration such as the zig-zag markings on an 16th-century bell at *East Down*. This type was commonly used by the early Penningtons, though some of their bells have tall crudely-made cannons with no moulding at all. The Bilbies' bells, and also the Evans's, have prettily-shaped cannons with an ovolo moulding,

---

11. The spelling of this word has been a matter of some controversy among bell historians, and I am aware that it is more often spelt "canon", and that some dictionaries support that spelling. "Canon" is derived from the Latin for a rule or order; "cannon" most commonly means a kind of gun , but there also is the "cannon-bone" in a horse's leg and the "cannon pinion" in a clock, and spelt thus the word seems to describe a shape or function, which is more applicable to the cannons of a bell. I can claim the support of the late H.B. Walters and of David Struckett's *Dictionary of Campanology* in persisting with this spelling.

and the Cornish Penningtons' are similar but usually less neatly moulded, but the Rudhalls frequently used decorated cannons, as at *Brixton* and (before they were removed and scrapped in the 20th century) *Pilton* and *Filleigh*. Most of the 19th-century founders made their cannons angular and square in section, though the Pannells continued to use the Bilbie patterns, and some Taylor bells of the later 19th-century have cannons which have a concave curve in the upright part and a convex curve in the top. However, when Taylors' recast some of *Pilton* bells for their patron Robert Chichester, they gave them magnificent cannons decorated with human and lion masks; it seems almost inconceivable that in 1969 the foundry which had created these beautiful cannons chopped them off and scrapped them. Finally both the Whitechapel and Cripplegate foundries adopted the "Doncaster" head designed by Lord Grimthorpe, which enabled a bell to be quarter-turned without any change in the supporting ironwork and was usually combined with an independent crown-staple. For some reason both foundries would sometimes use cannons on some of the bells and Doncaster heads on others in the same ring.

English bells almost always have six cannons, two in line with the argent on either side and four meeting it at right-angles [see 61], but John Taylor during his Buckland Brewer period occasionally made light bells with only four cannons, e.g. the front bells at *Dowland*. Small bells cast on the Continent, particularly in France, Spain and Italy, often have only an argent and two cannons in line with it, but a bell presumed to be Italian at the Royal Marines' camp at *Lympstone* has six beautifully decorated cannons arranged radially round a solid central pillar, and some of Llewellins & James's bells were cast with radial cannons in the 19th century. In the 1880s Taylors' devised a type of head consisting of four cylindrical pillars and a circular plate which was drilled for bolting to a metal headstock: however when once the founders had discovered that bells could be safely bolted direct to a metal headstock with only a wooden pad between, flat-headed bells rapidly came into fashion and are virtually universal in Britain today, though the Continental founders almost always cast their bells with cannons and take much trouble to decorate them. It may be noted that when the "Cobthorne" bell in Exeter Cathedral was cast in 1676, the cannons were incomplete and it was hung from four bolts; at the time Thomas Purdue had to sign an agreement with the Dean & Chapter of the Cathedral that the cannons of the "Cobthorne" bell were incomplete, stating that *the bell cannot be hung up by the canons or tenons thereof, as the same was formerly, and still ought to bee hung . . .* Purdue had to undertake to recast the bell gratis if it should fail within twenty years; in fact he was 200 years ahead of his time.

Until the later 19th century, any bell which was intended to be swung had a *crown-staple* cast into its head; this was made of iron, sometimes by the local blacksmith if the bell was cast on site. Most pre-Reformation bells have crown-staples which are round in section and U-shaped, but some, for instance on the William Chamberlain bells at *Dartmouth St Clement*, are square in the part which is cast into the head of the bell; others have the ends cut ragged to give them a firm hold in the bell-metal. The 17th and 18th-century founders in Devon continued to use U-shaped crown-staples, usually square, and their corners act as stress-raisers as the

Fig. 58. Marwood 3rd. A crack can be seen radiating from the corner of Bilbie's square-sectioned crown-staple which had been ground off but not drilled out when the independent crown-staple was fitted.

bell-metal shrinks more in cooling than the iron; bells by the Bilbies and Ambrose Gooding in particular have suffered badly through this; at *South Tawton, Welcombe, Holne* and *Shobrooke* for instance several of the bells in a ring have become crazed; sadly, the *Holne* bells, in 1974 the only surviving complete ring by Gooding, were found to be crazed just before bell welding had been perfected, and three of them were recast. 19th-century London founders adopted crown-staples looped into a single stem, and finally independent crown-staples replaced the cast-in type.

Repairs and Replacements

Apart from tuning, the commonest alteration made to bells is the replacement of the crown-staple because a cast-in staple had either come loose or been worn through. In early days this was done by fixing a wrought-iron staple through holes bored on either side of the head of the bell, using keys in early times and, later, square nuts. In recent times it has become routine to drill out cast-in crown-staples to prevent their cracking the bells, and fitting an independent crown-staple through a centre hole.

Cannons were occasionally removed before the 19th-century, but only when they had been broken or had been found unsafe through poor casting (as with "Cobthorne" at the Cathedral); however, once bells cast without cannons had been accepted in the late 19th and early 20th centuries they were very frequently removed, simply for greater ease of hanging. On occasion one finds false iron cannons fitted to replace broken ones, and at *South Pool* William Hambling repaired a broken cannon by drilling down through the upright part and fitting a long bolt through it.

At various times people have hoped to repair cracked bells; in 1578 at Braunton *bellemakers* were paid *for amending the Thyryd Bell,* and apparently used 19 pounds of tin in the process; in 1730 at *Littleham*, Sam Blacmore Senior was paid 2s 6d *to view ye Bell to see if ye crack could be repair'd without new casting*, and as late as 1904 the Guild report states that *"at Broadhembury the first attempt to repair a cracked bell in this country has been effected by Herr Ohlsson, of Lubeck, Germany. The original tone and note of the bell, which is upwards of a ton, has, apparently, been restored."* If the tone was restored, it was only for a very short time, and after nearly 90 years' very dismal sound the bell was recast. The "repair" was effected by cutting out butterfly-shaped recesses across the crack and rivetting into them inserts presumably of bell-metal. Cracks in the head of a bell were sometimes treated by shrinking an iron hoop round the shoulder; in some cases this prevented the crack from spreading, at least for some years, but in the case of *Powderham 5th* it only served to divert the crack, which over the years ran round unseen beneath the hoop until the bell fell off its crown, with very startling results, in the middle of a quarter-peal attempt: the tenor of our heaviest ring of six, at *Honiton St Michael*, has an iron hoop round its head, but the crack has reached the waist nonetheless and the bell is quite toneless. Another technique was to saw out the crack, as was done to "Big Ben" at Westminster and in 1884 to the tenor at *Staverton*. Fortunately for the future preservation of our ancient bells a technique for welding bells has now been developed, and has been successfully carried out in a number of towers, including *Brampford Speke, Halwell, Marwood* and *Shobrooke*, while the 15th-century former 3rd at *Awliscombe*, which had been kept in the church after being cracked and replaced with a new bell, was finally welded and hung as a service bell at Bishop's Lydeard in Somerset.

The Business Side

When it comes to the actual business of getting bells cast or recast, as well as the technology involved, church-wardens' accounts are by far the richest source; churchwardens' accounts can be utterly fascinating documents, especially when they date from the time when the Churchwardens' duties embraced practically every activity of a community, from arming the militia and relieving the poor to killing bullfinches and keeping the boys in order in church: those who research in church accounts for any particular topic need to maintain a rigid self-discipline if they are not to be lured away into delightful side-tracks.

Devon is comparatively rich in church accounts but not all are easy to read or interpret. Early examples, before about 1550, are often in Latin of a sort, though the writer would often use an English – or even a Devonshire dialect – word where he didn't know the Latin one, as in *Holy Trinity, Exeter*, 1462: *Item solut Iohne Ley carpentario pro labore suo supervidend le frame campanarum* (paid to John Ley carpenter for his work in supervising the bellframe). Later, the problem is often not only to decypher the handwriting of rustic churchwardens but to translate Devon dialect into standard English, as for instance at *Holne* in 1744: *Expended when the Parshner mite for to know wheer the wide have fouer or five bells* – try reading it phonetically in a broad Devon accent, and its meaning is clear enough: *Expended when the parishioners met to know whether they would have four or five bells*. "Ire" is often used for "iron", and quantities are often given in "seams", which were the pannier-loads of packhorses. "To Exeter" may mean, as it often does in Devon today, "at Exeter", but conversely in the 17th and 18th centuries "riding at Chudleigh" would mean "riding to Chudleigh".

Bellfounding operations came about because the parish wanted more bells or better bells, or because bells were broken. In the last case, the parish may have been "presented" by the Rural Dean in his annual visitation, as happened at *Dolton* in 1846 when the bell was *reported by the Rural Dean to be out of repair*; if they did not act the wardens might be summoned to the Archdeacon's Court and fined: *Ashwater* had to pay 10s *when the Church Bibell & Bell was presented*, and in *Clawton* in 1626 John Orchard the Apparitor (an official of the Archdeacon) was paid 3/7d *for carryinge of the Certifycate to the Lord Byshopps Court about the Bell* and John Kynsman was paid 9/2d by the wardens *for that he was excommunicated about the Certifycate of the bell* – which seems a drastic penalty for an error in the warden's paperwork. The Archdeacon could order the work to be done within a certain time; in 1681 the *Broadhembury* wardens *pd to ye Courte for that ye bell was not cast in season, 6s 10d* – they were to be presented again for their 4th in 1745 – and at *Feniton* they had to pay 10s *to the Cort of Exon for to grant ous time to finish our work*. As late as 1807 *High Bray*'s wardens *paid the a parater for sighting* (citing) *to Cort – 3s: Paid the Churchwardens for appearing to Cort – 3s: Paid the fees of the Court concerning the Bels – 2s 6d: Paid the a parater for sighting to Cort concerning the bells – 2s 6d*".

In most cases an enterprise as big as bell restoration required a meeting of the Vestry, usually attended by the principal payers of the Church Rate, and vestry minutes often record such a meeting, which might be the annual Easter Vestry or a specially called meeting at which the bellfounder might be present; he might already have come "*to view the bells*" with the wardens. There were at various times people who were regarded as experts in bell matters, who might be called in to inspect the bells and advise, or to meet with the bellfounder. One of the most active was Richard Beavis, a squire who lived at Sowton near Exeter, who was the Cathedral Chapter's designated expert in 1676 and also visited to advise about casting or tuning bells at *Colebrooke, Woodbury, Totnes, Cullompton, Tedburn St Mary* and *South Tawton* – he is actually described as tuning bells at *Cullompton*, but entries at *Tedburn St Mary* suggest that he supervised *his man* who was given 5/- *by consent of the parishners*", and *Totnes* paid £5 *in treating Mr Beavis and his retinue whilst he was in towne, and friends to accompany him about tuning the bells*. At *South Tawton* he and the bellfounder were provided with *a dinner and an extraordinary expense in beer* at the parish's expense – a custom which sadly for today's bell advisers seems to have lapsed. Other experts appear in church records in the same role; John Churley was paid 6d in 1617 *for coming hither* (to Halberton) *to talk with the pishoners & the bell founder*; Mr Collings was better rewarded by *Holbeton*; he received 12/6d in 1711 *at ye tryal of ye bells* and is described as "*Musicke Master*", receiving no less than a guinea *for Attendance & Tuning ye Bells* in 1723. Henry Mudge in 1727 gave *his opinion abt the new bell* at *Dawlish* and was paid 12/6 for his *journey and expences and expence att Jane Sennates in all* and 7/6d for a second journey, and he was at *Holne* in 1741 *to view the bells* [App.II:15], but the smaller (and less distant) parish paid him only 2/6d, with 3/6d *expended when Mr Mudge was heare to have his opinion abt ye bells*. *Bickington* paid 1/6 the same year in *Expences when Mr Mudge came out to see whether the Bell was tuneable*, and he returned to Holne in 1745 to *fewe the Timber*, when a Mr Shapily also came to *fewe the bells*. Henry Mudge lived at Dean Prior, whither Samuel Wills was sent from *Buckfastleigh* in 1743 to *give Mr Mudge Notice to meet ye bellfounder*, and where his name is inscribed on the waist of the tenor. Samuel Sanders was called in by *Dawlish* in 1741 *to vue the New cast Bell, where a* (whether it) *was in wth the other Bells or not*; a Mr Salter came to *Hemyock* from Honiton in 1750 to view the tower, with the ringers in attendance, but whether he was concerned with the bells or with the tower (which has a history of structural problems) is not clear. The framed account of the bells in the ringing-room at Bishops Tawton tells how the 3rd was recast at *Buckland Brewer* in 1831 and *the five hinder bells were tuned under the able superintendence of Mr Richard Passmore of Braunton, a musician of the most correct ear and first-rate ability in these matters*. Later on in the 19th century the Reverend H.T. Ellacombe was certainly the Diocese's most notable bell expert, and in the 20th another much-loved clergyman, Ernest Vyvyan Cox, was for years the bell adviser – by this time officially for the Diocesan Advisory Committee.

Almost invariably these meetings would involve "*expenses*" as well as the cost of the "*articles*" drawn up, perhaps, by the schoolmaster. The nature of these expenses is sometimes specified: at *Gittisham* in 1664 we have *Itm; laid out for beare at severall times when the bellfounder was heare About ye bell and when the bell was taken doune and when the bell was hanged up & when the bell was tried – 14s 8d* at Dawlish in 1741, *Pd at a parishe meeting by consent at Evan Sennetts and at ye same time at Mary Watson's for Beer when Mr Bayle* (Bayley of Bridgwater) *signd his agreemt – 1s 6d*: the agreement is still among the church records. Plying the bellfounder with drink seems to have been an almost universal and very long-standing custom, for as early as 1426 we find at *Holy Trinity, Exeter*: *iid in s'visia apd domu Robti Norton bellemaker* (2d for beer at the house of Robert Norton the bellfounder").

Until the 18th century there are few examples of parish vestries asking for estimates from more than one bellfounder; for much of the period there would have been only one bellfounder within practical reach of the client parish. However, we do have the example of *Cheriton Fitzpaine*, which drew up an agreement with William Evans and then gave the job to Thomas Wroth[12], and in 1773 the *Crediton* Governors obtained estimates for recasting their six into eight from five founders – Bilbie of Cullompton, Street & Pyke of Bridgwater, Thomas Rudhall of Gloucester, Jack Chapman of Whitechapel, and their final choice John Pennington of Stoke Climsland [App.II:17].

The Cathedral 1372 accounts show that there the bellfounder Thomas Karoun was paid for his work only; all the other expenses in material and labour were paid directly by the Chapter, including the bellfounder's expenses in travelling to buy metal; the long and complex operation at *Braunton* in 1591–1594, in which John Birdall, William Preston and William Poole were all involved [App. I:4], was paid for on a similar basis; both sets of accounts give us a wonderfully detailed picture of the process. Later, we find that different founders, and possibly different parishes, adopted different methods of paying; the parish might agree to supply a building, clay, wood, dung and various specified items, or it might agree simply on a price for the whole operation with an adjustment for any increase or decrease in weight after recasting; there might also be so much per hundredweight allowed for wastage and "tinning-up" – replacing the tin which vaporizes when bell-metal is melted. If the casting was to be done at some distance from the parish, transport was normally the parish's responsibility at least until the 18th century. The agreement might also stipulate where the work was to be done; the *Modbury* 1622 articles with Thomas Pennington I and II state that if any of them should fail they will be recast within the parish or within five miles of it; when *Crediton* got five estimates to have their bells recast in 1773, the job went to John Pennington of Stoke Climsland, whose estimate included "and I will Cast them at Crediton".

---

12. A decision which they may have regretted.

Here are some good examples of such agreements:

Sampford Courtenay, 1659
1. *First our Dsiere is*
2. *That Mr Pennington shall take downe the bell and hang him up againe after hee is new cast our pish ayding him wth helpe and conveniences for the hanging of her*
3. *To make him to be a tune able bell sufficiently to answer in tune with the second bell and the fowrth*
4. *To attend the plow in loading and helping him home to see there be noe wrong done to the bell in carriage*
5. *To give securitie sufficiently to maintayne the said bell pfectly sound and in good tune for the space of one whole yeare next after the casting of her at his owne p p cosst and charge And for the triall of the tune two men to be chosen one of each side*
6. *If the bell decrease of the waight you receive from us you are to allow us xijd for every pound*
7. *Wee exceipt the mettall of our owne bell to be imployed for the new macking of our bell*
8. *Also two brasses to be new cast and for the increase of weight upon them wee are contented to pay for every pound soe increased xijd*
9. *To gett us free libertie from the pish of Exborne to goe and come & to carry and recarry to & from the place where the bell is to be cast before the bell be cast and fetcht away*
10. *Not to lessen or abate the waight of our bell passing theirtie pounds*
11. *And wee to pay for every pound increased upon new casting xijd pvided that the increase exceed not lli if more to his owne cost*
12. *Wee the wardens of the pish of Sampfordcourteney wth the consent of others doe pmise for the pformance of these Articles aforesaid to pay unto the foresaid Mr Thomas Pennington*

August the 4th 1659	*The some of 8li - 0s - 0d*
This was done in the	
presents of us heere	
under written	
William Elles	*Thomas Pennington*
John Elles	*Richard yollam*
Hen: Weekes	*the signe of*
William Yolland	*Leonard A Aller*

Cheriton Fitzpaine, 1726

May 9th 1726. At a meeting of ye parishioners of the parish of Cheriton Fitzpaine

after publick notice given as usuall it was unanimously agreed by & with the consent of the Churchwarden That the Churchwarden for the present time being & his Assistant or successors shall contract with Mr William Evans of Chepstow in Monmouthshire for the Casting of the 2d 3d & 4th Bells according to his proposalls wch are as followeth:

Imps   That the Churchwarden & assistant shall sell to the sd Mr William Evans the sd three bells to be deliverd to him at Chulmleigh att the price of tenpence pr lb & that the sd Mr Evans shall deliver to the sd Church warden or successors three good new bells in true tune with the present Treble (& bring the present Tenor in due tune wth the rest) att the price of fourteen pence pr lb. The sd Churchwarden & parishioners finding draught & carriages for drawing home the Bells (when cast) under the care & inspection of the sd William Evans.

Item.   That the sd Churchwarden (with Assistant) or successors shall contract with the sd William Evans for the Furniture of the whole five Bells, viz: wheels, Clappers, Frames, Brasses, Stocks & Iron stuff at Price of twenty five pounds the sd Churchwarden & parishioners finding and allowing towards the same timber for the Frames &

Stocks to be delivered sawn at the Churchyard afores^d. The old Iron to be to the use of the s^d William Evans & the old Timber to s^d Churchwarden & parishioners. In witness of wch unanimous agreement we have subscribed our names att the time above s^d

Will Maunder	*Tho' Gibbs*
Andrew Hewis Chwarden	*Tho' Gibbs*
John Kingdon	*John Smart*
John Reed	*Rob Veasey*
William Bidgood	*Henry Waters*
John Gibbs	*John Hewish*

(After taking all this trouble to make an agreement with William Evans, the Cheriton Fitzpaine people finally had the work done by Thomas Wroth, a choice which they and their successors at Cheriton may have reason to regret.)

Ugborough, 1761:

Ugborough Novr. 17th: 1761.

In consequence of a notice given last Sunday in the Church for meeting to contract about taking down & new casting the Bells: We whose Names are hereunto subscrib'd have met at the Vestry, & agreed with Thomas Bilbie of Cullumpton Bellfounder for taking down the Five Bells and new casting the same of the same weight of Metal and adding one new one of a proper Size with the others for the Price or Sum of One Hundred Pounds Fifty Pounds of which to be paid on the 29th day of May next and the remaining fifty Pounds on the 19th day of May 1763 – the said Thos Bilbie to be allow'd Five Pounds out of every Hundred Weight of old Metal for wastage & fourteen pence per Pound for such new Metal as he shall have occasion to use not only for Five Bells but also for casting the additional new one – the said Thos Bilbie to be at the whole expence of Taking down the said bells carrying them away and – bringing the new ones and hanging them up and finding wheels, stocks, Bolts, Bell Ropes and all other necessarys except Framing Timber, Plank and Flooring Timber. The Bells to be Hung and fit for use on or before the 29th day of May next the said Thomas Bilbie to keep all the Bells sound for Twelve months from the said 29th day of May next, and if any accidents shall happen to repair them anew at his own expence – The Note of the Tenor Bell to be F natural.

John Savery	*William Jeffery*
John Pears	*Jonathan Gose*
Jno Hodder	*John Stentaford*
Philip Trenick	*Thomas Crocker*

Other examples of documents relating to bellfounding will be found in Appenix II.

Raising the Money

Once the decision had been made, the parish was faced, as it is today, with raising the money, which could be many times the church's average annual turnover. Until the beginning of the 17th century, most parishes raised the bulk of their income from Church Ales, which were usually held on the patronal festival of the church and its guilds or *stores* – *Clawton* had two, one at the feast of St Leonard the patron saint of the church, and one for St Katherine whose altar was in the North aisle, and *Morebath* had several. Many rural parishes had income from church sheep, and *Chagford* had a tin-working belonging to the church which was worked by the parishioners for a period each year; others had property in land or houses, or income from fair and market tolls – *Bampton*'s famous fair was given to the church in 1285 but was sold off with the endowments of the rectory when Buckland Abbey was dissolved, but much of *Chudleigh* church's income came from market tolls. These sources had to cover the upkeep of the church, roads and bridges, relief of the poor and all other parish needs, and could sometimes include quite large projects for the bells. In *Clyst St George* in 1596 Thomas Packer the churchwarden "*made his accompte before the pishe the money that he gott clere by the selling of a litl Ale withoute collectinge either money or malte came unto fower pounde viiis iiiid which was bestowed in castinge of the great bell*": as the price of ale at that time was certainly not more than 1d per quart, Thomas's "*litle Ale*" seems to have amounted to at least 130 gallons; one wonders what a lot of ale would be in his estimation.

Especially in the early 17th century, the parish might be "gathered" by one or two people going round to collect money. Our earliest example of this is at *Dartington* in 1488 – "*receptus Gervase ffoxe & Willelmus Myller collectoribus de moneta promisia campanis – summa iijli vis viijd*" (received from Gervase Fox and William Miller the collectors of the money promised for the bells – £3 6s 8d.) In this case, the parish also received 12d from the Prior of Totnes and another 12d from the bellfounder at Exeter; the bill for recasting was £20 10s 4d. An interesting feature of these "gatherings" in the early 17th century is that young people often took a prominent part; at *Widecombe-in-the-Moor* the new treble (now the 5th), dated 1632, is inscribed ROBEART HAMLYN SONNE OF IOHN HAMLYN OF CHITTELFORD GATHERED OF THE YONG MEN AND MAYDS FYFTENE POVNDS; at *Hartland* in 1613 the collector was John Blagdon who collected £3 12s *as a guift from the youth of the parish* [App.II:6]. Benoni Reeve at *Colebrooke* collected £3 13s 9d *as gift money collected by him* in 1627; he was a young man who five years later was raising a family. At *Halberton* in 1652 twelve young men, named in the account, gave a total of 5s 8d; at *Tedburn St Mary* the young men of the parish gave money for *repayring the great bell* in 1656. Before the Reformation many Devon country parishes had "Young men wardens" and "Maiden wardens" elected annually and raising money for their own "stores", and it seems that the idea of corporate action by the young people of a community lingered for at least two generations after the guilds and stores had ceased to exist in any formal way, people like John Hamlyn filling the role, perhaps, of today's Chairman of the Young Farmers' Club.

Not all the money necessarily came from within the parish; at *Aveton Gifford* we have a list of donations for the new bell in 1633; £13 8s came from within the parish in sums between £2 and 2s, and £5 11s 2d, including two of £1, came from outside. However, it was more often the local "quality" who were involved: for the bells of *St Petrox, Dartmouth* in 1754 Sir John Seale headed the subscription list with four guineas and Mr William Newcomen contributing 2/6d to raise £30 9s, – but *Mrs French in her Two shills gave one in Birmingham half pence which can make nothing of so the money Collected is no more than £30 8s*. In many instances the local squire was a major contributor to the bell fund; a ledger stone in the chancel at

Fig. 59. The Bampfylde ledger-slab at Poltimore, recording the gift of the tenor bell in 1390.

Poltimore records the gift of the great bell by one of the Bampfylde family, as we read on a ledger-slab in the chancel:

mcccxc   Hic iacent Johes Baunfeld & agnes uxor eius Pat & Mat Willi Baunfeld qui hac ecclia(e) maxima(m) campana(m) fieri fecerunt (*1390. Here lie the bodies of John Bampfylde and Agnes his wife Father and Mother of William Bampfylde, who caused the great bell of this church to be made.*) Coats-of-arms on mediaeval Exeter bells probably testify to the local landlord's contribution to them, though in some cases they may have been used on other bells simply as decorations. The 5th at *Molland* bears the arms of the local branch of the Courtenays who apparently gave it although they were recusant Roman Catholics at the time (1700), and at *West Alvington* it would appear that the Ilbert family paid the whole cost of recasting the bells in 1775. At *Ashburton* the bells, so legend has it, were lost at sea when the ship carrying them to London was taken by a French privateer; whatever the truth of that story, the new bells were paid for by the town's two Members of Parliament, John Harris of Hayne and Sir William Yonge, whose coats-of-arms were splendidly displayed on each of the ring of six cast by Thomas Lester. When the bells of *Bradstone* were recast at Buckland Brewer in 1827 by John Taylor, John Arundel the local squire footed the bill, as we have seen.

However, once the Church Rate became the standard method of raising church funds, the churchwardens raised the bulk of the cost of a bell restoration by levying as many church rates as might be needed – possibly many times the normal number. In some cases more drastic measures might be needed, as at *Buckland-in-the-Moor*: there the parish Feoffees, Churchwardens and Overseers of the Poor resolved in 1759 to have five new bells cast by Thomas Bilbie, with a new frame and gear; Bilbie's bill was about £30, and the meeting decided to borrow this sum from Richard Eales the younger of Ashburton, *the debt to be taken upon Riddiclift Estate* which belonged to the parish but was apparently in poor repair. The debt was later taken over by Robert Smerdon, one of the churchwardens, and eventually paid off in full, but it took 33 years, and Robert Smerdon stayed in office for the whole of that time, with only one short break; the year following the final settlement he resigned and became a Sideman[13] instead.

The parish might not contribute to the project in money only. As we have seen, when bells were cast on the spot much of the fuel, loam, dung and stone might be given, in addition to labour, and metal might also be collected locally. Indeed some parishes had stocks of bell-metal which they held for years, accounted for by succeeding churchwardens or some other official; the Mayor of *Plympton St Maurice* in 1668 held 235lb of bell metal on behalf of the parishioners, as collateral for a loan of £5. We have seen how in 1593 the Braunton wardens bought a "*great crok*"; 20s was paid as only one instalment for it, so it must have been a very large vessel, perhaps like the huge cauldron at Laycock Abbey.

A mutilated note in the *Braunton* accounts gives some idea of the complex transactions which went into recasting their five bells: it includes two lots of metal from Birdall, one of the three founders involved in the work; *a bell of Mr Richard Bellowes in wight ix^{li}*; six crocks altogether totalling 151½ lb; 10 lb of tin, and *ye hollinwater buckat wch was ye p'ishes, xiiijli in weight*. A certain amount of metal remained after the recasting, and was held by the churchwardens. The Braunton recasting [App.II:4] is one of the best documented in the county; it covered a period from 1581 to 1594, and involved three founders, John Birdall, William Preston and William Poole, who at times seem to have worked together, to create a ring of four bells of 10cwt 30lb, 13cwt 70lb, 19cwt 31lb and 25cwt 24lb (or 9cwt 22lb, 13cwt 14lb, 17cwt 26lb and 22cwt 60lb, if "c" stands for 100lb and not 112lb).

The *Plymouth* accounts for 1594, beautifully written in the "Widey Court Book" [App.II:5], show that the town bought nearly half a ton of tin from John Robbyns of Plympton (one of the stannary towns where the tin from Dartmoor was assayed), and over 5 cwt from Peter Edgecombe of Tavistock, another stannary town. They also paid

---

13. Most parishes had, in addition to the Churchwardens, a self-perpetuating group of men known variously as "Four men", "Six men", "Sidemen" &c, and who were much more influential in parish affairs than our sidesmen today.

for a gun either lying on the bottom of the harbour or stowed in the bottom of a ship as ballast. Other metal was bought from parishioners, and William Gill was paid 21s 8d *for a bell weighinge 70 pounde att vi^d pr pounde ie xxxv^s whereof he received xxx^s and thother v^s gave toward the bells*. The *Woodbury* wardens in 1720 bought a bell at "Bonehay" – Bonhay Island was still a site for metal dealing 250 years later – brought it back to Woodbury, and took it to Exeter again to be recast, presumably because it was out of pitch with the rest of the ring. The work was probably done by Thomas Pennington III, and it was recast again by Evans 18 years later.

The Casting site

Unless the work was to be done within a few miles of the foundry, it was common for the bellfounder, at least until 1700, to come to the bells rather than vice versa; his equipment would have been little more than one horse-load: in 1744 Oliver Langmaid was paid for carrying Mr Gooding's tools to *South Tawton*, presumably from Plymouth, and the following year the Holne people paid 4/10d for *one ganey to Southtowen* (going to South Tawton) *for to give Mr Gooding Account for mite* (meet) *the parish* – to arrange for him to cast their bells at Buckfastleigh [App.II:15]. However, it was often possible for the founder, once he had set up his foundry in one parish, to drum up work from other churches in the neighbourhood; so an unknown founder cast bells for *Georgenympton* at *Romansleigh* in 1680, Thomas Purdue cast a bell for *Colebrooke* in 1676 while he was working on the cathedral bells; the Evanses from Chepstow rented the Church House for a foundry when they cast the bells for *Braunton* in 1713 and kept it on for several years, [App.II:12] while William Evans in 1729 asked (unsuccessfully) for the Cathedral Chapter to provide him with a foundry site which he could use for three years, but in the end did keep a foundry going in Exeter after casting bells for the cathedral, and used it certainly for *Exeter St Edmund's* in 1731 and *Newton St Cyres* in 1733; *Holne* bells were cast by Gooding at Buckfastleigh with the ring for that tower in 1743–4; the Cornish Penningtons seem to have established temporary foundries at various places during the later 18th century; *Northlew* bells were recast in 1772, and *Ashwater* and probably *Black Torrington* there the same year; *Chudleigh* bells on site in 1781 and one bell for *Jacobstowe* there the same year, along probably with *Highweek*, while a local tradition has it that *Atherington, Burrington* and *Landkey* bells were all recast at Atherington.

All the same, people were not afraid to transport bells quite long distances to be recast, and at no small expense; the transport of two bells from *Woodbury* to Ash Priors and back can be traced in the wardens' accounts, and an epic journey it was, with 5 men and 14 oxen, three days each way (see App.II:2). They set off with the bells on a Sunday with *drinking for them that went forth that caried the bells to Aishe Priors before their going at Richard Bussells*; following the old ridge road by West Hill they had supper that day at Larkbeare near Whimple, and next morning stopped for a drink at Kentisbeare, reaching Milverton for supper where their number seems to have swelled to nine. They reached Ash Priors on the Tuesday evening, and spent four days there while their bells were recast – Roger Semson must of course have prepared the moulds beforehand, and along with John Langham provided *meate for the oxen four daies*: the oxen were also shod before starting on the return journey on the Saturday morning. First stop was Milverton, and on the Sunday they paid 12d *for going over the fermors ground at Harford Bridge* over the Tone near Langford Budville: they stayed the Sunday night in Kentisbeare, paid Thomas Farryn there for a yoke, and arrived home in Woodbury on the Monday, the account of the journey ending in the triumphant entry: *Pd att Jane Bussells homeward for drynkyng – iiijd*. In 1671 two bells went from *Awliscombe* to Closworth and back, and the cost of the transport and six journeys for the wardens came to nearly £10 against £33 for the recasting; in 1678 *Kilmington* paid Thomas Purdue £9 5s for recasting bells, and the bill for transport to Closworth and back came to £4 10s 6d, and *Cullompton*, even further away, sent their 3rd and tenor there in 1688; the transport cost £7, with 1/6d extra for men helping the bells up Black Down. Vehicles capable of carrying such loads were rare or non-existent in most Devon parishes – Celia Fiennes found that practically everything in Devon was carried on the backs of horses – and the word used is often "plow"; at *Gittisham* the account includes, *laid out for lent of a pair of weles to carry the bell at Exeter & for making a Boddy to the weles*: small wonder, then, that water transport was used wherever possible, for the whole or part of the journey. The *Braunton* accounts have a number of entries for bringing various cargoes by water – a "great crock" in 1593, bricks from Barnstaple for Evan Evans's furnace – brought to "the Vilata" which is now called Vellator; *Hartland* in 1613 paid Philip Nicholl *for carrying the Bells to Northam from Barnestaple in a boate* which belonged to William Skinner [App.II:6]. *Aveton Gifford* had a bell recast by Thomas Pennington II in 1633, and paid 5/- for *custome of the Bell at Exon*, 8d for *a let passe at ye custome house*, and 6/8d for bringing the bell to Kingsbridge, whence it apparently came by road. The people of *Chivelstone*, near the head of a beautiful creek on the Kingsbridge estuary, were well placed to use water transport for their bells; when in 1682 they paid *mordeca cockey for casting of our fouer bells* in Kingsbridge, they *paid the barge men for bringing of the bells from poole worthy*; when John Stadler recast them again in 1710 he did the work in Chivelstone, but in 1719 they had a new frame on seven foundation-beams for which they paid Thomas Willing £4 8s, 5/6d *for helping of this timber into the Boat at Dodbrooke Key*, 5/- to *the Boatmen for bringing of this timber from Kingsbridge* and 2/- *for helping of the tymber out of the Boat at Poole*. In 1798 one of their bells went to sea again, when Captain Gillard carried the 3rd to Plymouth for 7s 7½d and another vessel took it to Calstock to be carried by road to Stoke Climsland. Naturally, parishes which lay on or near the sea could look beyond their own county for foundries to cast their bells; mediaeval bells from the Bristol foundry can be found close to the North Devon coast at *Lynton, Brendon, Ashford, Horwood, Alwington* and *Yarnscombe*, while the South coast has London bells surviving at *Marldon, Dartmouth St Clement, Wolborough, Exeter St Petrock* and *St Mary Arches*, with others recorded but since vanished at *Dartmouth St Saviour* and *Plymouth*. After the Reformation this pattern continued until the coming of the railways; while the bells from the Devon and Cornish founders tend to cover the whole area, the Rudhalls of Gloucester established a strong connection in North Devon – *Pilton, Torrington, Filleigh, Ilfracombe, Georgeham* – with only a few examples, most of them near the sea, in the south, while the Whitechapel founders supplied *Ashburton, Newton Abbot, Dartmouth St Petrox, Ashprington, Kingsbridge* and *Dittisham*, all close to water. In 1762 and 1765 bells from *Axminster* were taken by road to Langport and thence by water to Bridgwater. Tom Chapman's estimate for *Crediton* bells specified that the founder would receive the old bells and deliver the new ones at Exeter Quay, but the parish was to cover the insurance of the new bells down to Exeter and the old ones up to London; evidently Chapman was planning to exchange the new ring for the old one, rather than actually recasting; Lester had done the same for *Dartmouth St Petrox* in 1754 and Thomas Mears for *Kenn* in 1826.

In fact, founders differed a good deal in the extent to which they itinerated. We have found no record to indicate that Ambrose Gooding had any permanent foundry site, and we have already seen that the Penningtons used temporary foundries in various places until almost the end of the 18th century in addition to their headquarters at Exeter, Tavistock, Lezant or Stoke Climsland; but there are few records of the Wroths casting anywhere except at Wellington, and once the Bilbies had made their temporary foundry at Cullompton a permanent one they seem to have expected the bells to come to them – when they recast the bells of Plymouth in 1748 they had yet to settle in Devon, and the on-site recasting at Beaminster seems to have been exceptional. The last bell cast on site in Devon was probably the former tenor at *Plympton St Maurice*, cast by William & Charles Pannell in 1833. No doubt the road network made a difference; Wellington and Cullompton were on the main road from Exeter to Bristol, but Chulmleigh, Lezant and Stoke Climsland are in comparatively remote and hilly country, and Plymouth's road communications were poor until the turnpike roads came into being.

If the bells were to be cast at a distance, it was often necessary for the founder to have an accurate note for a new bell to be, and in 1503 *Ashburton* sent *John Gye to ride to Exceter to take the tewne of the bell* [See App. II:1]. Likewise, when *Tawstock* had a bell recast by John Rudhall in 1794 the cost included *Paid for postage of Letters with the Receipts and pitchfork enclosed*. Bellfounders' agreements seldom specify the note of a new or recast ring, but *Ugborough*'s contract with Thomas Bilbie in 1761 states that *The Note of the Tenor Bell shall be F natural*.

In the event, the Ugborough people seem to have changed their minds, because they paid for a great deal of extra metal, and the note of Bilbie's tenor is below E flat.

One very important element in the business of casting or recasting was the weighing of the bells, for which the churchwardens were almost always present, even if they had not witnessed the casting itself. Normally this was done where the bells were cast, and if that was close to the church it might be necessary to borrow or make a beam and weights – *Plymstock* paid a shilling *for bringing up of the weights to weigh the bell from Or[e]ston* (where their regular use would have been on the quay), but *Kilmington* in 1677 evidently had no such facilities nearby and *laid out to Robert Hooper and Robert Damat for making a bame and wites to wite the beles*. *Dawlish* in 1742 spent a shilling on *Mr Elliott of Topsham for ye lent of his Beam in Beer & money*, another shilling to borrow a horse and a boy to carry the beam from Starcross to Dawlish and back, and 1/9d to bring the beam to Starcross and take it back to Topsham – evidently by boat. *Woodbury* in 1613 had their 4th weighed three times on the King's Beam in Exeter, and in 1731 a bell for *Ide* was weighed at Exeter Quay, where the scale-beam can still be seen.

4

THE BELLFOUNDERS: BEFORE THE REFORMATION

(Note: Although the Reformation took place in the middle of the 16th-century, the major change in bellfounding style and technique happened at the end of the century, and the mediaeval Exeter foundry continued in the old style until 1624, so bells cast before the change are commonly classed with "pre-reformation" bells.)

ONE FACT EMERGES VERY clearly from the written records about the people who cast our bells in former times, and that is that the trade carried considerable status. In an age when titles were not lightly conferred, when "Gentleman" or "Esquire" meant specifically a landowner with a coat-of-arms, the mason might be "John Spry" and the smith "Will Glandfield", but the bellfounder would almost always be styled "Mr Pennington or "Mr Bilbie". We know that William Wodeward of London, a bellfounder who also made cannon for Richard II, held the rank of King's Esquire,[14] and although no bellfounders are known to have been entitled to bear a coat-or-arms a number of them used armorial-style marks, apparently with impunity, and one branch of the Pennington family was armorial. Most bellfounders were literate (a remarkable exception is the great Thomas Purdue, who could write only his initials rather shakily), and it is noteworthy that in most cases a tradesman whose output might well be predominantly domestic metalware such as pots, skillets and cauldrons (which were usually cast in lead-bronze, not in bell-metal), would choose to style himself "bellfounder" – though the Birdalls almost always used the title of "brazier" and indeed the finds on their foundry-site show that they made a huge quantity of domestic vessels compared to their bell output: but the Pennington foundry in Exeter also produced much of the same kind of material, yet the Penningtons always called themselves bellfounders. This is not surprising; until the Industrial Revolution, bells were the largest and heaviest metal castings made by anybody – in fact, Thomas Newcomen had to go to a bellfounder for the cylinder of his first steam engine – and making them involved procedures which to most people must have seemed almost unbelievably alarming and mysterious, while most founders probably kept some of their trade secrets to themselves or at least in the family.

One has to ask how these craftsmen made their calculations in a process which demanded such accuracy and care. In this country there is virtually no detailed documentation of the techniques of bellfounding – a few diagrams and instructions survive on the Continent – so that one has to assume that our families or dynasties of founders had their own trade secrets passed down the generations, and there is evidence that most of the independent founders would have learnt their trade through an apprenticeship with another – Ambrose Gooding and John Stadler with the Penningtons and Thomas Wroth by his own testimony from Hodson. Many of our Engllish bellfoundries were run by family dynasties which lasted for generations – our own area was dominated by the Penningtons, the Bilbies and the Purdues, and elsewhere notably the Rudhalls of Gloucester: in the case of the Penningtons, the Cornish family alone was involved in bellfounding from the beginning of the 17th-century to the third decade of the 19th, covering seven generations, and the Bilbies, first at Chewstoke and later also at Cullompton, were working from

---

14. T.F. Tout, *Firearms in England in the 14th century*, Collected Papers II, p.148.

1698 to 1814. However, it is noticeable that in other Westcountry foundries there is very little evidence of the business passing down the family; as far as we know, Richard Russell was the only son of a mediaeval Exeter bellfounder to have inherited the business, and he may not have been closely involved with it; at Bridgwater, the foundry started by Thomas Bayley became a family business only when the Kingstons had it in the late 18th-century, and men like William Preston of Crediton, Mordecai Cockey of Totnes, Ambrose Gooding in Plymouth and John Stadler in Chulmleigh stood alone and their businesses died with them.

Bellfounding during the middle ages tended to be centred on the cities; in the Westcountry at Exeter, Bristol, Gloucester and Salisbury, while the London foundries sent bells to virtually every part of the kingdom. However, after the Reformation we find a great change, as founders appear in quite small towns and even villages; in Devon we had bellfounders working from Crediton, Barnstaple, Tavistock, Chulmleigh, Cullompton, Totnes and Blackawton as well as Exeter and Plymouth, and in Cornwall at Bodmin, Lezant, Stoke Climsland and Hayle. This may well be partly a result of the Reformation. By the end of the great tower-building period in the mid-15th-century, most of our churches had acquired rings of three of four, the normal number for the period, so that demand for new bells would have fallen: with the dissolution of the monasteries and the onset of Puritan ideas, there was certainly a further sharp drop in demand, so that bellfounders would be looking for other work such as the casting of domestic vessels to keep themselves in business, and this may have led to a wider distribution of foundries across the country.

One particularly interesting centre was near Yeovil. There, at Stoford (an interesting example of a mediaeval borough in Barwick parish, which never took off) but mainly at nearby Closworth, the Purdue family worked from the late 16th-century until the death of Thomas Purdue in 1711. In this quite small area during the 17th and 18th centuries there seems to have been a remarkable amount of metalwork going on, though there are no obvious reasons why this should be so, as there are no sources of non-ferrous metals in the vicinity. In addition to the Closworth foundry, the Wiseman and the Fathers families (who may have been connected by marriage or descent) worked at Montacute, the Pooles at Yetminster, the Sturtons at South Petherton and William Apsey at Nettlecombe.[15] After the death of Thomas Purdue the situation at Closworth becomes even more intriguing: William Knight, who during Purdue's declining years had worked with him, appears with a Thomas Knight who was probably his son, and a William Wright was also casting bells using the Closworth plant; he must be the founder whom "Young Bilbie" taunted in his inscription on Yeovil tenor (1728), YOU WRATH AND WRIGHT NOW SPEAK THE RIGHT COME SEE HOW I AM RUN . . . Then in 1749 we find William Elery, Thomas Roskelly, Richard Rock and James Smith, all of whom seem to have been casting bells, using the same plant, at about the same time. Elery and Roskelly are both Cornish names – in the 18th century there were Roskellys at Stoke Climsland. Perhaps William and Thomas were recruited on a tin-buying trip, but it almost seems as if the foundry was a community enterprise, operated as need arose by men who must have had some other source of income, perhaps on the land.

Some bellfounders operated on a wider scope still. We have documentary evidence of Thomas Pennington of Tavistock being a pewterer, and a silver chalice has also been attributed to him; other members of the Pennington family appear in documents relating to leadwork, as do Mordecai Cockey and his son. Willliam Hambling was a blacksmith and gunsmith, the Bilbies made both domestic and turret clocks, and the Bridgwater foundry produced a huge range of metal products including clocks, spinning jennies and cooking utensils.

The coming of the railways certainly hastened the demise of the local bellfoundries. As long as the major foundries had to rely on water transport to deliver bells over long distances, there would be a limit to their ability to compete with the local men; the distribution of Rudhall bells in Devon for example shows that they seldom

---

15. Roderick Butler, *English Bronze Cooking Vessels & their Founders, 1350–1830,* Butler, 2003.

occur more than a few miles from a seaport, but the railways soon brought almost every village within half a day's waggon-journey of a station, and their economies of scale were overwhelming. The Taylors' branch foundry at Buckland Brewer had come to an end before the railway reached Barnstaple, and the Pannells' attempt to build up their "West of England Bell Foundry" in Exeter in 1855 was too late; the line had reached the city eleven years earlier, and the field was left to London, Oxford (later Loughborough), Birmingham and Bristol.

Mediaeval Bellfounders: The Exeter Foundry

There may have been bellfounders working in Devon before the beginning of the Exeter foundry in the late 13th century, but only one is known by name – **Roger de Ropeford**, who in 1284 was appointed to cast bells for Exeter Cathedral in return for the lease of a property in Paignton (one of the Bishop's manors) at a rent of one penny per annum: his grandson is later recorded as holding the same property on the same terms. We have no bells which can be attributed to any of the family, but we do have entries in the Cathedral Fabric Accounts for 1286–7 for *rogero campanario et filio eius circa campanum qu vocatur Walterus et circa rotas faciend'* and *Rogero campanario et filio eius ad pendend' ij campanas*,[16] so we know that they were working on the bells at this time: they were also to be responsible for the organs. It is not clear that they had a permanent home in Devon; the holding in Paignton could have been no more than a source of income. However, it has to noted that Ropeford was an alternative spelling of the village named Rofford or Rufford, and that the Rufford family were to be notable bellfounders in London and in Bedfordshire during the 14th century.

The first bells which can be assigned to a Devon founder with any certainty are the group bearing inscriptions in a set of Lombardic lettering [Pl 2a], accompanied by a cross fleury [Pl 1a]. These bells almost all have the raised band on the shoulder, with moulding-wires above and below, which was used by London bellfounders from the second half of the 14th-century to the early 15th; 23 of these survive, and 8 more have been recorded but no longer exist. With one exception (at Zennor) the letters are evenly spaced around the inscription-band, sometimes with 3-dot stops between the words, and the quality of casting is almost always very good, with well-shaped cannons; one, at Dorchester-on-Thames, has cabled cannons.

A well-known feature of this group of bells is the raised line across the "M" and "N", showing that the matrix containing those two letters had been cracked and repaired if it was made of clay, or split if it was made of wood. Only one bell has so far been found without this crack, and that is at Chilthorne Domer in Somerset. In fact the distribution of this group of Exeter bells is by far

Fig. 60.　An early Exeter foundry bell (*c*1400) the 5th at Brompton Ralph in Somerset.

---

16. "to Roger the bellfounder and his son about the bell which is called Walter and about making the wheels", and "to Roger the bellfounder and his son for hanging two bells".

the widest of all; most of them are in Devon or Somerset, but others range from Dorchester-on-Thames in Oxfordshire to Zennor in Cornwall and from Brimpsfield[17] in Gloucestershire to *Seaton, Woodland* near Newton Abbot and Rame in Cornwall. The name of their founder or founders has not yet come to light, but the wide distribution and the occurrence of the earliest of the group in Somerset suggests the possibility that he was itinerating prior to settling in Exeter. Except for the very interesting English inscription at Brompton Ralph in Somerset, all the bells in the group are inscribed in Latin. The Zennor bell is in fact very strange and unique: the moulding-wires do not include the flat band; the letters are grouped into words; and the bell is decorated with two winged creatures with human faces, possibly "harpies" [Pl.1s], which appear nowhere else; for that reason its inclusion in this early group is uncertain. In addition to the bells, there is an account of a small mortar from St Just-in-Penwith, Cornwall,[18] bearing the same Lombardic lettering and cross, so we can be sure that this founder, like most if not all of the period, was making domestic metalware as well as bells.

Both the cross and the lettering of this group are very similar to a set used by the Gloucester foundry – so similar that only close comparison of casts can be certain of distinguishing them from one another. No doubt there was contact between these foundries, but whether one copied the lettering from the other, or both derived their matrices from the same engraver, is not immediately clear – nor which came first. However, Robert Hendley, the Gloucester founder who took over the set from his predecessor, is assigned by Sharpe and Bliss to the latter half of the 15th century, and from comparing the two crosses I suspect that the Gloucester cross, which is less boldly moulded [Pl 7p], is copied from the Exeter one and not *vice versa*: this would concur with the fact that the Gloucester moulds were apparently still in use towards the end of the century whereas we know that in Exeter they were superseded by black-letter inscriptions in the 1420s or 30s and later occur only very sporadically.

These Lombardic letters and their cross were taken over by **Robert Norton**, the first identifiable Exeter founder. Norton was enrolled as a freeman of the City in 1423, and in 1427 the churchwardens of *Holy Trinity, Exeter* were paying for beer drunk at his house: he is mentioned in a document of the early 1430s along with the churchwardens of *Brixham*, and in 1433 the parishioners of *Plymtree* brought a Chancery writ suing him and a Plymtree man named John Forde on the ground that they had by *ontrewe ymagynacion coneyne and desseit* claimed that three bells cast for Plymtree weighed 2,382lb, whereas the parishioners asserted that they were only 18cwt. (2016lb). The court issued a writ of *certiorari*, and there is no way of knowing the final outcome of the case. Ellacombe's opinion that this shows Norton to have been "a most dishonest tradesman" assumes far too

Fig. 61. Upton, Somerset: a beautiful casting by Robert Norton, *c*1430.

---

17. When I first saw this bell, I attributed it to Robert Norton, but having seen all the known bells of this group I am now satisfied that it belongs to an earlier founder.
18. Described in *Proceedings of the Society of Antiquaries,* Feb. 6, 1913. Apparently it has since disappeared.

much: at this period Chancery writs were a classic ploy used by embarrassed clients to put off payment – sometimes almost indefinitely. Norton used a foundry-mark of a bell in a rope circle flanked by his initials in black-letter [Pl 1i]. His bells are almost all very well cast. Norton and his successors probably worked in *Billiter Lane*, off Rack Street in Exeter, between South Street and Fore Street.

As long as Norton was using the Lombardic lettering he cast his bells very much in the style of his predecessor, but by 1423 the London founders had taken up the fashion for gothic "black-letter" script, and Norton was one of the first provincial founders to follow their lead – indeed he soon overtook them. As we have described earlier, Norton seems to have invented a technique for simplifying the process of making black-letter inscriptions by adopting a number of popular mottoes in the form of "Leonine" hexameters and making moulds which allowed a whole word or two short words to be made on one wax patera.

The six mottoes which he used on large bells were:

> Est michi collatum ihc istud nomen amatum
> *To me is given Jesus that beloved name* – on 75 bells by him or later Exeter founders

> Voce mea viva depello cun[c]ta nociva
> *With my lively voice I drive away all hurtful things* – on 35 bells

> Protege virgo pia quos convoco sancta maria
> *Holy virgin, Saint Mary, protect those whom I call* – on 33 bells

> Plebs o[mn]is plaudit ut me tam sepius audit
> *The people all applaud the more often they hear me* – on 30 bells

> Me melior vere non est campana sub ere
> *In truth beneath the sky there is no better bell than I* – on 15 bells

> Misteriis sacris repleat nos d[o]c[trin]a iohannis
> *May the teaching of John fill us in the holy mysteries* – on 12 bells.

The first and by far the most popular of these, "*Est michi collatum . . .*" declares the name of the bell to be the name of Jesus, and bells with this and similar inscriptions are often known as "Jesus bells": the devotion to the name of Jesus was growing very strongly in England at this period. In the case of the Exeter foundry, the motto does not seem to have been deeply significant, as more than one bell in a ring can be found with this inscription. Four of them have "Prte" added to the inscription; it may be that the founder was trying to give the bell the name of Peter, though in two cases the "ihc" also appears; the only survivor of these, at Over Stowey in Somerset, has only "PRTE Est michi", the last word inverted; one recorded at West Teignmouth by HTE was also corrupt.

"*Voce mea viva . . .*" refers to the belief that the sound of church bells would prevent thunderstorms, plagues, and so on, – a belief which in some places persisted until the 19th century. In other parts of the country (and indeed Europe) there are commonly found variants of "*Mortuos plango, vivos voco, fulgura frango*" – "I knell the dead, I call the living, I break the lightning".

"*Protege virgo pia . . .*", unlike the other Exeter stock inscriptions, can be found on an earlier bell in Devon – the tenor at *Petersmarland* by Richard de Wymbis, where it appears in Lombardic letters. The Exeter version in black-letter seems to have suffered some defect or damage in the matrix for "convoco": on some bells the "n" or "nv" are replaced by letters on separate paterae; on others the top of the "n" is covered by an oblong block showing that a piece was cut out of the matrix [Pl 4b]; and on a few a very close examination shows that this block on the wax pattern was carefully trimmed to form the top of the "n", very fine vertical lines revealing the final finishing with a knife-tip. No surviving bells with this inscription bear Robert Norton's mark, but it is almost certain that he created it along with the others, as we shall see.

"*Plebs ois plaudit . . .*" seems to have lost its initial "P", and often appears without it, or with the "P" on a separate patera. It was adapted by Robert Russell for his new, bigger "Peter" bell at Exeter Cathedral and reproduced by Purdue: "*Plebs patriae plaudit dum Petrum plenius audit*" – "The people of the land rejoice when they hear Peter more loudly".

"*Me melior . . .*", like the previous motto, is a boast by the bellfounder rather than a prayer or a dedication. It appears in two sizes of lettering, generally on comparatively large bells; as far as the 3rd at Torbryan is concerned, one can claim that it is true, but as much cannot be said for the treble of the old three at St Pierre du Bois in Guernsey.

"*Misteriis sacris . . .*", in smaller black-letter than the other five, appears only on bells by Robert Norton or probably by him, and it always appears with the cross which went with the Lombardic lettering – a cross which very seldom appears with any of the other stock inscriptions. Whether its sentiment became unfashionable after his time, or the patterns were lost or broken, one can only speculate. The abbreviation "dca" could stand for "dicta" or "doctrina", but I have preferred "doctrina" because "dicta" would be plural and "repleat" ought then to be "repleant".

One small bell, *Clyst St Mary* 1/3, has a set of small Lombardic capitals [Pl 2b]; another is described at Foxcott in Hampshire, but its present whereabouts is uncertain. There are two small bells, at *St Pancras, Exeter* and *Exeter Guildhall* with what appear to be stock inscriptions, though they survive nowhere else. Their lettering is very small [Pl 2c]: on the St Pancras bell, which has Norton's mark, it reads:

"Quamvis sum parva tamen audior ampla p[e]r arva"
Though I am small I will be heard over the wide fields

The Guildhall bell reads:

"Celi regina me p[ro]tege que[a]so ruina"
Queen of heaven, protect me I pray from ruin

It might seem strange for anyone to have taken the trouble to make the patterns for "stock" inscriptions which were unlikely to be used very often, but it may well be that the founder decided that making patterns for whole words would be less troublesome than applying dozens of tiny letters one at a time.

The patterns for these stock inscriptions appear to have been made by impressing the end of a suitably shaped stick into clay; in some cases strokes can be seen to overlap, which rules out the use of a carved wooden matrix. However, they were permanent, and some of the matrices apparently had a very long life; odd words such as "ois" and "convoco" were used perhaps as late as 1600 in jumbled inscriptions by the Birdalls: they must have been knocking about in the foundries at Rack Street and later in St Thomas for at least 160 years. This is not hard to believe when one sees boxwood matrices at Villedieu which have been in use there for over two centuries.

One advantage of a stock inscription was that it could be put on by an illiterate workman, provided he knew the order in which to apply the paterae and which way up to set them. There is no evidence that Norton ever took advantage of this feature of his invention, but it seems that later Exeter founders did, as a number of bells have words or even whole inscriptions inverted, words left out, or even words from different sets mixed in a meaningless jumble.

Along with his stock inscriptions, Norton introduced an alphabet of fairly large black-letter [4a] which he used to make up inscriptions to special order, but he and his successors would quite often save themselves trouble by using a word or part of a word from a stock inscription – the "Pro" of "Protege", for instance, in an "ora pro nobis" dedication. The most striking example of this is at St Erney, Cornwall [56 & Pl 4c]: there the remarkable and unique inscription, which occupies two lines round the bell, reads:

"Nomen campan[a]e pax anima[rum] ora p[ro] eis virgo virginum s[an]c[t]a[rum] quas purgatoris puniuntur quod prius per dei mi[sericordi]am liberentur"
"The name of the bell is 'peace of souls': pray, virgin of holy virgins for those who are being punished in purgatory that by the mercy of God they may sooner be set free" (the letters in brackets are abbreviated).

In this, a special symbol, [like a "l" with a bifurcated top] is used as an abbreviation for the genetive plural ending "..rum", but "[N]omen", "campan[e]", "virgo", "virg""in""um", and "quo[d]" are taken from various stock inscriptions, including "*Protege virgo . . .*" which does not appear in complete form on any bell bearing Norton's mark. The black-letter alphabet survived throughout the life of the Exeter foundry, and was still being used by John Birdall its last founder in the 1620s.

With the new lettering went a number of new initial crosses; one came in three sizes, [Pl 1b, 1c, 1d]; [Pl 1e] & [Pl 1f] were also used by Norton, and [Pl 1g], although it appears on only one bell and without a founders mark, at *Jacobstowe*, was probably originated by Norton as there is little evidence for much innovation by his mediaeval successors.

As we have seen in an earlier chapter, Norton also introduced, probably late in his career, a method of forming moulding-wires which results in identical patterns appearing on different bells. Whether this involved making a separate strickle for the moulding-wires, or a swage, perhaps heated, to create the notches in the strickle, is hard to tell. These too were continued by his successors, and for this reason the dating and attribution of Exeter foundry bells is extremely difficult; the lettering, crosses, moulding-wires and general style established by Robert Norton were continued by his successors, and there is little change before 1500 at least. Moreover, there is no clear evidence that Norton used his mark, a rope circlet containing a bell flanked by his initials in black-letter, on all his bells; however, the moulding-wires which he put on most of his bells are unlike those of his successors, and there are no bells which look like his but do not bear his mark. In all, 23 bells survive with Norton's mark, 6 are recorded but have been recast, and one has been stolen but its details are on record. Of the total, six were in the earlier Lombardic lettering, one in a small Lombardic, and 23 in black-letter.

"**I.T.**" used a mark very similar to Norton's [Pl 1j], but with a fine line outside the rope circlet and his initials – which indeed could possibly be "l t". Thirty-four surviving bells with his mark are probably by him, all inscribed in black-letter, and another 11 are recorded but have been recast or scrapped; as noticed above, a few more, perhaps half a dozen, are probably by him but do not bear his mark; some rings of three or four – Thurlbear, Somerset for example, – which appear to have been cast at the same time, have only one bell bearing the founder's mark. The identity of I.T. is a mystery still; although his output was so much greater than Norton's his name has so far been found on no document that can identify him as a bellfounder, and most of the Exeter freemen with suitable initials can be shown to have followed some other trade. His bells are not so consistently well cast as Norton's (though *Trusham* 5th is a most beautiful casting), and some of the inscriptions are corrupt, suggesting that as demand for bells increased, as it undoubtedly did in the middle of the 15th century with the building of so many of Devon's church towers, the master founder may have had to delegate work to journeymen who were illiterate or less skilled. Alternatively, his mark may have been used by other, later founders, as we know it was by the Birdalls some 150 years after his time.

THE BELLFOUNDERS: BEFORE THE REFORMATION

Fig. 62. Trusham 5th, by "I.T." of Exeter, mid-15th century.

The next bellfounder who appears in the documentary record is **William York**, described as a bellfounder in a lease of a tenement in Magdalen Street, dated 1454, and appearing in another deed of the previous year. Unfortunately nothing has so far enabled us to identify any of his bells, and it seems possible that he may have been a journeyman under I.T. or Robert Russell. He had been enrolled as a Freeman in October 1452.

In contrast to I.T., of whom nothing is known except his bells, **Robert Russell** is a notable and well-documented Exeter citizen, but his bells are not identifiable with any certainty. He was enrolled as a Freeman of the City in 1459, and came to own a number of properties in the city including the tower over the West Gate. In 1464 he was taken to court by the churchwardens of Stoke Climsland, who claimed that he had "falsely and fraudulently" sold them three bells which he knew to be "less strong and insufficient" – rather as the Plymtree wardens had dealt with Robert Norton. He did not appear, and the court ordered a distress to be levied on him by the County of Devon.[19] However, three years later he was one of the Bailiffs of Exeter, and in 1474 was named (under the title of Robert Belyet') as a Churchwarden of St Mary Major; he was involved in a number of lawsuits, including one for vexatious trespass against John Atwyll, in which he was associated with William Fundyng, a freemason; as Constable of the city some time between 1480 and 1483 he was again accused of a vexatious action for trespass by John Bounde of Denbury. His reputation remained high, and in 1485 he was chosen as mayor: this must surely have been in recognition of the casting of the "Peter" bell of the Cathedral, increased to four tons through the gift of Bishop Peter Courtenay, the previous year. At some time during the next few years he again appears in a Chancery suit, being sued by the churchwardens of *North Bovey* for £21, the price of a bell. In 1489 he was assessed for the "Tenth" at 4s, but the various ramifications of his business appear in other entries; John Shappecote, knight, was assessed for 5s 5d "by Robert Russell", and "Robert Russell by John Brian" at 4s 8d.

In 1496 his prosperity seems to have grown to the point where he could join Thomas Calwoodley, a very prominent citizen, in founding a charity for the poor, and the following year he made his will, in which he left a house in South Street to the Church of St Mary Major, with legacies for Richard Russell, described as his "servant", his daughters Rose and Alice, and his son John. One of the executors and residuary legatees was William Baker, husband of his daughter Rose. Other legacies were to his godsons, poor scholars at Oxford, the wardens of Bideford bridge, the Rector of St Mary Major "for forgotten tithes", the Chaplain and holy-water clerk, Simon Grendon's almshouses and the lepers of St Mary Magdalen. As one of the conditions of the gift of the South Street property, there was to be a Mass in St Mary Major on the anniversary of his death "for ever", with payments of 6d to the Rector, 4d each to five other priests, 4d to the holy-water clerk, 8d between four poor scholars attending and 1/- in bread and 2/- in ale to poor people attending. This trust continued for many centuries, and may be in

---

19. Noted by a Cornish antiquarian in the De Banco Rolls, and kindly brought to my attention by Dr Jo Mattingley.

Fig. 63. St Pierre du Bois, Guernsey: the treble of the old ring of three has groats impressed in the head.

existence in some form even today. The will was sealed with a seal depicting a bell, and was proved on Robert's death in 1502

Robert Russell's career coincides almost precisely with the dating of coin-impressions in one group of Exeter foundry bells. The coins are invariably groats (worth fourpence), and the impressions are in the heads of the bells between the roots of the cannons. One can attribute these bells fairly safely to Robert Russell, but the difficulty is that about half of the surviving Exeter foundry bells have had their cannons removed and have been hung on metal headstocks which make it impossible to know (without removing the bells from their headstocks) whether there are coin-impressions in them or not. That being so we can assign some 15 bells, from places as far apart as Guernsey, St Michael Caerhayes and Yeovilton, to Robert Russell, but also guess that at least as many again are probably his work. Apart from the coin-impressions (which have never been found in conjunction with Norton's or I.T.'s marks), there is no obvious feature to distinguish Russell's bells from those of other 15th-century Exeter founders.

Although Richard Russell was admitted a Freeman as Robert's apprentice, and seems to have been associated with the foundry after Robert's death, there is no evidence that he carried on the business, nor is it clear what was his relationship to Robert. He appears several times in the records, and the impression they give is not a good one; almost immediately after the proving of Robert's will he was sued by William Baker for detention of deeds; he became a Bailiff of the City in 1512, but was accused of allowing a miscreant to go free; and in 1522, when he was assessed in the Military Survey as being worth £40, he was accused of selling a property (apparently the one left to St Mary Major) of which he was a feoffee, and was dismissed from the Common Council. We hear no more of him, and Robert's son and heir John only appears in documents relating to property dealings. Robert Russell's son-in-law, **William Baker**, succeeded to the bellfoundry; he had become a Freeman in 1484, when he was living "Peter Plenty's House" in Rackhay, adjoining Billiter (Bellfounder) Lane and very close to the foundry site if not on it. William had been sued in 1482 for the return of some loose quires of a "portuas" or "portuose" of vellum, which a Friar, now deceased, had been writing for a priest named Thomas Dyer: it may be the same book for which Baker sued someone else in 1504. In 1489 William was one of the Collectors for the "Tenth" levy and on his own behalf paid 4s 8d. After Russell's death in 1502 we find him first described as "merchant" in his suit against "Richard Russell, bellfounder", but in 1504 he himself is described as a bellfounder. He may be the same William who appears in the Subsidy list for 1524, for St Lawrence parish, but this is more probably the William Baker who was admitted freeman in 1508 and whose will was proved in 1556 – surely too late for the bellfounder.

As the Exeter foundry's history is unbroken until the death of its last proprietor in 1624, we will include its later, post-Reformation period in this chapter. **John Sharke**, the next known Exeter founder, was listed in the 1522 Military Survey as an "alien" in St Mary Major parish, a servant to Richard Russell, "worth nil"; he was not admitted a freeman until 1544, but must by that time have been a man of some standing as he was assessed at £10 for his goods in the subsidy of that year and only five years later was one of the Churchwardens of St Mary Major, the premier parish church of the City – though it cannot have been a very propitious period for the bellfounding trade, with Puritanism growing in popularity and the spoils of the monasteries flooding the market: perhaps that was partly the motive behind John Sharke's one brief but colourful appearance on the stage of English history as we saw in Hoker's account of the siege of Exeter. The rebellion was suppressed and the ringleaders savagely punished, but it seems that John Sharke had sufficient standing in the city to get away with his defiance; in 1556 a document in the Exeter City Archives orders that some money be paid over *at the mansion of John Sharke the bellfounder*, and in 1563 he was appointed one of the attorneys of feoffment for none other than John Vowel alias Hoker, the man who had described him as a "bell-wether". Nevertheless, whatever John's standing in the City, one has to record the fact that in 1559 an Alice Trouffyld was accused of *her incontynent lyffe used with one John Sharke in a stable of his in Racke Lane*[20]: he must have died in 1563-4, as his wife is described as a widow in 1564.

Another bellfounder of this period was **John Savage**, who is described as such in 1555 in a grant of rents from the house in Holy Trinity parish in which he lived, and who may have been the *Savyge* who was paid for trussing the great bell at *Winkleigh* in 1550. His burial in Holy Trinity was recorded in 1570. His son or grandson John Savage was a clockmaker in Exeter in the early 17th century.

It is virtually impossible to attribute any surviving bells to Baker, Sharke or Savage except by guesswork; this period was one of low output in the trade, and also of great confusion and uncertainty. Such Exeter bells as can be placed in the years between 1502 and 1572 are characterised by rather rough casting, with badly-formed moulding-wires and often corrupt inscriptions. Three bells have "alphabet" inscriptions in Lombardic lettering which does not appear on earlier Exeter bells, and one at *Cookbury* has a series of letters which seem quite meaningless. However, some bells appear to date from the reign of Mary I, as they carry pre-Reformation-type inscriptions; these are inscribed in the earliest Exeter Lombardic lettering complete with the cross, but in quite a different style; the moulding-wires do not include the characteristic flat band, three of them have an additional cross saltire [Pl 1h], and the letters are grouped in twos, threes or fours, e.g. SANC TA MA RI A. *East Down* 4/4, which is one of these, has coin-impressions in the head which appear to belong to Henry VIII, suggesting that they may be the work of John Sharke. It is possible that the Zennor bell belongs to this group, though the standard of casting is superior to most.

The *Transactions of the Society of Antiquaries* for Feb. 6, 1916, contains an account of a mortar, presented by H.B. Walters and the property of Edgar Holman the Cornish mining engineer, which bears the Set 1 cross and lettering and the inscription OAI RAM ATCN SA, the groups of letters originally having been separated by handles which had been removed. In view of the inscription being back to front, which is most atypical of the earlier bells with this cross and lettering, it is probably best associated with this later group. It may be the same as the one described above from St Just-in-Penwith.

The Birdalls. Throughout all this period of over 160 years, the Exeter foundry appears to have been sited in Rack Street: the site was excavated during the 1970s, but had been so thoroughly and repeatedly dug over during its working lifetime that virtually nothing remained except a huge mass of used loam. However, the last phase of the old Exeter foundry saw it move across the river to a site near the western end of Exe Bridge in the parish of St Thomas, where it was operated by the Birdall family.

The first was Christopher Birdall, who appears to have been a brazier, though no bells can be attributed to him. He lived in St Thomas's parish, at Barrowhall which remained the family's home until the 17th century. **Thomas Birdall**, *c*1534–1609, first appears in the records in 1569 (just before John Savage's death) casting a bell at *Honeychurch* for the parish of South Tawton (see App. 1:3), and in 1572 **John Birdall**, his brother or possibly his cousin, agreed with the Four Men and Churchwardens of Holy Trinity, Exeter, to recast their Great Bell. In 1591 John was involved with William Preston and William Poole in the remarkable combined operation by three

---

20. Devon Record Office, ECA, Act Book, p.69.

Fig. 64. Bases for bell-moulds in the Birdall foundry, showing the holes for the pivots of the strickles. The soil is burnt red by the heat.

bellfounders at *Braunton*, and in 1594 Thomas was recasting in Exeter the little bell of *Chudleigh*. From this it would appear that John and Thomas were brothers working in partnership; both lived in St Thomas and raised families there during the 1560s and '70s. Both died in 1609 and the business was taken over by **John Birdall II**, Thomas's son, who had been born in 1568; in 1592 he married Wilmote Furse, who died in 1602 (probably in childbed with a daughter named after her) and in 1613 he married Margaret Fursdon. John Birdall died in 1624, and his family remained in Exeter for many years though no longer in the bellfounding business. The foundry site, close to the western end of Exe Bridge, was excavated in 1996 before the building of a supermarket, and again after the demolition of the supermarket in 1999–2000; it showed evidence of a very big metal-working operation with a number of bell-mould bases and large quantities of used loam; the site must have been ideal for the business, as it produced a suitable clay. The majority of the mould material found was from cauldrons and skillets, and one fragment, from the upper side of a skillet-handle, bore John Birdall's name and is now in the Royal Albert Memorial Museum in Exeter. Another find was half of a mould for a "manilla", a type of bronze armlet which was exported in large quantities to West Africa as trade goods, and has been identified as the raw material for the famous Benin bronzes. Many of the records refer to the Birdalls as "braziers", and the archaeological record confirms the fact that bellfounding was only a part of their business.

The bells from the last 70 years or so of the Exeter foundry give a confused picture; in addition to bringing back into use the old Lombardic lettering from the early 1400s and using some of the stamps first introduced by Norton, the Exeter founders seem to have acquired a collection of other stamps, including two other sets of Lombardic lettering which were long out of fashion in the late 16th century but have not been identified elsewhere. The smaller of these appears as a complete alphabet on *Puddington* 3/3, on *Templeton* 1/3 in the inscription SA NC TA MA RI A, partly inverted, and on the disused bell at *Beer* with the letters evenly spaced; it is possible that it was acquired by Sharke or Savage and used in the time of Mary I; the other examples are *Combeinteignhead* 6/6, a

Fig. 65. Aylesbeare tenor, probably by Thomas Birdall, inscribed in very large Lombardic letters.

part alphabet, *Cookbury* 1/3, apparently meaningless, the *Okehampton* bell now in the Sharpe Collection, a part alphabet, and *Honeychurch* 1/3, meaningless but including "onvoco" from the Norton stock inscription. It would seem almost certain the Honeychurch treble was cast by Thomas Birdall in 1569; the other two bells there are 15th-century. *Kingswear* 1/3 and 2/3 have inscriptions which include this smaller Lombardic lettering, fragments of Norton stock inscriptions and of Norton's black-letter alphabet, and also the "IT" mark; one of them bears also the initials T B.

Norton's black-letter was used for *Clyst St George* 5/6 (the inscription-band preserved in the church), with a Norton cross and the IT mark, and the inscription "Embrace trew museck" (the accounts date the bell at 1596), and for *Pinhoe* 8/8 "pres not thy self" [Pl 4e, f, g]; similarly Puritan-style inscriptions, "PRAISE GOD" on *Aylesbeare* 6/6 and PRAYSE NOT THY SELF on *Whimple* 6/6 are in very large, old-fashioned Lombardics [Pl 5d] which also appear as initials with black-letter smalls on two bells at *Kingston* dated 1601; one of these is inscribed "Thomas Byrdall made me". These bells also have a fleur-de-lys stop [Pl 6j] formed from one arm of a large cross of four fleurs-de-lys which appears on the Whimple and Aylesbeare bells [Pl 6b]. *Aylesbeare* 5/6, dated 1601, is all in black-letter with the churchwardens' names and the IT mark and a Norton cross; *Woodbury* 5/8, dated 1605, is similar, with Thomas Birdall's name, but on the head, between the cannons is a scratched monogram IB. (The black-letter "ll" on this bell was misread by H.T.Ellacombe as a "n", and, in spite of being aware of documentary evidence for "Birdall" or "Byrdall", he took their name to be "Byrdan".)

By the time he took over the business in 1609, John II had probably already being doing much of the work: although *Berry Pomeroy* 8/8 is dated 1607, it is probably the work of John II, as the initial capitals are from yet another set of letters. These are elaborately decorated with foliage, [Pl 6d,e,f] and the set seems to have been incomplete as in some cases the letters can be seen to be very skilfully pieced together [Pl 6g,h]. These letters, with the Norton black-letter, the fleur-de-lys and the IT mark, appear on all the remaining Birdall bells, *Clyst Hydon* 6/6 and *Exeter Cathedral* 4/12 of 1616, the Antony House bell, *Stockleigh English* 4/4 of 1622, *Woodbury* 5/8 of 1624, and a small undated bell, now in Exeter Museum, which evidently was cast for Sir Amyas Bampfylde's house at North Molton; none of these bells bears a cross.

With the death of John Birdall II the old Exeter foundry apparently ceased to exist, at least as a bellfoundry, and the field was open for Thomas Pennington II to migrate from Barnstaple and establish a new bellfoundry in the city.

Bells from the Mediaeval Exeter Foundry and the Birdalls.

(The entries in italics show bells which have been recast or otherwise lost, and those in bold type are in Devon.)

Pl.2a Capitals, Spaced

Ashbury	dis	*Germansweek*	*1/3*
Ashbury	**1/1**	Harford	1/3
Bridford	*2/4*	Harford	2/3
Brimpsfield Glos	5/5	**Knowstone**	**4/6**
Brompton Ralph So	4/4	**Loxbeare**	**1/3**
Chaffcombe So	5/6	**Meeth**	**2/4**
Chilthorne Domer So	2/2	**Meeth**	**3/4**
Dartington	*3/5*	Mylor Co	1/3
Dorchester Ox	7/8	**Seaton**	**8/8**
Fremington	**4/6**	**Southleigh**	**1/4**
Frithelstock	**4/6**	*Stockleigh English*	*1/4*

Stockleigh Pomeroy	*1/3*		Kingston	2/6
TremaineCo	1/2		Littlehempston	3/5
Trewen Co	*1/1*		*Mortehoe*	*2/3*
Uplowman	6/6		Payhembury	4/6
West Ogwell	2/3		Petersmarland	5/6
Whimple	5/6		St Erney Co	1/3
Woodland	1/3		*Sheldon*	*1/3*
			Strete	2/2
Pl. 2a Capitals, Words Together			Sowton Bishops Ct	1/1
Zennor Co	4/6		Upton So	2/3
			Warkleigh	5/6
Pl 2a Capitals, Grouped			*West Anstey*	*3/4*
Abbots Bickington	1/2			
Abbots Bickington	2/2		**Black-letter, IT mark**	
Alverdiscott	2/3		Bondleigh	2/4
Alverdiscott	3/3		Buckerell	6/6
E Down	4/4		Churston Ferrers	4/6
Martinhoe	2/3		*Clannaborough*	*1/4*
			Clyst St George	*3/6*
Pl.2a Capitals, RN Mark			Coffinswell	4/6
Broadwindsor Do	5/6		Crowcombe So	5/6
Hennock	1/4		E.Quantoxhead So	4/4
Kennerleigh	*3/3*		Farway	6/6
Knowstone	*3/3*		Gidleigh	1/5
Mortehoe	*1/3*		Hennock	3/4
Rame Co	2/3		Highampton	2/3
Romansleigh	*2/3*		High Bray	5/6
			Holcombe Burnell	4/6
Small Capitals, RN Mark			Kittisford So	4/4
Clyst St Mary	1/3		Loxbeare	3/3
Foxcott Ha	?		*Monkton*	*1/3*
			Monkton	*2/3*
Black-letter, RN Mark			*Monkton*	*3/3*
Beaford	3/6		Moreleigh	2/3
Churston Ferrers	5/6		Newton St Petrock	2/3
Colaton Raleigh	6/6		Newton St Petrock	3/3
Combe Florey So	*3/5*		Newton Tracey	2/3
Combe Raleigh	2/3		Northleigh	4/4
Dunterton	3/3		Offwell	2/6
Exeter S Pancras	1/1		Over Stowey So	3/6
Fremington	3/6		Ringmore	1/3
Exeter RAMM			St Decumans So	3/6
(ex Halse So 5/6)			Thorne St Mary So	1/1
Hittisleigh	3/3		Torbryan	4/4
Huish Champflower So	4/6		Thurlbear, So	4/4

Trusham	**5/6**	E.Quantoxhead, So	2/4
Upton Magna, Salop	?	*Egg Buckland*	*1/3*
Ven Ottery	**3/3**	Elworthy So	4/4
Wembdon, So	2/5	**Exeter Guildhall**	**1/1**
Wembworthy	**1/3**	**Exeter St Olave**	**1/2**
W.Worlington	**4/6**	*Feock, Co*	*1/3*
W.Worlington	**5/6**	*Feock, Co*	*2/3*
Whitestone	**5/6**	**Gidleigh**	**4/5**
Whimple	**3/6**	**Gidleigh**	**5/5**
Wilton, So	*2/5*	*Gunwalloe, Co*	*1/3*
		Gunwalloe, Co	*2/3*
Black-letter, IT mark, corrupt		**Highampton**	**1/3**
St Keyne, Co	*3/6*	**High Bray**	**3/6**
Seaton	***2/4***	*Hillfarrance, So*	*4/5*
Teignmouth St J	***2/4***	**Hittisleigh**	**2/3**
		Honeychurch	**2/3**
Black-letter, no Mark		**Honeychurch**	**3/3**
Angersleigh, So	2/5	**Huish**	**2/3**
Ashcombe	**2/3**	**Huish**	**3/3**
Aylesbeare	**4/6**	*Ideford*	*1/3*
Bicknoller, So	2/4	*Ideford*	*2/3*
Bradford-on-Tone, So	3/6	*Isle Brewers, So*	*2/4*
Broadwindsor, Do	4/6	**Instow**	**1/3**
Brompton Ralph, So	2/4	*Jacobstow*	*2/4*
Buckerell	*4/6*	**Jacobstow**	**4/5**
Buckerell	**5/6**	Kittisford, So	2/4
Cadbury	**4/6**	Kittisford, So	3/4
Cadbury	**6/6**	*Littleham N*	*3/4*
Churston Ferrers	**6/6**	**Loxbeare**	**2/3**
Clyst St George	*4/6*	**Luppitt**	**5/8**
Clyst St Mary	**3/3**	**Luppitt**	**7/8**
Coffinswell	**3/6**	**Manaton**	**6/6**
Colaton Raleigh	**5/6**	**Membury**	**4/6**
Corfe, So	*2/4*	**Membury**	**3/6**
Corfe, So	*3/4*	**Merton**	**2/6**
Corfe, So	*4/4*	**Monkleigh**	**4/6**
Coryton	**3/5**	**Monkokehampton**	**3/4**
Dalwood	**5/6**	**Monkokehampton**	**2/4**
Dartington	*5/5*	**Moreleigh**	**1/3**
Dowlish Wake, So	5/5	**Moreleigh**	**3/3**
Dulverton, So	7/8	**Okehampton St Jas**	**cl**
Dunchideock	**2/3**	Otterford, So	2/4
Dunchideock	**3/3**	Otterford, So	3/4
E.Anstey	**4/6**	Otterford, So	4/4
E.Portlemouth	**6/6**	Otterham, Co	1/6

Otterham, Co	3/6	W Quantoxhead, So	3/6
Pancrasweek	**3/5**	W Quantoxhead, So	4/6
Payhembury	**3/6**	**Whitestone**	**4/6**
Payhembury	**5/6**		
Pinhoe	**3/6**	**Black-letter, Coins in Head**	
Raddington, So	2/3	**Awliscombe**	**4/6**
Revelstoke	*1/2*	Bishops Lydeard, So	Cl
St Clether, Co	4/5	**ex Awliscombe**	**3/6**
St Clether, Co	5/5	Bradford-on-Tone So	2/6
St Ervan, Co	ex1/3	**Butterleigh**	**2/3**
St John, Co	1/3	St Pierre d B Guernsey	1/3
St Just-Penwith, Co	1/3	Hatch Beauchamp, So	4/6
St Just-Penwith, Co	2/3	Litton Cheney, Do	8/8
Salcombe Regis	**1/3**	**Northleigh**	**1/4**
Sampford Arundel, So	5/6	**Northleigh**	**2/4**
Sheldon	**1/1**	**Northleigh**	**3/4**
Sidmouth	cl	St Mich Caerhayes Co	4/6
S Huish	*3/4*	St Mich Caerhayes Co	5/6
Staple Fitzpaine, So	1/5	St Mich Caerhayes Co	6/6
Stawley, So	3/5	Stoke Abbot Do	4/6
Stawley, So	4/5	Yeovilton So	4/5
Stawley, So	5/5		
Stockleigh English	**2/4**	**Black-letter, no Mark,**	
Stockleigh Pomeroy	**2/3**	**no Coins, Corrupt**	
Stockleigh Pomeroy	*3/3*	**Aylesbeare**	**4/6**
Talaton	**4/6**	**Bondleigh**	**3/4**
Teignmouth St Jas	**1/4**	Brean So	2/3
Teignmouth St Jas	*3/4*	Burstock Do	2/3
Teignmouth St Mic	*1/3*	Chideock Do	3/5
Teignmouth St Mic	*2/3*	*Combeinteignhead*	*4/4*
Thurlbear, So	1/4	**E Anstey**	**5/6**
Thurlbear, So	2/4	*Exeter St Lawrence*	*1/1*
Thurlbear, So	3/4	**Holcombe Rogus**	**2/6**
Thurloxton So	6/6	**Huish**	**1/3**
Timberscombe, So	2/6	**Littlehempston**	**4/5**
Torbryan	**3/4**	Litton Cheney Do	7/8
Tresillian Co	1/3	**Martinhoe**	**1/2**
Twitchen	**1/3**	**Monkokehampton**	**1/4**
Upton Hellions	**1/1**	**Newton Tracey**	**3/3**
Vale, Guernsey	*1/3*	**Offwell**	**5/6**
Vale, Guernsey	*2/3*	Over Stowey So	5/6
Vale, Guernsey	*3/3*	Sampford Arundel So	4/6
Wembworthy	**3/3**	**Torbryan**	**1/4**
Westleigh	*2/4*	**Wembworthy**	**2/3**
West Ogwell	**3/3**	*Whimple*	*2/4*

Woodleigh	3/3		*Exeter St Mary Steps*	doc	*1572*
			Clyst St George	5/6	
No Inscription			**Kingswear**	1/3	
Columbjohn	1/1		**Kingswear**	2/3	
Cotehele House Co	1/2		**Pinhoe**	6/6	
			Aylesbeare	6/6	
Pl.5 Capitals			**Whimple**	6/6	
Beer	Dis		**Aylesbeare**	5/6	**1601**
St Colan Co	1/3		**Kingston**	5/6	**1601**
Combeinteignhead	5/6		**Kingston**	6/6	**1601**
Cookbury	1/3		**Woodbury**	5/8	**1605**
Sharpe Collection	1/1		**Berry Pomeroy**	8/8	**1607**
(ex Okehampton)			Exeter Museum	1/1	
Templeton	1/3		**Clyst Hydon**	6/6	**1616**
			Exeter Cathedral	4/12	**1616**
Birdalls			**Stockleigh Engllish**	4/4	**1622**
Exeter Heavitree	2/4		Antony House	1/1	1622
Honeychurch	1/3	1569	**Woodbury**	4/8	**1624**

Pre-Reformation founders from outside Devon

It is not possible to identify the founders of our very earliest bells: their founders probably came from outside the county. The five earliest of all, *Haccombe* 1/1, *Petton* 1/2 and 2/2, and *Bulkworthy* 1/2 and 2/2, are all uninscribed, but can be dated by their shape; they are all comparatively small, long-waisted bells, with flat heads, and probably all except Bulkworthy 2/2 were moulded in wax or tallow. The Haccombe bell has cannons moulded with a fine cable pattern; the Petton bells with a plait, and the smaller Bulkworthy bell with a cable, and all have very simple moulding-wires. All seem to date from between 1290 and 1320, and probably were the work of London founders, though there is just a possibility that some of them may have been cast by one of the **de Ropefordes**.

In 1372 one new bell was cast for Exeter Cathedral and another was recast by **Thomas Karoun**, about whom nothing else is known. As his name does not appear anywhere in Devon except the Cathedral Fabric Rolls, and he did the casting on site using labour supplied by the Chapter, one can make a fairly reliable guess that he was not a local man.

The oldest inscribed bells in Devon are the pair in *Okehampton, Museum of Dartmoor Life*, formerly in Tresmere, Cornwall, *Petersmarland* 6/6 and *Combepyne* 3/3. All three appear to date from the early 14th century: the Petersmarland bell is apparently by **Richard de Wymbis** [Pl 7a, 9a]; the lettering on the Combepyne bell is not known elsewhere, though the casting is of a high standard [Pl 10b]. The inscription on the Okehampton bells are in English as we have seen; the other two are Leonine hexameters. One wonders about the origin of the Petersmarland bell: did the founder come all the way to this tiny remote village to cast it, and if not, how was it brought here? One possibility is that it belonged formerly to one of the religious houses in the area – perhaps to Frithelstock Priory where we know that both the priory church and the parish church had towers.

Fig. 66. Wolborough: a beautiful bell by John Bird of London, preserved in the church with its original oak headstock.

The London Founders

Abbotsham 5/6 is the earliest bell which we can confidently assign to a known founder – **William Dawe** or **William Founder** of London, who is first recorded supplying 12 cannon to Dover Castle in 1385: his well-known mark [Pl 7c] shows two very large birds in a very small tree with "William ffoundor me fecit" round the circumference – the assumption being that the birds are (jack)daws. All surviving bells with this mark are inscribed in black-letter with Lombardic initials except this bell at Abbotsham whose inscription is all in Lombardics, so it may be assumed to be Dawe's earliest surviving bell. He also cast the ring of three – the oldest complete ring in the county – at *Brushford*. Two of these are inscribed; the treble has no inscription, but like the other two has laver-pot shields [Pl.7h] on the shoulders.

John Bird flourished between 1408 and 1418, and seems to have belonged, along with William Dawe, to the London Bellmakers' Guild. The mark of this guild was apparently the shield bearing a chevron and three laver-pots [Pl 7h]; another similar shield which often appears with it has a chevron with three trefoils. The laver-pot shield appears on the shoulders of the Brushford bells, and also on the old 2nd at *Wolborough* which, with the head of the treble and the inscription-band of the tenor, are now preserved in the church. They bear the crosses used by John Bird [Pl 7f,g] and are inscribed in black-letter Leonines with beautiful crowned capitals [Pl 9b]. Two mediaeval bells at *St Mary Arches, Exeter*, have the laver-pot and trefoil shields on the shoulder, but are otherwise uninscribed, and may be by either William Dawe or John Bird.

Johanna Hille was the widow of Richard Hille of London, who died in 1440 leaving her his business. Until recently it was believed that she remarried and was identified as Johanna the wife of John Sturdy who carried on *his* business after his death, but recent research by Caroline Barron[21] has proved that Johanna Hille died the year after her husband. No fewer than seven bells survive in various parts of England with her mark – her husband's mark of a shield with a bend, cross and annulet, with a lozenge, the heraldic symbol for womanhood, over it [Pl 7l]. Allowing for the normal loss through recasting one could estimate from this that her total output must have at least three times that number, which suggests that she may have been running the foundry (which her will shows that she certainly did) for some time during her husband's last illness, as well as the year of her widowhood. She cast two bells for *Manaton*, 4/6 and 5/6, which are arguably the most beautiful mediaeval castings in the county; they are

---

21. Caroline Barron, in *Mediaeval London Widows*, Hambledon Press, 1994, pp 99ff.

inscribed in black-letter with elegant Lombardic capitals, those on the 5th being crowned. Again one may well ask how these bells, the larger about 6 cwt., came to be bought from a London founder by a small, very remote community on Dartmoor. Were they cast on site, and if not how they were transported to such a place in a time when Devon had very few wheeled vehicles? There may be a hint in the dedication of the 4th to St George; the tinners' guild in Manaton had St George as its patron, and may well have had direct trading links with the London bellfounders. There is also evidence that in the 15th century the River Dart was to some extent navigable as far as Buckfastleigh, from which town the journey to Manaton would not be impossible – indeed there is an inn called "The Waterman's Arms" in Buckfastleigh to this day.

William Chamberlain had a very important business in London, for over 100 of his bells survive in an area running from Yorkshire to Cornwall; he is believed to have worked between 1426 and 1456. His bells always bear the beautiful cross with "ihu merci ladi help" around it [Pl 7n], flanked by two shields, one of them with crossed keys, a bell, a laver-pot, a fish and a sheaf (or *garb* in heraldic terms) [7m], and the other with a mark very like a typical merchants' mark of this period [Pl 7o]; the last two suggest that he may have had business interests outside the foundry trade. He left us *Marldon* 4/6 and *Dartmouth, St Clement* 4, 5 and 6/6.

"**The Successor to John Daniel**" is the title usually given to the unknown London founder of *Exeter, St Petrock's* 3/6. It is inscribed in black-letter with Lombardic initials, and bears the Royal Arms which were used by John Daniel [Pl 36a] and the "Brede mark" [Pl 7d]. The arms are assumed to have been used by Daniel for his recasting of the bells for King's College, Cambridge, in 1460; he may have continued to use them elsewhere as the equivalent of a "by appointment" claim.

Thomas Lawrence was a successor to William Culverden, whose name first appears in the records in 1523. Although we have no surviving bells by him in Devon, we know that he worked in the county, as a Chancery court case was recorded between him and the Mayor, Aldermen and Sheriff of London, relating to a bond given as security for money advanced for the repair of the bells of *Dartmouth*. There may be a link between this operation and the entry in Dartmouth Churchwardens' Accounts for 1529: *To Whittocke for his borde and drynkyng at strykyng of our bells with yervese* (Jersey) *men* – though how the Jerseymen were involved is not clear. Lawrence apparently moved to Norwich and left the bellfounding business in 1539 – probably a good time to leave it, with the Reformation impending and bells from monasteries and chantries flooding the market. He died in 1545.

The Bristol Founders

Just as mediaeval bells from the London founders are found for the most part along the south coast of Devon, so North Devon turned to Bristol when it looked outside the county for a bellfounder: the only surviving Bristol bells in the southern half of the county are at *Woodbury* and *Broadhembury*. Some of the Bristol

Fig. 67. Alwington 4th, an early 14th-century bell from the Bristol foundry, hung in a rather clumsy steel cannon-retaining headstock.

Fig. 68. Iddesleigh tenor, cast by the Bristol foundry in the 16th-century.

bells are very beautiful castings, notably *Alwington* 4/6 and the tenors at *Warkleigh*, *Iddesleigh* and *Molland*. Of the Bristol bells which have not survived, *Molland* and *Tetcott* (formerly at *Luffincott*) churches retain the inscription-bands. The bells from this foundry are not easy to date, as there are many variations: the most authoritative recent list is given in F. Sharpe's *Church Bells of Herefordshire*, and it is his groups and datings which are given below. The tenor at Molland is apparently the largest pre-Reformation bell in the county. In the list below the italics show bells which have been lost or recast.

Bells in Devon from the Mediaeval Bristol Foundry

Group	Founder	Date	Place	Bell
Group II		1350–80	Alwington	4/6
			Ashford	1/2
			Horwood	1/3
Group III		1380–1420	Ashford	2/2
Group IV(b)		1450–80	Molland	6/6
Group V(a)		1420–80	Yarnscombe	5/6
			Luffincott	2/3
			Sheepwash	1/1
Group VI1		480–1500	Warkleigh	6/6
			?Westleigh	3,4/4
Group VII(a)		1480–1500	Horwood	2/3
			Lynton	3/6
Group VIII	T Geffries	1505–45	Alwington	6/6
			Brendon	2/4
			Brendon	3/4
			Huntshaw	3/3
			Lynton	5/6
			Molland	4/6?
			N Tawton	saunce
			S Tawton	doc
Group IX(b)			Broadhembury	2/6
			Challacombe	2/4
			Iddesleigh	6/6
			ex Stevenstone Ho	1/1
Group XI	J White	1500–40	Woodbury	6/8

Unknown Pre-Reformation Founders

None of the oldest of Devon's bells can be identified with a known founder, the bells at *Haccombe, Petton and Bulkworthy* all being uninscribed, while the two Tresmere bells in *Okehampton* and *Combepyne* 2/3 and 3/3 are probably the work of founders from outside the county. An uninscribed bell at *West Ogwell* appears to date from about 1400 and may be from the Exeter foundry. Other uninscribed bells which suggest a later mediaeval date are listed below. The 2nd of the four at *Torbryan, Highampton* 3/3 and *Frithelstock* 3/6 probably belong to the time of Mary I, as their inscriptions are strongly pre-Reformation in style, but in Roman capitals.

Bells by Unknown Mediaeval Founders

Bulkworthy	1/2
Bulkworthy	2/2
Haccombe	1/1
Petton	1/2
Petton	2/2
Combpyne	2/3
Combpyne	3/3
West Ogwell	1/3
Torbryan	2/4
Highampton	3/3
Frithelstock	3/6
Barnstaple St Peter ex St Mary Mag	1/1
West Ogwell	1/3
Satterleigh	2/3
Tamerton Foliot, Warleigh House	1/1
Exeter College	1/1
Exeter, St Katherine's Priory	1/1
Abbots Bickington	3/3

5

THE BELLFOUNDERS: AFTER THE REFORMATION

SO DOMINANT IS THE PLACE of the Pennington family in the history of bellfounding in the South West from the Reformation to the early 19th-century that they will have to be awarded a chapter to themselves. Here we will deal with the other bellfounders who were active in that period, beginning with those who belonged in Devon itself.

Richard Tamlyn of Buckland Monachorum appears in the Bere Ferrers accounts, being paid for casting a bell in Buckland in 1620. This bell does not survive, but Ellacombe records two bells at *South Huish* with black-letter inscriptions, dated 1596 and bearing the initials R T in large Lombardics, and another at *Clyst Honiton* with the same initials, which may be his.

William Preston of Crediton appears in a number of written records, and seems to have been fairly active during the latter part of the 16th century. He appears in the *Crediton* accounts in 1551 when he bought a bell and some lead from the church; three years later, after the accession of Mary I he sold the parish a *morrowe masse bell* and a censer, and the following year he recast the second bell. He was paid 12d for drinks by the *Chagford* wardens in 1555, and was probably responsible for casting two bells for them at "Kerton". He rehung the *Crediton* bells in 1574 and recast the *great and litle* bells in 1598. In 1593 he was paid 2d *in earnest for the casting of ye bells* but all the succeeding payments for that work were made to William Poole so the parish may possibly have changed its mind. In view of the length of his working career it is remarkable that we have only one bell which can be attributed to him with any certainty. This is *Molland 2/6*, which is inscribed with impressions taken from the monumental brass of a Master Johannes Cooke, and the date 1591 scratched into the cope – all, including the date, being inverted and backwards [Pl 13a]: the Molland accounts show that William Preston was paid for casting this bell at North Molton in that year. Two other bells, inscribed in the same manner but bearing the single word "(e)lemosinary" [Pl 13b,c], at *Abbotsham* and *Torre Abbey*, are probably by this founder.

Mordecai Cockey. The name of Edward Cockey appears in the *Halberton* accounts for 1646 in connection with rehanging the 4th bell, and Christopher, son of an Edward Cockey, was baptized in St Mary's, Totnes in 1696; the Cockey family has a remarkable record of activity in various metalwork trades – pewterers, clockmakers, bellfounders, and braziers – in Frome in Somerset, Warminster in Wiltshire and Totnes and Dartmouth in Devon, and the various branches must all be connected, but this is the only clue; perhaps

Fig. 69. Torre Abbey clock bell, probably by William Preston of Crediton, 16th-century.
(*Photo by Christopher Dalton*)

Edward was here to learn the trade. In the branch of the family which lived in Dartmouth and Totnes, the name Mordecai was very popular; when **Mordecai Cockey** the bellfounder was baptized in Totnes in 1644 his name was given as "Mordecai or Marmaduke": his father was named Wlllliam, and trailed a pike in Totnes's Trained Band in 1635. In 1667 he was married at the neighbouring parish of Berry Pomeroy, to Elizabeth Langworthy, and in 1675 he was one of a group of tradesmen who paid *for using ye liberties of ye Towne not being free*. That same year he was one of a number of Totnes citizens presented for *not coming to Church (being resident Inhabitants in the Borough and Parish afs^d) for three Lord's days now last past* (this was a bad time for Totnes nonconformists; the Mayor in that year had a strong dislike of dissenters and presented his own wife when he found her in a conventicle). The birth of their son, another Mordecai, is not in the Totnes register; he may have been born while his parents were itinerating, and he had other sons, Samuel and Joseph, and daughters Mary, Jane, Demeris and Elizabeth, to whom he left equal shares in his estate when he died in 1702. A Mordecai Cockey was married at Dartington in 1694, but this could be the father or the son; Mordecai junior is named as a brazier in a bond of 1699 in which he and his father undertake to guarantee for twenty years a bell for *St Budeaux* which like the 9th at Exeter Cathedral had been hung from bolts (this does not necessarily mean that Mordecai junior was a bellfounder; there was no certainty that at the age of 55 the father would survive another 20 years, and in the event of his dying during the period of the guarantee his son would be responsible for having the bell recast). He moved to Plymouth, where he was engaged in the metal trade but usually appears in connection with deals in lead or iron; like his father he seems to have been a nonconformist. Samuel continued as a pewterer in Totnes, and was followed by a son William, the maker of fine pewter charger, bearing his mark of a double-headed eagle and W. COCKEY TOTNES. This is now in Totnes Museum, which also possesses a trade token issued by a James Cockey. The Totnes branch of the family seems to have attained some status in later generations: a ledger-slab now used as a threshold to the vestry door in Ashprington is to Mary the wife of Philip Cockey *Esqr* of Sharpham (a manor-house on the Totnes/Ashprington border), and was erected by her son Mordecai Cockey, *Gent*.[22]

Fig. 70. Teigngrace, a bell by Mordecai Cockey of Totnes, 1701.

Mordecai's earliest surviving bell is *Woodland* 2/3, dated 1678. Inscribed in bold Roman capitals with a small lozenge-shaped stop; it has a curious shape, with an equally curious tone; evidently the founder still had much to learn. In 1680 he cast a small bell for *Totnes*, bearing the name of the Mayor and almost certainly cast to hang in the bellcote on the roof of the Guildhall; it is now in St John's, Bridgetown. Like many of his later bells it bears a frieze of vine-leaves and grapes almost if not quite identical with the one used by Thomas Purdue, leaving one to wonder whether he had some connection with the Closworth foundry or could have learned his trade there. A larger bell

---

22. I am indebted to Ronald F. Homer and Alan J. Collins for their research into the Cockeys as pewterers, published in the *Journal of the Pewter Society,* Spring 2006.

cast in the same year for St Mary's chapel in *Highweek* parish is now preserved in St Mary's, Abbotsbury: another with the frieze was cast for *Churston Ferrers* the following year, when he also cast a small bell now in West Ogwell House. Bells which he cast in Totnes for *Chivelstone* in 1682 and *Chudleigh* in 1686 have since been recast, but two other bells cast in 1686 are still in use – *Ashcombe* treble and the one bell still hung at *Harford*. This last is a very good bell, well cast and of excellent tone. The only other surviving bell by him is *Teigngrace* 2/2, dated 1701; in 1699 he had recast the 3rd at *St Budeaux* as we have seen. Cockey's bells were often decorated with coin-impressions, as well as the vine frieze and lozenge. [See Pl 25a,b,c]

Bells by Mordecai Cockey of Totnes
1678   Woodland 2/3
1680   Totnes St John 1/2
1680   Newton Abbot Abbotsbury 1/1
1681   Churston Ferrers 3/6
1681   W Ogwell House Chapel 1/1
1682   Chivelstone doc 2-6/6
1686   Chudleigh doc
1686   Ashcombe 1/3
1686   Harford 3/3
1692   Ringmore 2/3
1699   St Budeaux doc [sen & jun]
1701   Teigngrace 2/2

John Stadler's date and place of birth have not been found; he worked in Chulmleigh but probably started as an apprentice or assistant to Thomas Pennington III of Exeter, though he first figures in the *Swimbridge* records working on his own, in 1684. In 1692 he was working with Thomas Pennington III on *Littleham* (Exmouth) 7/8, where his initials appear with Pennington's, and the first surviving bell with his initials alone is *Exeter St Petrock* 2/6, 1693. In the same year he apparently cast a bell which bore his name in full for St Paul's, Exeter – very curiously, as this was Thomas Pennington's home parish. In 1695 or 1696 he was married to Elizabeth Williams of Chulmleigh, and in 1698 he was working with John Pennington of Tavistock on a ring of four at South Hill in East Cornwall. His bells are inscribed in fairly small Roman capitals, often with coin impressions, and at first his initials appear either side of a bell mark with incised moulding-wires [Pl.25f]. In 1700 he cast two bells for *Littlehempston*, and in the 1701-2 *Kenn* accounts he appears again with Thomas Pennington, but the relationship is not clear; in 1701 John Stadler was paid for brasses; the following year Pennington was paid £3 *for casting the Bel*"; then we find "*pd Mr Uglow for Stadler*" and "*pd John Stadler for Castinge ye second bell – £3*", which may mean either that the two founders were working together, or that Pennington cast one (unspecified) bell and for some reason Stadler was employed either to recast it or to cast another. In 1710 Stadler "*of Chimney*" recast a four into a

Fig. 71.   Littlehempston tenor, by John Stadler of Chulmleigh, 1700.

complete ring of five for *Chivelstone*, apparently in the parish. Only the tenor of this ring survives, which is a pity as they bore a set of rhyming mottoes which are only incompletely recorded. By this time Stadler was using a handsome large oval mark with a bell in the centre and IOHANNES STADLER CHULMLEIGH round the circumference; it appears on all his later bells except one of two at *Meeth* and the small tenor bell at *Satterleigh* on which there was not enough room for it; *Alwington* 5/6 has a good example. [See Pl 25d - l]

In 1712 he recast *Buckfastleigh* 4th on site, as recorded in a very detailed set of entries in the wardens' accounts; the bell was recast by Gooding in 1743; in 1714 he recast two of the little four at *Meeth* and the tenor at *Satterleigh*, and his last known bell, later recast, was *Bishopsnympton* tenor, 1715. Unfortunately the Chulmleigh register for 1686–1725 has disappeared, so we have no record of John's death, but it probably took place before 1725 when an Elizabeth Stadler, presumably his widow, began to receive poor relief; she was buried in 1735.

Bells by John Stadler, Chulmleigh in Devon & Cornwall

1684	*Goodleigh 1 bell doc*	
1692	**Littleham 8/8**	with T Pennington
1693	**Exeter St Petrock 2/6**	
	Exeter St Paul 1/1	
1694	*Westleigh 3/5*	
1695	*Warkleigh 1/3*	
1698	South Hill Co 1-4/5	with J Pennington, Tavistock
1699	***Bickleigh (E) 6/6***	
1700	**Littlehempston 2, 5/5**	
1702	***Kenn doc***	*with T Pennington*
1703	***South Molton T H 1/1***	
1710	***Chivelstone 6/6***	
	Chivelstone 2-5/6 doc	
1712	**E Down 2/4**	
	Alwington 5/6	
	Challacombe 2/4	
	Buckfastleigh 4-8/8 doc	
1714	**Meeth 1, 4/4**	
	Satterleigh 3/3	
1715	***Bishopsnympton 6/6***	

Ambrose Gooding of Plymouth was a Cornishman, born in Bodmin in 1678, the son of William Gudding, He evidently learnt his trade with Christopher Pennington of Lezant, as his initials first appear with Pennington's at St Ervan in 1713. His earliest surviving bell is also in Cornwall, at Warbstow; 1714; he was working at *Holsworthy* in 1717, when he cast a bell which was eventually hung in *Tetcott*, and had bells at Little Petherick dated 1724 and Quethiock, 1725. At this time he may still have been living in Cornwall, but at some time he evidently settled in Plymouth. In 1728 he cast a ring of five for *Sherford* (now recast), and in 1731 four for *Welcombe* of which one survives; in the same year he is recorded as working with Christopher Pennington at St Cleer, and the following year he cast a ring of six for *Dartmouth St Saviour*, now all recast in facsimile. A small bell now at *Oldway Mansion, Paignton* is dated 1737; *Ringmore* tenor, 1740; in 1741 he made an agreement to recast *Dawlish* 3rd, but in fact the work was given to Bayley of Bridgwater; the Dawlish accounts include an entry *to Mr Thomas Tripe for going at Penton (Paignton) and Teignmouth to see ye new cast Bells*: it seems that Mr Tripe's report may have caused the Dawlish wardens to change their minds: in the same year he cast a small bell now in Totnes Museum for the owner of The Priory there. In 1743 Gooding had a busy year, casting rings of five for *Holne* [App.II:15] and *Buckfastleigh*, both in Buckfastleigh: the Holne bells survived intact until the front three were found to be cracked in 1974, and the Buckfastleigh bells have all been twice recast since. In 1744 he recast a five at *South Tawton*, of which four survive, and in 1748 *Thurlestone* 5/6. In 1750 he is recorded as working at St Cleer again, and in that year he cast *Berry Pomeroy* 7/8, his last surviving bell, though he cast a bell which hung in Buckfastleigh Vicarage in 1755, in Exeter.

Gooding's bells are not outstanding for tone, and they have suffered a great deal from crazing, which is understandable when one sees his crown-staples, which have large square-sectioned roots. It is very sad that the restoration of Holne bells, his last complete surviving ring, took place only a few years before new technology would have allowed them to be welded. His castings are generally handsome, with good clear lettering and a range of attractive decorations including a vine frieze, a human head, a dove (apparently as a symbol of the Holy Spirit), and a beautifully-executed oval mark, apparently an intaglio seal, depicting a cockerel. [See Pl 26j to r]

There is no evidence that he ever had a permanent foundry; and he seems to have been an itinerant throughout his long career; although he is described as belonging to Plymouth, no records have been found to show him casting any bells there.

Bells by Ambrose Gooding of Plymouth in Devon & Cornwall

1713	*St Ervan, Co doc with C Pennington*
1714	Warbstow, Co 3/3
1717	**Tetcott 1/1**
	Holsworthy doc
1724	Little Petherick, Co 4/6
1725	Quethiock, Co 1/3
1728	**Sherford 2-6/6**
1731	**Welcombe 5/6**
	Welcombe 3,4, 6/6
	St Cleer, Co doc with C Pennington
1732	**Dartmouth St S 4-8/8**
1737	**Paignton, Oldway Mansion 1/1**
1738	**Churchstow 1/4**
1739	Michaelstow, Co 4/5
1740	**Ringmore 3/3**
	St Blazey, Co 2/3
1741	*Dawlish doc*
	Totnes Priory (Museum) 1/1
1742	*Charleton 5/6*
1743	**Holne 3, 4/5**
	Holne 1,2, 5/5
	Buckfastleigh 1-5/5
1744	**S Tawton 3,5, 6/6**
	S Tawton 1,2, 4'6
1748	**Thurlestone 5/6**
1750	*St Cleer Co doc*
	Berry Pomeroy 7/8
1755	**Buckfastleigh Vicarage i/i**

Other Devon Founders of the 17th & 18th centuries

Samuel Baldwyn is so far known only from an indenture dated 15th May 1699, in which he and his wife Mary engaged with the Churchwardens and the Overseers of the Poor of St Mary Major, Exeter to take William Cheany, *being a poore Child and Destitute of able friends to mayntayne him* as an apprentice, *and will teach and instruct the said William Cheany (the said Apprentice) or Cause him to be taught or instructed in the art Trade or Mistery of a Bellfounder after the best manner they can or are able (under moderate and reasonable Correction).* There are no bells which we can confidently attribute to Samuel Baldwyn, and one assumes that he may have been working for Thomas Pennington III.

Thomas Drew, described as a bellfounder, had a son baptised at St Mary Steps in 1729. Robert Sherlock records a chandelier by him in the U. S. A., but as with Samuel Baldwyn no bells exist which can certainly be attributed to him.

William Howard was a brazier who became a Freeman of Exeter in 1734 by succession to his father who was a butcher. His only recorded bellfounding work appears in the *Chudleigh* accounts in 1752, when he was paid for recasting the treble and market bells which were taken to Exeter for the purpose: he was paid £1 8s per hundredweight for the casting, with 8 pounds in the hundred for waste and new metal at 1s 2d per pound.

William Bradford of Meshaw is known from an agreement which he signed in 1757 to rehang *Meshaw* bells in a new frame, in which he refers to himself as *William Bradford of Meshaw, Bellfounder.* He repaired the clock at *Cheriton Fitzpaine* at least three times, stocked a bell at *Shobrooke*, and at *Washfield* in 1760 was paid £4 14s 6d *for the bell*: the sum seems small for a recasting, and may have been for repairs of some kind, serious enough for the bell to have been "presented". No more is known about him, and no bells have so far been found which can be identified as his.

Unknown Founders. In addition the founders who are known by name from their bells or from documentary sources, there are a few who so far have not been identified. We know one of these by his initials "**W.K.**" His bells date between 1624 and 1640; some bear the inscription "SOLI DEO DETVR GLORIA" which suggests a possible connection with the Penningtons; they also bear several sets of initials which always include W.K.; on *Cookbury* 2/3 these two letters appear with a bell mark between them, showing them to be the founder's. The only decoration he used was a small fleur-de-lys frieze not unlike one of the Penningtons'. His bells survive in a swathe across the northern half of the county, from *Pancrasweek* to *Hemyock* and (formerly) *Sheldon*. The dates, the style of the bells, and their distribution suggest very strongly that he may have been an apprentice or journeyman under the Penningtons in Barnstaple, and stayed on there when Thomas II moved to Exeter. Six bells by him survive, and Ellacombe records two more, at *Sheldon*, 1628, and *Bulkworthy*, 1640. [See Pl 14d-g]

Fig. 72. Hemyock 3rd, by the unknown founder "W.K.", 1624, in a cannon-retaining headstock.

Bells by W.K.

1624	Hemyock 3/6	
1628	*Sheldon 3/3*	
1629	Cookbury 2/3	
1632	Torrington clock bell	
1634	Huntshaw 1/3	
1634	Pancrasweek 4/5	
1634	Pancrasweek 5/5	
1640	*Bulkworthy 3/3*	

Fig. 73. Georgenympton tenor, by an unknown founder in 1680.

A disused bell at *Cockington*, now preserved in the church, bears the date 1653 [Pl 14g] and an inscription all in reverse and very badly moulded. There are some initials on the bell, but none which unequivocally relate to the founder, and like most parishes Cockington has no surviving accounts from the Commonwealth period.

More frustrating are four bells in North Devon, two at *Georgenympton* and two at *Romansleigh*, which have nothing to identify their founder. The Georgenympton accounts contain several entries relating to the casting of their bells, even to the date – 4th September – but do not give the founder's name. They were evidently cast along with Romansleigh's, as the entries include *pd for ye bond concerning ye bellfounder with a large condition & expences at Romansleigh about signing it – 00 03 06*. They are well cast, with decoration in the form of an acanthus-leaf pattern stop and coin-impressions; Georgenympton's were apparently a complete ring of four, as a note in the flyleaf of the account-book reads: *The bells of Georgenympton tower were cast ye fourth day of September in y^e to and thirtieth year of the reign of Charles ye second* [23] *in ye year of our Lord 1680 . . .* [See Pl 26a,b]

Whether this founder was based in Devon or elsewhere is uncertain; there seem to be no other examples of his work in any other county. The same is true of the founder of the 2nd at *Instow* (1694), whose initials may have been I.C. as these appear either side of a mask-&-swag decoration [Pl 26h,i] along with the name FARMER DORMEN, the latter framed by small ring marks. The style of this bell is reminiscent of Robert Austen II of Somerset.

Fremington 5/6 is dated 1702 – apparently, as the final figure is set askew – and bears the initials R P with a bell mark between them; I P and W P also appear in the inscription. The stop is a roundel. [See 26c,d] None of these marks are recorded anywhere else; the date is too late for any of the Purdue family, and the initials do not fit any of the Penningtons, so this bell too has to remain a mystery, as must *Yarnscombe* tenor, dated 1709, with a wheel stop, a small roundel which looks like the impression of a button, and a small shield. [26e,f,g]

---

23. Charles II's reign was officially reckoned to have begun on the death of his father in 1649.

Fig. 74. Instow 2nd, by another unknown founder, 1694.

Post-Reformation Bells in Devon by Unknown Founders

?C16th	Exeter St Petrock 6/6	
1601	Hollacombe 2/3	
1625	Doccombe 1/1	
1653	Cockington dis	
1680	Romansleigh 4,6/6	
1680	Georgenympton 2,4/4	
1694	Instow 2/3	
?C17th	Teigngrace 1/2	
?C17/18th	Totnes ex Magdalen Chapel 1/1	
	Sydenham House, Marystow 1/1	
1702	Plymouth, Dockyard Museum 1/1	
c1705	Chudleigh Town Hall 1/1 ? Stadler	
1709	Yarnscombe 3/6	
1763	Princetown Tor Royal 1/1	
1769	South Brent Toll House 1/1	
1788	Blackhall House, Avonwick 1/1	
?C18th	Withleigh 1/1	
1827	Plymouth St Simon 1/2	
1828	Saltram House 1/1	
1838	Noss Mayo Village Hall 1/1	
?C19	Lee 1/1	
C19th	Ashford 1/3 ship's bell	
	Ash Thomas 1/1	
	Avonwick 1/1	
	Axminster Cemetery 1/1	
	Barbrook 1/1	
	Beaford, Yatton Court 1/1	
	Bere Alston 1/1	

Berrynarbor, Watermouth Castle 1/1
Bittadon 1/1
Brownston 1/1
Buckfastleigh St Luke 1/1
Buckland-tout-Saints House 1/1
Chudleigh, Ugbrooke House 1/1
Collaton St Mary saunce
Compton Castle, 1/1
Crediton, Knowle 1/1
Crediton, Knowle Barton 1/1
Credton, Yeoford 1/1
Dowrich House 1/1
Exeter, Countess Wear 1/1
Exeter, St James 1/1
Exeter, St Paul Burnthouse Lane 1/1
Gulworthy 1/1
Gunn 1/1
Harberton, Trisford House 1/1
Harbertonford 1/1
Dawlish, Holcombe 1/1
Hope Cove 1/1
Huccaby 1/1
Huxham 1/1
Ivybridge 1/1
Lee 1/1
Luton 1/1
Paignton, Christ Church 1/1
Plymouth, Devonport St Barnabas 1/1

Plymouth, Estover Ch Ch 1/1 ship's bell	Stoke Gabriel, Waddeton Court 1/1
Plymouth, Ford St Mark 1/1	Tedburn St Mary, Pathfinder Village 1/1
Plymouth, Devonport St Philip 1/1	Torquay, St John saunce
Plymouth, St Simon 2/2	Totnes, E gate 1/1
Plymouth, Devonport St Thomas 1/1	Upton Pyne, Pynes Home Farm 1/1
Sparkwell School 1/1	Whitford 1/2
Starcross 1/2 ?Mears	Whitford 2/2
Sticklepath (S Tawton) 1/1	Witheridge School 1/1
Sticklepath Methodist Church 1/1	

The Bilbies and the Cullompton Foundry

The Bilbies were one of the most prolific bellfounding dynasties in the South West of England, and shared with the Penningtons the bellfounding boom of the latter half of the 18th-century. The family hailed from Chewstoke, between the Mendip Hills and Bristol; Edward Bilbie cast for the church there the earliest surviving Bilbie bell, dated 1698. By 1714 he evidently reckoned that he had mastered his craft, and we find at Somerton the first of the Bilbies' well-known boastful (and badly-spelt) inscriptions: FRIND WROTH AND NIGHT FOR ALL YOURE SPIT(E) OVLD EDWARD BILBIE HATH ME RVND PVLL ME ROVND AND HEARE ME SOVND FRIND SVCH WORK YOV NEVER DON. Edward's business seems to have been confined to his own county; his son **Thomas Bilbie I** ("Thomas the Great") was more ambitious and extended his territory into Dorset, where the decline of the Closworth foundry would have been creating an opportunity for other founders, and later into Devon. He continued with his father's style of inscriptions, adapting the Somerton inscription for his recasting of the 2-ton Tenor at Yeovil:

> TAKE AND WEIGH ME RIGHT FOR I AM NEAR FIVE THOUSAND WEIGHT
>   SING PRAISE TO GOD
> WHEN I WAS NEW CAST SEPTEMBER THE 25 THE YEAR 1728
> STEPHEN HOOPER AND HIS WIFE IOANE WAS THE DONOR ALONE
> COME LET US SOUND OUT ILE KEEP MY PLACE NO DOUBT
> YOU WRATH AND WRIGHT PRAY SPEAK THE RIGHT
> COME SEE HOW I AM RUN
> TWAS YOUNG BILBIE THAT CAST ME SUCHE WORK YOU NEVER DONE

Thomas I took over the business on his father's death in 1725, and worked mainly in his own area until 1746. In that year the *Cullompton* churchwardens decided *that two of the Six Bells belonging to the Parish . . . .being Crack'd and that the Cage where in the Said Six Bells now hang is very much out of repair and that it is necessary to new cast the same and to hang them in a different manner . . . that all the said Six Bells shall be forthwith cast into Eight and that the Cage wherein they now hang shall be forthwith made fit and convenient for hanging the same . . .* A Vestry meeting four months later resolved *that the Bells of the Parish be Cast in some part of the Almshouse of this Parish, and that the parishioners of the same find the Bellfounder to carry on his work proper ffewell to run his mettle to dry his Moulds and sufficient Brick to build an Oven to compleat in lieu of the Expence of carrying the Bells to Taunton.* The parish had recently built a new workhouse, so the almshouse would have been untenanted at least in part: Richard Beavis, Esq. (apparently the son of the Richard Beavis who had adjudicated Purdue's work at the cathedral in 1676) and Mr Richard Harward were to *contract with some able Person for the compleating thereof.* There is no evidence that Bilbie was at that time working in Taunton, but he may have considered it as an alternative, because in 1747 he recast a bell for St James's, Taunton at Cullompton. In the event the cost of the materials for the 'oven' were provided by Richard Beavis; the bill for the work was £113 [App.II:16].

The work of the Wellington foundry had by this time been in serious decline, and this created an excellent opening in East Devon and West Somerset for a good bellfounder. Thomas Bilbie I took it with both hands; in addition to the Cullompton eight he recast a five at *Cadeleigh* and single bells at *Colebrooke* and *Broadhembury*; the following year *Kenton*'s six were recast and another six at *Bradninch* in 1748, while his area was extended in the other direction with a ring of six at N Bradley in Wiltshire. In 1749 in Cullompton he cast Devon's oldest surviving complete ring of eight for *Alphington*, a five for *Zeal Monachorum* and single bells for *St Michael's, Honiton*, *Littleham* [N] and *St Budeaux*; in 1751 bells for *Colebrooke, Talaton* and *Willand*. On some of these Thomas I used quirky, rhyming inscriptions: on Cullompton tenor we have, BILBIE THE FOUNDER, BUSH THE HANGER, HEATHFIELDS THE MAN WHO RINGS THE TENOR [24]: and on Kenton 5th, BILBIE THE FOUNDER, RUGG THE HANGER, CARTER THE SMITH AND TREBLE RINGER [51]. In 1749 he also cast a heavy eight for *St Andrew's, Plymouth*, in Plymouth, and the tenor for St Budeaux was probably also recast there: a letter survives, written from Plymouth in March 1748, from Thomas to the churchwardens of North Bradley, in which he says, *I am know in Plymouth and cannot come away for I am doing a peal of bells that doth come to two hundred and thirty pounds . . .*[25]. These bells are inscribed in neat, low-relief Roman capitals, and most of them bear two sizes of rose stamps [30b,c]; *Kenton* 3rd has between the founder's initials a bell mark in high relief [Pl 30a] which does not appear elsewhere in the county. In 1749 the Cullompton Vestry ordered that Bilbie should be permitted to use the foundry in the Alms House for another three years, at a rent of £1 3s 4d per annum, and in 1750 he was employed to set up a new chiming apparatus and repair the clock at a cost of £42.

Thomas Bilbie II was born in 1727, and in 1754 at the age of 26 he settled in Cullompton permanently at No 4, Fore Street, with his wife Mary, the daughter of Richard Castleman, a Bristol distiller (in succession to his father-in-law Thomas II received the freedom of the City of Bristol in 1769, and voted there in 1774). At Cullompton he was soon in business, casting fives for *Bow, Brampford Speke, East Budleigh* and *Upton Pyne* in the first two years. At Brampford Speke he seems to have been experimenting with his scale for light bells, as the diameters of the front three of the five were within 1½ inches of each other, and the 3rd was lighter than the treble. Until 1767 father and son worked in parallel, Thomas I's territory covering Somerset and Wiltshire, Thomas II's Devon and very occasionally Cornwall; both worked on occasion in Dorset, where Thomas II cast a fine eight, and built a big chime-barrel, for Beaminster. Murray T. Foster in the *Transactions of the Devonshire Association* vol. 42, p.168, wrote that the foundry was near Shortlands Lane, and until the 1980s at least there were ruins of a brick building with the base of a large chimney near the leat to the east of the High Street. Documents show that most of his casting was done at Cullompton, but the Beaminster eight were cast on the spot. The market areas of the Cullompton and Lezant/Stoke Climsland founders overlapped down the eastern flank of Dartmoor, and the Bilbies did a good deal of business all the way down the line of the Exeter-Plymouth road, with *Buckfastleigh, Ugborough, Modbury* and *South Brent*, and down into the South Hams with *Harberton, North Huish* and *West Alvington*: in the Plymouth itself were rings at *Egg Buckland* and *Stoke Damarel* as well as St Andrew's.

On the death of Thomas Bilbie I in 1768, Abraham Bilbie took over the Chewstoke foundry, and the division of the family territory continued, but when William Bilbie succeeded Abraham he cast a bell for South Brewham in Somerset in conjunction with Thomas II.

---

24. John Bush of Chewstoke was a noted bellhanger who often worked with Bilbie. In 1758 at Backwell William Evans made a riposte to the Chewstoke team: BILBIE AND BOOSH MAY COME AND SEE WHAT EVANS AND NOTT HAVE DONE BY ME
25. Bilbie & the Chew Valley Clock Makers, p69. This book is a very comprehensive account of the family.

Fig. 75. Bampton treble, by Thomas Bilbie III, 1800.

The bells from the Cullompton foundry are neatly inscribed in fine Roman capitals, and decorated at first with a shell [Pl 30f] similar to the one used by the Cornish Penningtons, and after 1761 with the small bell mark [Pl 30h] which continued in use well into the 19th-century. Thomas II's inscriptions do not have the lively local allusions or boastful claims of his father; they usually follow conventional 18th-century style, with the tenor very often bearing RELIGION DEATH AND PLEASURE MAKE ME TO RING, or I CALL THE QUICK TO CHURCH AND DEAD TO GRAVE. He spelt the name of his hometown in various ways; Cullompton, Collumpton, Cullumpton, all appear. The heads of his bells were usually made progressively flatter towards the heavy end of the ring, with sharply-angled shoulders (a fashion which the Penningtons also followed); his cannons are neatly shaped with an ovolo moulding. Some of his notable rings are the sixes at *South Brent*, 1759, *Harberton*, 1762, and *West Alvington*, 1775, and fives at *Exminster* (now eight), 1758, *Sourton*, 1775 and *Clyst St Lawrence*. Rings of six at *Broadclyst*, *Chagford* and *Northam*, and eight at *Tavistock* are among those which have been recast. Many of the surviving rings are very good, though some of the lighter rings such as *Rewe* are only mediocre in tone. His last work was the addition of a front five to Bayley & Street's tenor at *St Paul's, Honiton*.

Thomas Castleman Bilbie – Thomas III, the son of Thomas II, was born in Cullompton in 1758, and succeeded on the death of his father in 1780, continuing very much in the tradition which he inherited but achieving in his own right some of the Cullompton foundry's finest works. Many ringers regard the sixes at *North Molton* and *Modbury* as being the finest in the county; both are the work of Thomas Castleman Bilbie, the former in 1784 (the tenor has been recast), the latter, still complete, in 1806. Other good sixes include *Ipplepen*, 1799 (now 8) and *Bampton*, 1800. Thomas III continued also in the clockmaking side of the business, and supplied a new clock for Cullompton in 1811 for £55. The Cullompton foundry continued to be efficiently run and to produce work of high quality, while the Chewstoke branch of the family, under the eccentric and unreliable James and Thomas Webb Bilbie, went steadily to pieces. An advertisement in the *Exeter Flying Post* for 26 March 1812, while it suggests that the long war was having an effect on the market for bells, also makes it clear that Thomas Castleman Bilbie had little sympathy for the vagaries of his cousins:

THOMAS BILBIE, Bell-founder, Cullompton, Devon, returns his sincere thanks to his friends for the great support he has received for many years past in the Bellfoundery business, and assures those who may favor him with their orders, that they shall be executed with the best materials, with the utmost despatch, and on reasonable terms.

N.B. Church Bells cast and hung, also Ship and Gentlemen's Dinner and Factory Bells.

As there has been a complaint in different counties, especially that of Somerset and Dorset, of bells being kept too long at some founders, T.B. thinks it his duty to inform his friends and the public, that it shall not be the case at his foundery, and that all orders shall be compleated with all possible speed.

The last Chewstoke bell seems in fact to have been cast in 1811, but the records of Winford, Somerset, show that they were trying, unsuccessfully, to get the contract for recasting those bells as late as 1816.

THE BELLFOUNDERS: AFTER THE REFORMATION

Thomas Castleman Bilbie died in 1814; he left his house and working tools to his widow Elizabeth and, if she should remarry, to his son **John**. John kept the business going either during his father's last illness or until just after his death; he cast a ring of five for *North Bovey* in 1814 of which four survive, the only bells bearing his name. Soon after, the business was sold to William Pannell.

William Pannell is described as a tinman, but his family had apparently been in Cullompton for at least a hundred years; in 1721 and 1722 a Thomas Pannell was landlord of the inn where the parish discussed some recasting of the bells, and he was paid 2/6d for beer when the great bell was carried to be cast; when the bells were recast in 1746, £1 1s was entered in the receipts *of Joseph Pannell his subscription, out of his bill towards the bells*. If bellfounding matters were often discussed in the family inn, it would not be surprising for one of the sons to become interested in the craft and serve an apprenticeship in it. In any case, William Pannell continued at Cullompton, using largely the Bilbie stamps, though there seems to have been a gap of some six years before his first casting: Murray Foster *(op. cit.)* says that his foundry was at a house in the "New Cut" known as "Methodist Court", and the last bell by him was sold in 1901 to Mr Justice Eve at Bovey Tracey. He seldom maintained the Bilbie quality, and all his work consisted of single and recast bells, a high proportion of which have again been recast. One which well might have been recast but so far has survived is the 7th at *Ugborough*, which is notoriously out of tune and helps to give that ring its very peculiar sound. In 1828 William Pannell's name appears with that of his son **Charles Pannell**, and they placed the following in Trewman's *Exeter Flying Post* on March 13th that year:

DEVON
Cullompton Bell-Foundry
WILLIAM & CHARLES PANNELL,
Bell-founders, return thanks to the Gentlemen of
Dorset, Somerset, Devon and Cornwall, for their very
liberal support of that business, and trust that by attention to
merit future favours.

In 1833 they described their business in grandiose style as "The West of England Church Bell Foundry" on the tenor at *Plympton St Maurice*, the last bell in Devon to be cast on site. A few years before William's death, Charles, according to Ellacombe, went to London and worked at the Cripplegate Foundry where John Warner was developing casting techniques which are still in use in both British bellfoundries. There is a certainly a gap in the casting sequence between 1847 and 1851, though Christopher Dalton in *The Bells & Belfries of Dorset* describes four very strange bells at Little Bredy which were cast at Cullompton, perhaps by one of William's workmen. When William died in 1853 – his tombstone may be seen a little to the south of the tower at Cullompton – Charles set up a new "West of England Bell Foundry" in Exeter on a site in Longbrook Street, but by then the railway age in the West Country had advanced too far for a local bellfoundry (even a good one) to survive; after 1855 Charles produced no more bells, though curiously that last year saw the casting of the only complete Pannell rings surviving – the six at *Arlington* and the eight at *St Mary Magdalene, Upton, Torquay*: one other recorded ring was the six by William and Charles at *Lamerton*, described by Ellacombe as "poor bells" and destroyed by a fire in 1877. The Arlington bells are not notable in tone, but the Upton ring, tuned by Taylors', are pleasant enough. The quality of casting remained high throughout the Pannell period, though inscriptions on the later Pannell bells are characterized by some very idiosyncratic use of full-stops and colons. The *Exeter Flying Post* describes the opening of the Arlington ring in these terms:

CHURCH BELLS. Messrs Pannell and Co., bell founders of this city, recently put up a new peal of bells
in Arlington Church; on the 30th ult. These were what is technically called "rung out" by the Bratton,

Shirwill and Goodleigh ringers, on which the churchwardens of Arlington have written to Messrs Pannell and Co., bearing testimony to their talent and ability in the construction of the bells and expressing their unqualified satisfaction at the way in which they executed their contract.

The West of England Church Bell Foundry which came to an end in 1855 was the last local bellfoundry in Devon, but the Cullompton foundry, especially under the Bilbies, had left the county with some very fine rings. Under Thomas Bilbie I it cast 58 known bells for Devon of which 44 have survived: under Thomas II 168 from which 106 are extant: under Thomas III 145 with 98 survivors, and under the Pannells 95 of which 44 have been recast or lost – more than half the bells cast by William and Charles have been recast.

Bells by the Bilbies of Chewstoke and Cullompton

Year	Place	Founder	Year	Place	Founder
1698	Chewstoke So 5/6	Edward		Compton Martin So 4/6	J Badman
1699	Portbury So 3/6	Edward		Nailsea So 3,4,5/6	Edward
1705	*Wedmore So 4,6/8*	Edward		*Nailsea So 2,6/6*	Edward
	Wraxall So 3,4,7/8	Edward		Worle So 2/6	Edward
1707	Greinton So 4/6	Edward	1724	*Berrow So 3/6*	J Badman
	Meare So 4,5/6	Edward	1725	*Axbridge So 6/6*	Thomas I
1708	Hinton Blewett So 1-5/5	Edward		*Chewton Mendip So 5/6*	J Badman
	Hutton So 1,5/5	Edward		*Churchill So 6/6*	Thomas I
1709	Doynton Av 4/5	Edward		Clevedon So 8/8	Thomas I
1711	Bleadon So 2-6/6	Edward		*Publow So 5/6*	Thomas I
	Compton Bishop So 2,4,5/6	Edward	1726	Bristol Cath 1,2/8	Thomas I
	Compton Bishop So 3,6/6	Edward	1727	Mark So 6,8/8	Thomas I
1712	Shapwick So 5,6/6	Edward		*Bridport Do 2 bells doc*	Thomas I
	Wrington So 9/10	Edward	1728	Nempnett Thrubwell So 4/6	Thomas I
1713	Burrington So 2/6	Edward		Yeovil So 10/10	Thomas I
	Compton Martin So 2/6	Edward		*Yeovil So 7/10*	Thomas I
	South Petherton So 6/8	Edward	1729	*E Brent So 6/6*	Thomas I
	Portbury So 6/6	Edward		Compton Dundon o 3/5	Thomas I
1714	Charlton Adam So 1,2/5	Edward		Farmborough So 1,3,4,5/6	Thomas I
	Kingston Seymour So 5/6	Edward		*Farmborough So 2,6/6*	Thomas I
	Somerton So 6/6	Edward		W Harptree So 3/4	Thomas I
	Kingsbury Episcopi So 6/6	Edward		Bedminster St John So 1/1	Thomas I
	Abson Av So 4/6	Edward	1730	Stowey So 1-5/5	Thomas I
1716	Catcott So 1/1	Edward	1731	Chewstoke So 1/6	Thomas I
	Queen Charlton So 2/5	Edward		*Chewstoke So 6/6*	Thomas I
1718	Chewstoke So 2,3/6	Edward		Keynsham So 1,2/8	Thomas I
	Flax Bourton So 1/1	Edward		Meare So 1,6/6	Thomas I
	Abson Av 2/6	Edward	1732	*Chilcompton So 1/6*	Thomas I
1719	Compton Martin So 3,5/6	Edward		Dunkerton So 5,6/6	Thomas I
	Moorlinch So 1/6	Edward		*Dunkerton So 2,3,4/6*	Thomas I
1720	Cossington So 3/6	Edward		*Huntspill So 1/5*	Thomas I
1721	*S Petherton So 8/8*	Edward		Ilminster So 8/8	Thomas I
	Bristol, Temple So 8/8	Edward		*Merriott So 3/5*	Thomas I
	Bristol, Temple, 7/8	Edward	1733	Compton Martin So 1/6	Thomas I
1722	Churchill So 3/6	Edward		Kilmersdon So 3/6	Thomas I
1723	*Axbridge So 1-6/6*	Edward		*Merriott So 2,5/6*	Thomas I

	Shipham So 2,4,5,6/6	Thomas I		Bristol St Th 3/8	Thomas I
	Shipham So 3/6	Thomas I	1744	Steeple Ashton Wi 5/6	Thomas I
	Somerton So 5/6	Thomas I		*Steeple Ashton Wi 1/6*	Thomas I
	Weare So 2/6	Thomas I	1745	Mells So 3,8/8	Thomas I
1734	Banwell So 6,7,9,10/10	Thomas I		Worle So 3,/6	Thomas I
	Banwell So 5,8/10	Thomas I		*Worle So 5,6/6*	Thomas I
	Clutton So 4,6/6	Thomas I	1746	Evercreech So 5,8/8	Thomas I
	Croscombe So 3/6	Thomas I		Meare So 2,3/6	Thomas I
	Kewstoke So 4/6	Thomas I		**Broadhembury 5/6**	Thomas I
	Dorchester Do 3,5,8/8	Thomas I		**Cadeleigh 2-6/6**	Thomas I
	Dorchester Do 1,2,4,6,7/8	Thomas I		*Colebrooke 3/6 doc*	Thomas I
1735	*Chew Magna So 1,3,4,5,6/6*	Thomas I		**Cullompton 5,6,710/10**	Thomas I
	Haselbury Plucknett So 6/6	Thomas I		**Cullompton 3,4,,8,9/10**	Thomas I
	Haselbury Plucknett So 2,3,4,5	Thomas I	1747	**Kenton 1-6/6**	Thomas I
	Wookey So 3/6	Thomas I		*Kenton 4/6*	Thomas I
1736	*Loxton So 2/3*	Thomas I	1748	Kewstoke So 3/6	Thomas I
	Milborne Port So 3,4,5,6/8	Thomas I		Glastonbury St Jn So 7/8	Thomas I
	Milborne Port So 7,8/8	Thomas I		Taunton St M M So 11/12	Thomas I
	Stanton Prior So 1/1	Thomas I		N Bradley Wi 3,4,5,6,7/8	Thomas I
	Templecombe So 3,4/6	Thomas I		**Bradninch 3-8/8,x5**	Thomas I
	Wick St Lawrence So 4/5	Thomas I		*Bradninch 5/8*	Thomas I
1738	Charlton Adam So 4/5	Thomas I	1749	Wookey So 6/6	Thomas I
	Chelvey So 1/1	Thomas I		Taunton St Jas So 7/8	Thomas I
	Horsington So 4/6	Thomas I		**Alphington 1-8/8**	Thomas I
	Shepton Beauchamp So 8-12/12	Thomas I		**Honiton St M 2,6/6**	Thomas I
	Westbury s Mendip So 2/3	Thomas I		*Littleham (N) 3/6*	Thomas I
1739	Weston, Bath Av 3-8/8	Thomas I		**Plymouth St Andrew 3-9/10**	Thomas I
	Dorchester H Trin Do 1/1	Thomas I		***Plymouth St Andrew 10/10***	Thomas I
	Kingston Maurward house 1/1	Thomas I		*St Budeaux 6/6*	Thomas I
	Marshfield So 5,8/8	Thomas I		**Zeal Monachorum 2-6/6**	Thomas I
	Bristol SS P & J 1-5,7/8	Thomas I	1750	Dundry So 6/6	Thomas I
	Bristol SS P & J 6,8/8	Thomas I		Midsomer Norton So 5,6,7,12/12	Thomas I
1740	E Pennard So 4,5/5	Thomas I		Wrington So 8/10	Thomas I
	Radstock So 1,2,3,5/6,x4	Thomas I		*Wrington So 5,6,7,10/10*	Thomas I
	Radstock So 4/6	Thomas I		**Bishopsnympton 4,5/6**	Thomas I
	Caernarvon Gwynn 1/1	Thomas I		**Clayhanger 2/3**	Thomas I
	Bitton Gl 7/8	Thomas I		*Kenn 5/6 doc*	Thomas I
	Bristol Cath 4/8	Thomas I		Dorchester St P Do 1/8	Thomas I
1741	Newton St Loe So 1-6/6	Thomas I	1751	*Colebrooke 5/6*	Thomas I
1742	Banwell So 8/10	Thomas I		**Talaton 5/6**	Thomas I
	Dundry So 3/6	Thomas I		**Willand 2/3**	Thomas I
	Paulton So 1-5/5	Thomas I	1752	Bruton So 1,3/6	Thomas I
	Steeple Ashton Wi 6/6	Thomas I		Rowberrow So 1,2,4-6/6	Thomas I
1743	*Barrington 5/6*	Thomas I		*Rowberrow So 3/6*	Thomas I
	Glastonbury So 5/8	Thomas I		Stanton Drew So 2,3,4/5	Thomas I
	Glastonbury So 6/8	Thomas I		*Ston Easton So 1-4/5*	Thomas I
	Nempnett Thrubwell So 2,6/6	Thomas I		Tickenham So 4/6	Thomas I
	Stourton Caundle Do 3/4	Thomas I	1753	*Alford So 1/3*	Thomas I

	Babcary So 4/6	Thomas I		**Shobrooke 1-6/6,x5**	Thomas II
	Compton Martin So 6/6	Thomas I		*Shobrooke 5/6*	Thomas II
	E Brent So 2/6	Thomas I		Saltash Co 1,2,4/6	Thomas II
	Chewton Mendip So 4/6	Thomas I		*Saltash Co 3,5,6/6*	Thomas II
	Rode So 1-5/6	Thomas I	1761	*Bradford-on-Avon Wi 8/8*	Thomas I
	Rode So 6/6	Thomas I		Pilton So 4/6	Thomas I
	Ston Easton So 5/5	Thomas I		Wick St Lawr So 3/5	Thomas I
	Tickenham So 6/6	Thomas I		Keevil Wi 5,6/6	Thomas I
	Wellow So 2/6	Thomas I		*Bromham Wi 4/6*	Thomas I
1754	Congresbury So 3,8/8	Thomas I		**Rockbeare 4/6**	Thomas II
	Corston So ?	Thomas I		**Sampford Peverell 1-4/6**	Thomas II
	Halse So 2/6	Thomas II		**Shute 3-6/6**	Thomas II
	Bow 2,3/6	Thomas II		**Staverton 3,4,5/6**	Thomas II
	Bow 4,5,6/6	Thomas II		*Staverton 2,6/6*	Thomas II
	Down St Mary 5/6	Thomas II		Wayfor So 2/2	Thomas II
1755	Weare So 6/6	Thomas I	1762	Kelston So 3-6/6	Thomas I
	Brampford Speke 2-5/6	Thomas II		**Harberton 1-6/6**	Thomas II
	Brampford Speke 6/6	Thomas II		*Harberton 4/6*	Thomas II
	E Budleigh 4-8/8	Thomas II		**Ugborough 3,8/8**	Thomas II
	E Budleigh 4,7/8	Thomas II		*Ugborough 4,5,6,7/8*	Thomas II
	Upton Pyne 2-6/6	Thomas II		Cerne Abbas Do 2,4/6	Thomas I
1756	Beckington So 5,6/8	Thomas I		*Cerne Abbas Do 3/6*	Thomas I
	Beckington So 3,4,7,8/8	Thomas I	1763	Milverton So 3/8	Thomas II
	Winsley Wi 2/3	Thomas I		**Holcombe Rogus 5/6**	Thomas II
	Bristol St Th 1,2/8	Thomas I		**Mamhead 1-5/5**	Thomas II
1757	Leigh on Mendip So 1-6/6	Thomas I		Bristol, Redcliffe 8,10/12	Thomas I
	Leigh on Mendip So 2,3/6	Thomas I		*Bristol, Redclif 7,9/12*	Thomas I
	Corsham Wi 1/6	Thomas I	1764	Curry Mallet So 2,3/6	Thomas I
1758	*Pilton So 6/6*	Thomas I		W Harptree So 2/4	Thomas I
	Litton So 4/6	Thomas I		Witham Friary So 3/3	Thomas I
	Timsbury So 2,3,4,5/6	Thomas I		Tilshead Wi 1-3/3	Thomas I
	Timsbury So 1,6/6	Thomas I		**Powderham 6/6**	Thomas II
	Combe Raleigh 1/3	Thomas II		*Ugborough 5/8*	Thomas II
	Exminster 4-8/8	Thomas II		Longburton Do 2,3/4	Thomas II
	Exminster 5/8	Thomas II	1765	*Walcot, Bath 2/2*	Thomas I
	Corsham Wi 3,4,6/6	Thomas I		Dundry So ?4/6	Thomas I
	Corsham Wi 2,5/6	Thomas I		*S Petherton So 4/8*	Thomas I
1759	Cheddar So 8/8	Thomas I		Stogursey So 5/6	Thomas I
	S Brent 1-6/6	Thomas II		*Stogursey So 6/6*	Thomas I
	Buckland-In-the-Moor 4-8/8	Thomas II		Winsford So 3,5,6/6	Thomas II
1760	Batcombe So 1-5/6	Thomas I		*Winsford So 2,4/6*	Thomas II
	Batcombe So 6/6	Thomas I		N Wraxall Wi 1/1	Thomas I
	Castle Cary So 1-6/6	Thomas I		**Weare Giffard 2-6/6**	Thomas II
	Castle Cary So 2/6	Thomas I		*Weare Giffard 2,5/6*	Thomas II
	Doulting So 3/6	Thomas I		Beaminster Do 3-10/10	Thos I & II
	Hemington So 2/6	Thomas I	1766	Brislington So 6/6	Thomas I
	Somerton So 5/8	Thomas I		**Broadhembury 6/6**	Thomas II
	Gittisham 5/5	Thomas II		**Chagford 3-8/8**	Thomas II

	Chardstock bourdon	Thomas II		Compton Bishop So 6/6	Abraham
	Kingsteignton 4/8	Thomas II		*ComptonBishop So 1/6*	Abraham
	Batcombe Do 3/3	Thomas II		**Rewe 2-6/6**	Thomas II
	Durweston Do 3/5	Thomas II		*Abbotsbury Do 1,2,3/6*	Thomas II
	Doynton Av 2/5	Thomas I		Corscombe Do 1-6/6	Thomas II
1767	Long Ashton So 3/8	Thomas I		Horfield So 2-5/5	Abraham
	Ubley So 2,3/4	Thomas I	1774	**Brixham 8/10**	Thomas II
	Wrington So 7/10	Thomas I		**Kingsteignton 5/8**	Thomas II
	Brixham 6,7/10	Thomas II		**Widecombe-I-t-Moor 4/6**	Thomas II
	Broadhembury 3/6	Thomas II	1775	*S Brewham So 2/2*	Tho II & Wm
	Stoke Abbot Do 1/5	Thomas II		Uphill So 2,3,5,6/6	William
	Toller Porcorum Do 3/4	Thomas II		*Uphill So 4/6*	William
	Beaminster chime barrel	Thomas II		Wedmore So 8/8	William
1768	*Wanstrow So ?4/5*	Thomas I		Weston in Gordano So 3/6	William
	Yeovil So 3,4/10	Thomas I		**W Alvington 1-6/6**	Thomas II
	Broadclyst 3-8/8	Thomas II		**Colyton 5/8**	Thomas II
	Egg Buckland 6/6	Thomas II		**Dodbrooke 3,5/6**	Thomas II
	Chideock Do 4/5	Thomas II		**Sourton 1-5/5**	Thomas II
	Iwerne Minster Do 2/6	Abraham		Evershot Do 1-6/6	Thomas II
	Winterborne Whitch Do 5/5	Abraham	1776	Binegar So 4,6/6	William
1769	N Cadbury So 2,3,4,6/6	Thomas II		High Littleton So 6/6	William
	S Cadbury So 1,4/6	Abraham		Lullington So 1/1	William
	S Cadbury So 2,3/6	Abraham		Milverton So 5/8	Thomas II
	S Wraxall Wi So 1-6/6	Abraham		Publow So 1/6	William
	Tavistock 1-8/8	Thomas II		Queen Charlton So 5/5	William
1770	N Cadbury So 1/6	Abraham		N Stoke So 1/1	William
	E Coker So 3-8/8	Thomas II		**Kilmington 5/6**	Thomas II
	W Coker So 4/7,x8/8	Thomas II		**Sidbury 8/8**	Thomas II
	Whitchurch So 1/1	Abraham		Whitstone Co 2,5/6	Thomas II
	Winscombe So 3-8/8	Abraham		W*hitstone Co 3,4/6*	Thomas II
	Northam 3-8/8	Thomas II	1777	*Brent Knoll So 6/6*	William
	Shobrooke 4/6	Thomas II		Compton Dundon So 4/5	William
	Lyme Regis Do 5-1/10	Thomas II		*Freshford So 4/5*	William
	Poyntington Do 3/3	Abraham		*Maperton So ?2/3*	William
1771	E Coker So 1,2/8	Thomas II		Street So 3,4,6,7/8	William
	Crowcombe So 2,3/6	Thomas II		*Street So 5,8/8*	William
	Marwood 1-5	Thomas II		**Bridgerule 5,7/8**	Thomas II
	Marwod 6/6	Thomas II		**Otterton 2,3,4/6**	Thomas II
	Monkleigh 2/6	Thomas II		*Folke Do 1/2*	William
1772	Portishead So 3-8/8	Abraham		Wapley Av 2/5	William
	Portishead So 7/8	Abraham	1778	W Harptree So 4/4	William
	Wedmore So 3,5/8	Abraham		*Queen Camel So 1/6*	William
	Wells, St Cuth So 4/8	Abraham		**Clyst St Lawrence 1-5/5**	Thomas II
	Colyton 1/6	Thomas II		**Culmstock 6/8**	Thomas II
	Widworthy 2/5	Thomas II		**Topsham 1/6**	Thomas II
	Powerstock Do 2,4,6/6	Thomas II		*Mangotsfield Av 3*	William
	Thorncombe Do 5/5	Thomas II	1779	Cameley So 1/5	William
1773	Chelwood So 1/1	Abraham		W Coker So 3/8	William

	Middle Chinnock So 3/3	William		**Washford Pyne 4/6**	Thomas III
	Whitelackington So 2/4	Thomas II		Frome St Qn Do 1/2	Thomas III
	Corsley Wi 4/6	William		Sherborne Do 5/8	William
	W Anstey 2/4	Thomas II		Siston Av 1/6	William
	Thornbury 3/5	Thomas II	1788	Charlton Mackrell So 2/6	William
	Stalbridge So 6/6	William		Frome So 3/8	William
1780	Upton Lovell Wi 2/3	William		Greinton So 5/6	William
	Honiton St P 3-7/8	Thomas II		Keinton Mandeville So 3/3	William
	Pucklechurch Av 1/6	William		Mells So ?6/8	William
1781	Abbots Leigh So 1,6/6	William		Sandford Orcas Do 4/5	William
	Abbots Leigh So 5/6	William		**Morchard Bishop 2/6**	Thomas III
	Wellington So 6/8	Thomas III	1789	Keinton Mandeville So 2/3	William
	Wellington So 5/8	*Thomas III*		**Plymouth Stoke Damrel 1-6/6**	Thomas III
	Edington Wi 7/10	William		Symondsbury Do 2-5/6	Thomas III
	Cullompton 3/10	Thomas III		Bristol Ch Ch 1,2/10	William
1782	Chillington So 1/2	Thomas III		Tenby Dyv 3,5,7,8/8	William
	Downhead So 1,2,3/3	William	1790	Berkeley So 1,2/4	William
	Kingsdon So 4/5	William		Chard So 3,4,6,7,8/8	Thomas III
	Marksbury So 1-5/6	William		*Chard So 5/8*	Thomas III
	Marksbury So 6/6	William		Huish Chamflower So 2/6	Thomas III
	Somerton So 1/6	William		*Huntspill So 3/5*	Thomas III
	Thorncombe Do 7/8	Thomas III		Ilminster So 5/8	William
	Killerton House 1/1	Thomas III		Rodden So 1/1	William
1783	Ilchester So 4/5	William		**Calverleigh 6/6**	Thomas III
	Ilchester So 1/5	William		***Ottery St Mary 7/8***	Thomas III
	Milverton So 7/8	Thomas III		**Plymouth St Matthias 1/1**	Thomas III
	Colerne Wi 4,7/8	William		Broadwindsor Do 2/6	Thomas III
	Monkton Farleigh Wi 2/3	William	1791	Badgworth So 5/5	T W & Jas
	Tisbury Wi 4/6	William		Keynsham So 5/8	T W & Jas
	Clyst Hydon 2,/6	Thomas III		Odcombe So 2-6/6	T W & Jas
	Clyst Hydon 4/6	Thomas III		***Tiverton 6/8***	Thomas III
	St Erth Co 1,3/3	William	1792	**Talaton 3/6**	Thomas III
1784	Easton in Gordano So 1,6/6	William	1793	Kilmersdon So 6/6	T W & Jas
	N Molton Dn 1,2,3,5/6	Thomas III		Midsomer Norton So 11/12	T W & Jas
	N Molton Dn 6/6	*Thomas III*		Nailsea So 1,6/6	T W & Jas
1785	Othery So 5/5	William		Withypool So 4,6/6	Thomas III
	Pilton So 5/6	William		Bratton Wi 4/6	T W & Jas
	Wells St Cuth So 6/8	William		***Buckfastleigh 4-8/8***	Thomas III
	Musbury 1-5/5	Thomas III		***Coldridge 5/6***	Thomas III
1786	Farmborough So 2/6	William		**Whitestone 3/6**	Thomas III
	N. Perrott So 6/6	Thomas III		Buckland Newton Do 5/6	T W & Jas
	Atworth Wi 2/3	William	1794	*Chard So 5/8*	Thomas III
	Llangynwyd M Glam 1,2/6	William		*Sampford Arundel So 1/5*	Thomas III
1787	Wells St Cuth So 8/8	William		***Buckfastleigh 3/8***	Thomas III
	Colebrooke 6/6	Thomas III		***Exeter St Mary Major 1/1***	Thomas III
	Puddington 2/3	Thomas III		***Ilfracombe 7/8***	Thomas III
	Washfield 1-5/6	Thomas III		Gillingham Do 5/8	T W & Jas
	Washfield 2,3	Thomas III	1795	**W Down 2-6/6**	Thomas III

THE BELLFOUNDERS: AFTER THE REFORMATION

	Chideock Do 2/5	Thomas III		**Rackenford 1/6**	Thomas III
	Stalbridge Do 5/6	T W & Jas		*Rackenford 2,3,4,6/6*	Thomas III
1796	Compton Dundon So 5/5	T W & Jas		**Roseash 6/6**	Thomas III
	Dundry So 2/6	T W & Jas		Broadwindsor Do 1/6	Thomas III
	Weaverham Ches 1,6/6	T W & Jas	1807	**High Bray 6/6**	Thomas III
	Pucklechurch Av 3,4,5/6	T W & Jas		Golant Co 3,4,5/5	Thomas III
1797	**Ilsington 4,5,6/6**	Thomas III		*Golant Co 1,2/5*	Thomas III
	Ilsington 2,3/6	Thomas III	1808	**Coldridge 1,6/6**	Thomas III
1798	**Meshaw 3,4,5/6+2**	Thomas III		**Hockworthy 1-3/3**	Thomas III
	Meshaw 2/6	Thomas III		Maker Co 1-6/6	Thomas III
1799	**Ermington 4/6**	Thomas III		*Maker Co 6/6*	Thomas III
	Ipplepen 3-8/8	Thomas III		Dorchester St Pet Do 2/8	Thomas III
	Ipplepen 7/8	Thomas III	1809	Long Ashton 5/8	T W & Jas
	Lustleigh 2-5/6	Thomas III		*Yatton So 8/8*	James
1800	**Bampton 1-6/6**	Thomas III		**N Molton 4/6**	Thomas III
	Witheridge 7/8	Thomas III		Symondsbury Do 6/6	Thomas III
	Burton Bradstock Do 3/6	Thomas III	1810	Halse So 6/6	Thomas III
	Thorncombe Do 6/8	Thomas III		Langford Budville So 4/6	Thomas III
1801	Berrow So 5/6	T W & Jas		Runnington So 2/2	Thomas III
	Wedmore So 7/8	T W & Jas		**Clayhidon 2-6/6**	Thomas III
	Dalwood 2/6	Thomas III	1811	Chew Magna So ?date 3/8	T W & Jas
	Uffculme 3-8/8	Thomas III		Othery So 4/5	Thomas III
	Oldridge 1/1	Thomas III		**Hemyock 2/6**	Thomas III
1802	*Milverton So 8/8*	Thomas III	1813	*Hatherleigh 3-8/8*	Thomas III
	Bicton 1/1	Thomas III		**Ugborough 1,2/8**	Thomas III
	Hawkchurch 2-6/6	Thomas III	1814	**N Bovey 2,3,4,6/6**	John
1803	N Perrott So 2-5/6	Thomas III		*N Bovey 1,5/6*	John
	Staple Fitzpaine So 6/6	Thomas III	No	Nempnett Thrubwell So 3,5/6	?Thomas I
	Bishops Tawton 2,4/6	Thomas III	Date	Teffont Magna Wi 2/2	
	Sherborne Do 4/8	T W & Jas			
1804	E Harptree So 5/6	T W & Jas	**Bells by the Pannells of Cullompton and Exeter**		
	Hatch Beauchamp So 5/5	Thomas III	1820	*Uplowman 6/6*	William
	Minehead So 8/10	Thomas III	1821	*Axminster 6/6*	William
	Minehead So 10/10	Thomas III		**Hemyock 5/6**	William
	W Monkton So 5/6	Thomas III		**Stoke Gabriel** 6/6	William
	Wilton So 10/10	Thomas III		*Timberscombe So 8/8*	William
	Wilton So 8/10	Thomas III	1822	**Kentisbeare 6/6**	William
	Salcombe 2,3,4/6	Thomas III	1823	Porlock So 6/6	William
	Salcombe 5,6/6	Thomas III		Weston Zoyland So 6/6	William
	Ugborough 6/8	Thomas III	1824	**Brixham 9,10/10**	William
1805	Walcot St Swithun So 1/2	T W & Jas		**Hittisleigh 1/3**	William
	Drayton So 5/8 doc	T W & Jas		**Otterton 2/6**	William
	Cadbury 3,5/6	Thomas III		*Timberscombe So 4,6,7/8*	William
	Modbury 1-6/6	Thomas III	1826	**Bickleigh (E) 5/6**	William
	Paignton 4	Thomas III		**Dartmouth St Sav 1-3,5/8**	William
	Paignton 8/8	Thomas III		*Exford So 3,4,6/6*	William
	Uplyme 3,4,6/6	Thomas III		Huish Champflower So 3/6	William
	Uplyme 1,2,5/6	Thomas III		Loders Do /6	William

	Ugborough 7/8	William	1844	*Bickleigh [W] 3/6*	W P & Son
	Withiel Florey So 1/3	William		*Lamerton 1-6/6*	W P & Son
1827	St Ive Co 4/6	William		*Ashburton 7/8*	W P & Son
1828	**Cotleigh 5/6**	W & C	1845	**Killerton 1/1**	
	Ilsington 3/6	W & C		Landrake Co 1/1	T Pannell ?
1829	**Plymouth St Peter 1/1**	W & C		*Silverton 8/8*	W P & Son
	Wiveliscombe So 1,8/8	W & C	1846	**Denbury 1/5**	W P
1830	*Sampford Arundel So 3/6*	W & C		Loders Do 5/6	W P & Son
	Bishopsnympton 1,2/6	W & C	1847	**Littlehempston 1/5**	
1831	St Mellion Co 2,6/6	W & C		*Stoodleigh 2,3,4/6*	W P & Son
	South Hill Co 5/5	W & C	1848	Bolventor Co 1/1	T? P
1832	Bradford Abbas Do 1,4/6	W & C	1851	*Littleham [S] 5/8*	W P
	Pitminster So 7/8	W & C		**Newton Abbot Cemy 1/1**	W P
1833	*Ash Priors So 2,3,6/6*	W & C	1852	**Plymouth St George 1/1**	W & C P
	Plympton St Maurice 8/8	W & C	?	**Horrabridge 1/1**	W . . .
	Exeter St Edmund 5/8	W & C	1853	Churchstanton So 6/6	C P & Co
1835	**Cornwood 1/6**	W & C		*Culmstock 3/8*	C P & Co
1838	**Bickleigh W 1/6**	**W & C**		*Culmstock 4/8*	C P & Co
	Cofton 1/1	?		*Payhembury 6/6*	**C P & Co**
	Stanton St Gabriel Do 1/1			Pitminster So 8/8	C P & Co
1841	*Marshwood Do 1/1*	W & C	1854	**Colebrooke 3/6**	**C P & Co**
1842?	**Dunkeswell Abbey 1/1**		1855	**Arlington 1-6/6**	**C P & Co**
1842	Winsford So 2/6	W P & Son		**Torquay Upton 1-8/8**	C P & Co
1843	**Chevithorne 1/1**	W P & Son		Willand 1/3	C P & Co

Other Devon Founders of the 19th century

Samuel Kingdon of Exeter was a wealthy Unitarian ironmonger, whose formidable reputation gave him the nickname of "Iron Sam". He lived at Duryard Lodge – there is an unfounded tradition that his body was placed above the stone gateway at the entrance – and as a strong Conservative was elected to be the first mayor of the city under the Municipal Corporations Act of 1835, an office in which his "harsh voice and forthright manner were an asset on such occasions".[27] A small bell about 15" diameter was formerly in *Peamore House, Alphington*, bearing the inscription S. & W. KINGDON, EXETER and the date 1825: it was sold by auction in 1969 and its whereabouts are now not known.

John Abrahams of Tavistock left us two bells in churches, the 2nd at *South Zeal*, 1807, and the single bell at *Princetown*, 1821. We have seen two other bells by him, belonging to private houses, in an antique-dealers' in Tavistock, and there was another one at *Venn House, Lamerton*.

Jackson & Son of Tavistock may have succeeded John Abrahams. There is a bell bearing their name on the stable block at *Kelly House*.

Caleb Squire of Buckland Brewer probably learnt the trade from John Taylor (of whom more later): the name of a John Squire is recorded by HTE on a bell of 1825 at *Littleham* (N Devon), but could be the name of a churchwarden or donor. A certain C. Squire is on record as a clockmaker,[28] and Caleb (almost certainly the same

---

27. Robert Newton, *Victorian Exeter*, Leicester 1968.
28. Ponsford, *Devon Clocks & Clockmakers*, quoting *Devon Notes & Queries*, vol 8

man) is identified as a bellfounder from his name in full on the 5th at *Wear Gifford*, and from the signed receipt from 1843 in *Dolton's* accounts for recasting the 4th which bears his initials. The clock bell on the former Town Church of St John in *Hartland* also bears his initials, and all three bells carry a triangular mark. [See Pl 31d]

The Hamblings of Blackawton came from a family of blacksmiths, but James Hambling (1762-1837) expanded into the gunsmith's trade in the early 19th century. The history of the family's bellfounding activities is slightly confused inasmuch as the early bells bear only their surname; whether James was involved in bellfounding is not clear, as his son **William Bartlett Hambling** was already 34 when their earliest surviving bell was cast in 1821, and his eldest son (the eldest of twelve children, all of whom survived infancy) also had the initials W.B. However, Ellacombe writing in the next generation attributes the bellfounding to William.

The tenor at *South Pool*, dated 1821, seems to have been cast before William had acquired a means of inscribing his bells; instead there is a brass plate on the headstock bearing the names of the Vicar and Churchwardens with "Hamblings, Blackauton" and its weight. Two years later, he had equipped himself with a set of Roman capitals in two sizes, and decorations in the form of a small cross and a lozenge, which appear on *Halwell* 4/6. *Malborough* treble was also cast in 1823, but has since been recast. *Dartington's* treble and 2nd, cast in 1827 and also recast, had "Hamblings, Blackauton", as has *East Ogwell* tenor cast the following year, but in 1829 the tenor of the five at *Denbury* is inscribed "Hambling & Nott, Blackauton". We have the agreement for the recasting of *Stokenham* tenor in 1832 in App.II:19. The last recorded bell by the Blackawton founders was *Dodbrooke* tenor, cast in 1852. [See Pl 31f]

A trade card issued in about 1890 by Henry Hambling of Kingsbridge describes him as "Church & House Bell Founder"; he also seems to have kept an inn, probably the "King of Prussia" opposite his foundry in Duke Street. On the card, Henry, who was William Bartlett Hambling's fourth son, gives a list of "a few of the many Church Bells cast by my late Father and self", which is not entirely accurate. He also lists a new treble for *Dodbrooke*, 1876, a new ring of six at *Churchstow*, a new treble at *Bigbury* and a new bell at *Thurlestone*; these bells were all cast by Warner, and it would appear that Henry Hambling, like William Aggett, was a bell-hanger acting as agent for a founder and claiming the bells as his own. The bellframe at Churchstow is probably by him.[29]

Fig. 76. East Ogwell tenor, by William Hambling of Blackawton, 1823.

---

29. I am indebted to Dr Teresa Goatham of Gillingham, Dorset a descendant of the Hamblings, for valuable information about her family.

Bells by William Hambling of Blackawton
1821   *S Pool 6/6*
1823   **Halwell 4/6**
1823   *Malbrough 1/6*
1827   *Dartington 1,2/6*
1828   **E Ogwell 6/6**
1829   **Denbury 5/5**
1832   *St Martin by Looe Co 2/4*
1833   *Stokenham 6/6*
1836   ***Dean Prior 3/6***
1844   ***Buckfastleigh 6/8***
1844   ***Thurlestone 3/6***
1845   ***Stoke Gabriel 2/6***
1852   ***Dodbrooke 6/6***

James Moon is described in White's 1851 *Directory* as an ironmonger, and in the 1857 Billing's *Directory* as "ironmonger, tinman, brazier and agent to the Norwich Fire and Life Office", in High Street, Barnstaple. The only bell by him so far discovered is in the little mission church at *Burston Moor* near Welcombe, dated 1869.

Fig. 77. The bell of the chapel at Burston Moor, near Heartland, by James Moon, 1869.

Abbott & Co of Bideford were general founders who cast a few bells; only one is known to survive – the 2nd at *Weare Gifford*, 1878 – though others may be found in houses. Two trebles which they added to *Bideford* in 1876 have been recast. The Weare Gifford bell is inscribed in neat, small Roman capitals. [See Pl 31e]

Other Post-Reformation Bellfounders

As in the Middle Ages, the demands of the county for bells was never fully met by the local foundries, not only because of their capacity but also because the difficulties of transport often made it more economical to bring bells from outside the county, especially if this could be done by sea. In addition, the Devon founders inevitably had their high and low periods, and one can see how "foreign" founders of high repute and ability tended to be used when things in our own bellfoundries were not at their best. One of the earliest to appear is **Robert Wiseman** of Montacute in Somerset. He was in *Colyton* in 1611, casting the 5th of the present eight, and while there he cast a bell for *Honiton*. In 1622 he was in *Uffculme*, and cast a bell for *Halberton* there.

The Purdue Family

The Purdues were centred on the village of Closworth near Yeovil, but worked over most of the West Country. The earliest bells we have from them are by **George Purdue**, who cast bells for *Stockland* 1603, *Ashcombe* 1604, *Clayhanger*, *Dartington* (recast) and *Stockland* 1611, *Axmouth* 1612, *Plympton St Mary* 1614 and *Stoodleigh* (recast) 1615; of these the most notable is the fine tenor at Plympton St Mary which bears also the initials RP and may be the only known example of **George** and **Richard Purdue** working together. All are inscribed in broad, flat cut-out lettering. *Rockbeare* has a bell of 1613 by **William Purdue II**, and *Dalwood* 5/6 and *Axminster*'s "Brocas bell" are

Fig. 78. Farway 4th, by W & R Pudue, 1656.

Fig. 79. Exeter Cathedral 9th, "Cobthorne", one of the six bells cast by Thomas Purdue in 1676. It still hangs from four bolts, in spite of the Chapter's disapproval.

by **William Purdue III**, 1647. A bell of 1680 at *Kingswear*, recast in facsimile, is undoubtedly by a Purdue but remains something of a mystery as William III died in 1673. We also have another bell at *Farway* dated 1656 and carrying the initials WP and RP, the work of William III and Richard II.

In Devon by far the most important member of the family was **Thomas Purdue**, the greatest of the clan and among the greatest of all English bellfounders. His earliest bell in Devon was at *Cotleigh*, 1664 (now recast in facsimile); it was followed by the splendid tenor and 2nd of the six at *Awliscombe*, 1670, and then in 1676 by Purdue's masterwork at *Exeter Cathedral*. He set up his foundry in the garden of Canon Naylor's house in the Close – a departure for Thomas who did not often itinerate, but this was a huge operation. It consisted of one new bell, the present 6/12, and the recasting of the 9/12, 11/12 and 12/12 (the 5th, 7th and tenor of the eight as it was then), and the "Peter" bell, over 13 tons of metal in all: the 6th, which now bears Purdue's name, is undeniably a poor bell and "Grandison" the tenor has twice been recast since, but the 9th "Cobthorne", the 11th "Stafford" and "Peter" are all magnificent bells and play a major part in making Exeter Cathedral's one of the finest rings in the world. In the same year Purdue cast a bell for *Colebrooke*, and the following year he cast *Woodbury* 7/8 and *Kilmington* 4/6; the latter was cast at Closworth, but the Woodbury accounts contain no entry for transporting the bell, suggesting that it may have been cast on the Exeter site or even in the parish while Purdue was still in the area. Thomas Purdue came back to Exeter in 1693 to recast the 8/12, "Doom", assisted by **Thomas Knight** – Purdue was 73 by that time – and that was his last work in the county, but one of his successors, **Thomas Roskelly**, cast *Axmouth* 2/3 in 1755. Thomas Purdue died in 1711 aged 91, and his altar tomb can be seen in Closworth churchyard, with a large bell carved on the east end and on one side the verse:

Here lies the Bellfounder,
honest and true,
till the resurrection
named Purdue.

Fig. 80. Axmouth 2nd, a rare bell by Thomas Roskelly of Closworth, 1755.

On the other side is an inscription to Thomas Knight. A document in Exeter Cathedral Archives concerning the 9th bell, which was cast without cannons through shortage of metal, shows that Thomas could not write his name – he could manage only large, shaky initials – which makes his achievements the more remarkable.

The Closworth foundry poses a number of curious questions. Although before Thomas's day there are only sporadic records of the Purdue family in the parish itself – though Richard at one time lived nearby at Stoford in Barwick parish – there seems to have been a connection nevertheless from the time of William Purdue I in the late 16th century. After the death of **William Knight**, Thomas Knight's son, a number of people seem to have used the foundry and its plant, including **Thomas Roskelly**, **William Elery** (both of these with Cornish surnames, one notices: there are Roskelly tombstones at Stoke Climsland), **James Smith** and **Richard Rock**, each of whom cast a few bells in the period between 1749 and 1767 but not in succession, giving the impression that at any one time two or three founders had the use of the equipment, though none can have been full-time bellfounders.

The Purdue family and the other Closworth founders are very fully chronicled in Christopher Dalton's *Bells & Belfries of Dorset, p.880ff*. We will limit ourselves to listing only their bells in Devon.

William Purdue I

1610	*Exeter Heavitree 3/4*
1611	*Dartington 4/5*
1613	Rockbeare 6/6

George Purdue of Taunton

1603	Stockland 3/6
1607	Ashcombe 3/3
1611	Clayhanger 1/3
1611	Stockland 2/6
	Stockland 4/6
1612	?Axmouth 1/3
1614	Plympton St Mary 4/8 with Richard I
	Plympton St Mary 8/8
1615	*Stoodleigh 6/6*

Fig. 81. Thomas Purdue's tomb in Closworth churchyard. On the end is carved a bell.

William Purdue III of Salisbury, Bristol &c

1647	Axminster, Brocas bell
1647	Dalwood 5/6
1680	Kingswear 3/3

William III & Richard II

1656	Farway 1/3

Thomas

1664	*Cotleigh 4/6*
1670	Awliscombe 2,6/6
1676	Exeter Cathedral 6,9,11/12, Peter
	Exeter Cathedral 12/12
1676	*Colebrooke 2/6*
1677	*Kilmington 4/6*
1677	*Woodbury 7/8*
1681	Uplowman 5/6
1693	Exeter Cathedral 8/12

Among other Somerset founders, **Thomas Bickham** has no surviving bells in Devon, but the accounts of *Goodleigh* record his recasting a bell there in 1715. His only surviving bells are in Somerset and Dorset, and were cast in association with R. Apsey in the 1680s; they are inscribed R A T B.

The Wroths of Wellington

Thomas Wroth I of Wellington, probably the son of Sampson Wroth of West Buckland, yeoman, who died in 1656, seems to have begun as a clockmaker and general metalworker; his earliest record of work on bells is for recasting brasses, in 1679 at Nynehead and in 1680 at West Buckland (both in Somerset), and his earliest surviving bells are the 3rd and 4th at *Dunkeswell*, cast in 1684 and extremely poor-toned bells. He died in 1723, and was buried at West Buckland. **Thomas II** and Margaret Downing, both of Wellington, were married there in 1725. A "puff" in the *Sherborne Mercury* for 7 September 1742 – an advertisement for Thomas Wroth II printed under the guise of a news item – claims that the father learnt his trade from Hodson of Whitechapel:

> *Curry Rivel, In Somersetshire, Sept. 3. – Our peal of bells are compleated by Mr Thomas Wroth, bellfounder of Wellington, in such a curious & workmanlike manner that the performance will ever redound to his honour whilst the bells remain in the steeple. The art came to him originally from the most famous Mr Hodson, of Whitechapel, London, who did, in 1681, cast the Great Tom of Oxford, and from thence came to Wellington and erected a foundry for the late Mr Wroth, who, with the present Mr Wroth, in 1714, did new cast the first bell of St Andrew's in Wells, commonly called the Harebell (sic) bell, weighing 8,300 gross, which is the largest peal bell in England.*

It is hard to tell how much of this is true, though some of it certainly is not; Thomas Wroth cast two, at most, of the bells at Curry Rivel, three of the present ring being older than Wroth's, and the Harewell bell, Wells Cathedral Tenor, is now 56, not 74 cwt (it has been recast twice since Wroth's time, by John Rudhall and John Taylor), and has apparently never been as heavy as Exeter Cathedral's "Grandison". However, the connection with Hodson is quite likely. Thomas II probably took over the business 1721, when the initials "T W" with a bell outline between is replaced by "THOS WROTH" or "THOS WROTH FECIT".

Both father and son used fairly large Roman capital lettering, often with loops in the crossbars of "H" and "A", and knops in the uprights. The tenor at *Holcombe Rogus*, by Thomas I, 1691, has half-crowns as stops, but coin-impressions are not typical; the five at *Lympstone*, 1746, by Thomas II, are unusual in having a number of coin-impressions, some of them Portuguese. Thomas II introduced a 5-pointed star and an "eyebrow-and-dot" frieze which generally appears above the soundbow; he also used an arabesque ornament which appears in Devon first on a bell at *Southleigh*, cast, presumably by the father, in 1718. A number of Wroth bells also carry coats-of-arms of their donors, as at *Molland, Kentisbeare*, and *Sidbury*. [See Pl 27]

Fig. 82. Lympstone tenor, by Thomas Wroth II, 1746. The coin-impression are 400-reis pieces of John V of Portugal.

Most of the Wroths' bells are quite clean castings, but tonally they were extremely unreliable. *Holcombe Rogus* tenor is better than average for the period, but the five cast for *Feniton* are not at all good and reflect badly on the musical discrimination of the Churchwardens who paid Wroth a £1 bonus for *"his good work"*, and the two at *Dunkeswell* are among the worst in the county. *Uplowman* tenor is a fair bell, and the four remaining of the five at *Lympstone* are quite good, yet the 4th and 5th at *Cheriton Fitzpaine* are really quite bad; once again the parish can lay some blame on their Churchwardens, who had initially contracted to have them recast by William Evans and then for some reason gave the work to Wroth.

Both the Wroths seem to have been clockmakers, and the former clock of Wellington church, now in Taunton Museum, was made by Thomas I in 1706. It is a large, rather rangy-looking movement, and some of the details of the three-train clock at Bradford-on-Tone suggest that this was rebuilt by Wroth in a new frame, probably using some of the wheels of an earlier one. Bellchambers in *Somerset Clockmakers* gives the site of his workshop and foundry as being on the south side of the High Street (formerly East Street).

Unlike the Devon and Cornish founders and the Evanses, the Wroths seldom itinerated, and with the exception of the Harewell bell at Wells, which was cast in the Dean's coach-house, almost all the records which have so far been found refer to bells being taken to Wellington for casting; one exception is the former 4/6 at *Bickington* which ws taken to Kingsteignton in 1746 for recasting with the tenor there; another is the 6/8 at *Widecombe-in-the-Moor* which was cast on site in 1747 – no doubt the prospect of transporting it across the moor was not attractive; it was again recast by Bilbie 33 years later

We have already seen that Thomas Wroth II's public relations material was not by any means self-effacing, nor indeed very truthful. Another entry in the *Sherborne Mercury*, for 2nd March 1742, says: *Musberry, in Devon, Feb 27, 1742:*

Our old bells were sent on Saturday last to Mr Thomas Wroth, bell-founder, in Wellington, Somerset, to be cast & put in the same key with that most excellent, merry and harmonious peal he lately cast for St George's in the City of Oxford, which will ever redound to his honour so long as the bells remain in the steeple.

We have no way of knowing what his bells at Musbury were like as they were all recast by Bilbie only 43 years later, but we do know that there is not, nor has there ever been, a church of St George in Oxford, with or without a merry and harmonious peal of bells, nor are any bells by either of the Wroths known to have existed in Oxfordshire or Berkshire. In 1748 the same paper reported his work on the bells of his own parish:

Wellington, Somerset, Monday Nov 16th 1748. Our old heavy bells are, with an addition of metal, cast into a curious new peal of 8. Executed in every part of workmanship to the greatest perfection by Thomas Wroth bellfounder, of this place. They were opened this day by the gentleman ringers of Tiverton, who performed to admiration. They opened them again the morning following, and rung many curious peals, and went through with a variety of set changes to the truth of ringing, which gave inexpressible joy and satisfaction to all persons who had the pleasure to hear such beautiful music. The tone of every single bell perfectly good, their call to each other so exactly true to tone, that no peal of 8 in England (of their weight) is superior to them. They are without any fault, and will redound to the honour of Mr Wroth, whilst they remain in this lofty steeple, from whence their merry and harmonious tones will loudly and cheerfully sound forth his praise through the world, and happy they whom it may concern to employ so honourable, just and faithful a bellfounder.

It is not clear how many of the bells were recast at this time; the report implies that they all were, yet the 7th, by George Purdue 1609, was still in the ring until the 20th century. They have all been recast by Taylor so the only evidence for their tone (apart from the *Sherborne Mercury's*) was H.B. Walters's report that the 2nd was a very poor casting, heavily chipped around the rim, and the bells were difficult to ring, partly because the treble and 2nd sounded practically the same note.

The last Wroth bells which survive are at *Okehampton*, of 1750, two survivors of a ring of six. The line was not extinct with the death of Thomas II, because Elizabeth Wroth of Wellington, the daughter of Thomas Wroth, had been married to John Baily, tinman, of Taunton St Mary Magdalene, on 9 Dec 1710, and these were the parents of Thomas Bayley the first of the Bridgwater founders. In fact a vestry meeting in Bridgwater in 1752 discusses *employing Mr Bayly to put the Eight bells in Tune who has offer'd to do it (as it's supposed) for less than half its value on account his Unkle Wroths not doing it well.*

Bells by the Wroths of Wellington:

Thomas Wroth I

			Dartmouth St Clement 4/4
1684	**Dunkeswell 4,5/6**	1702	*Broadhembury 5/6*
1690	*Pitminster So 5/5*		*North Petherton So 4/5*
1691	**Holcombe Rogus 6/6**		Bicknoller So 2/5
1694	Buckland St Mary So 6/6	1704	*Chipstable So 4/4*
	West Buckland So 1/5		**Hemyock 5/6**
1695	Hillfarrance So 3/6	1706	**Cullompton doc**
1699	*Elworthy So 2/4*		*Uplowman 3/6*
1700	Badgworth So 1/5		*Uplowman 2/6*

	Yarcombe 3/6		*Cullompton 3 bells* doc
1707	*Cullompton 1 bell* doc		
	Bickleigh (E) 1/5		**Thomas Wroth II**
	Buckland St Mary So 5/6	1723	*Kilve So 1/3*
	Hillfarrance So 5/5		Weston Zoyland So 2/6
	Feniton 2-6/6	1724	*Combe St Nicholas So 3/6*
1708	**Sidmouth 6,9,10/10**		*Fitzhead So 5,6/6*
1709	**Offwell 3,6/6**		Taunton St James So 4/8
	Molland 5/6		*Thorne St Margaret So 1/3*
1710	Bagborough So 4/6	1725	Lyng So 4/6
	Combe Florey So 3/6		**Butterleigh 3/3**
	Combe Florey 6/6	1726	**Uplowman 6/6**
	Kentisbeare 2,5/6		**Stockland 5/6**
	Wembdon So 6/6	1727	**Cheriton Fitzpaine 4,5/6**
	Wootton Courtenay So 2,3/6		Rodhuish So 1/1
1711	**Yarcombe 4/6**	1729	Othery So 3/5
	Ashbrittle So 2,3/6		*Wiveliscombe So 1/5*
	Ashbrittle So 4/6	1730	*Ash Priors So 4/6*
	Ash Priors So 5/6		Bagborough So 1/6
	Wilton So ?/5 doc		Kingston So 1/6
	Trull So 3/6		*Monksilver So ?/4 doc*
1712	**Sidbury 7/8**	1732	**Dunkeswell 6/6**
	Crowcombe So 6/6		*Ide 4/4*
1713	Hillfarrance So 2,4/6		*Sutcombe 3/3*
	Stogursey So 4/6	1733	*Wiveliscombe So 1/5 (cf 1729)*
1714	**Broadhembury 4/6**	1734	**Cotleigh 6/6**
	Stoke St Gregory So 2/5		**Stoodleigh 4/5**
	Fitzhead So 2/5		Ashbrittle So 5,6/6
	Wells Cathedral So 6/6 doc		*Luccombe So 5/5*
1716	Broomfield So 5/6	1736	Dowlish Wake So 3/6
	Heathfield So 1/4		**Tedburn St Mary 4,5/6**
1717	Lydeard St Lawrence So 5/6		*Kingston So 2/6*
	Lydeard St Lawrence So 6/8		*Luccombe So 6/6*
1718	**Axminster 3/8**		**Woolfardisworthy E 1/3**
	Cullompton 1 bell doc	1737	**Cove (Salou, Spain) ex1/2**
	Southleigh 4/4		Milverton So 4,6/8
	Wellington So 4/6 doc		Otterhampton So 3/4
1719	*Dunster So 7/8*		**Twitchen 3/3**
	Honiton St Michael 3/6		Fiddington So 6/6
	Withycombe So 2/4	1738	Langford Budville So 2/6
1720	Winsham So 7/8		Ford Ho, Wiveliscombe 1/1
1721	Beer Crocombe So 4/4	1739	Durleigh So 4/6
	E Lyng So 5/6	1740	Ashbrittle 1/6
	Taunton St James So 4/8		*Exeter St John 2- 6/6*
1722	Old Cleeve So 3/3		**Woolfardisworthy E 2/3**

1741	*Halberton 4/?* doc		**Lympstone 2-6/6**
1742	*Combe Florey So 5/6*	1747	**Branscombe 5/6**
	Curry Rivel So 7/8		*Widecombe-I-t-Moor 4/6* doc
1742	Drayton So 4/8	1748	**Luppitt 6/8**
	Musbury ? bells advert		*Paignton 6/8*
1743	**Goodleigh 3,4/6**		*Wellington So 1,2,3,4,8/8*
	Goodleigh 2,6/6	1749	Bathealton So 1/4
	Luxborough So 3/5		**Yarcombe 2/6**
1745	Curry Mallet So 4/6	174?	**Farway 5/6**
	Stogumber So 5/6	1750	**Okehampton 5,6/8**
1746	***Bickington 4/6***		*Okehampton 3,4,7,8/8*
	Kingsteignton 8/8		

The Evans of Chepstow

It is noticeable that many of these founders were being employed by Devon parishes at the time of the Exeter foundry's downhill slide under Thomas Pennington III. Another business which profited from this was the Chepstow foundry in South Wales – at a time when the Bristol Channel was less a barrier than a highway for the transport of heavy freight, and the coal and metal ore trades were thriving. **Evan Evans I**, who probably learnt his trade with the Rudhalls of Gloucester, started on his own in Chepstow in 1686, and for the first 27 years his work was confined to South Wales, but in 1713 he came across the water to recast the bells of *Braunton*. The work was done on the spot, and the foundry site was kept in being; four years later the bells of *Ilfracombe* were being recast in Braunton, and although the accounts do not give the founder's name it must surely have been Evans, because the following year we have the first entry at Braunton of his paying rent for the Church House which still stands at the corner of the churchyard. In 1718 Evan was joined by his son **William Evans** in casting the very fine six (now the back six) at *Chulmleigh* – one of their most notable jobs in Devon – and a four at *East Buckland*. Work in Devon, especially in North Devon, increased from then on, with rings at *Chawleigh, Mariansleigh, Cruwys Morchard, Berrynarbor* and *Kentisbury*; in 1723 they worked their way further south to *Poltimore* and in 1724 they cast bells for *Morchard Bishop, Stoke Canon* and *Templeton* as well as an excellent ring for *Kingsnympton*: in that year Evan I died and William was joined by his brother **Evan Evans II**. In 1726 they were engaged to recast bells at *Cheriton Fitzpaine*, but as we have seen the parish for some reason changed its mind and gave the job to Thomas Wroth; in 1727 William and Evan II cast a ring for *Thelbridge*, but at *East Worlington* William's initials appear by

Fig. 83. Braunton Church House, rented as a foundry by the Evanses in the early 18th-century.

themselves, Evan II having quit the bellfounding trade to be a maltster; he died in 1730. In 1728 *Roseash* received a ring of four, and then in 1729 William took on what must have been the biggest commission of his life, at *Exeter Cathedral*.

Since Purdue's work in 1676 and the recasting of "Doom" in 1693, the Cathedral bells had suffered; "Grandison" the tenor was cracked, and so were the 33-cwt "Old Nine-o'Clock", and 15-cwt "Fox". In addition the Chapter wanted to have a diatonic ring of ten instead of a ring of eight in B flat and a six in E flat; there was at least one disused bell in the North tower. Evans's first specification was for *recasting ye 3 crack'd bells . . . viz. of ye 5th, 8th & Tenour, & likewise ye 3rd & 4th tho' sound. This being necessary to make a complete musical peal of Ten*. He proposed that *The Dean & Chapter to find ye Founder a proper Place for his Foundry, & to give him a Term of Three years in it: to be at ye Charge of covering, as Deals, Posts & Beams w^h may perhaps amount to £15 or 20^{ty} pds in Mr Lob's judgement*. **This usual**.

It was not usual enough, apparently, for the Chapter, and Evans put in another set of proposals, in a fascinating document, one which was clearly on the table at the Chapter meeting with emendations and additions written in the margins and between the lines as the meeting proceeded. This started with *To Recast the Three Cracked Bells*, but then added above the line *and the Little Nine o Clock Bell which is now in the One-Bell Tower*: this was to become the treble to make a ring of ten, now the 3rd of the twelve. The clause about providing a place for the foundry was crossed out, and instead the Chapter Clerk wrote in, . . . *and the Chapter shall give the Founder 25$^£$ to be paid in hand in full of all demands, Towards the Charge of his Foundery Mr Evans to find a Proper Place, pay the rent for etc*. The work was to be done before the 1st of January 1729; the fact that the bells are dated 1729 is explained by the fact that under the old calendar the year changed in April.

All did not go entirely according to plan. A letter in the Chapter archives, written in a very fair hand by William, tells of his problems:

> *I humbly present you with this, hoping you take it into consideration, the hard fortune I had in casting your Bells, especially the 9 o-clock Bell. I can't say but that you have paid me v. honourable according to my first a/c given in & to the extent of my agreement but however I was stinted to an impossibility as to weight, unless I had lessened them, which would have prejudiced them v. much & trusting to your Honours I ventured to keep them strong Bells notwithstanding I have over-runn'd my contract as to the addition of Mettal, yet there is not a pound too much in either of them, so I humbly submit myself to you, to do by me as you please, As to the additional Mettal of the Nine-a-Clock Bell I have left a note with Mr Webber of it, but as for ye waste mentioned int, I am very well satisfied to stand int, and as for the other if you please to consider me I shall be for ever obliged to you and always remain,*
>   *Rever'^{d} Sir your most obliged humble*
>   *Servt to comm'd*
>   *Wm Evans*

Nevertheless, the work was a triumph. We can only speculate about Evans's "Grandison", because it was recast in 1902, though some people at the time claimed that the recasting with half a ton of additional metal was unnecessary. Evans's "Old Nine-o'Clock", the 10th, still survives], and although the exceptional power of Purdue's "Stafford" gives that bell a special fame, one only has to hear the 10th rung singly to recognize her wonderful richness and smoothness of tone – what Devon country people call "plumm". Evans evidently kept his foundry in service for some years after 1729; the rings for *Exeter St Edmund* and *Newton St Cyres* were cast in Exeter in 1731 and 1733, and in 1736 the eight for *St Peter's Tiverton* were recast; the bill for carriage is not included in the account so they may have been cast in Tiverton, but when the 5th had to be recast again the following year there was an

Fig. 84. Exeter Cathedral 10th, "The Old Nine-o'-Clock", cast (not without some problems) by William Evans in 1729.

entry for "carriage journey". Like "Grandison", these bells have been recast, though a touring band of College Youths in 1869 had described the old bells as "fine".

William Evans gave us other good rings of six for *Shirwell, Chittlehampton, Tawstock, High Bickington* and *Silverton*, and a fine heavy one at *Witheridge*, and fives for *Charles, Morebath, Sandford, Swimbridge* and *West Buckland*, as well as a number of individual recastings; his bells are almost invariably good tonally, with a very solid strike-note: the castings are clean, with neat cannons and good lettering; inscriptions are sometimes in Latin, and almost always well spelt and literate. Some of his mottoes were reminiscent of the Rudhalls; "Peace and Good Neighbourhood", "Come let us ring for Church and King", "Prosperity to those who love good bells", "Prosperity to this Town and Parish". His most common decoration is a strip of arabesque ornament; he used the same bell mark between his initials as his father had done. [See Pl 28]

William Evans died in 1770 at the age of 80; his last bell was cast in 1767, so he had a remarkably long working life, but after the casting of the bells for West Buckland in 1756 he did no more work in Devon.

Bells in Devon by Evan Evans I & II and William Evans

Evan Evans I & William Evans

1713	Braunton 5,8/8	1723	Poltimore 1-6/6
	Braunton 3,4,6,7	1724	Kingsnympton 2-6/6
1716	*Ilfracombe doc*		
1718	Chulmleigh 3-8/8		
1718	E Buckland 3-6/6		
1720	Beaford 4/6		
	Cheldon 4/4		
	Chawleigh 2-6/6		
	Mariansleigh 3-6/6		
1721	Cruwys Morchard 2-6/6		
1722	Berrynarbor 1,2,4,5,6/6		
	Berrynarbor 3/6		
1723	Kentisbury 3-6/6		

William Evans & Evan Evans II

1724	Morchard Bishop 6/6
	Stoke Canon 6/6
	Templeton 2/3.
1727	Thelbridge 3-6/6
	E Worlington 4,5,6/6
	E Worlington 3/6

William Evans

1728	Roseash 2-5/6
	S Molton, Honiton Barton 1,2/2

1729	Exeter Cathedral 10/12	1742	Morchard Bishop 3,6/6
	Exeter Cathedral 2,7,12/12		Morebath 2-6/6
1731	Littleham S 6/8	1743	Morchard Bishop 5/6
	Washford Pyne 6/6		*Silverton 3-8/8*
	Exeter St Edmund 2-7/8	1748	Sandford 2-6/6
1733	Charles 1-5/6	1749	Clayhanger 3/3
	Countisbury 1/1	1753	High Bickington 3,4,6,7/8
	Newton St Cyres 3-6/8		*High Bickington 5/8*
	Shirwell 1-6/6	1753	Swimbridge 2-6/6
1736	*Tiverton St Peter 8/8*		Tawstock 3,5,7,8/8
1737	Tiverton St Peter 1-7/8	1754	*Chawleigh 1/6*
1737	Woodbury 3/8		Thelbridge 2/6
1739	Chittlehampton 3,4,5,7,8/8		R Butler (S Molton) 1/1
	Chittlehampton 6/8	1754	Witheridge 3,4,5,6,8/8
1739	Galmpton (Churston Ferrers)1/1		*Witheridge 7/8*
1739	*Morchard Bishop 4/6*	1755	Cruwys Morchard 1/6
1740	*Westleigh 2/6*	1756	W Buckland 2-6/6

THE BRIDGWATER FOUNDRY may have been making domestic castings some time before 1743 when its first surviving bell was cast for Charlynch in Somerset by **Thomas Bayley,** whose father, described as "Thomas Baily, tinman", had married Elizabeth Wroth at St Mary Magdalene, Taunton in 1710; at the time both were living in Bridgwater. He was admitted a Freeman of Bridgwater in 1738, and in 1742 was married at Wembdon to Betty Musgrove. In 1749 Bayley went into partnership with **Robert Street**, and the following year they cast four bells for Devon churches – *Sidbury* 6/8, *Topsham* 5/6 and 6/6, and a bell for *Sowton* which is now in *Holy Trinity Barnstaple*; later came bells for *Honiton St Michael, Honiton St Paul, Axminster, Torre* (these two now recast), *Widworthy* and *Challacombe*: after 1756 Thomas Bayley was working alone on bells until his death in 1774–5, though Robert Street was still making other castings including chandeliers until 1775. All these display the beautiful finish which is characteristic of Bridgwater bells, and the decoration which the foundry customarily used; often, as at Sidbury and Honiton St Paul, the founders' names appear in an elegant cartouche, and the inscription-bands are decorated with mask-&-foliage ornaments or swags. These ornaments on close examination reveal themselves to have been moulded from the patterns for domestic brass items; the mask-&-foliage is a cut-down version of a very popular spandrel-mount used on many long-case clocks, and the swag is probably from a drop-handle for a drawer. This liking for ornamentation was not confined to bells; some Bridgwater turret-clocks have highly ornamental frames as at the *Bluecoat School, Barnstaple*, and their brass wheels are often cast with ornamented crossings: these wheels may have been sold as blanks to other clockmakers, as they can be seen on a clock by Francis Pyle of Honiton and elsewhere.

As well as bells and clocks, the firm made a wide range of brassware, and bellmetal skillets bearing the names of Bridgwater founders can be found all over the country, while a number of churches retain splendid chandeliers from the foundry. **Thomas Pyke**, who succeeded Bayley and Street from 1775, advertised a very wide range of goods including Spinning Jennies and cooking stoves; he was mayor of Bridgwater in 1792 and again in 1810-11. He was still living in 1830, but seems not to have cast any bells after 1792. The back five bells at Bishops Lydeard in Somerset are good example of his richly-decorated bells. In Devon he cast another of the *Sowton* bells now in Barnstaple, one for *Dalwood* and two for *Stockland*, and also the 5/6, now recast, for *Membury* – there is an

Fig. 85. Beautiful decoration by Thomas Bayley on Honiton St Paul tenor, 1769.

interesting pocket of Bridgwater bells in the area south and east of Honiton. **George Davis** worked at Bridgwater from 1782 onwards, overlapping Pyke by some ten years; his only complete ring is the five at *Stoke Rivers*, and he also cast *Rockbeare* 2/5 – still showing the remarkably fine finish typical of his predecessors. His last surviving bell was cast in 1799; the year before this **John Kingston** has cast his first bell for the foundry. John and Isaac Kingston, and possibly other members of the family, kept the bellfounding side of the business going until 1832; their only surviving bell in Devon is *Holcombe Rogus* 3/6, for which in 1825 the parish paid a Mr Savery of Taunton, who must have been acting as middleman; a Richard Savery of Taunton cast three bells for Somerset churches in the next decade. Although visually the Bridgwater bells are among the most beautiful castings one can find anywhere in Britain – on one bell one can still read the date on the impression of a sixpenny piece – they are not outstanding tonally, and some, e.g. two of the five at *Widworthy*, are very poor. [See 29]

A complete list of the Bridgwater Foundry's bells can be found in *The Bells & Belfries of Dorset, p.930ff*. Here are the Devon bells from the Bridgwater founders:

Bells in Devon by the Bridgwater Foundry

Thomas Bayley & Robert Street
1742	*Dawlish 3/5 doc*
1750	Topsham 5,6/6
	Barnstaple Holy Trinity 2/2
	Sidbury 6/8
	Sidbury 3/8
1753	Honiton St Michael 4/6
1754	*Torquay Torre 5/6*
1755	Challacombe 1/4
1756	Widworthy 3,4/5
	Widworthy 1,2,5/5
1758	*Exeter S Kerrian 1/1*

Thomas Bayley
1759	Kilmington 2,3/6
1760	*Axminster 7/10*
1761	Honiton St Michael 5/6
1762	*Axminster 8/10*
1764	Barnstaple Bluecoat School 1/1
1765	*Axminster 5/10*
1769	Honiton St Paul 8/8

Thomas Pyke
1776	Barnstaple Holy Trinity 1/2
1780	Dalwood 3/6
	Stockland 1,6/6
1781	*Membury 5/6*

George Davis
1784	Stoke Rivers 1-5/5
1787	Rockbeare 1/5

John Kingston &c
1815	*Newton Poppleford 1/1*
1825	Holcombe Rogus 3/6
1826	*Countisbury 1,2/3*

THE TAYLOR FOUNDRY: Trevor Jennings in *Master of my Art,* tells the story of the Taylor foundry, which by virtue of a sojourn of eleven years in North Devon by one of the family must qualify to be at least half-way between the Devon founders and those from outside the county. The Taylor bellfounding business began in St Neots in the 18th century, but first figures in Devon in the early 19th, by which time **William** and **John Taylor** had moved their operations of casting bells and making clocks to Oxford. Their coming into Devon was the result of a personal contact; Robert Chichester of Hall, Bishops Tawton, a son of one of the leading landed families in North Devon, had been fascinated as an undergraduate at Oxford by visiting the Taylor foundry in St Ebbe's. As a result, while still an undergraduate, he commissioned William and John Taylor to recast the bells of his home parish church in 1823. In fact the *Bishops Tawton* bells were apparently cast in that parish, as the bells at Brill in Buckinghamshire are inscribed "W & J Taylor Founders Oxford and Bishops Tawton Devonshire". There can be no doubt that Chichester strongly influenced John Taylor's decision in 1825 to move to *Buckland Brewer* where he had been commissioned to recast a ring of six, and set up a permanent foundry there. The moment was opportune: John Pennington IV had died at Stoke Climsland two years earlier, and since Thomas Bilbie III's death the Cullompton foundry under William Pannell was not doing well: North Devon was an almost open market for an enterprising bellfounder. After Bishops Tawton the Taylors had already cast sixes at Oxford for *Roborough* and *St Giles-in-the-Wood*, and the Buckland Brewer foundry was soon busy enough with bells for Devon and East Cornwall. *Ashreigny*, 6, *Dowland*, 5, *Hartland,* 6 and *Woolfardisworthy*, 6 followed in 1826; *Bradstone,* 5, *Combe Martin,* 6 and *Lifton,* 8 in 1827. During his 11-year stay in Buckland Brewer from 1823 to 1833, John Taylor dominated the Westcountry bellfounding scene, with well over 100 bells cast for Devon and Cornish towers. It has to be admitted, though, that the musical quality was generally very poor: even the six which he cast for his own tower at *Buckland Brewer* were recast by his successors, as were *Hartland's*: Combe Martin and *Woolfardisworthy West* have also been recast, the last-named having been a quite unusually nasty-sounding ring. Of those which remain, *Dowland* and *Bradstone* are pleasant-sounding enough and in their original state; *Lifton* and *Bridestowe* have been tuned; *Halwill* and North Tamerton (Cornwall) are poor examples. The North Tamerton six has a curious history: the local tradition is that their treble came from *Tetcott* on the other side of the Tamar valley, yet Tetcott until 1966 possessed only a single cracked bell by Ambrose Gooding which was evidently second-hand. But the Tetcott church accounts show that Taylor did supply a new bell for Tetcott, in 1829, and the North Tamerton bells were a five dated 1830. Jennings says that "much extra time-consuming labour was essential on Tamerton's six bells and the single bells for Tetcott and *East Down* before they were considered fit for hanging", and the North Tamerton people were dilatory in paying for their hanging; it seems that Taylor failed to persuade the North Tamerton people to invest in a ring of six but cast a six and sold the treble to Tetcott; on hearing it across the valley the North Tamerton people changed their minds, so Taylor installed it in North Tamerton and provided Tetcott with a bigger, second-hand, bell in lieu.

Bells probably cast at Buckland Brewer by John Taylor I
1825   *Buckland Brewer 1-6/6*
1826   **Ashreigny 1,2,3,4,6/6**
          Ashreigny 5/6
          Dowland 1-5/5
          Hartland 1-6/6
          Winkleigh 6,8/8
          Woolfardisworthy W 1-6/6
1827   **Bradstone 2-6/6**
          Combe Martin 1-6/6
          Lifton 1-8/8

1828	**Beaworthy 1-3/3**
	Bridestowe 1-6/6
	Bridestowe 3/6
	Dolton 5/6
	Dolton 2,3,4/6
	Woodbury Salterton 1/1 (? from elsewhere)
1829	**Halwill 2-6/6**
	Heanton Punchardon 2-6/6
	Marystow 1,2,4,6/6
	Marystow 3,5/6
	Braunton 4/8
	Tetcott 1/1 doc
1830	**Braunton 6,7/8**
	E Down 3/4
	N Tamerton Co 2-6/6
1831	N Tamerton Co 1/6
1831	*Bradford 4/6*
1831	Advent Co 4,5/5
1833	**Monkleigh 5/6**
1833	Wendron Co 5,6/6

Bells for Boyton (Cornwall), *Bradworthy* and *Langtree* were cast in the two years following John's return to Oxford, and in all probability the foundry at Buckland Brewer continued to be used sporadically, either by Taylor or by Caleb Squire, until the 1850s, but after 1835 the Taylors' business in Devon fell very rapidly; there is only one surviving bell by them from the 1840s, and that (at *Paignton, St George's, Goodrington*) came from elsewhere as the church is a modern one. For some reason, John Taylor almost invariably put "Oxford" rather than "Buckland Brewer" on his bells, the only exception being *Braunton* 6/8 which was inscribed "Recast at the sole expence of Robt Chichester Esq and the Revd I W Landon Vicar by John Taylor at Buckland Brewer in the year of our salvation 1830". However, when he recast some of the *Pilton* bells in 1853 he inscribed the 6th "... John Taylor and Son late of Buckland Brewer". It is probably significant that both at Braunton and at Pilton Robert Chichester was a major benefactor. The Chichester papers include a number of letters from Taylor in Oxford begging for help, and it is recorded that Chichester several times kept Taylor afloat, and recommended him to possible customers, including Arlington in 1854 – unsuccessfully in that case as Pannell got the job. Taylor at this time used a neat but unremarkable Roman lettering on his bells, with "OXFORD" usually in large Italic capitals. His ornaments were usually a Star of David and a triangle, but at *Langtree* he used a handsome oak-leaf decoration on the waist. His inscriptions are normally laconic, seldom more than the names of the wardens and incumbent, but at *Pilton, Bradstone* and *Halwill* as we have seen he used doggerel verses and *Lifton* has more elaborate inscriptions than usual.

Taylor's work in Devon began to pick up again after 1851, when he recast one of the *Bishops Tawton* bells and added a treble for Robert Chichester, here again identifying himself as "late of Buckland Brewer". In the following year he recast the 4th and 6th at *Pilton* and added two trebles, decorating the new bells with some beautiful friezes and splendidly-moulded cannons bearing human and lion faces and inscribing the 4th with probably the worst doggerel of any bell in the county.

John William Taylor I had been born at Buckland Brewer in 1827, and took over the business in 1856, by which time the Loughborough foundry had been established and the Oxford site closed down. Under him the firm's fortunes in Devon began to revive, and once again a member of the landed gentry played a leading role. John, the brother of Charles Troyte of Huntsham Court, had learnt to ring at Oxford and Charles had caught his enthusiasm. In 1866, soon after he came of age, Charles had the *Huntsham* bells augmented and rehung, and the new bells were cast by Taylor, whose only recent work in Devon had been five clock bells for *St Paul's, Tiverton*. During the '70s more augmentations followed including one to eight at Huntsham, where the first peal was rung for the Guild: 14 bells came in the '70s and 32 in the '80s with complete sixes at *Egg Buckland* and *Westleigh*: in 1889 they installed Devon's first metal frame at *Stokenham*. The smaller Taylor bells of this period often have almost hemispherical heads with cannons curving sharply out to a point. Some of their bells cast at this time had radial cannons, e.g. the former hour bell at *St Paul's Tiverton*.

It was in the 1890s that the Taylor foundry made an immortal name in Devon, largely through its adoption of the new tuning methods advocated by Canon Simpson; one of their earliest efforts in "Simpson" tuning was at Werrington, then in the county of Devon, where a letter from Simpson is preserved in

Fig. 86. John Taylor's treble for Pilton, 1852.

the tower, describing the tone of the bells as "perfect". In 1892 and 1894 they recast and augmented the bells at *Clyst Honiton*, first to a six and then to an eight, but in 1897 they installed in the newly-rebuilt tower of *St Michael's, Heavitree* a 25-cwt eight which is still regarded as one of the finest in the kingdom. This was not only a triumph in itself but almost certainly led to Taylors' being given the contract for restoring and rehanging the ring of bells with the world's heaviest tenor (at that time) at *Exeter Cathedral*. Until this time the Cathedral bells, a ring of ten with Evans's tenor of 62 cwt., had been hung in a very high oak frame, the eleven bells all swinging the same way and requiring at least 14 men to ring the ten. In 1902 the tenor and 5th of the ten were recast, the other bells tuned, and all were hung in a massive cast-iron "H" frame for twelve; the tenor was given an additional half-ton of metal, and the outcome was one of the great rings of bells in the world, and a remarkable feat of bellhanging; even before it was hung in ball-bearings the tenor "Grandison" could be rung by

Fig. 87. "Grandison", Exeter Cathedral's tenor, recast by Taylor's in 1902.

one man although it is normally handled by two. A recast and augmented ring of eight at *Bovey Tracey* was cast in the same year.

Between 1902 and the First World War the Loughborough foundry, in addition to a number of augmentations, cast an excellent light six for Bradford, 1912, a front five for a six at *East Portlemouth*, a six at *Sherford* and a good eight at *Chagford*. After the war the business, now under **John William Taylor II,** really took off in Devon; the 1920s saw 82 bells cast for the county, as well as a great number of augmentations and rehangings such as those at *Cullompton, Sidbury, Northlew, Georgeham, Churston Ferrers, Luppitt, Braunton* and *Whimple*; complete rings of eight were cast or recast for *Northam, Tiverton St Peter, Tavistock, Wolborough, Uffculme* and *Bideford*, and a six at *Mortehoe*. In 1923 two new Taylor bells augmented *Exeter Cathedral* to a twelve.

Taylors' Devon total in the '20s was exceeded by Gillett & Johnston's, but in the '30s the Loughborough foundry took the lead with no fewer than 94 bells. Augmentations in this decade included *Buckland-in-the-Moor, Exbourne, St Budeaux, Dean Prior, Torrington, Welcombe, Down St Mary, South Molton, Ashburton, Silverton* and *Tawstock*: pride of place in the complete rings went to *Buckfast Abbey* with 14 ringing bells and Devon's biggest bell of all, "Hosanna"; there were also eights at *Ilfracombe Holy Trinity, Buckfastleigh, Plympton St Maurice* and *Broadclyst*, and sixes at *Sutcombe* and *Mariansleigh*. During this period Taylors' became firm favourites with most Devon ringers, many of whom would hear of nobody else, delighted by the splendid tone of such rings as *Tavistock, Broadclyst, Tiverton* and *Wolborough* and also by the beautifully silky "go" which Taylors' achieved through good engineering and the use of ball-races for main bearings and pulleys.

After the Second World War Taylors' hegemony continued: the eights at *Ottery St Mary, St Mark's, Exeter* and *Sidmouth* (later made a ten) and the fine six at *Hartland* are theirs, followed by a recast eight at *Appledore*, a pleasant six to replace the horrible Buckland Brewer-cast ring at *Woolfardisworthy West*, another six at *Kentisbeare* and a new ring of six at *St Paul's, Tiverton*, cast from five clock bells. In 1979 they added to their work in *Exeter Cathedral* with a new extra treble.

One particularly interesting bell from the Taylor foundry is the single bell at *St Helen's, Bucks Mills*, with inscription and decoration cast by the *cire perdu* method, and described in Chapter 3. Taylors' cast a few more bells using the *cire perdu* method, but soon returned to using bell-cases with stamped lettering. After World War II their bells bear foundry numbers, usually two 3-figure numbers stamped on the head. The foundry is still flourishing, under the name of Taylors Eayre & Smith Ltd.

THE LONDON FOUNDERS: Lawrence Wright of London was brought to Plymouth in 1594 to recast the bells of St Andrew's; the operation can be followed in great detail in the "Widey Court Book" [App.II:5]. Not much is known of Wright, and very few of his bells survive; according to Stahlschmidt his "work was evidently cheap and nasty"; Lawrence's bells for Plymouth were recast again in 1708. London bellfounders do not seem to have been employed again by Devon parishes until 1740, when **The Whitechapel Foundry** was responsible for the six at *Ashburton*; they were commissioned from **Thomas**

Fig. 88. An experimental bell by Taylors', 1899, with lost-wax decoration and lettering.

Lester of Whitechapel by the town's two M.Ps, after (according to a local tradition) the earlier bells had been captured by a French privateer. The two donors had their coats-of-arms very splendidly cast on the waists of the bells, and it may be that they selected a metropolitan founder for the work because of their London connections. There followed three rings by **Lester & Pack**, all in the South Hams at *Dartmouth St Petrox* [5, 1754], *Kingsbridge* [5, 1761] and *Malborough* [4, 1753-4, augmented to 5 1765]. **Pack & Chapman** supplied a six for *Newton Abbot* in 1772 and eight for *St Sidwell's, Exeter* in 1773, but failed to get the recasting of the eight at *Crediton* the following year. In 1782 **Chapman & Mears** cast an eight for *Charles, Plymouth*, and in 1790 **Thomas Mears** cast the five for *Ashprington*, styling himself "Thomas Mears, late Lester, Pack & Chapman" as if he was not yet confident of his own reputation; through all this period the distribution of London bells is very close to that before the Reformation – never far from the Channel coast. Once the 19th century began, the Whitechapel Foundry steadily increased its business in Devon; for a short period the Taylor foundry at Buckland Brewer checked its business, and for some time in the later 19th century it had a strong competitor in Warners', but at the end of the century it far outpaced its rivals. It popularity declined sharply during the 20th century, however, and it was only in the period after World War II that it began to recover.

Devon apparently possesses one unique bell from the Whitechapel Foundry's work in the 2nd of the three at *Ringmore*. It bears the only known example of the very handsome stamp of **Robert Stainbank**, a timber merchant who owned the foundry between 1865 and 1883 but usually used the title "Mears & Stainbank" on his bells [Pl 33b]. The designer of this mark was almost certainly William Kimber, a man with a fine artistic talent who for many years was chief moulder at the foundry; another version of it exists with blank spaces instead of the initials "R S", and was used for medallions to commemorate the first peals on new rings from the foundry, with the names of the ringers engraved in the blank spaces; its use has been revived lately, and medallions were cast from it to celebrate the Crediton project. Another remarkable Whitechapel bell hangs on the gallery of the Breakwater Lighthouse at Plymouth. It was apparently cast for the ring of ten at the parish church in Montreal – now presumably the Roman Catholic Cathedral – to replace the 9th which had been sent back for recasting in 1861, and having proved to be too flat to tune safely was sold off to Trinity House. It weighs about 33 cwt. In the 20th century the Whitechapel Foundry was eclipsed by Loughborough until after the Second World War, but since then, under Albert H. Hughes, William and Douglas Hughes and in the present generation Alan Hughes, has done some fine work including the recasting of the war-damaged six at *Clyst St George*, the light eight recast from a Bilbie six at *Stoke Damarel, Plymouth*, and most recently a new ring of eight at *Plymouth, St Mary's, Laira* and the magnificent ring of ten at *Crediton*.

A very rare survival is the bell in the former *Royal Naval Hospital, Plymouth*, which is now hung in an iron frame in the central courtyard. It was cast by **Weare & Savill** in 1776 for the cupola above the clock in the central block of the Hospital, and is 33" diameter. As far as we can discover, there are only three bells recorded by William Savill, and this may be the only one to bear his name with that of William Weare, with whom he served his apprenticeship. [See 32a]

Fig. 89. The bell of the Royal Navy Hospital, Stonehouse, Plymouth, by Weare & Savill of London, 1776.

Fig. 90. Warners' lombardic lettering (and "lombardic" arabic numerals) at Revelstoke, 1889.

The Cripplegate Foundry of the **Warner** family first started casting church bells in about the late 18th century, and the earliest castings by the Warners are brass measures which can be found in several Devon museums. The church bell business began in earnest in 1850, and the first bell cast by them for Devon was probably the former tenor at *St Saviour's, Dartmouth*, 1854. Until 1867 the only work they secured was in single bells (a large proportion of the single bells in our Victorian churches were cast by Warners'), recastings or augmentations, but in 1867 they cast the six for *Stoodleigh*, with a six for *Monkton* the following year. They seem to have established something of a bridgehead in the rapidly-growing resort of Torquay; in 1874 they cast a ring of eight for *All Saints', Babbacombe* – the elaborate and idiosyncratic lettering suggests that the architect William Butterfield may have had a good deal to do with this ring – and three years later they cast a ring of eight for *St Marychurch*: in the same year the six at *Churchstow* were cast – Henry Hambling being the hanger and apparently the middleman. Other rings by them include the six at *Dartington* 1879, eight at *Revelstoke*, 1881–2 where they used a set of very fine Lombardic lettering which includes Arabic numerals, and *Withycombe* Raleigh 1889. They also recast the 5th and tenor of the Rudhall eight at *Totnes* 1863, and in 1897 recast the 4th and rehung the eight in an iron frame. Their bells are not to everyone's taste, tending to have a rather hard timbre, but often respond very well to modern tuning – *Withycombe Raleigh* and *St Marychurch* are excellent examples. Their last ring in Devon was the little six at *Meshaw* 1914, which was hung in one of their riveted steel "cantilever" frames with self-aligning plain bearings.

Warners' made two important contributions to bellfounding technology in the 1850s; one was the introduction of the cast-iron cope case which obviated the use of a clay model. After Charles Borham Warner had patented this in 1853, and the firm had been appointed bellfounders to Queen Victoria, Warners' usually placed the Royal arms on the waists of their bells, with "PATENT" beneath them. The other British bell-founders followed Warners' lead in the use of iron bell-cases, but it seems to have remained a uniquely British practice. The other Warner innovation was the "Doncaster" pattern for cannons, which had been designed by Edmund Beckett Denison[30] for a ring of bells at Doncaster with the idea that a bell could be quarter-turned without the need to alter the headstock or ironwork, especially if an independent crown-staple were used. This design was used by the Whitechapel foundry, but never adopted by Taylors'

THE CROYDON FOUNDRY: The Croydon Foundry grew out of the clockmaking firm of **Gillett & Bland**, which began work in Croydon in the middle of the 19th century, making excellent flat-bed turret clocks, often with

---

30. Edmund Beckett Denison, later Lord Grimthorpe, was endowed with wealth, inventiveness and ingenuity, opinionatedness and irascibility in more or less equal measures. For a time Warners' were his favourite bellfounders and were much influenced by his theories, but after the failure of the first "Big Ben" which they cast to his design, he fell out with them and gave the recasting of the bell to George Mears – with whom he fell out in turn.

the new double three-legged gravity escapements invented by Lord Grimthorpe. Their earliest example found in Devon is at *Collaton St Mary*, which is a little unusual for a Gillett clock in having a Graham escapement and rack striking; Gillett & Bland clocks at *Ottery St Mary* 1874 and *Ashwater* have the more uncommon 15-legged gravity escapements. From 1883 the firm called itself Gillett & Co., but in 1877 Arthur Johnston became a partner and the firm expanded into bellfounding. We have no bells in Devon bearing the name of Gillett & Bland, the earliest in the county from the Croydon foundry being three at *Cotleigh*, dated 1886 and signed Gillett & Co., followed by bells for *Stokeinteignhead* and (now vanished) *St Edmund's, Exeter*. In 1889 the firm became Gillett & Johnston, under which name it has traded ever since.[31]

The firm's first ring of bells for Devon was the six at *Littleham* near Bideford, 1913, and this was their only ring in the county before World War I, but soon after the end of the war their popularity in Devon grew rapidly and deservedly. The first major post-war casting was the little 8-bell chime for *Kennerleigh* in 1920, followed by the good eight at *Moretonhampstead* 1922, the front five at *Chudleigh* in a new fabricated steel frame, eight for *Exeter, St Thomas* and six for *Lustleigh* in 1923, both in new frames. The '20s and '30s were very productive for them – we have 96 Croydon bells cast in the decade 1920–29 – with *Bridgerule*, 8, 1926-8, chimes at *Clannaborough* and *Brixham All Saints*, 1928-9, and probably their finest work in Devon, the noble eight at *Kingsteignton*, 1929, with good sixes at *Broadwoodkelly*, 1931 and *Clovelly*, 1933. In the same period they augmented and restored rings at *Littleham* near Exmouth, *Ilsington*, *Highweek* and *Okehampton* among other work. After World War II they recast the tenor and augmented *Buckland Monachorum* and recast *Holsworthy*, 8, and *Bishopsnympton*, 6; the last is a very fine ring of six but the splice at Buckland Monachorum was less successful. After the death of Cyril Johnston the business declined rapidly, and by 1957 it was in receivership. The clockmaking side of the work is still in business, and although Gillett & Johnston still supply bells they no longer cast them but their influence is still with us: the magnificent ring of ten at Crediton was cast by the Whitechapel Foundry to Gillett & Johnston profiles.

Fig. 91. Two of the chime by Gillet & Johnston (1920) at Kennerleigh.

Bells from the Croydon foundry were cast to very high standards, and the quality of casting, and design of lettering and decoration are consistently excellent. Cyril Johnston took a great interest in carillon bells – the chimes at *Kennerleigh, Clannaborough* and *Brixham All Saints* are cast to carillon dimensions – and some of his ringing bells sound almost like carillon bells, but the best are as good as any; there can be very few 15-cwt rings of eight anywhere to match Kingsteignton. Gillett & Johnston bellhanging was also consistently good with well-designed cast-iron frames of low-side or "H" pattern, usually in cast-iron but occasionally in steel.

THE GLOUCESTER FOUNDRY of the **Rudhall** family dominated the northern half of the county during the 18th century as the Bristol foundry had done before the Reformation; they have only a few bells in the south, all of

---

31. The clock in the clock tower in Newton Abbott, dated 1887, bears the name of Gillett & Bland; possibly the frame casting was a pre-1883 one taken from stock.

Fig. 92. Brixton 4th, by Abel Rudhall of Gloucester, 1737.

them close to the coast. **Abraham I** (fl 1684–1718) gave us four at *Filleigh*, 1703, five at *Broadwoodkelly* 1705 (recast), the heavy back six at *Pilton* 1712 (2 recast) and a fine six at *Great Torrington* 1716. **Abraham II (**fl 1718–35) cast six for *Bideford* (recast) and one for *Landcross* 1722, and the heavy eight for *Totnes*, 1732 (4 recast) which were probably the first ring in Devon cast as a complete octave; they bear the arms of the town on their waists. **Abel Rudhall** (1736–50) supplied bells for *Brixton, Exeter St Petrock, Ilfracombe, Bradworthy, Georgeham* and *Loxhore*; **Thomas** (1760–83) one at *Georgeham*, and **John** one at *Tawstock*. An additional bell, by Abraham I, can be seen in the *Hoops Inn*, near Clovelly; it was cast in 1722 for Weare Gifford Hall, and evidently came down by sea with the Torrington bells. A full account of the Gloucester foundry can be found in *Church Bells of Gloucestershire* by Mary Bliss & Frederick Sharpe.

BRISTOL FOUNDRIES. From Bristol in the 19th-century we have a single bell by **Thomas Hale**, hanging in *Bradley Manor*, Newton Abbott, and the old workhouse bell at *Tiverton* by **John Packer,** now in Tiverton Museum and probably dating from about 1838. **Llewellins & James** of Bristol began casting bells in 1854; their earliest surviving in Devon is the single one at *Leusdon*, 1863, which is unusual in having radial cannons. In 1876 they added five bells to a single one by Warner for *St Philip & St James, Ilfracombe*, and a good deal of their work between then and 1900 was in North Devon, with augmentations at *West Down, Abbotsham, Alwington,* and *Frithelstock*, but their bells are also found at *Petertavy, Jacobstowe, Stoke Canon, Whitestone, Whimple, Clyst Hydon, Sampford Spiney* and *Broadhempston* where they added a treble which is a semitone flat. Some of Llewellins & James's bells were evidently cast as stock with their inscription-bands recessed, so that the inscription could be cast on a separate strip of metal and rivetted on: *Ilfracombe St Philip & St James* has one such, and from the ground the two bells at *Lynmouth* appear to be the same, but being exposed to the weather their inscription-bands have for the most part fallen off. The only complete ring in the county by this foundry is the eight at *St Michael's, Teignmouth*, 1897; they were not tuned when they were rehung, and have a rather harsh tone like many of the bells from this foundry.

OTHER ENGLISH FOUNDRIES. Only three bells by **James Barwell** of Birmingham have been found in Devon – the treble and 2nd at *St Peter's, Barnstaple* and a single bell, since scrapped when the church was closed, at *Holy Trinity, Torquay*.

William Dobson of Downham Market has only a single bell in Devon – the tenor at *Withycombe Raleigh* cast in 1831 for Peterborough Cathedral and acquired from there to be added to the ring in 1991.

William Blews of Birmingham set up a bellfoundry in about 1852, and later used the title of William Blews & Sons. All the bells which he sent to Devon were single bells or augmentations, beginning in 1868 with the single bell (a particularly nasty one) at *Brooking, St Barnabas*. In 1870 he cast two for *Dunkeswell* and recast the tenor for *Powderham*, and the following year recast *Paignton's* present 3rd and added a treble at *Thelbridge*. None of the Blews bells in the county is very distinguished: two added to the mediaeval three at *Buckerell* in 1872 have been

Fig. 93. The oldest dated bell in Devon, at Walrond's Almshouses, Tiverton, cast in 1539 by Albert Hackman of Kleve.

Fig. 94. The bell formerly in the Royal Clarence Hotel, Exeter, a French casting dated 1694.

recast, and the two trebles at *Ashburton* would have been if funds had been available. The single bell which hung in the tower at *Blackborough* has been scrapped, but *Westward Ho!* has two in its bellcote. William died in 1887, and his business was sold to Charles Carr.

Charles Carr of Smethwick cast the ring of eight for *Lundy Island* in 1897; those who heard them in their original form described them as being indifferent in tone, but they have been tuned into an excellent ring and have now been augmented to ten. They were hung in a composite frame of Carr's distinctive design which was reduced to ruin by rust and has been replaced; another example in the county is the frame at *Littlehempston*.

John Bryant of Hertford was chosen to recast the six at *Barnstaple St Peter* in 1803, and at the same time recast the former 6th for *Tawstock*.

During the 19th century the firm of **Vickers** in Sheffield did some experimenting with cast steel bells. These have the characteristic of a deep tone for their weight and a distinctly mournful sound – at worst sounding like a tin bath. Only one such bell has been found in a Devon church – at *Herner* Chapel near Barnstaple – but there are three in the former Roman Catholic Priory at *Abbotskerswell*.

FOREIGN BELLS. A surprising number of bells in Devon private houses prove to have been cast overseas. The earliest, at *Walrond's Almshouses, Tiverton*, is dated 1539 (the oldest dated bell in Devon) and was cast by **Albrecht Hachman** of Kleve near the Dutch/German border. It is a beautiful casting, evidently acquired second-hand by John Walrond on one of his business trips to the Low Countries, and may have hung originally in a monastery or convent which became a victim of the Wars of Religion. At a private house near Kingsbridge is another beautifully cast bell dated 1691 by **Quirinus de Visscher** of Rotterdam. *Colleton Barton* near Chulmleigh has a bell with a very prominent soundbow and 3-looped cannons, with a cross formed of stars and strips of letters from an alphabet; it appears be about contemporary with the bell which hung in the foyer of the *Royal Clarence Hotel, Exeter*, which was dated 1694 and probably came from southern France. Another French bell hanging in a mansion near Honiton is dated 1733 and bears the name of **F. leGros** of Rochefort. At a house near Kenton I saw a small bell, uninscribed, bearing on the waist a cross on three steps which had been moulded with strips of wax pressed into a pattern with an incised arabesque pattern. The same type of cross can be seen on the bell of the Spanish flagship *San Josef*, captured by Nelson at Cape St Vincent, and date 1782, so the Kenton bell is probably also from late-18th-century Spain. *Bampton* School has a bell decorated with figures of putti playing musical instruments; similar figures can be found on bells from the **Villedieu-les-Poeles foundry** in Normandy, from the 19th century. A farmhouse near Ugborough has another bell, undoubtedly French 19th-century, with figures of saints on the waist, and the Royal Marines' depot at *Lympstone* possesses a beautiful casting with decorated radial cannons and figures of saints, which almost certainly came from Italy; it first appears in the records of the Corps after the second world war.

Foreign-cast bells in churches are less common, but *St Peter's Ilfracombe*, built in 1903, has a small bell dated 1868 and bearing decorations including angel figures, which is almost certainly French; how it got to Ilfracombe is not recorded; it was evidently a ship's bell. The *Church of Ascension, Crownhill, Plymouth* has a small bell which is inscribed LAN 1741 – L'An being French for "the year". It is reported to have come from Widey Court (the old mansion which belonged to the City until its demolition after World War II) and probably came from a prize captured during the wars against France. The Dockyard at *Devonport* has a bell hung near the Morice Town gate, which was recast from another prize – Spanish this time.

Two more ship's bells are the bell on the stables at *Bigadon House, Buckfastleigh*, bearing the name of the *Estrela*, a Portuguese schooner wrecked on Lundy Island in 1811, and the bell at *Beesands* church, which bears the name JANUS and the date 1813, although it is said to have belonged to the schooner *Lunesdale* which was wrecked therein the great blizzard of 1891. A schooner named *Janus* was registered in 1814 in New York, so this bell may have been cast in the United States.

The Roman Catholic Church of the Sacred Heart in South Street, Exeter, has a bell by **Murphy** of Dublin, and there are probably other bells by this founder in Roman Catholic churches in the county.

Finally, we have two beautiful modern bells from the **Eijsbouts** foundry at Asten in the Netherlands, cast to augment the three at *Gittisham* in 1991.

Foreign Bells in Devon

1539	Tiverton, Walrond's Almshouses	A Hachman, Cleve
C16	near Ugborough	French
1691	near W Alvington	Q de Visscher, Rotterdam
1694	Exeter, Royal Clarence Hotel	?French
C17	Colleton Barton, Chulmleigh	?French
1733	near Honiton	F le Gros, Rochefort
1741	Plymouth, Ascension	French
175?	Tapeley Park, Westleigh	?Dutch
1788	Clyst St George School	Spanish
C18	near Kenton	Spanish
C18	W Ogwel House	?Dutch
c1798	BigadonHouse, Buckfastleigh	Portuguese
1813	Beesands	?New York
C19	Bampton Primary School	Villedieu foundry
C19	Lympstone, Royal Marines	Italian
1868	Ilfracombe St Peter	French
1991	Gittisham	Eysbouts, Asten
1991	Gittisham	Eysbouts, Asten

6

THE PENNINGTON FAMILY

THE PENNINGTONS MUST SURELY be one of the most prolific and most productive bellfounding dynasties in Britain – and one of the most puzzling. Their output between 1600 and 1823 must rival that of the Rudhalls of Gloucester; we know of over 750 bells by them which are still surviving, and at least another 300 have been recast. For two centuries branches of the family dominated the trade in Devon and Cornwall (another branch operated in Monmouthshire), in their heyday casting five, six or even seven rings of bells in a year. However, their family history presents a number of problems of which the most important are, first, that the Cornish branch and the two Devon branches were already separated before we have reliable church registers; second, that until quite a late date the Cornish Penningtons tended to itinerate, so that many of their children were born away from home; and third, that they showed a deplorable lack of enterprise in the naming of their male children, so that one can find two or three Thomases, Johns or Christophers in a single generation.

The earliest records for the family in Devon and Cornwall may begin in Crediton in the 1560s; a bellfounder whose name is given as "Pemerton" was casting a bell for Crediton in 1578, though this may well have been a misspelling for Preston – and other Penningtons appear in the records there though not in connection with bells. In 1580 Robert Pennington appears on the bellfounding scene in Bodmin and Thomas I in Barnstaple, buying bell metal from the Northam churchwardens. A bell at Minehead dated 1607 bears the motto "Soli deo detur gloria", which was later to be a favourite with the Devon Penningtons, with a small rectangular mark with a bell and the initials T P. The same motto and the same mark appear on *Yarnscombe* 5th along with the initials R P in flat letters with a flat cut-out bell, and this seems to identify the founders as Thomas I and Robert. However, by this time Robert had made his home in Bodmin, where he was married to Mary Wallkye in 1594: we shall meet him again when we come to consider the Cornish branch of the family.

It seems likely that Robert of Bodmin and Thomas I of Barnstaple were brothers. In Barnstaple, there were a Richard and a William Pennington in the 1590s; Thomas's elder son Thomas II was probably born there, but the first of his children registered there is John, born in 1606.

The Barnstaple & Exeter Penningtons

Except for the Minehead and Yarnscombe bells which were inscribed using old Lombardic and black-letter stamps, apparently second-hand, **Thomas Pennington I of Barnstaple**'s bells are characterised by flat "cut-out" type lettering and marks; some of the later ones were decorated with coin-impressions; the most important surviving are *Eggesford* tenor [54], 1618, *East Anstey* 6/6 and Dulverton, Somerset 4/8, 6/8 and 8/8, 1619. In 1620 he travelled from Barnstaple to *Tiverton* to recast the bells of St Peter's, and in 1622 he and his son Thomas II signed a bond to recast the four bells of *Modbury* into five, the work to be done within five miles of Modbury church: we also have the 3rd at *Iddesleigh*, 1620, and *Hollacombe* treble, 1622, both with impressed lettering, and probably the work of Thomas II. **Thomas Pennington II of Exeter** was married in Barnstaple in the same year to Dorothy Lucas; there is no record that they had any children, and he may have been widowed and married again, as a memorial in St Paul's,

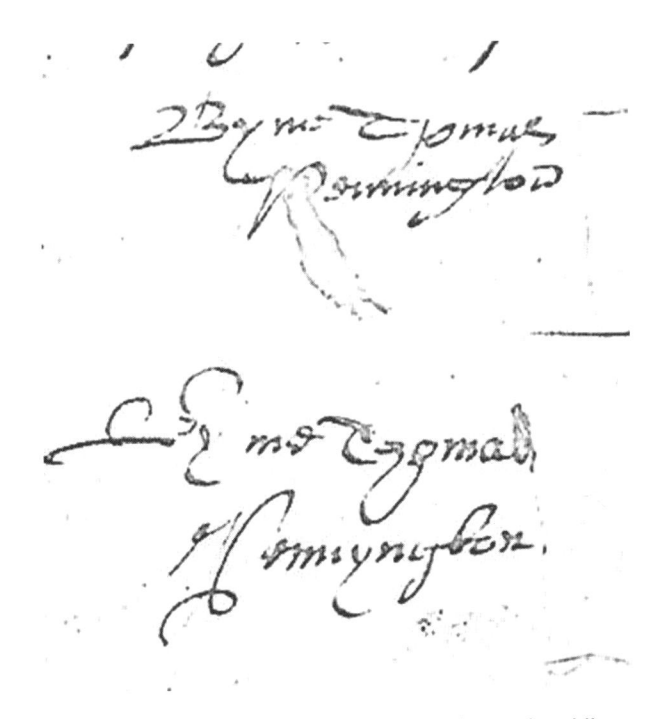

Fig. 95. The signatures of Thomas Pennington I and II on the contract to recast Modbury bells, 1622.

Fig. 96. Iddesleigh 3rd, by Thomas Pennington II (note the impressed lettering), 1620.

Exeter is recorded to Alice, "wife of Thomas Pennenton", who died in 1640. The use of impressed lettering indicates that Thomas was using the new technique for inscribing his bells, which has been described in Chapter 3.

In 1623 Thomas II seems to have been in charge, using his initials with the skeleton bell mark which his brother, nephew and great-nephew continued to use for nearly a century, and the bolder, neater impressed lettering. By 1626 he had moved to Exeter (no doubt to fill the space left by the death of John Birdall), where he acquired a house in Paul Street with a yard running back to the city wall, and there he established his foundry, at first outside the North Gate but later inside the wall. His name was by now well-known over a wide area, for in that year he was given one of his most prestigious commissions, the recasting of three bells, now the 6/10, 8/10 and 9/10, at Yeovil, and while he was in Somerset also cast bells for Taunton St James, Kilton, Muchelney, Trent and Loders, the last-named described by Christopher Dalton as "one of the loveliest-sounding bells in the county": no doubt he established a temporary foundry in Somerset (probably in Yeovil) for much of this work. His fleur-de-lys friezes first appear in 1625, and from then until his death in 1642 his work went on steadily. Many of his bells carry the inscription SOLI DEO DETVR GLORIA; another which he often used was DRAW NEARE VNTO GOD, sometimes with the addition AND GOD WILL DRAW NEARE VNTO YOV; other bells by him give the names of the

Fig. 97. Holcombe Rogus 4th, by Thomas Pennington II of Exeter, 1626, with coins of Henry IV of Navarre.

churchwardens or "sidemen"; a few, such as the Yeovil bells and two at *Payhembury* obviously cast to special order, have elaborate inscriptions in Latin. In 1627 he was given the job of casting the bronze head of the "nail" in Axbridge, its inscription giving the exact day on the month and year of its casting, as does that of *Colebrooke* 4/6, a particularly fine casting from the same year – a significant expression of confidence in his skill. In 1622 and 1623 his stop between words is a cross in an oval; from 1624 to 1632 he normally used coin-impressions – usually shillings but sometimes something more exotic like the half-écu of Henri IV of Navarre at *Holcombe Rogus*. From 1632 almost all his bells have the 5-dot stop which was used thereafter by the Penningtons until the late 18th-century. In 1642 he died; his last surviving bell, the tenor at *Burlescombe*, is a notable casting, with an elaborate cartouche of the donor's arms on the inscription-band. His agreement with the people of Tiverton for recasting their "great bell" in 1629 can be seen in Appendix II:7.

John Pennington of Exeter, the youngest son of Thomas I, was born in Barnstaple in 1612 and married in 1635 to Philippa Fuegins or Friggens, in St Paul's, Exeter, just across the road from the family home and foundry; she apparently came from St Mabyn in Cornwall, which suggests that there may have been regular contact between the Bodmin and Exeter families. Their first two children, Elinor, 1636–40 and Thomas, 1638–41, died in infancy; the third, born the following year, was also given the name Thomas; the last was Alice, 1646–72.

Until Thomas II's death in 1642, John presumably worked with him; his initials appear along with his brother's only once, on *Payhembury* 2/6, 1635. The John Pennington who was working in the Gloucestershire area and cast Gloucester Cathedral 11/12 in 1626 remains a mystery, but cannot be the John who was born in 1612 – indeed the connection between that founder, the Cornish and Devon Penningtons, and the Monmouth branch of the family is still obscure, though there must surely be one.

Fig. 98. Exeter Cathedral 5th, cast during the Commonwealth by John Pennington but with impressions of Charles I shillings.

In 1658 John recast the 5/12 at *Exeter Cathedral*; it would be interesting to know how this was paid for, as the cathedral was at that time shared between the Presbyterians and the Independents; even more remarkable are the impressions of Charles I shillings on the bell. In his own parish of St Paul's, things were far from happy; the Rector before the Civil War, Robert Oland, was described as *a person extremely vicious and ignorant* who *rifled the church . . . and fled to the Parliamentary Army*, though he is listed as Rector until 1662. In 1652 St Paul's was one of the thirteen churches which the City Chamber ordered to be sold off for secular use, but John Pennington bought the chancel for £16 to save it from profanation; nevertheless, as his son reported later, *the Anabaptists violently broke in and held their assemblies there, and one Byfield a Fifth Monarchy Preacher sometimes also usurped it*. John Pennington apparently took charge of the church Register, and his 17-year-old son used a blank half-page at the end of Volume I to practice his handwriting and show off his school Latin:

Thomas Pennington eius liber Anno Dommini 1659
Cum plebe plebit, dum deus audet, Thomas Pennington 1659.
  John Pennington
  Edward Wills

It is interesting to note in the line of Latin verse an echo of the mediaeval Leonine couplets which Thomas must have read on old bells; translated it means: "When the people plead, God will be listening."

John used the same lettering, skeleton bell and 5-dot stop as his brother, and on a bell at *Spreyton*, as at the cathedral, used a coin-impression – apparently Spreyton was remote enough for him to risk a coin of Charles I – but on two of his bells, *Eggesford* 2/3 [47] and *Holcombe Burnell* 6/6 he decorated the inscriptions with impressions of seals or signets, using the seal itself as pattern, not a wax impression. After the Restoration, business picked up as one might expect – 1664 was especially good with eight bells surviving or recorded. Many of John's bells at this period are inscribed I P EXON on I P X to distinguish the Exeter founder from his namesake in Tavistock.

In 1659 the City renewed John's lease of the foundry site in Paul Street, described as *all that plott or parcel of grounde wth the app'tenances adjoyning to the Walles of the said cittye sett lying and being wthin the Parishe of St Paules in the said cittye of Exeter nowe in the tenure or occupation of the said John Pennington and lyeth betweene two gardens & plotts of ground in the severall tenures or occupations of John Butler and Mathew Lant or their Assignes, contayning in length Thirtye & five foote and in breadth eighteen foote or thereaboute.*

The lease ran for 99 years or the lives of John, Philippa his wife and his son and daughter Thomas and Alice; the rent was four shillings a year – leases for the lives of three named people were customary in Devon at this period. John had to undertake to repair and maintain the premises and the *Barbigan of the cittye walles adjoyning the same in all manner of needfull and necessary repa'tions When and soe often as need shall require at his and their owne proper costs and charges,* and give the *Mayor, Bailiffs and comynaltie their Successors and Assignes and their workmen* right of ingress and egress to view and repair the walls and mural walk. Failure to do this, or to *comitt or doe or willinglie suffer to bee done . . . any Act or thing wch may be p'iudiciall and hurtfull to the walls of the said cittye* without repairing it within twenty days would mean forfeiting the lease. The site was excavated in 1982, when a well-preserved furnace firebox [52] was found in the slope of the bank which backed the city wall. About 8 feet away to one side was a large casting-pit with the remains of some 20 mould-bases in it; the bowl of the furnace, which must have been between the furnace and the casting-pit, had disappeared along with the upper part of the furnace. Between this and the back of the house in Paul Street had been a yard with buildings in it; the ground contained significant quantities of copper residue, and a path along the E side of the plot had been covered with successive layers of used loam.

John Pennington died in 1668, and was buried in the centre aisle of the church which he had cared for during its dark days. He was succeeded by his only son.

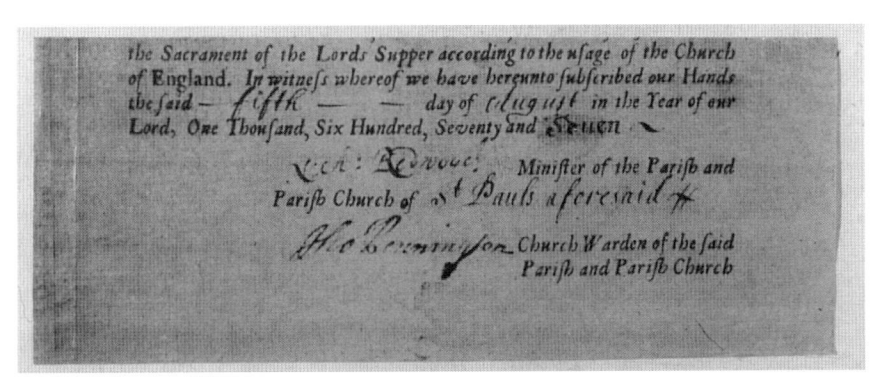

Fig. 99.   Thomas Pennington III's Sacrament certificate.

Fig. 100. Exeter St Martin. The bell by Thomas Pennington III, with satirical medal impressions, 1675.

Thomas Pennington III of Exeter was born in the year that his father took over the foundry, and himself succeeded in the year when his own eldest child was born, having married Sara Quarrell at St Thomas's in the previous year. Like his father he usually added EXON to his initials to distinguish himself from the Tavistock branch of the family, and the style of his bells is virtually indistinguishable from his father's. He seems to have been married four times; Sara his first wife, whom he married at St Paul's in 1667, died in 1673; only one child, John, is recorded of this marriage, but a son Thomas who was buried in Thorverton church in 1680 may have been hers; in the same year 1673 he married Margaret Rydler of St Thomas at Dunchideock. This marriage seems to have come to an untimely end, as a licence was issued in 1675 for the marriage of Thomas Pennington and Joan Pooke; a Thomas Pennington was married in that year at Cadeleigh, but the bride's name is given as Mary Pooke. We have his signature on a Sacrament Certificate dated 1677. His bells carried on very much the style of his predecessors, with coins often used as stops; at *Exeter, St Martin* and *Ottery St Mary* he used a satirical medal as a stop.

About this time Thomas settled in Thorverton, where three sons, Thomas, George and Samuel were born and all died in infancy. Some time before 1691 he married for the fourth time, his wife this time being Mary the daughter of Zachary Travers, one of Thorverton's wealthiest inhabitants. Zachary left some rents to *the children of Mary, wife of Thomas Pennington of Thorverton, bellfounder, my daughter, at 21, the said Thomas not to meddle therein*. It was not uncommon for a clause such as this to be included in a legacy to a married daughter, but in Mary's case there may have been a particular reason for it: Thomas III seems to have been hitting the bottle. Entries for drink for the bellfounder appear in almost every church account-book of the 17th and 18th centuries, but Thomas's case looks different. We have seen how the South Tawton wardens paid for *an extraordinary expense in beere* when they met with Thomas III and Richard Beavis, and in 1683 the wardens of *St Petrock's, Exeter* spent the large sum of 4/6d *at the Myter and Black Dogg in wyne and ale in agreeing with him* (the bell which he cast carried only his initials, the figure "83" and some frieze). Towards the end of his career the habit apparently got worse; at *Bishopsteignton* in 1717 the parish spent the extraordinary sum of £1 8s 6d *at severall parish meetings and other times for beer & Cyder for the Bellfounder & all ye Labourers yt attended the worke*, and in 1718 the *Rewe* wardens found their bellfounder very expensive indeed:

for licker Mr Pennington had when he came to take the Bell att Castin	4	9
Philip Thomas (the local publican) *for licker in taking down the bell*	4	6
Phillip Thomas *for Mr Pennington and his men for Vittells & Beare which they left to pay*	5	6
Phillip Thomas *for Vittells Mr Pennington and his men had*	2	0
Phillip Thomas *for Beare Mr Pennington had*	2	6

Phillip Thomas for Vittells & Lika Mr Pennington and his three men had
in ording the Bell to hang it on	6	6
for to Qurte of ale Mr Pennington had		6
for licker Mr Pennington had and Vittells	4	6
for hanging oup of the Bell in licker the first time	4	6
expense for one hanging the Bell when the Cannons broak and hanging it oup Agane the secken time	3	6
Expense in Tuning the Bell for Vittells & Beare	17	6

(The full bell account for 1718 is shown in App.II:13.)

The fact that ale was apparently three-halfpence a pint, and that the sum of these entries, £2 16s 3d, was equivalent to 56¼ gallons of ale, is significant, as may be the fact that Thomas failed to pay for some of his "vittells". Whatever the reason, Thomas III's work gradually tailed off, in quality as well as quantity; in the 1690s he and John Stadler, who had probably learnt his trade with him, were working intermittently together, but Stadler after 1702 seems to worked on his own from Chulmleigh. We have knowledge of only 13 possible bells by Thomas III between 1690 and his death in 1721, almost all of them close to Exeter, and of these only four remain; the last cast is the single bell at *Shillingford St George*, of 1716. The family remained in Thorverton for some time after Thomas III's death, but played no part in the bellfounding business: the bulk of the work in East Devon was already going to the Wroths in Wellington, Gooding in Plymouth and the Penningtons in Tavistock and Lezant were dominant in the South and West of the county, and the Rudhalls were beginning to find work along the North coast. Until the Pannells established their short-lived foundry in the 1850s, bellfounding in Exeter was at an end: there are 133 bells from the foundry surviving in Devon, Cornwall, Somerset and Dorset, and at least another 64 have been recast or scrapped, making a total of 197.

(Note; The Exeter Mayor's Court Book records on October 20, 1673, the admission as a Freeman of "Thomas Pennington, bellfounder, son of Thomas Pennington, by succession." This poses several problems; Thomas Pennington I had died in 1642, apparently childless; Thomas III had been born in the same year, and would have been 30 or 31, so could not hardly have had a son old enough to be admitted as Freeman, in 1673. We have conjectured that "Thomas" was entered as the father's name in error for "John", which seems to be the most likely explanation, but another possibility is that this was Thomas III's son who died young in 1680, and that he was enrolled as Freeman in 1673 at a very tender age, along with some 300 others, because there was a hotly contested by-election in Exeter that year.)

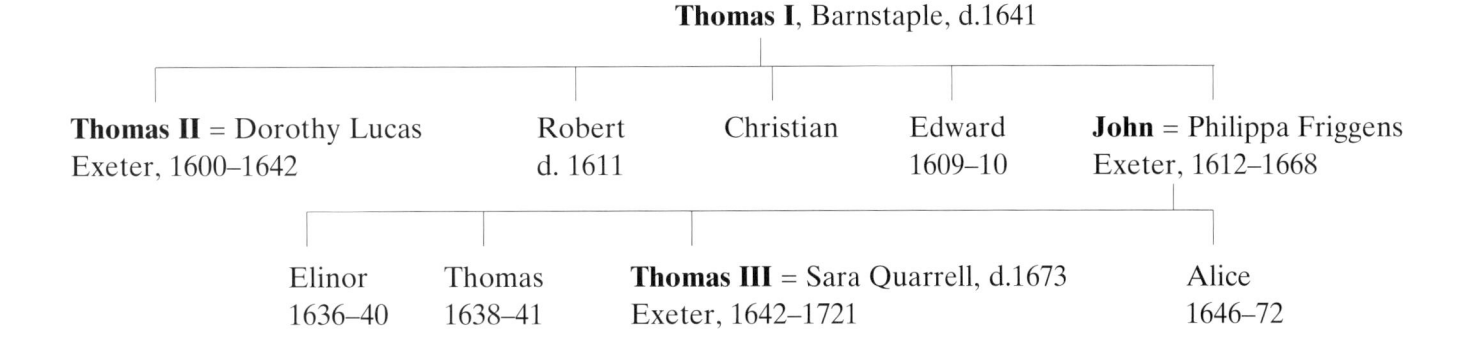

Thomas I, Barnstaple, d.1641

Thomas II = Dorothy Lucas   Robert   Christian   Edward   **John** = Philippa Friggens
Exeter, 1600–1642   d. 1611   1609–10   Exeter, 1612–1668

Elinor   Thomas   **Thomas III** = Sara Quarrell, d.1673   Alice
1636–40   1638–41   Exeter, 1642–1721   1646–72

The Penningtons of Tavistock

For a long time there were puzzles concerned with bells bearing the initials "T.P." (e.g. *Sampford Spiney* 3/5 and the notable tenor at *Thurlestone*), cast in 1653-4 when Thomas Pennington III of Exeter was twelve years old, and with later "I.P." bells cast between 1669 (the year after the birth of Thomas III's son John) and the end of the century. As research went on, indeed, it became increasingly apparent that this John the son of Thomas III was a not a bellfounder at all; Pennington bells in the Exeter area are marked "TP" to the end of the business in 1720, and the "I.P." bells which do appear in that period are different in style with a different skeleton-bell mark. When a member of the Devon Record Office staff pointed me in the direction of a whole new family of Penningtons in Tavistock (where the parish registers are not included in the I.G.I. database) this clarified the matter to a great extent.

Thomas Pennington of Tavistock is described in some documents as a pewterer or a brazier. He and his wife Margaret had two sons, John and Thomas, and at least one daughter, Thomazin, who died in 1638. A bell at Sampford Spiney, dated 1653, which bears the initials "TP IP" [Pl 16f] with the Exeter version of the skeleton bell mark may have been cast by this Thomas in cooperation with John of Exeter, and is probably the first surviving bell bearing his initials; Thurlestone's remarkable tenor also bears the Exeter bell mark with the initials TP and IP and the date 1654, but Thurlestone 4/6, now recast, bore only Thomas's initials, if Ellacombe's account is correct. We have no other bells which can be attributed to him until 1669, when he and his son John made a sally into North Devon to cast bells for *East Down, Parracombe* and *Merton*. Thomas died in 1670, and a document relating to his estate describes him as a pewterer, with "brazier" crossed out.

Thomas of Tavistock's son **John Pennington I of Tavistock** was married in 1656 in Buckland Monachorum, to Katherine Farley (one notes that Bernard Pennington of Bodmin was married in 1663 to Charity Farley, who may have been a relative). John's brother, Thomas the younger, was probably not a bellfounder, and he may prove to have stayed in the pewter side of the business, but John joined his father, and although no surviving bells appear to bear his initials before 1669, it is noticeable that during this period John of Exeter usually signed himself "I.P.EXON", apparently to avoid confusion with this other John. When Thomas the elder died in 1670; John carried on the business, with bells at *Newton St Petrock,* 1671, *Abbotsham* (recast), *Stoke Gabriel, Sampford Spiney, Cookbury* and *Wembury* (cast in Tavistock as the records show and since recast again) 1674, *Instow* [App.II:10] and *Egg Buckland* (recast), 1682, *Bondleigh,* 1683, *Coryton* and *Hollacombe,* 1684, and *Kingston,* 1690. These bells are usually good castings, often using as stops coin-impressions or a lozenge, and fleur-de-lys, four of which are sometimes made up into a cross. The founder's initials are set either side of a skeleton bell [Pl 22i] smaller and squatter than the Exeter one. One other bell can be attributed to John – a small one in the Victoria & Albert Museum, London, the provenance of which has so far not been discovered, inscribed I P with a small solid bell and dated 1670. The 5-dot stop strongly suggests that it was cast by one of the

Fig. 101. Kingston 3rd, by John Pennington I of Tavistock, 1690.

Fig. 102. A bell originally in St Marychurch, later in the Roman Catholic church there, and finally cracked and scrapped. It was cast by John Pennington I & II of Tavistock in 1702.

Westcountry Penningtons, and John I is the most likely candidate. John I was an alderman in Tavistock in 1684; a Sacrament Certificate of 1688 survives for John Pennington, bell founder, of Tavistock, and John I witnessed the certificate for David Burchinshaw, clerk, of Lydford.

The story of John and Katherine's family is a heart-breaking one. They probably had at least 14 children; Dorothy died aged 6, Thomas 8, John in infancy, Peter 1, Katherine 2, Samuel 1, Elizabeth in infancy, four un-named in infancy: brother Thomas fared no better, with possibly only one out of his nine surviving. Joan survived to marry William Hutchings, and John, the second child with that name, joined his father in the business. Two other children of John and Katherine, Daniel and Francis, may have survived, but do not appear in the registers again. Katherine died in 1682 – not surprisingly – after the birth of Elizabeth, who survived her by only six months. John I probably married again; a daughter Susanna was born to him in 1688, and *Mary the wife of John* appears in the burial register for 1704.

John Pennington II of Tavistock was born in 1668 and his initials appear with those of his father, IP IP, in 1697 on *Thurlestone* 2/6. In 1702 the initials IP^s IP^i appeared on the former bell of *St Marychurch* (later hung in the Roman Catholic church there and eventually cracked and scrapped), and in 1706 at *Charleton* on the 5/6 (recast) and tenor: the St Marychurch and Charleton bells both carried a fleur-de-lys cross, and the initials have between them a small solid bell with moulding-wires.

"Mr John Pennington" (John I) was buried at Tavistock on January 13th, 1709: *Coryton* 4/5 is dated that year, and it is probably by John II as the bell mark is a new one which does not appear elsewhere, but John II does not seem to have continued in the business after his father's death, though he lived until 1754. A document of 1729 refers to "premises late in the occupation of John Pennington, pewterer", so one can assume that he concentrated on that trade for the latter part of his life, leaving the Lezant branch of the family to continue with the bellfounding. His first wife Jane Edmond, whom he married in 1692, died in 1718, and he was married again to Elinor Hornbrook five months later; she lived until 1748. He had a son Thomas and a daughter Thomazin by his first wife.

Twenty-two bells by the Tavistock Penningtons survive, and we know of another nine which have been recast or scrapped.

Not far away on the Cornish side of the Tamar at this time, Christopher Pennington was working in Lezant, and the bells of the two branches show a marked contrast. Christopher's bells are usually rather crude castings with ungainly cut-out lettering; John of Tavistock's are much neater, and were stamped into a groove filled with soft loam, as Thurlestone 2/6 clearly shows.

The Cornish Penningtons

The first record of the Pennington family in Cornwall is the marriage of **Robert Pennington** of Bodmin to Mary Wallkye in 1594. In the same year Anne, daughter of Humfrie Pennington, was baptised at Lanreath, and there seems to have been another brother or cousin, William, married to Loveday, whose daughter Alice was baptised at Lanhydrock in 1607. Robert left few bells that can be definitely attributed to him; the initials RP in cut-out letters flanking a bell appear with a TP mark on Yarnscombe 6/6, 1608, and a note in the Blisland register records that he cast the Treble and 2nd on the 9th March 1632, *betweene fower and five of the clocke in the afternoone...the price five poundes*, and in Devon we have a record of him at Kenton casting a bell for *Dawlish* in 1618. Two bells at *East Ogwell* dated 1633, one with the initials R.P., are almost certainly his, along with *Denbury 3/6* also dated 1633 [Pl 17a]; all three have cut-out lettering. The former tenor at *Wembury*, dated 1631 and also inscribed "R.P", was another which can be assigned to him, and there are several bells in Cornwall similarly initialled. The Liskeard accounts show that he recast the front three of four in 1632–3 and the tenor four years later.

Robert and Mary had three children. The elder son **John Pennington I of Bodmin,** born in 1596, was married at Bodmin in 1628 to Wilmot Rickard. He remained in Bodmin – all his nine children were baptized there – and died there in 1660, leaving his fairly modest goods and chattels, worth £19 4s 6d (£19.22) to his wife [App.I:1]. Robert's second child Elizabeth was born in 1605, and his son **Bernard Pennington** in 1607. Bernard was described as a bellfounder and was mayor of Bodmin in 1666 and 1680: his initials appear on a fine gallon measure dated 1646 in Bodmin Museum and a bell formerly at St Dennis in Cornwall, with the initials B.P. and dated 1657, was probably his. He evidently prospered; he died in 1674, leaving goods worth no less than £105 5s 4d including *new brasse potts & new brase panns* worth £20, and bequeathing his *woorkehouse*, moulds and tools to his son **Christopher Pennington I** [App.I:2]. Christopher I was born in 1631 and was also described as a bellfounder in his will. Bells at St John, Cornwall, 1682, *Frithelstock*, 1686, and *Monkokehampton*, 1687, rather rough castings with the initials "C P" and a mixed set of letters, are probably his [Pl 17h,i,j,k]. Christopher I made his will in 1697 and died in 1699; he left his work-house to his wife Susanna and after her death to his son Robert

Fig. 103. Cut-out lettering on East Ogwell 4th, by Robert Pennington of Bodmin.

Fig. 104. Frithelstock 5th, probably by Christopher Pennington I of Bodmin, 1686.

Fig. 105. One of a pair of silver goblets bearing the Pennington arms.

Fig. 106. Bondleigh tenor, by Fitzantony Pennington I of Lezant, 1656.

[App.I:3], but none of his children seems to have continued in the trade; his third son William took holy orders and became Vicar of Davidstow. This William's son, another William, was tutor to the children of the Marquis of Bute and prospered enough to purchase Bodmin Priory and build the present house: on his death it passed to Nancy, the daughter of his sister Susanna and Anthony Hosken, the Vicar of Bodmin; she married a member of the Gilbert family, and a pair of silver goblets bearing the Pennington arms – or, five lozenges in fess azure – are still in the possession of descendants of this branch of the family. The same arms were used on the seal of Bernard Pennington in 1674, and resemble those carried by the Penningtons of Cumbria.

Robert's wife Mary died in 1625, and the following year he married Agnes Williams at Bodmin, but she died in 1630 without issue and in 1632 he married a Jane Blacallow. By her he had two children, **Edward** and Jane. Edward raised a family in Bodmin, and may have worked with his half-brothers John and Bernard in the bellfounding business; he witnessed the will of John I in 1660. Much later he appears in his own right, casting three bells for St Veep in 1682, one for *Upton Hellions* in Devon in 1690 [App.II:11] and one (the only one still extant) for Camelford Town Hall in 1699.

John I's first child, **Fitzantony Pennington I**, was born in Bodmin in 1631, the same year as his cousin Christopher I: the name Fitzantony was to become a tradition in the family. At some point Fitzantony moved to Lezant not far from Launceston; he married Ann Gloyn at Launceston in 1655, and three children, Anne, 1655, John, 1657 and Richard, 1660, were baptized there. In 1656 Fitzantony I cast bells for *Bondleigh* and *Frithelstock* [Pl 17b-e] and the following year bells at *Parracombe* and *Mortehoe* were cast, almost certainly by him as they bear similar marks and lettering to the bells of 1656 marked "F.P". In 1668 he was working at Sheviock with his cousin Christopher I; in 1676 the *Goodleigh* accounts show a bell recast by "Mr Pennington" at Swimbridge, and *Mr ffitz Antho: Pennington*

Fig. 107. Fitzantony Pennington I's monument on the wall of Lezant church tower.

Fig. 108. Buckland Monachorum 6th, cast in Tavistock in 1723 by Christopher Pennington II and John II.

coming to receive the money [App.II:8]; he had presumably done the casting: in 1690 Fitzantony I was buried at Lezant, and a fine slate monument can be seen on the south exterior wall of the church there.

The baptism of **Christopher Pennington II** has not yet been found in the records; there is a gap in the Bodmin registers between 1653 and 1661, no doubt due to the Commonwealth: a child of that name, son of Christopher I, was baptized at Bodmin in 1665 but died two years later. The most likely theory is that Christopher II was a son of Fitzantony I, born possibly after Richard, as he lived till 1749. He probably cast the bells marked "C P 3" at *Stoke Canon* and *Pinhoe* – they do him little credit, and most of the bells that can be attributed to him are rough castings, with a rather sprawling skeleton bell and flat letters [Pl 18a-f]. Christopher II and his wife Joan had five children including three sons, all baptized in Lezant, of whom **Christopher Pennington III**, 1697–1764, and **John Pennington II of Lezant**, 1700–c1745, became bell-founders. Two bells at *Thrushelton* inscribed CP IP 1718 are probably by Christopher II and his son John II, as are three at *Marytavy*, 1720, but the next few years saw a complete change in style which may indicate that the two sons were now in charge. At *Buckland Filleigh*, 1722, is a ring of four by John, with a smaller, neater bell mark and smaller but bolder lettering [Pl 19b,c]; at *Petertavy* in the same year Christopher III and John II worked together using the same lettering [Pl 19a]. The following year the brothers produced some of the most handsome castings ever made by the Cornish Penningtons, a five at *Buckland Monachorum* and a four at *East Allington*. All are beautifully inscribed, with a fine scribed line below the letters, and both have finely-detailed coats-of-arms of their donors in roundels; at Buckland there are also trade-mark roundels with a bell and "C P" or "I P", and a neat frieze like fern-leaves [Pl 19d-l]. The Buckland bells also display what became a characteristic mark of the family – slim oval stops which we will term "grains", either singly as stops or arranged into crosses, saltires, stars or sunbursts.

Christopher III appears in the Lezant wardens accounts as paying 2d a year in the Church Rate for Trekenner Mill, beside the swift-flowing River Inny, and it would appear that he may have been a miller as well as a bellfounder. His eldest son James and grandson John continued in the milling business, and a John Pennington was

Fig. 109. Trekenner Mill, which was occupied by the Penningtons from 1756 to the 1840s.

still tenant of the mill when the Tithe Award was made in the 1840s. There are no visible signs of bellfounding activity there today, but there are traces of quite extensive outbuildings either side of the road.

In 1724 John II was at *Winkleigh* recasting a ring of five, and there he married Pascha Bulled, the daughter of a well-to-do local farmer; he seems to have stayed in Winkleigh for a year or two, as *Spreyton* sent a bell there to be recast by him in 1726 [Pl 20a] and in the same year the first of five sons, John III, was baptized there. His second son was almost certainly Fitzantony II, though the record of his baptism has not yet come to light; Richard, the next, did not join the firm but moved to Maker and raised a family; Christopher IV was born in Lezant in 1737 and William in 1740 – these became the future "John Pennington & Co". After his stay in Winkleigh it appears that John II tested the bellfounding market in Exeter, now without a bellfounder since the death of Thomas III in 1720. A paragraph in *Brice's Weekly Journal* for May 10th 1728 states:

John Pennington, Bell Founder, is lately come to settle in the City of Exon, and casts Church Bells of any size, either in Rings, or in Part, and will perform all his work on reasonable Terms, in such a manner as shall be judg'd by the nicest Ear to be exactly in Tune, and a good Tone, otherwise he expects no Reward. He is ready to give Satisfaction to any Person that may question his Ability, by a proof of the Exactness of his Method and Rule in working several Rings he has cast in this County, which prove to fall exactly in Tune from the Mould, without Chipping or Barbing; which frequently spoils the Bell.
Direct for him near Nroth (sic) *Gate.*

It may be that John had hopes of getting the prestigious contract at the cathedral which was won by William Evans; in fact, none of his bells survive in the Exeter area, and the following year he was working with his brother Christopher at South Petherwin.

From 1731 to 1739, only John II's initials appear on the bells, but he must have died about 1740: his last surviving bells were cast for Menheniot in 1739, his last child was born in 1740, and by 1746 Pascha was a widow and had gone home to Winkleigh to marry a Thomas Heal, apparently leaving her children at Lezant with their uncle Christopher and his wife Mary – but Mary died in 1745, and it isn't clear who thereafter looked after Christopher, 8 and William, 5 and a baby, Mary. Christopher II came back into the business, casting a four at *St Giles-on-the-Heath* in 1740 [Pl 20d] (they bear no initials but are unquestionably his) and in 1742 working together with Daniel Masters to cast three into five at Laneast. His bells in this later period are once again rough castings with crude lettering, confirming that it was John II who had aspired to a fine finish; a poorly-cast bell at St John's near Torpoint dated 1743 has CPs CPi for Christopher II and III, but bells cast for Cuby and Mabe in 1744 have the initials TC with his. Between 1744 and 1750 we have only one surviving ring from the Lezant foundry, at *Ermington* where in 1748 we find CP IP on three bells remaining from a ring of five, far better cast with a larger version of the Buckland Monachorum fern-leaf frieze [Pl 20e,f,g] and a big medallion of Admiral Vernon. Christopher Pennington II was buried in Bodmin and his will was proved in 1749, so we can assume that his son Christopher III is now in charge, assisted by his nephew, John II's son **John Pennington III,** 1726–1790: Christopher III's own son James did not join the business, but worked as a miller at Trekenner Mill.

John Pennington III of Lezant's initials do not appear again until after his uncle's death, and all bells cast between 1749 and 1756 have C P only for Christopher III [Pl 20h-l]. However in 1756 **Fitzantony Pennington II,** c1740-1768, who as we have seen was probably the second brother, was working on his own at *Newton Ferrers*, casting a ring of four and also recasting a bell for *Holbeton*: he may have been living in Landulph, near the Tamar. His initials appear on most of the family's bells until 1761, including fives for *Pyworthy*, St Breward, St Stephens-by-Saltash and *Belstone*, where we first find the shell mark [Pl 21f] which was used by the family for the next fifty years; in the same year he seems to have been joined by his brothers **John Pennington III** and **Christopher Pennington IV**, 1737–1799, and in a very busy five years they sign their bells "IP FAP", or "Pennington fecit" "Penningtons fecit" or (more correctly) "Penningtons fecerunt"; from 1766 they are "Penningtons makers" or "IP FAP", and are using a neat, round-sectioned lettering [Pl 21a,b]. This was the beginning of a boom period for the Westcountry bellfounders; ringing was extremely popular in Devon and Cornwall, as a number of ringers' songs testify, and old rings of three and four were being recast or augmented to fives and sixes; the Penningtons' output steadily rose from 1765 onwards, with two fives in 1765, three in '66, three sixes and a four in '67, two fives and a six in '68, three sixes and a five in '69, four sixes and a five in '70. But in 1768 tragedy struck the family when a boat carrying Fitzantony and one of his bells capsized in the river and he was drowned. His monument in the tower at Landulph depicts an angel sounding the Last Trump and at the same time, appropriately, ringing a bell, with the inscription:

> *NEAR* this place, Lies
> The Body of Fitz Anthony
> Pennington; Bellfounder,
> of the Parish of Lezant, in
> Cornwall. who departed
> this Life, April 30; 1768.
>   Aetatis Suae 38.
>
> *Tho Boistrous Winds, & Billows sore,*
>   *Hath Tos^d me, To and Fro;*
> *By God's Decree; in spite of both:*
>   *I Rest now; here below.*

Fig. 110. Fitzantony Pennington II's monument in the tower of Landulph church.

There is a tradition in the Pennington family that the tragedy happened as Fitzantony was taking a bell for Landulph across the Antony Passage. This seems unlikely: Fitzantony lived, and presumably worked, either in Landulph or in Stoke Climsland; there was no reason to take a Landulph bell across any river, let alone the Lynher, unless it was a scrap bell to be recast for Landulph. However, the *Plympton St Maurice* bells were recast in that year (with John's initials) and would have had to cross the Tamar at Saltash or at Torpoint (in the latter event the Lynher as well) – or indeed could have been taken virtually all the way by water: the accident may have happened as one of these bells was being brought to the quay at Antony Passage, or possibly the Landulph bells were recast at Plympton. When he died so tragically, Fitzantony had just completed the recasting and hanging of the Landulph bells, and on June 12th 1768 the Vestry agreed to pay the money owing for the job, £57 0s 7d, to his brother John. One of the signatories was Thomas Wymond, who the previous year had had his name inscribed on the new sundial over the porch and whose daughter Ann the following year married Fitzantony's younger brother Christopher IV; their first child, Thomas Wymond Pennington, was christened at Landulph in 1770.

The three surviving brothers, **John III, Christopher IV** and **William**, 1740–1781 now continued the business, usually signing themselves "I.P & Co", or "IP CP WP". Their bells at this period are inscribed in the lettering of rounded section, with "grains" forming stops, crosses and other patterns, and the shell mark which had first appeared in 1761. In 1773 a John Pennington was married to Elizabeth Leach at Stoke, where both are described as "sojourners"; this may have been John III, who by this time was in his mid-40s, but Elizabeth's name does not appear on John's tombstone and the register entry for John's death describes him as "single". Four years later, John was witness to a marriage at Stoke. As we have seen, Christopher IV had married Ann Wymond in 1769 at Landulph, where their first three children were baptized – Thomas Wymond (1770), John (1771) and Ann (1776); but the last three, Elizabeth (1782), Christopher (1786) and Mary (1789) were baptized at Stoke Climsland, and as *Broadwoodwidger* bells were cast at Stoke in 1774 it seems that John III and William had by then probably moved the foundry site to Stoke and that Christopher IV later moved to join them there. There is little trace of the

Fig. 111. The entrance to Foundry House, Stoke Climsland, with traces of old outbuildings on the right.

Fig. 112. Crediton: the 7th of the old ring of eight, by John, Christopher & William Pennington, 1774.

Fig. 113. Ann Pennington & Christopher Pennington III's tombstone, Stoke Climsland, 1792.

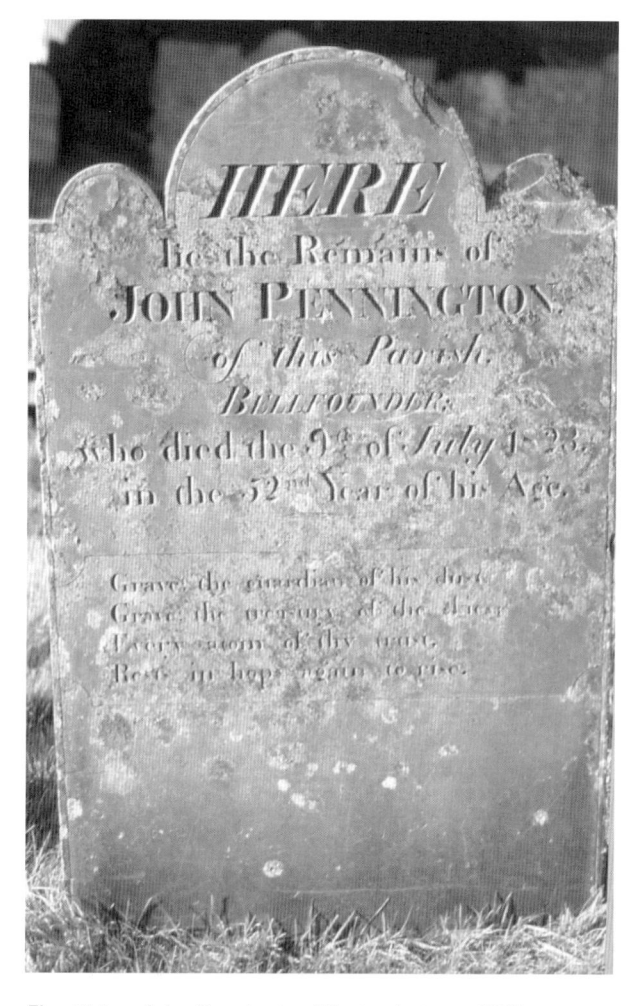

Fig. 114. John Pennington IV's tombstone, 1823.

foundry today, apart from a modern building called "Foundry House", and traces of outbuildings on the right of the entrance, but people remember a ruined building on the site of Foundry House which must have been the foundry.

Business was still plentiful, with at least 36 rings of five or more cast or recast in the ten years from 1771, including their only three known rings of eight, Stoke Crimsland, St Columb Major and *Crediton* – the latter was also their heaviest, and perhaps somewhat beyond their competence. William Pennington died in 1781 – he was buried at Gowan – and Pennington bells from 1783 to 1789 are signed "IP CP": the demand for new and augmented rings may have been declining a little, as the number of known rings of five or more in the 1781–91 decade was 17. In 1790 John III died and was buried at Stoke Climsland; his tombstone in the churchyard carries also the names of his nephews, Christopher IV's sons Thomas Wymond Pennington and Christopher, who died aged 9 years and 6 months respectively. The register gives the cause of his death as "palsy". Two years later Christopher IV's wife Ann died, "hurt in her knee", and her headstone, now sited just west of the tower, also bears the name of her husband.

Christopher Pennington IV and his eldest surviving son **John Pennington IV of Stoke Climsland** sign themselves "CP IP" until Christopher's death in 1799 of "consumption of the flesh". John IV, who had married Ann Rundle the previous year, continued the work, but by now the French wars were having their effect on trade in general and perhaps particularly on non-essential trades like bellfounding; rings of bells amount to fewer than one per year, the last known being the six for *Bovey Tracey* (since recast) in 1816. The latest surviving bell is Liskeard 3/8, 1819, and John IV died in 9th July 1823. His tombstone, marking the end of a remarkable dynasty of bellfounders in the Westcountry, stands next to Christopher & Ann's, and reads:

HERE
lie the remains of
JOHN PENNINGTON
of this Parish
BELLFOUNDER
who died the 9th day of July 1823
in the 52nd year of his age.

Grave! The guardian of his dust
Grave! The treasury of the skies:
Every atom of thy trust
Rests in hope again to rise.

As far as we know John IV and his wife had no children, and the stone makes no mention of a wife, though John Birkle, a descendant of the Stoke Climsland family, cites a Fanny Pennington, born in 1806, as a daughter of John IV and Ann Rundle. Evidently John IV was an active member of the community at Stoke; he was one of the 22 men and 8 women who in about 1821 signed a document committing themselves to practice "pious Psalmody" every Saturday evening at 7 o'clock from October to May and at 8 o'clock from May to October (with one month off for hay and corn-harvests) and to sing in the church at 6.0 every Sunday evening. 40 strokes on the tenor were the signal for their assembly, and anyone who did not arrive after they had finished singing one Psalm-tune was to be fined 2d – those who lived more than one mile from the church had 10 minutes' grace. Being intoxicated, cursing, swearing or blaspheming were punishable by a one-shilling fine, but by far the most serious offence, worth ten shillings and sixpence, was *disposing of any tune which shall be sung in any neighbouring parish*. Rivalry between villages has always been a feature of life in Cornwall (it is not unknown in Devon) and seems to have extended even to pious Psalmody. A monument in the church porch commemorates Thomas Calvert, who in 1746 *introduced into this church four part Psalmody and with indefatigable Pains and perseverance not only encouraged but in a great measure supported it with great reputation upwards of 30 years*: evidently his influence was still alive in 1821.

From 1778 onwards, the round-section lettering was replaced by neat, flat Roman capitals with bold serifs but very little relief [Pl 21h-j]; the shell mark was used almost to the end of the foundry's career, and the 5-dot stop often appears. Quite common also is a 9-dot diamond; coin-impressions were occasionally used including a Swedish copper coin at Lydford in 1789 and a 3-shilling silver bank token at Kingskerswell in 1815. In 1782 two rings of bells, probably cast locally, at *Blackawton* and *Loddiswell*, carried a flat bell mark [Pl 21k] which seems not to appear again, and in 1790 with the arrival of John IV in the firm we see a circular seal-impression bearing two scallop-shells with small sprigs of foliage above and below [Pl 21l]. This mark appears intermittently until at least 1806, and was evidently made by impressing the seal itself in the mould, as the mark on the bell is a "negative"; it may have been a personal seal of John IV. Like the Bilbies, the Penningtons at this period cast their bells with heads which become progressively flatter and squarer towards the heavier end of the ring, no doubt to make the heavier bells turn more quickly. An analysis of weights and diameters shows that Pennington bells of this period are cast to a fairly thin scale, which gives them a deep strike-note for their weight and typically a husky but not unpleasant tone: the late Bishop Wilfred Westall used to say that the bells in North-west Devon has a specially distinctive sound, citing towers like *Sampford Courtenay, Northlew, Belstone* and *Broadwoodwidger* – all rings by the Cornish Penningtons. *Drewsteignton's* tenor of 13cwt 3qr 7lb, (without cannons), 44½" in E, is a good example; until it was rehung, tuned and accurately weighed in 1970 its weight was estimated at "nearly a ton". Pennington bells of the later 18th-century often show the fine grooves of scratch-tuning. There are a few bellframes from this period which from the church records can be definitely attributed to the Penningtons: examples at Poundstock, Cornwall, 1791, and *Dolton*, 1813, show that the family's skill at bellfounding was not matched by their ability as bellhangers; both frames have braces which are too slight and too upright to be effective; a characteristic of both is the use of double tenon-and-mortice joints in the frame-heads and bottom sills. The undated frame at Crediton though massive showed many of the same characteristics, and was probably also by the Penningtons, though it was not part of the 1774 specification.

Between their beginnings in the early 17th century and the death of John IV, the Cornish Penningtons cast well over 900 bells which are either extant or known from the records, of which over 600 survive: from the decade between 1771 and 1780 we know of at least 222 bells were cast by John Christopher & William – a remarkable output for any foundry at that time, and one which has left Devon and Cornwall incomparably richer.

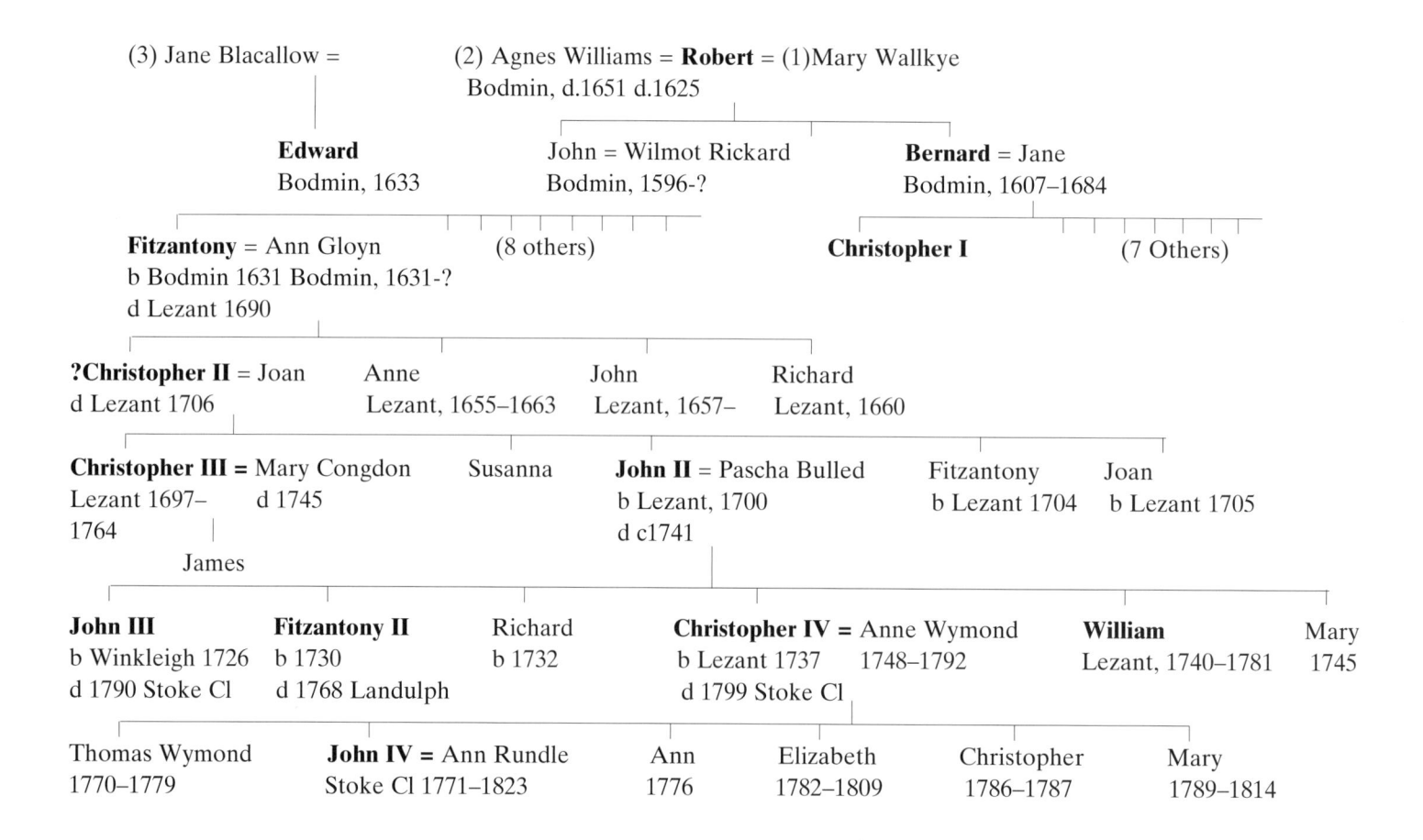

```
(3) Jane Blacallow =            (2) Agnes Williams = Robert = (1)Mary Wallkye
                                                Bodmin, d.1651 d.1625

        Edward              John = Wilmot Rickard            Bernard = Jane
        Bodmin, 1633        Bodmin, 1596-?                   Bodmin, 1607–1684

Fitzantony = Ann Gloyn         (8 others)         Christopher I          (7 Others)
b Bodmin 1631 Bodmin, 1631-?
d Lezant 1690

?Christopher II = Joan    Anne              John            Richard
d Lezant 1706             Lezant, 1655–1663 Lezant, 1657–   Lezant, 1660

Christopher III = Mary Congdon   Susanna    John II = Pascha Bulled   Fitzantony         Joan
Lezant 1697–      d 1745                    b Lezant, 1700            b Lezant 1704      b Lezant 1705
1764                                        d c1741
         James

John III        Fitzantony II      Richard    Christopher IV = Anne Wymond   William              Mary
b Winkleigh 1726 b 1730            b 1732     b Lezant 1737    1748–1792     Lezant, 1740–1781    1745
d 1790 Stoke Cl  d 1768 Landulph              d 1799 Stoke Cl

Thomas Wymond   John IV = Ann Rundle   Ann      Elizabeth       Christopher      Mary
1770–1779       Stoke Cl 1771–1823     1776     1782–1809       1786–1787        1789–1814
```

The Penningtons of Monmouth

A number of bells in Gloucestershire and SE Wales bear the initials I.P. with a skeleton bell mark so similar to the one used by the Tavistock Penningtons that one would assume their founder to have been a member of the clan, even if the 1626 accounts of Gloucester Cathedral did not include the payment of £8 *to John Pennington for Casting the Bell*, for the 11th of the present ring. Bells bearing these initials, often with the skeleton bell, range from 1626 to 1682; **John Pennington I** of Monmouth died in 1665 – he was described as "Gent", and the family had farming interests as well as their bellfounding: we have also heard of a silver chalice dated and hallmarked 1622, bearing the initials I.P. over a bell, which strongly suggests that John I was a silversmith, just as Thomas of Tavistock was a pewterer. John I was succeeded by his son **John II**, who gave up bellfounding in 1682 though he did not die until 1713. Many of the earlier bells from this foundry were inscribed with the familiar motto, "SOLI DEO DETVR GLORIA": the Gloucester Cathedral bell bears an inscription made from a squeeze from (presumably) a Latin Leonine verse on the earlier bell, so that it reads backwards, with the letters recessed into their paterae, but the founder's initials and bell mark are normal.

An account of the Monmouth Penningtons can be found in *Church Bells of Gloucestershire*, by F. Sharpe and M. Bliss, but it was written just before the researches of John Eisel located the family's base at Monmouth. John Eisel has published an account of the family in his *Church Bells of Breconshire* (Logaston Press, 2002).

The existence of three John Penningtons in the same generation (born about 1600) suggests that the connection must have been at least two generations back – possibly through an unrecorded brother of Robert Pennington of Bodmin.

Altogether, surviving bells cast by the Westcountry Penningtons come to over 750, with over 430 which are known to have existed but have been recasst or scrapped; a total output of at least 1,180. In the lists which follow, we have listed the bells chronologically, as with the Cornish family it is often difficult to be sure which Christopher or John was responsible for them. Those listed as "Pennington" were cast by Fitzantony II, in most cases with John III. "JP CP WP" are John III, Christopher IV and William.

Bells by the PENNINGTON FAMILY:

Penningtons of Barnstaple & Exeter

Year	Bell	Founder
1607	Minehead, Som ex7/10	Thomas I
1608	**Yarnscombe 6/6**	Thomas I
1609	*Cullompton* doc	Thomas I
1611	*Sutcombe 5/6*	Thomas I
1616	**Templeton 3/3**	Thomas I
1617	Stoke Pero Som 1/3	Thomas I
	Halberton doc	Thomas I
	Brendon 1/4	Thomas I
1618	**Eggesford 3/3**	Thomas I
1619	Dulverton, Som 4,6,8/8	Thomas I
	East Anstey 6/6	Thomas I
1620	**Iddesleigh 3/6**	Thomas I or II
	Iddesleigh 4/6	Thomas I or II
	Washford Pyne 5/6	Thomas I
	Cheldon 3/4	Thomas I
	Tiverton doc	Thomas I
1621	**Braunton** doc	Thomas I or II
1622	*Modbury 2-6/6* doc	Thomas I & II
	Hollacombe 1/3	Thomas I
1623	*Kingsteignton 7/8*	Thomas II
	Torquay, Torre 6/6	Thomas II
	Trusham 4/6	Thomas II
	Coldridge doc at Lapford	Thomas II
	Lapford doc	Thomas II
1624	Withypool, So **5/6**	Thomas II
	Elworthy So 3/4	Thomas II
1625	*Exeter St Stephen 1,3/3*	Thomas II
	Payhembury 2/6	Thomas II
	Tetcott 1/1	Thomas II
	Milton Damarel 2/3	Thomas II
	Yarcombe 5/6	Thomas II
1626	Yeovil Som 6,8 & 9/10	Thomas II
	Exeter St Olave 2/2	Thomas II
	E Portlemouth 5/6	Thomas II
	Holcombe Rogus 4/6	Thomas II

	Coffinswell 5/6	Thomas II	1640	**Dulverton So 5/8**	Thomas II
	Loders Do 6/6	Thomas II		**Topsham 4/6**	Thomas II
	Trent Do 5/5	Thomas II		**Woodleigh 3/5**	Thomas II
	Kilton So 4/4	Thomas II		**Woodleigh 4/5**	Thomas II
	Muchelney So 5/5	Thomas II		*Lapford doc at Chawleigh*	Thomas II
	Taunton St James 6,8/8	Thomas II	1641	**Paignton 6/6**	Thomas II
	Yarcombe 6/6	Thomas II		**Stoke Canon 4/6**	Thomas II
1627	**Colebrooke 4/6**	Thomas II	1642	**Burlescombe 6/6**	Thomas II
	Colebooke 3,5,6/6	Thomas II	1648	**Stoke Gabriel 4/6**	John
	Awliscombe 5/6	Thomas II	1650	**Spreyton 5/6**	John
1628	*Totnes doc 2*	Thomas II		*Clyst Honiton 5/8*	John
	Tiverton 5/5 doc	Thomas II		*Littleham (S) doc*	John
1629	**Woodbury 8/8**	Thomas II	1652	*Ottery St Mary 5/8*	John
	Doddiscombesleigh 4/6	Thomas II		*Eggesford 2/3*	John
	Iddesleigh 5/6	Thomas II	1653	**Sampford Spiney 4/5**	John & Tho (T)
1630	**Gittisham 3/5**	Thomas II	1654	**Thurlestone 6/6**	John & Tho (T)
	Exeter Cathedral 6b/12	Thomas II		*Thurlestone 4/6 J*	ohn
1631	*Yarnscombe 4/6*	Thomas II		*W Anstey 4/4*	John
	Abbotsham 3/6	Thomas II		*Doddiscombesleigh 5/6*	John
	Churchstow 2/3	Thomas II		*Lit Torrington Taddiport 1/1*	John
1632	**Widecombe-I-t-Moor 5,7 & 8/8**	Thomas II		**Holcombe Burnell 6/6**	John
	Widecombe-I-t-Moor 3,5/5	Thomas II	1655	**Pinhoe 7/8**	John
1633	**Combeinteignhead 6/6**	Thomas II		**Withycombe St John 1/1**	John
	Aveton Gifford doc	Thomas II	1656	*Bickleigh 3/6*	John
	Willand 3/3	Thomas II		*Zeal Monachorum doc*	John
	Salcombe Regis 2/3	Thomas II		**Exeter St Mary Steps 1,2,3 4/4**	John
	N Tawton doc 2	Thomas II	1656	*Goodleigh doc*	John
1634	*Revelstoke 2/2*	Thomas II	1657	**Ven Ottery 2/3**	John
1635	**Branscombe 4/6**	Thomas II	1658	**Exeter Cathedral 5/12**	John
	Payhembury 1/6	Thomas II	1661	*Talaton 2/6*	John
	Berry Pomeroy 5/8	Thomas II		**Culmstock 8/8**	John
	Combeinteignhead 1/4	Thomas II		**Exeter Liverydole 1/1**	John
1636	**Burlescombe 5/6**	Thomas II		*Lapford doc, at Chulmleigh*	John
	Marldon 3.5/6	Thomas II	1662	**Thorverton 9/10 J**	John
	Woodland 3/3	Thomas II		*Sidbury 4/8*	John
	Holcombe Burnell 3/6	Thomas II	1663	*Sidbury 5/8*	John
1637	**Abbotskerswell 6/6**	Thomas II		**Gittisham 4/5**	John
	Coffinswell 6/6	Thomas II		**Rockbeare 3/6**	John
	Burlescombe 2,3 & 4/6	Thomas II		**Huntsham 7/8**	John
	Eggesford 1/3	Thomas II		*Cruwys Morchard doc*	John
	Salcombe Regis 3/3	Thomas II		*Langford Budville So 3/6*	John
	Hennock 4/4	Thomas II		**Seaton 5,7/8**	John
	Hennock 2/4	Thomas II		St Keyne Co 6/6	TP JP
	Bridford 6/6	Thomas II		*Southleigh 3/4*	John
1638	*Burlescombe 6/6*	Thomas II	1664	*Bickington 5,6/6*	John
1639	*Culmstock 7/8*	Thomas II		*Petersmarland 3/6*	John
	Ayshford Chapel 1/1	Thomas II		*Fremington 6/6*	John
	Marldon 6/6	Thomas II		*Abbotskerswell doc*	John

	Bridford 3/6	John	1696	*Powderham 5/6*	Thomas III
	Horwood 3/3	John		*Branscombe 3/6*	Thomas III
	Colebrooke doc	John	1700	**Dunchideock 1/3**	Thomas III
1665	**Cheriton Fitzpaine 6/6**	John	1702	*Kenn* doc	Thos III & JS
	Huntshaw 2/3	John	1705	**Abbotskersell 5/6**	Thomas III
	Exeter Heavitree 1/4	John	1709	*Bickleigh (E) 4/6*	Thos III & NT
1666	**Ideford 6/6**	John		**Topsham 2,3/6**	Thomas III
	Kentisbeare 4/6	John	1710	*Cheriton Fitzpaine* doc	Thomas III
	Harpford 3/3	John	1711	*Kenn* doc	Thomas III
	Nynehead So 3/6	John	1712	**Doddiscombesleigh 3/6**	Thomas III
1667	*Sidmouth 7/10*	John		Powerstock Do 3/6	Thomas III
	Colyton 6/8	John		*Askerswell Do 1, 5/5*	Thomas III
	Exeter Heavitree 4/4	John	1713	**Clyst Hydon 3/6**	Thomas III
1669	**Branscombe 2/6**	Thomas III	1714	*Southleigh 2/4*	Thomas III
	Plymtree 5/6	Thomas III	1716	**Shillingford 1/1**	Thomas III
1670	**Knowstone 5/6**	Thomas III	1717	*Bishopsteignton* doc	Thomas III
	Ottery St Mary 3/8	Thomas III	1718	*Rewe* doc	Thomas III
	Clyst Hydon 3/6	Thomas III		**Exeter Museum**	Thomas III
	Crediton doc	Thomas III	1720	*Ide 4/6*	Thomas III
	Runnington So 1/2	Thomas III			
1671	*Ottery St Mary 6/8*	Thomas III		**Penningtons of Tavistock:**	
	Axmouth 3/3	Thomas III	1653	**Sampford Spiney 4/5**	Tho & JP Ex
	Combe Raleigh 3/3	Thomas III	1654	*Thurlestone 4/6*	Thomas
	Gidleigh 3/5	Thomas III		**Thurlestone 6/6**	Tho & JP Ex
	Branscombe 6/6	Thomas III		*Plymstock* doc	Thomas
1672	**Kilmington 6/6**	Thomas III	1658	**Milton Damarel 3/3**	Tho & JP Ex
	Calverleigh 4/6	Thomas III	1659	*Sampfod Courtenay* doc	?
1673	*Exeter St Stephen 2/3*	Thomas III	1663	St Keyne Co 6/6	Tho & John I
	Thorverton 8,10/10	Thomas III	1668	**Cookbury 3/3**	John I
1674	**Thorverton 7/10**	Thomas III	1669	**E Down 1/4**	Tho & John I
	Clyst St Mary 2/3	Thomas III		**Parracombe 4/6**	Tho & John I
	Cheldon 2/4	Thomas III		**Merton 4/6**	Tho & John I
	Littleham (S) 7/8	Thomas III	1670	**Torrington Market House**	John I
1675	*Exeter St Martin 1/1*	Thomas III	1671	**Newton St Petrock 1/3**	John I
1676	**Trusham 6/6**	Thomas III	1674	**Stoke Gabriel 5/6**	John I
	Stokeinteignhead 5/6	Thomas III		*Stoke Gabriel 3/6*	John I
	Powderham 4/6	Thomas III		**Abbotsham 5/6**	John I
	Netherexe 1/1	Thomas III		**Sampford Spiney 3/5**	John I
1677	**Down St Mary 6/6**	Thomas III	1675	**Wembury 4/6**	John I
	Exeter St Petrock 5/6	Thomas III	1682	**Instow 3/3**	John I
	Woodbury doc	Thomas III		*Hartland* doc 4	John I ?
1678	**Spreyton 3/6**	Thomas III		*Plymouth Egg Buckland 2/3*	John I
1680	*Ottery St Mary 4/8*	Thomas III	1683	**Bomdleigh 1/4**	John I
1683	**Exeter St Petrock 4/6**	Thomas III	1684	**Hollacombe 3/3**	John I
1684	**Trusham 3/6**	Thomas III		*Coryton 5/5*	John I
1687	Langford Budville So 5/6	Thomas III	1689	*Bridford 5/6*	John I
1692'	**Littleham (S) 8/8**	Thos III & JS		*Tedburn St Mary* doc	John I
1695	*Twitchen 1/3*	Thos III & JS	1690	**Kingston 3/6**	John I

Year	Place	Founder	Year	Place	Founder
1693	*Bow* doc	John I		Morval Co 3,4/4	John II
1697	**Thurlestone 2/6**	John I & II	1717	**Thrushelton 4,6/6**	Chr II & J II
1698	South Hill Co 1-4/5	John I & JS	1718	**Thrushelton 2,5/6**	Chr II & J II
1702	**Torquay St Marych'ch RC 1/1**	John I & II		*Lawhitton Co 1,3,4/4*	Chr II
1706	**Charleton 6/6**	John I & II	1719	St Enoder Co 5,6/8	J II ?
	Charleton 5/6	John I & II		Dodbrooke 4/6	Chr II & J II
1709	**Coryton 4/5**	John II	1720	**Marytavy 1,2,4/5**	Chr II & J II
				Marytavy 3/5	Chr II
Penningtons of Cornwall:				*Sutcombe 5/6*	? Chr II
1622	St Allen Co 2/3	Robert	1722	**Buckland Filleigh 2-5/5**	John II
1631	*Wembury 6/6*	Robert		St Mellion Co 4/6	Chr II & John II
1632	*Blisland (2) doc*	Robert		*St Mellion Co 3/6*	Chr II & John II
1633	**Denbury 2/5**	Robert		Lezant Co 2,3/6	Chr III
	E Ogwell 4,5/6	Robert		*Clannaborough 2/3*	John II
1637	Mylor Co 2/3	Robert		**Petertavy 5/6**	Chr III & John II
1656	**Frithelstock 6/6**	Fitzantony I	1723	Rame Co 3/3	John II
	Bondleigh 4/4	Fitzantony I		**E Allington 3,4,5/6**	Chr III & John II
1657	*St Dennis 5/8*	Bernard		*E Allington 2/6* C	hr III & John II
1657	**Mortehoe 6/6**	Fitzantony I		**Buckland Mon 3 - 7/8**	Chr III & John II
1658	**Parracombe 6/6**	Fitzantony I		**Buckland Mon 8/8**	Chr III & John II
1664	**Virginstow 1/1**	?		*Holbeton doc 3*	John II
1668	Sheviock Co 2/2	Chr I & Fz I		Lezant Co 1/6	John II
1671	*St Colan Co 3/3*	Fitz I	1724	**Winkleigh 4 - 8/8**	John II
1675	St Mawgan in Pydar 8/8	JP RP	1725	**Plympton St Mary 5,7/8**	Chr III
1676	*Goodleigh doc*	Fitz I		*Plympton St Mary 6/8*	Chr III
1678	*St Veep Co doc*	John I		***S Milton* doc**	Chr III
1680	Warbstow Co 2/3	Chr I	1726	**Coldridge 4/6**	John II
1681	St Buryan Co 1/4	Chr I		*Coldridge 2,3/6*	John II
1682	St John Co 2/3	Chr I		**Nymet Rowland 1/1**	John II
	St Veep 1,2,3/3	Edward		**Spreyton 6/6**	John II
1686	**Frithelstock 6/6**	Chr I or II		*Kingsteignton 3/5*	John II & ES
1687	**Monkokehampton 4/4**	Chr I or II	1727	**Ashbury 3/3**	John II
1689	*Bodmin Co doc*	Chr I or II		Botus Flemng Co 3,6/6	Chr III
1690	**Upton Hellions doc**	Edward	1728	*Stokeinteignhead 3/6*	John II & ES
1691	**Stoke Canon 3,5/6**	Chr II	1729	*Putford 5/6*	Chr III
	Pinhoe 6/8	Chr II		S Petherwin Co 2,3,5/6	Chr III & John II
1699	Camelford T H 1/1	Edward		S Petherwin Co 4/6	Chr III & John II
1700	E Looe Co 1/1	Pennington	1731	St Cubert Co 1,2/3	John II
1703	*Feock 3/3*	Chr II		*St Keverne Co 6/8*	John II
1705	**Dunterton 2/3**	Chr II		*St Martin by Looe Co 4/4*	Chr III
1707	Davidstow Co 2,3/6	Chr II		**Ashburton Town Hall 1/1**	John II
1710	**Stowford 2-5/6**	Chr II		*St Cleer doc*	?P with A G
	Stowford 6/6	Chr II	1733	St Eval Co 3,4,6/6	John II
1712	*Treneglos Co 1,2,3/4*	Chr II		*St Eval Co 5/6*	John II
1713	*Clawton 6/6*	Chr II		**Plymouth St Andrew doc**	John II
	Putford 6/6	John II	1734	**Dean Prior 4,5,6/6**	John II
1714	*Cardynham Co 1-5/5*	Chr II		**Dean Prior 2,3/6**	John II
1715	Morval Co 1,2/4	Chr II		St Juliot Co 5/6	John II

	St Juliot Co 6/6	John II	1757	*St Columb Minor Co 4 – 8/8*	Fitz II
	Whitchurch doc	Mr Penn'n	1758	**Pyworthy 2-6/6**	Fitz II
1735	Liskeard Co 7/8	John II		**Lewtrenchard 5/6**	Fitz II
	Tintagel Co 2/6	John II		St Breward Co 2 – 6/6	Fitz II
1736	*Altarnun Co 4 - 8/8*	John II		*St Clether Co former 4/4*	Fitz II
	Lawhitton Co 4/6	John II		**Clovelly 3 – 6/6**	Chr III
1738	*St Dennis Co 7/8*	John II		**Milton Damarel 1/3**	Chr III
	St Buryan ?	?	1759	**Petersmarland 4/6**	Fitz II
1739	**Clawton 4/6**	John II		Sancreed Co 1/3	Fitz II
	Clawton 5/6	John II	1760	*St Stephens/S'ash Co 2 - 6/6*	Fitz II
	Plymstock 4,5,6,8/8	John II	1761	**Belstone 2 – 6/6**	Fitz II
	Plymstock 7/8	John II		*Petertavy 2/6*	Pennington
	Launceston St Th Co 2/6	?	1762	**Moretonhampstead 3 - 8/8**	Pennington
	Menheniot Co 2, 5,6/6	John II		**S Huish 2/4**	Pennington
	Menheniot Co 3,4/6	John II		**S Pool 1 – 5/6**	Pennington
1740	**St Giles-on-the-Heath 1 - 4/5**	? Chr II or III		*S Pool 6/6*	Pennington
1741	**Pancrasweek 1,2/5**	? Chr II or III	1763	**Halwell 1,2,3,5,6/6**	Pennington
	Withiel Co 4,6/6	William		*Halwell 4/6*	Pennington
	Withiel Co 5/6	William		**Rattery 2,3,5/5**	Pennington
1742	*Laneast Co 3/6*	Chr II or III &		*Rattery 4/5*	Pennington
		D Masters		**Throwleigh 2,3,6/6**	Pennington
1743	St John Corn 3/3	Chr II & III		*Throwleigh 4,5/6*	Pennington
	S Petherwin Co 6/6	Chr III	1764	**Sampford Spiney 5/5**	Pennington
	Petertavy 6/6	?Chr II or III		Fowey Co 8/8	Pennington
1744	*Mabe Co 3 – 6/6C*	hr II or III & TC		*Lostwithiel Co 2 – 6/6*	Pennington
1748	**Ermington 2,5,6/6**	Chr III & Jn III		Luxulyan Co 6/6	Pennington
	Ermington 3,4/6	Chr III & Jn III		*St Issey Co 3,6/6*	Pennington
1750	**Dunterton 2/3**	Chr III		Antony Co 1 – 5/6	Pennington
	Michaelstow Co 5/5	Chr III	1765	**Bickleigh (W) 2,4,5,6/6**	Pennington
1751	Philleigh Co 3/3	Chr III		*Bickleigh (W) 3/6*	Pennington
	Philleigh Co 1,2/3	Chr III		**Filleigh 5/6**	Pennington
1752	*Merton 6/6*	Chr III		**N Tawton 3 – 7/8**	Pennington
1753	Duloe Co 2,6/6	Chr III		*N Tawton 8/8*	Pennington
	Duloe Co 3,4,5/6	Chr III		**Bow 5/6**	Pennington
1754	**Plympton St Mary 5/8**	Chr III		St Ive Co 6/6	Pennington
	St Martin by Looe Co (?)	Chr III		**Plymstock ,Saltram Ho 1/1**	Pennington
	St Winnow Co 5/6	Chr III		Quethiock Co 3/3	Jn III & Fitz II
	Lezant Co 4/6	Chr III	1766	**Plympton St Mary 3/8**	Jn III & Fitz II
1755	Duloe Co 2,6/6	Chr III		**S Milton 2 – 6/6**	Jn III & Fitz II
	Duloe Co 3,4/6	Chr III		St Erme Co 2 - 4/6	Pennington
	Liskeard Co 4/8	Chr III		*St Erme Co 5,6/6*	Pennington
	Liskeard Co 6/8	Chr III		Lamorran Co 1/1	Pennington
1756	**Alverdoscott 1/3**	Chr III		St Newlyn East Co 2 – 6/6	Pennington
	Tresillian Co 2/3	Chr III		Botus Fleming Co 2/6	Pennington
	Ruan Lanihorne Co 1/2	Chr III	1767	Gwinnear Co 1 – 4/6	Pennington
	Newton Ferrers 3 – 6/6	Fitz II		*Gwinnear Co 5,6/6*	Pennington
	Trevalga Co 2/3	Fitz II		Crantock Co 1,2,3/6	Pennington
	Holbeton doc	Fitz II		*Crantock Co 4/6*	Pennington

	Bratton Clovelly 1 – 6/6	Jn III & Fitz II		Veryan 6/6	JP CP WP
	Chertion Fitzpaine 3/6	Jn III & Fitz II	1773	**Tamerton Foliot 1 – 6/6**	JP CP WP
	Rockbeare 4/5	Jn III & Fitz II		Lanreath Co 1 – 6/6	JP CP WP
	Perranzabuloe Co 3/6	Jn III & Fitz II		Pelynt Co 4/6	JP CP WP
	Lewannick Co 1 – 6/6	Jn III & Fitz II		*Talland Co 3/6*	JP CP WP
1768	**Exbourne 2 – 6/6**	Penningtons		Trevalga Co 3/3	JP CP WP
	Landulph Co 1,2,3,6/6	Penningtons		St Dominic Co 1 – 6/6	JP CP WP
	Landulph Co 4,5/6	Penningtons		Calstock Co 1 – 6/6	JP CP WP
	Plympton St Maurice 3-8/8	Jn III	1774	Tywardreath Co 1 – 6/6	JP CP WP
1769	**Lewtrenchard 3/6**	JP CP WP		**Crediton 1- 8/8**	JP CP WP
	Milton Abbot 1 – 6/6	JP CP WP		Lanteglos-by-Fowey Co 5,6/6	JP CP WP
	Shaugh Prior 1 – 5/6	JP CP WP		*Lanteglos-by-Fowey Co 1 – 4/6*	JP CP WP
	Shaugh Prior 6/6	JP CP WP	1775	**Bere Ferrers 1 – 6/6**	JP CP WP
	Sheepstor 2 – 6/6	JP CP WP		**Broadwoodwidger 2,3,5,6/6**	JP CP WP
	Werrington Co 1,2/2	JP CP WP		*Broadwoodwidger 4/6*	JP CP WP
	Walkhampton 1,3 – 6/6	JP CP WP		St Ive Co 3/6	JP CP WP
	Walkhampton 2/6	JP CP WP		St Germans Co 4 – 8/8	JP CP WP
	Landrake Co 1/3	JP CP WP		*St Germans Co 3/8*	JP CP WP
1770	**Cheriton Bishop 2 – 5/6**	JP CP WP		**Slapton 3,5,6/6**	JP CP WP
	Cheriton Bishop 6/6	JP CP WP		*Slapton 4/6, former 5/5*	JP CP WP
	N Tawton 8/8	JP CP WP	1776	St Columb Major 3,4/8	JP CP WP
	Cheriton Fitzpaine 2/6	JP CP WP		*St Columb Major 1,2,5-8/8*	JP CP WP
	Cornwood 2,3,5,6/6	JP CP WP		St Mellion 5/6	JP CP WP
	Cornwood 4/6	JP CP WP		**Stokenham 2,3,4/6**	JP CP WP
	Devonport Dockyard 3-8/8	John III		*Stokenham 1,5,6/6*	JP CP WP
	Stowford 1/6	John III	1777	Redruth Co 3,6,7/8	JP CP WP
	Tedburn St Mary 2,3/6	JP CP WP		St Allen Co 2,3/3	JP CP WP
	Sampford Courtenay 1 – 5/6	JP CP WP		St Neot Co 1 – 6/6	JP CP WP
	Sampford Courtenay 6/6	JP CP WP		St Wenn Co 1 – 5/6	JP CP WP
	St Veep Co 1 – 6/6	JP CP WP		*Callington Co 2 –6/6*	JP CP WP
1771	Jacobstow Co 1 – 6/6	JP CP WP		*Perranzabuloe Co 4/6*	JP CP WP
	Breage Co 2/2	JP CP WP		**Stoke Fleming 1,2,3,5,6/6**	JP CP WP
	Sithney Co 1 – 3/3	JP CP WP		*Stoke Fleming 4/6*	JP CP WP
	St Winnow Co 2,6/6	JP CP WP	1778	**Parkham 1 – 6/6**	JP CP WP
	St Winnow 3,4,5/6	JP CP WP		**Heanton Punchardon 1-6/6**	JP CP WP
	Stoke Climsland Co 1 – 8/8	JP CP WP		**Sydenham Damarel 2 – 6/6**	JP CP WP
	St Nectans Ch Co 1/1	Jn III		*Stratton Co 4 – 8/8*	JP CP WP
	St Blazey Co 3/3	JP CP WP	1779	**Aveton Gifford 1 – 6/6**	JP CP WP
1772	**Ashwater 2,3/6**	JP CP WP		**Yealmpton 1,3,5,6/6**	JP CP WP
	Ashwater 4,5,6/6	JP CP WP		*Yealmpton 2,4/6*	JP CP WP
	Kelly 1 – 4,6/6	JP CP WP		**Meavy 5/6**	JP CP WP
	Kelly 5/6	JP CP WP		*Meavy 1 – 4,6/6*	JP CP WP
	Northlew 2 – 5/6	JP CP WP		St Colan Co 2/3	JP CP WP
	Northlew 6/6	JP CP WP		**Chivelstone 5/6**	JP CP WP
	Black Torrington 1,2,3,5/6	JP CP WP		*Kingsbridge 1/6*	JP CP WP
	Black Torrington 4,6/6	JP CP WP		North Petherwin Co 2 – 6/6	JP CP WP
	Gorran Co 1,3,4,6/6	JP CP WP		St Stephens/Laun Co 3 – 8/8	JP CP WP
	Gorran Co 2, 5/6	JP CP WP		**Buckland-tout-Saints 1/1**	JP CP WP

1780	**Ashton 2 – 6/6**	J P CP WP	1789	*Exeter St Thomas 3 – 8/8*	Jn III & Chr IV
	Holbeton 1,2,3,5/6	JP CP WP		**Lydford 2 – 6/6**	Jn III & Chr IV
	Holbeton 4,6/6	JP CP WP		St Cleer Co 1 – 4,6/6	Jn III & Chr IV
	Plymouth St Budeaux 3,4/6	JP CP WP		*St Cleer Co 5/6*	Jn III & Chr IV
	Plymouth St Budeaux 2,5,6/6	JP CP WP	1790	**Loddiswell 5/6**	Chr IV & Jn IV
1781	**Broadhempston 2 – 6/6**	JP CP WP		Blisland Co 1 – 6/6	Chr IV & Jn IV
	Chudleigh 6,7,8/8	JP CP WP		**Petetavy 3,4/6**	Chr IV & Jn IV
	Chudleigh 3,4,5/8	JP CP WP		St Ive Co 5/6	Chr IV & Jn IV
	Cornworthy 1 – 6/6	Jn III & Chr IV		St Winnow Co 3/6	Chr IV & Jn IV
	Highweek 4 – 8/8	JP CP WP		*Welcombe 4/6*	Chr IV & Jn IV
	Highweek 3/8	JP CP WP		*Poughill Co 2,6/6*	Chr IV & Jn IV
	Jacobstowe 2/5 J	P CP WP	1791	Poundstock Co 2 – 6/6	Chr IV & Jn IV
	Probus Co 6/8	Jn III & Chr IV		St Gennys Co 1 – 4/4	Chr IV & Jn IV
1782	**Blackawton 1 – 5/6**	Jn III & Chr IV	1792	**Shebbear 2 – 5/6**	Chr IV & Jn IV
	Blackawton 6/6	Jn III & Chr IV		*Shebbear 6/6*	Chr IV & Jn IV
	Loddiswell 2/6	Jn III & Chr IV	1793	**St Giles-on-the-Heath 5/5**	Chr IV & Jn IV
	Loddiswell 3 – 6/6	Jn III & Chr IV		*Tremaine Co 2/2*	Chr IV & Jn IV
1783	Tresillian Co 3/3	Jn III & Chr IV		Laneast Co 4/6	Chr IV & Jn IV
	Davidstow Co 4/6	Jn III & Chr IV		*Newton Ferrers 2/6*	Chr IV & Jn IV
	Fowey Co 3/8	Jn III & Chr IV	1794	North Hill Co 1,3,4,6/6	Chr IV & Jn IV
	Lanteglos/Camfd Co 2,4,5,6/6	Jn III & Chr IV		*North Hill Co 2,5/6*	Chr IV & Jn IV
	Lanteglos/Camfd Co 3/6	Jn III & Chr IV	1797	**Lapford 1 – 6/6**	Chr IV & Jn IV
	St Juliot Co 3/6	Jn III & Chr IV	1798	*Dodbrooke 2/6*	Chr IV & Jn IV
1784	**Dawlish 3 – 8/8**	Jn III & Chr IV		*Sherford 5/6*	Chr IV & Jn IV
	Drewsteignton 1 – 6/6	Jn III & Chr IV		*Chivelstone 4/6*	Chr IV & Jn IV
	Botus Fleming Co 1/6	Jn III & Chr IV	1799	**Northlew 6/6**	John IV
	St Martin/Looe Co 1/4	Jn III & Chr IV		**Thrushelton 3/6**	John IV
1785	**Christow 3 – 8/8**	Jn III & Chr IV		St Keyne Co 5/6	John IV
	Dunsford 1 – 6/6	Jn III & Chr IV		*Sherford 3/6*	John IV
	Tintagel Co 4/6	Jn III & Chr IV	1801	*Poughill Co 6/6*	John IV
1786	**Whitchurch 1 – 6/6**	Jn III & Chr IV	1802	**Kelly 5/6**	John IV
	Atherington 1 – 4,6/6	Jn III & Chr IV	1803	**Cheriton Bishop 4/6**	John IV
	Atherington 5/6	Jn III & Chr IV		St Pinnock Co 1 – 4/4	John IV
	Quethiock Co 2/3	Jn III & Chr IV	1804	**Little Torrington 2 – 6/6**	John IV
1787	**Ashton 1/6**	Jn III & Chr IV		**Lewtrenchard 6/6**	John IV
	Brixham 5/10	Jn III & Chr IV		**Stowford 6/6**	John IV
	St Mabyn Co 3,5,8/8	Jn III & Chr IV		Talland Co 2,3/6	John IV
	St Mabyn Co 4,6,7/8	Jn III & Chr IV	1805	*Helland Co 1/1*	John IV
	St Cuby 1/1	Jn III & Chr IV		Linkinhorne Co 1,2,4 – 6/6	John IV
	St Enoder Co ?8/8	Jn III & Chr IV		*Linkinhorne Co 3/6*	John IV
	Tregony Town Hall Co 1/1	Jn III & Chr IV		Lesnewth Co 4/6	John IV
1788	**Bigbury 2 – 6/6**	Jn III & Chr IV	1806	**Petrockstowe 2 – 4/6**	John IV
	Landkey 1 – 6/6	Jn III & Chr IV		*Petrockstowe 5,6/6*	John IV
	Burrington 1 – 4,6/6	Jn III & Chr IV	1807	**Jacobstowe** De **5/5**	John IV
	Burrington 5/6	Jn III & Chr IV	1808	**Inwardleigh 6/6**	John IV
	Pilton clock	Jn III & Chr IV		Lanivet Co 3 – 7/8	John IV
	Talland Co 5/6	Jn III & Chr IV		*Lanivet Co 8/8*	John IV
	Kenwyn Co 5/8	Jn III & Chr IV		St Juliot Co 2,4/6	John IV

	St Erme 5,6/6	John IV		Fowey Co 4,5/8	John IV
1809	Pillaton Co 1,2/6	John IV		St Minver Co 1/6	John IV
	St Stephens/Saltash Co 3/6	John IV		*Sancreed Co 2/3*	John IV
	Marytavy 2/5	John IV	1815	**Kingskerswell 2,3,4/6**	John IV
	Marytavy 5/5	John IV		*Kingskerswell 5,6/6*	John IV
1810	**Petrockstowe 5/6**	John IV	1816	**Langtree 2,3,6/6**	John IV
1811	***Bradford 3 – 6/6***	John IV		*Langree 4,5/6*	John IV
1812	***Lewtrenchard 2,4/6***	John IV	1818	***Bovey Tracey 3 – 8/8***	John IV
1813	***Dolton 1 – 5/6***	John IV		***Bridgerule 8/8***	John IV
	Laneast Co 5/6	John IV	1819	Liskeard Co 3/8	John IV
1814	***Meavy 4/6***	John IV		*Lezant Co 5/6*	John IV

7

BELLHANGING & BELLHANGERS

A SWINGING BELL CREATES powerful forces both vertically and horizontally, and the structure in which it is mounted needs to be as rigid as possible if the bell is to be controlled and the building is not to be damaged. So bellhanging always demanded a high standard of engineering skill and carpentry, while the gear also needed expert ironworking if it was to be safe. A bell is hung between a pair of trusses to which the bearings are fixed, and a bellframe for more than one bell is laid out with the trusses making a series of "pits" arranged ideally so that the loads on the tower are imposed evenly, and the ropes fall in something close to a circle. The historical development of bellframes can be seen primarily in the evolution of the trusses or frame-sides, which consist of horizontal bottom sills and frame-heads, king-posts and other uprights, and canted braces.

Devon is not rich in early bellframes, thanks largely to the enthusiasm of our ringers in the 18th and 19th centuries. The earliest are constructed with king-posts braced with curved braces, and long frame-heads; the curved braces, being cut from grown crooks, had the advantage of having their tenons at either end cut on the straight grain. Such frames [115A] survive at *Ashcombe*, *Hennock* (much altered) and *Upton Hellions*. The next group also has king-posts, but the braces are mortised into the junction of the king-posts and the frame-heads, – an example at *Newton St Petrock*. This type is followed in turn by trusses with the braces (curved or straight) meeting the frame-heads only [115B], as at *Horwood* and *Puddington*, where one frame-side is preserved in the church. Finally the king-post was found to be unnecessary, and we find frames with braces deeper than before but still curved [115C] (although there was now no structural advantage in the curvature). The dating of these changes is far from certain, and there are wide regional variations across Britain in both the design of frames and the dates at which developments occur; no early bellframes in Devon are dated, but we can assign a fairly definite date to the abandonment of the king-post in Devon – at least in Exeter which one might expect to be in the lead. *Exeter, St Mary Steps* had a ring of three in 1552, and a frame with curved braces but without king-posts was built to house them between that date and 1656 when the bells were recast into four and the frame was modified accordingly. A bell of 1655 at *St John-in-the-Wilderness (Withycombe Raleigh)* is hung in a similar frame, and there is another of 1675 at *St Martin's, Exeter*. On the basis of this we can conjecture that braced king-post frames in Devon probably date from before, say, 1550 and

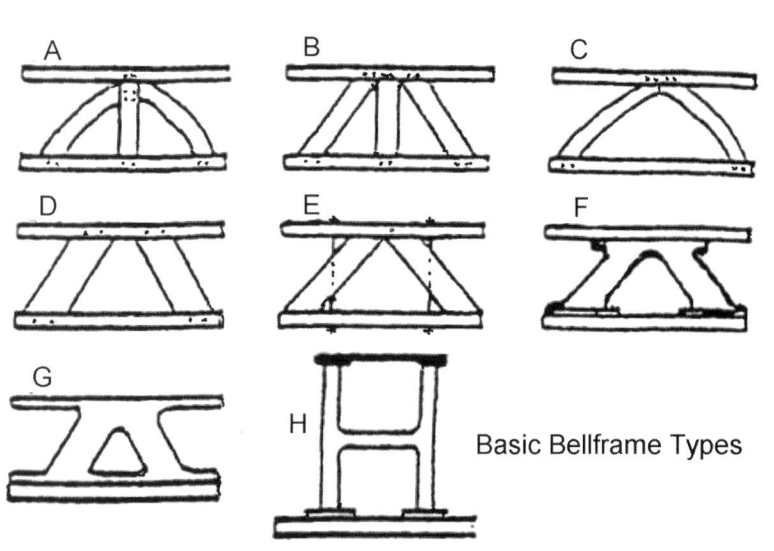

Basic Bellframe Types

Fig. 115. Basic bellframe types.

153

Fig. 116. Part of the early bellframe at Hennock, a braced-king-post frame much modified. Note the mortices, for struts to support an earlier short frame-head.

Fig. 117. Puddington old bellframe, with braces meeting the frame-head and the king-post.

Fig. 118. St John-in-the Wilderness, Exmouth. The king-post has been dispensed with, but the braces are still curved. The frame is probably of the same date as the bell, 1655.

frames with king-posts and braced frame-heads between 1550 and 1650. By the beginning of the 18th-century it seems to have been recognized that straight braces were as effective as curved if not more so, and the familiar braced-frame-head frame [115D] has been the norm for timber frames ever since: the frame at *Brushford* has straight braces and is dated 1741 (Ellacombe missed the inscription and believed the frame to be mediaeval). Another important change which took place in the 17th or early 18th century was in the foundation of the frame. Early frames are usually supported by the horizontal bottom sills into which the posts and braces are mortised, with the sills spanning the tower and their ends resting on an offset or on corbels: this was satisfactory for rings of three or four bells hung side-by-side, but as bell numbers increased and layouts became more complex, a set of main foundation-beams came to be used below the bottom sills, which were reduced in size accordingly and jointed together to form a grillage. Bellhangers in those days – and indeed until the 19th-century – could be fairly cavalier

Fig. 119. One side of a bell-pit wedged into a window opening, at St Mary Steps, Exeter, probably 1656.

Fig. 121. Most of the brackets under the frame at Crediton are made from gown forks of oak, and have been dated to the early 16th century.

Fig. 120. The Axmouth bellframe; each pair of braces is made from a forked piece of oak.

in their treatment of belfries; at *St Mary Steps, Exeter* one frame-side is jammed into a window opening, and the same expedient was used by John Barrett in 1845 to cram eight bells into the tower at *Sowton*.

Timber bellframes for full-circle ringing are almost invariably built of oak, but there are pitch-pine frames at *Kenton* and *Powderham*, and *North Bovey* has a magnificent frame made by Mears & Stainbank of Burma teak, and in the 19th-century some single bells and a few rings of three (e.g. *Hittisleigh*) were hung for full-circle ringing in softwood frames.

One very unusual, if not unique, bellframe in the county is at *Axmouth* where each pair of braces is made in one piece from an inverted section of a forked tree. Dating such a frame as this without using dendrochronology is very uncertain, but it was

Fig. 122. The bellframe as Dolton, just before it was dismantled. Built by John Pennington IV in 1813, it was fastened with trenails, and tiebolted in the 19th-century.

Fig. 123. A tiebolted oak frame by Harry Stokes, 1897, at St Michael's, Teignmouth. The mortises in the frame-heads were for a hoisted frame which was later replaced by a cast-iron upper tier.

probably built in the 17th century; the treble of the three dates from 1612 and the tenor from 1661. A similar use of natural forked timbers can be seen under the foundation-beams at *Crediton*.

Until the 19th-century bellframes were fastened with oak pins or trenails [115D], and the final development in the design of timber bellframes was the use of vertical tiebolts passing through the frame-heads, braces and bottom sills, and often through the foundation-beams as well [115E]. These obviate the need for trenails to fasten the joints, and allow the frame to be tightened as the timber shrinks. Tiebolted frames were almost universally used from the 1850s onwards, except in a few cases where local carpenters copied the frames which they were replacing, as for example at *Dunterton*. Another locally-built frame was that for the ring of six at *Huntsham*. In a letter written to Taylors', C.A.W. Troyte wrote: "The bellframe, of which you sent me a model – and I put up – is one of the most perfect pieces of woodwork I have ever seen", indicating that here too the estate workmen were responsible.

Timber bellframes are extremely durable, provided they were well designed in the first place, and have been given some care. Their enemies are damp (for which Devon towers are notorious) and death-watch-beetle, which feeds on the fungus caused by damp and unlike furniture-beetle can reduce large timbers to powder. The eggs and

Fig. 125. A cast-iron frame by Harry Stokes at Hemyock, 1908.

Fig. 124. Stokenham, the first cast-iron bellframe in Devon, by Taylors', 1889.

larvae of these beetles are probably brought into towers in sticks by jackdaws – one very good reason for excluding these birds.

The first metal bellframe in Devon was installed at *Stokenham* in 1888 by Taylors' of Loughborough – a frame with A-shaped trusses, the bearings set on the cross-bar of the "A". This pattern was superseded by the "low-side" type [115G], with the bearings carried on the tops of the trusses, and the "H" frame [115H] with the bearings on the cross-bar of the "H": the latter were especially useful for two-tier frames as low-side frames could be mounted on top of the "H"s, but they do not make access at all easy in cramped towers. Thomas Blackbourne of Salisbury followed at *Morchard Bishop* in 1897, and Warners' of London at *Totnes* and *Berry Pomeroy* in the same year. Composite frames, with cast-iron braces bolted to timber bottom sills and frame-heads, were used by Doble of Taunton [115F]. Harry Stokes's first iron frame apparently based on Blackbourne's, was at *Lympstone* in 1902, and he went on to build many, including Hemyock, 1908: William Aggett's first was in 1904 at *Pyworthy* (since replaced). Many of the local hangers set their cast-iron frame-sides on timber bottom sills, but the bellfounding firms quickly adopted all-metal frames. Fabricated steel frames were pioneered in 1913 by Warners' with their "Dreadnought" and "Cantilever" frames – one of the latter survives at *Meshaw* and there is a "Dreadnought" frame at *Stoke Climsland* in Cornwall – and Gillett & Johnston installed a rivetted steel frame at *Chudleigh* in 1923; welded steel frames came into use after World War II, but are less rust-resistant than cast-iron, though nowadays they are usually hot-dip galvanized. Ringers endlessly discuss the merits of metal bellframes, some maintaining that they affect the bells' tone; the fact is that when a metal frame replaces a timber one, the bells are almost inevitably

Fig. 126. The steel bellframe for Crediton at Andrew Nicholson's works, 2005.

also rehung (possibly at a different level in the tower) in different headstocks, fitted with different clappers, and often retuned, all of which can affect the sound quite as much as the material of the bellframe. By far the most significant problem with metal frames is their tendency to rust, especially the steel foundation-girders (cast-iron is far less vulnerable to corrosion) and particularly near to the sea. A number of installations of the inter-war period have had to be rebuilt at very great expense because they were not kept painted and the ends of their steel foundations were destroyed by rust, and one in Cornwall was found to have lasted only just over fifty years; it is to be hoped that with galvanizing the future may be better.

Bell Gear

A bell which is to be swung is fastened to a **headstock** which has **gudgeons** at either end working in **bearings** on the frame (when a bell is hung "dead" and not swung, this is known as a "deadstock"). Attached to the headstock are a **wheel** or lever by which the bell is swung, and, if the bell is to be rung full-circle, the **stay** which prevents it from going more than a few degrees over the balance and by engaging with the **slider** enables it to be set mouth-upwards. Thanks once again to the enthusiasm of Devon's ringers, we have few examples of very early bell fittings in the county, and those are found in 3-bell towers, most of them nearing dereliction. The most complete early installation is at *Ashcombe*, where the bells are hung in a braced king-post frame from oak headstocks, secured with nailed shearbands and keyed U-bolts. There are ¾-wheels; the clappers are stirrup-topped with long flights, now no longer hung from baldricks but "boxed" with elm tops. Apart from the clapper-tops, the gear appears to be almost all 16th century or earlier.

Another early installation was the three at *Huntshaw*, where the frame is slightly later in type. The headstocks were oak, but most of the ironwork was nutted. One of the clappers still had its iron baldrick collar and wooden busk-board; when the installation was found to be unsafe and the bells were hung dead for chiming, this clapper with one of the headstocks was given to the Royal Albert Memorial Museum, Exeter.

A: Headstock
B: Wheel
C: Wheel stay
D: Stay
E: Slider
F: Clapper
G: Bellframe
H: Gudgeon & Bearing

Fig. 127. A bell hung for ringing on a timber headstock (from Ellacombe's *Church Bells of Devon*).

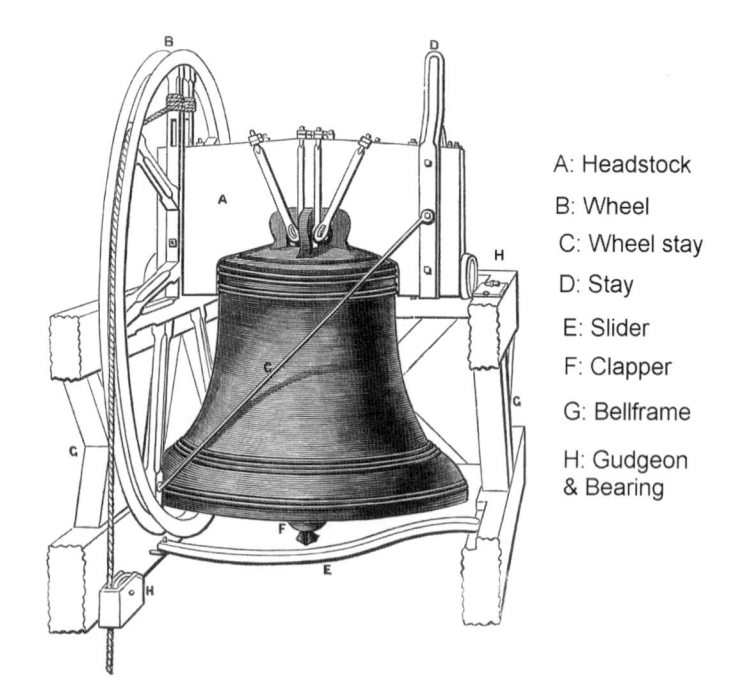

Fig. 128. Oak headstocks, nailed and keyed ironwork and three-quarter wheels at Ashcombe.

A good example of a mediaeval headstock and ironwork can be seen at *Wolborough* [66], where the middle bell of the old three is preserved in the church with its headstock. The headstock is oak; the shearbands and straps are nailed and the argent-bolt is keyed with "forelocks" passing through slots in the bolt with many washers (once known as "followers" or "flowers") to take up the slack: there are many sets of nail-holes where the bell was "trussed", tightening the ironwork by nailing the straps in fresh areas of the timber. The gudgeons are driven into bosses at each end of the headstock and centred with wedges; the bosses have iron stock-hoops to prevent them from being split.

One problem of early bellhanging was the tendency of the smaller bells to swing faster than the larger, and one attempt to remedy this was by hanging the bells as far as possible at the same distance from their bearings. At *Horwood* the 2nd has its gudgeons half-way up the headstock, and at *Clyst St Mary* before the bells were rehung the treble's gudgeons were high in the headstock,, while the 17th-century 2nd had a high crown which had a similar effect. These bells had three-quarter wheels and had iron spikes projecting from the frame-sides to prevent them from being turned right over the balance.

At the end of the 17th century screws and nuts began to replace nailed straps and keys, and by the middle of the 18th century they were universal, though usually hand-wrought by the smith so that each screw had to be matched to its own nut. In the 19th century driven-in gudgeons were superseded by plate gudgeons which are secured to cast-iron plates fitted on the underside of the headstock and secured by bolts or U-bolts. These remain properly centred as long as the bolts are kept tight, and can be more easily replaced

Bells in the type of gear used before the 17th century could be controlled only on one stroke; the first full wheels had the rope attached at the top of the wheel, and were rung "dead-rope", but in the early 17th century, with full wheels, it was found that by fastening the rope to the wheel about half-way between the pulley and the top of the wheel both strokes could be controlled, the rope being provided with a woollen "sally" so that it could be gripped on the handstroke: with a stay and slider, a bell could now be set mouth-upwards, and changed at either stroke. The earliest record of ringing "**sally-way**" in Devon is at *Exeter Cathedral*, where the bells were hung to ring on the sally by a hanger named Warren in 1678, twelve years after their restoration by Purdue and Hart. There is an intriguing entry in *Spreyton*'s accounts for 1680 for *cords & thongs . . . to tie aboute our bell wheeles*, and the Ringers' Rules of *St Andrew's, Plymouth* dated 1700 clearly indicate sally-way ringing as they include the phrase "*now up on end at stay*". In 1737 Samuel Rowe was evidently hanging the five at *Colebrooke* sally-way [App.III:4], surprisingly ahead of *Cullompton* where the bells were sallyed in 1742 [App.III:5], followed by *Talaton* in 1745. The big boom in ringing of the mid-18th-century was probably driven partly by the greater ease of good striking brought about by

Fig. 129. An iron stay and latchet slider by Thomas Bilbie's hanger at Hockworthy, 1808.

ringing sally-way, so that by the time that Ellacombe made his survey in 1864–5 very few bells are recorded as being hung dead-rope. He recorded *Bridford, Clyst St Mary, Dunchideock, Combeinteignhead, Harford, Horwood, Kingston, Northleigh, Satterleigh, Southleigh, West Ogwell, Venn Ottery* and *Woodland* had half-wheels of which only Satterleigh's now survive today but *Ashcombe* also has three-quarter wheels, which he didn't mention, while *Charleton, Coffinswell, Frithelstock, Kingsteignton* and *Stokeinteignhead* were recorded as being hung dead-rope; all of these five have since been rehung.

An important requirement for a wooden headstock is that it should resist splitting, and most surviving oak headstocks are cut from knotty and cross-grained pieces of timber. Elm, which is very difficult to split, seems to have come into use for headstocks during the 17th or early 18th century; the four at *St Mary Steps, Exeter*, dated 1656, are apparently in their original oak headstocks, and most headstocks which can be assigned to earlier dates are of oak: as late as 1737 Samuel Rowe was rehanging *Colebrooke* bells on oak headstocks [App.III:4]. By the mid-17th-century screwed ironwork was coming into use, and some of the larger churches were having their bells hung for full-circle ringing with full wheels; there is evidence that in many 18th-century installations iron peg stays and latchet sliders were used; these were specified for *Colebrooke* in 1737 and can still be seen on Bilbie's three at *Hockworthy*. The cast-iron headstock still preserved in the church at *Crediton* was made for the tenor by William Underhill, a local millwright, and dated 1838. It is arched so that the bell could be hung by its cannons in conventional ironwork, and is very massive, so that one is not surprised to know that the bell was notoriously heavy-going: it is probably the earliest iron headstock in existence, and metal headstocks did not come into general use until towards the end of the 19th century: at that time they were almost always made of cast-iron, except for very large bells; "Grandison" at Exeter Cathedral and "Hosanna" at Buckfast Abbey were hung from rivetted steel headstocks, though the former has since been given a cast-iron one. Since the 1970s there has been a steady increase in the use of fabricated steel headstocks, but the bellfounders generally prefer to use cast-iron as being less prone to rust.

A bell-wheel has oak spokes supporting the rim, which consists of the "sole" on which the rope rests and the "shrouding" which keeps the rope on the sole. Most of the half- or three-quarter wheels surviving are made with the main spoke running from the top to the bottom, sometimes cranked but often straight and sloping with the upper part housed into the face of the headstock. The beautiful three-quarter wheel at *Dunchideock* illustrated by Ellacombe was replaced when the bells were rehung by Stokes, but a replica of it is fitted to the fine Robert Norton bell on the roof of *Bishop's Court, Sowton*. As we have seen, when full-circle ringing first began, the rope was passed through a hole in the top of the wheel and the bell could be controlled only on one stroke – "dead-rope" ringing; to create a sally or handstroke pull a lashing was tied round the rim of the wheel, and this was known as the "fillet" – the term "fillet-stroke" is still used by some Devon ringers instead of "handstroke". Late 18th and early 19th-century wheels are sometimes made with the rope passing through a hole in the top of the wheel and passing under a bobbin set in the shrouding at the appropriate point to create a sally pull: the A*xmouth* wheels have bobbins, and some early Warner wheels are fitted in this way. Since sally-way ringing came into use, bell-wheels have been made in two halves divided horizontally so that they can be taken off and replaced without having to lift the bell.

The very earliest bells probably had no **bearings** as such; their gudgeons worked in notches in the frame – indeed the east belfry opening at *Trusham*, which was originally a bell-cote on the gable, has projecting stone corbels with grooves which still show traces of grease from gudgeons which seem to have worked directly in the stone but may have been lined with metal. However, some of our earliest documents mention bearing brasses, which were at first let directly into the frame-heads, with wooden covers (called "clapses" in Devon wardens' accounts): at *Tedburn St Mary* in 1691 we have a payment *for staples for to drive into the bell frames to keep down the clapses that ye Bells might not leap out of ye frame* – something that happened when one of the authors of this book was ringing a bell with a *clapse* missing from one bearing. In the early 19th-century it became the custom to fit bearing brasses in cast-iron plummer-blocks secured to the frame-heads with coach-screws. During the 19th century various bellhangers experimented with bearings which were self-aligning to allow for distortion in the frame-heads; *Meshaw* bells are hung on Warners' self-aligning plain bearings which are mounted on trunnions, and several towers still have William Aggett's "Patent" bearings which were designed to be self-aligning.

Stays were traditionally made of ash as they are today, but before the early 19th century bells were often fitted with short iron peg stays working with iron latchet sliders or short iron sliders pivoted in a king-post. These can still be found in some towers, e.g. *Exeter St Mary Steps* where they probably date from 1656 and *Hockworthy* [129] where they were probably fitted by Thomas Bilbie III in 1808; they are specified in Samuel Row's 1737 contract for *Colebrooke*. Before stays were fitted, when bells were rung "dead-rope", a spike could be driven into the frame-side to stop the bell from overturning; the old frame at *Clyst St Mary* was fitted in this way. Ash is by far the most suitable timber for stays, as it does not normally snap but bends, allowing the ringer some warning before the bell goes over the balance and the rope disappears through the ceiling boss.

When bells were rung "dead-rope" the ropes generally ran over **rollers**; these were replaced by **pulleys** for sally-way ringing. Early pulleys ran on wooden spindles in their boxes, which were often solid blocks of timber.

Clappers were traditionally made from wrought-iron, one of the few materials which will stand the repeated battering involved with a minimum of fatigue: on a visit to *St Andrew's, Plymouth* we saw a clapper which had been made locally from mild steel, turned from a solid billet; it lasted for one practice-night and broke the following Sunday morning. A mediaeval clapper was made with a stirrup-shaped top and was hung from the crown-staple of the bell with a leather strap or "baldrick": *bawdricks* or *bawders* appear very often in wardens' accounts; they were also sometimes called "collars" – *Clawton* in 1608 paid 2s for *"a payre of bootes to make a bell coller"*. The

fig. 130. An early 19th-century pulley at Hockworthy; housed in a solid block.

Fig. 131. A boxed clapper. Note also the chip-tuning marks on the soundbow of the bell.

baldrick was buckled, and when full-circle ringing was introduced a wooden "busk-board" was lashed to it, to prevent the clapper from falling back into the bell. Later, iron collars lined with leather came into use, and in the 18th century the "boxed clapper", with two blocks of elm housed to take the crown-staple and the head of the clapper and bolted together, supplanted the baldrick and collar. Boxes were often fitted to the old stirrup-topped clappers, but later clappers had "T"-shaped heads which were easier to fit. In the 19th-century the strap-topped clapper, with a flat head bolted to a leather-lined iron strap, became fashionable, and since the introduction of the independent crown-staple the clapper with an eye top and a fitted pivot-pin running in a bush has become the norm. Although boxed clappers look primitive, they are remarkably durable, and we have never heard of a boxed clapper breaking through metal fatigue. When true wrought-iron became virtually unobtainable, in the 1960s and 70s, there was an urgent need to find a material for clappers which would not suffer from metal fatigue; eventually spheroidal graphite cast iron was found to be suitable, and it is now used for the great majority of new clappers. In France, where bells are rung only to frame height, leather baldricks are still commonly used. An early clapper usually has a long "flight" below the ball, and clappers may be found with a twist in the shank; this may have been made when the clapper ball got worn, to bring another face in contact with the bell.

Bellropes were evidently made locally and, judging by the frequency with which churchwardens had to replace them, were not very long-lasting. There are examples of parishes buying three ropes, laying them up as a cable for hoisting the bells into the tower, and then unlaying them for use as bellropes as at *Bere Ferrers* [App.III:1]

Bellhangers

Bellfounders usually also worked as bellhangers; the **de Ropefords** in the 13th-century were rehanging bells at the Cathedral. The earliest mention of a specialist bellhanger to have been found so far is in 1462, when *Holy Trinity, Exeter* suffered something of a calamity – *item in takyng downe omnis trina campane quae cadebat in strata . . .* – a bell falling into the street must have been quite spectacular. **John Ley** *carpentarius* was paid *supervidend le frame campanar*. In 1543 **William Westbrook** (Westybroke) was paid for *le bellframe* at *Ashburton*; he was a local man (he was paid for making a bier in 1551) but the initial payment of 53s 4d suggests that he built a complete new frame. *Crediton* had its bells worked on in the 1570s by **William Preston** the bellfounder and another hanger named **Blakedon.** In 1580 **George Downe** was at *North Molton* to see the bells, and was given his dinner; later he was there with his boy for six days, so his work must have been fairly extensive. Other workers whose names appear in church accounts may have been professional bellhangers, or may have been local carpenters rather than specialists; one can sometimes, but not always, discover whether or not they were engaged on other woodwork in the church. But in the early 17th century we meet the first definitely identifiable family of bellhangers, the Chubbs of Cullompton.

Edward Chubb and his men were working among the bells at *Cullompton* in 1609; he was at *Talaton* the following year, *mending the little bel*, and in 1617 he was at *Halberton* with his *ropes & tackling* to hang a bell which Thomas Pennington had been casting on site. In 1622 *East Budleigh* wardens paid 2s *for carrying home Chubes tooles & his rope being two horse burthens*, and in 1627 "Chubb", presumably Thomas, hung the new ring which Thomas Pennington had cast for *Colebrooke*; the work cost £6 1s, against Pennington's bill of £16 1s. In 1630 a **Thomas Chubb**, perhaps Edward's son, hung the fine Pennington tenor at *Woodbury* for £1 3s 4d, and 3s was paid for *carrynge of Chubbs takell and toules*.

Richard Sherland or Sharland was working in the Tiverton area at about this time, at *Colebrooke* in 1642, at *Zeal Monachorum* in 1651 and 1666, and at *St Peter's Tiverton* in 1671.

In 1646 we find that an **Edward Cockey** was rehanging the 4th bell at *Halberton* – as we have seen, the Cockeys were involved in a number of metalworking trades including bellfounding from the 17th century to the 20th, though where this member fits into the family tree is not yet certain. The Harts from Somerset were also working in Devon during the 17th century, in association with Thomas Purdue; in 1676 the Dean & Chapter agreed for the restoration of the Cathedral bells with Thomas Purdue of Closworth and **Thomas H[e]art** of Long Sutton, and in the same year Purdue recast a bell for *Colebrooke* and **John Hart** was paid there "*for his father*" for 28 days and for himself for 37 days: this must have been quite a major rehanging, though the bells were to be rehung in a new frame and gear 70 years later. In 1678 John Hart was working at *Kilmington*, and in 1688 at *Cullompton*, each time in association with Purdue.

In the Cullompton area another family appears in the next century, beginning with a **Robert Pope** repairing the chimes at *Woolfardisworthy East* in 1708 and **Joseph Pope** of Bradninch stocking the bells of *Cullompton* in 1709, where ten years later the wardens spent 2/6d on *beer when Pope came to agree for righting the bells*. In 1723 we have the first record of the Murches of *East Allington*, **John Murch** at *Modbury*, John Murch and his brothers at *Holbeton* in 1726, and **John, William** and **John Murch** junior at *Ugborough* in 1730. In 1738 the *Buckfastleigh* people spent 2s 6d on a *Wakinton man* (i.e. a man from Walkhampton) *Concerning y*^{e} *bells*, and later the warden claimed 2s *for a Journey for my Self to Wackington*. The hanger in this case may have been **Charles Wickett**, who was paid for a fortnight's work and 4s *for his journey comeing first*, so evidently he was not one of the local Wycott family who feature in the recasting of the bells in 1743. Another craftsman whom one is surprised to find fitting a new headstock at *Modbury* in 1732 is **William Stumbels**, born in Aveton Gifford later living in Totnes, one of Devon's most celebrated clockmakers and renowned for the fineness and delicacy of his craftsmanship, a far cry from bellhanging.

A particularly rare and important document is the contract between **Samuel Rowe** of Spreyton and the churchwardens of *Colebrooke* for rehanging their bells in 1737 [App.III:4]. He is to make a *new cage or frame* to replace the existing one *being now very dangerous and become ruinous & much decayed*. The new frame is to be built *exact to a platt form or draught which he the said Samuel Row hath drawn out*, in heart oak for the cage and also the stocks and wheels (it is interesting that at this time elm had not replaced oak for headstocks), and dry sound elm for the *fells & featherings* of the five wheels. He is to fit *substantial stays or stops of iron to and for the said bells in such manner that the Ringers may take them off or on at their wills and pleasures*, showing that at this time iron peg stays and latchet sliders were being used, as they were by the Bilbies until the early 1800s. There are also to be boxes for the ropes to run in, and a *guide or new fframe* about 13 or 14 foot high from the belfry floor, evidence that the bells were to be rung sally-way, possibly for the first time in this tower. Samuel Row is also *to paint the cage, wheels and stocks,* and leave all *so that six ringers may easily and orderly ring the said five bells in peal, that is six men to rise and fall them as usual*. He is also to protect the clock from damage while the work is being done, box in the clock-weights, and guarantee to make good *any or either of the said bells that shall happen to be dampnified or crazed on the ffourth and ffifth day of November next ensuing and no longer*. The Churchwardens are to appoint an accomplished craftsman to inspect and view the work, and the whole work is to cost £36; the contract includes a maintenance agreement for 21 years at £1.5s per annum. It would be wonderful to have his "platt form or draught", but it has not survived with the contract.

When the Bilbies first established a foundry to recast the bells at *Cullompton* in 1746, they brought their favourite hanger, **John Bush**, from Wrington to hang the bells, and recorded the fact on the tenor – BILBIE THE FOUNDER BUSH THE HANGER HEATHFIELD'S THE MAN WHO RINGS THE TENOR. Bush also worked on the bells at Broadhembury where Thomas I recast a bell the same year, but at *Kenton* the following year they were using a different hanger, named **Rugg** or **Rudge** – BILBIE THE FOUNDER RUGG THE HANGER CARTER THE SMITH & TREBLE RINGER. In 1765 we find **William Searle** working with Thomas Bilbie II at *Broadhembury* and later rehanging the bells of *Exeter Cathedral* as Bilbie's sub-contractor.

Another known 18th-century hanger was **William Bradford** of Meshaw, whose contract to rehang the bells of his parish church in 1757 survives. He describes himself as "bellfounder", but no bells survive which can be assigned to him. The contract to rehang the bells *in the newest and best manner* originally included the bellframe, but that was later erased.

The Penningtons worked as bellhangers as well as bellfounders: Christopher of Lezant rehung the *Holbeton* bells in 1711, and Fitzantony built a new frame for *Buckland Monachorum* in 1767 [App.III:6]. The former frame at *Dolton* [117] was made by John IV in 1814, as the church accounts testify, and survived until 1998; its design, and that of frames at Poundstock and North Hill in Cornwall, has made it possible to identify some others, including probably the old frame at *Crediton*, as Pennington frames. They are made of timber almost all of the same scantling, which means that the frame-heads are rather over-large and the braces, which are often insufficiently canted, too slight: one characteristic is the use of double through-mortise joints for the frame-heads and bottom sills. **Samuel & Robert Turner** of Whitechapel rehung the *Exeter Cathedral* bells in the 1770s, according to their list, though the mediaeval frame seems to have remained in use until 1902; we are indebted to Christopher Pickford for this information.

The 19th century saw the dominance of the **Taylors** and the London foundries in Devon as far as casting was concerned, but most of the bellhanging was still being done by local people until the early 1900s. One known local hanger was **Moses Luxton** of Winkleigh, who is recorded as providing new brasses for that church in 1818 and is reputed to have rehung the bells in a new frame subsequently. The *Winkleigh* frame, which was replaced in 1963, was very badly designed, and other work attributed to Luxton (including *Dunsford* and *East Worlington*) confirms the suspicion that he was not a very good bellhanger. **John Barrett** of Exeter acted as agent for Thomas Mears and is described as such in an advertisement in the *Exeter Flying Post*, 6th October 1836. He is recorded as hanging new Mears rings at *Sowton* and *Holsworthy*, and also rehanging the bells at *Alphington, Tawstock* and *Widecombe-in-the-Moor*, and fitting Ellacombe chiming-hammers to the bells of the cathedral: in the Whitechapel record for the augmentation at Litton Cheney in Dorset, 1848, he is described as belonging to Venn Ottery; he died in 1850. In 1865 we have the first records of the notable Woodbury hangers, in the name of **Thomas Hooper**, who rehung the heavy six at *North Molton* in that year, though he may have built the frame for *Merton* in 1858. In the next ten years we have surviving frames by him at *Kentisbeare, Kelly, Poltimore, Buckerell* and *Cadbury*, most of them characterised by very generous scantlings and jack-bracing above and below the main braces. All his frames are tiebolted. The first Thomas Hooper died in 1872, and in 1877 **Thomas Hooper II** and **Harry Stokes** were in partnership, and worked with together until 1883. In 1886 we find Hooper working independently again; his last surviving frame, at *Kenton*, was built in 1888. Along with Harry Stokes he had built a similar frame in 1879 at *Powderham*; both were built for the Earl of Devon, and curiously a plaque in Kenton ringing-room states that the oak for the frame was given by the Earl from the Powderham Estate, though in fact both frames are unusual in being entirely of pitch-pine.

Harry Stokes's first rehanging without Hooper was in 1881, at *St Giles-in-the-Wood*. He worked very much in the same style as Hooper, though he less often used jack-bracing: like Hooper he hung his "hoisted" bells with long braces mortised into the frame-heads of the main frame, with long tiebolts. His wheels are very easily identifiable from the shaped cheeks at the fillet-holes to lead the ropes over a more gentle curve – a design advocated by H. T. Ellacombe. All Harry Stokes's work is carried out using the best materials available and the largest scantlings which the tower will accommodate; main braces for large bells may be over 15 inches deep and 41/2 inches thick, and foundation-beams are usually 10 x 10" or more. Harry Stokes was clearly a very major employer in Woodbury: many of his business records still survive, and show that he was involved not only in bellhanging but in general building & decorating, joinery, undertaking and transport: he owned a fleet of heavy waggons which operated around the Exmouth area. His bellhanging took him as far as Land's End to the west and into Dorset and Somerset to the north and east, and the very high survival rate of his bellhanging work speaks volumes for the quality of his workmanship. In 1902 he embarked on building frames in cast-iron, probably emulating Thomas Blackbourne of Salisbury who had rehung *Morchard Bishop* bells in an iron frame and whose pattern he closely copied: his cast-iron frames, like Blackbourne's, are very fine and are almost all built on a grillage of oak bottom sills – a type which has been described as unsatisfactory, though Stokes's have given very little trouble down the years. The First World War was clearly a heavy blow to local bellhangers, and Stokes did little bellhanging after 1918; his last new job was probably *Thurlestone* in 1928.

Fig. 132. William Aggett, in his billycock hat, posing beside the cast-iron frame for Wembury in 1909.

Roughly contemporary with Harry Stokes was **William Aggett** of Chagford. The first job which can be definitely be assigned to him was the four at *Kingston*, 1875, a rather flimsy frame which was replaced, none too soon, in 1978. The earliest surviving frame which is certainly by him is probably a very slight one for three at *Woodland*. The survival rate of Aggett's timber frames is very poor; the total known is probably 34, of which only 18 have not been replaced, and three of those are rings of 3 or 4 which are not now fit for ringing full-circle. His cast-iron frames have survived a little better, but they are very slight compared with those of other hangers, and generally inadequately fastened: a photograph of the iron frame for *Wembury* was taken in his workshop. William Aggett took great pride in the Patent "Ball" bearing which he designed and fitted in many of his later installations from 1898 onwards. It was not a ball-race, but a brass ball with the gudgeon running in a hole in the middle, housed in a cast-iron casing in which the ball could move so that (in theory at least) it was self-aligning. Though it does allow for some natural twisting in a frame-head, this bearing performs badly when the gudgeons come out of alignment (as Aggett's often do), and very severe friction takes place as the ball constantly moves in its housing. Details and drawings of this bearing can be found in Jennings, *The Development of British Bell Fittings*, 1991. Both his iron frames and his bell ironwork often shows a notable lack of engineering sense; the braces of the frames are set some two feet apart at the top, leaving the bearing supported only by the frame-head, and the strap-bolts securing bells to their headstocks are often shaped like an elongated "S" – elegant rather than efficient. Aggett's advertisements in the reports of the Guild of Devonshire Ringers are very florid, and headed by the statement, "By Royal Letters Patent Bell Hangers for H.M.Government Devonport Dockyard". In 1914 his advertisement stated *"We are the Only First-Class Bell Hangers and Bell-founders in the West of England"* and appeared on the opposite page to Stokes's. As to his being a bellfounder, he may have cast house-bells, but the only church bells bearing his name were cast by

Taylors' or Mears & Stainbank, with "W.AGGETT, CHURCH BELL WORKS, CHAGFORD" inscribed on them.

Other firms who did occasional work in the county were **Doble** of Taunton, who used wooden frame-heads and bottom sills with cast-iron braces at *Halwill*, **Thomas Blackbourne** of Salisbury who installed a fine cast-iron frame at *Morchard Bishop* in 1897, and **Henry Hambling** of Kingsbridge, who built several frames for Warners' of London.

After these two firms had ceased business, until the 1960s, the three national bellfoundries carried out all the bellhanging work in Devon, apart from one rehanging by White's of Appleton. Taylors' had already pioneered metal frames in Devon, the first being at *Stokenham*, and followed up with magnificent installations at *St Michael's, Heavitree* and *Exeter Cathedral*, the latter replacing a timber frame ten feet high with the bells all swinging in the same direction, which had required fifteen ringers for the ten bells. In 1963 two former employees of Taylors', **Arthur Fidler** and his father John, came from Loughborough and set up a bellhanging business in Bow. Later, after his father's death, Arthur moved into Cornwall and worked at Rame until his retirement in 1999. More recently **Andrew Nicholson** of Bridport has steadily built up a bellhanging business, and rehung the new ten at *Crediton* in a new steel frame, and **Robert Parker** of Taunton has rehung the ten at *St Andrew's Plymouth*, **Eayre & Smith** of Melbourne have rehung the ten at *Withycombe Raleigh*, **Hayward Mills Associates** have restored the six at *Fremington*, and **Peter Bazley of Tavistock** has also worked in the county; these hangers often work in cooperation with the bellfounders who supply them with frame components, headstocks, clappers &c.

Chime-makers

Chimes appear in church accounts as early as 1472 (*St Petrock's, Exeter*), and in 1582 we learn that the cathedral bells were equipped with a "cheime" by **Hugh Chapingdon** of South Molton; he had been paid 20s by the *Braunton* wardens in 1571 and received 6/8d a year for some time thereafter, possibly for the clock, and in 1582 *North Molton* wardens sent a *"messenger to go to molton for Hugh Chappingdon*. The *Cathedral* chimes were repaired in 1612 by **John Savage** whose father or grandfather we have already met as a bellfounder and who was also a clockmaker. **Robert Grinking**, also a watchmaker and clockmaker, and **Thomas Poling** contracted in 1655 to *formerly and substantially fframe erect and sett goinge the Chymes on the fowre bells* of *Holy Trinity, Exeter*. Robert Grinking had in 1643 given evidence against one John Bond, a barber, for expressing approval at the Parliamentarian losses in the battle at Stratton, so unlike John Pennington he seems to have supported the Puritan cause. **Thomas Bilbie I** made a set of chimes for *Cullompton* in 1750, just after his recasting of the bells, and his son Thomas II also made chime-barrels; there is a very fine example in Beamister, dated 1767, and another at East Coker, 1772; some parts of the *Tavistock* chime-barrel have many similarities to these, and are also probably by him.

8
BELLRINGING AND BELLRINGERS

RECORDS OF BELLRINGING AND bellringers before the Reformation are very scarce in England, and Devon is no exception. Victorian writers sometimes created a picture of mediaeval ringers as godly and devout men, almost a religious order, but there seems to be very little evidence for anything of the kind. The Exeter Cathedral regulations include detailed instructions for the ringing and chiming of the bells, and it appears that this was done at first by the *annuellarii*, the chantry priests whose duty it was to celebrate masses for the dead; but by Bishop Oldham's time in the early 16th century it was permitted for servants of the Cathedral clergy to assist in ringing, and the likelihood is that this was an official confirmation of an established practice. In most parish churches, of course, there would not have been spare clergy to ring the bells, and the ringers would have been laymen from the outset.

Fig. 133. The "Judas Bell" at Bourges Cathedral. It was used during Holy Week instead of the tower bells.

The rules for ringing at the Cathedral in Exeter were elaborate and detailed, with different types of ringing for the various classes of feasts and ferial days. They include *"pulsatio"*, which probably means tolling or swing-chiming, and *"classicum"* which presumably means ringing all the bells at once; the term may have survived into post-reformation usage in the phrase *an honour clash*. In the early 16th-century Bishop Oldham's statutes suggest that the custom seems already to have been established whereby, before the daily offices, the bells are chimed singly in turn, and then chimed in rounds, as is the custom today. Simpler rules probably applied in parish churches. The bells were not rung on Good Friday and Holy Saturday, and this was generally the rule in all churches, as it is in most churches still; we have two references in early church accounts to what was used instead, the "Judas bell" or "Judas clapper", at *Exeter St Petrock's* in 1439 and 1522, and at *Exeter St Mary Steps* in 1534. This was a set of thin wooden slats fastened to a frame and vibrated by a series of cams on a shaft, like a huge version of the old football-supporter's rattle. We know of none surviving in England, but the remains of one can be seen in France, preserved in the Cathedral in Bourges.

There is no doubt that ringing was an important factor in the life of every community before the Reformation, and was not by any means restricted to what today we would call "religious" occasions; indeed it is impossible to understand many aspects of the life of church and community in past centuries unless one accepts that there was virtually no distinction between church and community, religion and everyday life, sacred and secular, before the 18th century. Before the Reformation the trade and craft guilds were dedicated to saints and shared in the life of the parish church; in *Totnes* for example the rebuilding of the parish church in the 15th century (including the Priory's part of it) was undertaken and largely paid for by the town, and in the 18th century the name of the mayor was inscribed on the new bells, along with the town's coat-or-arms; after the Reformation the Vestry and the churchwardens were responsible for roads, poor relief, control of vermin, equipment of the militia, and many more affairs which today seem to have nothing to do with the church; people would have been astonished that anyone could disapprove of ringing the church bells to welcome a visiting nobleman or celebrate a military success, while all the national and local holidays and festivals were identified with Christian holy days, though much of what went on, even in the churchyard or church house, would have little or no relevance to religion, by today's standards at any rate.

One ringing occasion which clearly was specially important in the later Middle Ages was All Saints' night and the following day, the Feast of All Souls, and such church records as survive from before the Reformation contain references to this ringing, often all night and all day. It was accompanied by the lighting of bonfires, and whether this was a survival from some pre-Christian festival is not certain, but it seems likely. We see in *Ashburton*'s accounts that money was given for ringing on that day, and in some cases people gave hemp for the making of new bellropes [App.IV:1]. The ringers also collected money for ringing for All Souls, some of which may have been given to the church but some no doubt retained by the ringers. In addition to the ringing for the dead on All Souls' Day, people in most parishes paid to have the great bell rung for the dead, and these payments could be a significant part of the church's annual income: that custom of course was perpetuated after the Reformation in the ringing of the Passing Bell. Service ringing is often described today as being done "to call people to church", but in mediaeval practice it was not always solely to give notice of services; it could also form part of the worship, and in Exeter Cathedral the bells were rung during the services; indeed to this day the custom is for "Peter" to be tolled during the installation of a Dean or Canon or the enthronement of a Bishop. Bells were also believed to be effective in warding off danger: *The Golden Legend* states that *it is said that the evill spirytes that ben in the regyon of th'ayre doubte moche whan they here the belles rongen. And this is the cause why the belles ben rongen whan it thondreth, and whan grete tempeste and outrages of wether happen to the ende that the fendes and wyckd spirytes shold be abashed, and flee and cease the movynge of tempest*: as the popular pre-Reformation bell motto has it, *Voce mea viva depello cuncta nociva*, (with my lively voice I drive away all harmful things). There are records of ringing to drive away thunderstorms in *South Tawton* in 1527 – *sol pro pulsac' temporibus tonitui* (paid for ringing in time of thunder), in *Chagford* in 1480 – *pd William Taverner for ringing when it thundered* – and also from *Ashburton* [App.IV:1] and elsewhere; indeed as late as 1899 the *Torquay Directory* reported that *in conformity with an old usage, the bells of Dawlish Parish Church were rung during the recent thunderstorms . . .* Whether the use of bells to give warning of disasters derived from this prophylactic usage, or whether it was the other way round, we may never know. Linked with this may be the custom of ringing the bells "backwards" ("rounds" in reverse, up the scale from tenor to treble) as an alarm, which was probably the signal used for calling out the Rebels in 1549.

Much of this came to an end at the Reformation. In Ashburton we know that the All Souls ringing started again as soon as Mary I came to the throne [App.IV:1] but after her death and the accession of Elizabeth I this custom persisted in many places despite the crown's repeated efforts to suppress it: ringing for All Souls, the lighting of bonfires and other local customs, were seen as survivals of Popery and forbidden by statute more than once during the reign of Elizabeth I, yet apparently proved impossible to stop. As Ronald Hutton writes: *The ritual which the Elizabethan reformers found most tenacious was the ringing of bells for the dead on All Saints' Night. It got people into trouble all through the 1560s in both villages and towns and in all regions. The custom continued to be condemned in the visitation articles of the bishops of Lincoln and Hereford in the 1580s, and individuals were still prosecuted for it during that decade in the courts of the dioceses of York and Oxford. In 1587 at Hickling in Nottinghamshire's Vale of Belvoir some men not only kept up the custom but used violence against the parson at that time to maintain their ringing*[32]. But when the Gunpowder Plot was discovered three days after the old pre-Reformation ringing day – the time when anyone moving combustible materials about would attract least notice – James I's government in an astonishing coup succeeded, in a single year, in establishing November 5th as the universal day for bellringing and bonfires throughout England, turning a defiant papist survival into a piece of anti-Roman triumphalism – or was it perhaps simply a survival of a tradition which was more deeply ingrained than either, as the *Shebbear* custom (described below) suggests?

The Curfew continued to be rung, apparently in every parish, and because a single bell could not be heard throughout the city the Chamber in Exeter during the reign of Elizabeth I issued detailed instructions about the ringing of certain bells in the city. In 1591 it was *ordered that the parishe of St Lawrence shall ring their great bell for a Curffew Bell in the morninge and eveninge, & that they toward the same shall have and receve yerly 10s, viz. of the parishioners 2s, of the parishioners of St Stephens 2s6d, do of All Hallows in Goldsmyth Streate 2s6d do of St Johns Bowe 2s, do of St Pancras 12d. The Parishe of St Petrocke shall ringe one other Bell as aforesaid, and for the same shall receve as follows, viz. of the parishioners of St Petrocke 6s8d, do of St Paule 3s4d, do of St Martyn 2s8d, do of St George 3s4d, being in the whole 16s. Also an other bell shall be rung at St Mary Steppes at a cost of 20s, to be paid for by the parisheners of St Mary Steps, St Mary Arches, St Olaves, St Edmunds and All Hallows (on the Walls). Also an other bell at Trinity, 10s for the parishes of Trinity and St Mary the More, and that the ringers of the saide parishes shall have paymente accordingly.* It was ordered that nobody was to walk about the streets *after the last bell named the bowe bell*, rung at 9 o'clock, unless he carried a light.[33] At the cathedral a bell was rung at 8 o'clock every evening; according to John Pare, who in 1691 petitioned for his pension for ringing it[34], it was *chiefly rung for the intelligence of the tyme to the whole city and county*: he made the petition because his chief source of income, for ringing for burials in the Cathedral Yard, had diminished since the opening of St Bartholomew's Churchyard. It would appear that at this time the Curfew was not rung at the Ccthedral as it is today.

From 1605 until the middle of the 19th century, virtually every ring of bells in the country was rung on November 5th and this ringing was paid for by the church officers. In many places the payments begin almost immediately: for instance the *Bere Ferrers* sidemen in 1606 *bestowed on the Ringers to drinck in remembrance of thancks to Godd of the daie the Kings ma^ty escaped his daungers wrought towards him – 2s*, and more generously at *Braunton, To the Ringers appoynted to the day of Preservation – 12s*: *Crediton, Honiton, Chudleigh* and *Shobrooke* begin the following year, but *Crediton*'s account for 1604/5 also contains the entry, "*pd the Bell Ringers the 12 of november ye daie of his ma^ties blessed deliverance from Piercies bloudy Treason – 7s 10* – apparently as soon as the news of the Gunpowder Plot arrived in the town: *Cullompton, Dawlish*, and *South Tawton* all begin in 1613. By the time of the execution of Charles I it is quite clear that ringing on the 5th November had lost any associations it may have had for supporting the monarchy, for in *Clawton* and other parishes the payments continue through the 1650s, and *Gittisham*'s and *Cockington*'s actually first appear during the Commonwealth – though just how many parishes continued in this way is not easy to discover, as many church accounts are missing for this period. Once again it appears that fundamentally it was neither a monarchical nor a Protestant demonstration but simply the persistence of a cherished tradition.

This continued until the second quarter of the 19th century, when, as we shall see, the clergy succeeded – to some extent – in establishing a new regime among their ringers. However, one curious and puzzling entry in the *Combe Martin* accounts for 1742 records, *"pd for ale for the Ringers ahallant Eive, 1/-"*. It would be interesting to know whether Combe Martin really continued with All Souls-tide ringing, or simply kept the old name for the ringing on

---

32. *Merry England, the Ritual Year 1400-1700,* OUP 1994.
33. *Devon Record Office, ECA, Act Book of the Chamber, 1587–1601.*
34. *Historic Manuscript Commission report on Exeter City Records*, 1916, p. 217.

the 5th of November: these old titles do persist; in north-west Devon people still call Epiphany "Old Christmas Day", as they have done since the calendar was changed in 1752.

We get a glimpse of the 17th-century daily and weekly routine of ringing and chiming in *Exeter Cathedral* from the Injunctions issued by Bishop Lamplugh at his Visitation in 1679. He laid down *that a little bell be rung out att nine a clock in the morning as the first peale to the forenoone prayers, and the same to be rung againe att three a clock in the afternoone, as the first peale to evening prayer; And that the bells be tolled out at tenn a clock in the morning and at fower in the afternoone, as hath been accustomed heretofore. Also that the bell (which upon Sundays, Holy days and other Sermon days hath been accustomed to be tolled att the first lesson to give warning of a Sermon) be tolled upon those days immediately after the bells have been chimed all into the prayers, some continued tolls to the number of fifty-one or thereabouts.* These customs evidently derived from the regulations issued by Bishop Oldham in the early 16th-century, which in turn were a modification of rules going back to Grandison's statutes in the 14th.[35] The present custom is apparently a partial return to the pre-Reformation practice.

It would appear that most Devon bells were hung with half- or three-quarter-wheels until at least the 17th century, and in many cases much later, though very few examples survive today. Bells hung in this manner can be controlled to the extent of being rung in "rounds" (i.e. ringing in order down the scale from treble to tenor); we know this because in 1549 the Prayer Book rebels were called out by ringing the bells backwards.[36] However the order could only be changed with difficulty, and probably during the 16th century the change took place to "dead-rope" ringing, in which the bell is fitted with a full wheel: the bell could now be controlled better, but only at one stroke – what ringers call the backstroke. Full control, enabling the bells to change their order at will and at either stroke, came with the invention of "sally-way" ringing; at first this was done by tying a lashing, the "fillet", round the wheel so that on one stroke the rope, which is now given a woollen "sally", rises again part-way, and can be checked and pulled on both strokes; the bell can now be "set" mouth-upwards and set in motion again by pulling on the sally, as described in the last chapter. This had become widespread by the mid-18th century, and was the beginning of the great period of enthusiasm for bells in which so many rings of three and four were recast into fives and sixes, which kept the Bilbies and the Penningtons busy for the rest of the century, and which saw ringing competitions begin to proliferate all over the south-west.

We can get some idea of the kind of people who were ringing bells at this time from some of the songs which were composed in the West Country to extol the skill of ringers in one place or another. The Egloshayle ringers' song gives a vivid picture of the band in their tower:

> There was Craddock, the cordwainer, he rang the treble bell,
> John Ellery was the second man, and few could him excel;
> The third was Pollard the carpenter, the fourth was Thomas Cleave,
> And Goodfellow was the tenor man, that rang his round so brave.
>
> Now Craddock was the treble man, he titched 'long with his toe,
> And casting of his eyes around, commanded them to "Go".
> They pulled away with courage bold, which did their hearts revive,
> Sweet music then was quickly heard, from one, two, three, four, five.

---

35. Exeter Cathedral Archives, Exeter Cathedral Chapter Clerk's Minute Book, 1676–1882.
36. *Devon & Cornwall Notes & Queries*, 1900, p. 18.

Baring-Gould, in *Cornish Character & Strange Events* wrote that Humphry Craddock died in 1839, John Ellery in 1845 aged 85, John Pollard in 1825 aged 71, Thomas Cleave in 1821, aged 78, and John Goodfellow in 1846 aged 80, so a likely period for the song would be 1780–1800. One notes that the two ringers whose trades are mentioned were both craftsmen. Exactly what "titched 'long with his toe" means is not certain, but I have known call-change ringers who would adjust the rope so that the bight just touched their toe, and this may be what Craddock was doing. A cordwainer was a shoemaker; a cobbler merely repaired shoes. The *Dolton* song is reputed to date from about 1850, and Samuel Lyne is listed as a blacksmith in the 1851 Directory; the best-known of all Devon ringing songs, from Northlew, (given in full in App.IV:5) may very likely also date from the late 18th-century; the bells of *Northlew, Ashwater, Broadwoodwidger,* St Stephen's-by-Launceston and Callington were all recast by the Penningtons between 1772 and 1779, and by the 19th century gold-laced hats would have been old-fashioned even for Devon.

In Dolton two verses of the local ringing song "Dolton Boys" likewise describe the occupations of the ringers:

> The first he was a butcher,
> And Bissett was his name,
> The second Lyne the Blacksmith
> A ringer of great fame.
> The third was William Folland,
> A mason was by trade,
> The fourth was a cordwainer
> And he a clever blade.
>
> The fifth he was a thatcher,
> His name was Richard Scott;
> He'd ring a bell for half an hour
> And never be at fault.
> The sixth was brother to the fifth
> A ringer of renown;
> He'd ring a bell with any man
> In country and in town.

A *Torrington* ringers' song lists the ringers as follows:

> Good ringers we be that in Torrington dwell,
> And what that we are I will speedily tell;
> The first is called Turner, the second called Swete,
> The third is a Vulcan *(blacksmith)*, the fourth Harry Neat,
> The fifth is a Doctor, and man of renown,
> The Tenor, a Tailor that clothes all the town.

In the larger communities, and often in the villages, it seems, the ringers were mainly drawn from among the craftsmen and professional classes. The beautiful candelabrum which was given to hang in the ringing-room "for ever" (it now hangs in a side chapel) by the *Totnes* ringers was made by one of them, and lists the ringers, one of whom was Benjamin Kennicott, who became Professor of Hebrew at Oxford University. Kennicott's Articles for Totnes ringers, often quoted but printed here in Appendix IV:4, give a very good light on the ethos underlying

Fig. 134. The Ringers' candelabrum at Totnes, 1732.

ringing in the 18th-century, especially in larger communities. Notwithstanding his eminence as a Divinity scholar, Kennicott describes ringing not as a religious activity but as a healthy physical and mental exercise, and a sociable pastime, a *"manly . . . employment at vacant hours"*. He obviously regarded his Totnes colleagues as a little superior to bands in less genteel societies, who needed *"rules for conversation"* and *"penalties for any misbehaviour"* such as are laid down in the Ringers' Rules at *St Andrew's, Plymouth* and elsewhere:

   Let awful silence first proclaimed be,
And praise unto the Holy Trinity.
Then honour give unto our valiant King,
And so with blessing raise this Noble Ring.
   Hark how the chirping Treble rings most clear
And covering Tom comes rowling in the Rear:
Now up on end at stay come lett us see
What laws are best to keep sobriety,
Then all agree and make this their decree.
   Who swear or curse or in an hasty mood
Quarrel and strike altho' he draw no blood,
Who wears his hatt or spurs, or turns a bell
Or by unskilful handling marrs a peal
Lett him pay Sixpence for each several crime
T'will make him cautious 'gainst another time.
But if the Sexton's fault an hindrance be
We claim from him a double penalty.
If any should our Parson disrespect
Or Wardens' orders any time neglect,
Lett him be always held in Foul Disgrace
And ever after banished from this place.
   Now round lett goe with pleasure to the ear
And pierce with echo through the yielding air.
And when the bells are cease'd then lett us sing
     GOD BLESS OUR HOLY CHURCH
        GOD SAVE THE KING
            1700

Several sets of ringers' rules can still be seen in Devon towers; the St Andrew's, Plymouth version is almost the same as that at *Stoke Damarel* and also appears in some Cornish towers; in *Drewsteignton* we have:

THE RINGERS ARTICLES
I
Whoever in this place shall swear
Sixpence he shall pay therefore.
II
He that ringers here in his hat
Threepence he shall pay for that.
III
Who overturns a bell before
Threepence he shall pay therefor
IIII
Who leaves his rope under feet
Threepence he shall pay for it.
V
A Good ringer and a true heart
Will not spare to spend a quart.
VI
Who will not these rules agree
Shall not belong to this belfree.
JOHN HOLE, WARDEN
1816–1824

What is clear from the tenor of these and most sets of ringers' rules before about 1830, and from other evidence, is that the ringers were making their own rules and regarded their company as being almost autonomous. They might warn against neglecting the Wardens orders, but the documentary material shows that they were quite ready to negotiate terms with, or sometimes defy, the wardens, and even the parson, on occasion, when their interests conflicted. Contrast these examples with the rules which were displayed in the ringing-room at *Kingston* in 1875:

Fig. 135. The Ringers' Rules at Drewsteignton.

KINGSTON
CHURCH BELLS

RULES FOR THE RINGERS

The use of the Bells is to be strictly confined to
Ecclesiastical Purposes
as they were always intended to be, that is, they are
not to be rung for
POLITICAL MATTERS
SUCH AS
ELECTIONS, LAWSUITS, RACES &c
NOR FOR ANY
Unusual Special Purpose
Without the consent of the Minister and Churchwardens
And no ringing shall continue later in the Evening
Than Nine o'Clock, except on the Evening of the
OLD YEAR

---

1. The Belfry is a part of the Church, the house of God, and the Ringers being officials thereof, they ought to be persons of good character and respectability whatever their station in life may be.

2. As it the practice in the Church of England that no man should wear his hat in God's house, every ringer should abide by this pious custom, and no swearing, bad language, irreverent conduct, drinking, or smoking shall be allowed in the belfry.

3. The Four Bells shall be rung every Sunday before Divine Service at the usual hours, also Christmas Day; and all ringers shall appear clean and orderly in their persons, and attend to the Divine Service.

4. Should any dispute arise between any of the ringers, it shall be decided by the Churchwardens. A copy of these rules shall be hung up in the Vestry and Belfry.

      Rev. C. BULTEEL, Vicar
      Messrs. BROOKING & HELMER, Churchwardens

 It was almost inevitable that local rivalry would enter the picture, and competition ringing became very popular in the 18th and 19th centuries, often promoted by the landlord of the local inn who stood to do very good trade on the day of a ringing match even if he didn't run a book on the result. An advertisement in *Trewman's Exeter Flying Post* for 18th March 1847 announces prizes of two guineas (£2.10) and one guinea (£1.05), and ends: *Further particulars may be obtained on application at THE CASTLE INN.* A report on the event (at *Bradninch*) in the same paper on April 4th notes *The ringers assembled at that hospitable and well-conducted house, Govier's Castle Inn . . .* Prizes were not always in money: the famous Northlew ringing song records that the ringers in the first contest between Northlew and Ashwater *rang for a belt and a hat laced with gold*, but in the second match the prize was *a note of five pound*.

It is difficult to discover just how much service-ringing was taking place in ordinary parish churches during the 17th and 18th centuries, because it was not paid for and so does not appear in the church records; Ellacombe does not give us much evidence of bell customs in Devon, but North in his surveys of Leicestershire and Northamptonshire provides a wealth of information about the local practice in those counties, where ringing the bells on Sundays was very unusual and in almost all churches it seems to have been the custom for the bells to be chimed on Sundays either by the ringers or by a different set of "chimers", or even by a machine such as can be seen at *Colyton* or *Branscombe*. Indeed there is evidence from Devon accounts that in many parishes ringing on Sundays was expressly disallowed; at *South Tawton* in 1660 the dogwhipper was paid 5 shillings annually for several years for *taking up ye belropes Sabbaths days*; at *Chivelstone* in 1712 they paid 2/6d a year *for taking care of ye ropes one ye Sundayes*, and by 1726 this was recorded as *"loking in the bell rops"* and included in the Clerk's regular duties; in *Cullompton* in 1822 the vestry voted 2 guineas per annum for chiming the bells on Sundays, and at *Stokenham* we learn that the ringers were paid *for chiming the day of Confirmation*, while after the sacking of the *Buckland Monachorum* ringers in 1815 a new band was recruited to *ring when they think proper* and *to Chime before Divine Service*. In *Cornwood* the rules of the mid-1850s provided for six of the ringers to chime the bells on Sunday mornings (with a fine of 2d if they did not stay for the service); there was to be no ringing on Sunday mornings without the Vicar's permission, and we have seen in other dioceses ringers' rules from the early 19th century that ringing on Sundays was expressly forbidden by the incumbent; H. T. Ellacombe's rules for the ringers at Bitton in 1848 included the following rule XIX: *There is to be no ringing on Sundays, for any person or thing – excepting it be a wedding, if there is time before ten o'clock: and on the Sunday mornings stated in the next rule.* The next rule allowed ringing before 8 o'clock on Easter Day and Whitsunday, and other great festivals if they happened to fall on a Sunday. Ellacombe commented: *It should have been noticed, that the ringers to whom these rules apply have nothing at all to do with the service bells and chiming: the sexton attends to all that. It is certainly desirable that the ringers, as officers of the church, should be in attendance at those times: but that cannot be expected of men of that grade, unless they are paid for it . . .* It was expressly to avoid the necessity of having the ringers in the building on Sunday that Ellacombe designed his famous chiming apparatus. However, *Kingston* at least had set up a routine of service-ringing by 1875.

Among the regular occasions for ringing in the 17th and 18th centuries was, still first and foremost, November 5th, which as we have seen was established almost immediately after the discovery of the Gunpowder Plot as the nation's great outpouring of loyalty and anti-Popery. The ringers were always paid for this, as they had been for the All Souls'-tide ringing which preceded it; payment for this ringing varied greatly, but in some places the ringers were treated very lavishly indeed, as the *Cullompton* accounts for 1698 show:

for Candles beere & tobacco ye 4th of november	0	11	0
the fifth of November for Rolles	0	1	0
for Cheese	0	1	6
for beere at breakfast	0	3	6
more for beere after breakfast	0	1	10
for a rump of beefe a shoulder of mutton a legg of lamb bread & Dressing	0	13	10
for beere at Dinner	0	9	0
more after Dinner	0	5	0
more after	0	6	0
for the Gentlemens Dinner	0	4	0
for beer wine fire & tobacco	0	17	8

A total of £3 14s 4d (£3.72). However, by 1736 the 5th November ringing was down to 30s (£1.50), though there were several other ringing days which brought the ringers' annual income to nearly £7, so it is not surprising to find that in 1742 the Vestry resolved that there should be only four ringing days, May 29th (Oak-apple Day), the King's birthday, November 5th and the King's Accession, and payment for each was not to be more than 12s. However, it didn't last: by 1768 they were paying *Tho: Serle 2 bills for Ringers liq^r – £4 11s 8d* (£4.58), and the following year they ordained that total payment for ringing was to be not more than £2 10s 6d (£2.52) per annum. By contrast, in *Bickington* the payment was only 1s 6d (71/2p) and in *Goodleigh* 2s (10p).

Another usual paid ringing day after the Restoration was May 29, "Oak-apple Day", and the King's birthday was celebrated with paid ringing in most parishes, but November 5th was the ringing day of all days. The unique importance given to it is shown in the many parish accounts which record a regular payment for overhauling of the bells each November 4th; in the contract for rehanging *Colebrooke* bells in 1737, there is a special clause requiring the work to be completed by the next 4th November, and the hanger is to guarantee the bells against damage on that first 5th November. The "Peter" bell of Exeter Cathedral was cracked on November 5th, 1610. Monarchist enthusiasm seems to have been less marked in some places than elsewhere; at *Great Torrington* in 1751 a special meeting of the Corporation decided *that there shall be no Ringing for the future on the present or any future King's Coronation Day.* In *Axminster* there was much activity at the time of the Monmouth Rebellion (after which Judge Jefferies visited the town) and the accounts show that ringing was an important part of it [App.IV:2].

The special occasions for ringing were many and very various; victories and royal births are probably the most common, but the freeing of the Seven Bishops (who of course included Exeter's Bishop Trelawny), of John Wilkes (*Widecombe-in-the-Moor*) and Dr Sacheverell (*Kenn*), the repeal of the cider tax in 1766 (*Great Torrington & Bickington*) and Prince Maurice's coming (*Honiton* 1643) were all celebrated with ringing, and in 1826 the bells of *Alphington* were being rung to celebrate the result of an election when the tower was struck by lightning and a boy killed (the vicar, who doubtless supported the party which had lost the election, declaring it to be a divine judgement). Alphington was clearly a place with a strong tradition for ringing on special occasion, and the entries in the accounts include the discovery of the Rye House plot (1683/4), *nuse of His Majesty's recovery*, (1684), *when Argile was taken*, and *when Monmouth was taken* (1685/6, after Sedgemoor),*when the Lord Bushup past by* (frequently, as it was on his road out of Exeter to his residences at Chudleigh and Paignton), *rejoycing day when the Queen was with child* (1687), *at the brith* (sic) *of the Prince* (this was the future young Pretender), and *for the King* (William III) *entering London* (both in 1688: Alphington was not slow in recognizing the new regime), *when the King came home and the French were worsted* (1692), and *when the tower was finished* and *when good news came from Spine* (both 1706). Not surprisingly, perhaps, the Vestry in 1723 minuted a resolution that *for the future the Parish doth allow no more than three ringing days in the year, that is to say the King's Birthday, the 29th May, the 5th November and that there be paid to the Ringers each of the said days seven shillings and sixpence and no more* – but they still paid for the battle of Dettingen in 1743 and *Victory gained by the King of Sardinia over the Spaniards in 1746*. The arrival of a high-ranking visitor would often be greeted by bell-ringing, paid by the community or sometimes perhaps by the visitor, as in *Great Torrington* where the Town Wardens paid for ringing when Lady Walpole was in town in 1726. It was understood, though, that any member of the local gentry could have the bells rung at his own expense and for his own gratification: an illuminating entry in the *Plympton St Maurice* Vestry Book for 1755 goes as follows:

> *Agreed on Easter Monday March 31st Day 1755 by we whose names are hereunto subscribed being the parishioners then present at the Vestry then held: that only five persons shall and are by the authority of the said Vestry allowed to ring the bells of this parish for the future and that they shall ring only on such public days as the Parishioners shall from time to time agree to and approve of and that the said five persons that shall undertake to ring shall be obliged likewise to Chime the said bells on every Sunday in the forenoon*

and the afternoon at the proper season for Divine Service and that they shall be obliged to give their due and regular attendance both in the fore and afternoon of every Sunday upon the Service of the Church and that they be at liberty to ring for George Treby Esqr and the other Gentlemen belonging to the Corporation as often as the said Gentlemen shall signify it to be their pleasure and have the bells rung and that the said ringers are never to ring after eight of the clock in the evening or before seven in the morning.

In fact there was clearly a mounting resentment among hard-pressed or parsimonious churchwardens from the latter part of the 17th century onwards, at the amount which was being paid to ringers for their paid ringing days. Already in 1688 the *Chivelstone* vestry had passed a memorandum *that wee the pishoners will not for the future allow to be spent on the fifth of november not above eight shillings* – in 1686 it had been 14/6d: at *Feniton* the Churchwardens in 1693 *Spent uppon the ringers the 5th of November & at other reioyceing daies 12^s which ye pishoners looks upon to be to muche & very extravigant & hardly alow it* (but then the Feniton wardens were not noted for open-handedness; in 1689 they had paid 6/- to Mr Churchill for keeping the register *which we look upon as not due to him*, and in 1718 they were to pay the "Dean Ruler" (Rural Dean) *2^s ye which we deem to be a incroachment on the parish*). In 1707 some of the *Holsworthy* ratepayers noted that *Wee whose names are subscribed doe not allow of the two shillings charged on ye fifth of November being contrary to the pysh Agreement. Dawlish* passed a similar resolution in 1712, and in 1717 *Lympstone* decided that *the Churchwardens for the time to Com shall not exceed five shillings in expence one the 5th of Novemb^r. Cullompton's* reaction to this problem can be seen in App.IV:3 – but it has to be said that like many economy measures then and since, the new order didn't last long. Not everyone approved of the custom: at *Bickleigh* (W), the churchwardens in 1773 made a memorandum that *As it hath been found by experience that ye money heretofore given by the Parrish for ringing the Bells on the night of the 4th of November occasions many irregularities & disorders of families among servants, it is now agreed by the concurrent consent of the Parishioners now met to discontinue that custom for the future & ease the Parish of expence productive of many evils*. This was signed by the vicar and four of the leading ratepayers. The ringers had hitherto been paid 5 shillings for this ringing; enough for half a hogshead (36 gallons) of cider. In fact two years later the four lay signatories signed the accounts which included 2/6d for ringing on the 5th November. At *Dolton* in 1843 the annual payment of 12/6d was discontinued and added to the sexton's salary.

One of today's best-known annual ringing customs, ringing the old year out and the new year in, very seldom appears in church records, but that only implies that it was not paid for from church funds. So far the only record we have found is at *Chittlehampton* in 1721 and 1723 – *pd to the Ringers at the End of the old year and the Beginning of the New – 3s 4d*. This was half the sum paid at that time for November 5th. In Chittlehampton as in several other parishes, the ringers were paid for ringing when the new churchwardens took up their office.

The picture which we have seen so far is in many ways similar to the one which we saw before the Reformation – the bells as part of the community's equipment and the ringers as the community's functionaries. At *Ottery St Mary* in 1670 there was a dispute as to whether the parishioners (through the Church Rate) or the Governors were responsible for the bells, and one of the witnesses alleged that *Ever since he can remember the Bells in the Tower of the Church of Ottery whether of the Collegiate or parochial Church there – which are both joyned together – have constantly been reputed to belong and appertaine to the parishioners and inhabitants of the said parish in generall and have accordingly been used and imployed for the generall use of the whole parish . . .* As long as the community and the church remained virtually different aspects of the same entity, this caused no problem, but from the middle of the 18th century the situation began to change. Several factors combined to bring this about: the Evangelical and Methodist revivals had emphasized personal religion and tended to belittle what we would call "folk religion" as an empty formality; the rise of nonconformity and Catholic emancipation meant that in towns and in an increasing number of villages the Parish Church was no longer the place of worship for everybody; the organization of rural communities had changed so that the Churchwardens' and the Vestry's business was more and more confined to specifically ecclesiastical matters and less involved with poor relief, roads and other "secular" matters which concerned the community in general; and, especially in the second quarter of the 19th century, a new class of parish clergy, better educated, more cultivated, more earnest and often more affluent, was coming on to the scene, while the "lower orders" were becoming less deferential to the leaders of what Max Weber has called "the ceremonial society". Eventually there would be a show-down between the ringers and the clergy, as the latter became less tolerant of the old order and the former came to feel increasingly threatened by the new one.

One of the first examples appears in 1805 in *Cullompton*, where the ringers, who may have been spoilt by their very generous treatment in earlier generations, *positively refus'd to ring on this Day (being Easter Monday) and when requested impudently behav'd themselves*; the Vestry ordered that they might no longer ring without the express consent of the Churchwardens [App.IV:6]. In 1815 the *Buckland Monachorum* ringers were in the habit of ringing late at night, and when the key was refused them they got into the tower where a carpenter was putting a new lock on the gallery door and rang the bells in defiance, using "illiberal language" to the parishioners. The Vestry agreed to choose nine ringers *who was not concerned with the Mutinous Setts*; some of the ringers who were also in the choir *showed their Malice and Hatred* by leaving it *with a view to Distress the Singing* and were *discarded and never join the Choir any more* [App.IV:7] These disputes very often centred on the church key; John Skinner, that strange and tormented Somerset parson whose depression eventually led to his suicide, had a long-running battle with his ringers: significantly, they were supported by the local Squire, who clearly recognized their traditional function as part of the historic structure of the village, and saw Skinner as someone who was bent on destroying it.

The arguments were not invariably with the clergy: a MS note in the *Winkleigh* records says that *during the middle of the last century the squire of the village (self-appointed churchwarden) locked the ringers into the belfry one evening for the 'crime' of ringing a peal contrary to his instructions. Charged, acquitted and compensated at South Molton Police Court for breaking the lock, the ringers composed a song in which occurs this couplet: "The ringers went up and made a good peal, they got five shillings and a gallon of ale"*.

The disputes rumbled on through the 19th century; one serious row broke out in *West Worlington* as late as 1882 and was fully reported in the *South Molton Gazette* [App.IV:8]. The ringers had reportedly been in the habit of getting drunk every year on Revel Sunday, and the rector tried to enforce some new rules on them. They refused, and subsequently the rector's outbuildings were set on fire; on November 5th he was burnt in effigy, his gate was unhung, and the police had to be called to protect him from *other indignities*, while *horrible language was used*. One of the ringers broke into the church, stole a bronze cross, two brass candlesticks and vases (could there have been an anti-ritualistic element here?), and three bell clappers; he was arrested and the landlord of the inn was also arrested when the clappers were found hidden in his well. The two were tried at the Assizes but acquitted for lack of evidence. The innkeeper published a song which went:

Remember, remember the Fifth of November,
For fifty years the bells have been rung,
But now the old Guy does strictly deny
That any such thing should be done.

One suspects that prize-ringing had now become an important factor in these arguments. A report in the *Exeter Flying Post* for 16th August 1849 gives a vivid picture of the kind of activity which went with ringing a generation earlier in West Worlington; if the same attitudes were still around in the '80s their new rector's action is perhaps not so surprising:

The lovers of the science of bell ringing, in this part of the county, were highly gratified with a ringing match which took place on Wednesday, the 7th inst., on the musical peal of six bells, in the spire of West Worlington Church. It being the revel week, a very large number of persons were present, and who appeared highly to appreciate the treat afforded them. At 9 o'clock the trial peals commenced and lasted till 12, when the ringing for the prize of four sovereigns began and terminated about 8 o'clock; in the course of which it was asserted by competent judges that better ringing had never been heard in Worlington. At the conclusion of the ringing the prizes were awarded as follows. – Morchard Bishop 30s., Witheridge 20s., Chulmleigh 15s., Oakford 10s., and Coldridge 5s., which distribution has given dissatisfaction to the Witheridge ringers, who have challenged to ring any of the parishes. About 60 persons then adjourned to Lee's Stuckley Arms Inn, and partook of an excellent dinner, the Churchwardens of East and West Worlington presiding, and on the removal of the cloth, the healths of the rectors, the Rev. B.Clay and the Rev. W.M. Bruton, were enthusiastically received; the evening was spent in a truly convivial manner, to the gratification of all; in the course of the evening six treble men, from six different sets of ringers rung a beautiful peal of changes. – The ringers of Morchard Bishop were so elated at their success, that on their return the inhabitants of the village were awoke by a peal of victory but with what precision rung we will not venture to state.

In 1885 there was another row between a vicar and his ringers at *Modbury . . . the ringers wanted to ring for the arrival of the local Conservative candidate, who was, incidentally, a generous contributor to their funds. They added that they would also ring for the Liberal candidate when he arrived the following week. The Vicar refused, saying that he would not let the bells be rung for any type of political demonstration. The ringers were upset and instead of ringing they chimed for three services the following Sunday . . . They claimed that they had the majority of villagers behind them, whilst the Vicar said that the influential inhabitants supported him. The latter won, of course, and the bells remained silent*[37]

It was not only the ringers who were involved in this kind of confrontation with the reforming clergy, though their resistance was usually the most organized: in many places zealous incumbents were sweeping out box-fpews which had been allocated to particular farms or families for generations, scraping off plaster inside and roughcast outside, re-ordering chancels and replacing the village musicians – doubtless lacking in artistry and often fiercely independent – in a gallery with a harmonium or organ played by someone under close clerical control. A sad example was at *Thurlestone*, where the Vicar, having consulted the parishioners and learnt that they were totally opposed to his plans, closed the church for a week and had the whole church stripped and refurnished with new-style benches which he had had built during the preceding winter in the Vicarage barn by a deaf-mute carpenter from Kingsbridge. Most of the men in the congregation walked out, and swore never to enter the church again. Clergymen were free to do this kind of thing in the second half of the 19th century because with the abolition of the Church rate and the increase in clerical incomes there was no effective lay control over incumbents: the clergy would often pay for major rebuilding or refurbishing out of their own resources, or call on their wealthy relations, friends and allies to subscribe. Of all the lay groups in the church, the ringers had hitherto been least subject to clerical control; they resented this clerical take-over, and in many parishes the result was a stand-off between ringers and parson which has survived to this day. One symptom of this was the obstinate survival of prize-ringing into the last decade of the 19th-century, aided in some parishes by a dwindling band of clergy who were still wedded to the old order. By the middle of the 19th century, it would appear that paid ringing had virtually died out in Devon, with the exception of the Cathedral where the ringers continued to be paid until the early 20th century. Ringing for weddings is of course normally still paid for, and provides many bands of ringers with a useful fund to pay for new ropes, outings, and the like.

Incumbents who sought more control over their ringers found this difficult as long as the ringing-room was upstairs and out of sight, and one popular tactic was to bring the ringing floor down to ground level where the ringers could be seen from the body of the church – and might have to file past the congregation if they wanted to

---

37. From the church guidebook, by the Modbury Local History Society.

leave before the service – and where only the most defiant would venture to smoke or bring in a barrel of cider. In some towers one can still find a row of pegs in the middle stage of the tower where the ringing-room used to be, and in many more the ringers still have to cope with 60- or 70-foot ropes – and still have to file past the congregation – because of a 19th-century reforming vicar, though no Devon ringers have to negotiate the external near-vertical ladder and 4-foot-high doorway which the Vicar at Launton in Oxfordshire installed to ensure that his ringers remained stone-cold sober.

The prize-ringing scene, which we have already noticed at West Worlington, became increasingly unpopular with the church authorities, not least because it was associated with gambling and usually sponsored by a local pub. It also seems often to have given rise to unpleasantness among the ringers themselves; we saw how the *Witheridge* band grumbled about the result at Worlington; in the previous year, 1848, the *Exeter Flying Post* had reported: *The match for a bet of £5 each side, between the Tedburn St Mary and Drewsteignton ringers, came off on Monday afternoon, at Exminster, and was won by Drewsteignton. It appears the Drewsteignton men felt dissatisfied with the decision of the tryers at the recent Exminster match, and Tedburn having challenged any set of ringers who had taken part on that occasion, this match was the result.*

In *Bradninch*, which had been the scene of a major ringing match in 1847 [App.IV:7], organized by *that hospitable and well-conducted house, Govier's Castle Inn*, the ringers in 1863 featured in two reports in the Flying Post: *The Churchwardens of this parish have withdrawn the yearly advance of 30s. to the ringers: and on Sunday morning none of her Majesty's lieges heard the sound of the churchgoing bell. The chimes, as well as the general ringing, ceased with the cessation of pay to the ringers. We are informed that the youths who visited the belfry on Monday for practice were ordered out by the parish authorities.*

. . . and the following week: *The paragraph which appeared in our paper of last week stating that the churchwardens had withdrawn the yearly allowance of 30s. to the ringers is incorrect. The ringers themselves have refused, without giving proper notice to the churchwardens, to chime the bells on Sundays unless their pay is increased. W.H.BESLEY and W.FROST, Churchwardens.*

A good picture of the working of a local village band in the 1880s can be gathered from the *Kenn* Ringers' Book, now in the Devon Record Office. Prior to 1880 the six ringers had received gifts (probably solicited) from individual parishioners each year at Christmas, varying between 6d and 10 shillings, with an additional £2 from the Vestry meeting, which they shared out to give each ringer about 12 shillings. In 1880 a new band was formed, with six ringers and four supernumeraries, none from the old band; one assumes that there had been a typical 19th-century ringers' row. The new ringers were to be paid 10s for special evening ringing, 30s for morning and evening, and when ringing caused loss of earnings an additional 5s. Practices were on Wednesdays from 8 till 9, and (unusually) on Sundays from 4 till 5, and the ringers were to pay 2d per week to the general fund, which was disposed of each year as the members decided – with the consent of the President (the Vicar). The band joined the Guild four years later.

Call-changes and "Scientific"

Until the middle of the 19th century, there is virtually no evidence of "scientific" change-ringing in Devon or Cornwall, and the bells were rung to rounds or call-changes, with much attention to raising and lowering in peal. Some reports and advertisements from the 19th century suggest that unlike Devon call-changes today, the changes were sometimes double, but there is very little surviving record of the "peals" which were in use. Certainly today by far the most popular peals on six bells is "Sixty on Thirds", and on eight "The Queen's Peal", and these are virtually universal in competition-ringing, which sometimes seems to be a pity, as there is much scope for invention and variety in call-change composition, and a competition in which the changes were issued to the contestants a month beforehand would be a good test of all-round ringing competence. Most callers prefer to call the changes from memory, but in some towers they are called from boards or from cards placed on the floor; one of the cards used in the Cathedral before the Guild took over the tower is preserved in the Guild Library.

Raising and lowering bells in peal is a skill highly rated among all Devon ringers, but especially in call-change bands, for a well-performed rise can be really exhilarating to hear – the late Tommy Darch of Torrington said "I love to hear them spread out like a flock of birds" – and a good ring of bells never sounds so fine as half-way down in a good lower. Devon custom varies from the "up the line" practice, in that instead of starting the rise by chiming first the treble, then treble and 2nd, then treble, 2nd and 3rd, and so on, the bells are "pitched" together, usually on the third swing, to strike in a closely-packed round. Likewise in lowering, instead of the bells being brought down to chime and then missed for one round and caught on the next, they are simply stopped on a signal, usually when the treble-man stamps his foot. The very terminology varies between the two schools of ringing; among call-change ringers the handstroke or sally stroke is still sometimes called the "fillet", a memory of the change to sally-way ringing when as we have seen the handstroke was created by tying a lashing or fillet around the rim of the wheel; the backstroke likewise is often called the "rope's-end". "Treble's going . . . She's gone", the command for pulling the bells off the balance, is often replaced by "Go . . . Here they go", the warning call before starting a peal of changes is "Look out", and the command to begin a lower is usually "Downwards". A "peal" is a set of changes, possibly including the rise and lower, the bells are changed only on the handstroke, and changes are always called "up", i.e. the two bells making the change are called, so that the change from 123456 to 124356 would be "Three to four". In competition ringing the teams raise the bells, ring a peal of changes, and lower them again: the judges (usually three) are installed where they can hear the bells clearly but cannot see who is going into the tower, after which the teams draw for the order of ringing. Quarter-, half- and full faults are awarded for a clip, a bad clip and a blow out of place or a "chitter" – a bell striking before the start of a rise or after the finish of a lower; Broadwoodwidger ringers would have been awarded a full fault for "*a blow on the tenor should never have been*".

This style of ringing, at its best, produces very good striking, and one reason for the Devon ringers' resistance to "method-ringing" is that it is rare to hear it struck as well as most call-changes. For that and other reasons, "scientific" has not spread to very many places outside the cities of Exeter and Plymouth. However, since the early 17th century ringers in other parts of the country, particularly in London and the big cities, had been experimenting with changes made at every round. Before long they had discovered how to ring all the possible changes – 5,040 – on a ring of eight with the tenor "covering" behind, and a "peal" for change-ringers came to mean over 5,000 changes (which takes about 3 hours), rung non-stop without repeating a change: any set of changes shorter than a peal is a "touch". "Scientific" change-ringing did not penetrate the far west until the advent of the railways made it possible for bands of ringers from "up the line" to visit Devon and Cornwall.

Four men were specially important in the development of change-ringing, coupled with belfry reform, in Devon. **H.T. Ellacombe,** Rector

Fig. 136. The Rev. H.T. Ellacombe, with a model bell and frame which he made. (Picture courtesy of Richard Bowden).

of *Clyst St George*, was probably the greatest bell pundit of the Victorian era. Born in 1790 to a long-standing Devon family at Alphington where his father was Rector, he was intended to follow his father into the the Ministry and graduated at Oriel College, Oxford, but his keenness and skill at engineering drawing brought him to the attention of Marc Isambard Brunel, who took him on as assistant engineer in Chatham Dockyard. When the Admiralty ended this appointment Ellacombe returned to Oxford to study divinity before being ordained, and after a curacy at Cricklade he went on to serve for 33 years, first as Curate and then as Vicar, in the parish of Bitton in the South Gloucestershire coalfield, where he had to fit the windows of his vicarage with iron shutters to protect himself and his family from the local thugs; he said that anyone meeting a stranger there on a dark night would simply hand over his money without any argument – and some of the local thugs were among his bellringers. Although he was one of the leading exponents of the belief that method-ringing was an essential adjunct to belfry reform, he was not in favour of having the bells rung for Sunday services; "It is certainly desirable," he wrote, "that the ringers, as officers of the church, should be in attendance at these times: but that cannot be expected of men of that grade, unless they are paid for it . . .".[38] For that reason he designed the chiming apparatus which still bears his name, by which the bells can be sounded (albeit rather feebly) by one person. In 1850 he succeeded his eldest brother William as Rector of Clyst St George, and had the bells augmented to six in 1867. They were opened by a change-ringing band from Bristol,[39] but there is no evidence that there was a change-ringing band there until 1886, the year after his death. When over 70 he visited all the church towers in Devon except one (where the churchwarden refused permission) in four years, and in 1867 published *The Church Bells of* Devon, followed by *The Church Bells of Somerset* in 1875 and *The Church Bells of Gloucestershire* in 1881; the last two being largely compiled from information sent to him. As well as being a leading authority on bells, Ellacombe was a celebrated botanist and gardener, a skilled craftsman, and a mine of information on many subjects, and his standing as an authoritative figure in the diocese and outside it was immense: there can be no doubt that his opinion on the superiority of "scientific" was extremely influential with the clergy and some of the landowners in the county, and made a huge contribution to the early growth of the Guild of Devonshire Ringers.

Fig. 137. The Rev. Maitland Kelly of Kelly, one of the founders of the Guild of Devonshire Ringers.

Maitland Kelly had shown an interest in ringing from an early age – he claimed to have tolled the bell for death of the Duke of Wellington. Encouraged by his brother-in-law Harry Trelawny of Calstock who had raised a change-ringing band among his estate workmen and tenants, he trained a band at *Kelly* (where his family have been squires since at least the 13th century) to ring Grandsire Doubles in 1865. After taking holy orders and serving in Salcombe and Ottery St Mary, he inherited the Kelly estate in 1899 but did not become a "squarson" as he always had a vicar to run the parish: however, he made sure that his tenants and estate workmen learnt method-ringing. In later years he once advertised for a coachman, and one applicant was a man named Boucher. When he came to be interviewed, Kelly asked him why he'd chosen to apply: "Well, sir," said Boucher, "I heard you was

---

38. *Practical Remarks on Belfries and Bellringers,* 5th Ed., London, 1884
39. A hymn for the dedication service was specially written by the Rev. Francis Kilvert.

Fig. 138. Charles A.W. Troyte, squire of Huntsham and author of *Change Ringing*.

a keen ringer." "Are you a ringer?" "Yes, sir." "A method-ringer?" "Yes, sir" "You've got the job," said Kelly: he never asked Boucher if he could drive a coach. In 1917 he lost a foot in an accident with a gun, but later made his way up to the Cathedral ringing-room, pulled by Boucher (by now his chauffeur) in front and propelled from behind by G. F. Coleridge, President of the Central Council of Church Bell Ringers[40].

Charles Troyte (born Acland) of *Huntsham* was another village squire and like Kelly an Oxford graduate. In 1863 he inherited the Huntsham estate on condition that he changed his name to Troyte and lived there for six months of every year, so he abandoned his army career and threw himself into the role of a devoutly Christian country landowner. He had the old ring of three at Huntsham augmented to six in 1866 by Taylors', and in the process was introduced to change-ringing by John Taylor; he taught himself and five of the Huntsham ringers to ring Grandsire Doubles, and in 1869 on the strength of that experience he wrote and published *Change Ringing*, one of the most celebrated manuals of method-ringing, which was still in print forty years later:[41] in 1874, wishing to ring peals which at that time were not recognized on six bells, he had the ring augmented to eight, and the first peal, of Grandsire Triples, was rung for the Guild of Devonshire Ringers.

William Banister was born in 1790, the same year as Ellacombe; he came to Devon from Woolwich, where from his boyhood he had worked in the Royal Dockyard and where he had been a member, with his father and five brothers, of the Woolwich band of ringers, ringing, composing and conducting peals in Surprise methods in the 1840s and '50s and also ringing with the College Youths in the City. As a foreman caulker he was transferred in 1865 to Devonport; though he must have been dismayed to arrive in a change-ringing desert he took charge of the ringing in the *Dockyard Church* and established change-ringing there, and helped Harry Trelawny at Calstock and Charles Troyte at Huntsham; in 1874 he published a book on change ringing, which ran to three editions but never attained the popularity of Troyte's.

An early missionary venture in "scientific" ringing is described in the notebook of James R. Haworth. In August 1869 a party of ten College Youths took Brunel's broad-gauge railway for a visit to Devon; they were: H. W. Haley, J. Pettit, J. R. Haworth, G. Ferris, M. Hayes, M. A. Wood, H. Booth, J. Dwight, G. Muskett and W. Cooter. After visiting the Rev. H. T. Ellacombe at Clyst St George they were met by Charles Troyte at Tiverton (where they described the old Evans eight as "fine", which makes one wonder why the bells needed to be recast by Taylors' in

---

40. Information from the late Wilfred Boucher, the coachman's son, and from *The Kelly Book* a duplicated family history shown me by the late Michael Kelly.
41. Inspired by finding a copy of this book in the bargain-box of a second-hand bookshop, Dorothy L. Sayers went on to write her detective novel *The Nine Tailors*.

1923). Two days later they heard the Cathedral bells rung in rounds by the local band, and then tried to ring them to methods. A large number of ringers from Exeter and the villages around had gathered to hear the demonstration, but the result was a complete failure; the party reported that they were "not in a proper condition to allow of changes being rung on them", but a letter to the Exeter and Plymouth Gazette the following day from Charles Troyte and William Bannister of Plymouth virtually accused the Cathedral band of having sabotaged the bells – *if any tricks have been played upon the bells, we hope the persons who played them enjoy the disappointment of the numerous persons who assembled to hear the ringing of some of the best ringers in England . . .* It may well be that, as Jim Phillips has suggested, the Devon ringers were tired of the ranting of Ellacombe, who had for some years been trying (with no small success) to convince his fellow-clergy, the church authorities and the "great and good" in Devon that "scientific" ringing and respectable churchmanship were inseparably linked, and round-ringing was morally and socially inferior.

The situation in most towers in Devon was evidently very unsatisfactory, with prize-ringing still widespread and the ringers hardly recognizeable as part of the Church. Whether things were worse in Devon than elsewhere is uncertain, but here there was clearly an urgent need for reform. Today the whole kingdom is covered by ringers' guilds and associations which were founded to reform the Exercise, but it was here in Devon that it all began. On March 21st, 1874 a meeting was held in the office of an architect and member of a long-established landowning and clerical family, R Medley Fulford, in Cathedral Yard, Exeter. The Revs. James and Langdon Fulford, father and son from Woodbury, were there, and another Fulford, Bartholomew who was an Exeter merchant and a ringer at St Sidwell's; also present were the Rev. W.F.Gore of Feniton, Samuel Mardon and John Sharland, both school-masters, Richard Merson of Uplowman and Augustus Southey of St Sidwell's. The chair was taken by the 84-year-old H. T. Ellacombe. They proposed the foundation of **The Guild of Devonshire Ringers** to spearhead a strong attack on prize ringing; the founders, clerical and lay but mainly middle-class, believed that belfry reform was possible only if it were linked with "scientific" change-ringing. The proposed objects of the Guild were: "the cultivation of change-ringing, the promotion of belfry reform and the abolition of prize-ringing", but the last clause was not passed; there were a number of clergy and influential people who thought prize-ringing was a good old custom, and perhaps a frontal assault was thought to be unwise.

The first need was to canvass support in influential quarters, and an impressive list of forty Honorary Members was soon compiled, including one Earl, one Baron, two Colonels, one Admiral, one Captain R.N., seventeen squires and seventeen clergymen, who, to quote the sermon at the first Annual Meeting, "by a liberal expenditure of their wealth, as well as by their own zealous efforts, have been the pioneers of change-ringing in this county". Only three of them were active ringers. The aims of the Guild were soon enthusiastically embraced by the Bishop and the Archdeacons, and for some years the Guild's reports printed extracts from episcopal sermons and archidiaconal charges condemning prize-ringing as a desecration of sacred buildings. In 1886 the Guild introduced a rule which made any member who took part in a competition for prizes subject to immediate expulsion, and this was still in force over 50 years later, despite the fact that call-change ringers had long since reformed competition ringing under their own initiative..

Devon method-ringing has always been centred mainly in the towns, and particularly in the cities of Exeter and Plymouth, but in the early days there were method-ringing bands in some very out-of-the-way places – usually because of the enthusiasm of a squire or clergyman. *Huntsham* and *Kelly* we have already seen, but for the first few years of its history the Guild had a band at *Merton*, thanks to Prebendary J.A.Kempe who installed Seage's silent ringing apparatus there; *Uplowman*'s Vicar, C.S.Bere, was another enthusiast who converted his ringers to "scientific", and the parish had a pioneering band of lady ringers before the end of the 19th century; Richard Merson was one of his parishioners and the parish was part of Charles Troyte's Huntsham estate. At *Monkleigh* a band was led by William Willett, and encouraged by the Vicar, C.S.Willett. All three bands were ringing Grandsire and Stedman Doubles in 1881, but by 1886 they no longer figured in the reports. William Willett became incumbent of Monkleigh and revived the band in 1890, but in 1899 it once more vanishes from the Guild record. In 1896, the Guild tried a new tactic of admitting Associate Bands, most of which continued to ring call-changes but subscribed to the Guild's opposition to competition-ringing; some of them eventually took up change-ringing, but others, such as *Totnes* and *Torrington*, apparently never did. In 1903 another missionary venture was launched in the shape of the Exeter Ringers' Cycling Club, which visited 32 towers in that year. It *"hoped in this way to spread a knowledge of change ringing in the immediate neighbourhood of the City, and gain recruits for the Guild."*. The Cycling Club was soon making three-days tours to *"the remotest parts of the county where it has been the privilege of the Club to bring the Guild to the doors of those who, from various causes, have perhaps never heard half-pull ringing accomplished"*. It also rang some notable peals, including the first non-conducted peal for the Guild in 1905. The following year it hired a motor car so that some of the party could arrive early and *"have a good chat about bells and ringing with the local men"*, and the members were joined by the notable F.E. Robinson for a week's ringing. *"Five peals were rung,"* he reported, *"under difficulties of bad weather and long distances, (some men having to cycle 10 miles out and home, and to be at their work next morning); but 'Devonshire grit overcame all difficulties'"*. The Cycling Club ceased to function after 1912, but one of its members, Arthur W. Searle, was still ringing at the Cathedral well into the 1950s, where with his wing-collar, pince-nez glasses and flowing moustache he cut a fine Edwardian figure. The Guild for its first hundred years did not advance very rapidly in experimenting with new methods; Grandsire, Plain Bob and Stedman were the usual fare: it was not until 1955 that a resident band rang a peal of Surprise Major, but since then, thanks probably to greater mobility in the population generally which has brought more experienced ringers to live in the county, there has been a remarkable increase in peal-ringing especially in more complicated methods, and the Guild numbers some very progressive ringers among its members. No doubt the development of the University of Exeter and St Luke's College, which have their own Exeter Colleges branch of the Guild, has been a good influence.

Call-change ringing's own reformation began to take shape in 1902, when a rally at *Kingsteignton* led to the formation of the **South Devon Association for the Encouragement of Round Ringing**. This received some support from the rural clergy, who believed, as one speaker at the rally put it, that "the shifting of the population in the rural districts made change-ringing an impossibility." There was probably some truth in this, as the days were passing when a squire like Maitland Kelly could engage a coachman without discovering whether he could drive a carriage, on the strength of his being a method-ringer, and as we have seen method-ringing towers in the country areas were few and scattered. The **South Devon Association** was followed by others in different parts of the county, and by 1924, probably because the motor car and the "charabanc" had made the whole county accessible to village ringers, the **Devon Association of Bellringers** was founded at *Zeal Monachorum*. The main object of these societies was to encourage good service-ringing, which they sought to do by organizing competitions which were rung not for gold-laced hats or

Fig. 139. Call-change ringers at a competition for the reopening of Broadhempston bells in 1967. In the centre is the figure of the legendary Bill Miners of Widecombe-in-the-Moor.

money but for certificates, and many individual parishes ran their own annual competitions and festivals as well, so that a full programme of competitive ringing was soon in being for keen call-change bands, and dedications and re-openings in call-change towers are usually accompanied by a competition.

It was not until after the Second World War that the Guild and the Association began to draw together. Until then, there was a feeling among the call-change ringers – fostered to some extent by the Church hierarchy's declared preference for the Guild – that they were regarded as inferior and ignorant by the "scientific" people, and that method-ringing was almost invariably badly struck compared with call-changes and (especially when the tenor was turned in) difficult to listen to. This was not helped by the fact that in other parts of Britain call-change ringing, nicknamed "stoney" or "churchyard bob" was associated with rustic yokels who had no interest in developing their art; when the Association was finally affiliated to the Central Council of Church Bell Ringers it came as a surprise to many ringers "up the country" to hear the quality of Westcountry call-changes and particularly rising and lowering in peal: a Christmas broadcast in the '50s, of *North Tawton* ringers ringing a faultless "Queen's Peal", created a notable stir in other parts of the kingdom. In the 1950s the Guild band at *Newton St Cyres* made history by ringing well-struck methods and also taking high places in the Devon 6-bell call-change competitions, and a new joint venture for the two bodies was the founding of the Devon Church Bell Restoration Fund, which receives money and has committee members from both; more recently the Devon Ringers' Council has taken cooperation a step further.

Few historic **Ringing Customs** are maintained today in Devon. The ringing of the Curfew is still kept up at the Cathedral, where the "Peter" bell is tolled each evening, the number of strokes being the number of days in the month. John Hoker in his *History of Exeter* tells us in 1562: *For the sundry & manye comodyties aswell to artyficers and inhabitantes of this Citie, and to the Compforte of all straunges & travellors to & from this Citie especyally in the tyme of wynter, it is therefore ordered that as in the Citie of London so also yn this Citie of Exon there shalbe one Bell ronge everye mornynge & everye Evenynge yn the pishe of St Marye the Mor* . . . at 4 a.m. in summer at 5 a.m. the rest of the year. A newspaper article from the 1870s describes the customs in *Totnes*: "The curfew is still tolled every night at 8 o'clock, on the 3rd bell, except during the twelve days of Christmas, and on Sundays. After the curfew has been rung the day of the month is tolled on the 7th bell; every morning during the summer months the 3rd bell is rung at 6 o'clock, the day of the month being similarly tolled on the 7th bell; in the winter (namely from about 9 weeks before Christmas to Valentine's Day); this is done at 7 o'clock. The bell rung on Sunday mornings at 7 o'clock seems to be a relic of the early mass or Communion now discontinued, just as the bell which formerly rung immediately at the close of the morning service was a relic of the sanctus bell; of late this has been discontinued." The curfew continued to be rung at Totnes until the Second World War ban on ringing, but was not revived when the ban was lifted, and the same happened in many other places. Nicholls in *Bells thro' the Ages*[42] mentions *Lifton* and Totnes, and also mentions the ringing of the Calling Bell at Totnes at 6 a.m. and a Market Bell at 10, and an article in the *Gentleman's Magazine* in 1816 mentions two "curious customs" in *Hatherleigh*, where "every morning and evening, soon after the church-clock has struck five and nine, a bell from the same steeple announces, by distinct strokes, the number of the day of the month, intended, perhaps for unlearned villagers. The other is, that after a funeral, the church bells ring a lively peal, as in other places after a wedding; and to this custom the parishioners are perfectly reconciled, by the consideration that the deceased is removed from a scene of trouble to a state of peace." In *Kingsbridge* a bell was rung every morning to indicate the date. James Cossins in *Reminiscences of Exeter Fifty Years Since* wrote: *At eight o'clock* (on Sunday morning) *the bells of the different parish churches would toll for short time to announce there would be a morning service, as occasionally out of the seventeen parish churches open, from illness or other causes, a clergyman could not be found to do the duty; and the*

---

42. Published by Chapman & Hall, 1928.

same process was gone through after service was over. The ringing of the passing bell seems to have died out with the ban on ringing in World War II – if it still survived so long. H.H. Harvey in his *History of Clawton* says "the strange custom of ringing a peal of bells after the reading of Banns for the first time was an old custom only recently given up", and he cites an example of the same custom from Lincolnshire. One custom which does survive is the ringing at *Clyst Honiton* every 26th November in accordance with the will of Edward Trapnell, who died in 1710 leaving instructions for the ringers to be paid five shillings for ringing on his anniversary. When the five bells were augmented to eight, another parishioner provided another 3s for three more ringers. Each bell is chimed three times in turn before the bells are raised; then three peals are rung, and after lowering the tenor is chimed three times three. Another is the ringing which precedes the turning over of the Devil's Stone at *Shebbear* every 5th November: the bells are jangled anyhow before the ringers take their crowbars and turn the boulder over; the custom certainly antedates the Gunpowder Plot and was probably a pre-Christian ceremony to drive away evil, "christened" and linked with All Souls' tide. It was stopped in the first year of World War II, but the news was so bad that the people decided to carry it out a week later.[43] In several towns and some villages it is customary to ring the bells for the "Mayor-choosing" every year, even when the "Mayor" is more of a joke than anything else. A ringer who was recruited to ring for the Mayor-choosing at *Woodbury* was surprised to know that such a comparatively small village had a Mayor, and asked what his duties might be. "Well, he don't do much really", was the reply. "He may turn up at a football match now and then, but he gets served pretty rough if he do".

The *South Brent* ringers still keep up the custom of electing a Lord Chief and a Crier at their annual meeting, and entering their names in a book which dates from 1789. The rules include most of the usual ones about cursing and swearing or striking another ringer, and also the following: *That when any Ringer is chosen Lord Chief or Crier, every ringer shall behave in a sober and decent manner, penalty for breaking this rule 6d. If any Ringer talks in the Society in a ridiculous manner, penalty 2d.* The book records the ringing for the opening of the South Devon Railway (which passes through the village) in 1848, with *Breakfast for 10, 7/6d; Cider and Tobacco, 3/6d; Loaf 1/1d; Beef, 5/6d; Pint of Porter, 2½d; 8 quarts of beer, 2/-.*

Ringing Superstitions include the belief that the sound of bells can drive away evil – always supposing, of course, that that is a superstition and not a fact – who knows? We have seen that ringing against thunder was certainly done right to the end of the 19th century in some parishes; it had been ordered by Pope John IX in 900 a.d. The late Theo Brown, collector of Devon folklore, gave me three references for bells which rung of their own volition, at *Netherexe*, where the bell rang for the death of the Lord of the Manor,[44] at *St John-in-the-Wilderness* where it tolled three times for the death of the squire[45] and at *Portledge House* near Bideford, where tenants heard the bells of the church tolling, apparently for a member of the Pine-Coffin family which owned the house[46] – but the church is over a mile away over the hill.).

---

43. Mrs H.W. Oliver in *Transactions of the Devonshire Association*, Vol 80, p. 161.
44. Frank Curzon, *Lays & legends of the West*, 1847.
45. *Western Miscellany*, 1849.
46. Alasdair Alpin MacGregor, *The Ghost Book*, 1955.

9

THE CHURCH CLOCKS

CHURCH CLOCKS ARE LITTLE different from turret clocks in other buildings, and the turret clocks of Devon have been so well chronicled by Clive Ponsford in his *Devon Clocks & Clockmakers* that we will not seek to cover too exhaustively ground that has been very well covered already. Properly speaking, a *clock* has a striking mechanism, as opposed to a *timepiece* which only has a dial, and for the most part people notice the striking of a public clock more than the dial. *Ipplepen, Pilton* and *Cockington* all have dial-less clocks, and *Exeter Cathedral* and *Exeter, St Michael, Heavitree* have clocks without external dials. A timepiece has only a *going train;* a clock which strikes the hours has also a *strike train;* and a clock which strikes the quarters has a *quarters train* and is commonly known as a *three-train* clock.

A remarkable number of churches, including some in quite remote villages, possessed church clocks by the early 17th-century – indeed there is evidence for clocks in some places which do not possess them now – *Rewe, Dawlish, Exeter St Petrock* and *St Olave*, and *Feniton* all have documentary evidence of clocks but have none today, and the tenor at *Culmstock* is indented by a now-vanished clock-hammer. Incidentally, the existence of a sundial on a church does not mean that there was no clock; before the coming of the telegraph, clocks had to be checked and set by a sundial.

Our earliest church clocks have no documentation, and dating is far from easy, but we can at least assign a fairly definite date to the striking train of the *Exeter Cathedral* clock, for the "Peter" bell on which it was designed to strike was recast on a very much heavier scale than its predecessor, in 1484, and so would have needed a heavier hammer and likewise a more powerful strike train. Moreover, the design of the train is very similar to that of the Cotehele House clock in Cornwall which can fairly confidently be dated to 1485 when the chapel was built with a recess expressly designed for it.

These two movements were both mounted on a vertical post secured to the wall, and have *flail locking*; the Cathedral movement was mounted separately at some distance above the going train, and let off by a wire, but the Cotehele clock had an underslung *foliot* (a weighted horizontal bar which rotates to and fro) with a *verge*

Fig. 140. Exeter Cathedral: the going-train of the ancient clock, dating from 1484.

THE CHURCH CLOCKS

Fig. 141. Cothele House, Cornwall. The clock in the chapel which was built in 1485, with the trains one above the other and a foliot instead of a pendulum.

escapement; no doubt the Cathedral going train would have been very similar, and it seems likely that, in the West Country at least, the earliest turret clocks had this type of movement.[47] Flail locking, in which the train is locked and released by a long arm some 3 or 4 feet long, requires a locking-plate which has notches on the inside and teeth on the outside of its rim: similar locking-plates are found, recycled, in the clocks at *Ipplepen* and *Ottery St Mary*.

Fig. 142. St John's, Hartland Town. The clock by John Morcombe, 1621, in a "field-gate" frame. It formerly had a foliot but was converted to a pendulum and re-wheeled. It is wound by hand, using the bars on the barrels.

The vertically-mounted movement was supplanted in the South-west by the *field-gate* frame in which the trains are mounted end-to-end. The clock in the former *St John's, Hartland Town*, made by John Morcombe in 1621, is of this type (another can be found at Porlock and there is a group in Dorset) with clear evidence that it was originally built with an overhead foliot; the rivet-holes for the cock and the opening for the verge in the top rail are still there. The clock was re-wheeled and converted to a pendulum and anchor escapement in the 18th century, when

---

47. This may be true of the country as a whole, if one shares the opinion that the Salisbury Cathedral clock, whose late-14th-century dating rests on very dubious documentary evidence, is contemporary with the 16th-century clock at Rye, and probably by the same maker.

Fig. 143. Ipplepen. The oak-framed clock, probably late 17th-century but incorporating parts from an older movement. Most of the wheels are of wrought-iron, and the pendulum-bob is cast in lead from a handbell pattern.

Fig. 144. Modbury. The movment by Ambrose Hawkins, 1705.

practically all our existing turret clocks were updated for the sake of the pendulum's vastly superior timekeeping. It is wound using capstan-bars on the barrels.

The old clock at *Ottery St Mary* has a four-posted frame, but the trains are set end-to-end, the only one of this type in the county. It may have been wound with capstan-bars but has for centuries been wound using counter-wound ropes which run to winding barrels at ground level, and this arrangement may be original. However, as has been mentioned, the present movement incorporates parts from an earlier, flail-locking clock, and the astronomical dial, similar to that at Exeter Cathedral, may predate it.

Ipplepen has the county's only known turret clock with a wooden frame and shows many signs of great age even in its present form, though some of its parts may be even older; the 78-toothed main wheel of the going train has internal notches showing that it was originally made to be the locking-plate of a flail-locking movement. Its pendulum's hung from a cock above the frame, and linked to the pallets by a horizontal rod (a feature it shares with the old *Exeter Cathedral* clock and *St Mary Steps, Exeter*), and is wound from ground floor level by counter-wound ropes, like the former clock at *Denbury* and the old *Ottery St Mary* movement. It has a four-posted frame, made of oak with turned finials to the posts; the pivot-bars are wrought-iron. Devon has no four-posted-frame clocks which show clear evidence of having been converted from either a foliot or a verge escapement.

The wrought-iron-framed, four-posted movement with the trains side by side probably reached Devon in the late

THE CHURCH CLOCKS

Fig. 145. The clock by Lewis Pridham, 1711, at Newton St Cyres, restored and auto-wound.

Fig. 146. Brixham St Mary. The preserved movement by William Stumbels of Totnes, dated 1740. The count-wheel has projections instead of the more usual notches.

17th century, when many new clocks with pendulums and anchor escapements replaced the earlier types. Among the makers of these were some of Devon's most celebrated makers: **Ambrose Hawkins** made clocks for *Dartmouth* and *Modbury* and **William Stumbels** of Aveton Gifford and Totnes, built a church clock at *Brixham*; both are well known for exceptionally fine domestic clocks, including Stumbels's magnificent month-going, musical and astronomical long-case clock at Powderham Castle; while **Jacob Lovelace**, who probably built a new going train for *Exeter Cathedral* made the famous "Exeter Clock" with its multitude of automata, musical and astronomical features, fragments of which are preserved in Liverpool. However, a number of far less sophisticated makers, such as **Lewis Pridham** of Sandford, **John Cole** of Barnstaple and **Francis Pile** of Honiton, whose domestic clocks are for the most part simple, 30-hour movements, made excellent turret clocks which (unlike Hawkins's and all but one of Stumbels's) are still running to this day. These movements were also 30-hour, with anchor escapements; those installed in churches were almost always set by sliding the pallets out of engagement, though private-house clocks, which usually had shorter leading-off work and smaller dials, were sometimes fitted with friction clutches. Pendulum rods were iron, and pendulum beats often run to curious figures; Pridham's *Newton St Cyres* clock of 1711, for example, has a 78-tooth main wheel driving a 9-leaf pinion and a pendulum beat of 46.2 a minute: the rod has a weld half-way up, and it seems likely that the gear ratio was chosen to equalize the wear on the teeth of the wheels and pinions, and the pendulum rod was made in two sections, adjusted until it was the right length, and then forge-welded (in another clock which had a 80:10 ratio, the wear was found to be so uneven that the wheel and pinion would bind unless they were meshed as they had been before). The frames were normally made of iron bar about 2 x ½", which was imported from Sweden in quantities at this period (the old clock at *Broadhembury* displayed the trade-mark of its Swedish iron-master), but William Stumbels and a few others showed great skill and artistry in their ironwork, and most early 18th-century clock-frames have finials in the shape of knobs or scrolls.

These early pendulum clocks were comparatively crude pieces of machinery. Their weights were hung from hemp (or occasionally leather) ropes which were bulky and limited the number of turns that could be

Fig. 147. Colyton. The main movement is probably by Pridham, *c*1710: the quarter-clock on the right has iron wheels and is probably older.

Fig. 148. Exeter, St Mary Steps. The movement of "Matthew the Miller", 1725: the pendulum on the extreme left is linked to the pallets by a horizontal rod.

accommodated on a barrel. They were lubricated with "train-oil" or grease, which in time became hardened; hence the rather surprising entry in the accounts of *Gittisham* in 1725, *for boiling ye Clock & brasses 1s*.[48]

Until the early 18th-century it would seem that quarter-chimes were operated by separate *quarter-clocks* let off by the going-train of a two-train movement; such quarter-clocks still exist at *Colyton* and *Otterton*; the earliest clock in Devon with three trains in one frame is the famous one at *St Mary Steps, Exeter*, 1725, by **Joseph Robertson**; like most quarter-chiming clocks of this period it uses "ting-tang" quarters, in this case sounded by jacks on two hemispherical gongs. *Thorverton* has a three-train clock of 1751 by **John Tickle** of Crediton which sounds ting-tangs on the tower bells. Rarely, one finds 18th-century turret clocks which sound a passing single stroke at the half-hour; the disused movement at *Talaton* was one such.

Thanks to the work of Abraham Darby in the middle of the 18th century a cheap and plentiful supply of cast-iron led to a great improvement in turret clocks. Until that time there had been a limit to the power that could be

---

48. However, Joshua Slocum in *Sailing Alone Around the World* describes his tin clock as going better "after I had boiled her".

Fig. 149. Talaton. Movement by Francis Pyle of Honiton, 1752, now superseded.

Fig. 150. The first cast-iron-framed clock in Devon, at the Royal Naval Hospital, Plymouth, signed by Grignon & Son, London but probably by Thwaites.

applied to a wrought-iron frame without distorting it, and this was the chief reason for the short running-time of any large movement, but the far greater rigidity of cast-iron made it possible to used heavier weights and heavier pendulum-bobs, so that four-wheel trains could be used, running for several days on a winding, and with greater accuracy than before. This greater accuracy, and the less frequent winding, led to the fitting of *maintaining-power* to keep the clock running while it was being wound, and this in turn encouraged makers to offer *dead-beat escapements*, the earliest being Graham's type, as alternatives to the anchor (recoil) type, though in practice these more up-to-date escapements do not offer much better timekeeping in a turret-clock. Another refinement was the use of *rack striking*, which was regarded as superior to *locking-plate* or *count*-wheel striking in domestic clocks as it allowed the clock to be advanced through the hour without waiting for the strike to be completed – a feature which is in fact very seldom important in a church clock. The earliest cast-iron turret-clock in Devon was at the *Royal Naval Hospital, Stonehouse, Plymouth* built by a London maker, but by the end of the century local makers like the **Pollards** were offering cast-iron-framed clocks though the simpler, cheaper wrought-iron clocks, mostly with a 30-hour running period, were still being supplied to those who wanted them until at least 1813, when Pollard of Crediton supplied one to *Ashreigny*. Many of these are still running, since electric auto-winding has eliminated the need for daily winding; indeed several 30-hour clocks, out

Fig. 151. The beautiful clock of 1852 by T.J. Pollard of London (but from Devon) at Combeinteignhead.

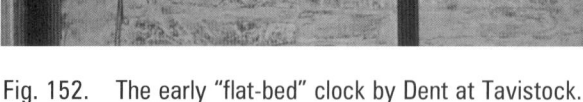

Fig. 152. The early "flat-bed" clock by Dent at Tavistock.

Fig. 153. A fine early "flat-bed" movment of 1851, at St Paul's, Honiton, signed by Matthew Murch but probably imported from France.

of use because nobody could be found to wind them, have been restored and set going again with auto-winding. It should be noted, however, that auto-wound clocks still need someone to look after them and keep them adjusted.

As with bells, so with clocks, as the 19th-century went on the local makers were gradually eclipsed by the big city firms, and by the 1840s most of our church clocks, though often bearing the local clock-maker's name, were bought in from Bristol or London makers and installed by local men. The remarkably fine clock at *Combeinteignhead*, indeed, was made by **Thomas C. Pollard**, of a well-known clockmaking family from Crediton, who had moved to London and for some time worked for Dent.

The design of turret-clocks was revolutionized in the 19th century by the development of the *flat-bed* movement to replace the 4-posted frame. This was a French invention; the first in Devon was made by **Benjamin Vulliamy** for the *Royal William Victualling Yard, Stonehouse* in 1831, and later a simpler form was introduced by **E.J.Dent** whose great clock in the Palace of Westminster, "Big Ben", 1860, established it as the dominant type for thenceforward. Dent had supplied *Woodbury* in 1846 with the first flat-bed church clock in Devon, a rather light example, probably one of a number imported from France – though Dent strongly denied doing this. In 1851, **Matthew Murch**, a Honiton clockmaker, installed a splendid flat-bed clock in *St Paul's, Honiton*, which he almost certainly imported from France, and from that time onwards flat-bed clocks, which are very much easier to service and repair than clocks with posted frames, steadily supplanted the earlier type; some 4-posted clocks such as the one at *Swimbridge*, installed in the 1880s, were evidently second-hand.

The other innovation which enabled Dent to secure the contract for the Westminster clock was the brilliant double-3-legged *gravity escapement* invented by Lord Grimthorpe – a device which, like all the greatest inventions, is in essence wonderfully simple. By making the impulse delivered to the pendulum entirely independent of the power which drives the going train, it allows a turret clock to maintain very accurate timekeeping despite rain, wind, ice, snow or birds sitting on the hands, and most makers adopted it very quickly, particularly for clocks with more than one dial – Smiths' of Derby normally fitted single-dial clocks with a pinwheel escapement. A variant of the more common double 3-legged escapement is a 15-legged one at *Ottery St Mary*.

Fig. 154. The gravity escapement at Ottery St Mary, by Gillett & Bland, 1874.

Fig. 155. Exeter, St John. The two minute-hands, for local and "railway" time, can just be seen in thie early photograph.

Another fashion which stemmed from the fame of the Westminster clock was the "Westminster" quarter-chimes – which in fact had been composed by Dr Crotch for the clock of Great St Mary's, Cambridge and are more accurately called "Cambridge" quarters. They became so popular as to be almost universal, even in 6-bell towers, and *Yarcombe* used a curious adaptation for five bells. *Tiverton St Peter* is notable in having "Whittington" quarters.

The coming of the railways created an increased demand for accuracy in public clocks, and the development of the telegraph made it possible for the whole kingdom to be put on a single standard time, where before each town or village had kept its own time, regulated, more or less, by a sundial – hence the appearance on churches of sundials of later date than the clock in the tower. It is possible to see in several places in Devon (*Sidmouth* is one example) how a new clock come to be installed in the church just at the time soon after the railway reached the town, though in *Exeter* there was a strong resistance to giving up "our" time in favour of "railway time". Because of the resulting confusion, with Exeter people frequently missing their trains, the clock of *St John's* church, which with its dial overhanging Fore Street was the most prominent public clock in the city, was fitted with an extra minute-hand, 14 minutes ahead of the existing one; as the *Exeter Flying Post,* 16 October 1845, has it, "the railway

Fig. 156. Braunton. The movement is signed by Ford of Barnstaple, but was made by a London maker, probably Sainsbury of Walthamstow.

Fig. 157. Stoke Gabriel: a typical late-19th century or early 20th-century flat-bed movement by Smith of Derby.

time is shown by a silvered hand, the minute hand denoting *the true time* (our italics) being gilt." *Tavistock* had equipped its church with a new clock from Dent in 1849 which was specifically "to keep Tavistock time", but in 1859 a Town Meeting voted "that the Portreeve be instructed to entrust Mr Snell (a local watchmaker) to keep the town clock by railway time", the Great Western Railway having reached the town the previous year.

The development of flat-bed movements, involving even more specialized castings, virtually eliminated local makers from the field of turret clocks, but they continued often to act as contractors and installers, so that the names of **Ford** of Barnstaple, **Squire** of Bideford, **Depree, Ellis & Young** of Exeter, and **Page, Keen & Page** of Plymouth appear on movements built by **Gillett, Gillett & Bland** and **Gillett & Johnston** of Croydon, **Smith** of Clerkenwell, **Thwaites & Reed** and **Benson** of London and **Sainsbury** of Walthamstow. So far we have not found any clocks by **Smiths' of Derby** bearing any name but their own.

In the early years of the 20th century Gillett & Johnston introduced a new type of movement, which had essentially a plate-&-spacer frame carrying the barrels, main-wheels and second wheels, with the other pivots mounted in bolted-on units above, usually with a double 3-legged gravity escapement. The same escapement modules were also mounted on electrically rewound movements, as at *Paignton St John*.

Fig. 158. A "plate-&-spacer" framed clock by Gillett & Johnston, 1910, at Kenton.

During World War I it was believed (possibly with reason) that German Zeppelins were coming over Britain and lurking above a low cloud-base with their engines stopped to listen for a striking clock to give them the location of a town or village. As a result many if not all clocks were silenced; there are pencilled notes inside the cases of the clocks at *Whimple* and *Cullompton Old Police-station* recording this: the former also notes the beginning of Daylight Saving:

The Clock was advanced one hour (Daylight saving time) on May 20th 1916.
The Clock was stopped from striking (on account of Air Raids) on August 19th 1916.
The Clock was put back one hour (old time) on September 30th 1916.

Electric auto-winding has been increasing in popularity over the last fifty years, not only because it no longer requires someone to climb the tower – sometimes up steep or vertical ladders – to wind the clock at frequent (even daily) intervals, but because it allows much smaller weights to be used: some turret-clock weights can weigh as much as a quarter of a tonne, and present quite a hazard in the event of a weight-line breaking; it must be remembered that any extra vibration can cause a weakened weight-line or anchorage to fail, so that there is quite a strong likelihood that it will happen when the bells are being rung, as has happened in fairly recent years at *Holsworthy* and at *Crediton*, causing much alarm but luckily no injury to the ringers. Early types of auto-wind based on endless chains, adapted from the Huygens system, are simple and efficient, but involve long runs of chain some of which is usually exposed to dirt and damp; the same disadvantage applies, rather more acutely, to the so-called "monkey-up-a-stick" types in which the motor itself acts as the weight and winds itself up an endless chain. Units using epicyclic gearing, which are now most prevalent, have the advantage that the weights themselves can be hung on wires and therefore can be positioned more conveniently in the tower.

Mechanical turret-clocks are now no longer in regular production, and new installations are almost invariably synchronous electric or quartz movements with electric motors or solenoids used to operate the hammers: the last pendulum-driven clock in the county – and probably in the country – was installed at *Widecombe-in-the-Moor* in 1979; it has an auto-wound going train with a direct-drive strike. In some cases these devices have been installed in place of mechanical movements, but although they are cheaper to install they promise a much shorter working life and quicker obsolescence than the movements which they replace, and a good mechanical turret-clock movement seldom becomes so badly worn that it is impossible to restore. Today the code of practice issued by the Council for the Care of Churches makes it unlikely that Faculties will be granted for replacing mechanical clocks except in exceptional circumstances.

Chime-barrels

From quite early times, devices have been made to allow several bells to be sounded without the need for one or more ringers for each bell. These machines normally consist of a drum or barrel with pins which raise and release levers linked to chiming-hammers, rather in the manner of a musical-box: the barrel may be driven by a hand-crank, or more often by a weight and set off by a clock. These machines, often referred to as "carillons", but more correctly chime-barrels, were much commoner in the 18th and 19th-centuries than they are today: we have several still, though not many are in regular use. Our earliest surviving tune-playing chime-barrels are those at *Thorverton* and *Otterton*, the former still in use and using *flail-locking*, a system which probably dates the movement to the 17th-century or even earlier: it plays the hymn-tune, "York" on six bells, and must have been brought here from some other church as until the mid-19th-century Thorverton had only four. Otterton's is probably 18th-century, but also seems to have come from some other tower, it is no longer working. *Ottery St Mary* has a chime-barrel which also is not now working, but *Tavistock's* (which may have been built originally by Thomas Bilbie II, who built a fine one for Beamister in Dorset) is still in working order, and plays seven different tunes; Tavistock had chimes back in 1574. *Crediton* has one, probably by Thwaites & Reed, 1838, which may one day be restored to use; *St Andrew's, Plymouth*, still possesses a fine Gillett & Johnston machine with very sophisticated trigger-action, but it has been superseded by an electronically-operated one; a similar machine at *All Saints', Brixham*, is still working, and was installed to commemorate the Rev. H.F. Lyte, whose hymn *Abide with Me* is included in its repertoire. *Holsworthy* has one, also by Gillett & Johnston, which is pneumatically driven and among other tunes plays S.S.Wesley's *Holsworthy Church Bells*. Among the churches which once had chime-barrels but have them no longer are *Exeter St Petrock*[49] where chimes are mentioned in records as early as 1472, and *Exeter Cathedral*, where chimes were installed by Hugh Chapingdon of South Molton in 1582, *Chudleigh*, 1584, *Cullompton*, 1610, *Exeter Holy Trinity*, 1655, *Exeter St Sidwell's*, 1691 and *South Molton*, 1699 (where they were "righted" by Ambrose Hawkins). There is also evidence for them at *Honiton St Michael's*, where until a few years ago the barrel of a chiming machine was standing on end outside the church, *Axminster*, where one used to play the Fiftieth Psalm and "Britons Strike Home", and *Barnstaple St Peter*. It is sometimes possible to deduce the former existence of a chime-barrel from the pins on the locking-plate of the clock which used to release it; conversely, it was presence of such pins on the clock at *Bishop's Tawton* which

Fig. 159. The chime-barrel at Thorverton, with iron wheels and flail locking.

---

49. A footnote to Brice's *Mobiad*, written in 1738 and published in 1770, states that *at 8, 12, and 4 o'clock St Petrock's chimes play Sternhold's queer old Tune of the Fourth Psalm.*

enabled us to deduce that it had once belonged to *Barnstaple*, and also confirmed our suspicions that that the *Exminster* clock had come from Crediton.

A mention of chimes in the accounts of *Woolfardisworthy East* in 1708 is surprising as there were (and are) only three bells there, but this probably refers to a simple hand-driven machine for ringing rounds on the bells: such machines still exists at *Branscombe* and *Colyton*. As we have seen, it was customary between the 17th and the 19th-centuries for the bells to be chimed on Sundays, rather than rung, and this no doubt encouraged the use of these hand-driven barrels which normally chime the bells in rounds. The invention of the chiming apparatus which H. T. Ellacombe devised with the specific purpose of dispensing with the Bitton ringers on a Sunday, is no doubt one reason for the disappearance of these machines; another, of course, is the happy revival of Sunday service ringing thanks to the reforms of the later 19th century.

Appendix I

PENNINGTON DOCUMENTS

1. The Will of John Pennington, 1659 CCRO P995/1

In the name of God Amen. I John Pennington of Bodmin in the Countie of Cornwall Belfounder being sicke and weeke of Body but of sound and pfect memory praysed be God, doe make and ordaine this my last will and Testament in manner followling (sic)

   Imprimis as every Christian man ought to doe I commend my soule into hands of Almighty God my maker and redeemer and my bodie I commit unto Christian buriall

   Item I doe give unto every of my children both sonnes and daughters twelve pence a piece when they shall lawfully demaded (sic).

   All the rest of my goods and chattells not formerly given nor bequeathed I do give and bequeath and make and devise unto Wilmoth Pennington my wife, my debts and legacies payd and my funerall expences discharged I doe make and ordaine her my whole and sole executrix In witness hereof I have hereunto set my hand and seale hearin the eleventh day of September in theyeare of our Lord Christ 1659

Sealed signed in the p'sence of   *The signe of*   X   *John*
John Harrys   *Penington*
Edward Penington
The signe of X Amies Leay

Probate Inventory of John Pennington, 1660 P995/2

An Inventorie of the goods and Chattels of John Pennington Belfounder of Bodmyn in the County of Cornwall praysed the twenty third day of June 1660 praysed by Sampson Crabb Joseph Richards

Imp^s his purse girdell and wearing apparrel	xxx^s
Beds bedsteads boulsters pillows and all other things belonging to the same	iij^{li}
In puter	x^s
2 brass crocks and 2 kittells	xxx^s
1 Cubbert 2 table boards and 2 chaires	x^s
2 Cushings	ij^s vi^d
1 ould Coffer & 2 boxes and all other timber stuffe	viij^s viij^d
4 ? . . . brasses	xxx^s
In Bill Bonds & Chattells	x^{li}
For all other things not thought on	iij^s iiij^d
	xix^{li} iiij^s vj^d

Sampson Crabb
Joseph Richards

2. Probate Inventory of Bernard Pennington of Bodmin, 1674 P1339/2

An Inventory of the goods & Chattles late of Bernard Pennngton late of Bodmyn deceased taken and appraised the 22nd of September 1674 by us William Brabyn of the sayd Borrough Tanner & William Armld of the same Taylor

Imprimis his purse and notary apparell	20-00-00
In the parlor two bedds & furniture thereunto belonginge	10-00-00
In the deep chamber two bedds & furniture thereunto belonginge	06-00-00
In the litle chamber two bedds & furniture thereunto belonginge	03-00-00
In the higher Buttery one bedd & furniture thereunto belongnge	02-05-00
The furniture of the hall tenn joint stooles and one paire of Andirons one paire of doggs one Chaire one Chest two musketts one sword & a paire of bandoleers	01-15-00
In the higher chamber one featherbedd one flockbedd	02-15-00
One dozen of pewter one dozen & halfe of brasse candlesticks one dozen and three flaggons three salts five pewter chamber potts on dozen of pewter plates three pewter butter plates	08-00-00
The new brasse potts & new brase panns	20-00-00
The old brasse potts & old brasse panns & suchlike things	10-00-00
The brewing pann & brewing Ceeve & Coolers	03-00-00
In the kitching three brasse potts two brasse kittells three spitts one jack one . . . . one gridiron one board one small paire of handirons two paires of pothookes two paire of pothangings one sillett	03-00-00
Two silver bowles half dozen of silver spoones one litle tankard & one sugar dish	03-00-00
The cellar & hogsheds & barrells & materialls	01-10-00
Two horses & their tackell	05-00-00
One cow & one hefer	05-00-00
One half dozen of pewter spoones & half dozen of . . . dishes on . . . Two bucketts & three piggs troughs one barrow one ladder two piare of Paniers two piare of dung potts one shovell two paire of . . . One short pick one Evill 2 hayrakes	01-00-04

105-05-04
Willliam Brabyn
Will Arnold

(A "ceeve" or "kieve" is a sieve. An "evil" or "heavel" is a four-pronged pitchfork. Dung pots were containers with hinged bottoms which were carried by a pack-horse.)

3. The Will of Christopher Pennington of Bodmin, 1697 P2044/1

In the name of God Amen I Christopher Pennngton of ye Borrough of Bodmin the ye County of Cornwall being by ye good will of God visited with sicknes but by his mercy of fit memory and understanding and beinge truly sensible of my unstable state and condition, do hereby make and constitute this my last will and Testament.

First I humbly render back my soul into the hands of Almighty God who made it hoping for Salvation in and through ye merits of Jesus Christ my Lord and redeemer and desire yt my body may have a decent and Christian buriall, and as to what belongs unto the goods and chattels yt God hath been pleased to bless me wth I doe hereby ordain as followeth.

First I give and bequeath unto each of my Children whether Son or Daughter the sum of five shillings.

Itm I doe ordaine that my executrix shall pay unto my son Robert ye sum of ffower pounds to further his trade out of the Roul *of my work house of . . . . . . shall soe do if ye estate wch I have therein shall continew soe long as that ye Roul be suffisal to pay him.*

Item I doe Ordayn that after ye decease of Susanna my Wife my three best panns shall remain to my three daughters my wife havinge the use of them during her life but in case my wife shall in her life tyme have occasion to dispose of them . . . . . soe to doe, then my will is y^t ye price be equally divided into fowre parts whereof my wife shall have one part and my three daughters ye remaining . . . Soe in case y^t either or any of my said daughters . . . . . . to dye . . . . . .

Lastly all my goods and chattles not hereby before disposed of . . . . unto my wife Susanna whom I hereby make and appoint my sole and only executrix of this my last will and Testament hereby re . . . oninge all other herebefore made whether by word or in writing in witness whereof I have signed sealed and Acknowledg'd
In the p'sence of
    Will Wood   *Chris Pennington*
    George Ffrench

The Probate Inventory of Christopher Pennington, 1699 P2044/2

Aprill 27th An^o Domini 1699
Inventory of the Goods and Chattels of Christopher
Pennington late of the Borrough of Bodmin and taken by John Pennington and
Nicholas Bradley of the s^d Borrough.

Imprimis	his purse and wearing apparell	02-00-00
	His Chattell right in his house ye work house & sleye	08-00-00
	An old horse and a mare	02-10-00
	Four Bullocks and a young Calfe	07-00-00
	Goods and things belonging to his trade in the shop	11-08-08
	4 small milk panns	00-12-00
	3 kettles	00-12-00
	4 old brasse panns	01-00-00
	3 skilletts	00-03-00
	1 brasse pann	00-10-00
	Brasse candlesticks & a small mortar & lye pott	01-00-00
	3 old Chaufors, a Skimmer, a skillett & a dripping spoone	00-03-00
	a warming pann	00-03-00
	2 dozen of old pewter plates	00-08-00
	one dozen & 7 old platters, two pw' plates	02-02-00
	5 basons and a Cullander	00-05-00
	6 flaggons	00-03-00
	4 small old tanketts a bottle & 2 cupps	00-03-00
	4 candlesticks	00-03-06
	2 butter plates & 6 porringers	00-04-00
	4 fether bedds	04-00-00
	4 bolsters	00-16-00
	5 pillows	00-05-00
	2 ~~Truckle~~ bedsteads wth ~~courtains & Vallances~~	00-16-00
	1 presse and a small table	00-08-00
	2 Truckle bedsteads	00-03-00
	1 presse or chest	00-10-00
	An old Trunke & 2 boxes	00-02-00
	6 old joynt stooles	00-06-00
	2 tables & 1 forme & a Livery table	00-07-00

7 Chaires	*00-05-00*
An old presse	*00-05-00*
3 p^r of Andirons	*00-04-00*
4 p^r of sheets 2 board cloathes & 2 dozen of Napkins	*01-05-00*
6 jacks & 3 spitts	*00-06-02*
4 pillow drawers	*00-02-00*
the goods in the work house	*05-00-00*
Lumber & small things y^{at} may be omitted	*00-10-00*

57-19-02
John Pennington
Nicholas Bradley

Appendix II

BELLFOUNDING DOCUMENTS

1. Bell Exchange at Ashburton

Alison Hanham, ed., *Churchwardens' Accounts of Ashburton, 1479–1580*, Devon & Cornwall Record Society, NS 15, 1970. The early accounts are written in a mixture of Latin and English.

1503–4

for belcoleres		2s	8d
for yreworke to the belles and frankincense, and a nother belcoler		4s	6d
for mending of a bell to William Schaptor			8d
For the bell change at on tyme	£3	4s	6d
For John Gye to ride to Exceter to take the tewne in the belle			20d
For carige of the bell and thechyng of the waye		10s	4d
For havyng up of the bell and belcoleres		2s	6d
For the chaunge of the bell at a nother tyme		44s	8d
For caryge of the same bell and a man to schew hym the waye		7s	
John Prediaux and Noseworthe ther labour and coste at Exceter		3s	
For havyng up of the saide bell and yreworke to the same		2s	4d
For caryng of the bell to Exceter		6s	8d

1508–9

To John Mayne & John Frubber to turne a bell	4s	8d

1509–10

23^d and 10^{lb} of hemp (calibis) *received from and for ringing on the night of the Feats of All Saints less the expenses of the ringers on that night.*

73^s 4^d paid in full payment for the exchange of the great bell weighing 1816^{lb}., nearly 1613½ ^{lb} of olde metall abated. And so the same bell is greater in weight by 202½ ^{lb}, paiyng for each 100^{lb} of new metal 28^s. Sum 56^s 10^d. And for le castynge of every 100^{lb} of old metall 7^s. Sum 113^s 4^d and for a reward to the bell founder 20^s Sum total £9 10^s 2^d Whereof the Wardens paid on this account 73^s 4^d. Besides 40^s paid from the account of the Grene Torches by Thomas Mathewe, with 24^d which remains in the hands of the said Thomas from the same account. And besides 48^s 9^d paid by the said wardens from the account of last year.

8^d for carriage of metal for weighing the said bell.

2. TakingWoodbury Bells to Ash Priors: Woodbury Wardens' Accounts, 1557–8

1557

Gift to the Belles by the Pishoners	*Itm receyved of Xpofor* (Christopher) *Wescott and George Seyward* of the gift of the pishe to the casting of the bells for the Est pte of Wodbury*	*xlvj^s*	*viij^d*

Itm receyved of John Wescott of Combe and Thoms
Yong receyvers of the pishe for the gifts to the casting of
the bells for the Weste pte of Wodbury — iij^{li} xiij^s iiij^d
Som of the gifts to the belles — vj^{li}

Sum tole of all the receipts and gifts of the dead with the gifte of the pishoners
 to the belles — xx^{li} viij^s

Payments for the charges of the Bells
Pd to Willm Bond and his brother for striking of the bells — xx^d
paid for their bourding — iiij^s iiij^d
pd for drinking for them that went forth that caried the bells to Aishe Priors before
 their going att Richard Bussells — v^d
paid att Larksbere the Sonday, for v mens supper & fetching of a yoke — xxj^d
pd there for oxen meate (fodder for oxen) — ij^s iiij^d
paid for showing (shoeing) of the Wardeyns horse — vj^d
paid at Kentisbeare the Monday in the morning for their drinking — ix^d
Itm paid att Milv'ton (Milverton) the same day att supper for ix men — iij^s
Itm paid for oxen meate there that day — iij^s
paid at Halse the Tewesday — vj^d
paid the same day att Aish Priors for denr (dinner) — ij^s
pd for their supper there that day — ij^s
paid for their denar there the Wednysday — xviij^d
paid for their supper there the same day — iij^s iiij^d
paid for their denar there the Thursdaye — ij^s
pd there the same day for their supper — xvj^d
paid for their denar there the Frydaye — xvj^d
pd the same day there att supper — xij^d
paid the Satterday att brekefast — viij^d
paid for their bedding — viij^d
paid for meate for the oxen four daies to Roger Symson & John Langham — xvij^s iiij^d
pd for showing of oxen there — xvj^d
paid for the showing of Thoms Halls eight oxen — v^s iiij^d
pd att Milv'rton homeward the Satt'day att night for supper — x^d
paid the same night for oxen there — ij^d
Itm for brekefast there the Sondaye — xvj^d
pd for going over the fermors (farmer's) grounde att Harford Bridge — xij^d
paid the same night at Kentisbeare for supper — v^s vj^d
pd the Monday for brekefast there — xj^d
paid to Thomas Farryn for a yoke — iiij^d
Itm paid att Jane Bussells homeward for drynkyng — iiij^d
paid to Baldewyn, carpenter, his two men, and his bwaye (boy), thre dayes — vj^s
paid for their table, and theym that were helping of them — xj^s
paid to the same Baldwyn carpenter and his bwaye for half a daye — vi^d
paid for their table the same half daye — xij^d
pd the same Baldwyn for a whele for the bell — v^s
pd to Richard yate for a staple & a pegon and nailes for locke and keyes — vj^s
pd to John Lee for showing of his oxen — ij^s viij^d
pd for the lone of a pulley & cariage home of the same pullie agayne — viij^d

pd to ffraunces Gale for the lone of a roope to trusse up the bells   ij^s viij^d

pd for the laying againe of the thre flowers (floors) *after the bells were had up and for nayles to fasten the bourds*   xj^d

to Joan Eliott for grese for the bells   iij^d

pd to Roger Symson the Belluter in pte of payment of a more some   x^{li}

paid to Willm Roper for making of two clappers att Busshoppes liddiard   xlvij^s viij^d

1558

Paid to Henry Toune for making a paier of Indentures and an Obligacon betwene the parishe aforesaid and one Roger Symson of Aishe Priors bellfounder for the casting of two bells for Woddebury   iij^s

First paid unto Roger Sympson bellfounder att his second payment   v^{li}

paid to the same Roger att hys third payment   v^{li}

paid for four cruitches for the bells and for the yerne (iron) *worke thereto appteinyng*   vj^s

paid for making the clapsis to cover the bells and for staples of yron thereunto belonging wt the workmanship   xviij^d

paid to John Baldwyne for a whele for the great bell   v^s

paid for a staple for the great bell   viij^d

paid for trussing of the fourth bell and the newe making of one of the stiropes and for nailes for the same bell   ij^s

3. SouthTawton Wardens' Accounts

1533

6^{li} *solut Tho Geffray belfounder* (Thomas Geffries of Bristol)

1534

iiii^{li} *solut the Belfounder in pleno* (in full)

1535

vi^s *sol pr campana voc a lechebell* (a bell called a Lychbell – a handbell rung in front of a funeral procession)

1561

Item paid unto Kettletree for his paynes taken and for his labor beyng here to see the bell   ii^s

1570

(The bell involved in this account was recast at Honeychurch, where there is a 16th-century bell which must have been cast at this time; this account identifies it as the work of Thomas Birdall.)

    The delyverye of the great bell delyvered to Thomas Byrdall yn the yere ad 1570. Item delyvered out yn the presence of John Blakedon Wyllyam Ffrende Henrye Dawe and lawrance ffursman yn weyght of the great bell 1944^{li} and receyved agayne 2491^{li} ther ys mettall then to be payde yn the great Bell 547^{li}.

Item delyvered yn weyght to Thomas Byrdall for the lytell bell yn the presence of the men above named - 624^{li} and the bell ?? broken mettall 102^{li}.

    So the hole somme delyvered ys 726^{li} and receved 805^{li} so there ys to be payde yn mettall yn the lyttell bell 74^{li} So the hole mettall of both bells that ys dew to be paide amount 621^{li} at v^s the pound.

(The account below is all written consecutively, but is transcribed here in columnar form.)

It vi^d payed	to John Blakedon for the dynnr when he first did vewe the bells
It vi^s & vi^d payed	to John Blakedon for takyng downe of the bells
It iiii^s iiii^d payed	to iiii^{or} men for ther labor wth meate & drinke for ii dayes for ther helpe towards the takynge downe of the saied bells
It ii^d payed	for a mans labor to bete barres of iron
It iiii^d payed	for fettyng & delyveryng a Cabull (cable) rope at Ingwardleigh
It ii^s payed	for the wretyne (writing) betwyne the caster of the bells & wardens
It iii^s iiii^d payed	for weynyng (loading on a waggon) of the sayed bells & mens labor to go with them to honychyrche (Honeychurch) & for haye for the oxen wch caryed them
It ii^s vi^d	for ther meate & drynke wch carryed the bells to honychyrche
And i^d payed	for spooks of iron to staye the bells
It iii^s payed	to John Blakedon to se the bells weyed (see the bells weighed) at honychyrche & to iii men to go wt hym thether
And to iii^d payed	for a mans labor to cawse the saied blacdon to come to wey the saied bells
And iiii^s iiii^d payed	for tymber wch made the planchyn (planking) yn the towre
And iiii^{li} payed	to the belfounder at northwyke (North Week near South Tawton)
And iii^s iiii^d payed	for carryng of tymb (timber) ffrom northwyke to Tawton
And ii^d x^d	for John Blakedon & ii men to way the bells at honychyrche
And vi^d payed	for a mans labor to go to Chagford to fett wights to wey the bells & for bearing of them thether agayne
And xii^d payed	for ii dayes labor & charges at honychyrche when the bells were yn castyng
And xii^d	for weying of the lytell bell
And xxi^d payed	for carryng home of the lyttell bell yn expences
And ii^d payed	for A buckell for the therde bell
And x^s iiii^d payed	for iii newe bell ropes
And iiii^s iiii^d payed	for three newe bell collers
And v^s viii^d pay	to iiii^{or} men for iiii^{or} dayes labor for makyng of the bell wheles & for workyng of tymb
And viii^s payed	for meate & drynke for the sayed iiii^{or} men for iiii^{or} dayes

(much more for carpenters & helpers.)

And xii^d payed	for for weyng of the greate bell
And iiii^s payed	for mens labor to fett home the greate bell wth ther meate & drynke
And v^s payed	for iron worke for the greate bell & mendyng of a clapper
And vi^d payed	for lone of a powlye (pulley)
And ii^d payed	for Carryng of a yowke (yoke for oxen) to honychyrche
And iiii^{li} payed	to Thomas Byrdall at Exeter for his seconde payment
And xii^d payed	for rydyng to exeter to paye the saied some of iiii^{li}
And xii^d payed	for Iron worke for the bell wheles
And xiiii^d payed	for mendyng of the stocke of the greate bell for one dayes labor with his meate
and xi^{id} payed	to iii men wch trussed & untrussed the greate bell
And vii^{li} payed	to Thomas Byrdall for the iii^{rde} payment of the bells & for mettall
And xi^d payed	to ryde to exeter for payment of the saied vii^{li}
And iiii^d payed	to exell (axle) a Weyne for fettyng home of the greate bell
And xvi^d payed	for iron work for the greate bell
And v^s iiii^d payed	for a whele for the greate bell
and vi^d payed	for fettyng home of the greate bell whele
And xviii^d payed	for mendyng of the clocke & the stocke of the greate bell

and xviii^d payed	*to John Rowe for his meate & drynke for iiii^or dayes aboutt the mendyng of the clock & the stocke of the greate bell*	
And xii^d payed	*for a mans labor to helpe the foresayd Rowe*	
and xviii^d	*for meate & drynke of the other man for iii dayes*	

4. A Recasting involving Three Bellfounders: Braunton Churchwardens' accounts

1581 (Headwardens' account: the parish still had a number of different "stores", as most parishes had before the Reformation.)

to the Belluter	xxiiiis	
for caredge of Clay		xid
for Carridge of stones	iis	
for iii dossen of wood		xxviid
for carridge of the same		xiid
for bearing the same wood to the house		iiid
for delving of stones		ixd
to one to attend the belluter vi dayes	iis	vid
for a borde of oke for the belluter		vid
to Robert Tollen for a Barr of yron which the Belluter hadd		xvd

(A inventory of 1581 includes "i grett rope for ye steeple")

1581 (another account following the accounts of the store of St John & St George.)

Itm to the bellfounder for casting the bell	vli iis	
to wm Heddon for the wast of his yron wch was at the herthe of the furnace		xviiid
for carridge of mettall from yearnescombe		xiid
to James browne for delving of stones to buyld the furnace		iiid
for carridge of the stones		viiid
to Symon Gilbert for stones		viid
to Robartt Tollen for a new staple for the new bell	iis	vid
to the same Robert for amending the new bell clapper		?
~~*cutting shorter of the little*~~		
to make them drink wch did help downe the old bell		xviiid
to make them drink wch did help the new bell upp	iiis	iiiid
Wm Greenway for fetching a pully & a rope at Aish for the hoisting of the bell		iiid

1582 (a/c as above)

to John Allen for filling the pitt wherein the bell was cast	vid

1591 (Four men' account.)

pd to John Birdall Belfonder the first of maye in pte of payment for new castinge of the third bell	xxxs	
for 42 pounde of mettell and halfe at v^d the pound of the said Birdall the xv^th daye of Maye	xviis	viiid
pd to the said belfounder one assention daye	vs	
pd to him againe the xviii^th of may	iis	
againe the xx^th of maye	xxs	
more to him the xxii^th of maye	xs	
pd to the belfound^r againe the xxiii of maye	xxixs	vid
pd to the belfond^r in Iron soe much as came to	xiiis	vid

to the belfond^r the xth of June	xls	
spent in meat & drinck & for the labor of the watchmen for the safe keeping of the metall the first night aft^r casting ye bell		xviid
to John Kent for Riding at Barnestable ii tymes for fetching of metall		xvid
pd to the Belfounder Wm Poole the xix^th of August in earnest for the casting of the 2 greatest bells	vs	
pd to Richard Woode for i daies worck about the tymbring of the howse for casting the bells in		xd
pd for 40 sheves of reed for the said howse	iis	
pd to Symon Hamont for 2 daies worck in delving stones for the belfounders		xxd
pd to Philipp Reed ye yong^r for his labor 5 daies about carrying of stone & wood for the belfounders	iiis	iiiid
pd for labor of his horsses one daie & halfe		ixd
pd to Richard Payne for wood for the belfounder	iiis	
pd to Arthur Lock for his labor 7 daies & half to attend the belfounders		xxid

(many more entries for wood and labour.)

pd for halfe a pound of frankyncense for ye bells		vid
pd for turpentyne for ye same		viiid
pd for Rasome for the same worck		iiiid
pd for Allam		iid
pd for Ashes		vid
pd for 2 pounde of Seame for the Belfounder		xd
pd for 2 pounde of wax for ye same worcke		xxd
pd for xl sheves of wood for ye bellfounders		vid
pd for a pound & half of hempe for ye belfounder		vd
pd for a myll brass for the bells	vs	ixd
pd to the belfounder	xs	
pd to Wm Poole Belfounder for his expenses & paynes when he went to Annery to see metall for ye bells		xiid
pd for Drinck & Dreggs for ye belfounders worck		vid
pd for furses for ye belfounder		iid
pd more unto 2 watchmen Anoth^r night		viiid
pd to Phillipp houghe for pewter vessels for the bells		xixd
in ale for the ringers at the setting up of the bell spent for the Dinner of the Poore People		iiiid
pd to John Singe for making of a Iron Pynne for m^r richard Bellewes great Pullye & other Irons about the bells		xixd
for making the obligation between the pishe & the belfounders		iiiid
pd to John Peter for the Carriadge of a Crock from Wysham for the foresaid bell		iiid
for the expensis of William Bowden ii daies when hee went at Barnestable to buy metall for the bell		viiid
memorandm ye said wardens received for metall that was left at the casting of the bell since this account iiii^li iii^s iiii^d wch mony was paid by them as followeth		
Imprimis pd to John White for potmetall bought of him at casting of ye bell		xls
Itm to Mr Bellews for collens		xs
Itm to John Wheale for pot metall		xxxiiis

APPENDICES

1593 (Headwardens' account.)

Imprimis paid to John Wheak for belmetall	*iiis*	*vid*
pd to John Singe for Iron & Iron worck about ye new bells	*vis*	*viiid*
pd to Robert Aclond for 5 daies worck at setting upp ye bells	*iiis*	*viiid*
pd to Preston belfonder in earnest for casting of ye bells		*iid*
pd for bread & drinck for those that did helpe downe ye bells	*iis*	
pd for ye labor of 3 marriners that did sett up ye tacle		*xiid*
pd to Willima Beare & Phillip Wooly for the fetching of a great crock for the bells at Annery	*iis*	*vid*
pd for the lent of the bote that carried the said crock		*iiiid*
pd for the labor of a man & 2 horsses that did fetch up the said crock from the vilata		*iiiid*
pd to Wm Brook for his charges when he went to anery for to see the weighting of the great crock		*viid*
pd to Edward Garland for 4 seames of wood for ye bells	*iis*	*iiiid*
pd to Gilbert Harris the 23 of September for belmetall	*xxs*	
pd to Peter Knill for 4 daies worck about helping up ye bells	*iiis*	*iiiid*
pd to Richard Wood for worck about helping upp ye new bells & mending the weenlace	*iiis*	*viiid*
pd to Arthur Lock for 5 daies worck attending ye belfounder		*xviiid*
pd to Phillip Reed for 5 daies worck about ye bells	*iiis*	*iiiid*
pd to Wm Brook & Peter ffosse monye to helpe pay for a new hosser for helping up the bells	*vis*	
pd to Mr Richard Bellow in pte of paymt for ye great crok	*xxs*	
pd to Wm Poole belfonder the last of October	*xvs*	
pd for the breakfast of those that did helpe to weene upp the bells	*iis*	*vid*
pd to Phillipp Marck for ye wast of his iron in the belfounders furnice & for breaking of his sledg		*xid*
pd ye watchmen that watched ye bells one night		*xiid*
pd for drinck for ye belfonder at casting of the bells		*iid*
pd to the belfonder the 3 of October	*xxs*	

1593 (Brannock store account.)

paid to John Sing for making a new Pegg for ye Second Bell and alsoe for a chucking iron for driving out the broken pegg		*xviiid*
pd to antonie morrishe for setting upp of the same		*iiiid*
to Mr Richard Bellew in pte of paymt for the great crock that was bought at annery		*xiid*
to Mr Bellews reve		*ob*
for thetching of the belhowse & lathing it	*xvs*	
to William Poole Belfonder	*iis*	*vid*

(probably same date but not on an adjoining page)

to Jo. Singe for arighting of Iron for removing of the Clock from the great Bell to the Little bell		*viiid*
pd Jo. Hodge the viiith of September for a crock that the pishe had of him for the third bell	*iiiis*	*iiiid*

1594 (Headwardens' account.)

Received of the pishe of Fremington for Bell metall	*xxxiis*	
pd to John Marck Peter Crampe & John Toker monye the pishe owed them for helping upp ye bells the last yeere		*xid*
pd for 2 pounde of morte for the Belfounder		*xd*
pd for 2 pounde of hempe for the Belfounder		*xd*
pd to Wm Symons of beere for vi seames of wood for ye Belfounder	*iiis*	*vid*
pd to Alice Payne for wood likewise	*iiiis*	
pd to Thomas Quick likewise for woode		*xvid*

pd to Phillip Reed for carriadg of Wood & Cley for the Bell		xxiid
pd to John Cock for carrying of woode likewise		iiiid
pd for the Carriadge of more wood for the same purpose		xvid
pd to Robert Dallen for cleving of wood & one to helpe him	iis	iiiid
pd to John Galsworthie for clevinge of woode		viid
pd to a weeks worck to him that attended the belfond^r & delivered wood		xiid
pd for Rasome Turpintyn Allome and drawsens for ye Belfound^r		xiiid
pd for 2 pounde of wax likewise		xxid
pd for barck Ashes for the Bell & the Carriadge		vid
pd for halfe a Quarterne of Rewd for the Belhowse		viiid
pd for Reftering the said howse		iiiid
to Symon Longe for Thetching the same howse		iiiid
to one that did serve him & gathered rodds & neeles		iiiid
for Sparrs for the same howse		iid
pd to Phillip Marck for a hatchet for the Belfounder		xd
for a Buckat for the Belfounder		iiiid
pd to Gilbert Harris for Belmetall	iiili	xs
for carriadge of the same Metall		ixd
for Carriadge of the Pullies from Ashe		iid
for Candells for the Belfounder		id
to Robert Aclonde for 2 halfe dayes worck about Ripping the seats for carriadg out of the bell & setting upp againe of the same seats in the Church		viiid
to John Schore & Jo. Pickard for a dayes worck about Trussinge the new bell & the third bell		xxd
pd to Arthur Lock for all his labor about tending ye Belfound^r	ixs	
pd for Candells when the aforesaid Carpenters wrought uppon the bells	iiis	
for charges at Takinge downe of the Great bell		viiid
for expensis at Castinge of the Bell		viiid
for expensis at Taking up the bell of the pitt and Bringing of him into the Church		viiid
for expensis at hanging upp of the Bell and to the Maryners John Clogg & Phillip Weat the same tyme		ixd
to John Singe for the Iron Ringe about the cannells of the great Bell & for keys & varlocks for ye same	iis	iid
to John Singe for worcking 16 pounde of old Iron into Braces for the said Bell		xvid
to Jo Singe for the wast of his iron in the belfounder furnis		xvid
pd to Richard Stephin for the Belfounder	xls	
pd to the Belfounder another tyme		vid
pd to the Belfounder at his depture	vis	viiid

1594 (Brannock store account)

pd to John Singe for the belfounders tooles	xis	viiid
to the belfounder in pte of his waigis	vis	viiid
in drowsens for the belfounder		iid
to Richard Stephins for drinck & drowsens for ye belfounder	vis	
at takinge downe of the bell in drinck & meat		xviiid
in drinck at breakinge abroad the bell		iid
in drinck at casting the bell		iid
for ye supper for them that helpe the bell in ye tower	iis	iid
to John Sing for 3 staples for the Clapses of the bells & nayles		iiiid

to Phillip Marck for shorting the great bell clapper   ixd
for turninge ye 3 bell clapper & making a new eare on him   xxd
for an iron to picke the bells wth all   iid

(A note, undated and badly mutilated, between the headwardens' accounts & others.)
A note taken manye yeres past at ye buying of . . .
Cage of Bells wth in the Tower of Braunton as . . .
& what wight each of the said bels then was.

Imprimis the formost bell in wight	x^c and xxx^{li} for ye hundred xxviii^s
	Summa xiiii^{li} vii^s vi^d
Itm the Second Bell weyeth	xiiii^c lxx^{li} for the hundred xxviii^s
	Summa valu xix^{li} xiiii^d
Itm the Third Bell weyeth	xix^c and xxx^{li} for the hundred ut sup
	Summ xxvi^{li} xii^d
Itm the Great bell weyeth	xxv^c xxiiii^{li} for the hundred ut sup
	Summ xxxv^{li} v^s ix^d
Somma tot valu dict iiii^{or} campanar	lxxxxvi^{li} xv^s vi^d

M^o against every hundred weight in a bell ther must be iii^{li} of
iron in the clapper (that is to weete) a bell of x^c weight
the clapper must be xxx^{li} and for after that rate.

(Incomplete note, undated, apparently c1591.)

In primis of Birdall ye Belfonder	69^{li} & half
and a bell of Mr Richard Bellowes in wight	xi^{li}
And more metall of Birdall	v schore xiiii^{li} & half
ye hollinwater buckat wch was ye pishes	xiiii^{li} in weight
Jo. Bennet iii crocks conteyning	75 pound
Jo. White crock	40^{li} & half
Jo. Hodges crock	13^{li} . . .
another crock of Jo. White	xxiii . . .
Tynne of Jo. White	x^{li} . . .
	Some total 24 schore 17^{li} & h . . .
	at v schore the hundred

Glossary:

dossen	dozen
rasome	resin
allam	alum
seames	? (normally packhorse loads, but evidently not here)
hosser	hawser
weenlace	windlass
weene	wind (up)
morte	lard or grease
drawsens, drowsens	?
rewd	reed
sparrs	thatching spears

cannells	cannons
keys & varlocks	different types of keys
clapses	bearing covers

5. A Major Recasting at Plymouth: Plymouth & West Devon Record Office

The "Widey Court Book", a beautifully-written account book of Plymouth town council. Apart from giving a detailed description of the whole operation, in which two of Plymouth's most celebrated citizens had a part, this document casts a sharp light on the daunting prospect of 16th-century accountancy, when £2.37½p could be expressed as £2 7s 6d, 47s 6d, ii^{li} vii^s vi^d, or xlvii^s vi^d, and when c^{li} could mean 100 pounds sterling or 112 pounds in weight – or perhaps 100 pounds in weight.

1594

Charges disboursed for the bels appearing as followithe

Imprims payed to Mr Goddart for Tymber as by the bill of perticulers appeareth	vi^{li}	iii^s	ix^d
Itm pd to Robert Myco for sixe beames at Yealme	ix^{li}	xii^s	
Itm pd to John Haymes as by his bill of pticulers appeareth		liii^s	
Itm pd to Mr Sparcke for a pece of elme beinge 4 foote		iiii^s	
Itm pd him for a pece of tymber to make the bell stocks		xxxvi^s	viii^d
Itm pd him for fyne winscotte		xxv^s	
Itm pd Mr Hitchins for twoe beames		xxvi^s	viii^d
Itm pd Hugh Sampson for one beame		xxvi^s	viii^d
Itm pd for fetchinge the six beames from Yealme		xxxiv^s	x^{xd}
Itm pd for three bellstocks wch came from Armyngton		xx^s	
Itm pd for bringing them to the water side			xviii^d
Itm pd for carryenge of tymber & beames to the church		x^s	iii^d
Itm pd for makynge the takell to hoyse uppe the tymber into the Tower			xii^d
Itm pd to certayne marriners for hoyestinge uppe of tymber into the Tower & for 13 Irishe bords		vii^s	ix^d
Itm pd for beare when the first beame was hoysed up			xii^d
Itm pd for fetchinge the blocke abord shippe to make the takell withall			xiii^d
John Moxye for a hawser waieing 400 and qt att one pound fower shilling three pence pr li(/)	l^{li}	ii^s	?
Itm pd to John Facye for a hawser for more than his guift was for the bells		xl^s	ii^d
Itm pd John Scobell for a roppe waienge 23^{li}		l^s	ix^d
Itm pd John Robbyns of Plympton for nyne hundred three quarters & Nynetyne pounde of tynn at iii^{li} xii^s pr ^{cli} wth waienge & carriadge thereof	xxxv^{li}	xvi^s	vii^d
Itm pd to Peter Edgecombe of Tavystocke for fyve hundred twenty & six pound of Tynn att iii^{li} xiii^s iiii^d pr ^{cli} wth the carriage thereof	xxx^{li}	v^s	viii^d
Itm pd for morestones to John Trounce for the bottom and mouth of the furnysse		v^s	
Itm pd for one and twentye seames of stones		x^s	iiii^d
Itm pd Reyle for a boat of stones		iiii^s	
Itm pd for iiior busshells of lyme		ii^s	
Itm pd for 7 busshels of sand & carriadge thereof			xii^d
Itm pd for iiii^{or} (four) horses hier (hire) to carrye stones & claye		iiii^s	
Itm pd for bricke for the furnice		viii^s	
Itm pd John Trounce for makinge the furnice		xxxii^s	ix^d
Itm pd to divers laborers for riddinge the furnice and the place where the bells were cast		xlvii^s	vi^d
Itm pd to Shipherd and Luke for carryenge of earth and clay		xvii^s	
Itm pd for carrienge a boat of stones from the water syde unto the same furnice		iii^s	iii^d

Itm pd laborer for attending the worckmen one whole weeke		11^s	vi^d
Itm pd for six seame of Claye			xii^d
Itm pd for one pounde & three quarters of wax to make the townes armes in the bells			xix^d
Itm pd laborers to rame earth about the mooles (moulds)		vii^s	vi^d
Itm pd for carrienge of deale bordes to cover the furnice			vi^d
Itm pd two laborers for fyve days & two neights worke when the mettell was meltinge		vi^s	
Itm pd for rommagenge & bringing to shoare of a broken peice of ordynance wch Sr Francice Drake and Sr John Hawkins gave towarde the bells		vi^s	viii^d
Itm pd for carryenge five broken bares to the furnace		iiii^s	ii^d
Itm pd for carryenge the waights when the metell was waied & for beare then		ii^s	vi^d
Itm pd the flemynge for woode more then the founder allowed		xiii^s	
Itm pd for wyne when the greate bell was taken downe out of the tower		iii^s	viii^d
Itm pd for wyne and beare at divers sevrall tymes		iiii^s	x^d
Itm pd Lampen & his man for one weeke worke att xiiii^d a daie ech of theym		xiii^s	vii^d
Itm pd him more the seconde weeke for himself		xxii^s	x^d
Itm pd him more the third weeke for himself and his mens labor		xlv^s	viii^d
Itm pd him the fowerth weeke as by the perticuler appeareth	iii^{li}	vii^s	i^d
Itm pd him the fyveth weeke as by the perticulers appeareth		lvii^s	vi^d
Itm pd Sallamon and his twoe men for one weeke worke		xviii^s	
Itm pd Lampen the sixeth as maye appeare by bill of prticulers		lii^s	ix^d
Itm pd Lampen the 7th weeke as appeareth by a bill of prtyculers		xxii^s	xi^d
Itm pd Lampen the 8th weeke as by a bill of the prtyculers appeareth		lviii^s	ix^d
Itm pd Lampen the 9th weeke as by the prticulers appeareth		xlvii^s	vii^d
Itm pd Sallamon & three men for sawinge of timber two dayes		viii^s	
Itm pd a leven laborers for carryenge of timber to the Church		viii^s	ii^d
Itm pd Cornishe for drawinge of timber to the church			x^d
Itm pd for charges in castinge of the litle bell		xv^s	i^d
Itm pd to George Shere for iron worke over & above allowance of old iron as by his bill appeareth	xiii^{li}	xvi^s	x^d
Itm pd for floxe (flux)			xv^d
Itm pd for carrienge awaye of robbell (rubble)		xiii^s	
Itm pd Nicholas Blake for a drie (??)		iii^s	
Itm pd Mr Goddard for bringinge the fyve bases and landing of theym			x^d
Itm pd for exchange of ffrench monie & pistolette			xx^d
Itm pd to Laurence Wreight Belfounder for meltinge of Twelve thousand seaven hundred and one quarter of mettell at x^s pr c^{li}	lxiii^{li}	xii^s	vi^d
Itm pd him more for fyve paire of bases (? brasses)	v^{li}		
Itm pd him more toward his charge in comynge downe from London		l^s	
Itm pd John Scoble wch Wreight left unpayed for wch Mr Maior gave his word	v^{li}		
Itm pd Wreights men for castinge the five paire of brases		xiii^s	iiii^d
Itm pd his two men toward theire comynge		vi^s	viii^d
Itm pd John Trounce and his men for makinge of a hole throughe the vaut in the Tower		vi^s	i^d
Itm pd Mr Goddard for two litle bells weighenge thre hundred three quarters & fower pound at liii^s iiii^d pr ^{cli}	x^{li}	x^s	ii^d
Itm pd him more for three quarters & two pounds of shruffe (scrap brass)		xxxv^s	x^d
Itm pd him more for one brasse base weighenge eight hundred three quarters & seven pound abating for iron two quarters and fowertene pound at l^s pr c^{li}	xx^{li}	vi^s	iiii^d

Itm pd Wm Sowneman for fortie poundes of shruffe at v^d pr pound			...
Itm pd John Scoble for feiftie nyne pounde of mettell at v^d the pounde		xxiiii^s	vii^d
Itm pd Henrie Lawrie for ffortie poundes of mettell at v^d the pounde		xxi^s	viii^d
Itm paied Wm Gill for a bell weighinge 70 pounde att vi^d pr pounde ie xxxv^s			
whereof he received xxx^s and thother v^s gave toward the bells		xxx^s	
Itm pd lawrence Wreight for 556^li of mettell at xl^s pr c^li	xi^li		
Itm pd Joseph Gubbes for 17 pound of mettall at v^d pr li		vii^s	
Itm pd Dennys for three pound			xii^d
Itm pd John White for lvii pound at v^d pr pound		xxiii^s	ix^d
Itm pd a Tyncker for 33 pound		xiii^s	ix^d
Itm pd Wreights man for lvi pound of mettell at v^d pr li		xxv^s	viii^d
Itm pd for 44 pounde of mettell to a Brasier at v^d pr li		xx^s	
Itm pd William Haynes for 22^li at v^d pr li		viii^s	vi^d
Itm pd M^r ffownes for mettell	v^li	iii^s	iiii^d
Itm pd Mr John Trelawny for mettell	iiii^li	xvi^s	x^d
Itm pd Vincent Scoble for mettell		xlvi^s	viii^d
Itm pd John Meicke for mettell			xxv^d
Sum	xxxiii^li	iii^s	iiii^d
Sum – total pr solutione campan	cclxxxxiiii^li	xii^s	iiii^d

(In receipts)
Collected by Peter Antonye & Wm Neyle   cxix^li   iii^s   x^d

6. Hartland: Water Transport and a collection from the Youth of the Parish

1613

Receaued of John Blagdon as a guift from the youth of the parish towardes		
the Casting of the Bells	iij^li	xij^s

(John Blagdon was also one of the Collectors for the main church rate that year.)

R' of Mr Docton & M^res Docton as a gift from them for the same purpose	xxviij^s	
R' of M^res Elizabeth Docton as a gift from her for the said purpose	ij^s	
Itm pd to Alse Popham for drinke when the 3 bells were let downe		iij^d
Itm to the Belfounder at earnest		xij^d
Itm pd to Alse Popham for drinke when the 4th Bell was let downe		x^d
Itm pd to John Colman to hoise out ye Bells at Barnestaple key	ij^s	
Itm pd to William Skinner for carrying ye Bells vp & Downe	xxxviij^s	
Itm for being at Barnestaple when the Bells were carryed vp, for 2 daies expences	ij^s	
and for my horse meat (fodder for horses)		vj^d
Itm when Thomas Cholwill and my selfe were to Barnestaple 3 daies to see the Bells cast	vj^s	
And for horse meat the same tyme		xviij^d
Itm when I was at Barnestaple to fetch home the Bells when he did appoint to new cast the		
4th Bell for 3 daies & horse meate the same tyme	iiij^s	vj^d
Itm pd to Philip Nicholl for carrying the Bells to Northam from Barnestaple in a boate	vij^s	vj^d
Itm to Honor Strange men to hoyse out the Bells into Skinners boate	ij^s	vj^d
Itm when I was to Northam to receaue ye Bells from Barn'		vj^d
Itm pd to Hugh Nicholl of Brounsham for 6 daies to helpe ye Bells		
to Barnestaple and home for his expences and labour	iiij^s	vj^d
Itm paid to William Pollard to helpe vp the Bells and Beames		xviij^d

Itm pd to Pollards men for the like helpe   vj^d

Itm pd to John Juell for his helpe   xvj^d

Itm pd to James Meye for his helpe   iij^d

Itm pd to Sampson Prust for his helpe   iiij^d

Itm pd to Abraham Bond and his man for a daies worke about the beames and Bells   iij^s ix^d

Itm pd to Richard Meye for 2 daies worke   xviij^d

Itm pd to William Meye for 2 daies worke   ij^s

Itm pd to Alse Popham and for drinke ye same 2 daies   xviij^d

Itm pd to William Holloford for makeing ye iron about ye Bells & nailes for the same   iij^s

More defraied about the casting of the Bells and mettall for the same to the Belfounder as appeareth by 2 severall acquittances for the same   xxj^{li} xv^s

more laid out   iij^{li} x^s

7. Tiverton, 1629

Articles of covennte indented had made concluded and agreed upon the fower and twentieth daye of ffebruarye Ano 1629. Between the ffeoffees of Mr Robert Chilcott good uses in Tiverton and the Churchwardens of Tiverton aforesaid of one pte. And Thomas Pennington of the Citye of Exon Bell founder of the other pte. As followeth.

   imprimis It is agreed upon between the said pties, And the said Thomas Pennington doth hereby covennte and promise that he shall and will new caste the ffiveth or great Bell that is now crazed in the Tower of Tiverton aforesaid, and make another new Bell of the said mettall, sounde, agreeable, and tuneable to and with the other fower bells that are now in the aforesaid Tower according to the order of Musicke: And if it happen that the new Bell made of the said mettall doe or shall craze or breake within the space of one whole yeare next after it shall the hanged settled and runge in the Tower of Tiverton aforesaid that then the said Thomnas Pennington shall and will caste again the said Bell at his own proper coste and charge, and make and deliver him sounde, agreeable and tuneable according to the other ffower bells as aforesaid.

   Item it is also agreed upon by and between the said pties that the said Thomas Pennington shall receive the said Bell mettall by weight, and to redeliver the Bell made of the said mettall according to the same weighte that it is delivered unto him, And if it happen that the said Thomas Pennington doe adde and putt more mettall of his own to make the said bell tuneable as aforesaid, that then the said Thomas Pennington shall have twelve pence for every pounde weighte of the mettall soe added and putt to: And if the said Thomas Pennington doe caste the said Bell to be to great burthen and not tuneable to the rest, that then the said Thomas shall sett and putt him in tune as aforesaid, and such mettall as shal be clipped or hewen out of the Bell, to have and take payinge for the same unto the said ffeoffess and churchwardens Twelve pence a pounde, for every pounde soe clipped and hewen out of the said Bell.

   Item the said Thomas Pennington doth likewise covennte and promise that he shall and will caste the said Bell mettall by itself and without mixture of any other Bell, and what metall shalbe therunto added shalbe of the like goodnes, and that it shalbe caste and done with the concent and in the view of the said ffeoffees and churchwardens and their assignes, And to give notice to the said ffeoffees and churchwardens seven days before the said Thomas doth intend to caste the said Bell, And to newe caste the said Bell of the same mettall as aforesaid with two days next after the receite thereof, and deliver the Bell soe new caste unto the said ffeoffees and churchwardens or to their assignes within seaven daies next after he shall receive the said mettall.

   Item the said ffeoffees and churchwardens doe covennte and promise that they shall and will at their coste and charge carrie the said Bell mettall to Exon aforesaid, and recarrie the said Bell (when it shalbe new caste) from the said Thomas Pennington's castinge place without Northgate in Exon aforesaid; and alsoe shall and will paie unto the said Thomas Pennington seaven shillings lawful English money for every hundred of merchante weighte that shall be sent to him at Exon aforesaid for the new castinge thereof; and paie the said money within tenne dayes next after the Bell shalbe handed upe settled and tuneable as aforesaid in the said Tower of Tiverton. In witness whereof the pties aforesaid to these pntes their handes and seales interchangeable have set the daie and year first above written.

    Signed sealed and delivered   By me Thomas
    in the Pnse of   Pennington
    Thomas Cogan
    Geo. Bryse
    William Marks

8. Goodleigh: John Pennington, Fitzantony Pennington and John Stadler

1656
Rec'd
Gift money £8 for new casting of our bell from John Skinner & John Pasmore[50]

Imprimis pd Mr John Penitent for Casting of our bell	8	0	0
pd to Mr John Penitent for the Mettle which was put into our bell the some of	xi^{li}	08	8
pd to George Brothers for wood	0	6	0
pd to Richard carder for Raghters and hard wood to dry the Molds and melting of the Mettle	1	3	0
pd to William ? ? for the great Rope and one Bell Rope and ? Marly and Hempe	00	16	8
pd to fetch the Cabinge (cable) Rope	0	1	0
pd to John Brother to thetch it	0	3	10
pd to fetch Rude and other things for Rud (thatching reed) and speres (spars) of Ruds	0	2	0
pd Taken down & up the Bell	0	6	0
pd to John Toker for makinge Ire worke a Bout the Bells and all other things	1	16	6
pd for two Blockes	0	2	6
pd to Thomas Knight for ston	0	1	0
more for stone	0	0	4
pd to John Harres for horse Donge	0	2	0

1676

pd Mr Pennington for casting of the second bell	6	0	0
pd for 66li of mettell a 1s 2d pr li comes to	3	17	0
pd in expences when the pishioners made the bargaine with Mr Pennington	0	10	0
pd for taking downe of the bell	0	6	0
pd in expences when we carryed the bell at Swimbridge	0	8	0
pd Thomas Budd for carrying the bell at Swimbridge & home againe	0	10	0
pd for making the Covenants with the bell founder	0	2	0
pd in expences for find sevall dayes before the bell was cast	0	5	0
pd for lent of the grates & the bell stapell	0	6	6

---

50. John Passmore was born in 1622, and married Margaret Berry at Swimbridge in 1657. John Skinner was married to Christian Somer at Chittlehampton in 1658. They seem to have been fulfilling the function of the "young men", cf Widecombe, Hartland and Colebrooke.

APPENDICES

pd for 4 dayes and two nights at Swimbridge for dyett & in expences for the wardens and the bell founder & his man & Giles ffrost & others of the pishoner for taking the bell out of the pitt & for carrying him into the Church	0	15	8
pd for taking up the bell into the tower	0	5	0
pd Giles ffrost for being at Swimbridge two dayes & two nights when the bell was cast	0	4	0
pd when mr ffitz Antho: pennington came to receive his money twice	0	6	7
pd for amercement for the bell	0	2	6

(The last surviving bell by Fitzantony I is dated 1671, and the "Mr Pennington" mentioned may have been Christopher I: a bell with his and his father's initials is dated 1668.)

1684

Rec'd for wood wch was left of w^t was Bought for casting of the bell & the house	0	17	0
Rec'd for the Iron wch came from out of the furnice	0	1	7
paid homphrey Stribling for Diging the pitt for to Cast the bell in	00	02	00
paid Robert Stribling for one days work for himself and his men to Build the house to cast the bell in	00	02	04
paid for 16 sheves of Rude	00	03	00
paid Bartholamew Lee for Thatching the house	00	01	06
paid homphrey Stribling for Diging the Loung pitt	00	01	00

(more entries for stones, clay, drawsens & beer, horse dung, *to Sabyna Breach for carring of water*, cleaving of wood, &c.)

One pound of cannells & one li of tallow	0	0	9
pd for a bord for ye Moulds, & for ye hier of A beame for ye pitt & bords for beating ye Clay one & A planke to Draing in ye Bell upon & other things he used	0	1	6
more paid for ye mending of Tho: Striblings Sladg wch was Broken in Break the Mettell	0	1	6
paid for expences when the pishoners made A Bargain wth Mr Stadler for Casting ye Bell	0	3	6

9. Ashwater Churchwardens' Accounts: Casting a bell locally in 1671

1671

pd to John Ellery for expenses & horses meat to Mter Penitent when he came to see the bell	3	6
pd to John Holman for 14 seames of wood & for caryinge the same into the Church	10	0
pd for beere for y^m y^t did help take downe the bell	1	6
pd Jo Holman for 4 dayes worke	4	0
pd Jo Holman for 13 rige to make the bell house	3	6
pd Jo Holman for 3 dayes worke	3	0
pd to him againe for wood	1	0
pd to Alexander Hockaday for 2 dayes worke	2	0
pd to Tobias & Edward Striblin for worke about ye bells	5	0
pd for beere for them y^t did help the bell from the Church to the pitt		6
pd for candels when the bell was cast		6
pd to Jo Holman for ashes		2
pd for beere to them y^t did help weight the bell	1	0
pd for my owne labour for 10 dayes	10	0
pd to Jo Holman & Alexander Hockaday for takeing up the earth about the bell	1	0
pd for beere for them y^t did help the bell from the pitt into the Church	1	0

pd for beere for them y^t did help in the bell into ye tower		1	0
pd to Mr Penitent for casting the bell	10	0	0
pd for makinge 4 new brasses of the old & adding 3^lb of metell		16	10
pd for two new brasses	1	3	4
pd to Arthur Bassett for 56lb of iron and bringing the same from Holsworthy		9	4
pd to Willm Collins for workinge up the same for ye bells		16	8
more for workinge of the old iron		8	0
pd to him for mendinge the clapper		9	0
pd him more for mending the second time		5	0
pd more for mending the clapper			6
pd for 14 days attendant about the bell worke		14	0
pd to Ed Bastin for thetching the bell house			6
pd to Jo Short Esq for 5 loade of stones & caryinge the same		7	6
pd to him for reed & strawe		1	6
pd to Willm Ball for drawinge of stone		1	9
pd to Willm Ball for drawinge of stone		3	3
pd to Willm Ball for lent of 4 posts for ye bellhouse			6
pd to Michael Davy for carrying one seam of bolmet			6
pd to Tobias & Edward Striblin for carrying of clay & for weighing the bell for lettinge downe & taking up & hanginge the bell for mendinge the frame & puttinge in the brasses & making the bellhouse & for a roller for the littel bell	3	0	0
pd to Jo Holman for attendinge Mr Penitent when he mended the leade		1	0
pd to Jo Ellery for 3 seames of horse dung & two bundles of hay		2	8
pd to Gideon Crocker for 12 seames of horse dung & carryinge the same		6	0
rige	softwood planks from Riga		
bolmet	?		
seames	packhorse loads		

10. John Pennington of Tavistock casting Instow bells across the Torridge at Littleham

1683

*An Acct of George Punchard & Anthony Nickell Deputy Churchwardens
for Mr Edward Fleming & Roger Burges given in and made
up to the prish this 9th of Aprill 1683 of their Disbursmts
on casting of the third bell as followeth viz:*

Imps pd the bellfounder for his coming heare	00	10	00
pd for board when the belfounder came heare	00	02	02
pd for beare when the belfounder came heare	00	01	00
pd for beare when the bell was caryed away	00	1	00
pd for beare when the bell was weighed	00	1	6
pd for beare when the bell was caryed to the Boate	00	0	4
pd for beare when ye bell was brought ashoare of the Boat	00	0	8
pd for beare when ye bell was brought out of the Church	00	1	0
pd for bere when ye bell was brought into ye Church	00	1	6
pd to Anthony Nickell for goeing to Littleham when ye bell was Cast and for expences	00	6	0
pd to a shipcarpenter of Bitheforde (Bideford) for a plainke to make stocks for the wheeles	00	18	00
pd for bringing ye plainke from Bitheforde to the keye	00	2	0
pd for bringing ye plainke from the keye to the Church	00	1	6

pd for beere when the plainke was brought up	00	1	0
for goeing to Bitheford to buye the plainke	00	1	0
pd James Downman for peeces	00	2	0
pd Mr Prince for A plainke	00	1	0
pd John Kent for Cake	00	7	0
allowed Anthony Nickell for one daye to goe to Littleham when ye bell was cast	00	1	0
pd for a wan lace (windlass)	00	2	0
pd John Rude for A Board	00	1	0
pd for Carpenters passage to goe to Bideford	00	0	2
pd for board for the Carpenters when ye prish mett	00	1	6
pd for leather for the bell	00	1	0
pd for a bell roape	00	2	0
pd for beere when the bell was hangd up	00	0	3
pd to Jordan Reeve for carying home ye roape	00	0	3
pd to Christopher Limbury for Iron worke	02	4	5
spent in beare when ye agreemt was made wth Littleham men	00	1	3
pd to Littleham men	3	14	0
pd to the Carpenters	3	11	0
pd for casting the Bell to the belfounder	7	00	0
pd ye bell founder for mettall	11	19	2
pd for beare when ye bellfounder received ye money	00	1	0
for my goeing to Bideford twice to make an agreemt wth Littleham men	00	2	0
for Drawing the windelace to ye Church	00	0	6
pd to Tho: Stoyle for carying ye bell in ye boate to Littleham & home again	00	8	0
pd to Downman for Drawing ye bell	00	4	0
pd for a pound of mort to grease ye brasses	00	0	6
pd for carying ye takell & ye block	00	0	4
pd Tho: Stoyle for wresting (straining) *his roape*	00	1	0
	32	15	9
More Disbursments since the account wt was forgotten for beare to Littleham & the waye homeward when ye bell was boated at Littleham		1	2

(The tenor at Instow, which was cast in 1682, bears the initials AB, IP, ID, IR, TS. Mr Prince, James Dowman, John Rude or Jordan Reeve and Thomas Stoyle probably fit some of these.)

11. Edward Pennington: Upton Hellions Wardens' Accounts, 1690

(In the flyleaf of the book)
   An agreement made ye 22th (sic) day of April 1690 with Mr Edward Penniton for ye Casting of our second Bell! (sic)
   ye conditions hereof are those following
Imprs We are to pay him 1li 2s & 6d for every hundred weights casting:
Itm wee are also to pay him 1s & 2d for ye mettall he shall add unto ye sd Bell; & if any of ye metall of ye sd Bell be Diminished Mr Edward Penniton is to allow us 1s pr pound, wee allowing five pound's pr 100 for wast; and ye sd Mr Edward Penniton faithfull (sic) promises to make ye sd Bell sound & tunable

Witness his hand
ye day & yeare above
written the marke

Witnesses John Davie   of
            Samuell Woollway Rectr

Edward E P Penniton

1690

Impr pd for taking down ye bell from ye tower	00	03	06
pd for Drawing ye bell to Exeter & home againe	00	14	00
pd for founding ye bell & for 39^li of Mettle put to ye bell	09	01	00
pd for weighting of ye bell before & after its founding	00	08	00
pd for a new stock for ye bell & puting up in ye tower	00	17	00
pd ye Smith for Iron stuff for ye bell & an iron collar	01	00	00

(There is no record of an Edward Pennington working in Exeter at this time; Thomas III who was the founder had no recorded son of that name. There was an Edward Pennington, born in Bodmin in 1633, who was the son of Robert Pennington by his third marriage, and this may be a rare instance of his work.)

12. Braunton Churchwardens' Accounts: Evan Evans come to Devon, 1713

1713

pd Henry Incledon Esqr for one Tun & halfe of Timber & Sixth pte of a tun of Timber for Beams & piggons for the planching a New Belferry in the Steeple & free Stone for ye Steeple window	5	0	0
for 9 days worke to break out a window in the wall of ye Steeple & walling in ye Beams		10	6
To Charles Thomas for going to Barnstaple with his Boat for 1500 Bricks		6	0
& for going another time for 1500 Bricks		6	0
& for going another time for 800 Bricks		4	0
& for fetching ye weights		3	0
& for carring them home		3	0
& for fetching of 200 Bricks from Appledore in his Boat		0	6
& for fetching of Dell boards for Bytheford		5	0

(Further entries include making of a freestone window, laying the belfry floor with beams and piggons, carrying earth, fetching weights, fetching freestone from Buckland, and wood.)

It Pd to Mr Evan Evans Belfounder for Casting 6 bells & for 409^li of Mettall 20^li 9^s 0^d	113	9	0
The 20th of July on a Vestry held for casting of the Bells pd for Beer and Cyder for ye Parishioners	0	9	6
pd for Carriage of 1500 Bricks 11 horses & 6 men in Beer	0	1	6
pd for carriage of 1500 Bricks more 11 horses & 6 men	0	1	6
pd for the Carriage of 1000 Bricks 7 horses & 4 men	0	1	0
pd for the carriage of Lime for ye Bellfounders 8 horses & 4 men	0	1	2
November ye 27th 1713 when we took downe 2 of our 4 Bells pd	0	1	4
November ye 30th 1713 for Carriage of 700 Bricks Earth Beams Scales & weights 14 horses & 7 men	0	2	0
when the Bells were Drawn out	0	3	6

1717

Recd of the Bellfounders for the Church House	01	10	00

(this rent appears annually until 1720 inclusive.)

piggons ? joists

13. Thomas Pennington III's Bill for Drinks

Rewe Wardens' Accounts, 1718

for licker Mr Pennington had when he came to take the Bell att Castin		4	9
Mr Burranton for Lent of a Rope to Let down the Bell		3	6
Philip Thomas for licker in taking down the bell		4	6
Philip Thomas for Loading of theBell		1	6
Expenses for one loading the Bell at Exon		3	6
For lent of A horse to fech the Rope to Let down the Bell			6
for the Eye of the Bell		2	6
Mr Pennington for 50 wast of Mettell 6 pound to the hundred	2	10	0
Mr Pennington for Casting the Bell	8	0	0
Mr Pennington for 40 pound of Mettell aded	2	0	0
for waying the Bell twice		6	6
Expense in Casting the Bell at Exon		5	6
Expense in loading the Bell when cast at Exon		4	6
Philip Thomas for licker in one loading the Bell		3	0
Robert Chowne for draing the Bell at Exon about the Church		10	0
Phillip Thomas for Mr Pennington and his men for Vittells & Beare which they left to pay		5	6
Phillip Thomas for Vittells Mr Pennington and his men had		2	0
Phillip Thomas for Beare Mr Pennington had		2	6
Phillip Thomas for Vittells & Lika Mr Pennington and his three men had in ording the Bell to hang it on		6	6
for to Qurte of ale Mr Pennington had			6
for licker Mr Pennington had and Vittells		4	6
for hanging oup of the Bell for Licker the first time		4	6
expense for one hanging the Bell when the Cannons broak and hanging it oup Agane the secken time		3	6
Expense in Tuning the Bell for Vittells & Beare		17	6
John Tare's bill for eier work used A boute the Bells	5	6	5
farthin [Ferdinando]Comb for tuning the Bells	1	1	0

14. South Milton, 1725: Christopher Pennington of Lezant recasts a bell in the churchyard

ARTICLES *of Covenante and Agreemente indented had made concluded & fully agreed upon this Eighth day of May – Anno Dni 1725. By and between Christopher Pennington of Lezant in Cornwall Bellffonder of the one parte and Thomas Cornish Churchwarden of the parish of South Milton in the County of Devon Gent of the other parte are as follow. (viz.)*

   IMPs *The said Christopher Pennington Doth for himself his Executrs Administratrs & Assigns Covenant pmise and agree to & w*th *y*e *s*d *Thomas Cornish his Heirs & Successors and to & w*th *every of them by these presents in manner & form following (that is to say) that he y*e *s*d *Christopher Pennington for & in consideration of the sume of Twelve pounds of Lawfull money of Great Brittain to him well & truly paid or secured to be paid by y*e *s*d *Thomas Cornish his Heirs or Successors in manner and at such time as is hereafter mentioned shall & will att & before the first day of August next ensuing the Date hereof make or new cast one good sound and in every respect a Compleat Bell and well tuneable w*th *them w*ch *are already hanging & being in the Tower of South Milton afores*d*. And that he y*e *s*d *Christopher Pennington his Executors Adm*rs *or Assigns shall & will at his own p'per Cost & Charges take down from the Tower afores*d *the old crackt Bell there and when the same shall be so compleatly new made & Cast as aforesd shall & will at his like Cost & Charges Replace & Compleatly hang up the same there and shall & will find & p'vide all & all manner of Materialls for doing the same Except what hereafter is mentioned to be done & performed on the part & on behalf of y*e *s*d *Thomas Cornish his Exec*rs *or Administ*rs *And that he y*e *s*d *Christopher Pennington his Executors*

Administratrs or Assigns shall & will take all the Bell Mettall wch shall be left & not used in recasting the s^d Bell and pay ye s^d Thomas Cornish after the Rate of One shilling ye pound that shall be so left as afores^d And that he ye s^d Christopher Pennington shall not nor will purloin Deminish or any way voluntarly wast or spoil the Mettall belonging to the parishonrs afores^d and wch is now contained in the old crackt Bell And that such Mettall as he shall add to or in the Casting of ye s^d Bell shall be ye best & finest sort of Bell Mettall which is used in Casting Church Bells for wch he is to have fourteen pence ye pound.

ITEM The sd Thomas Cornish Doth hereby for himselfe his Executrs & Admrs Covent p'mise & agree to & wth ye s^d Christopher Pennington his Exec^{rs} Adm^{rs} & Assigns in manner & form following (that is to say) That he ye s^d Thomas Cornish his Execrs or Adm^{rs} shall & will well & truly pay or cause to be paid unto ye s^d Christopher Pennington his Exeec^{rs} adm^{rs} or Assigns the sume of Twelve pounds of Like Lawfull money of Great Brittain when & as soon as the afores^d Bell shall be so Compleatly Cast made tuneable & finished as afores^d. And that he ye s^d Thomas Cornish his Exec^{rs} or adm^{rs} shall & will p'vide for him ye s^d Christopher Pennington of his ye s^d Thomas Cornish's own p'per Cost & Charges Six seams of Clay or thereabte Six seams of horse Dung or thereabte four gallons of Beer Lees, an Hundred weight of Hay, a Truss of Straw, Three Knitches of Reed in order for ye making the Mould & Casting ye s^d Bell and shall & will p'mitt ye s^d Christopher Pennington to have ye use of ye house wch is already Built in ye Churchyard of ye s^d Parish for the Compleating & finishing the s^d work And shall & will Likewise certify the Clapper & ye Irons wch at p'sent support ye s^d Crackt Bell and for the true & faithfull p'formance of all & every the Covent & Agreemt aforesd each of the partys afores^d Doth bind himselfe unto the other of them in the penalty of Thirty pounds of Lawfull mony of Great Brittain In Witness whereof the partys to these p'sents (being duly Stampt) their hands & seales Interchangeably have set the Day & year first above written.

  Sealed & Delivered after the sevrall Razures & Intrlineations . . .
  in the p'sence of   Jno Arundell   Christopher Pennington

15. Holne Wardens' Accounts: Henry Mudge the Bell Expert and Ambrose Gooding

1741

Expended when Mr Mudge was heare to have his opinnion abt ye bells	00	03	6
pd Henry Mudge when he was heare to view the bells	00	02	6

1742

A Journey to plymouth about the Bells & posteds (postage) *of a Letter*	00	06	09
Edward Collings Bill			
Expended on the Bellfounder	00	04	00
Andrew Weight Bill expended when Henery Mudge was her (here) *a bout the Bells*	00	03	06

1743 (Thomas Tolsher & John Hoett Churchwardens)

Expended on ye bellfounder	0	5	0
for keping of ye bell founder horse	0	2	0
fore his meat	0	2	0
fore his drink	0	4	0
Left when you made ye barging [bargain]	0	12	0

1744

At a Vestry meeting held the thirtieth day of May 1743 Pursuant to publick notice in the Church, in order to Agree and Contract for haveing the Bells in the Tower of Holne new cast there being proper occasion for the same, one of them for Instance being Crazed and unfitt for use, we whose names are hereunto subscribed do Consent and agree, being all that are present at this Meeting, that the said bells now in the Tower shall be new Cast & made five Bells and we do hereby desire the Churchwardens for the present year to Contract under their hands with Ambrose Gooding of Plymouth Bellfounder for the Casting & founding of the

said Bells in such manner as shall be mentioned in such Contract for the sume of threescore Pounds witness our hands the day and year abovementioned.
(16 signatures)

pd Mr Gooding towards part Cassing (casting) *of the bells*	40	00	00
Expended when the Parshner mite for to know wheer the wide have fouer or five bells (when the parishioners met to know whether they would have four or five bells)	00	07	06
Expended when the bell whear brock up (were broken up)	00	02	00
Expended when the beams whare weighted (were weighed) *the last time*	00	04	00
Expended upon the that drawed beam from Brook wood	00	02	06
Expended when us brought the timber And give ouer ateannance (our attendance) *when the bell whear* (were) *cast*	00	03	00

(The bells were almost certainly cast at Buckfastleigh.)

1745

Payed Mr Ambrose Gooding in full of his Last Payment	25	00	00
Expended when Mr Shapily was heare to fewe (view) *the bells*	00	04	10
One ganey to Southtowen (South Tawton)* *for to give Mr Gooding Account for mite* (to meet) *the parish*	00	04	00
Payed Mr Mudge when he fewe the Timber of the bell & Expendeds	00	08	06
Expended when the parisher mite for to Paye Mr Gooding the Last paymant	00	07	06
Expended when the parisher mite Mr Gooding About the Mitle (metal)	00	02	00

(*South Tawton bells were recast by Gooding in 1744)
These accounts are written in very broad Devon dialect some of which we have translated.

16. Thomas Bilbie I arrives in Devon

1745 – Vestry Minute Book.
At A Vestry Meeting regularly conven'd and held by adjournment at the Salutation Inn the Town of Cullompton this 24th day of June 1745 it appearing unto us whose names are hereunto subscribed that two of the Six Bells belonging to the Parish of Cullompton aforesaid being Crack'd and that the Cage where in the Said Six Bells now hang is very much out of repair and that it is necessary to new cast the same and to hang them in a different manner it's unanimously agreed by us whose names are hereunto subscribed that all the said six Bells shall be forthwith cast into Eight and that the Cage wherein they now hang be forthwith made fit and convenient for hanging the same And that Richard Beavis Esqr and Mr Richard Harward shall forthwith contract with some able Person for the compleating thereof….
(Beavis is among the signatories, though he does not sign any other documents in Cullompton and was apparently not a resident.)

1745 – Vestry Minute Book
At a Vestry Meeting held by adjournment at the White Hart the 7th day of October 1745 its Resolved that the following Rules and Orders be Observed.
First Tis ordered that the Bells of the Parish be Cast in some part of the Almshouse of this Parish, and that the Parishioners of the same find the Bellfounder to carry on his work proper ffewell to run his mettle to dry his Moulds and sufficient Brick to build an Oven to compleat in lieu of the Expence of carrying the Bells to Taunton.
2^d Richard Beavis Esqr for the better Support of the Workhouse makes a present of Materials towards the Erecting an Oven there the Parish being at the Expence of Erecting the Same, ordered that the Chairman returns him thanks in the name of the whole Vestry.

3ᵈ Ordered that the House late in the Possession of the Wido Gratland part of the Premes belonging to the Workhouse be forthwith put in tenatable repair as Mʳ Harward and Mʳ Cross shall think proper and that they sett same for any Term of Years for the Benefit of the Poor.

1746 – Wardens' Accounts.

Recd of the Subscription Money towards the Bells	28	10	0
Do of Jospeh Pannell his subscription, out of his Bill towards the Bells	1	1	0
Paid Mr Belby the Belfounder for Casting Eight Bells for the Parish of Cullompton	113	0	0
Do for eight new Bellroops	2	2	0
Do Mrs Williams for 42lb of Bellmettle	1	8	0
Do to Will Martin for woode for Casting the Bells	0	17	0
to Robt Reed for 15 hundred of hard wood	0	8	9
to Mr Wm Palmer for 30 hundred of Do for Casting the Bells	0	17	6
for Drawing of the bells to the Foundry, & for Drawing of 'em home when Casted	0	10	0
Eliza Rabjohn for 12 hundred of hard wood for the bells when casted	0	8	0
To Geo: Rossiter for Ingrossing the Articles for Casting the Bells	0	3	6

17. Crediton: Five estimates for recasting the bells, 1773

Jack Chapman, London. (Not verbatim except the last paragraph.)

If the Tenor to be 26 cwt., total weight 5 tons @ £6 pr cwt.		£630	0	0
8 clappers		10	10	0
Hang with stocks, wheels, rollers, ironwork, nuts & screws,				
and recast brasses		60	0	0
		700	10	0
For the old bells, reputed weight 81 cwt.				
@ £4 12 0 pr cwt.		372	12	0
		327	18	0
If the Tenor to be 24 cwt., total 96 cwt.		576	0	0
clappers		9	9	0
hanging		58	0	0
		643	9	0
old bells		372	12	0
		270	17	0
If the Tenor to be 22 cwt., total 90 cwt.	540 0 0			
clappers		8	8	0
hanging		55	0	0
		603	8	0
old bells		372	12	0
		230	16	0

The new bells to be deliver'd at Exeter key, and we to receive the old bells at the same place* but may keep the old Bells if requested till the new are deliver'd. One half of the ballance to be paid at the delivery of the new Bells, and the other half in six months after.

  * *Provided the Parish insure the New Bells down to Exeter & the old ones up to London.*

Thomas Rudhall, Gloucester

Thomas Rudhall of the City of Gloucester Bellfounder do propose to the Gentlemen of the parish of Crediton in the County of Devon, to take down the Six Old Bells belonging to the parish afores^d:he will receive them at Topsam with the Old Stocks Clapper Bras's & Iron Work, & also the s^d: Thos Rudhall will for the Sum of Two Hundred & Seventy Pounds Deliver at Topsam a good Musical peal of eight the Tenor of which shall weigh about 26 Cw^t: the other Bells in proportion to s^d Tenor he will erect the Bells in the Tower.£270.

Street & Pyke, Bridgwater

New Casting the Old Bells 21^s pr hundred weight, compleat fit to be Rung - which is 2¼^d pr pound.

Addition of new Metal 13^d pr pound, the Composition of the Purest Graind Tin and Copper, if an inferior quality from 13^d to 10^d pr pound – the whole deliverd and taken at Bridgewater at the expence of the Parish of Crediton. If it be expected to Cast the bells on the spot, it will be expected a Pit and necessaries be provided at the expence of the Parish.

(Recasting 81 cwt would have cost	85	1	0
19 cwt of additional metal would have cost another	115	5	4
	200	6	4)

Thomas Bilbie, Cullompton

Proposals of Thos.Bilbie of Cullompton for Casting a Peal of Eight Bells for the Town of Crediton taking Down the Old & Hanging up the New Eight & finde wheels stocks Iron Brasses & all Other materials & Compleat the whole in a good workmanlike manner having the Old Materials I will do it for a Hundred and five pounds & I will add what quantity of New Mettell that shall be thought proper for six pounds pr Hund. gross.

(13d a pound = £6 1s 4d per cwt. Adding 19 cwt would have cost £114 on Bilbie's estimate, and the whole would have been £219.)

John Pennington

Sep^t y^e 24th 1773.
Gentlemen
I will take down your Six old bells now in the Tower of Crediton and Cast them into a Peal of Eight good Sound Tuneable Bells and find all new wheels, Stocks, Iron and Brasswork (having the old to my use) and one set of new Ropes, and put them up in the Tower in a workmanlike manner for the sum of one Hundred and twenty Pounds, and return weight for weight, & I will render ye mettle that shall be Added for six Pounds pr Hundred W^t. and If any of the Bells shall hapen (sic) to break in one Year, I will Cast them a gain and put them up an my own Cost as before, and I will leave thirty Pounds in hand for one year after they are finish'd, and I will Cast them at Crediton.

The mettle to be Added according to my estimate to make the Tenor 26 hundred in ye whole may be about 10 hund w^t and am Gentlemen with the utmost respect your Obedient Humble Servant
  John Pennington

N.B. I cannot do it Till this time twelve Month at least
no Money till the work is Finish'd
N.B. Srs According to my rule of working the Tenor or biggest Bell shoud be ¼ part of the whole or something more.

18. John Taylor agrees to recast the bells at Winkleigh: entry in the Wardens' Accounts, 1825

Copy of an agreement and so forth at a Vestry meeting held at the Barnstaple Inn November 28th 1825

Winkleigh November 28th 1825
Pursuant to a regular notice in the Church on the two preceding Sundays, a Vestry Meeting is this day held by the Church Wardens and the Principal Inhabitants of the Parish aforesaid for the purpose of having new bells and putting the same in order when the following agreement with Mr John Taylor of Oxford was enterd into and that the expense of the same be risen out of the Church Lands in Winkleigh aforesaid.

Memorandum of an agreement made this 28th day of November 1823 Between the Inhabitants of the Parish of Winkleigh of the one part and John Taylor of Oxford Bellfounder.

This witnesseth that the said John Taylor has agreed with the Churchwardens &c to take down the old Tenor and Third bells and put up in their place two new bells to agree with the other in proper tone – also to new hang the Five (that is to say new Wheels, Roll Blocks, Brasses, Clappers, iron work and all complete including carriage one way (that is, from Buckland Brewer where the bells are to be cast) for the sum of sixty six pounds –, and whereas some difference in point of weight may happen between the old and new bells the Taker agrees to allow the Parish one shilling per pound for any Deficiency and on the other hand the Parishioners agree to allow him one shilling and fourpence per pound for any surplus – the Taker agrees to perform the whole of the above agreement against Lady (sic) next 1826 when one half of the aforesaid sum is to be paid and the other half on Lady day 1827 (being the sum of Thirty Three pounds of one year and 4 per cent interest) and to which time the Taker binds himself to keep the said two new bells in good order. The parties to the aforesaid agreement have on subscribed their names the day and year above written.

Signed:
Samuel Denning
Tho. Molland } *Churchwardens*   *John Taylor*
                                          Bellfounder
(about 20 other names)

Weight of the Bells

		lbs		lbs
			Old Tenor	1661
			Do Third	1094
New Tenor		1780		2754
Do Third		1066		2846
				91 lbs overplus

19. William Hambling agrees to recast Stokenham Tenor: Stokenham Wardens' Account Book, 1832

Stokenham
At a Vestry meeting held (by adjournment) this 2oth day of Feby: 1832 for the porpose of recieveing proposuals for new casting the damaged Bell.

William Cole in ye Chair.

William Bortlet Hamling undertakes and agrees with the Parishioners of the sd Parish to new Cast the sd Bell on the following terms.

viz. To take down convey and new cast ye sd Bell, and new make every thing belonging to the same, and allso return and hang up the same in a proper state, for the sum of Thirty Pounds, one half of the Money is to remain in the Churchwardens hand for three months after the Bell is hangd by way of Indemnity for the Parish as to the Perfectness and tune of the sd Bell.

And in cause there is any thing amiss the Bell is to be new cast again at the undertaker expence or the Money (last said) to be forfeited to the Parish. –

The Bell is to be returnd the same size, weight and metal and the new metal wanted to be of the first quality and to be repaird one year by the undertaker.

Mr Hamling agrees to make new and repair the Timber work belonging to the sd Bell and if any damage is done to ye Planck or any thing in the Tower by removing the sd Bell it is to be repaird by the undertaker.

The Bell to be hung and the whole to be finished by ye 7th June next.

Witness } W. Cole Ch: Man } *Churchwardens*

N. OLdrey   Richd Oldrey

W.B. Hambling

Appendix III

BELLHANGING

1. Rehanging at Bere Ferrers: Churchwardens' Accounts, 1638

paid for a new dobble blocke to hoist up and down the Beelles	0	1	6
paid to Lampire the cappenter for a dayes jornye to Plimoth to inquire for Timber for the Beells	0	1	6
paid for timber plaunkes & borde wch we boughte at Plimoth to make the frames the wheeles and other use for the Beells	3	0	0
paid the cappenters for squarringe the ... cuttinge & sawinge of it there att Plimoth the M^r (master) workman 18^d a day & his 2 men 14^d a pice a day all three did worke there two days a pece which comes too	0	7	8
pd to Thomas Clarke & Raffe Willes to bringe the same timber in there Boate from Plimoth of Beere cause(way)	0	6	0
paid for cappenters work about the Beells the M^r workman 18^d a day for nine weeks	4	1	0
paid to one of his men for the like time 14^d a day wch comes too	3	3	0
paid to the other of his men 14^d a day for seven weeks	2	9	0
paid for new ropes for the Beells and the fetching of them the(y) were something bigger and longer then ordinarie because the did serve first to hoiste up and downe the Beells	0	12	0
Paid for a pownde of twine to tie the Ropes in the top of the Tower	0	0	4
Paid for new casting and makine of the Brasses for the Beells and for carringe of them to bockland and fetchinge of them againe	0	13	0
Paid to James Spries for Irework for the Beells first for 4 new pigges and 2 crampes weainge 39^{li} wch came to	0	15	0
paid for an other new pigge	0	3	0
paid for twelve flowers (washers) and twelve forelocks (keys)	0	4	6
paid for bolts	0	1	4
paid for twelve staples	0	3	0
paid for ringe & a staple	0	2	1
paid for a hundred of borde neles	0	1	2
paid for twelve brasses	0	3	4
paid for a hundred of hache nailes	0	0	10
paid for fower flowers and fower forelocks	0	1	2
paid for sixte spukes	0	0	9
paid for Beere to make them Drinke that did helpe down the beells wth the cappenters	0	0	6

2. A general overhaul at Goodleigh, 1658

1658

paid for taking off the stock of the little bell the canons being broken & for setting him downe	00	02	06
paid for a new stock for the little Bell	00	04	06
paid Oliver Striblyn for Stocking and hanging up the little bell & for hire of roves & for bords & nailes to make the wheele of the fourth bell new & for mending the other wheeles	00	16	00
paid to John Davie for a peece of tymber to make a stem for the great Bell wheele	00	01	06
paid John Tooker for making 4 holes in the little bell & for bolts & keyes to hang her up & for adding more weight to the great Bell clapper	01	13	06
paid for bolts keyes & forelocks to new hang the second and third Bells & for new hanging of them & repairing them against the 5th of November	00	03	00

(there were four bells at this period.)

3. William Smale Rehangs Spreyton Bells: Spreyton Wardens' Accounts, 1677

paid to William Smale the Carpenter and his men that hee brought with him for takeing downe of or bels & beames & other timber of or tower it being 16 days work	1	8	0
pad to William Smale & Marke Hill for 12 days in the same worke	0	17	0
pd to John Smale for lent of his horse for to ride to South Tawton & to Cheriton for to git a Capell (cable) roope	0	0	8
paid to Mr Risdon for A tree to make plankes and one beeme for our tower	1	10	0
paid to an other person for ffower scoare of fiften ffoote of timber which wase housed in or tower	4	15	0
paid to Mr Cann for drawing of this timber neere to or tower dore	0	13	4
paid for A pully for to fich up & doune the timber in our tower	0	3	0

(entries for hooks, crosbose? spukes, bordnils, brads, hatchnils, smalle nils, a stapple to draw up the beams, &c, all to Leonard Beere.)

paid unto William Smale for new timbering of the hayeyr (higher) plancking in or (our) tower and for mending of or bell wheales & for hanging up of the bels	10	0	0
paid to John Smale for halfe inch boards to make faythering (feathering, i.e.shrouding) for our bell wheels & for a peice to make fast the foot of a winleise (windlass)	0	3	6
paid for a Capple roape being 54 pounds 4 pence halfe penny A pound	1	0	3
pd for bringing home of or (our) Capple roape	0	1	6
pd for the Caring hoame of Sowth Tawton Caple roape	0	0	8
pd for 10 (or "to") pounds & three quarters of grease for to grease or (our) Caple roape withall	0	1	6
pd to Coldridge for fewing (viewing) the worke of or tower	0	0	8
pd for gitting hither of Coldridge	0	0	4
pd Moses Langford for A beame of twelve foote brought in place	0	13	0
pd Moses Langford for a pece of timber brought in place to make a roler to fich up & doune or bels & timber in or tower	0	8	0

(The "cable rope" was an important investment, and three years later the wardens had trouble when it was lent to William Man and they had to go with witnesses before the justices in Crediton to get it returned.)

4. Samuel Rowe contracts to rehang Colebrooke bells in a new frame and gear, 1737

ARTICLES OF AGREEMENT Indented made and concluded upon and entred into the fourteenth Day of September and in the Eleventh Year of the Reign of O^r Sovereign Lord George the Second by the Grace of God of Great Britain Ffrance and Ireland King Defender of the ffaith and soe forth, and in the Year of O^r Lord One thousand Seven hundred thirty and Seven By and between William Pidsley Gent. And Thomas Southcott p'sent Churchwardens of the parish of Colebroke in the county of Devon and Richard Hole of and within the said Parish of Colebrooke and County of the one part and Samuel Rowe of the parish of Spreyton in the County aforesaid of the other part ———————————————————————————————————————

WHEREAS notices was publicly given in the said parish Church by the said Churchwardens ordred on the Sabbath Day before the date of these p'sents ffor the said Churchwardens and parishioners to meet on the Day and year aforesaid at the sign of the Bell being the house of William Eeles to consult and advise with one another for new making All the cage or fframe of the five Bells which now stand or are in being in the Tower of the said parish Alsoe to new make and putt five new Stocks and five new wheels to the said five Bells And alsoe to putt or fix two new Beams to the two middle floors or Chambers in the said Tower, All as aforesaid having been thoroughly inspected into and is found to be very dangerous and become ruinous and much decayed And having several meetings been called and held on the same account for the repairing the Tackling timber and Chambers of the said five Bells of the Tower On which Day and place Them the said Churchwardens and parishioners meet at the house aforesaid And mutually consented agreed and concluded upon to bargain putt and to sett the said Cage or fframe together with the Stocks wheels and Beams as aforesaid To be new made and erected fixed and putt in the said Tower Unto the said Samuel Rowe to new make erect compleat and to finish A new cage or fframe in the place of the fformer to be endurable and serviceable p'suant And exact to a platt form or draught which he the said Samuel Rowe hath drawn out to witt for the number of pieces of timber As alsoe the length breadth and thickness of which are to be used and converted to and for the said cage or fframe which in the said platt form or draught he the said Samuel Rowe hath hand delivered to the said Churchwardens with his name subscribed thereunto having even date of these p'sents As also five new Stocks and five new wheels and Beams to and for the said five Bells and Tower, ffinding and providing all materials and necessaries at his own proper cost and charges as also the brass and iron that there shall be Occaslon for or expended about the p'fecting and finishing of the said Bargain and work As alsoe to make the forementioned things of good and substantial and of new Sufficient and well seasoned timber of heart Oak for the Cage or fframe and as alsoe for the said Stocks and wheels And alsoe well seasoned sound Elm for making the fells and featherings of the said wheels Alsoe to fix or erect substantial Stays or Stops of Iron to and for the said Bells in such manner that the Ringers may take them off and on at their wills and pleasures Alsoe to make and erect Boxes for the ropes to run in Between the Chambers aforesaid Alsoe to putt or erect a Guide or new fframe about thirteen or fourteen feet high from the Bellfry floor Alsoe to Colour or paint the said Cage or fframe wheels and Stocks of the said Bells with proper Oils and Colours to prevent the perishing and Decaying of the said timber which may be done and truly p'formed within Six months after the date of these p'sents All which said work bargaine and undertaking &c the said Samuel Rowe doth here by these p'sents contract covenant promise and agree to with the said Churchwardens and parishioners of the parish aforesaid ffaithfully to make and p'fectly to compleat ffinish and truly p'form as Aforesaid at or before or on this side the ffourth day of November next ensuing the date hereof and in right order Soe that Six Ringers may easily and orderly to Ring the said Bells in in (sic) peal, that Six men to rise and fall them as usuall on the said Occasion provided and always Excepting and reserving in case it soe happen any or other of the said Bells shall or do chance to be crack'd craz'd or are damnified by means of taking them down or the erecting or putting them up in the said intended Tower cage or fframe and in proper places by him the said Samuel Rowe or his order p'curement or Assistant as he shall or may Employ in making compleating and p'forming of the said work and undertaking That then the said Samuel Rowe forthwith and immediately shall and with all convenient Speed cause any or either of the said Bells soe damnified as Aforesaid to be new casted rectified or amended and made good within the space and time of Six Calend^r months from the date of these p'sents and from the time and space that it shall soe happen and upon and at his own proper cost and charges, And after the due p'formance and compleating of the said bargain contract work and undertaking when soe well done and finished They the said Churchwardens to choose at their Discretion An accomplished craftsman who is well advised and thoroughly Experienced in such undertaking work and p'formance to Inspect and to view the said work whether it be made done and p'formed to the Art rule and practice of good workmanship in Such cage And if soe allowed by the said p'son soe Indifferently Chosen that it is faithfully made and p'fectly p'formed and fulfilled as Aforesaid That then they the said Churchwardens covenant bargain and Agree and do here by these *p'sents promise to pay or cause to be paid Unto the said Samuel Rowe the sum of Six and thirty pounds of good and lawful money of Great Britain at or on Easter Monday next ensuing the date hereof And the said Samuel Rowe doth by these p'sents Except and reserve All the old materials or ruins now in the said Tower for and to his own use and benefitt, And the said Samuel Rowe doth also covenant promise and Agree to keep and preserve the Clock which now stands or is in the said Tower from all accidents or Damages that may happen or Accrue on the said Clock during and the performing and undertaking as Aforesaid, And at the End of compleating and perfecting the said work and performance to leave the said Clock weights and what is right unto thereunto belonging, As also to sett or fix the Striking part of the said Clock to strike or warn on the fifth or Greater of the Bells in the said Tower as usuall, As alsoe to fix and erect the Box or house in a proper place or corner of the Bellfry floor as Aforesaid to receive the lighting or descending of the weights of the said Clock provided the said Clock was in repair at the Executing and delivery of these p'sents He the said Samuel Rowe to leave it soe at the end of the work as Aforesaid, and the said Samuel Rowe is not to hurt or damnifie the said Tower or anything thereunto appertaining or belonging unless it is by the approbation and consent of them the said Churchwardens and parishioners as Aforesaid And further the said Samuel Rowe doth promise contract and Agree to undertake and p'form at his own proper cost and charges to support uphold sustain and to keep the Aforesaid Cage or fframe ffloors & chambers in timber & ropes as alsoe brass and ironwork of and in the said Tower thereunto appertaining or belonging to the said Bells for and during the Term and whole time of one and twenty years next unexpired and to come from the date of these p'sents if it soe happen that the said Samuel Rowe fortune to survive the said term yearly and every year providing materials and necessaries for the doing thereof and as often as need or occasion shall or may require They the said Churchwardens to acquaint or give the said Samuel Rowe timely notice of it at his respective dwelling house or abode And upon such notice the said Samuel Rowe shall and will attend or cause some p'son or p'sons to attend which are well skilled and p'fectly accomplished in the Rule and performance in such case to give his or their Attendance within the space or time of five days if need or Occasion may be And alsoe the said Samuel Rowe doth promise covenant and Agree to and with the said Churchwardens and parishioners That he the said Samuel Rowe shall and will make good any or either of the said Bells that shall happen to be damnified or crazed on the ffourth or ffifth day of November next ensuing the date hereof and no longer, And further the said Samuel Rowe doth covenant promise and Agree to and with the said Churchwardens and parishioners to leave the said cage or fframe and wheels ffloors chambers & ropes of & in the said Tower in good and sufficient repair and in right order at the End and Expiration of the Term Aforesaid As always well maintaining and keeping of them in repair during the term as Aforesaid And lastly upon the due p'formance & attendance maintenance continuance and repairing the said timber and Iron and brass work of and for the said five Bells together with the fframes ffloors chambers wheels and ropes as Aforesaid Then they the said Churchwardens and parishioners pay or cause to be paid unto the said Samuel Rowe or his order the sum of one pound and five shillings of good and lawfull money of Great Britain the ffirst payment to be made and paid at or on the twenty ninth day of September next come twelve Calend^r months which will be in the year of our Lord One thousand and Seven hundred and thirty Eight and soe yearly and every year during the Term of one and Twenty Years as Aforesaid, if the said Samuel Rowe shall soe fortune to live, In witness whereof the said parties have hereunto sett their hands and Seals ffirst written*

Sealed Signed and Delivered	
After the several Interlineations	*Samuel Rowe [seal]*
being first duely stampt	
in the p'sence of	
William Wallin	
John Brutton	

Notes:
Several interesting points arise from this very verbose and pettifogging document, drawn up by John Brutton, who was paid no less than 16 shillings for it – perhaps he was paid by the line?:

1. As it is an indenture, the signatures of the Churchwardens would have been on Rowe's half of the document.
2. The bells had probably been at least partly rehung in 1676, when the 2nd had been recast by Thomas Purdue and John Harte, Purdue's hanger, had spent 37 days, and his father John 28, working on them, at a cost of £7 8s 6d.

3. Samuel Rowe had been paid 2/6d earlier in the year for *fastning the Gudgins of ye fourth bell*; it seems likely that on that visit he told the parish that the bells needed rehanging.
4. The bellhanger is to supply a drawing of the frame.
5. The deadline is November 4th, for the most important ringing day of the year – and the one for which the ringers were paid most generously.
6. The headstocks are to be of oak, not elm as would have been the case in the 19th or 20th centuries.
7. The stays are to be iron, presumably with latchet or swinging sliders.
8. The height of the rope-guide shows that the bells are evidently to be rung sally-way; it is not clear whether they had been hung so previously, but the detailed description here suggests that they had not.
9. The contract provides for an annual service and a guarantee covering the bells against being cracked at least over the first November 5th ringing after completion.
10. The clock had been installed by Robert Blackwell in 1659; in 1737 it was being serviced by John Tickell of Crediton.

(There is also a bond between Samuel Rowe and the Churchwardens in which Rowe is bound in £20 to carry out the work)

5. Cullompton Wardens' Accounts & Vestry Minute Book: Hanging the Bells sally-way

1742 – Vestry Minute Book.
At a vestry Meeting Held by Adjournment at the White Hart this 10th day of Novemb 1742

It is Agreed by we whose names are hereunto Subscrib'd that the Bells belonging to our Parish Church of Cullompton shall be hanged Sally and that the Same shall be got done by Mr John Martin and Mr Anthony Heathfield the present Churchwardens Provided the Expense of Sallying the same does not Amount to No More then 25 pounds and when such Bells are Sallyed that then all orders heretofore made by the Parishioners of the s^d Parish for paying persons for Ringing of the s^d bells shall be Void and of None Effect.

1742 – Wardens' Accounts.
Paid to Mr Wrath for Sallying the Bells	25	0	0

6. Fitzantony Pennington rehangs Buckland Monachorum bells

Buckland Monachorum Wardens' Accounts, 1767

Paid Mrs May for 232¼ feet of oake timber	11	12	3
Paid for drawing home ye same	3	00	0
Paid for Elm for the stocks of the Bells	1	11	3
Paid Mr Wm Billing for Deal plank	1	05	0
For Drawing home ye same from Dock (Devonport) *& Expence*	0	12	0
Paid for Oyl and Colers for the wheels	0	11	2½
Paid for a Bottell of Oyl for ye Bells	0	01	3
Paid the Smiths Bill for ye Bells	12	14	7
Paid Mr Anthony Pennington his Agreement for takeing down and New hang ye Bells	32	12	0
Paid for Stones for the Sound holes of ye tower	0	19	10
For attendance three days takeing down timber with Mr Penington and makeing ye Agreement	0	07	6
A Mistak in Drawing the timber	0	6	6

Appendix IV

BELL RINGING

1. Ringing at Ashburton, at All Hallowstide and against Thunder

Ashburton Wardens' Accounts, 1479-1580, DCRS 1970.

1485–6
13^d rec. from Thomas Drewiston collected among the men on the Vigil of All Souls
14^d rec. from Richard William & John Luce collected on the Vigil of All Souls.

1509–10
23d and 10lb of hemp (calibis) *received from and for ringing on the night of the Feats of All Saints less the expenses of the ringers on that night.*

1510–11
Paid the Ringers when there was thunder	2d
Paid the Clerk for ringing against thunder	8d

1513
3^s 1½^d and 6^{lb} hemp as reward from various parishioners for ringing on the night of the Feast of All Saints.

1537–8
2^s 4½^d in gifts for ringing on the night of the commemoration of souls (*and on the next day* added)

1554–5
20^d for ringing on All Souls' night collected by Henry Lang and John Froude
(Evidently the custom had been revived on Mary I's accession, and the the years following 1558 tell the rest of the story . . .)

1558–9
for ryngyng Quenez Mary ys knyll   8d

1559–60
for there labor that carryed the images to be burnt and there drynkyng   8d

1570–1
for ale for the ringing at th rejoicing for the coronation and divine continuation of the reign
   of the Queen (Elizabeth I)   *12d*

235

2. Monmouth's Rebellion at Axminster

Axminster Wardens' Accounts, 1685

pd for Ringing when yᵉ Earl of Bathe past by	00	05	00
paid to yᵉ Ringers yᵉ 29th of May	00	14	00
paid to Mary Flood for cleansing the churchyard after the Kings Armie	00	01	00
To ye Ringers at yᵉ Colonells coming into yᵉ Towne	00	4	6
To ye Ringers when yᵉ Justices sate at yᵉ taking of Monmouth	00	10	0
To ye Ringers when yᵉ Colonell & yᵉ Major came from Lyme	00	5	0
To ye Ringers when yᵉ Duke of Albemarle passed by	00	4	6
To ye Ringers yᵉ 5th of November	00	14	0
To ye Ringers yᵉ 6th of ffebruary	00	19	0
To ye Ringers when yᵉ Lrd Bishop was here	00	5	0
March 20 To yᵉ Ringers when Major Bragg came to Town	00	4	6
To yᵉ Ringers at yᵉ Colonel's coming another time	00	3	6
Paid out for fuell for a Bonfire & Beere for yᵉ Soldjers (by yᵉ justices order) when Monmouth was routed (July 10th)	00	10	6
Paid for Ringing when Colonell Pole came from Parliamt	00	2	6
Paid for Ringing when yᵉ Justices past through yᵉ Town March 15	00	03	00

3. Cullompton Vestry decides to economize

Cullompton Vestry Minutes, 1741

At a Vestry Meeting held by Adjounment this 30ᵗʰ day of March 1741 at the White Hart in Cullompton It is Agreed by us whose Names are here Subscribed Principall Inhabitants and payers of the Pish Aforesᵈ That Whereas it has been for time past a great Expence to the Pish in Respect of Ringing, Now we do hereby Order Consent and Agree that there shall be Ringing for the future But four days In the Year att the Expence of the Pish as it is hereafter Mentioned And for wᶜʰ days the sᵈ Ringers shall have 12s Each day and no More wᶜʰ is as follows the first day is the 29ᵗʰ of May the 5ᵗʰ of Novembʳ the Kings Accession Day and the Kings Coronation Day.

And it is further agreed upon that for the future there shall be But Ten Shillings Spent at any Pish Meeting on any Occasion Relating or Concerning the Sᵈ Pish.

4. Dr Benjamin Kennicott's Ringers' Articles for Totnes, 1742

Among the many recreations approved of by the sons of pleasure, ringing is a diversion that may be emphatically said to bear away the bell, and so much does it engage the natives of Great Britain, beyond all other nations, that it has been the distinguishing appellation of "the ringing isle". The art then, for which this kingdom is renowned, shews a judicious taste in those of its inhabitants who have by their performances contributed thereto, since this art wants no foreign encomiast, but the harmonious bells are the heralds of their own praise. The ingenuity required for the diversion administered in, and the health subsequent upon this exercise, give it a particular sanction among mankind and recommend it as an employment at vacant hours, worthy of the regard of all denominations.

We therefore, whose names are subscribed, taking into consideration the great pleasure that results from this manly employment, the innocence with which it is performed, and the advantage enjoyed from so healthy an exercise of our bodies, and also having the peculiar satisfaction of ringing with ease a set of eight bells, of established fame, and applauded excellence, do hereby agree to meet together in the usual place of ringing, every Monday evening, at six o'clock, for our improving this science; and for the greater certainty of attendance, we do hereby severally promise to forfeit the sum of three-pence, if not attending at the hour aforesaid, and six-pence if not present at seven o'clock, to be deposited in the hands of the treasurer for the time being, and spent as the major part of the Society shall seem fit. And for the better regulation of this our fraternity, we do also hereby agree that we remain in the belfry during pleasure, and then for the further pleasure and benefit of conversation adjourn to any house the company shall choose, and there tarry till the hour of ten, and no longer.

And whereas the stays supporting the bells are liable to damage from unskilful hands, we agree that whoever hurts shall repair the same, at his own proper charge. We make no rules for conversation, nor penalties for any misbehaviour in it, resolving to render it innocently agreable to each other, and whenever a breach of this rule is committed, that a reprimand be admitted from the Society. In all cases and disputes not hereinbefore decided, the majority of the company shall determine, that so this Society amicably begun, may be amicably carried, and not meet the fate of others that have gone before it.

[signed] *BENJ. KENNICOTT.*

Totnes, November 8th, 1742.

5. The Northlew Ringing Song

One day in October, neither drunken nor sober,
O'er Broadbury Down I was wending my way,
When I heard of some ringing, some dancing and singing,
I ought to remember that jubilee day.
'Twas in Ashwater town, the bells they did sound,
They rung for a belt and a hat laced with gold;
But the men of Northlew rang so steady and true
That there never was better in Devon, I hold.

'Twas misunderstood by the men of Broadwood,
With a blow on the tenor should never have been,
But the men of Northlew rang so faultlessly true,
'Twas a difficult matter to beat them, I ween
'Twas in Ashwater town, &c.

They of Broadwood being naughty then says to our party,
"We'll give you a challenge again in a round.
We'll give you your chance in St Stephens or Launceston
The prize to the winner a note of five pound.
'Twas in Callington town the bells next did sound, &c.

The match then came on in good Callington,
And the bells they rang out o'er the valleys below;
And old and young people, the hale and the feeble,
Came out for to hear the sweet bell music flow,
'Twas in Callington town, &c.

They of Broadwood once more were oblig'd to give o'er,
They were beaten completely and done in a round;
But the men of Northlew rang so steady and true
That never their like in the west could be found.
'Twas in Ashwater town and Callington town, &c.

6. The Cullompton Ringers on Strike, 1805

Cullompton Vestry Minutes.

The Ringers having positively refus'd to ring on the Day (being Easter Monday) and when requested impudently behav'd themselves, it is order'd that in future they ring on no Occasion whatever, without the express Consent of the Churchwardens or one of them.

7. The Buckland Monachorum Ringers in Revolt

A Memorandum of 1815 in the Buckland Monachorum Account Book.

Whereas some of the Ringers have lately made a Practice of frequently ringing in a Week at a late hour to the disturbance of the Neighbors often being in Bed, the Churchwardens desired Mr Mark Tucker, in future not to spare the Key of the Belfry Door, unless they begin to Ring and leave off early, on Saturday Evening 6th May 1815, between Eight and Nine o'CLock, they ask'd for the Key and was very properly refused, not coming at an earlier Hour. They understanding a Carpenter was putting on a lock on the Door which leads from the Gallery into the Ringing Loft, they went to the Church door and got admittance, and rang the Bells in defiance. For their illiberal Language to the Parishioners in several instances, and by one in particular, in saying they may take the Bells and Ropes to stop their . . . , No Ringing, no Chiming, therefore for their Mutinous and Riotous behaviour, shall be discarded as Ringers.

X John Smith	*We the Minister, Churchwardens, Overseers, Parishioners, holding*
Peter ?Thearle	*a Vestry in the Church this Tenth day of May1815 for settling and*
Charles Bloy	*Ballancing the Church accounts, do agree to choose Nine Men for*
John Lethbridge	*Ringers and Chimers as pr Margin who was not concerned with the*
Simon Lethbridge	*Mutinous Setts, to take upon them the care of the Tower and Bells,*
William Hooper	*to Chime before Divine Service, as usual, to be allowed the money*
Thomas Lethbridge	*yearly, commonly called Ringing Money, and may Ring whenever*
	they think proper, but not at a late Hour, unless it should so happen
	to be on any particular Rejoicing day, or Wedding day.

Also the Young Men who are Learners to have a Ringing Evening on Wednesdays and if two Setts of them to take Week and Week, or, Peal and Peal on the said Wednesday Evening, but to leave off early.

We also agree that those Ringers who were Singers, who have shown their Malice and Hatred by leaving the Choir, and doing it with a view to Distress the Singing, shall be so discarded and never join the Choir any more.

8. A Ringing Competition at Bradninch, 1847

Exeter Flying Post, 18th March 1847.

BRADNINCH
PRIZE RINGING ON EASTER TUESDAY
To be rung for on Tuesday the 6th day of
APRIL next, on a Peal of Six bells, a PURSE OF
THREE GUINEAS, by any Set of Practical Ringers, of one
Parish or any other Parishes, who would like to compete for
First Prize . . . Two Guineas
Second Prize . . . One Guinea
to be awarded as three competent Judges may decide. The Bells will
be at liberty for the practice fortnight previous to the day of
ringing. Further particulars may be obtained on application at
the CASTLE INN.

8th April, 1847.
RINGING – BRADNINCH. The Ringing Match at Bradninch took place yesterday, (Tuesday) and this ancient Borough presented all the appearance of Holiday on the occasion, so great was the influx of company, and so exceedingly gay and spirited the whole affair. The ringers assembled at that hospitable and well-conducted house, Govier's Castle Inn, the competition for the prizes being the ringers of St David's, Exeter, Broadclist, Clayhidon, and Exminster, and the ringing was opened at 5 o'clock in the morning. The peals for the prizes were rung in the order in which the parishes have already been mentioned, and the many judges present as well as the public generally were delighted with the science displayed. At the close the prizes were declared as follows: First Prize of £1 17s to Exminster: Second Prize of 18s 6d to Broadclist: third ditto of 7s 6d to St David's, Exeter. Good humour and hilarity prevailed and a hope was expressed that an amusement like this may at some proper period be repeated.

9. "Extraordinary Sacrilege at West Worlington": a Ringers' Revolt

From the *South Molton Gazette*, 1882.
The village of West Worlington has been the scene of some extraordinary occurrences of late in connection with the Church and the Rector, the Rev. C.W.Moloney. During the last year a dispute arose between the Rector and the Church bell-ringers in consequence of the latter refusing to abide by certain rules which the Rector wished to introduce. Subsequent to this the Rector's out-buildings were set on fire and then on November the fifth 1881 his effigy was burnt, his gate unhung and he was subject to other indignities so much so that extra police were stationed in the village. No one was brought to justice for these outrages, but a man named Leach was bound over to keep the peace towards the Rector.

On the third instant further crimes were committed; and for one of them a Smith, named Edward Holmes, an elderly man and one of the old ringers, was brought up on bail before the South Molton magistrates, the charge being that he broke into the Parish Church and stole one bronze cross, two brass candlesticks, two brass vases, one surplice, the clappers of three bells and the screw nuts of another bell.

Summary of the Court Report
Evidence was given by Sarah Lee, the Sextoness. The evidence was that she had found certain things which indicated that the Church had been broken into; she had then called at the Rev. Moloney's house.

Next the Rev. C.W.Moloney gave evidence, he said that he also found evidence that the Church had been broken into, and that several large stones had been taken forcibly from the wall and were left lying on the ground. He also found that the Harmonium had been smashed in at the back and some keys taken from it. It could also be seen that entrance to the Church was gained through a small ventilator near the side window in the Tower.

During the investigation of the Church robbery by P.C.Yelland the Special Constable for West Worlington and Sergeant Wellington of Witheridge and P.C. Christopher, a toe-cap had been found beneath the bells.. but, a South Molton Shoemaker said that Mr Edward Holmes had lost his toe-cap but it was not the right size for his boot.

The Bench then committed the prisoner for trial at the next county assizes.

Another Report from the Court Room
A warrant was obtained to search the premises of Mr William Hosegood, Landlord of the Stucley Arms. The house and the Arms were very thoroughly searched; but nothing was found. The well was emptied by bucket and two of the missing clappers were found. So Mr Hosegood was arrested and admitted to bail for fifty pounds and two sureties of twenty pounds each.

The bench then committed the prisoner, Mr Hosegood, for trial at the next Devon Assizes.

A Report on the Devon Assizes, Exeter, on July 29th, from the *South Molton Gazette*.
Evidence was given, and it was found that the cause of the trouble was, that on Revel Sundays, all the Ringers got very drunk every year. So, the Rev. C.W.Moloney, being Custodiam of the bells, didn't think it right to allow the proceedings to be sanctified by the bells. He drew up some rules, stopping drunkenness. All the ringers protested and some even left. On top of these rules the Ringers were not allowed to ring on Revel Sunday.

In spite of this the bells were rung, the Rector went up to the bellfry and turned all the ringers out, he then locked the door. But later they returned and started ringing again, the Rector returned to remonstrate with them, but, from a sign given from Mr William Hosegood the Ringers continued, directly against the Rector's wishes.

It appears that Mr William Hosegood was the ring-leader, because he had the notices about November the Fifth printed by a man named Mr Nott. Luckily for Mr William Hosegood and for Mr Edward Holmes there was insignificant evidence to convict either man, and therefore the Jury acquitted them and they were discharged.

An Account of Bonfire Night.
Before Bonfire Night a notice was put up in the Village which read:–

    The Bonfire for poor Guy will be
    held in a field near the Village
    The Procession will take place at
    Six-o-clock; and the Bonfire to
    Start at Seven-thirty precisely.
    N.B. All Ringers should buy the newest set of changes,
    of ten doubles in rhyme, one and a half penny each.
    Address: Mr Cock
        Hen and Chicken Yard,
        Poultry Square,
        West Worlington 1881.

Verse	*Remember, remember the Fifth of November,*
	For fifty years the bells have been rung,
	But now that old Guy does strictly deny
	That any such thing should be done.
Chorus	*Guy Forks, Guy, poke him in the eye,*
	If you can't do it first, you must have another try.

On the actual night the effigy of the Rev C. W. Moloney was burned and it is reported that "Horrible language was used".

BIBLIOGRAPHY

Primary Sources: Churchwardens' Accounts and Vestry Minutes, &c. for the parishes of Abbotskerswell, Alphington, Ashprington, Ashwater, Aveton Gifford, Awliscombe, Axminster, Bere Ferrers, Bampton, Bickington, Bickleigh (W), Bishops Tawton, Bishopsteignton, Bow, Braunton, Brixham, Broadhembury, Broadhempston, Broadwoodkelly, Broadwoodwidger, Buckfastleigh, Buckland-in-the-Moor, Buckland Monachorum, Cadbury, Chagford (transcript), Cheldon, Cheriton Bishop, Cheriton Fitzpaine, Chittlehampton, Chivelstone, Chudleigh, Clawton (transcript), Clyst Hydon, Clyst St George, Cockington, Coldridge, Colebrooke, Colyton, Combeinteignhead, Countisbury, Crediton, Cruwys Morchard, Cullompton, Dartington (transcript), Dartmouth St Petrox, Dawlish, Dean Prior, Dolton, Drewsteignton, East Budleigh, Exeter Cathedral, Exeter All Hallows Goldsmith Street, Exeter Holy Trinity, Exeter St John's, Exeter St Mary Steps, Exeter St Petrock's, Feniton, Frithelstock, Georgenympton, Gidleigh, Gittisham, Goodleigh, Halberton, Hemyock, High Bickington, High Bray, Highweek, Holbeton, Holcombe Rogus, Holne, Holsworthy, Honiton, Ide, Ilfracombe, Instow, Jacobstowe, Kelly, Kenn, Kentisbeare, Kilmington, Landcross, Landulph (Cornwall), Lapford, Lewtrenchard, Littleham (S), Lympstone, Marytavy, Meshaw, Modbury, Molland, Newton St Cyres, Northam, North Molton, North Tawton, Offwell, Otterton, Ottery St Mary, Paignton, Plymouth (the Widey Court Book), Plymouth St Budeaux, Plympton St Maurice, Plymstock, Rewe, Sampford Courtenay, Shobrooke, South Milton, South Tawton, Spreyton, Staverton, Stoke Climsland (Cornwall), Stoke Gabriel, Stokenham, Stoodleigh, Talaton, Tavistock (transcript), Tawstock, Tedburn St Mary, Teignmouth St James, Tetcott, Tiverton St George, Tiverton St Peter, Topsham, Ugborough, Upton Hellions, Warkleigh, Washfield, Wembury, West Buckland, West Down, Whitchurch, Widecombe-in-the-Moor, Winkleigh, Woodbury, Woolfardisworthy (E), Zeal Monachorum.

Parish Registers of Births, Marriages & Burials for the parishes of Barnstaple St Peter, Bodmin, Chulmleigh, Dartmouth, Exeter St Paul, Exeter St Thomas, Landulph, Lezant, Plymouth St Andrew, Stoke Climsland, Stoke Damarel, Tavistock, Totnes and Winkleigh.

Davidson	*Church Notes*, MS in Exeter Westcountry Studies Library, 5 vols.

Published sources:

Baring-Gould, S.	*Old Devon Characters & Strange Events*
Beeson, C.F.C.	*English Church Clocks, 1280-1850*, 1971
Bellchambers, J.K.	*Devonshire Clockmakers*, 1962
Betty,	*Records of Mediaeval Church Building in the South-west*, D.C.R.O., 1989
Berman, Gideon	*An Essay on Church Clocks*, 1974
Biringucchio, Vanucchi	*Pirotechnia*, Trans. Smith & Gnudi, 1943
Blagg, T.F.C.	*An Umbrian Abbey, San Paolo di Valdiponte*, British School in Rome, 1974
Blaylock, Stuart R.	*Bell and Cauldron Founding in Exeter*, Journal of the Historical Metallurgy Society, Vol 30, 1996.
" "	*Excavation of an early post-mediaeval bronze foundry at Cowick Street, Exeter, 1999-2000*. R.A.M.Museum, Exeter, 2001
Bliss, M. & Sharpe, F.	*Church Bells of Gloucestershire*, 1986
Brown, Colvin & Taylor	*The History of the King's Works*, 1963
Butler, Roderick, & Green, Christopher	*English Bronze Cooking Vessels and their Founders, 1350-1830*, 2003
Cannon, A.C.,	*Church Bells of Cornwall*, 1978
Central Council of Church Bell Ringers	*Tower and Bells: a Handbook*, 1990
Cherry & Pevsner, N.	*The Buildings of England: Devon*, 2nd Ed., 1989
Chope, R. Pearse	*Early Tours in Devon & Cornwall*, 1918

Colchester, W.E.	*Hampshire Church Bells*, 1920
Copeland, G.W.	*The Church Towers of Devon.* Transactions of the Plymouth Institution & Cornwall Natural History Society, 1937
Cossins, James	*Reminiscences of Exeter Fifty Years Since*, 1878
Crossley, F.H.	*English Church Design*, 1947
Cox, J.C. & Ford C.B.	*The Parish Churches of England*, 1935
Cresswell, Beatrix	*Exeter Churches*, 1908
Curzon, Frank	*Lays and Legends of the West*, 1847
Dalton, Christopher	*The Bells and Belfries of Dorset*, 3 vols, 2005-2005
Dalton, J.N.	*The Collegiate Church of Ottery St Mary*, 1917
Denison, Edmund B., (Lord Grimthorpe)	*Clocks, Watches and Bells*, 1860
D.C.R.S.	Vol 15, *Churchwardens' Accounts of Ashburton*, 1479-1580
"	Vols 10 13, 15,16, 18, *The Register of Edmund Lacy, Bishop of Exeter*, 1420-1455 Ed. G.R. Dunstan.
"	Vol 22, *Tudor Exeter – Tax Assessments 1489-1595*.
"	Vols 24 & 26, The Accounts of the Fabric of Exeter Cathedral, 1279-1353
"	*Extra Series 1, Exeter Freemen, 1266-1967*
Devonshire Association	*Transactions*, Vols 1-137
Diderot,	*Encyclopedie*
Donn, Benjamin	*A Map of the County of Devon*, 1765. Reprinted 1965
Duffy, Eamonn	*The Voices of Morebath*, 2001
Dunkin, E.H.W.	*Church Bells of Cornwall*, 1878
Early Chancery Proceedings, HMSO.	
Eisel, John	*Giants of the Exercise*, 1999
Ellacombe, H.T.,	*Church Bells of Devon*, 1867
"	*Bells of the Church*, 1872
"	*Church Bells of Somerset*, 1875
"	*The Bells of the Cathedral Church of St Peter, Exeter*, 1874
"	*Church bells of Gloucestershire*, 1881
"	*Practical Remarks on Belfries and Ringers*, London, 1884
Elphick, George,	*Sussex bells and Belfries*, Phillimore, 1970
" "	*The Craft of the Bellfounder*, Phillimore, 1988
Exeter Flying Post	
Fiennes, Celia	*The Journeys of Celia Fiennes,* ed. C. Morris, 1947
Francis, David	*Discovering Exeter: Lost Churches,* 1995
Gray, Todd	*The Lost Chronicle of Barnstaple*, 1998
" "	*Exeter Engraved*, 2001
" "	*Lost Exeter*, 2002
Gray, Todd, Ed.	*Devon Documents*, 1996.
Gregory, I.L, Ed.	*Hartland Church Accounts, 1597-1706,* 1950
Harris, Helen	*The Industrial Archaeology of Dartmoor*, 1986
Harvey, H.H.	*History of Clawton*, 1939
Harvey, John	*Gothic England*, 1947
Harvey, Sir Robert	*Harberton Church Bells*, 1917
Hemery, Eric	*Historic Dart*, 1982
Heywood, Sir A.P.	*Bell Towers and Bell Hanging*, 1914
Hine, James	*Notes on some Moorland and Border Churches*, n.d.
Historic Manuscript Commission,	*Exeter City Records*, 1916
HMSO	*Early Chancery Proceedings*
Hodgson, H.L.	*The Churches of Chulmleigh Deanery,* (articles from the Chulmleigh Deanery Magazine, 1924ff
Homer, Ronald & Collins, Alan	*The Cockey Family of Metal Workers* in the *Journal of the Pewter Society*, Spring 2006

Hoskins, W.G.	*Devon*, 1854.
"	*Old Devon*, 1966.
"	*1000 Years in Exeter*, 1960, new ed. 2004
Hunt, Peter	*Payne's Devon*, 1986.
Hutton, Ronald	*Merry England, the Ritual Year*, 1994
Ingram, Tom	*Bells in England*, 1954
Jennings, T.	*Bellfounding*, Shire Albums, Aylesbury, 1988
	The Development of British Bell Fittings, 1991
"	*Master of my Art, The Taylor Bellfoundries*, Loughborough, 1987
Jewett,	*History of Plymouth*, 1873
Lloyd, W.S.	*The Musical Ear*, 1939
Loomes, Brian	*Great British Clocks*, 1978
Lukis, W.C.	*Church Bells*, 1857
Moore, J, Rice, R, & Hucker, E.	*Bilbie & the Chew Valley Clockmakers*, 1995
Morris, E.,	*The History and Art of Change Ringing*, 1937
Museo di Verona	*Fonditori di Campane a Verona dal Xi al XX secolo*, Verona, 1979
Newton, Robert,	*Victorian Exeter*, 1968
Oliver, George	*The History of Exeter*, 1821.
Pearson, C.,	*A Ringer's Guide to the Church Bells of Devon*, 1888
Pickford, C.N.	*Bellframes*, 1993.
Ponsford, C N.	*Devon Clocks and Clockmakers*, 1985
"	*Time in Exeter*, 1978
Ponsford, C.N. & Scott, J.G.M.	*A New Look at the Dating of Early English Clocks*, in Antiquarian Horology, Vol 12 No 1, 1980
	Wells and Salisbury, in Antiquarian Horology, Vol 12 No 5 1981
Ponsford, C.N., Scott, J.G.M, & Authers, W.P.	*Clocks and Clockmakers of Tiverton*, 1977
Prince, John	*Worthies of Devon*, 1810
Pugsley, David	*Old Cullompton*, 1986
Pullman	*Book of the Axe*
Raven, J.J.	*The Church Bells of Dorset*, 1906
"	*The Bells of England*, 1906
Robinson. F.E.	*Among the Bells*, 1909
Rose-Troup, Frances	*The Western Rebellion*, 1913
	The Lost Chapels of Exeter, 1923
Salter, Mike	*Tne Old Parish Churches of Devon*, 1999
Scott, J.G.M.	*Devon Bellringing, 1874-1975*, 1975
"	*Some Dating Features for Turret Clocks*, in Antiquarian Horology, Vol 12 No 5, 1981
Selleck, A. Douglas	*Cookworthy*, 1978
Sellman, R.R.	*Illustrations of Devon History*, 1962
Seymour, Robert	*Torre Abbey*, 1977
Sharpe, Frederick	*Church Bells of Radnorshire*, 1947
" "	*Church Bells of Oxfordshire*, 1953
" "	*Church Bells of Guernsey, Alderney & Sark*, 1964
" "	*Church Bells of Cardiganshire*, 1965
" "	*Church Bells of Berkshire*, 2nd ed. 1970
" "	*Church Bells of Herefordshire*, 1976
" "	Article in *Isles of Scilly Parish Year Book*, 1971
Sherlock, Robert	*West Country Chandeliers and their Makers*, Journal of the Antique Metalware Society, 2002
Shorto, Edward	*Some Notes on the Church of St Petrock, Exeter*, 1878.
Simmons, Jack	*A Devon Anthology*, 1971
Skinner, John	*Journal of a Somerset Rector, 1772-1839*, Ed. J. Coombes & A. Bax, 1930

South Molton Gazette	
Stabb, J.	*Some Old Devon Churches,* 3 vols, 1932-4
Stoyle, Mark	*From Deliverance to Destruction*, University of Exeter, 1996
Swete, Rev. J.	*Travels in Georgian Devon*, Ed. Todd Gray, 4 vols, 1997
Tavistock's Yesterdays.	
Theophilus,	*De Diversis Artibus*, trans. Dodwell, 1961
Thrupp, Sylvia	*The Merchant Class of Mediaeval London*
Tout, T.F.	*Firearms in England in the 14th Century*, Collected Papers, II
Van Heuven, E.W.	*Statistical Measurements of Church Bells*, 1948
Vowell, als Hoker, J.	*An Account of the Sieges of Exeter, the Foundation of the Cathedral Church and the Disputes between the Cathedral and the City Authorities,* 1911
Walters, H.B.	*Church Bells of England*, Oxford, 1912
"	*Church Bells of Wiltshire*, 1929, reprint 1969
Warne, Arthur	*Church & Society in 18th-century Devon*, 1969
Watkin, H.R.	*Dartmouth: Pre-Reformation*, 1935
"	*The History of Totnes Priory and Mediaeval Town*, 1914-17
Western Antiquary, The	
Williamson, Henry	*Life in a Devon Village,* 1945
Worth, F.N.	*The Rings of Bells in the City of Plymouth*, 1953
Worth, R.N.	*Tavistock Parish Records*
"X. Y.Z."	*Bells and Bellfounding*, 1879
Youings, Joyce	*Devon Monastic Bells*, in *Devon Documents*, ed. Todd Gray, D & C N Q 1996

GENERAL INDEX

[Note: The Indexes refer to Volume 1 only: Volume 2 is virtually in index in itself. In the General Index, we have not included the names of people (e.g. churchwardens or signatories to documents) who do not appear elsewhere in the text. In the Index of Places, we have not included places which appear only in the lists of bells by various founders, and not elsewhere.

Abbott & Co, Bideford, founders, 106
Abrahams, John, Tavistock, bellfounder, 104
Access to towers, 8-12
Accession Day ringing, 176, 236
Advertisements, 96, 97, 109, 116, 164, 165
Advisers, 57-9, 132
Aggett, William, Chagford, bellhanger, 105, 157, 161, 165
Agreements, (indentures) for casting bells, 57-60, 207, 208, 217, 221
Aishford family, 40
All Souls' Day ringing, 168, 169, 175, 235
Albemarle, Duke of, 236
Alphabet bells, 34, 51
Alum, used in casting bells, 210
Annuellarii, Exeter Cathedral, 167
Apparitor, 57
Apsey, William, Nettlecombe, Som, brazier, 67, 109
Archaeology, 42, 76, 131
Archdeacon's court, 57
Argent, 45, 54
Arundell, John, Bradstone, squire, 40, 62
Arundell, Thomas, 31
Ashes, 46, 210, 212, 219
Ashworth, Edward, architect, 25, 26
Astronomical dials, 190
Atwyll, John, Exeter, 73
Austen, Robert, Somerset, bellfounder, 92
Auto-winding, 193, 197
Axbridge, Somerset, "nail", 130

Baker, William, Exeter, bellfounder, 73, 74,
Baldricks, 161
Baldwyn, Samuel, Exeter, "bellfounder", 91

Bampfylde family, 40, *f59*, 62
  Amyas, N. Molton, 77
Banister, William, Plymouth ringer, 183, 184
Banns, ringing after calling, 187
Barn-owls, 3
Barrett, John, Exeter, bellhanger, 155, 164
Barwell, James, Birmingham, bellfounder, 125
Basilican church plan, 1
Bats, 2
Battlements, 1
Bayley, Thomas, Bridgwater, bellfounder, 58, 67, 89, 111, 116
Bazley, Peter, Tavistock, bellhanger, 166
Bearings, 158, 161, 165
Beauchamp, Joanna de, 49
Beavis, Richard, bell adviser, 47, 57, 94-5, 132, 225
Beer lees, 45, 224
Beer stone, 15, 20, 22
Bees, 2
Belfry openings, 20
Bell-case, 49
Bell collar, 161, 205, 208, 222
Bellcotes, 28
Bellfounders, status, 66
Bellfounder's ague, 47
Bellframes, 57, 105, 144, 153ff, 232-3
  Metal, 120, 124, 157
Bell gear, 158ff, 165
Bellhanging, 153ff
Bell-house, 44, 210, 211-2, 219-20
Bell-hutches, 28
Bell-metal, 205, 207, 209-213, 216, 217, 218, 220, 223, 224, 226
Bell-ringers, 170ff

245

Bellropes, 162, 221, 226, 230
Bell wheels, 160-1, 207, 208, 232
Bellowes, Richard, Braunton, 62, 211
Bellows, 46
Bere, Rev C.S., Uplowman, 184
Bickham, Thomas, Somerset, bellfounder, 109
Big Ben", Westminster, 194
Bilbie family, bellfounders, 39, 52, 54, 56, 66, 67, 94ff, 143, 163, 164, 170
  Edward, 94
  Abraham, 95
  James, 96
  John, 97
  Thomas I, 39, 44, 52, 94, 166, 225
  Thomas II, 51, 58, 60, 62, 64, 95-6, 198, 227
  Thomas III (Thomas Castleman), 96-7, 118, 161
  Thomas Webb, 96
  William, 95
Bird, John, London, bellfounder, 50, 82,
Birdall family, bellfounders, 38, 42-4, 50, 51, 66, 71, 75-7
  Christopher, Exeter, brazier, 75
  John I, Exeter, bellfounder, 75, 209
  John II, Exeter, bellfounder, 51, 58, 62, 72, 76, 129
  Thomas, Exeter, bellfounder, 51, 75, 207, 213
Bissett, Dolton ringer, 171
Blackawton bellfoundry, 105
Blackbourne, Thomas, Salisbury, bellhanger, 157, 166
Blackwell, Robert, clockmaker, 234
Blacmore, Sam, senior, 56
Blagdon, John, Hartland, 61, 216
Blakedon, bellhanger, 162, 208
Blews, Willliam, Birmingham, bellfounder, 125
Bolmet, 46, 220
Bonhay Island, Exeter, 63
Boniface, St., 53
Bottles, 21
Boucher, H., Kelly ringer, 182-3
  Wilfred, ringer, 183n
Bounde, John, Denbury, 73
"Bow bell", 169, 186 Boxed clapper, 162, *f131*
Boxes for ropes, 232
Bradford, William, Meshaw, bellhanger, clockmaker, 91, 164
Brakspeare, Harold, architect, 26
Brasiers, Norwich, bellfounders, 31
Brasses, bearing, 59, 88, 109, 161, 164, 192, 201, 215, 220, 230
"Brass-foundry" bells, 48
Breaking up bells, 46, 212, 219, 225
"Brede mark", 83

Brian, John, Exeter, 73
Brice's Weekly Journal, 139
Bricks, 64, 214, 222
Bridgwater foundry, 52, 53, 54, 58, 64, 67, 89, 111, 116-7, 227
Bristol bellfoundries, 31, 36, 64, 67, 83-5, 124, 125
Brocas, Abisha, Exeter, bookseller, 52
Brown, Theo, folklorist, 187
Brunel, Isambard Kingdom, 7
  Marc Isambard, 182
Bryant, John, Hertford, bellfounder, 126
Buckland Brewer bellfoundry, 55, 58, 62, 68, 118-9, 122, 228
Bulteel, Rev. C., Kingston, 174
Bush, John, Wrington, Som, bellhanger, 95n, 164
Busk-board, 162
Butterfield, William, architect, 16, 25, 123
Butterflies & moths, 2, 3
Buttresses, 6-8, 10, 11-13, 14, 15, 27

Cable rope, 162, 208, 218, 223, 231
Cachemaille Day, N.F., architect, 27
Call-change ringing, 180f
Calwoodley, Thomas, Exeter, 73
Cambridge quarter-chimes, 195
Candles, 175, 212, 219
Cannons, "cannells", 45, 54, 119, 212, 223
Canute, 30
Carew, Sir George, 31
Caröe, W.D., architect, 26, *f42*
Carr, Charles, Smethwick, bellfounder, 126,
Casting bells on site, 43ff, 63, 95, 209-16, 218, 219, 223
Cast-iron clock frames, 192-3
Castleman, Richard, Bristol, 95
Central Council of Church Bell Ringers, 186
Centralized plan for church, 1, 4
Chamberlain, William, London, bellfounder, 31, 50, 55, 82
Change Ringing, by C.A.W.Troyte, 183
Chapingdon, Hugh, South Milton, chime maker, 166, 198
Chapman, Jack, Whitechapel, bellfounder, 58, 64, 226
Chapman & Mears, Whitechapel, bellfounders, 122
Cheany, William, Exeter, apprentice, 91
Chepstow foundry, 113
Chichester family, 40, 49
Chichester, Robert, 55, 118-9
Chime-barrels, 95, 166, 198ff, *f159*
Chiming, 175
  Apparatus, 164, 182, 199
  Machine, 175

INDEX

Chubb family, Cullompton, bellhangers, 162-3
   Edward, 163
   Thomas, 163
Church Ales, 60-1
Church Rate, 57, 62, 179
Church sheep, 60
Churchwardens, 3n, 36, 38-9, 47, 56-7, 62-3, 65, 69, 73, 86, 89, 168, 176-8, 180
  parsimony of, 36, 176-7, 236
Churley, John, bell adviser, 57
Cider Tax, 176
Cire Perdu (lost wax) casting, 36, 42, 48, 49, 121, *f88*
Civil War, 34, 130
Clappers, 161-2
"Clapses", 161, 207, 212
Clarke & Holland, architects, 25
Clay, 42ff, 209, 212, 214-5, 219, 220, 224
Cleave, Thomas, Egloshayle ringer, 170-1
Cluster-flies, 3
Closworth bellfoundry, 54, 63, 67, 87, 94, 106-9
Clyst St Mary, battle, 32
Coats-of-arms, 40, 45, 53, 62, 66, 125, 168
Cobthorne, John, dean, 40
Cockey family, 86-8
   Edward, 86, 163,
   Mordecai, Totnes, bellfounder, 47, 51, 52, 64, 67, 86f
Coin impressions, 49, 51ff, 74, *f63*, 110, 130, 143, *Pl 38-9*
Cole, John, Barnstaple, clockmaker, 191
Coleridge, Rev G F, 183
Collens, 46, 210
Collings, bell adviser, 57
Combe, Ferdinando, bell tuner, 48, 223
Comers ashes, 46
Commonwealth, 35-6, 49, 52, 53, 92, 138, 169
Competition ringing, 36, 170, 174, 180-1, 184-6, 239
Confiscation of bells & clappers, 33-4
Continental bells, 55, 126f
Cooke, Master John, 51, 86
Cookworthy, William, 47
Cope, 42ff
Cope-case, iron, 123
Core, 42ff
Coronation Day, 176, 236
Count-wheel striking, 193
Courtenay family, 38, 53, 62
  Bishop of Exeter, 40, 73
Cox, Rev. E.V., bell adviser, 58
Cracks in bells, 55, *f58*

Craddock, Humphrey, Egloshayle, ringer, 170-1
Crocks, used for metal, 46, 62, 64, 210-1, 213
Cromwell, Thomas & Oliver, 35
Crown-staple, 45, 55, 90, 209, 218
Crotch, Dr, composer, 195
Croydon bellfoundry, 49
Crediton Barns, battle, 32
Croydon bellfoundry & clock works, 123ff
Crutches for bells, 207
Crymes family, 40
Culverden, William, London, bellfounder, 83
Cullompton bellfoundry, 44, 94ff, 118
Curfew, 169, 186

Dalton, Christopher, bell historian, 129
Daniel, John, successor to, bellfounder, 83
Darby, Abraham, ironmaster, 192
Darch, Tom, Torrington ringer, 181
Dart, River, 83
Davidson, James, 28
Davie family, 40
Davis, George, Bridgwater, bellfounder, 117
Dawe, Wlliam, London, bellfounder, 31, 50, 82
Daylight Saving, 197
Dead-beat escapement, 193
Dead-rope ringing, 159, 170
Death-watch beetle, 3, 156
Decoration on towers, 20-1
Decoration on bells, 51ff
Denison, Edmund Beckett, Lord Grimthorpe, 123, 194
Dent, E.J, London, clockmaker, 194
Depree, Ellis & Young, Exeter, clockmakers, 196
Dettingen, Battle of, 176
Devil's Stone, Shebbear, 187
Devon Association of Bellringers, 185
Devon Church Bell Restoration Fund, 186
Devon Ringers' Council, 186
Dialect, Devon, 57
Dial-less clocks, 188
Dinham family, 53
Disputes, between ringers & clergy, 177ff, 239-40
Dissolution of monasteries, 31, 67
Doble, Taunton, bellhanger, 157, 166
Dobson, Downham Market, bellfounder, 125
Donations for bells, 61-2
Doncaster cannons, 55, 123
Downe, George, bellhanger, 162
Drake family, 40

Drake, Sir Francis, 40, 46, 215
Drawsens, 46, 212, 219
Dregs, 45, 210
Drew, Thomas, Exeter, "bellfounder", 91
Drink, involved in bell work, 58, 132, 206-225 *passim*
Dyer, Thomas, Exeter, 74

Earle, Arthur, Dean of Exeter, 40
Eayre & Smith, Melbourne, bellhangers, 166
Edgecombe, Peter, Tavistock, tin merchant, 62
Edward VI, king, 31
Eisel, John, bell historian, 145
Eysbouts, Asten, bellfounders, 36, 127
Ellery, John, Egloshayle ringer, 170-1
Elery, William, Closworth, bellfounder, 67, 108
Elizabeth I, Queen, 34, 168, 169, 235
Ellacombe, Rev. H.T., 28, 39, 58, 69, 77, 97, 134, 154, 160, 175, 181, *f136*, 183, 184, 199
Elphick, George P., bell historian, 48
Estrela, schooner, 127
Evangelical revival, 36, 177
Evans family, Chepstow, bellfounders, 41, 44, 52, 54, 113
  Evan I, 113, 222
  Evan II, 113-4
  William, 47, 53, 58, 59f, 63, 95n, 110, 113-6
Exchange of bells, 64, 205, 226-7
Exeter Archaeological Field Unit, 42
Exeter mediaeval bellfoundry, 30, 37, 39, 42-3 ,45, 46, 50-1, 52, 54, 62, 66, 67, 68-81, 85
Exeter Colleges Guild, 185
Exeter, Dean & Chapter, 57, 63, 114
Exeter Flying Post, 96, 97, 164, 165, 174, 178-9, 180, 195
Exeter Ringers Cycling Club, 185, 239

Fathers family, braziers, 67
Fenny Bridges, battle, 32
Ferrers family, 53
Fidler, Arthur, Bow & Rame, bellhanger, 166
Field-gate clock frames, 189, *f142*
Fiennes, Celia, 63
"Fillet", 161, 181
Fireplaces in towers, 2
Flail locking, 188, 198
Flat-bed clock frames, 194
Fleur-de-Lys, 53
Flock, 45
"Flowers" (washers), 159, 230
Flux, 215

Foliot, 188
Folland, William, Dolton ringer, 171
Ford, Charles, Barnstaple, clockmaker, 196
Forde, John, Plymtree, 69
Forelocks (keys), *varlocks*, 159, 205, 206, 212, 230, 231
Fortescue family, 40
Foulston, John, architect, 24
Four-posted clock frame, 190
Fowler, Charles, architect, 24
Fox, Richard, bishop, 40
Frankincense, 46, 205, 210
Friezes, 51
Fulford, Bartholomew, Exeter, 184
  Rev James, Woodbury, 184
  Rev Langdon, Woodbury, 184
  Robert Medley, Exeter, architect, 25, 184
Fulford & Harvey, architects, 26
Fulford, Tait & Harvey, 26
Fundyng, William, Exeter, 73
Furnace, *f53*, 43, 46, 64, 131, 209, 214, 215
Furniture beetle, 3, 156
Furze, 210

Galleries, 12
Gargoyles, 19, 21
Geffries, Thomas, Bristol, bellfounder, 31, 207
Gilbert, Com. W.R., 40, 53
Gillard, Captain, 64
Gillett & Bland, Croydon, bellfounders, clockmakers, 123, 196
Gillett & Johnston, Croydon, clockmakers, bellfounders, 52, 121, 124, 157
Gloucester, Glos, bellfoundr, 50, 67, 69, 124
Goatham, Dr Teresa, 105n
Goodfellow, John, Egloshayle ringer, 170-1
Gooding, Ambrose, bellfounder, 44, 47, 52, 54, 56, 63, 64, 66, 67, 89f, 118, 133, 224-5
Gore, Rev W.F., Feniton, 184
Grandison, John, bishop, 40, 170
Granite, 8, 10, 14, 15, 16 ,22
Gravity escapement, 194, *f154*
Green, James, architect, 24
Grimthorpe, Lord, *see Denison*
Grinking, Robert, chime maker, 166
Growdon, Roger, Master mason, 11, 15
Gudgeons ("*pegs*" or "*piggs*"), 158-9, 211, 230, 234
Guild of Devonshire Ringers, 182, 184-5
Guille family, 53

Gunpowder Plot, ringing for, 169-70, 175, 176, 177, 231, 233-4, 235

Hachman, Albert, Kleve, bellfounder, 51, 126
Hair, 45
Hale, Thomas, Bristol, founder, clockmaker, 125
Half-wheels, 160, 170
Hambling, James, 105
  Henry, Kingsbridge, bellhanger, 123, 166
  William, Blackawton, bellfounder, 52, 56, 67, 105f, *f76*, 228-9
Hamlyn, Robert, Widecombe-in-the-Moor, 61
Harbottle, E.H., architect, 11, 27
Harris, John, M.P., 40, 53, 62
Hart, Thomas & John, Long Sutton, Som, bellhangers, 159, 163, 233
Harward, Richard, Cullompton, 94, 225
Hawkins, Ambrose, Exeter, clockmaker, *f144*, 191, 198
  Sir John, Plymouth, 46, 215
Hawkins, Rohde, architect, 25
Hawser, 211, 214
Hay, 45, 224
Hayle, Corn., bellfoundry, 67
Hayward, John, architect, 25, 27
Hayward Mills Associates, bellhangers, 166
Headstocks, metal, 160, *f67, f72*
  Timber, 158, *f127, f128*, 234
Hemp, 44, 45, 168, 205, 211, 235
Hendley, Robrt, Gloucester, bellfounder, 69
Herald moth, 3
Hille, Joanna, London, bellfounder, 31, 50, 82-3
Hine & Odgers, architects, 25, 27
Hodson, London, bellfounder, 66, 109
Hoker, John, 32, 75, 186
Holy-water bucket, 213
Hooper, E.F., architect, 27
Hooper, Thomas I & II, Woodbury, bellhangers, 164
Horse dung, 44, 218-9, 220
Howard, William, Exeter, brazier, 91
Hugall, J.W., architect, 2, 25
Hughes family, Whitechapel, bellfounders, 42, 122
Hunkapunks, 7-8, 21
Hurdwick stone, 23
Huyshe family, 40, 53

Ilbert family, 40, 41
Inscriptions, 36ff, 48ff,
  Stock, 50, 70ff

Inventory of Church Goods, 1552, 31
Iron, used in furnace, 208, 209, 211-12, 215, 218-9
I.T., bellfounder, 31, 53, 72-3, *f62*, 78

Jackdaws, 3
Jackson, Gordon, architect, 27
Jackson & Son, Tavistock, founders, 104
Janus, schooner, 127
Jefferies, Judge, 176, 236
Jersey men, 83
"Jesus bells", 70
Johnston, Cyril, Croydon, bellfounder, 124
Judas bell, 167, *f133*

Kaolin, 47
Karoun, Thomas, bellfounder, 43, 58, 81
Kelly, Rev Maitland, 182
Kempe, Preb J A, Merton, 184
Kennicott, Dr Benjamin, Totnes ringer, 171, 236-7
Kettletree, 207
Key of belfry, 238
Kilvert, Rev. Francis, 182n
Kimber, William, Whitechapel, 122
Kingdon, Samuel, Exeter, 104
Kingstons, Bridgwater, bellfounders, 67, 117
Knight, Thomas, bellfounder, 67, 107
  William, bellfounder, 67, 108
Knowles, J.T., architect, 25

Ladders, 8, *f11*,
Lamplugh, Thomas, Bishop of Exeter, 170
Latin, 37-8, 41, 57, 115, 130
Lawrence, Thomas, London, bellfounder, 83
Le Gros, Rochefort, bellfounder, 126
Leofric, Bishop of Exeter, 30
Leonine verses, 37, 50, 70
Lester, Thomas, Whitechapel, bellfounder, 64, 121-2
Lester & Pack, Whitechapel, bellfounders, 122
Lettering, Black-letter, 41, 48, 50-1, 70-2, 77, 82, 83, 128
  Cut-out, 48, 51, 106, 128, 135, 136
  Impressed, 48, 128, 129
    Lombardic, 37, 50-1, 68-9, 70, 71, 75, 76-8, 82-3, 123, 128
Ley, John, carpenter, 57, 162
Lezant, bellfoundry, 137ff
Limestone, 20, 22
Living quarters in towers, 2
Llewellins & James, Bristol, bellfounders, 55, 125

Lob, Mr, Exeter, adviser, 114
Locking-plate, 189
Loughborough bellfoundry, 36, 49, 118, 119, 157
Louvres, 20
Lovelace, Jacob, Exeter, clockmaker, 191
Lowering bells in peal, 186
Lumber, deposited in towers, 2
Lunesdale, schooner, 127
Lussey, Mr, bell tuner, 48
Luttrell family, 53
Luxton, A.C., architect, 28
Luxton, Moses, Winkleigh, bellhanger, 164
Lychbell, 207
Lyne, Samuel, Dolton ringer, 171
Lyte, Rev H F, Brixham, 198

Mackintosh & Abbot, architects, 25
Maintaining power, 193
Manillas, 76
Mardon, Samuel, 184
Mariners, helping with lowering and hoisting bells, 211-2, 214
Market bell, 186
Mary I, Queen, 31, 34, 51, 75, 76, 85, 86, 168, 235
Maufe, E., architect, 27
Maurice, Prince, 176
Mayor-choosing, 187
Mears, Thomas, Whitechapel, bellfounder, 64, 122, 164
Medals, 49, 53
Merson, Richard, Uplowman, 184
Metalware, domestic, 66-7, 76, 116
Methodist revival, 177
Miners, William, *f139*
Mitchell, William, bell tuner, 48
Moloney, Rev C W, West Worlington, 239-40
Monmouth Rebellion, 176, 236
Moon, James, Barnstaple, ironmonger, 106
Morcombe, John, clockmaker, 189
Morrow Mass bell, 32, 86
"Morte" (grease), 211
Moulds, 215, 218, 219, 221, 224
Moulding-wires, 45
Mudge, Henry, bell adviser, 57-8, 224-5
"Mulley groove", 49
Murch, J W & J, E Allington, bellhangers, 163
    Matthew, Honiton, clockmaker, 194, *f153*,
Murphy, John, Dublin, bellfounder, 127
Mutiny, ringers', 178f

Name of Jesus, 70
Naylor, Canon, Exeter, 107
Neat, Harry, Torrington ringer, 171
New Year, ringing for, 177
Newcomen, William, Dartmouth, 51
    Thomas, 66
Niches, 21
Nicholson, Andrew, Bridport, bellhanger, *f126*, 166
Nicholson & Corlette, architects, 26
North, Thomas, bell historian, 175
Norton, Robert, bellfounder, 31, 45, 50-1, 58, 69,
Note of bell, 60, 64
Nott, Hambling &, Blackawton, bellfounders, 105
Nott, bellhanger, 95

Oak-apple Day, 176
Ohlsson, Herr, bell "repairer", 56
Oland, Rector of Exeter St Paul, 130
Oldham, Hugh, bishop, 40, 167, 170
Openings & windows, 20
Orleans (Bollée) bellfoundry, 43, 44, 47
Oxen, 63, 206-7, 208
Oxford bellfoundry, 36, 116,

Pack & Chapman, Whitechapel, bellfounders, 39, 122
Packer, John, Bristol, founder, 125
Page, Keen & Page, Plymouth, clockmakers, 196
Pannel family, bellfounders, 52, 64, 68, 97
    Charles, bellfounder, 97
    Thomas, innkeeper, 97
    William, bellfounder, 39, 97, 118
Pare, John, Exeter, 169
Parker, Robert, Taunton, bellhanger, 166
Passing Bell, 168, 187
Passmore, Richard, bell adviser, 58
Pattern bell, 45
Peals, 181
Pearn & Proctor, architects, 28
Pearson, J.L., architect, 25, 27
"Pemerton", bellfounder, 128
Pendulum rods, 191
Pennington family, 38, 53, 66, 128ff, 164, 170, 171
    In Monmouthshire, 128, 145,
    Bernard, Bodmin, (1607–1674), 134, 136, probate inventory 202
    Christopher I, Bodmin, 1631–1699), 136, 137, will 202-4
    Christopher II, Lezant (?–1706), 54, 89, 135, 138,

INDEX

Christopher III, Lezant, 1697–1764), 44, 45, 47, 53, 138-40, 223-4
Christopher IV, Stoke Climsland, (1737–1799), 140ff, *f113*
Edward, Bodmin, (1633–?), 137, 201, 221
Fitzantony I, Bodmin & Lezant, (1631–1690), 53, 137, *f107*, 218
Fitzantony II, Lezant (1730–1768), 47, 140-1, *f110*, 234
John, Exeter (1612–1668), 35, 47, 52, 130, 134
John I, Bodmin (1596–1660), 136, 201, will 201
John II, Lezant, 1700–c1741), 48, 52, 53, 138-40
John III, Stoke Climsland, (1726–1790), 58, 139, 140ff, 227
John IV, Stoke Climsland, (1771–1823), 53, 118, 142ff, *f114*
John I, Tavistock (?–1709), 47, 88, 134, 218
John II, Tavistock (1668–1754), 47, 135,
Robert, Bodmin (?–1625), 48, 51, 128, 136, 145
Thomas I, Barnstaple (?–1641), 48, 51, 52, 58, 128, *f95*
Thomas II, Exeter (1600–1642), 34, 38, 48, 51, 52, 58, 64, 77, 91, 128-31, *f95*, 217
Thomas III, Exeter (1642–1721), 41, 53, 63, 88, *f99*, 113, 131, 132-3, 223
Thomas, Tavistock (?–1670), 52, 67, 134,
William, Stoke Climsland, (1740–1781), 141ff
William, Rev., Davidstow, 136
Pewter vessels, added to bell metal, 210
Pewterers, 67, 86-7
Pickford, Christopher, bell historian, 164
Pidcock's Menagerie, 53
Pigeons, 3
Pile, Francis, Honiton, clockmaker, 191
Pine-Coffin family, 187
Pinnacles, 8, 10, 11, 12, 13ff, 21, 22, 25, 26
Pinnacles, removed, 15
Pious psalmody, 143
Poling, Thomas, Exeter, chime maker, 166
Political reasons for ringing, 174, 176, 179
Pollard family, clockmakers, 193
  John, Egloshayle ringer, 170-1
  Thomas C, London, clockmaker, 194
Poole family, braziers, Yetminster, 67
Poole, William, bellfounder, 58, 62, 75, 86, 210
Pope, Robert & Joseph, Bradninch, bellhangers, 163
Portledge House, Bideford, 187
Portobello, capture of, 53
Pot metal, 210
Potter & Hare, architects, 28
Prayer Book Rebellion, 32, 74-5

Preston, William, Crediton, bellfounder, 49, 51, 58, 62, 67, 75, 86, 162, 211
Pridham, Lewis, Sandford, clockmaker, 45, 191
Prynne, G H Fellowes, architect, 25, 26, *f38*
Pulleys, blocks, 161, *f130*, 206, 208, 209, 210, 212, 214, 218, 230
Purdue family, bellfounders, 48, 67, 106ff
  George, 106, 111
  Richard I, 106
  Richard II, 107
  Thomas, 47, 51, 53, 55, 63, 66, 67, 71, 87, 107, *f81*, 114, 159, 163, 233
  William II, 106
  William III, 107
Puritanism, 38, 67, 75, 77
Putlog holes, *f14*, 21
Pyke, Thomas, Bridgwater, bellfounder, 116ff

Quarter-clocks, 192
Queen's Peal, 180

Rack striking, 193
Railways, 36, 64, 97, 181, 195
Rain-water disposal, 19
Raising & lowering bells in peal, 180, 181
Reed, *rude*, 45, 218, 219, 224
Reeve, Benoni, Colebrooke, 61
Reformation, 32, 67, 167-8, 177
Religious houses, 31
Rendering, 21
Repairs to bells, 56
Resin, Rasome, 210
Rige, planks, 44, 219
Ringing Customs, 175, 186
Ringing Days, 36, 175
Ringing room, 2, 12, 171, 173, 179-80
Robbyns, John, Plympton, tin merchant, 214
Rock, Richard, Closworth, bellfounder, 67, 108
Robbyns, John, Plympton, tin merchant, 62
Robertson, Joseph, Exeter, clockmaker, 192
Robinson, Rev. F.E., 185
Rogers, T C, architect, 26
Rolle family, 40
Rope, used in casting bells, 45
Rope-guides, 233-4
Ropeford, Roger de, bellfounder, 68, 81, 162
Rose & crown, 54
Roskelly, Thomas, Closworth, bellfounder, 54, 67, 107

Rowe, John, bellhanger & clockmaker, 209, 232-3
   Samuel, Spreyton, bellhanger, 159, 161, 163-4
Roughcast, 21
Rudhall family, Gloucester, bellfounders, 39, 51, 55, 64, 66, 67, 113, 115, 124ff, 128, 133
Rudhall, Abraham I, (fl.1684–1718), 53, 125
   Abraham II, (fl. 1718–1735),125
    Abel, (fl.1736–1750), 125
   Thomas, (1760–1783), 58, 125, 227
   John, (1737–1835) 64, 109, 125
Rufford family, bellfounders, 68
Rugg, bellhanger, 164
Rules, Ringers', 171ff, 236-7
Rural Deans, 57, 177
Russell, Sir John, 32
   Richard, Exeter, 67, 73-4
   Robert, Exeter, bellfounder, 45, 52, 71, 73
Rye House Plot, 176

Sacheverell, Dr,, 176
Sainsbury, Walthamstow, clockmakers, 196, *f156*
St Antony, 21
Salisbury bellfoundry, 67
Sally-way hanging & ringing, 36, 159, 170, 234
Salter, Mr, adviser, 58
Salvin, Anthony, architect, 25
Sampford Courtenay, battle, 32
Sandeers, Samuel, adviser, 58
Sandstone, 23
San Josef, Spanish ship, 126
Savage, John, Exeter, bellfounder, 75
   John, Exeter, clockmaker, 166
Savery, Richard, Taunton, 117
Savill, William, London, bellfounder, 122
Sayers, Dorothy L, writer, 183n
Saxon towers, 4n, 5, 6, 9, 30
Scallop-shell, 53-4
"Scientific" change-ringing, 180
Scratch tuning, 48, 144
Scott, Richard, Dolton ringer, 171
Sea, churches close to, 2
Seage's silent ringing apparatus, 184
Seals, 35, 49, 53, 143
Seame, 210
Searle, Arrthur W, Exeter ringer, 185
   William, bellhanger, 164
Sedding, E.H., architect, 26
Semson, Roger, Ash Priors, bellfounder, 49, 51, 53, 63, 206-7

Service ringing, 168, 199
Servington, John, 31
Seven Bishops, 176
Shapily, Mr, bell adviser, 58, 225
Shappecotte, Sir John, Exeter, 73
Sharke, John, bellfounder, 32, 74-5
Sharland, John, 184
Sharpe, Frederick, bell historian, 84
Sharpe Collection, Oxford, 77, 81
Sherborne Mercury, 109, 110, 111
Sherland, Richard, bellhanger, 163
Shruff (scrap brass), 46, 215-6
Shutters in belfry openings, 20
Sidemen, 62
Silver, 46-7
Simon Grendon's almshouses, Exeter, 73
Simpson, Canon, 120
"Simpson" (true harmonic) tuning, 120
"Sixty on Thirds", 180
Skinner, Rev J, 178
Skirting, 48
Sliders, *f127*
   Latchet, *f129*
Slocum, Joshua, 192n
Smerdon, Robert, Buckland-in-the-Moor, 62
Smith, James, Closworth, bellfounder, 53, 67, 108
Smiths of Clerkenwell, London, 196
Smiths of Derby, clockmakers, 194, 196, *f157*
Somerset style towers, 20, 21, 27
Sound lanterns, 7, 20
South Devon Association for the Encouragement of Round Ringing, 185
South Devon Railway, 187
Southey, Augustus, Exeter, 184
"South Hams" towers, 11-12
South Molton Gazette, 178
Spinning jennies, 116
Spires, 17-19
Squire, Caleb, Buckland Brewer, bellfounder, clockmaker, 104, 119
Stadler, John, Chulmleigh, bellfounder, 39, 48, 52, 53, 64, 66, 67, 88f, 93, 133, 218, 219
Stafford, Edmund, bishop, 40
Stahlschmidt, J C L, bell historian, 121
Stainbank, Robert, Whitechapel, bellfounder, 122
Stairs, 9ff
Statues, 21
Stays, 161, 236

iron peg, 160, 233-4
Stoke Climsland, Corn, bellfoundry, 31, 64, 67, 95, 141ff, *f111*
Stokes, Harry, Woodbury, bellhanger, 157, 164-5
Stooke, John, 34-5, 40
Stores, 60-1
Straw, 45, 224
Street, G.E., architect, 26, *f41*
Street, Robert, Bridgwater, bellfounder, 116
Street & Pyke, Bridgwater, bellfounders, 58, 227
Strickle, 42, 44
String-course, 8
Stumbels, William, Totnes, clockmaker & bellhanger, 163, 191, *f146*
Sturdy, John & Joanna, London, bellfounders, 52
Sturton family, S Petherton, braziers, 67
Sunday, ringing and chiming on, 175
Sundials, 188, 195
Superstitions, 187
Swete, Torrington ringer, 171
   Rev. John, 9n

Tallow, 42, 45
Tamlyn, Richard, Buckland Monachorum., bellfounder, 86
Taylor family, 55, 49, 68, 97, 109, 111, 118f, 122, 123, 156, 157, 164, 166
  John, bellfounder, Oxford & Buckland Brewer, 40-1, 55, 62, 104, 228
  John William I, 119f, 183
  John William II, 121
Theophilus, 42
Thunderstorms, 70, 168, 187, 235
Tickle, John, Crediton, clockmaker, 192
Telegraph, 195
Thwaites, Thwaites & Reed, London, clockmakers, 196
Tiebolts, 156
Tin, 46, 58, 60, 62, 213, 214
Tin glass (bismuth), 46
Tower roofs, 16
Tower walls, thickness, 6
Towers, central, 1, 4, 13
Towers, dating, 3
Towers, near the sea, 2
Towers, transeptal, 4
Towers, western, 5
Tractarian movement, 36
Trade tokens, 49, 52

Transport, by land, 63, 82, 205-7
  by water, 64, 82, 216, 220, 222, 230
Trap (volcanic stone), 23
Trapnell, Edward, Clyst Honiton, 187
Travers, Zachary, Thorverton, 132
Treby, George, Plympton St Maurice, 177
Trekenner Mill, Lezant, 138
Trelawny, Col Harry, Calstock, 183
  Jonathan, Bishop of Exeter, 176
Trenails, 156
Trouffyld, Alice, Exeter, 75
Troyte, Charles A.W., Huntsham, 120, 156, 183, 184
Trussing, 159, 207, 208, 212
Tuning, bell, 47, 217, 223
Turner, Torrington ringer, 171
Turner, Samuel & Robert, Whitechapel, bellhangers, 164
Turpentine, 46, 210

Underhill, William, Crediton, millwright, 160

Verge escapement, 188-9
Vermin, payment for, 56, 168
Vernon, Admiral, 53, 140
Vickers, Sheffield, makers of steel bells, 126
Victoria & Albert Museum, London, 134
Vincent, John, 32
Villedieu-les-Poëles, France, bellfoundry, 43, 45, 51, 71, 127
Visscher, Quirinus de, Rotterdam, bellfounder, 126
Vulliamy, Benjamin, London, clockmaker, 194

"W.K.", bellfounder, 52, 91-2
Walrond, John, Tiverton, 126
Walshe, Robert, priest, 33
Walters, H.B., bell historian, 54n, 75, 111
Ware, Charles, & Partners, architects, 28
Warners, London, bellfounders, Cripplegate, 49, 55, 97, 105, 122, 123, 125, 157, 161, 166
Warren, bellhanger, 159
Watching bells after casting, 47, 210, 211
Wax, 42, 45, 210, 212, 215
Weare & Savill, London, bellfounders, 122, *f89*
Weighing bells, 65, 205, 208, 223
Weight-lines, 191
Weights, clock, 191, 234
Wellington bellfoundry, 94, 109
Wesley, Samuel Sebastian, composer, 198
Westbrook, William, bellhanger, 162
"Westminster" quarter-chimes, 195

West of England Church Bell Foundry, 97
Whitechapel bellfoundry, 49, 54, 55, 64, 121ff
Whites of Appleton, Oxon, bellhangers, 166
"Whittington "quarter-chimes, 195
Wickett, Charles, bellhanger, 163
"Widey Court Book", Plymouth, 62, 121, 214
Wildlife in towers, 2
Wilkes, John, 176
Willett, Rev. C.S., Monkleigh, 184
   William, Monkleigh, 184-5
Windlass, 211, 221, 231
Wiseman family, Montacute, braziers, 67
   Robert, bellfounder, 106
Wodeward, William, London, bellfounder, 66
Wokingham bellfoundry, 52
Wood (for firing), 46, 210-215 ,218, 219, 226

Woolcombe family, 40
Wright, Lawrence, London. Bellfounder, 45, 121, 215-6
   William, Closworth, bellfounder, 67
Wroths, Wellington, bellfounders, 52, 53, 64, 109ff, 133
   Thomas I, 38, 66
   Thomas II, 39, 58, 113, 234
Wymbis, Richard de, bellfounder, 54, 70, 81
Wymond, Thomas, Landulph, 141

Yarde family, 40, 49
Yonge, Sir William, 40, 53, 62
York Minster, 42
York, William, Exeter, bellfounder, 73
Young people, 38, 61, 206, 216

Zeppelins, 197

INDEX OF PLACES

[Note: This index gives the names of towers and other places where bells or clocks are found. The main entry may normally be assumed to refer to the parish church. Places outside Devon which are named only in lists of bells are not indexed.]

Abbots Bickington, 78, 85
Abbotsbury, St Mary, Newton Abbot, 26, 87, 88
Abbotsham, 4, 12, 38, 49, 50, 82, 86, 125, 134, 146, 147
Abbotskerswell, 146, 147
  Priory, 126
Alphington, 23, 95, 99, 164, 176, 182
Alverdiscott, 78, 149
Alwington, 7, 8, *f9*, 10, 20, 64, *f67*, 84, 89, 125
Antony House, Corn, 77, 81
Appledore, 121
Arlington, 41, 97-8, 104, 119
Ashburton, 3, 11, 40, 45, 49, 53, 62, 64, 104, 121-2, 125, 162, 168, 205, 235
  St Lawrence, 18
  Town Hall, 148
Ashbury, 77, 148
Ashcombe, 3, 20, 79, 88, 106, 108, 153, 158, *f128*, 160
Ashford, 4, 64, 84, 93
Ashprington, 1, 64, 122
Ash Priors, Som, 63, 206
Ashreigny, 4, 118
  clock, 193
Ash Thomas, 93
Ashton, 151
Ashwater, 10, 44, 46, 57, 63, 124, 150, 171, 175, 219, 231
Atherington, 21, 63, 151
Aveton Gifford, 4, 9, 13, 61, 64, 146, 150, 163, 191
Avonwick, 93
Awliscomb, 32, 51, 56, 63, 80, 107, 109, 146
Axbridge, Som., 130
Axminster, 4, 13, 64, 103, 106, 109, 112, 116, 117, 176, 198, 235
  Cemetery, 93
Axmouth, 106, 107, 108, *f80*, 147, 155, *f120*, 161

Aylesbeare, 51, 77, 79, 80, 81
Ayshford Chapel, Burlescombe, 146

Bampton, 8, *f10*, 60, *f75*, 96, 103
  School, 127
Barbrook, 93
Barnstaple, Holy Trinity, 25, 116, 117
  St Mary Magdalene, 85
    St Peter, 4, 17, 18, 125, 126, 198-9
    Abbey, 31
    Bluecoat School, 116, 117
Beaford, 4, 78, 115
Beaminster, Dorset, 64, 95, 166, 198
Beaworthy, 18, 119
Beauvais, France, 1
Beer, 19, 20, 76, 81
Beesands, 127
Belstone, 47, 140, 144, 149
Bere Alston, 93
Bere Ferrers, 2, 86, 150, 162, 169, 230
Berrynarbor, 8, 21, 113
Berry Pomeroy, 20, 51, 77, 81, 87, 90, 146, 157
Bickington, 57, 110, 113, 146, 176
Bickleigh (E), 89, 103, 112, 146, 147
Bickleigh (W), 10, 15, 16, 104, 149, 177
Bicton, 103
Bideford, 28, 106, 121, 125
Bigadon House, Buckfastleigh, 127
Bigbury, 2, 12, 105, 151
Bishop's Court, Sowton, 78, 160
Bishops Lydeard, Som., 56, 80
Bishopsnympton, 16, 89, 99, 104, 124
Bishops Tawton, 4, 18, 58, 103, 118, 119, 198
Bishopsteignton, 4n, 9n, 132, 147

Bittadon, 18, 93
Bitton, Glos., 175, 182
Blackawton, 11, 105, 143, 151
Blackborough, 25, 126
Blackhall House, Avonwick, 93
Black Torrington, 14, 63, 150
Blisland, Corn., 136, 148
Bondleigh, 78, 80, 134, 137, *f106*, 147, 148
Bourges, France, Cathedral, 167
Bovey Tracey, 34, 52, 121, 143, 152
Bow, 95, 100, 148, 149
Bradford, 53, 119, 151
Bradford-on-Tone, Som., 12, 49, 79, 80, 110
Bradley Manor, Newton Abbot, 125
Bradninch, 95, 99, 174, 180, 239
Bradstone, 3, 20, 23, 40, 62, 118, 119
Bradworthy, 14, 16, 119, 125
Brampford Speke, 28, 56, 95, 100
Branscombe, 2n, 4, 9, 10, 20, 113, 147, 175, 199
Bratton Clovelly, 4, 10, 150
Bratton Fleming, 97
Braunton, 3n, 4, *f2*, 18, 44, 45, 46, 56, 58, 62 ,63 ,64, 76, 113, *f83*, 115, 119, 121, 145, 166, 169, 209-14, 222
  clock, *f156*
Brendon, 7, 64, 84, 145
Brentor, 37
Bridestowe, 6, 15, 118, 119
Bridford, 77, 146, 147, 160
Bridgerule, 2, 14, *f17*, 101, 124, 152
Bridgwater, Som. , 111
Brill, Bucks, 118
Brimpsfield, Glos. 69, 77
Brixham, All Saints, 124, 198
Brixham, St Mary, 2n, 20, 69, 101, 103, 151
  clock, 191, *f146*
Brixton, 39, 51, 55, 125, *f92*,
Broadclyst, 8, 21, 96, 101, 121, 239
Broadhembury, 10, 48, 56, 57, 83, 84, 95, 99, 100, 101, 111, 112, 164, 191
Broadhempston, 3, 12, 125, 151, *f139*
Broadway, Som., 53
Broadwindsor, Dorset, 49, 78, 79
Broadwoodkelly, 124, 125
Broadwoodwidger, 10, 144, 150, 171, 181, 237
Brompton Ralph, Som., 37, *f60*, 69, 77, 79
Brooking, *f37*, 25, 125
Brownston, 93
Brushford, 17-18, *f25*, 38, 50, 82, 154

Buckerell, 12, 32, 43, 78, 79, 125, 164
Buckfast Abbey, 20, 31, 121, 160
Buckfastleigh, 7, 11, 18, 31, 44, 45, 46. 47, 58, 63, 83, 89, 90, 95, 102 ,106, 121, 163
  St Luke, 93
Buckland Brewer, 3, 7, 58, 118
Buckland Filleigh, 138, 148
Buckland-in-the-Moor, 11, *f15*, 62, 100, 121
Buckland Monachorum, 3, 10, 12, 15, 16, 53, 86, 124, 138, *f108*, 148, 164, 175, 178, 234, 237
  Abbey, 31, 61
Buckland-tout-Saints, 151
  House, 93
Bucks Mills, 49, 121, *f88*,
Budleigh Salterton, 26
Bulkworthy, 28, 42, 54, 81, 85, 91, 92
Burlescombe, 10, 53, 130, 146
Burrington, 4, 63, 151
Burston Moor, Welcombe, 106
Butterleigh, 12, 80, 112

Cadbury, 79, 103, 164
Cadeleigh, 21, 95, 99, 132
Callington, Corn., 171, 237
Calstock, Corn, 64, 183
Calverleigh, 147
Cambridge, King's College, 83
Camelford, Corn, Town Hall, 137
Canonsleigh Priory, 31
Chagford, 60, 86, 96, 100, 121, 168
Challacombe, 84, 89, 116, 117
Chardstock, 25
Charles, 115,116
Charleton, 2, 90, 135, 148, 160
Chawleigh, 113, 115, 116
Cheldon, 17, 24, 38, 115, 145, 147
Cheriton Bishop, 14, 150, 151, 231
Cheriton Fitzpaine; 8, *f11*, 48, 58, 59f, 91, 110, 112, 113, 147, 150
Chevithorne, 104
Chewstoke, Som., 94-6
Chilthorne Domer, Som. 50, 68, 77
Chipstable, Som., 111
Chittlehampton, 3, 6, *f30*, 20, 21, 40, 115, 116, 177
Chivelstone, 7, 15, 39, 47, 64, 88, 89, 150, 151, 175, 177
Christow, 23, 151
Chudleigh, 61, 63, 76, 88, 124, 151, 157, 169, 198
  Town Hall, 93

INDEX

Chulmleigh, 3, 7, 8, 15, 41, 64, 67, 113, 115, 179
Churchstow, 21, 90, 105, 123, 146
Churston Ferrers, 2, 5, 53, 78, 79, 88, 121
Citta di Castello, Italy, 54
Clannaborough, 78, 124, 148
Clawton, 12, 16, 57, 60, 148, 149, 161, 169
Clayhanger, 9, 106, 108, 116
Clayhydon, 103, 239
Closworth, Som, 63
Clovelly, 2n, 124
Clyst Honiton, 20, 86, 120, 146
Clyst Hydon, 77, 81, 102, 125, 147
Clyst St George, 61, 77, 78, 79, 81, 122, 182
  School, 127
Clyst St Lawrence, 3, 96, 101
Clyst St Mary, 5, 50, 71, 78, 79, 147, 159, 160, 161
Cockington, Torquay, 2, 52, 92, 93, 169
  clock, 188
Coffinswell, 53, 78, 79, 146, 160
Cofton, 104
Colaton Raleigh, 53, 78, 79
Coldridge, 48, 102, 103, 145, 148, 179
Colebrooke, 52, 57, 61, 63, 95, 99, 102, 104, 107, 109, 130, 146, 147, 159, 160, 161, 163, 176, 232-3
Collaton St Mary, 93, 124
Colleton Barton, Chulmleigh, 126, 127
Columbjohn, 81
Colyton, 4, 13, 19, 20, *f29*, 101, 106, 147, 175
  clock & chime-barrel, 192, *f147*, 199
Combeinteignhead, 51, 76, 80, 81, 146, 160
  clock, *f151*, 194
Combe Martin, 2n, 7, 21, 118, 169
Combe Raleigh, 78, 100, 147
Combpyne, 16, *f22*, 20, 37, 50, 81, 85
Compton Castle, Marldon, 93
Cookbury, 5, 18, 75, 77, 81, 91, 92, 134, 147
Cornwood, 104, 150, 175
Cornworthy, 31, 151
Coryton, 79, 134, 135, 147, 148
Cotehele House, Corn., 81, 188, *f141*
Cotleigh, 104, 107, 109, 112, 124
Countisbury, 116, 117
Cove, 28, 112
Cowley, 28
Creacombe, 28
Crediton, 4, 13, *f19*, 15, 20, 23, 46, 53, 58, 64, 67, 86, 122, 128, f112, 142, 147 150, *f121*, 156, *f126*, 160, 162, 164, 169, 226-7

clock & chime-barrel, 198,199
Cruwys Morchard, 17, 41, 113, 115, 116, 145
Cullompton, 3, 8, 21, 39, 44, 48, 57, 63, 64, 94-96, 99, 102, 111, 112, 121, 124, 144, 145, 159, 163 ,164, 166, 169, 175, 177, 178, 197, 198, 225-6, 234, 236, 238
  Old Police Station, 197
Culmstock, 19, 101, 104, 146, 188
Curry Rivel, Som., 109

Dalwood, 79, 103, 106, 109, 116, 117
Dartington, 2, 27, 61, 77, 79, 105, 106, 108, 123
Dartington old church, 12
Dartmouth, St Clement, 31, 38, 55, 64, 83, 111
  St Petrox, 19, 23, 61, 64, 122
  St Saviour, 12, 64, 89, 90, 103, 123
    clock, 191
Dawlish, 2n, 10, 57, 58, 65, 89, 90, 117, 151, 168, 169, 177
  clock,188
Dean Prior, 53, 58, 106, 121, 136, 148, 190
Denbury, 3, 49, 51, 52, 104, 105, 106, 136, 148, 190
Diptford, 12, 18
Dittisham, 2, 64
Doccombe, 93
Dodbrooke, 19, 64, 101, 105, 106, 148, 151
Doddiscombesleigh, 146, 147
Dolton, 20, 57, 105, 119, 144, 152, *f122*, 164, 171, 177
Dorchester, Oxon., 68, 69, 77
Dowland, 55, 118
Down St Mary, 100, 121, 147
Dowrich House, Sandford, 93
Drewsteignton, 7, *f7*, 14, 52, 144, 151, 173, *f135*, 180
Dulverton, Som., 79, 128, 145, 146
Dunchideock, 53, 79, 147, 160
Dunkeswell, 109, 110, 111, 112, 125
  Abbey, 31, 104
Dunsford, 10, 151, 164
Dunterton, 3, 15, 22, *f32*, 54, 78, 148, 149, 156

East Allington, 53, 138, 148, 163
East Anstey, 79, 80, 128, 145
East Buckland, 5, 113
East Budleigh, 95, 100, 163
East Down, 4, 54, 75, 78, 89, 118, 119, 134, 147
East Ogwell, 2, 51, 105, *f76*, 106, 136, *f103*, 148
East Portlemouth, 53, 79, 121, 145
East Putford, 28
East Quantoxhead, Som, 53, 78
East Worlington, 25, 113, 115, 164

257

Egg Buckland, 22, 79, 95, 101, 120, 134, 147
Eggesford, *f48*, 36, 48, *f55*, 49, 128, 131, 145, 146
Egloshayle, Corn., 170-1
Ermington, 18, 31, 53, 103, 139-40, 149
Exbourne, 121, 150
Exeter, Cathedral, 5, 6, 9, 13, 17, 55, 57, 71, 159, 162, 163, 164, 166, 168, 169, 170, 179, 181, 184, 186, 187
Exeter Cathedral bells: 30, 35, 31, 35, 36, 40, 43-44, 51, 52, 53, 58, 63, 68, 77, 81, 94, 107, 109, 114-5, *f84*, 120-1, *f87*, 121, 130, *f98*, 139, 146, 166
  "Cobthorne", 55, 56, 87, 107, 109
  "Old 9 o'Clock, 47, 114-5
  "Stafford", 51, 107
  "Grandison", 53, 107, 109, 114-5, 120, 160
  "Peter", 51, 71, 73, 107, 109, 168, 176, 186
Exeter Cathedral clock & chimes, 166, 188-9, *f140*, 190, 191, 198
Exeter, All Hallows, Goldsmith Street, 169
  All Hallows-on-the-Walls, 169
  St Andrew, 28
  St Boniface, Whipton, 28
  St David, 24, 26, *f42*, 239
  St Edmund, 63, 104, 114, 116, 124, 169
  Emmanuel, 26, *f39*,
  St George, 169
  Holy Trinity, 24, 28, 57, 58, 69, 75, 162, 166, 169, 198
  St James, 27, 93
  St John, 112, 169, 195-6, *f155*
  St John's Hospital, 31
  St Kerrian, 117
  St Lawrence, 80, 169
  St Luke, Countess Wear, 93
  St Mark, 27, 121
  St Martin, 53, 132, *f100*, 147, 153, 169
  St Mary Arches, 33, 64, 82, 169
  St Mary Major, 5, 9, 25, 33, 42, 44, *f52*, 73, 74, 91, 102, 169, 186
  St Mary Steps, 35, 81, 146, 153, 155, *f119*, 160, 161, 167, 169
    clock, 190, 192, *f148*
  St Matthew, 26
  St Michael, Heavitree, 11, 27, 81, 108, 120, 147, 166
    clock, 188
  St Michael, Mount Dinham, 25, 27
  St Olave, 79, 145, 169, 188
  St Pancras, 71, 78, 169
  St Paul, 41, 88, 89, 128-9, 130, 169
  St Paul, Burnhouse Lane, 28, 93
  St Petrock, 19, 25n, 37, 52, 53, 64, 83, 88, 89, 93, 125, 132, 147, 166, 167, 169, 188, 198
  Sacred Heart (R.C.), 127
  St Sidwell, 122, 184, 198
  St Stephen, 145, 147, 169
  St Thomas, 20, 33n, 124, 151
  Polsloe Priory, 31
  St Katherine's Priory, 85
  St Nicholas Priory, 31
  College, 85
  Guildhall, 71, 79
  Liverydole, 146
  R.A.M.Museum, 78, 81, 147
  Royal Clarence Hotel, 126, 127
Exminster, 23, 96, 100, 180, 199, 200, 239
Exmouth, Holy Trinity, 25, *f38*, 26
  St John, Withycombe Raleigh, 25

Farway, 78, 107, 109, 113
Feniton, 52, 57, 110, 112, 177, 184, 188
Filleigh, 25, 55, 64, 125, 149
Ford Abbey, now Som., 31
Fowey, Corn., 47
Foxcott, Hants, 71, 78
Fremington, 4, 52, 77, 78, 92, 146, 166, 212
Frithelstock, 5, 31, 51, 53, 54, 77, 81, 85, 125, 136, *f104*, 137, 148, 160

Galmpton, Churston Ferrers, 116
Georgeham, 64, 121, 125
Georgenympton, *f35*, 24, 52, 63, 92, *f73*, 93
Germansweek, 77
Germigny-des-Prés, France, 1
Gidleigh, 22, 78, 79, 147
Gloucester Cathedral, Glos., 130, 145
Gittisham, 41, 58, 63, 100, 127, 146, 169, 192
Goodleigh, 5, 28, 39, 44, 45, 46, 89, 98, 109, 113, 137, 146, 148, 176, 218-9, 231
Guernsey, 74, 80
Gulworthy, 93
Gunn Chapel, Swimbridge, 28, 93

Haccombe, 42, 54, 81, 85
Halberton, 48, 57, 61, 86, 106, 113, 145, 163
Halwell, 7, 21, 52, 56, 105, 106, 149
Halwill, 40, 118, 119, 166
Harberton, 95, 96, 100
Harbertonford, 93

INDEX

Harford, 77, 88, 160
Harpford, 147
Hartland (Stoke), 2, 6, 12, 21, 40, 61, 64, 118, 121, 147, 216-7
 Abbey, 31
 Town, St John, 105
Hatherleigh, 17-18, *f26*, 103, 185
Hawkchurch, 103
Heanton Punchardon, 119, 150
Hemyock, 4, 39, 58, 91, *f72*, 92, 103, 111, 157, *f125*
Hennock, 47, 51, 78, 146, 153, *f116*,
Herner Chapel, Bishops Tawton, 126
Highampton, 51, 78, 79, 85
High Bickington, 5, *f3*, 115, 116
High Bray; 21, 57, 78, 79, 103
Highweek, 3, 31, 63, 87, 124, 151
Hittisleigh, 78, 79, 103, 155
Hockworthy, 28, 103, 160, *f129*, 161, *f130*
Holbeton, 18, 57, 140, 148, 149, 151, 163, 164
Holcombe, Dawlish, 93
Holcombe Burnell, 36, 49, 78, 131, 146
Holcombe Rogus, 52, 80, 100, 110, 111, 117, 130, *f97*, 145
Hollacombe, 16-7, 93, 128, 134, 145, 147
Holne, 46, 56, 57-8, 63, 90, 224
Holsworthy, 2, 15, 22, 89, 90, 124, 164, 177, 197, 220
 chime-barrel, 198
Honeychurch, 51, 75, 77, 79, 81, 207-8
Honiton, St Michael, 56, 95, 99, 106, 112, 116, 117, 169, 176, 198
 St Paul, 24, 54, 96, 102, 116, 117, *f85*,
  clock, 194, *f153*
Honiton Barton, South Molton, 115
Hoops Inn, Clovelly, 125
Hope Cove, Malborough, 93
Horrabridge, 104
Horwood, 52, 64, 84, 147, 153, 159, 160
Huccaby, Princetown, 93
Huish, 3, 28, 79, 80
Huntsham, 28, 120, 146, 156, 183, 184
Huntshaw, 84, 92, 147, 158
Huxham, 93

Iddesleigh, 38, 52, 84, *f68*, 128, *f96*, 145, 146
Ide, 65, 112, 147
Ideford, 79, 147
Ilfracombe, Holy Trinity, 4, 64, 102, 113, 115, 121, 125
 St Peter, 26, 127
 SS Philip & James, 27, 125
Ilsington, 103, 104, 124

Instow, 79, 92, 93, 134, 147, 220-1
Inwardleigh, 151
Ipplepen, 8, 11, 12, 21, 96, 103
 clock, 188, *f143*, 189, 190
Ivybridge, 93

Jacobstowe, *f13*, 14, 53, 63, 72, 79, 125, 151

Kelly, 150, 151, 164, 182-3, 184
 House, 104
Kenn, 23, 64, 88, 89, 99, 147, 176, 180
Kennerleigh, 78, 124, *f91*
Kentisbeare, 103, 110, 112, 121, 147, 164
Kentisbury, 113, 115
Kenton, 12, 21, *f31*, 23, 39, *f51*, 52, 95, 99, 126, 127, 136, 155, 164
 clock, *f158*
Killerton House, Broadclyst, 102, 104
Kilmington, 28, 63, 65, 101, 107, 109, 117, 147, 163
Kilton, Som., 129, 146
Kingsbridge, 4, 18, 64, 105, 122, 150, 185
Kingskerswell, 2, 53, 143, 152
Kingsnympton, 8, 17, 18, 113, 115
Kingsteignton, 20, 101, 110, 113, 124, 145, 148, 160, 185
Kingston, 52, 77, 78, 81, 134, *f101*, 148, 160, 165, 173-4, 175
Kingswear, 28, 77, 81, 107, 109
Knowle, Crediton, 93
 Barton, Crediton, 93
Knowstone, 77, 78, 147

Lamerton, 97, 104
Landcross, 28, *f45*, 125
Landkey, 63, 151
Landscove, 25
Landulph, Corn., 140-1, 150
Langford Budville, Som., 63, 103, 112, 146, 147
Langport, Som., 64
Langtree, 7, 12, 119, 152
Lapford, 10, 52, 145, 146, 151
Lee, 93
 School, 93
Leusdon, 125
Lewtrenchard, 149, 150, 151, 152
Lezant, Corn., 148, 149
Lifton, 118, 119, 185
Liskeard, Corn., 136, 143, 149, 152
Little Bredy, Dor., 97
Littleham (N), 7, *f8*, 79, 95, 99, 104, 124, 220-1

Littleham (S), 2n, 56, 88, 89, 104, 116, 124, 146, 147
Littlehempston, 15, 16, 78, 80, 88, *f71*, 89, 104, 126
Little Torrington, 151
Litton Cheney, Dor., 80, 164
Loddiswell, 143, 151
Loders, Dor., 129, 146
Loxbeare, 6, *f4*, 77, 78, 79
Loxhore, 125
Luffincott, 24, 84
Lundy Island, 126
Luppitt, 79, 113, 121
Lustleigh, 103, 124
Luton, Ideford, 93
Lydford, 15, 52, 151
Lympstone, 28, 52, 110, *f82*, 113, 157, 177
  R.M. Camp, 55, 127
Lynmouth, 125
Lynton, 2n, 64, 84

Malborough, 12, 18, 106, 122
Mamhead, 100
Manaton, 31, 79, 82-3
Mariansleigh, 113, 115, 121
Marldon, 20, 31, 40, 53, 64, 83, 146
Martinhoe, 8, 78, 80
Marwood, *f58*, 56, 101
Marystow, 119
Marytavy, 138, 148, 152
Meavy, 150, 152
Meeth, 77, 89
Membury, 79, 116, 117
Menheniot, Corn., 139
Merton, *f6*, 7, 79, 134, 147, 149, 164, 184
Meshaw, 91, 103, 123, 157, 161, 164
Milton Abbot, 23, 150
Milton Damarel, 145, 147, 149
Milverton, Som., 63, 206
Minehead, Som., 51, 103, 128, 145
Modbury, 3, 18, *f27*, 58, 95, 96, 103, 128, 145, 163, 179
  clock, *f144*, 191
  Priory, 31
Molland, 38, 49, 51, 53, 62, 84, 86, 110, 112
Monkleigh, 79, 101, 119, 184-5
Monkokehampton, 28, 54, 79, 80, 136, 148
Monkton, 78, 123
Montreal, Canada, 122
Morchard Bishop, 102, 113, 115, 116, 157, 165, 166, 179
Morebath, 16-17, 20, 33, 60, 115, 116

Moreleigh, 78, 79
Moretonhampstead, 3, 124, 149
Mortehoe, 2n, 4, 53, 78, 121, 137, 148
Muchelney, Som., 129, 146
Musbury, 102, 110-1, 113

Netherexe, 147, 187
Newnham Abbey, now Som., 31
Newton Abbot, clock tower, 20, 39, 64, 122, 124n
  Cemetery, 104
Newton Ferrers, 15, 140, 149, 151
Newton Poppleford, 10, 117
Newton St Cyres, 1, 9, *f12*, 12, 21, 23, 41, 63, 114, 116, 186
  clock, 191, *f145*
Newton St Petrock, 78, 134, 147, 153
Newton Tracey, 78, 80
Northam, 39, 64, 96, 101, 121, 128, 216
North Bovey, 73, 97, 103, 155
North Bradley, Wilts., 95
North Hill, Corn., 164
North Huish, 18, 95
Northleigh, 78, 80, 160
Northlew, 63, 121, 144, 150, 151, 171, 174-5, 237
North Molton, 15, 77, 86, 96, 102, 103, 162, 164, 166
North Tamerton, Corn., 118, 119
North Tawton, 52, 84, 146, 149, 150
Noss Mayo Village Hall, Revelstoke, 93
Nymet Rowland, 148
Nynehead, Som., 109, 147

Oakford, 28, 179
Offwell, 78, 80, 112
Okehampton, All Saints, 77, 111, 113, 124
  St James, 79
  Museum, 37, 50, 81, 85
Oldridge, 103
Oldway Mansion, Paignton, 89, 90
Otterton, 5, 28, 101, 103, 192, 198
Ottery St Mary, 3, 5, *f5*, 6, 17, 53, 102, 121, 124, 132, 146, 147, 177, 182
  clocks, 189, 190, 194, *f154*, 198

Paignton, St John, 103, 113, 125, 146, 176
  clock, 195
  St Andrew, 26
  Christ Church, 93
  St George, Goodrington, 27, 28, 119
  St Paul, Preston, 27, 28

INDEX

Pancrasweek, 80, 91, 92, 149
Parkham, 150
Parracombe, 134, 137, 147, 148
Pathfinder Village, Tedburn St Mary, 94
Payhembury, 38, 51, 78, 80, 104, 130, 145, 146
Peamore House, Alphington, 104
Peterborough Cathedral, 125
Petersmarland, 37, 50, 54, 70, 78, 81, 146, 149
Petertavy, 10, 15, 125, 138, 148, 149, 151
Petrockstowe, 151, 152
Petton, 28, *f46*, 42, 45, 54, 81, 85
Pilton, 4, 10, 41,55, 64, 119, *f86*, 125, 151
  clock, 188
Pinhoe, 77, 80, 81, 138, 146, 148
Plymouth, St Andrew, 2n, 3, 8, 15, 22, 31, 44, 45, 46, 62, 64, 95, 99, 121, 148, 159, 161, 166, 172, 214-6
  chime-barrel, 198
  St Andrew, Stoke Damarel, 28, 95, 102, 122, 173
  Ascension, Crownhill, 28, *f43*, 127
  St Aubyn, Devonport, 24
  St Barnabas, Devonport, 93
  St Bartholomew, 28
  St Budeaux, 52, 87, 88, 95, 99, 121, 151
  St Catherine, 28
  St Chad, Whitleigh, 28
  Charles, 24, 122
  Christ Church, Estover, 93
  Dockyard Church, 150, 183
  Emmanuel, 26
  St Francis, Honicknowle, 28
  St George, 104
  St Jude, 27
  St Mark, Ford, Devonport, 94
  St Mary, Laira, 26, *f40*
  St Matthias, 25, 27, 102
  St Paul, Efford, 28
  St Paul, Stonehouse, 24
  St Peter, 2, 26, 104
  St Philip, Weston Mill, Devonport, 26, 94
  St Simon, 93, 94
  St Thomas, Keyham, Devonport, 26, 94
    Breakwater Lighthouse, 122
    Devonport Dockyard, 127,
    Dockyard Museum, 93
  Royal Naval Hospital, 122, *f89*, 193, *f150*
  Royal William Victualling Yard, 194
Plympton, Abbey , 31
  St Mary, *f20*, 15, 22, 40, 106, 108, 148, 149

  St Maurice, 3, 49, 62, 64, 97, 104, 121, 140, 150, 176
Plymstock, 65, 147, 149
Plymtree, 10, 69, 147
Poltimore, *f59*, 62, 113, 115, 164
Porlock, Som., 189
Portledge House, near Bideford, 187
Poundstock, Corn., 164
Powderham, 23, 56, 100, 125, 147, 155, 164
  Castle, clock, 191
Princetown, 104
Puddington, *f47*, 76, 102, 153, *f117*
Putford, 148
Pynes Home Farm, Upton Pyne, 94
Pyworthy, 1, 19, 140, 149, 157

Rackenford, 103
Rame, Corn., 69,78
Rattery, 18, *f28*, 52, 149
Revelstoke, 41, 80, 123, 146
Rewe, 96, 101, 132-3, 147, 188, 223
Ringmore, 5, 18, 78, 88, 89, 90, 122
Roborough, 118
Rockbeare, 100, 106, 108, 117, 146, 150
Romansleigh, 28, 63, 78, 92, 93
Roseash, 103, 114, 115
Rye, Sussex, clock, 189n

St Austell, Corn., 15. 47
St Breward, Corn., 140, 149
St Colan, Corn., 81, 148
St Columb Major, Corn., 142, 149
St Dennis, Corn., 136, 148
St Erney, Corn., 50, *f57*, 72, 78
St Ervan, Corn., 80, 89, 90
St Giles-in-the-Wood, 118, 164
St Giles-on-the-Heath, 139, 149, 151
St John-in-the-Wilderness, Withycombe Raleigh, 146, 153, *f118*, 187
St Just-in-Penwith, Corn., 69, 75, 80
St Martin-by-Looe, Corn., 106, 148, 149
St Michael Caerhayes, Corn., 53, 74, 80
St Pierre du Bois, Guernsey, 71, 74, 80
St Stephen-by-Launceston, Corn., 171
St Stephen-by-Saltash, Corn., 140
St Veep, Corn., 137, 148
Salcombe, 25, 103, 182
Salcombe Regis, 80, 146
Salisbury, Wilts, Cathedral clock, 189n

Salou, Spain, 112
Saltram House, Plymstock, 93, 149
Sampford Courtenay, 8, 32, 59, 144, 147, 150
Sampford Peverell, 19, 100
Sampford Spiney, 15, 125, 134, 146, 147, 149
Sandford, 115, 116
Satterleigh, 28, *f44*, 85, 89, 160
Seaton, 2n, 10, *f14*, 21, 69, 77, 79, 146
Shaugh Prior, 15, 150
Shebbear, 151, 169, 186
Sheepstor, 3, 22, 150
Sheepwash, 84
Sheldon, 78, 80, 91, 92
Sherford, 11, 89, 90, 121, 151
Sheviock, Corn., 137, 148
Shillingford St George, 133, 147
Shirwell, 4, 115, 116
Shobrooke, 56, 100, 101, 169
Shute, 4, 13, 100
Sidbury, 5, 6, 18, 20, 52, 53, 54, 101, 110, 112, 116, 117, 121, 146
Sidmouth, 20, 80, 112, 121, 147, 195
Silverton, 104, 115, 116, 121
Slapton, 18, 20, 150
Sourton, 96, 101
South Brent, 4, *f1*, 19, 95, 96, 100, 187
  Toll House, 93
South Hill, Corn., 88, 89, 104, 148
South Huish, 80, 86, 149
Southleigh, 77, 110, 112, 146, 147, 160
South Milton, 15, 44, 45, 46, 149, 223-4
South Molton, 121, 166, 198
  Town Hall, 89
South Petherwin, Corn., 139
South Pool, 15, 56, 105, 106, 149
South Tawton, 7, 56, 57, 63, 75, 84, 90, 132, 168, 169, 175, 207-9, 225, 231
South Zeal, 104
Sowton, 25, 41, 57, 116, 155, 164
Sparkwell School, 94
Spreyton, 36, 52, 131, 139, 146, 147, 148, 159, 231
Starcross, 65, 94
Staverton, 12, 56, 100
Stevenstone House, St Giles-in-the-Wood, 84
Sticklepath, S Tawton, 94
  Methodist Church, 94
Stockland, 106, 108, 112, 116, 117
Stockleigh English, 77, 80, 81

Stockleigh Pomeroy, 78, 80
Stoford, Som., 67, 108
Stoke Canon, 6, 28, 113, 115, 125, 138, 146, 148
Stoke Climsland, 73, 108, 142, 150, 157
Stoke Fleming, 2, 150
Stoke Gabriel, 103, 106, 134, 146, 147, *f157*
Stokeinteignhead, 124, 147, 148, 160
Stokenham, 105, 106, 120, 150, 157, *f124*, 166, 175, 228-9
Stoke Rivers, 117
Stoodleigh, 104, 106, 108, 112, 123
Stowford, 15, 22, *f33*, 53, 148, 150, 151
Sutcombe, 112, 121, 145, 148
Swimbridge, 17, *f24*, 18, 88, 115, 116, 137, 218-9
  clock, 194
Sydenham Damarel, 150

Taddiport Chapel, Little Torrington, 146
Talaton, 21, 48, 49, 51, 80, 95, 99, 102, 146, 159, 163
  clock, 192, *f149*
Tamerton Foliot, 10, 16, *f22*, 150
Tapeley Park, Westmeigh, 127
Taunton, St James, Som., 95, 99, 112, 129, 146
Tavistock, 3, 20, 23, 96, 101, 121
  clock & chime-barrel, *f152*, 166, 196, 198
  Abbey, 31, 33n
Tawstock, 4, 13, 15, 64, 115, 116, 121, 125, 126, 164
Tedburn St Mary, 47, 57, 61, 112, 147, 150, 161, 180
Teigngrace, 88, 93
Teignmouth, St James, 28, 70, 80
  St Michael, 4n, 9n, 25, 27, 80, 125, *f123*
Templeton, 51, 52, 76, 81, 113, 115, 145
Tetcott, 22, 23, 84, 89, 90, 118, 119, 145
Thelbridge, 113, 115, 116, 125
Thornbury, 102
Thorverton, 23, 132, 145, 147
  clock & chime-barrel, 192, 198, *f159*
Throwleigh, 149
Thrushelton, 52, 138, 148, 151
Thurlbear, Som., 72, 79, 80
Thurlestone, 15, 16, 36, 48, *f56*, 52, 90, 105, 106, 134, 135, 146, 147, 148, 165, 179
Tiverton, St Andrew, 28
  St George, 24, *f36*, 28
  St Paul, 120, 121
  St Peter, 3, 21, 48, 102, 111, 114, 116, 121, 128, 130, 145, 146, 163, 183, 195, 217-8
  Museum, 125
  Walrond's Almshouses, 51, 126, 127

INDEX

Topsham, 5, 28, 65, 101, 116, 117, 146, 147
Torbryan, 11, *f16*, 21, 51, 71, 78, 80, 85
Torquay, All Saints, Babbacombe, 25, 27, 41, 123
  Holy Trinity, 27, 125
  St John, 26, 27, *f41*, 94
  St Marychurch, 2, 25, 27, 47, 123, 135, *f102*, 148
  St Mary Magdalene, Upton, 25, 52, 97, 104
  Torre, 116, 117, 145
  Torre Abbey, 2, 31, 49, 86
Torrington, Great, 5, 17, 52, 64, 92, 121, 125, 171, 176, 185
  Market House, 147
Tor Royal, Princetown, 93
Totnes, St Mary, 3, 11, 15, 21, 23, 31, 45, 53, 57, 61, 67, 86-7, 123, 125, 146, 157, 168, 171-2, *f134*, 185, 236
  St John, 24, 87, 88
    East gate, 94
    Museum, 89, 90, 93
Trent, Dor., 129, 145
Tresmere, Corn., 37, *f49*,
Trisford House, Harberton, 93
Trusham, 28-9, 34-5, 40, 72, *f62*, 79, 145, 147, 161
Twitchen, 80, 112, 147

Uffculme, 19, 25, 27, 103, 106, 121
Ugborough, 15, 60, 64-5, 95, 97, 100, 103, 163
Ugbrooke House, Chudleigh, 93
Uplowman, 78, 103, 109, 110, 111, 112, 184
Uplyme, 10, *f13*, 103
Upton, Som., *f61*, 78
Upton Hellions, 80, 137, 148, 153, 221
Upton Magna, Salop, 79
Upton Pyne, 21, 95, 100

Vale, Guernsey, 80
Ven Ottery, 79, 146, 160
Venn House, Lamerton, 104
Verona, Italy, 54
Virginstow, 148

Waddeton Court, Stoke Gabriel, 94
Walkhampton, 10, 15, *f21*, 150, 163
Warbstow, Corn., 89, 90, 148
Warkleigh, 78, 84, 89
Warleigh House, Tamerton Foliot, 85
Washfield, 102
Washford Pyne, 17, 49, 102, 116, 145
Watermouth Castle, Berrynarbor, 93

Weare Gifford, 100, 105, 106
Welcombe, 56, 89, 90, 121, 151
Wellington, Som., 12, 64, 111
Wells, Som., 109
Wembury, 2, 15, 16, 134, 136, 147, 148, 165, *f132*
Wembworthy, 80
Werrington, Corn., 120
West Alvington, 40, 41, 62, 95, 96, 101, 126, 127
West Anstey, 78, 102, 146
West Buckland, 28, 115, 116
West Buckland, Som., 12
West Down, 24, 102, 125
West Hill, 63
Westleigh, 12, 80, 84, 89, 116, 120
West Ogwell, 78, 80, 85, 160
  House, 88
Westward Ho!, 28, 126
West Worlington, 18, 79, 178-80, 239-40
Whimple, 51, 77, 78, 79, 81, 121, 125, 197
Whitchurch, 149, 151
Whitestone, 2, 79, 80, 102, 125
Whitford, Shute, 94
Widecombe-in-the-Moor, 8, 15, 22, 38, *f50*, 61, 101, 110, 113, 146, 164, 176, 197
Widworthy, 8, 101, 116, 117
Willand, 95, 99, 104, 146
Winkleigh, 75, 118, 139, 148, 164, 178, 228
Witheridge, 103, 115, 116, 179, 180
  School, 94
Withleigh, 93
Withycombe Raleigh, Exmouth, 25, 123, 125, 166
Wolborough, 31, 38, 64, 82, *f66*, 121, 159
Woodbury, 34, 48, 57, 63, 65, 77, 81, 83, 84, 107, 109, 116, 146, 147, 163, 164f, 187, 205-7
  clock, 194
Woodbury Salterton, 119
Woodland, 11, 69, 78, 87, 88, 146, 160, 165
Woodleigh, 81, 146
Woolfardisworthy East, 45, 112, 163, 199
Woolfardisworthy West, 118, 121

Yarcombe, 112, 113, 145, 146, 195
Yarnscombe, 4, 12, 48, 51, 64, 84, 92, 93, 128, 136, 145, 146
Yatton Court, Beaford, 93
Yelverton, 26
Yealmpton, 150
Yeoford, Crediton, 93

Yeovil, Som., 38, 67, 94, 95, 101, 129, 130, 145
Yeovilton, Som., 53, 74, 80
York Minster, 42

Zeal Monachorum, 95, 99, 146, 163, 185
Zennor, Corn., 51, 68, 69, 75, 78

Subscribers

All Saints Church Bellringers (East Budleigh)
Anzab Library
Alan Bagworth
Reverend Dr John Baldwin
Madeline Baldwin
Alan Barnes
Garry Barr
Mark Bertram
Peter Bill
Jonathan Bint
Dr Stuart Blaylock
Mary Bliss
Owen J. Borlase
Richard Bowden
Leslie Boyce
Alan Brown
Marjorie Buley
A. M. Bull
Keith Burrow
Roderick Butler
William Butler
Hazel Cardwell
Derek J. Carr
Reverend David L. Cawley
Central Council of Church Bell Ringers' Library
D. W. Chaffe
Tony Clayton
Richard Coley
Colonial Williamsburg Foundation
Shirley Colquhoun
Alan Cooper
Canon Christopher Dalton
George A. Dawson
Philip Denton
Devon & Exeter Institution
John Dietz
Peter Dyson
Dr John C. Eisel

John Ellacombe
Daphne Empson
John Enderson
Exeter Diocesan Advisory Committee
Judith Farmer
Jean & David Gay
Dr Teresa Ann Goatham
Dr Tom Greeves
David and Jeanette Harris
James Hedgcock
Paul Heighway
Geoffrey C. Hill
Julia Le Messurier House
Rosemary Howson
Dr & Mrs P. A. Hughes
D. A. Hutton
Bryan Tuckett Ipplepen
T. C. Jackson
Nigel Jackson-Mack
Pat Johnstone
Richard L. Jones
David J. Kelly
John Kelly B. E. M.
Andrew King
David Kirkcaldy
J., P. L. & L. J. Kirkcaldy
Chris McKay
Mary Mack
Peter Mack
Peter L. F. Martin
George Massey
Keith Matthews
Margaret Mattingley
Michael Mears
Reverend Darren R. Moore
Rosemary Anne Morgan
Brian V. Mountjoy
Graham Naylor

Andrew Nicholson
North Devon Athenaeum
Richard Offen
Russ Palmer
Paul J. Pascoe
Stephen D. Pettman
Chris Pickford
David Pike
Michael Platt
Laith Reynolds
Jonathan Rhind Architects
Roy Rice
Christopher Ridley
Donald John Roberts
Michael Rose
St Mary's Hemyock Ringers
Kristin and Roger Saunders
Susan Sawyer
Sheila Scofield
Ian Self
Richard Shere
Neil Skelton
P. A. Sloman

Anthony P. Smith
Dr Arnold J. Smith
Ian V. J. Smith
Clare Stagg
Andrew J. Stevens
Terry Sturtevant
Taylors, Eayre & Smith Ltd
Neil Trout
Truro Diocesan Guild of Ringers
Lesley Tucker
Colin M. Turner
Malcolm Upham
John Walling
Ken and Pauline Webb
Michael Webster
Oliver West & John Scott
Michael V. White
P. M. Wilkinson
Michael A. Williams
Neil Williams
Anne Willis
Michael and Elaine Wycherley
Lester Yeo

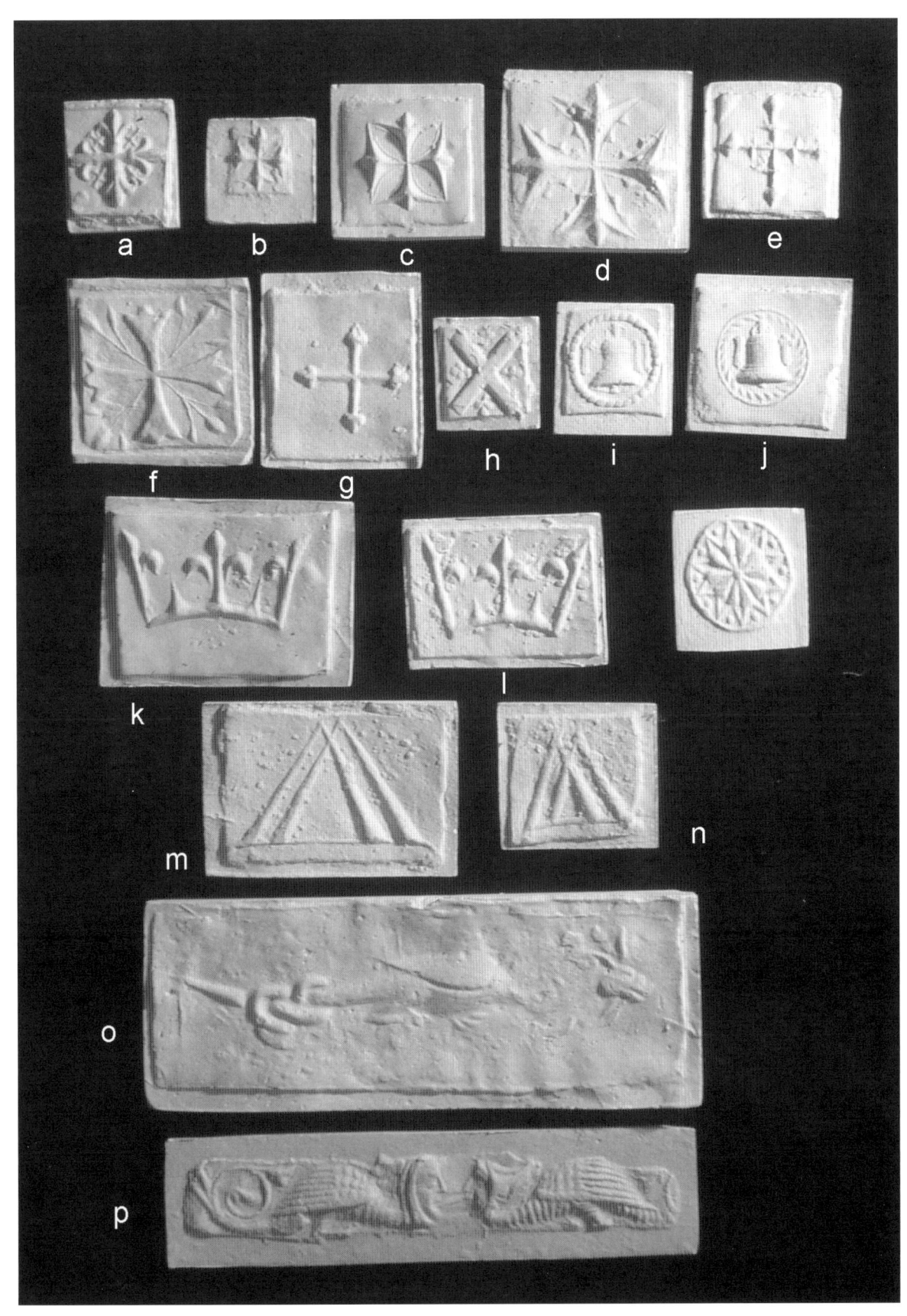

Plate 1.
Exeter Mediaeval Foundry.
Crosses, foundry marks
and decorations.

Plate 2.
Exeter Mediaeval Foundry.
a, b: Lombardic capitals;
c: Small black-letters stock inscription, Exeter St Pancras.

Plate 3.
Exeter Mediaeval Foundry.
Examples from "stock" inscriptions.

Plate 4. Exeter lettering.
a: "protégé" in single letters; **b:** "convoco", showing damaged top of "n"; **c:** "per die" made up from pieces of stock inscriptions (St Erney, Co.); **d:** "IT" thumbprints (Northleigh 4/4); **e:** Norton's black-letter used by Birdalls (Aylesbeare 5/6, 1601); **f:** dittto (Kingswear 2/3); **g:** ditto (Pinhoe 8/8); **h:** Birdalls' Arabic numerals (Aylesbeare 5/6, 1601).

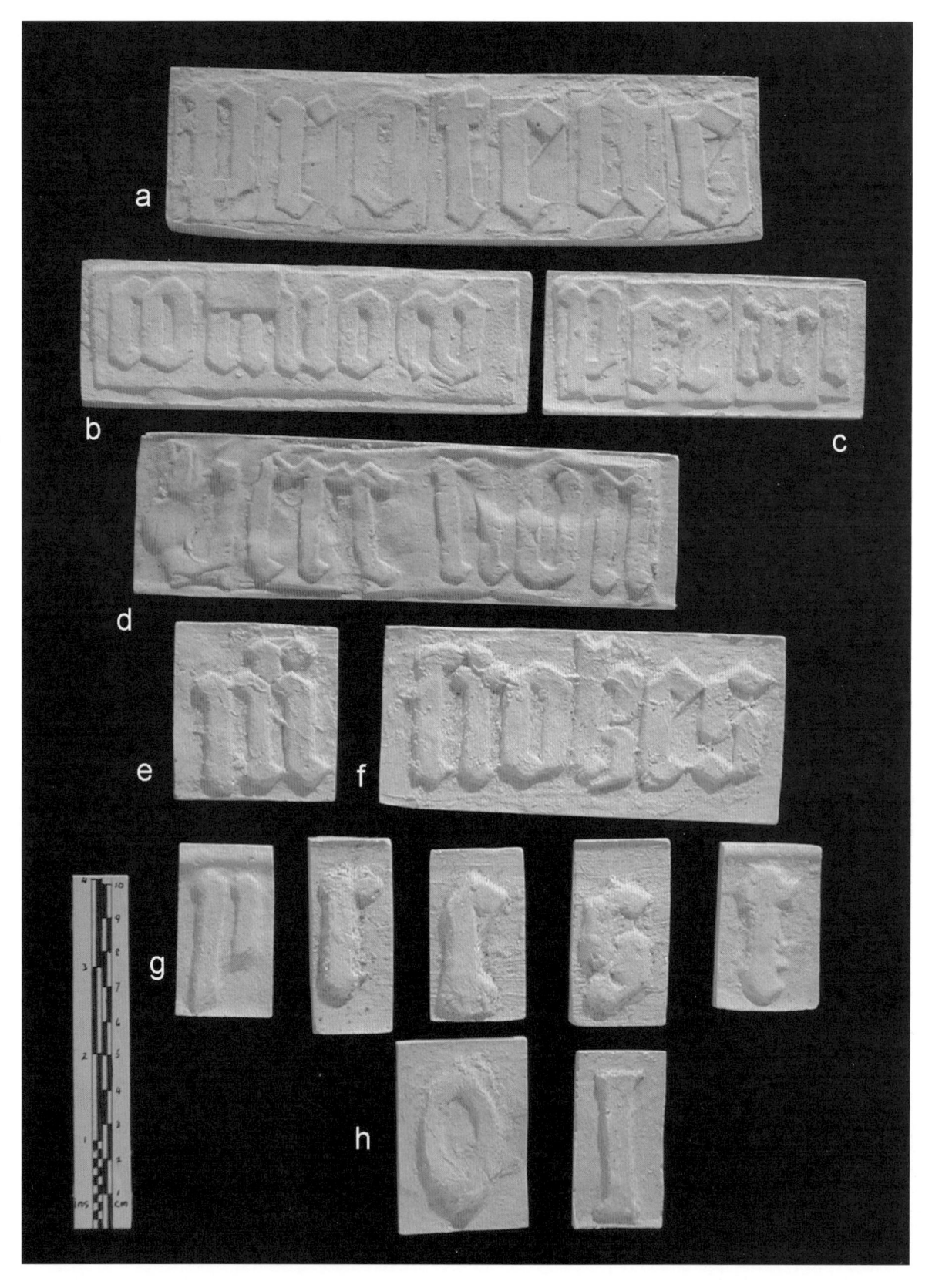

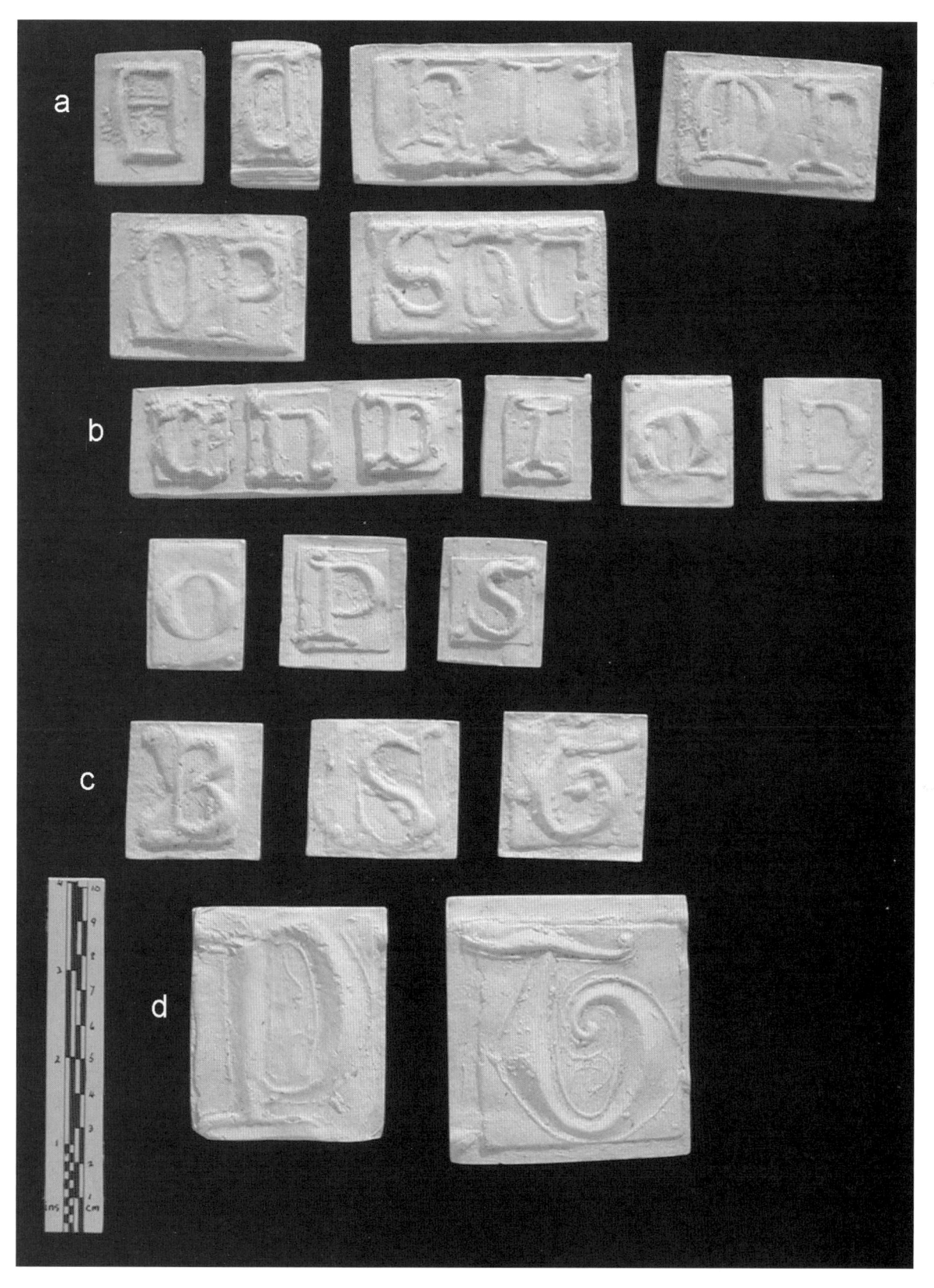

Plate 5.
Exeter Foundry:
The Birdalls.
Lombardic capitals.

Plate 6.
Exeter Foundry: The Birdalls.
a-c: Crosses; **d-i**: John Birdall's floriated capitals, the "N" & "G" pieced together; **j**: Fleur-de-lys; **k**: IT mark used by John Birdall.

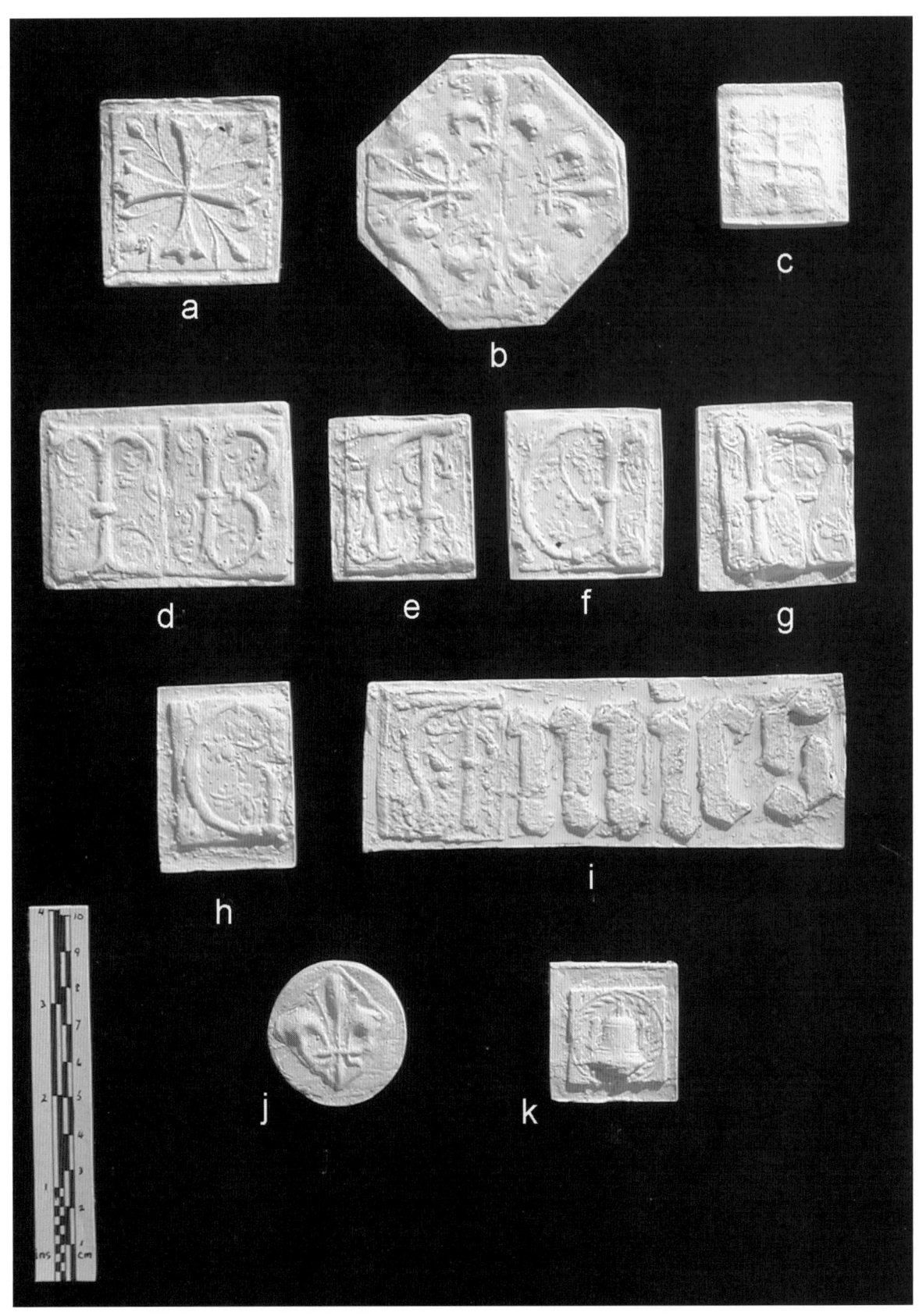

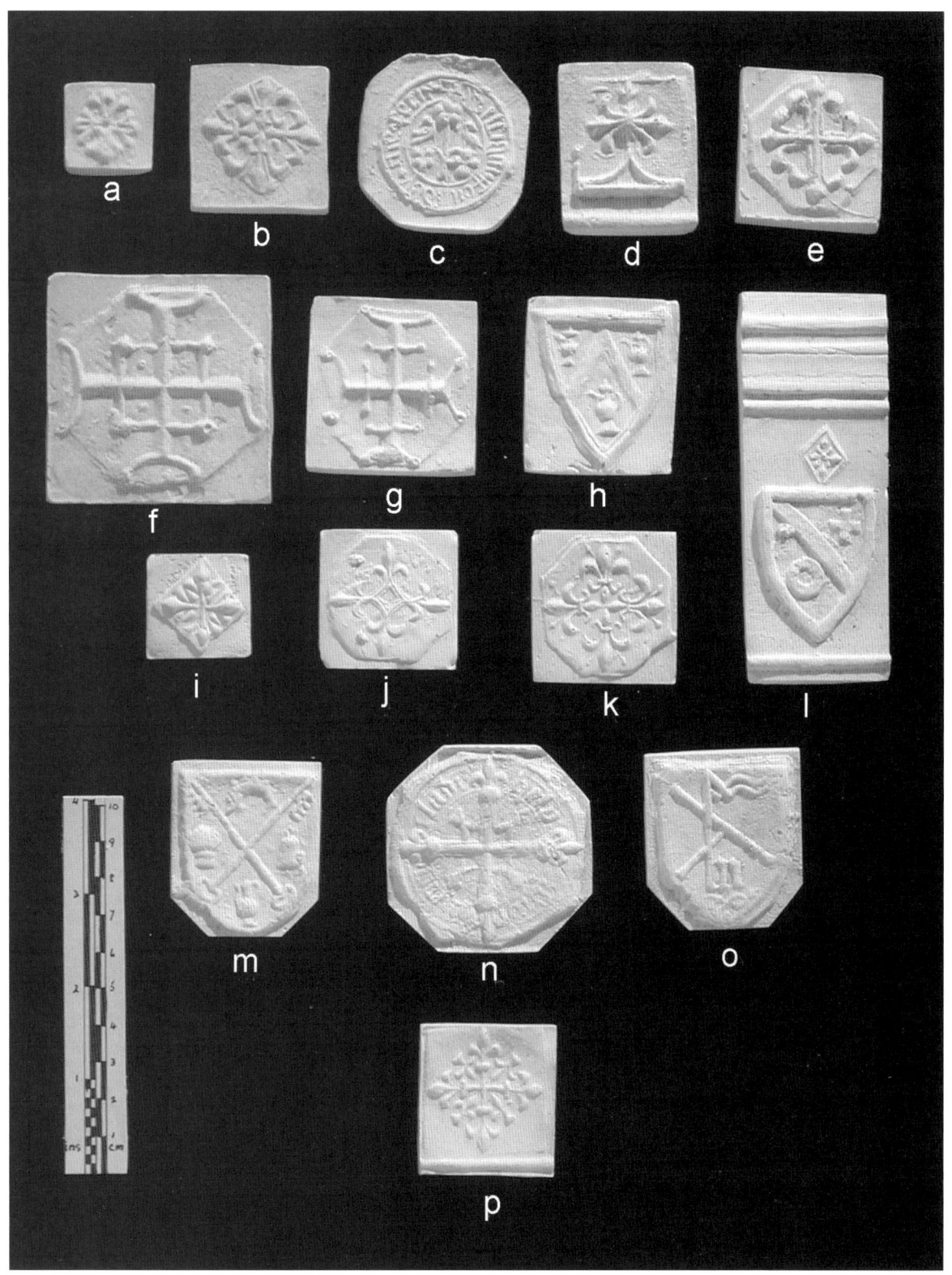

Plate 7.
London founders.
a: Richard de Wymbis, *c*1340 (Petersmarland 6/6);
b,c: William Dawe, *c*1390 (Abbotsham 5/6);
d,e: "Brede mark" founder (Exeter St Petrock 2/6);
f,g,h: John Bird (Wolborough old bells;
i,j,k,l: Joanna Hille (Manaton 4/6 and 5/6);
m,n,o: William Chamberlain (Marldon 3/6);
p: Gloucestor foundry cross (for comparison with Exeter cross 1a).

Plate 8.
Bristol foundry marks.
a: (Ashford 2/3);
b: (Molland 6/6);
c: (Ashford 3/3);
d: (Warkleigh 6/6);
e,f: (Yarnscombe 6/6);
g: The Bristol Ship (Northover, Som);
h: Ship & castle (Yarnscombe 6/6);
i: (Broadhembury 2/6);
j,k,l: (Woodbury 6/8).

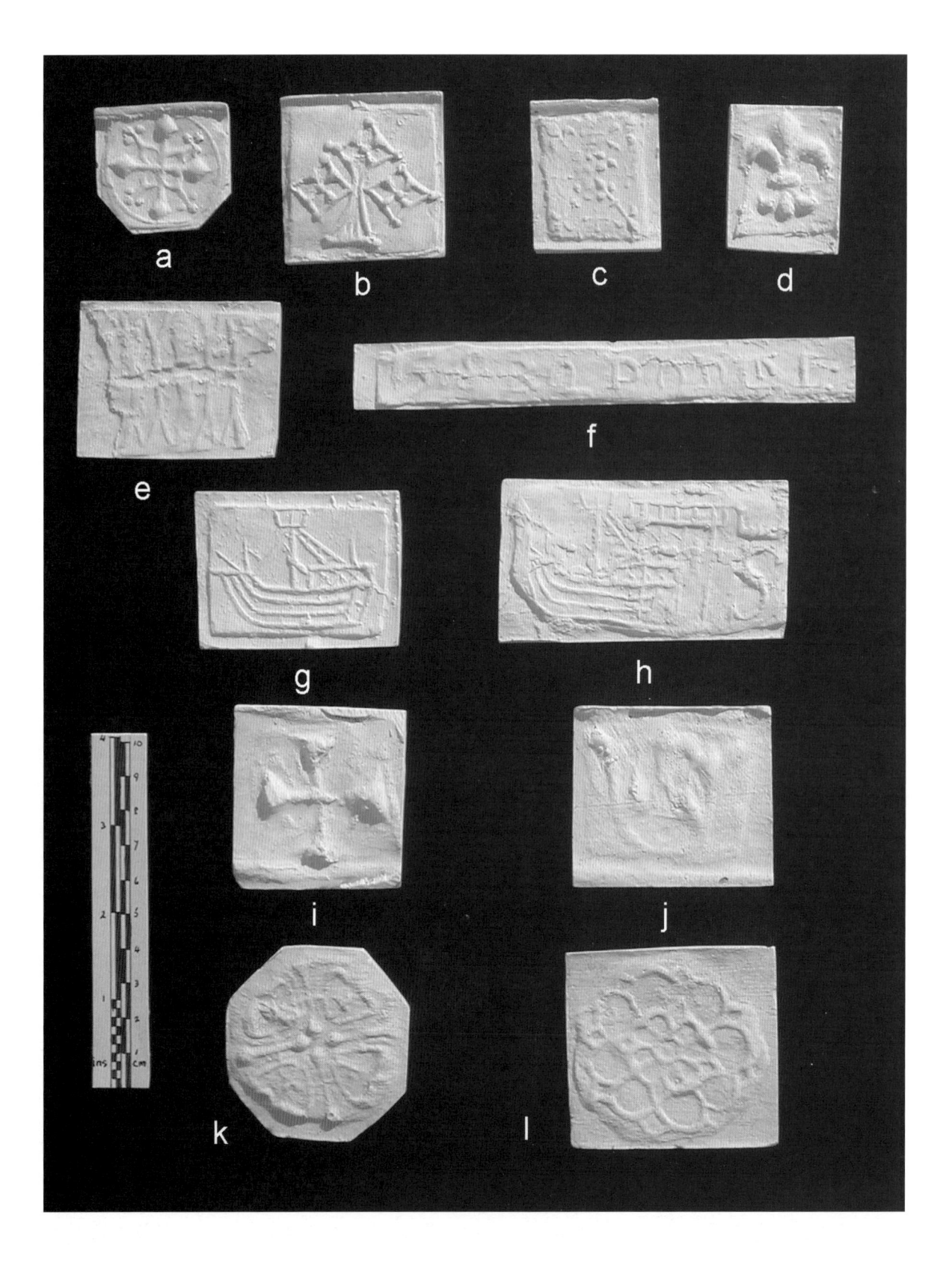

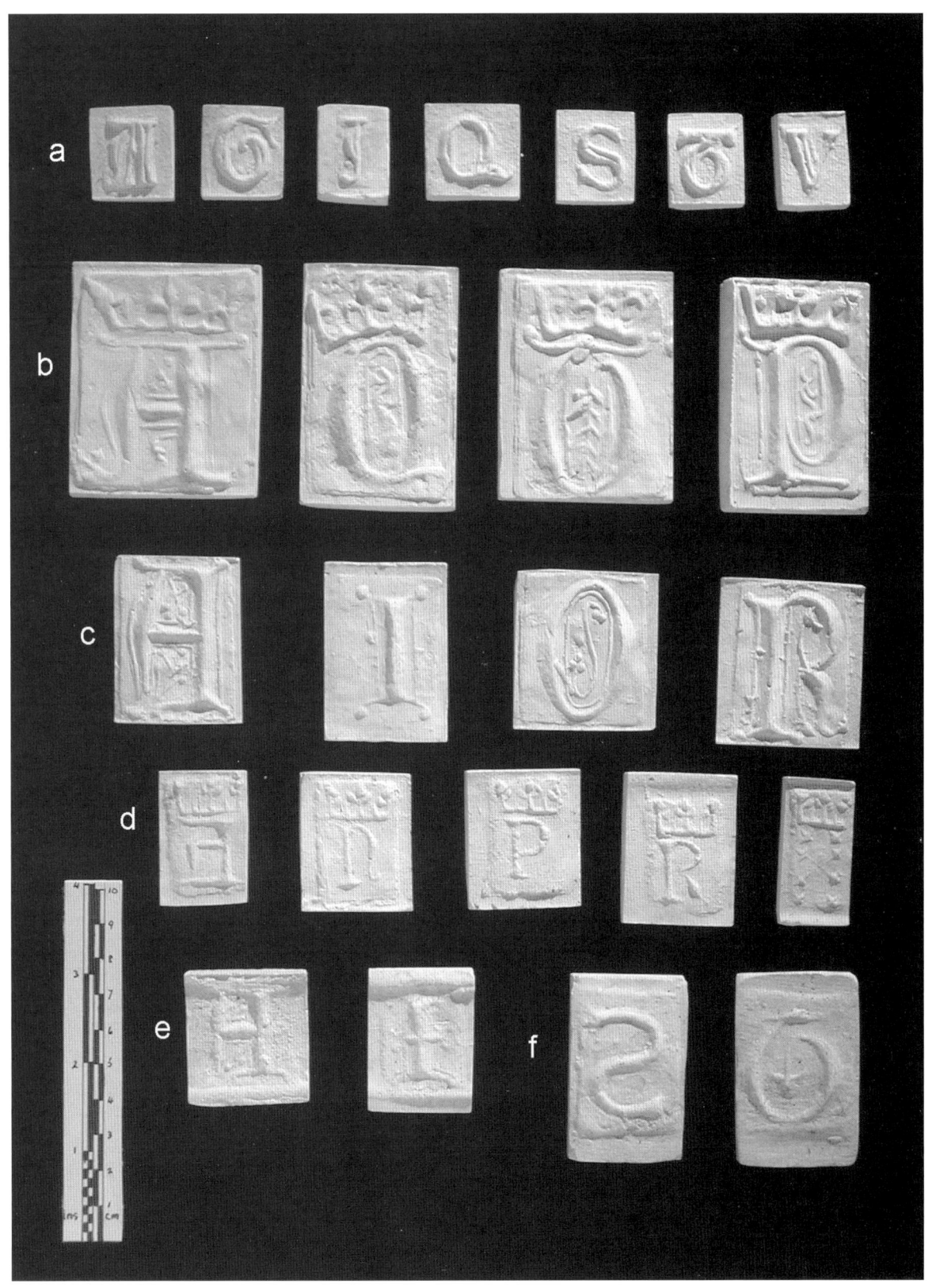

Plate 9.
London and Bristol lettering.
a: Richard de Wymbis (Petersmarland 6/6);
b: John Bird, London (Wolborough old bell);
c: Bristol foundry (Molland 6/6); **d:** ditto (Alwington 4/6); **e:** ditto (Horwood 1/3); **f:** ditto (Yarnscombe and Woodbury).

Plate 10.
14th-century bells by unknown founders.
a: Inscription (Tresmere 1/2, now in Okehampton Museum); **b:** Part of inscription (Combpyne 3/3

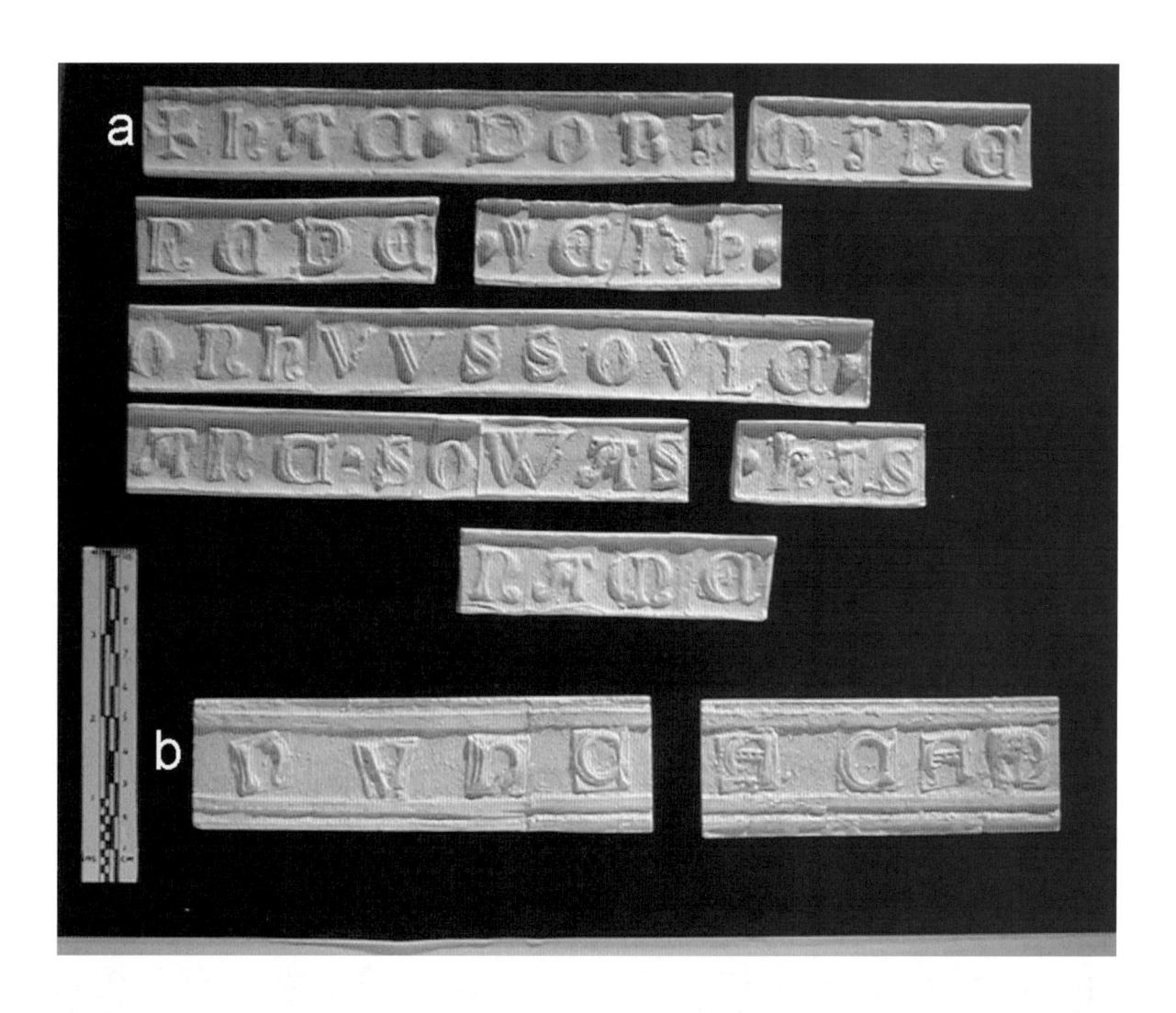

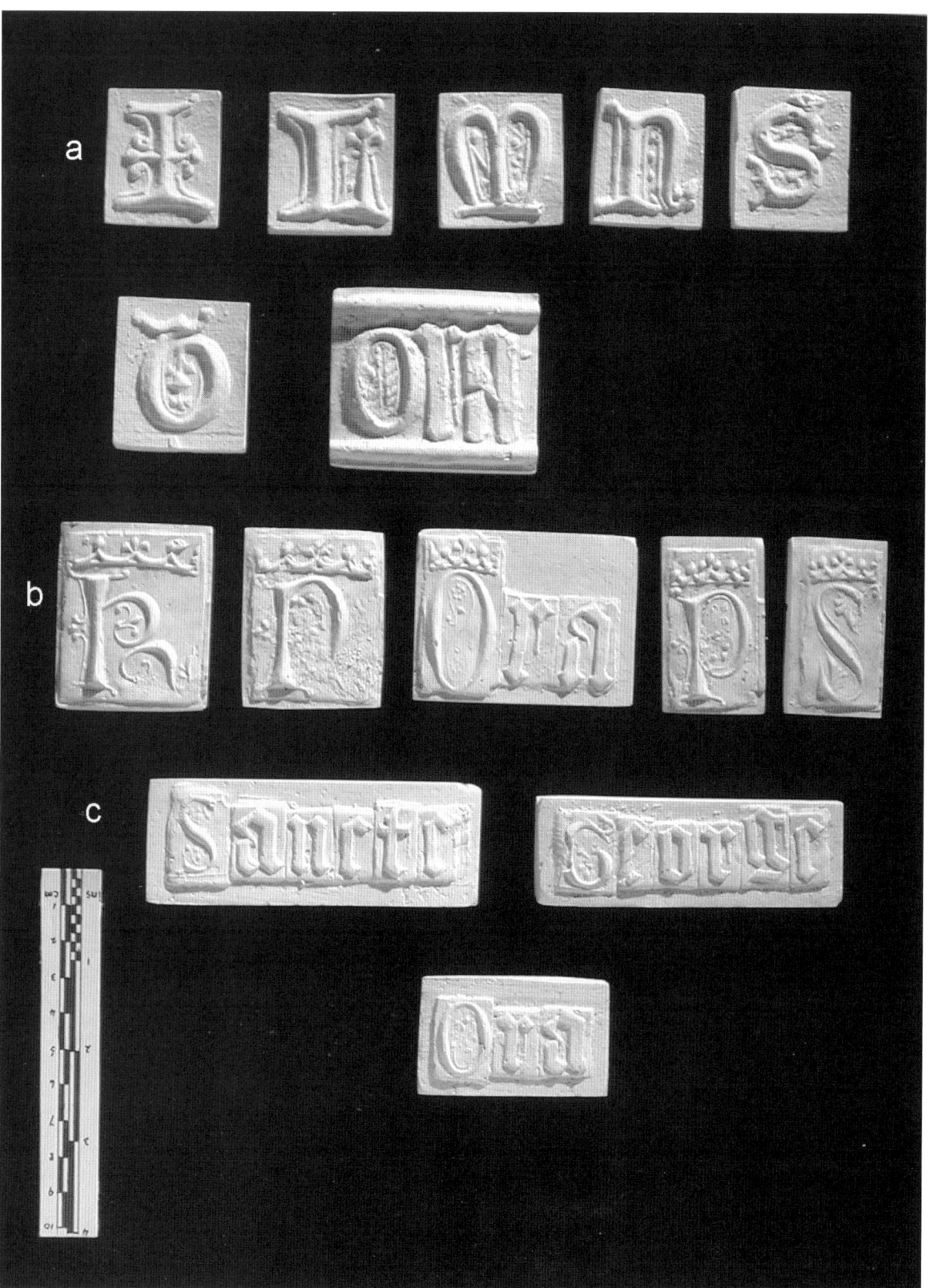

Plate 11.
William Dawe and Joanna Hille lettering.
a: William Dawe (Abbotsham 5/6);
b,c: Joanna Hille (Manaton 4 & 5/6).

Plate 12.
Roger Semson.
a,b,c: (Talaton 6/6);
d,h,i: (Plymtree 4/6;
e,f,g: (Luppitt 8/8).

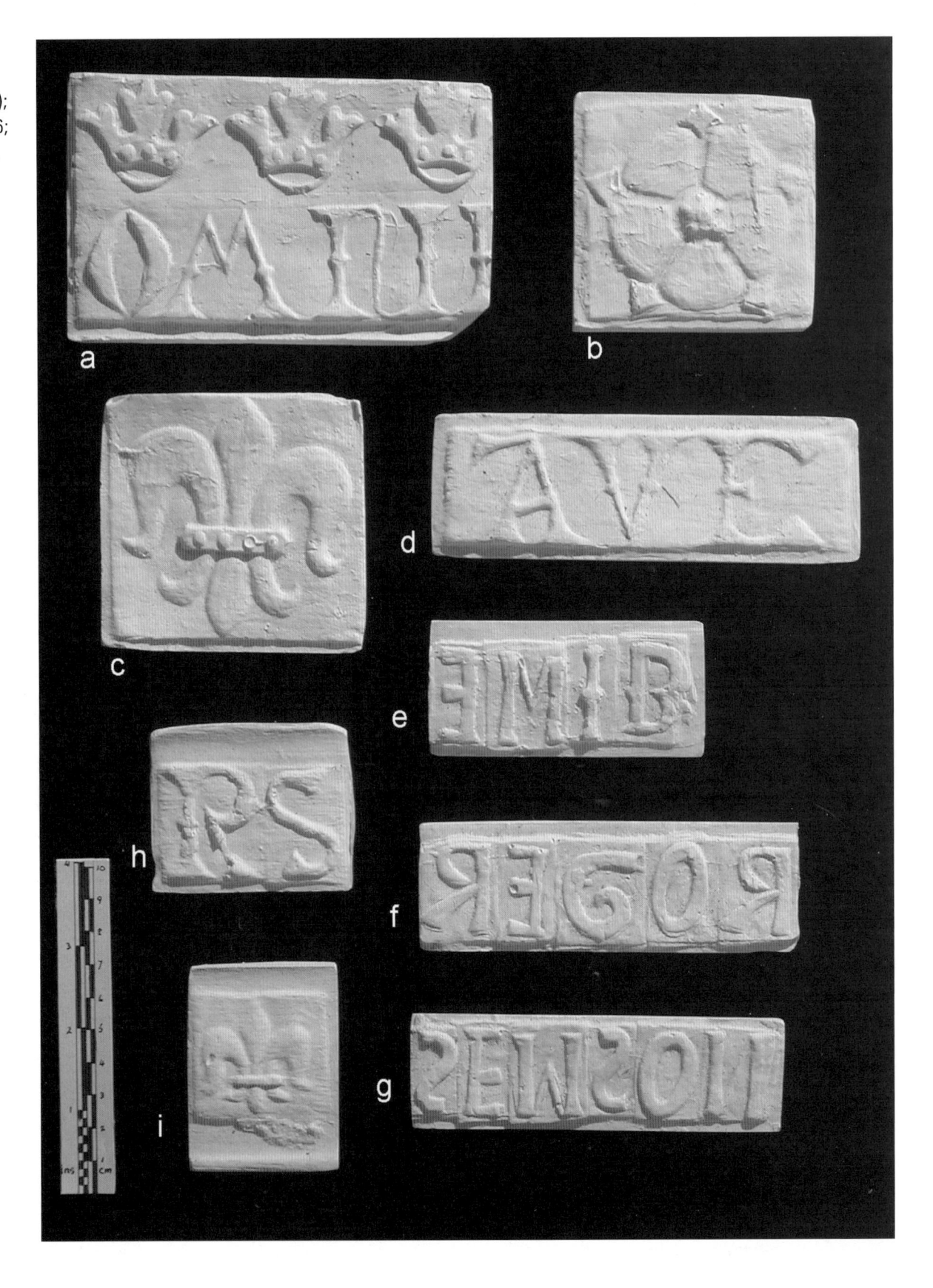

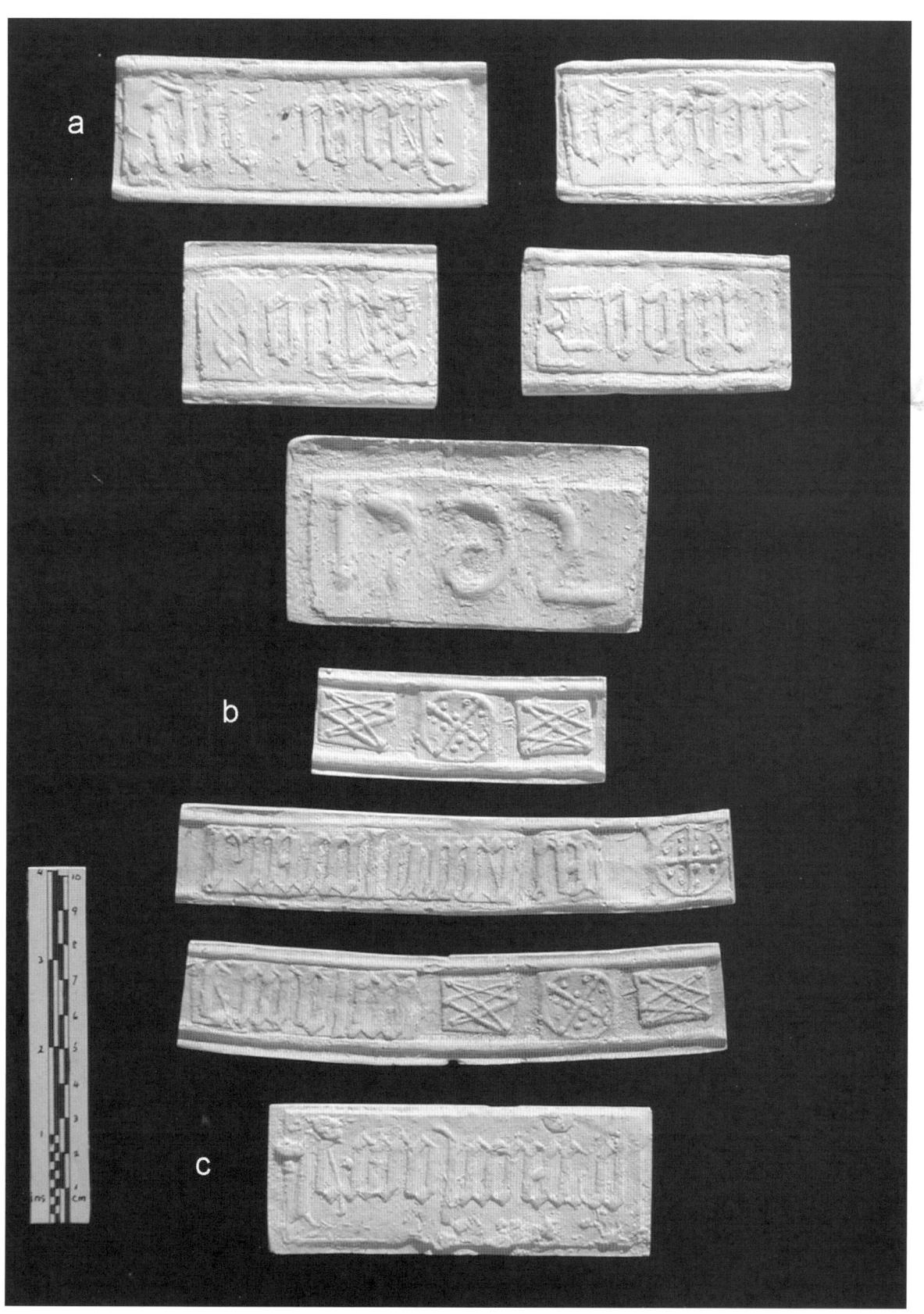

Plate 13. William Preston.
a: Impression from monumental brass (Molland 3/6, 1595); **b:** (Abbbotsham 6/6); **c:** (Torre Abbey).

Plate 14.
Unknown founders, 15th and 16th centuries.
a: (Highampton 3/3);
b: (Torbryan 2/4);
c: (Denbury 4/5 1631);
d,f: W.K., 1629 (Cookbury 2/3); **e:** W.K., 1634 (Pancrasweek 5/5);
g: (Cockington disused 1653).

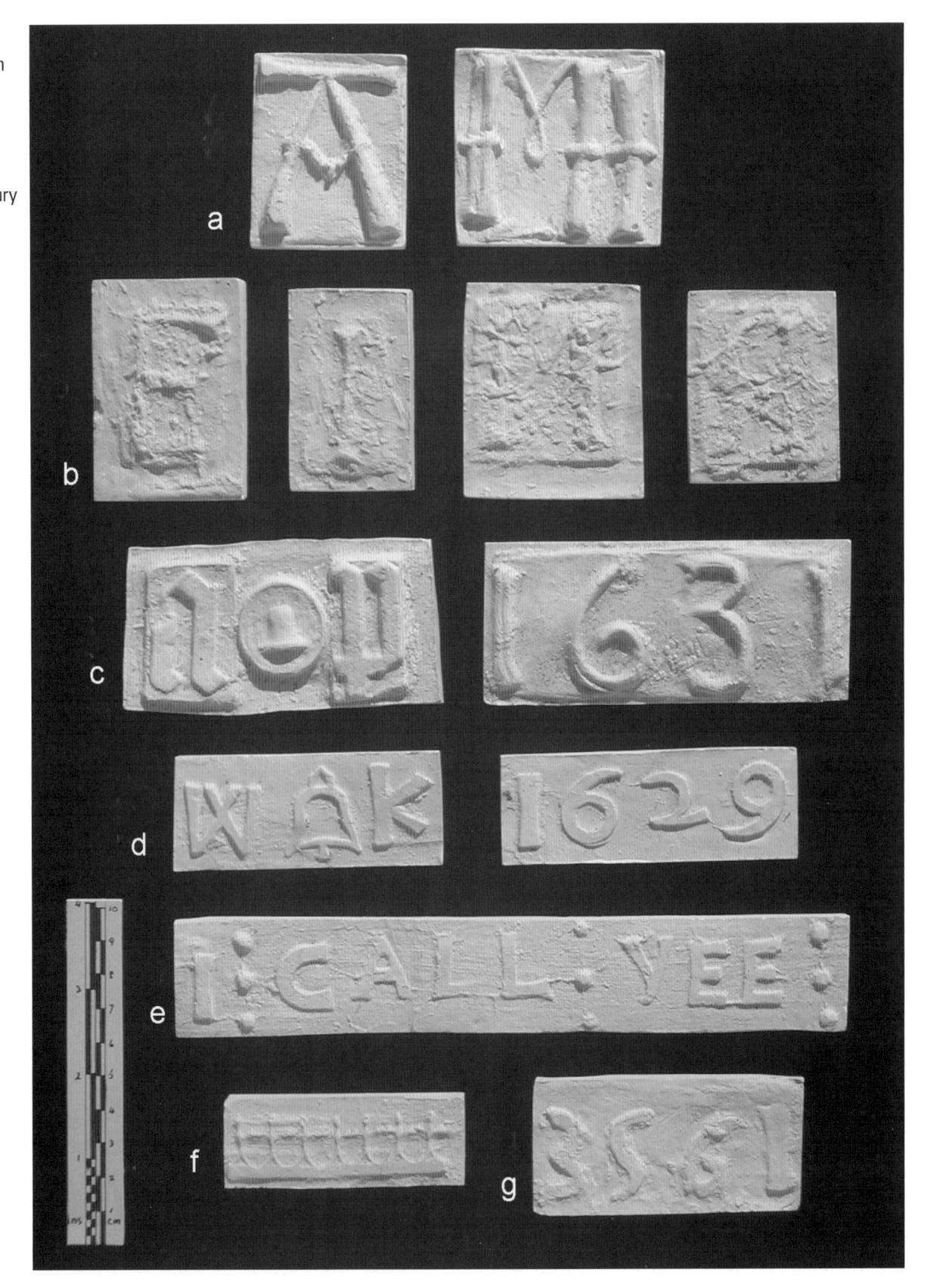

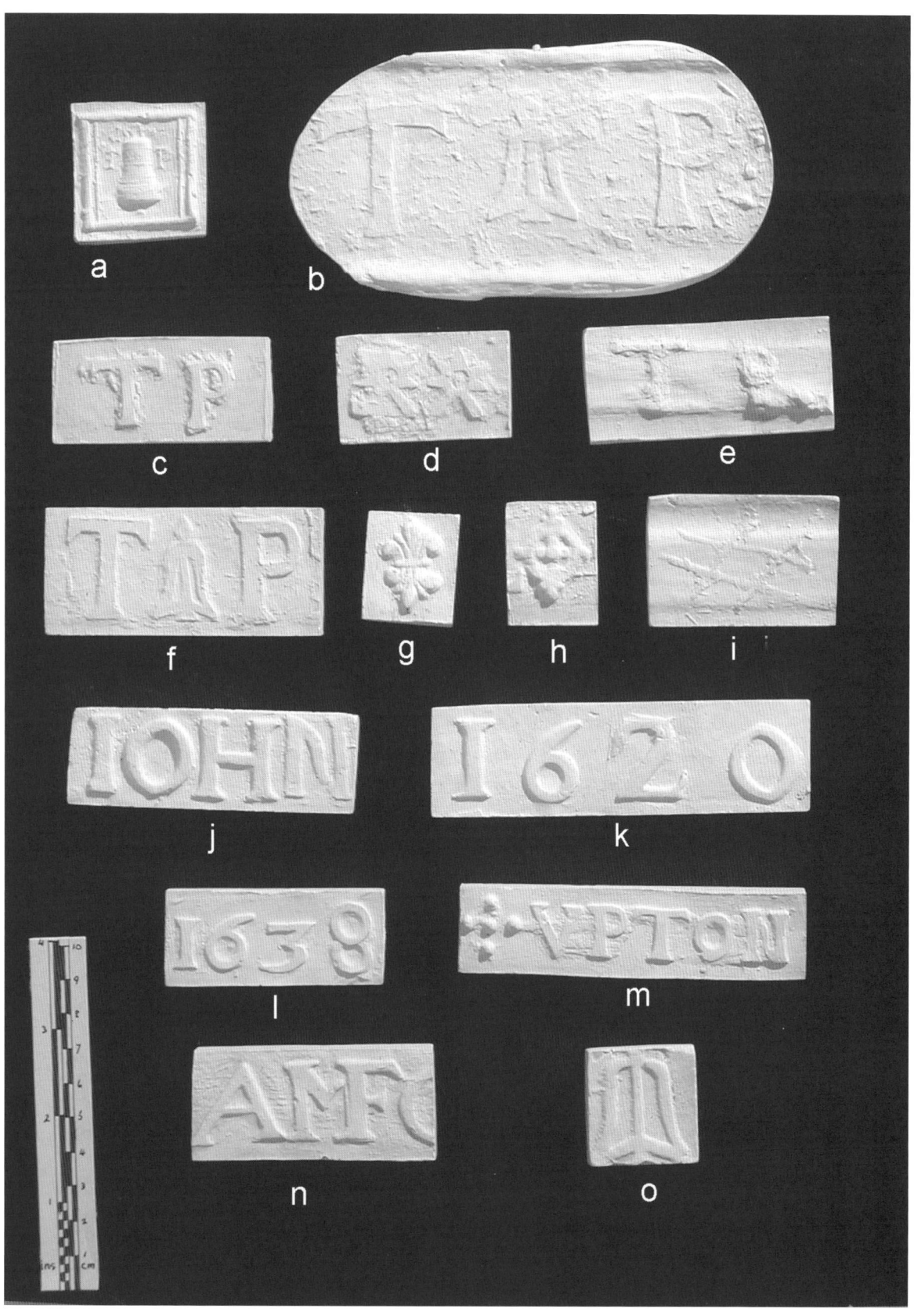

Plate 15.
Thomas Pennington I of Barnstaple, Thomas Pennington II of Exeter.
Thomas I. a: (Yarnscombe 5/6, 1608); **b:** (Eggesford 3/3, 1613); **c,d:** (Templeton 3/3, 1616); **e:** (Washford Pyne 5/6, 1620); **f:** (East Anstey 6/6, 1619).
Thomas II. g,j,k: (Iddesleigh 3/6, 1620); **h:** (Trusham 4/6, 1623); **i:** (Washford Pyne 5/6, 1620); **l,m:** (Burlescombe 6/6, 1638); **n:** (Trusham 4/6, 1623); **o:** (Trusham 6/6).

Plate 16.
John Pennington and Thomas Pennington III of Exeter. **a,b,c:** Fleur-de-lys friezes, large, small and very large; **d:** John (Culstock 8/8 IP 1661); **e:** John (Sidbury 5/8, 1663); **f:** John of Exeter and Thomas Pennington of Tavistock (Sampford Spiney 4/5, 1653); **g,i:** Thomas III, satirical medal and foundry mark (Exeter St Martin 1/1, 1675) **h:** Thomas III (Exeter St Petrock 4/6, 1677); **j,l:** Thomas III and J. Stadler (Littleham (S) 8/8, 1692); **k:** Thomas III (Clyst Hydon 3/6, 1713).

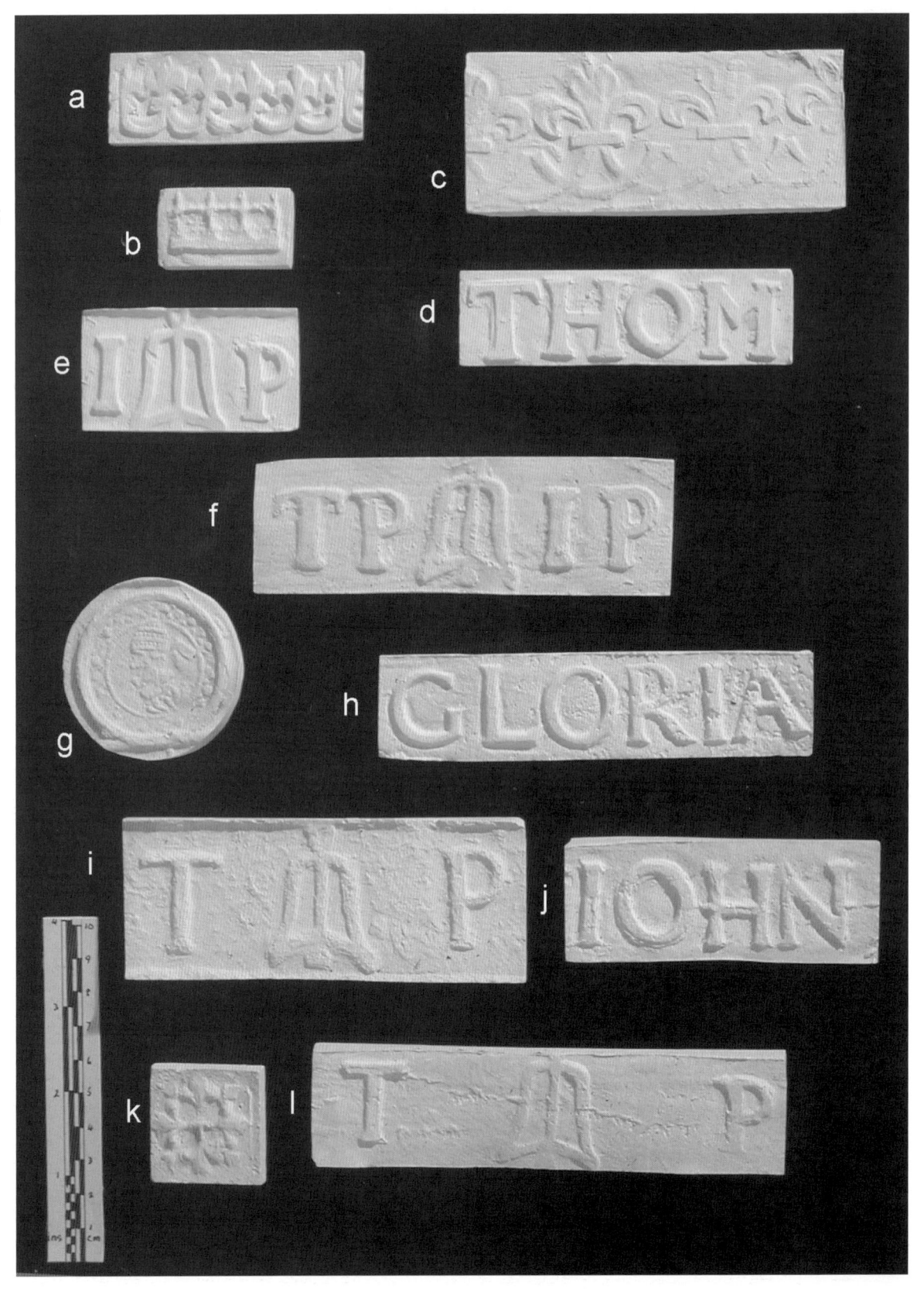

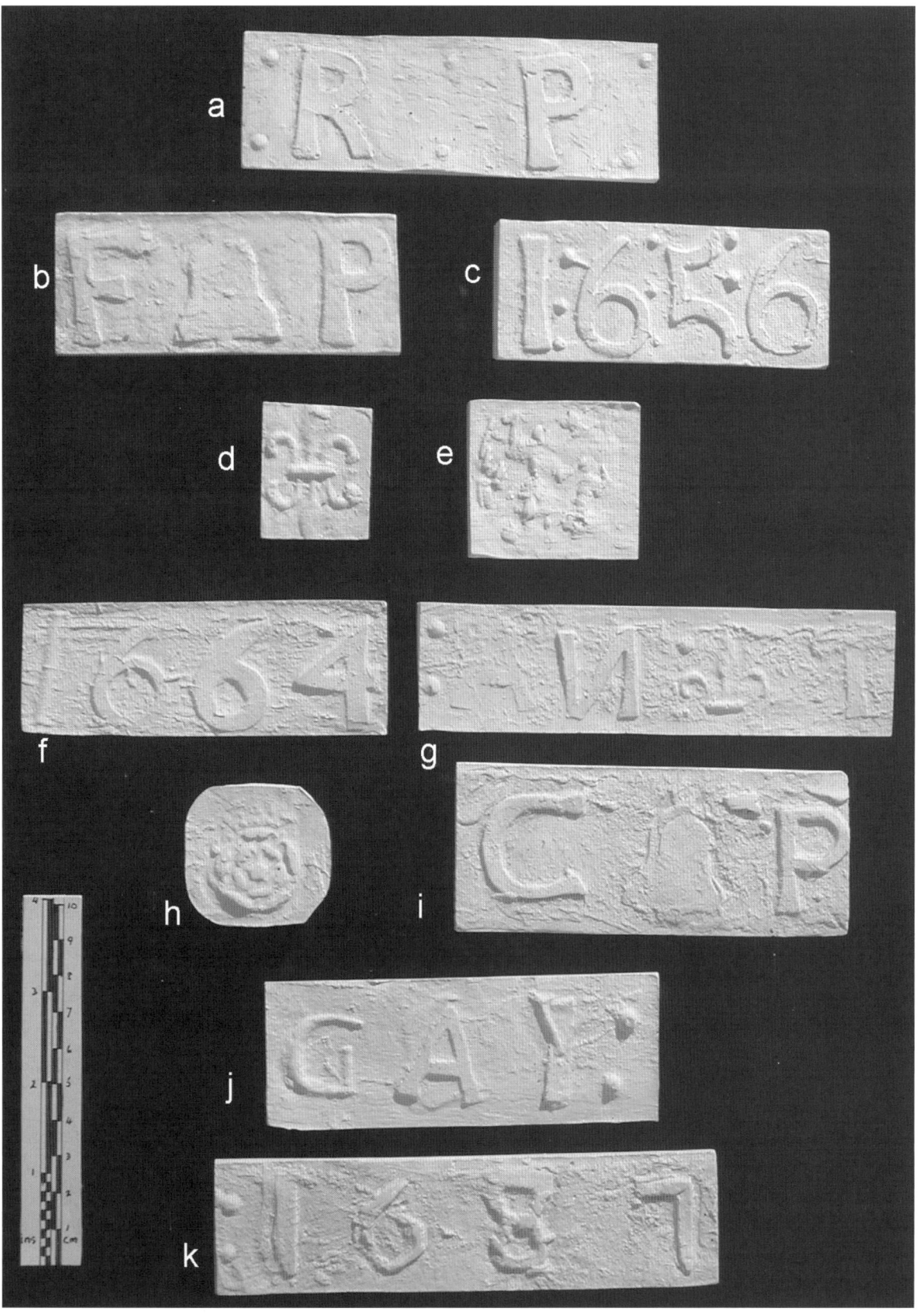

Plate 17. The Cornish Penningtons, 17th cemtury.
a: Robert Pennington, (E. Ogwell 5/6, 1633);
b,c,e: Fitzantony Pennington I (Frithelstock 6/6, 1656);
d: Fitzantony Pennington (Bondleigh 4/4, 1656);
f,g: ? Pennington (Virginstow, 1664);
h,i: Christopher Pennington I (Frithelstock 5/6, 1686);
j,k: Christopher Pennington I (Monkokehampton 4/4, 1687).

Plate 18.
The Cornish Penningtons, 1700–1720.
a,b,c: Christopher II (Stoke Canon 4/6, 1691);
d,e,f: Christopher II (Dunterton 1/3, 1705);
g: Cloth seal from Exeter Museum; **h,i:** John II (W. Putford 6/6, 1713);
j,k: Christopher II and John II (Thrushelton 5/6, 1718);
l,m: Christopher II or John II (Dodbrooke 4/6, 1719).

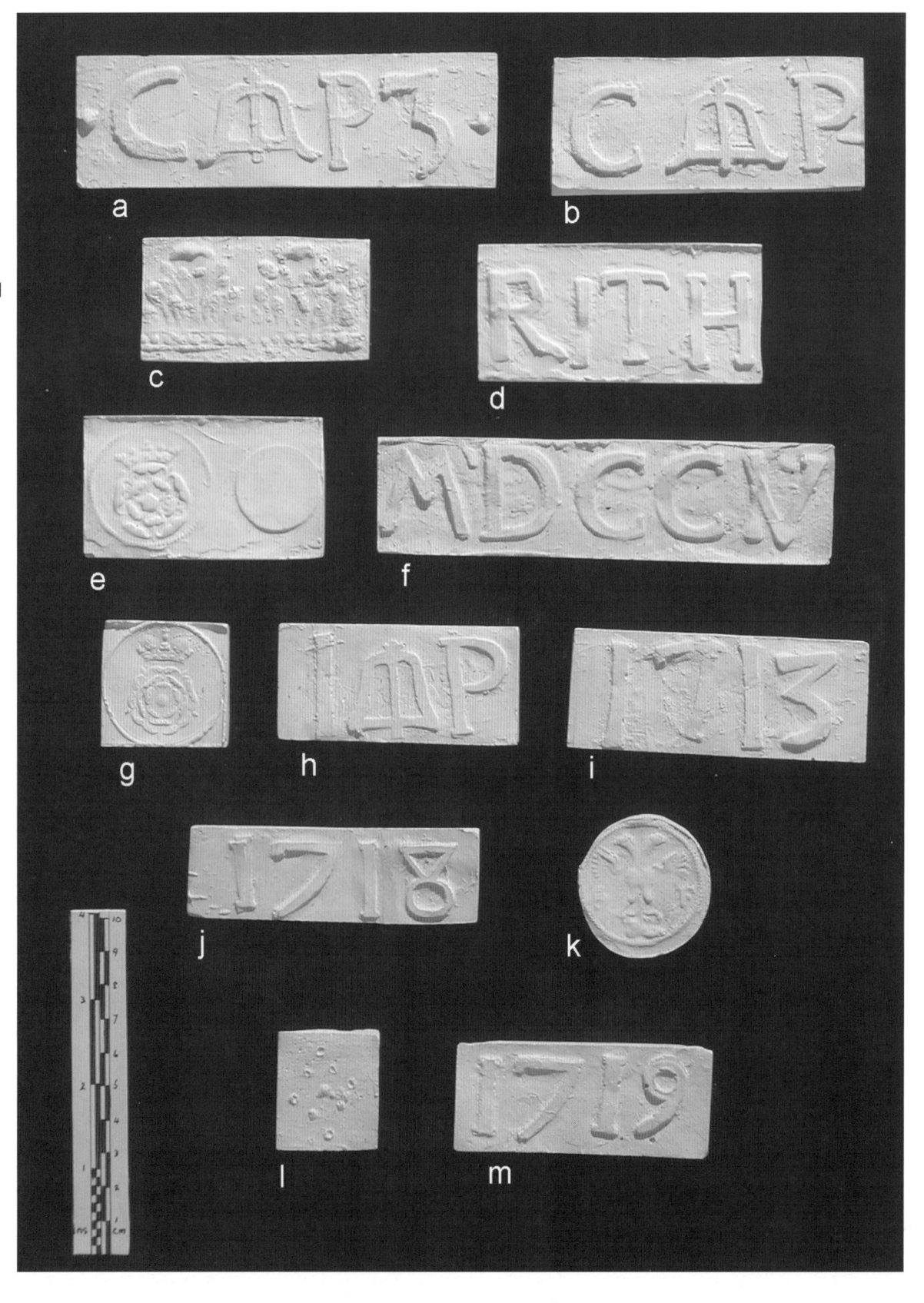

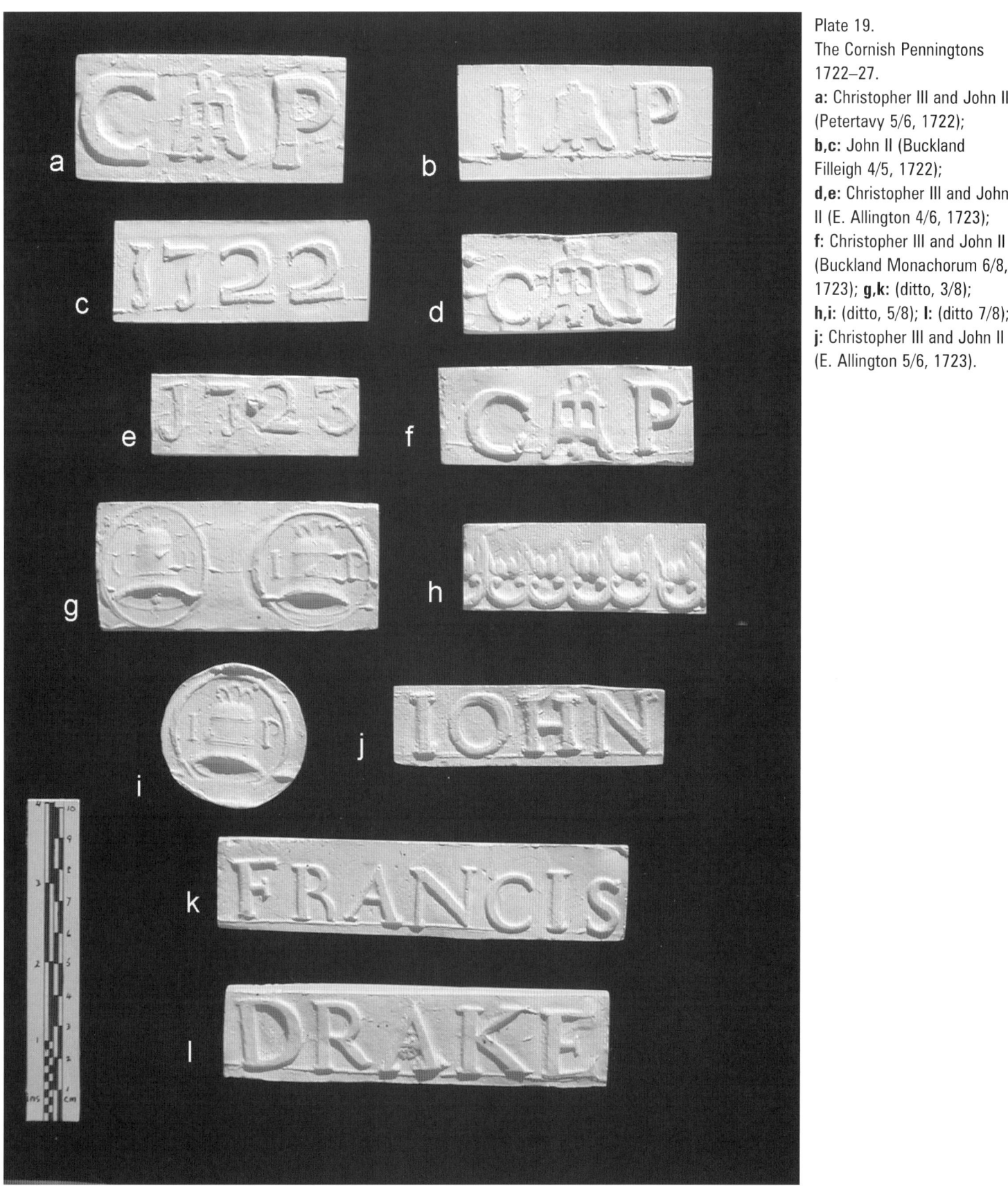

Plate 19.
The Cornish Penningtons 1722–27.
a: Christopher III and John II (Petertavy 5/6, 1722);
b,c: John II (Buckland Filleigh 4/5, 1722);
d,e: Christopher III and John II (E. Allington 4/6, 1723);
f: Christopher III and John II (Buckland Monachorum 6/8, 1723); **g,k:** (ditto, 3/8);
h,i: (ditto, 5/8); **l:** (ditto 7/8);
j: Christopher III and John II (E. Allington 5/6, 1723).

Plate 20.
The Cornish Penningtons 1727–1758.
a: John II (Spreyton 6/6, 1726); **b:** John II (Ashbury 3/3, 1727); **c:** John II (Dean Prior 5/6, 1734); **d:** Christopher II (St Giles on the Heath 4/5, 1740); **e,f,g:** Christopher III and John III (Ermington 6/6, 1748); **h,i:** Christopher III (Dunterton 2/3, 1750); **j,k,l:** Christopher III (Milton Damarel 1/3, 1758).

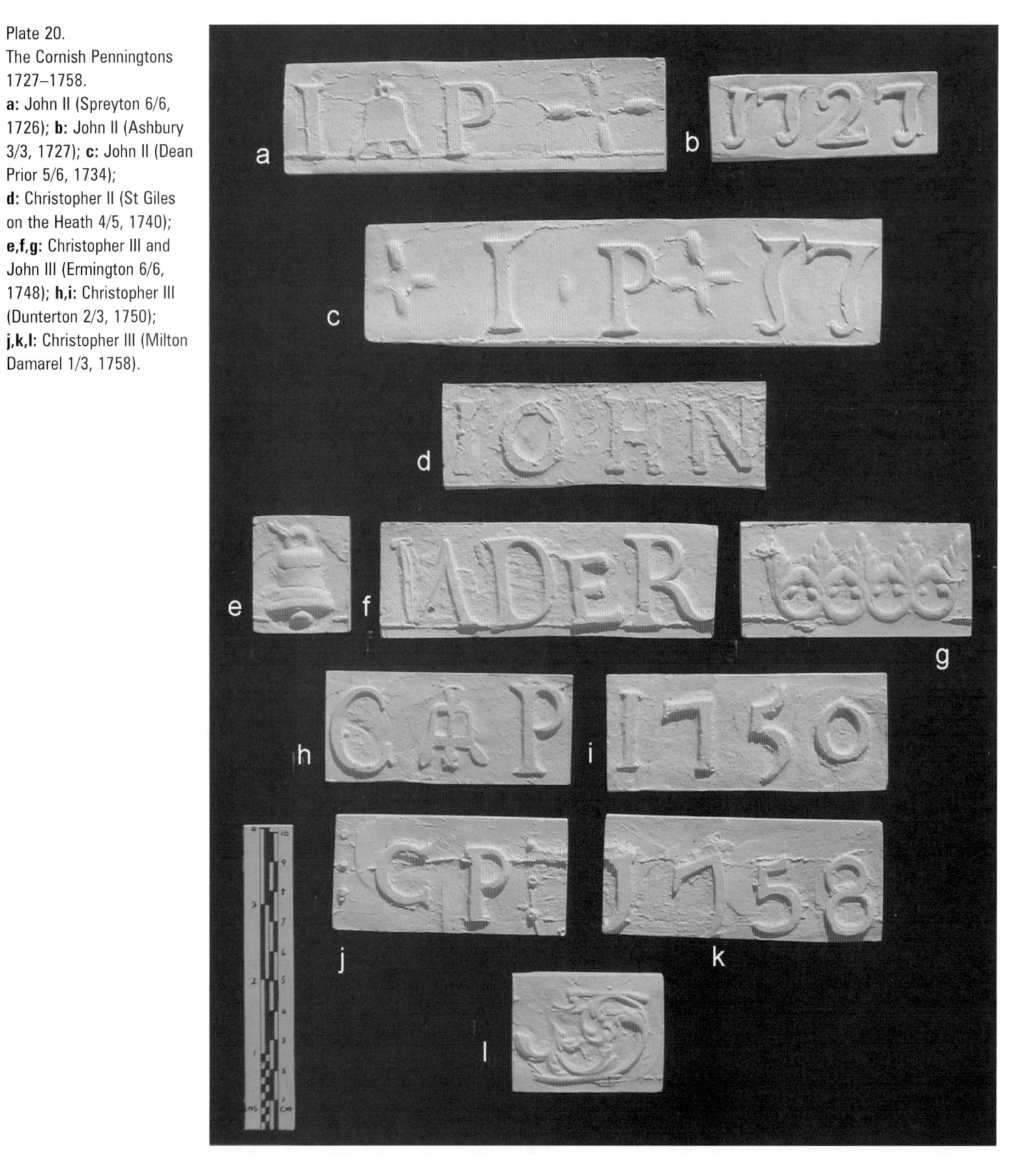

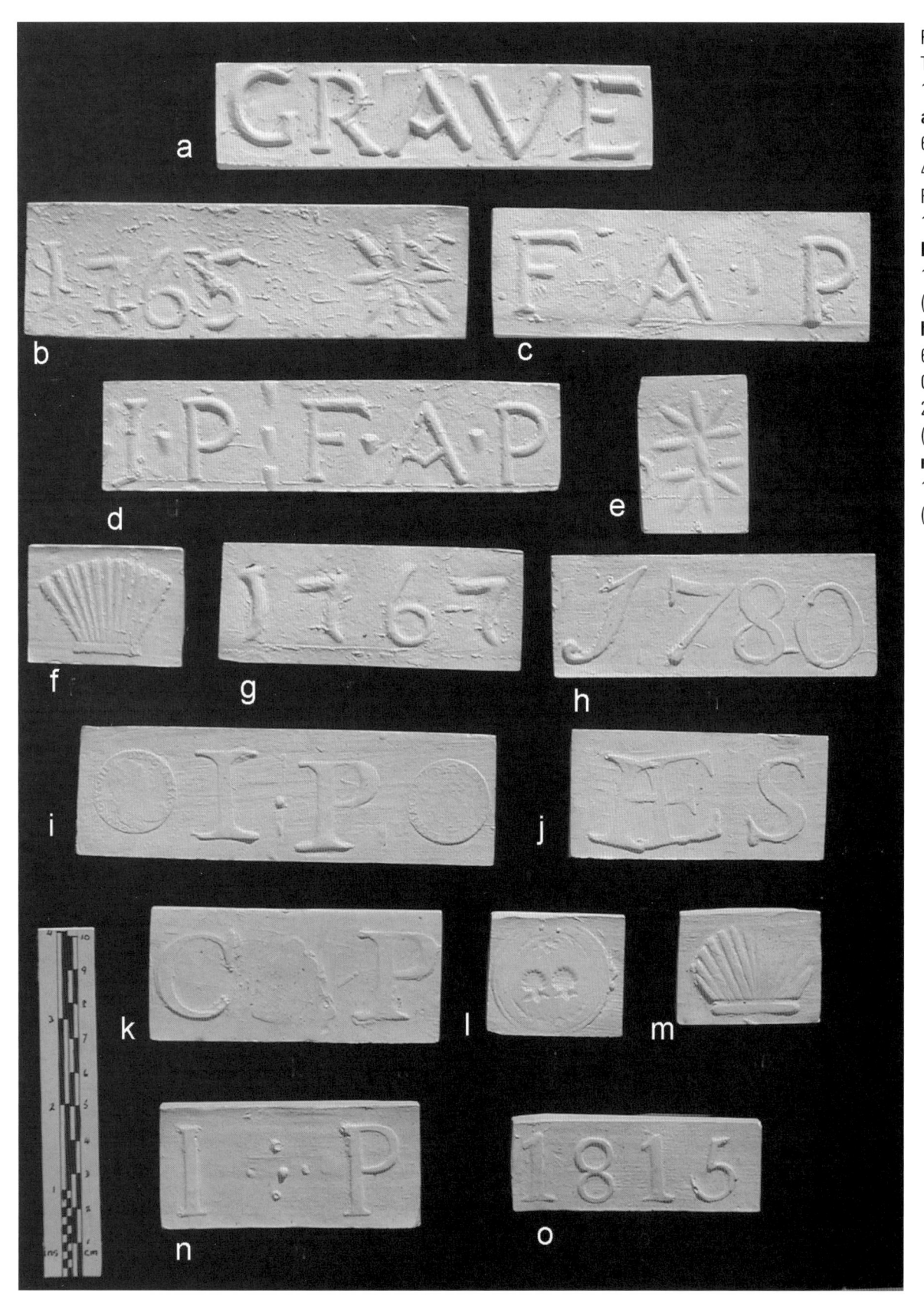

Plate 21.
The Cornish Penningtons, 1763–1813.
a: Penningtons (Throwleigh 6/6, 1763); **b:** (N. Tawton 4/8, 1765); **c,g:** John II and Fitzantony (Rockbeare 5/6, 1767); **d,e: John II and Fitzantony II** (S. Milton, 1766); **f:** Fitzantony II (Belstone, 1761); **h,i,j:** I.P & Co. (St Budeaux 6/6, 1780); **k:** John II and Christopher IV (Loddiswell, 2/6, 1782); **l:** John IV (Petrockstowe 4/6, 1806); **m:** John IV (Langtree 6/6, 1816); **n,o:** John IV (Kingkerswell 5/6, 1815).

Plate 22.
Tavistock Penningtons 1.
a: Thomas of Tavistock and John of Exeter (Thurlestone 6/6, 1664);
b,c,d: John I (Cookbury 3/3, 1667); **e:** Thomas and John I (Merton 4/6, 1669);
f,g,h: John I (Stoke Gabriel 4/6, 1674); **I,k:** John I (Instow 3/3, John I, 1682);
j: John I (Bondleigh 1/4, 1683).

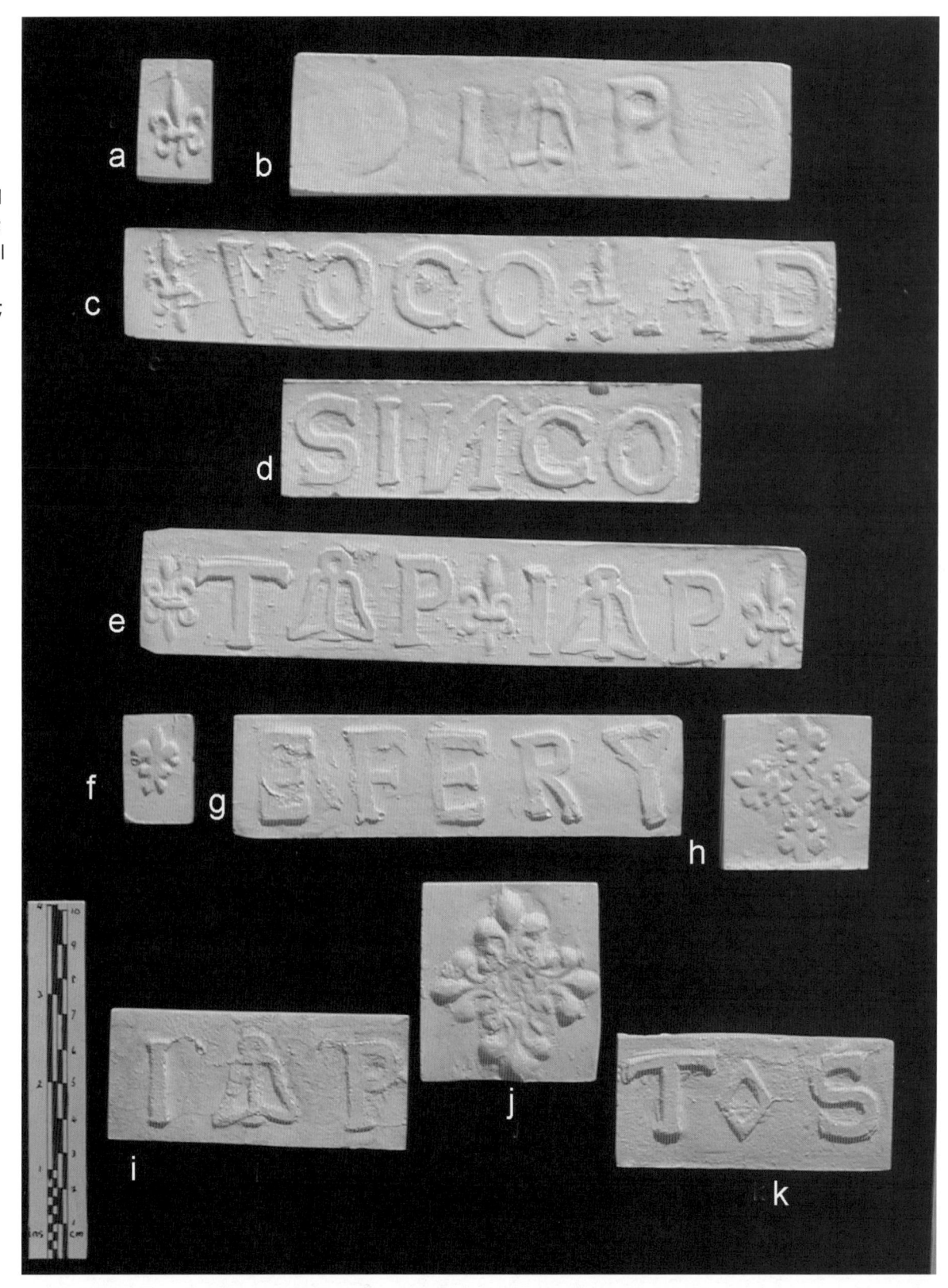

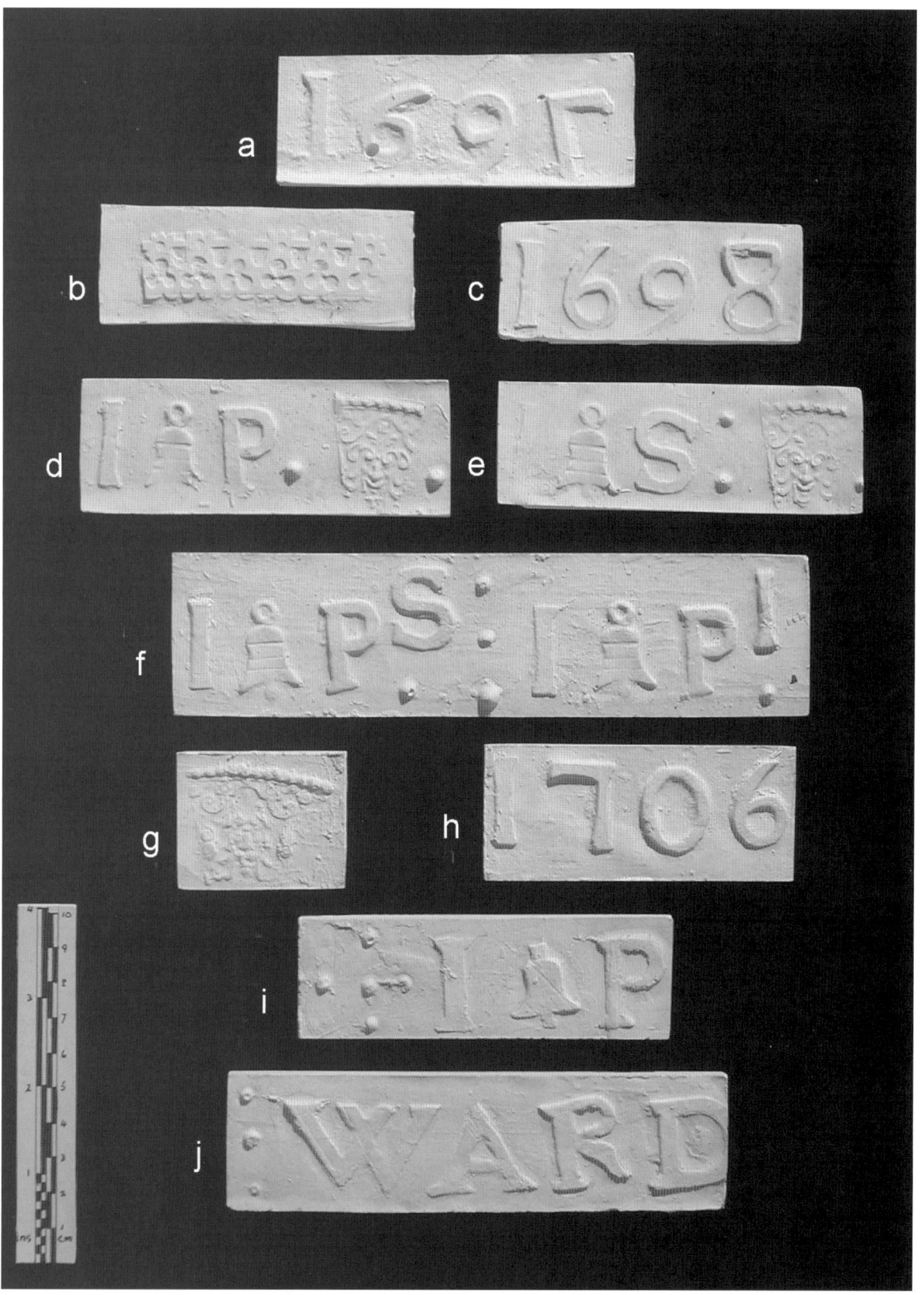

Plate 23.
Tavistock Penningtons 2.
a: John I and II (Thurlestone 2/6, 1697);
b,c,d,e: John I and John Stadler (South Hill, Cornwall, 3/5, 1698);
f,g,h: John I and II (Charleton 6/6, 1706);
i,j: John II (Coryton 4/5, 1709).

Plate 24.
The Closworth foundry.
a: Thomas Purdue (Awliscombe 6/6, 1670);
b: William Purdue (Rockbeare 6/6, 1613);
c,g: William Purdue III and Richard II (Farway 4/6, 1656);
d: W. Purdue III (Dalwood 4/6, 1647);
e: Thomas Purdue (Exeter Cathedral 6/12, 1676);
f,h: Thomas Purdue (Awliscombe 6/6, 1670);
i: Thomas Purdue Exeter Cathedral 8/12, 1693);
j,k: T. Roskelly (Axmouth 2/3, 1755).

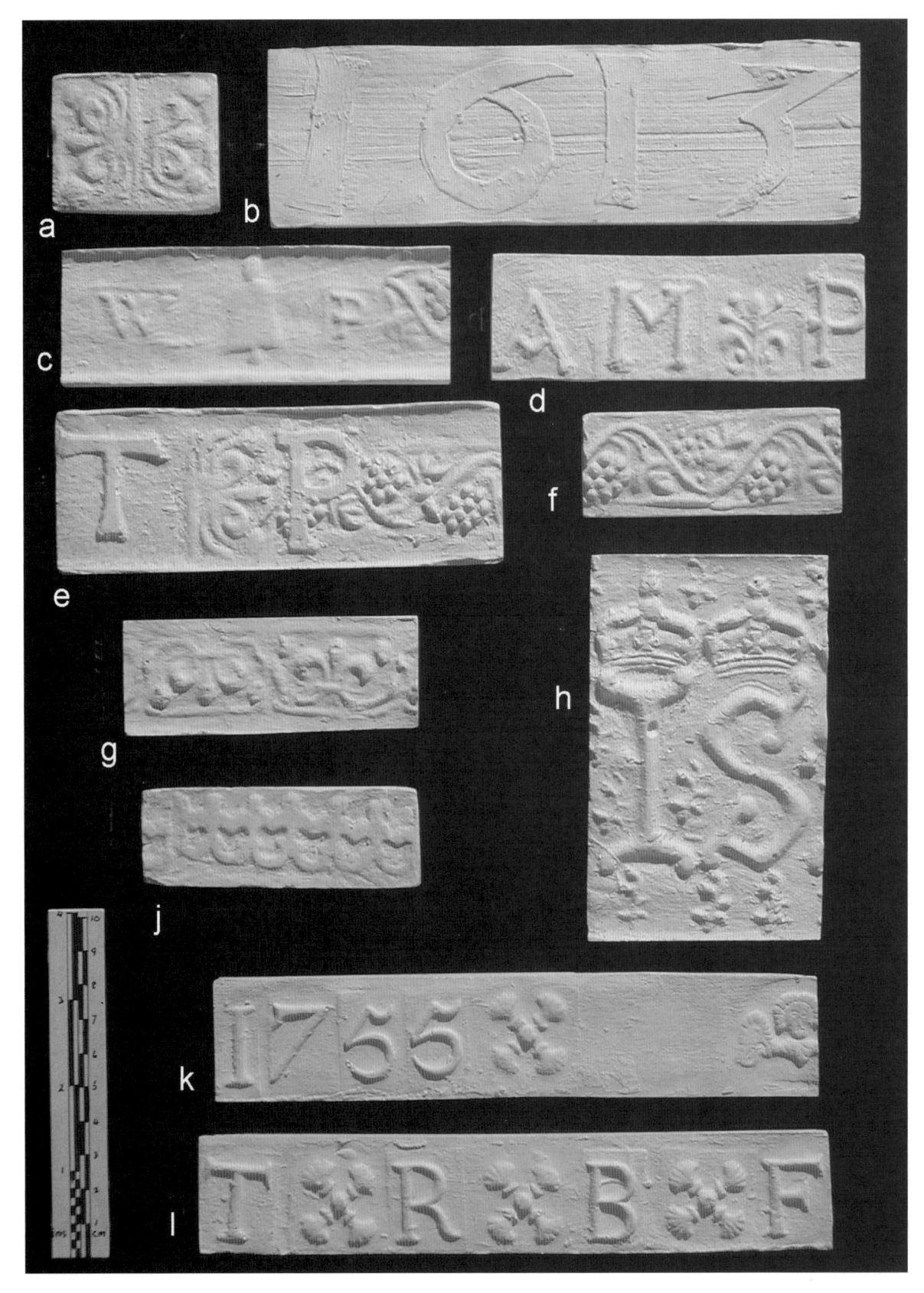

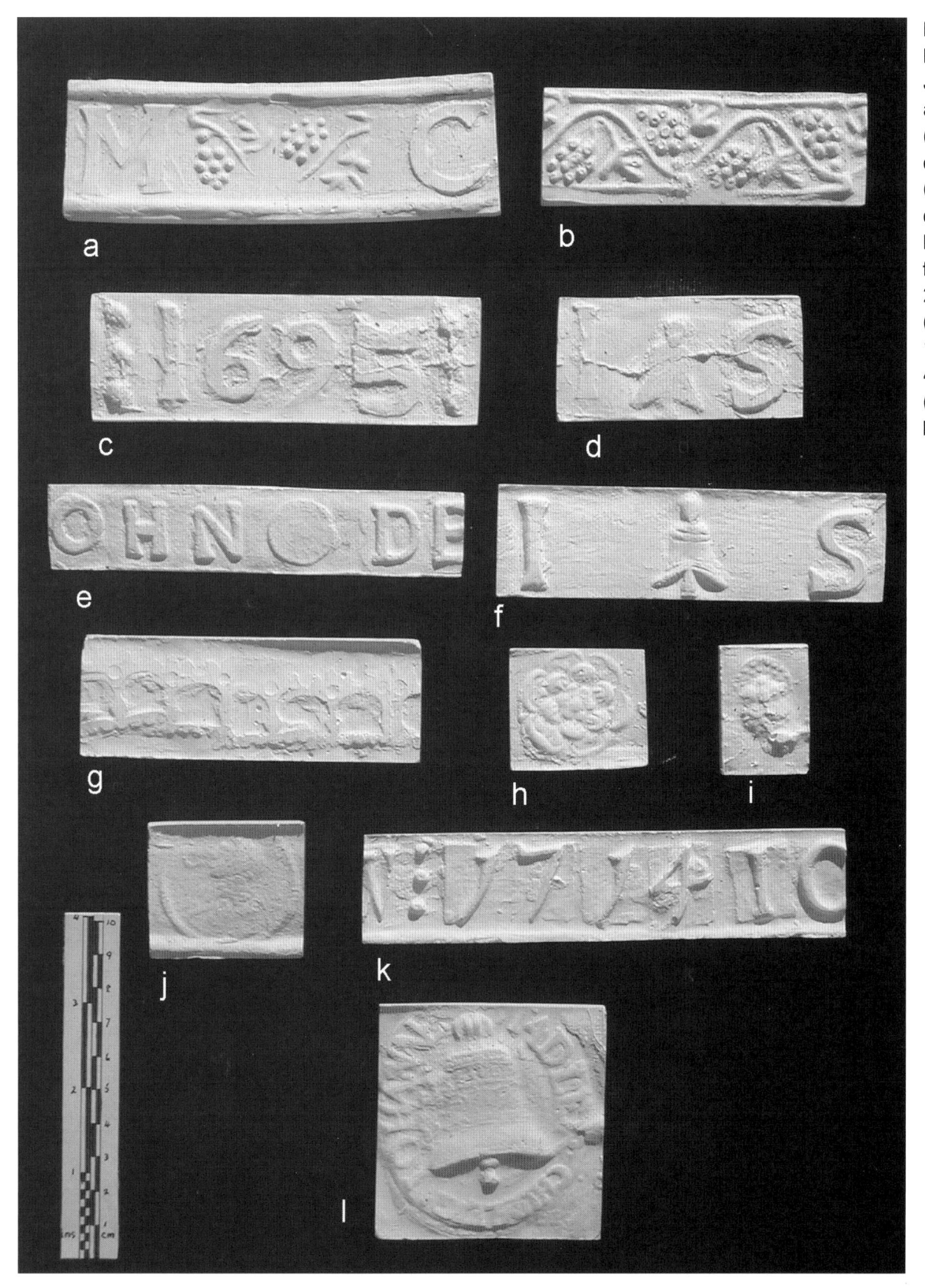

Plate 25.
Mordecai Cockey and John Stadler.
a,b: Mordecai Cockey, (Teigngrace, 2/2, 1701); **c,d:** John Stadler, (Warkleigh 4/6, 1695); **e,j:** ditto (Exeter St Petrock 2/6, 1693); **f:** ditto (Littlehempston 2/5, 1700); **g,h:** ditto (Littlehempston 5/5, 1700); **i:** ditto (Warkleigh 4/6, 1695); **k:** ditto (Satterleigh 3/3, 1714); **l:** ditto (Alwington 5/6).

Plate 26.
Ambrose Gooding and others.
a: Unknown founder (Romansleigh 4/6, 1680);
b: Same unknown founder (Georgenympton 4/4, 1680); **c,d:** RP (Fremington 5/6, 1702 or 5);
e,f,g: Unknown founder (Yarnscombe 3/6, 1709);
h,i: Unknown founder (Instow 2/3, 1694);
j,l,p: Gooding (Ringmore 1/3, 1740); **k:** Gooding (Welcombe 3/6, 1731 facsimile); **m,n,q:** Gooding (Holne ex 3/5, 1743);
o: Gooding (Berry Pomeroy 7/8, 1751); **r:** Gooding (Welcome 5/6, 1731).

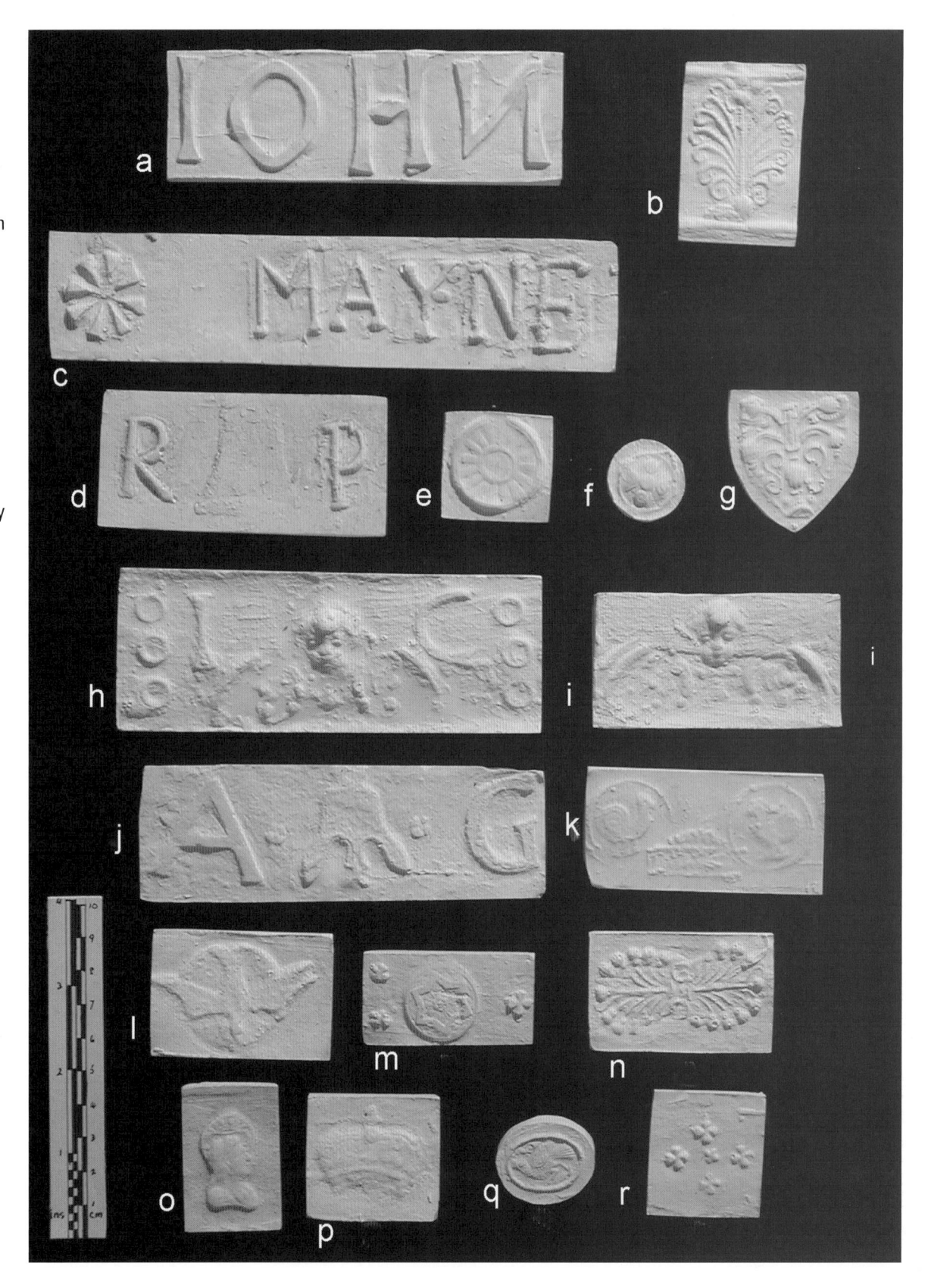

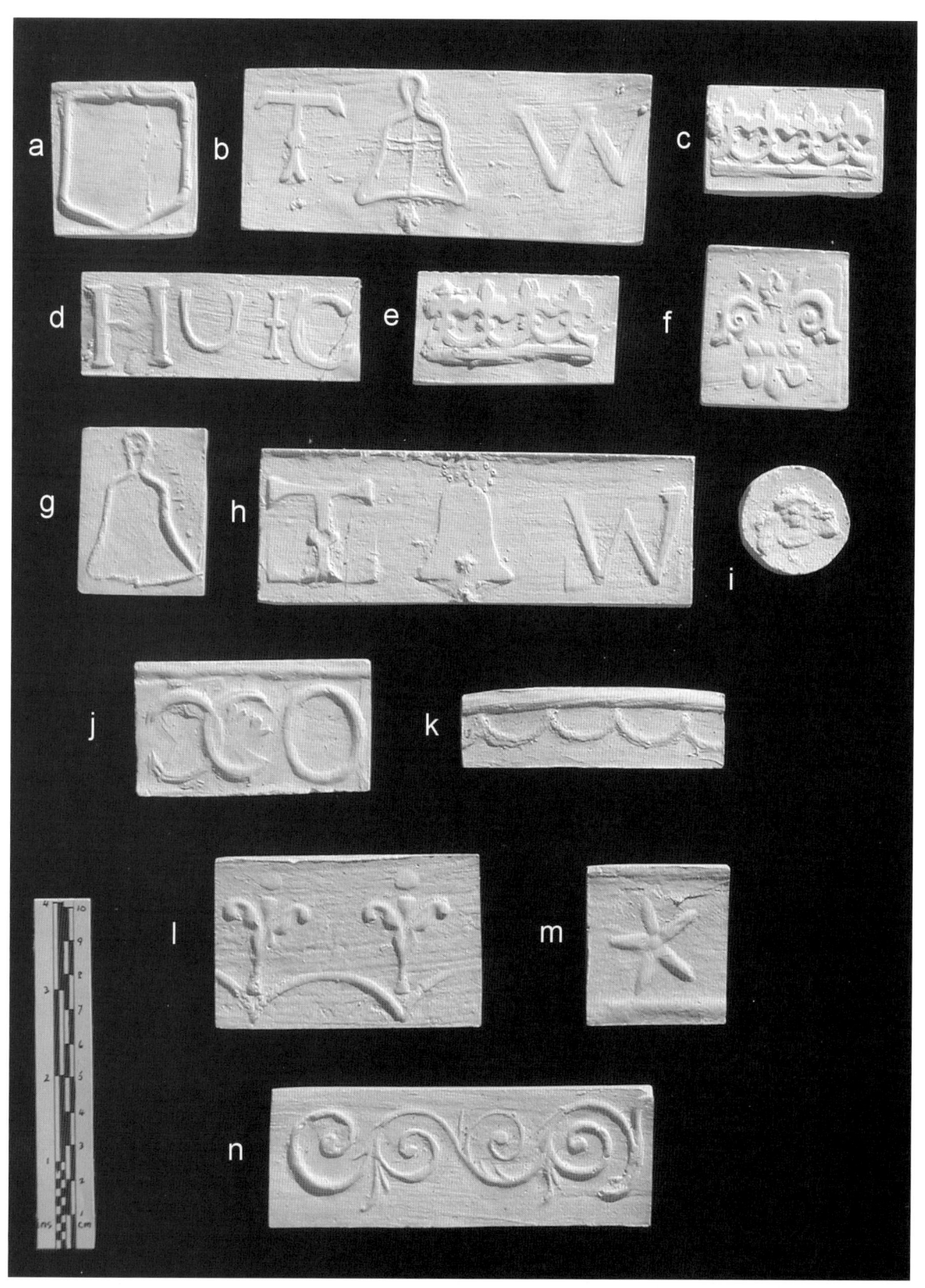

Plate 27.
The Wroths.
a: T. Wroth I (Offwell 6/6, 1709); **b,d,e:** ditto (Offwell, 3/6, 1709); **f:** ditto (Molland 5/6, 1709); **g:** ditto (Sidbury 7/8, 1712); **h,i,j:** ditto (Southleigh 4/4, 1718); **k,m:** T. Wroth II (Butterleigh 3/3, 1725); **l:** ditto (Butterleigh 1/3, 1732); **n:** ditto (Branscombe 5/6, 1747).

Plate 28.
The Evanses.
a: Evan I and William Evans (Braunton 5/8, 1713); **b:** ditto (Braunton 8/8, 1713); **c:** ditto (Berrynarbor 6/6, 1722); **d:** William Evans (E. Worlington 6/6, 1727); **e:** ditto (Honiton Barton, S. Molton, 1728); **f:** ditto (Countisbury 1/1, 1733); **g:** ditto (Honiton Barton, S. Molton, 1728); **h:** ditto (Exeter St Edmund, former 2/8, 1731); **i:** ditto (Tawstock 5/8, 1757).

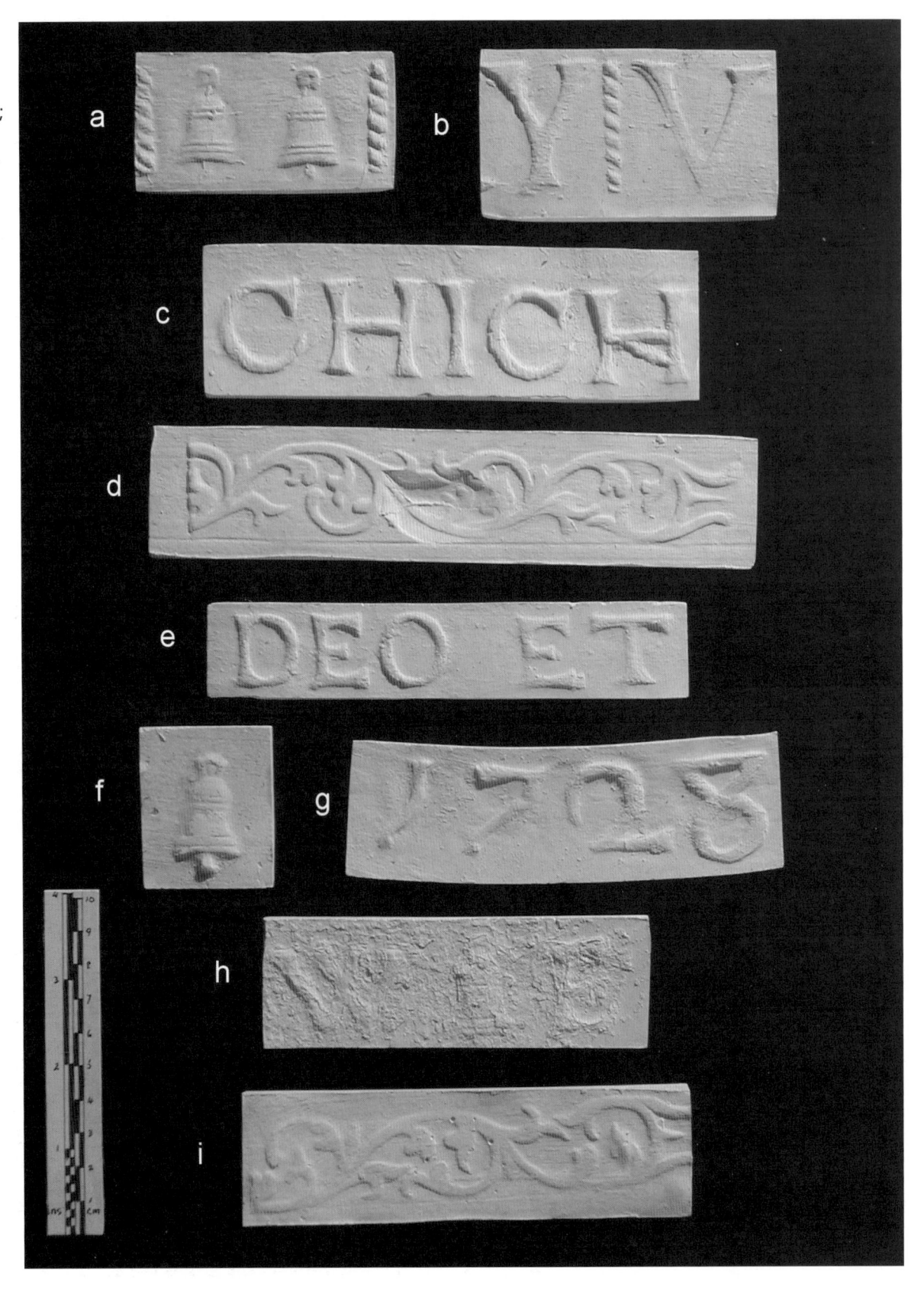

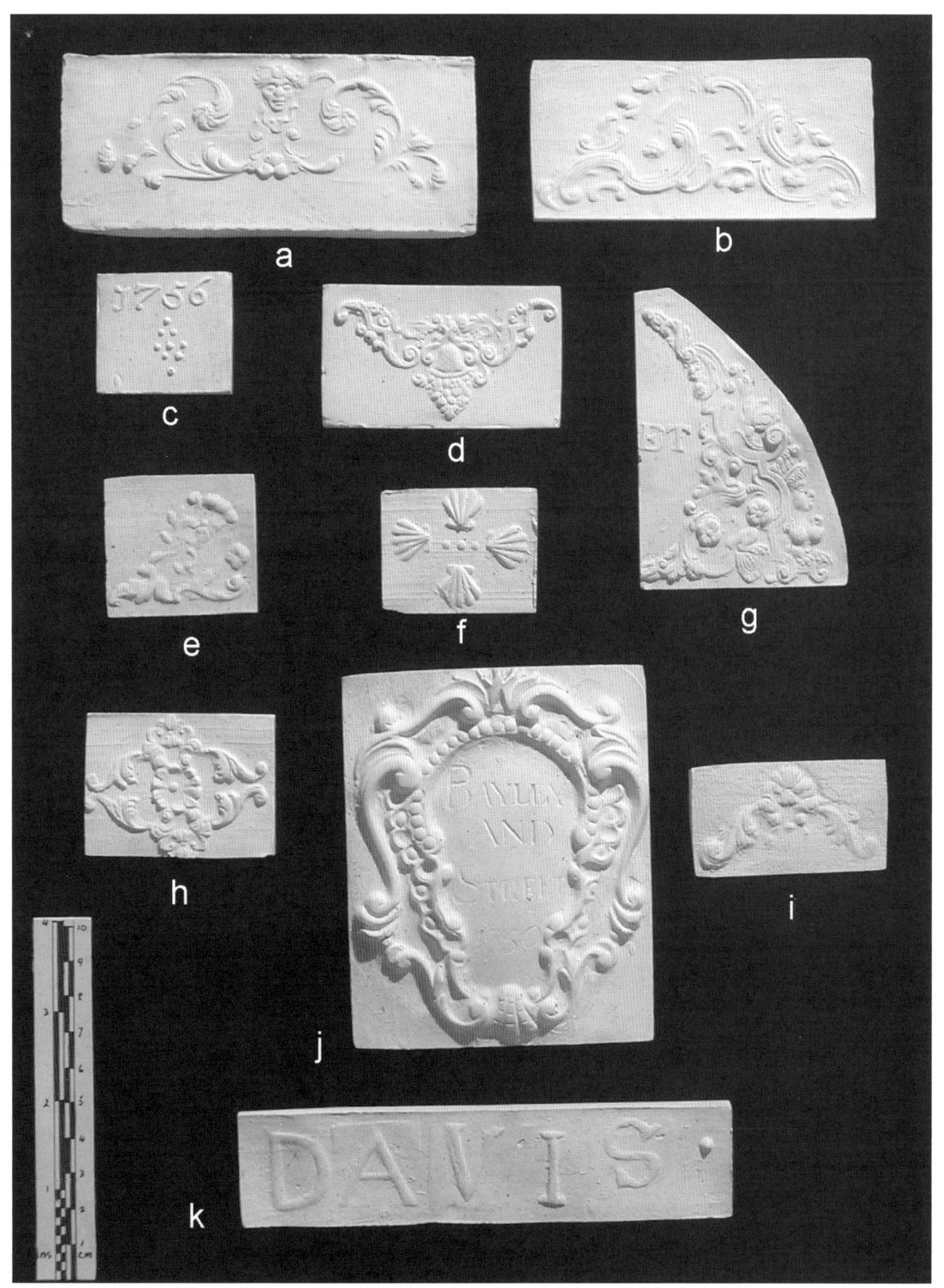

Plate 29.
Bridgwater Foundry.
a: Bayley & Street (Challacombe 1/4, 1758); **b:** ditto (Huish Champflower, Som., 5/6, 1763. This is included because an identical spandrel-mount is illustrated in Brian Loomes, *Complete British Clocks*, fig. 9:16; **c,d,e,f:** ditto (Widworthy 3 and 4/5, 1756); **g,h,i:** ditto (Sidbury 6/8, 1750); **j:** T. Pyke (Dalwood 3/6, 1785); **k:** G. Davis (Rockbeare 2/6, 1887).

Plate 30.
The Bilbies.
a: Thomas Bilbie I (Kenton 4/6, 1747); **b,c:** T. Bilbie I (Talaton 5/6, 1751); **d:** T. Bilbie II (Ugborough 8/8, 1762); **e,g,j:** ditto (Clyst Hydon 1/6, 1778); **f:** ditto (Staverton 4/6, 1761); **h:** Thomas Bilbie III (Talaton 3/6, 1792); **i:** T. Bilbie II (Ugborough 8/8, 1762); **k:** Thomas Bilbie II (Ugborough 6/8, 1804); **l:** ditto (High Bray 6/6, 1807).

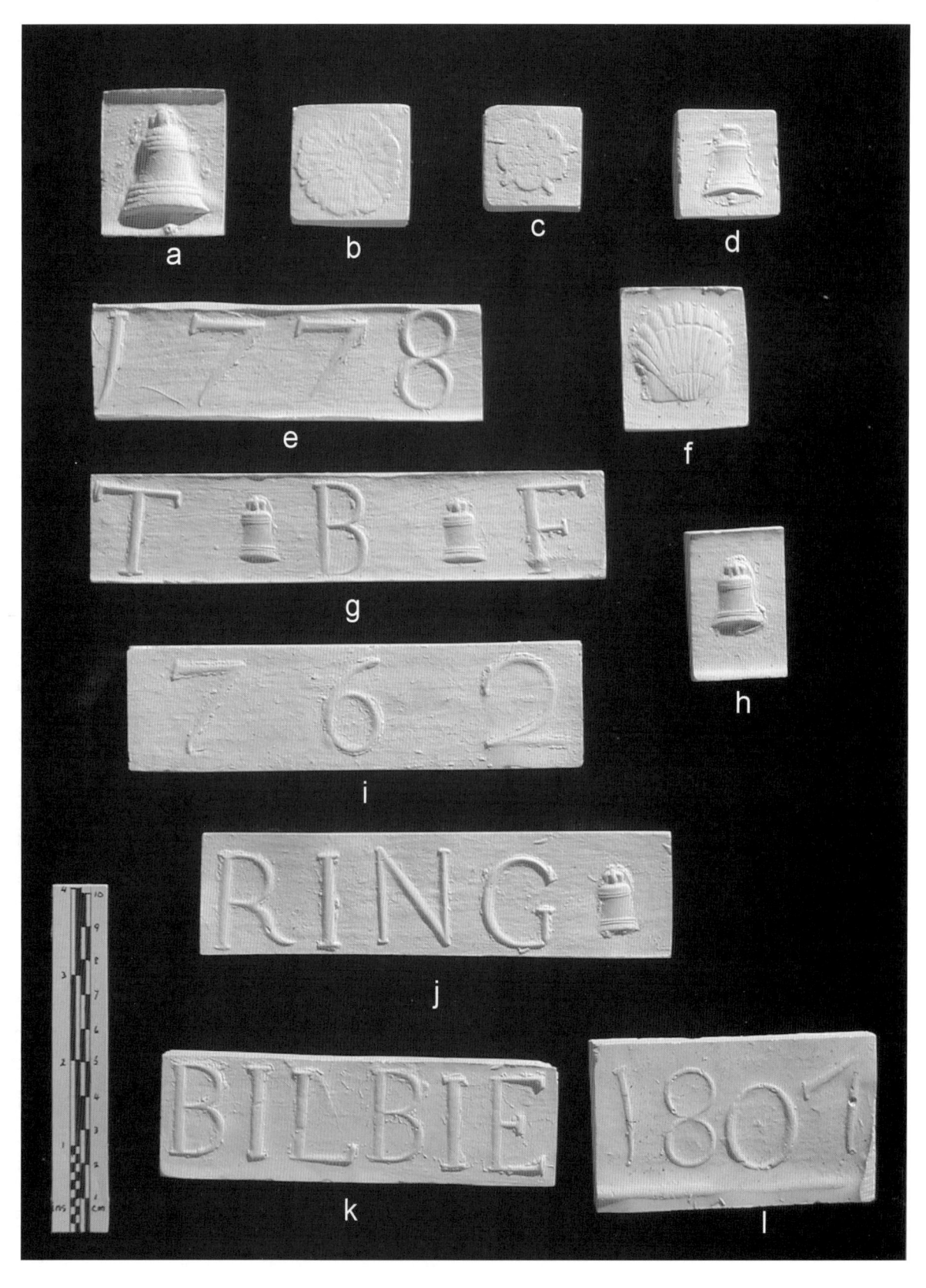

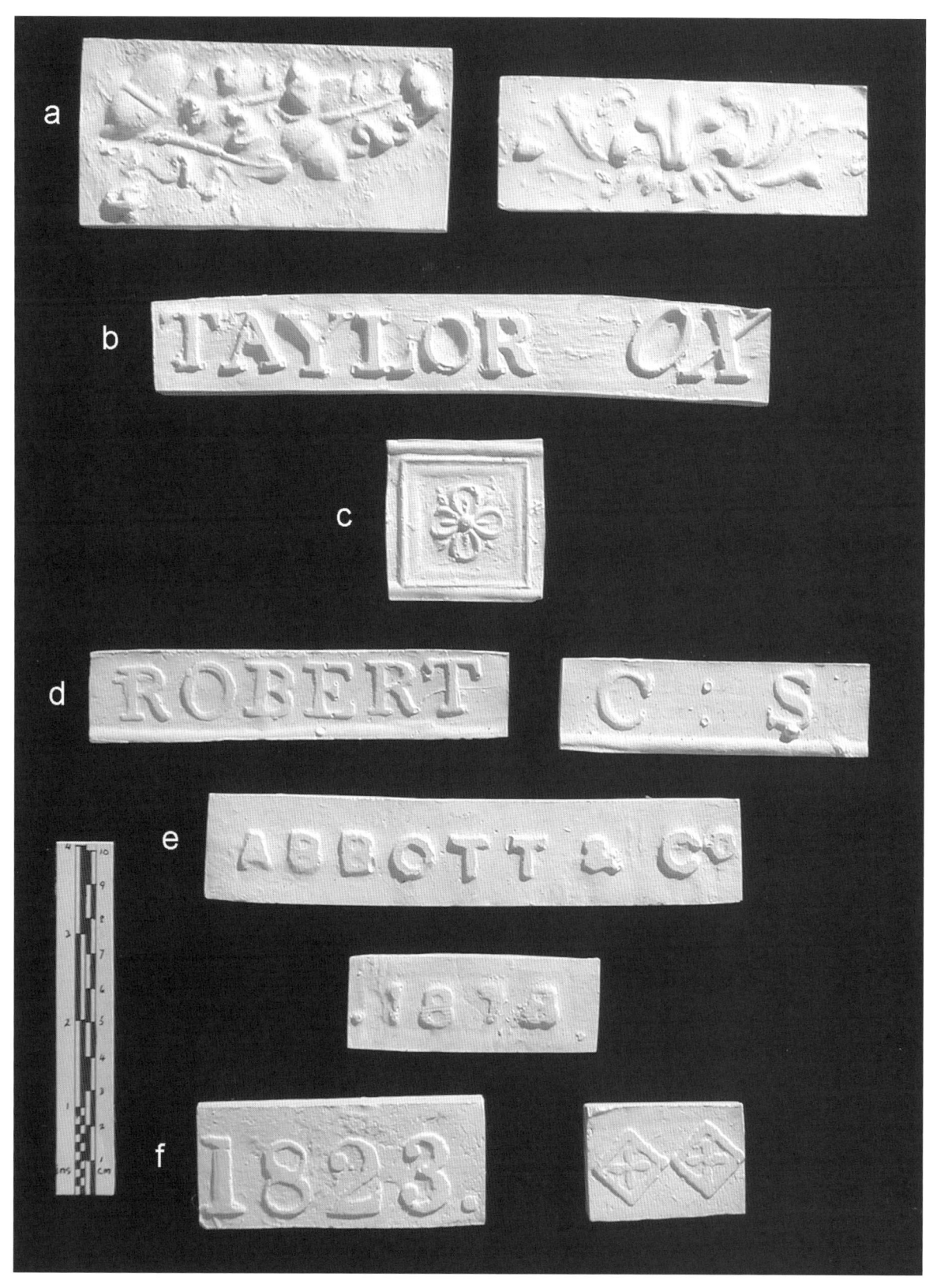

Plate 31.
Taylor at Buckland Brewer, Squire & Co.
a: J. Taylor (Langtree 5/6, 1835); **b:** J. Taylor (Dolton 5/6, 1828); **c:** J. Taylor, Halwill 2/6, 1829); **d:** Caleb Squire (Dolton 4/6, 1846); **e:** Abbot & Co (Weare Gifford 2/6, 1878); **f:** W. Hambling (Malborough ex 1/6, 1823).

Plate 32.
Weare & Savill: Warner.
a: Weare & Savill (R.N. Hospital, Plymouth, 1776);
b,c,d,e: J. Warner (Revelstoke, 1881);
f,g: J Warner (Harpford 4/6, 1900).

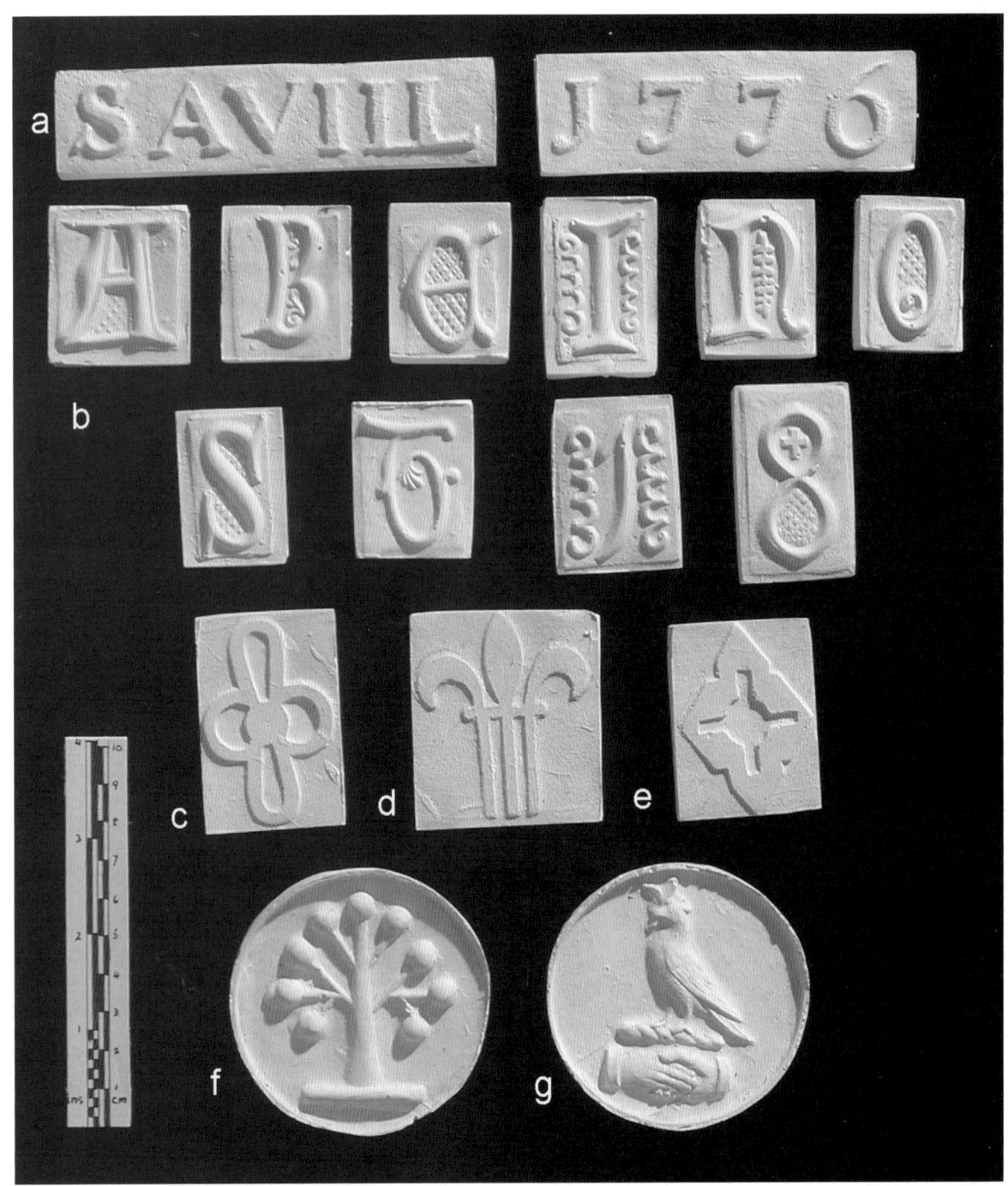

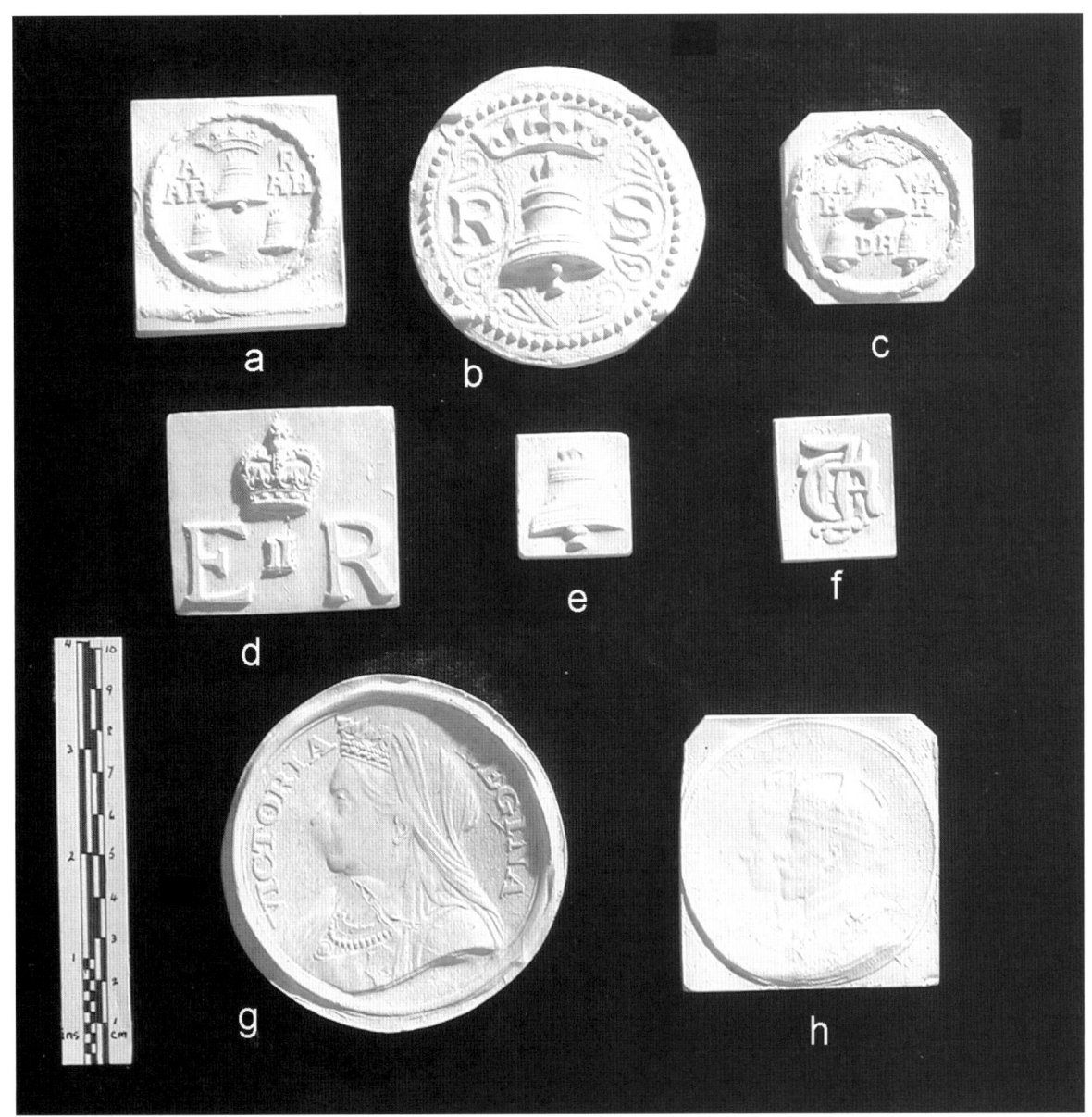

Plate 33.
Whitechapel, Croydon and Loughborough foundries.
a: Mears & Stainbank (Combe Martin 5/8, 1922); **b:** John Stainbank (Ringmore 2/3, 1869); **c,d:** Mears & Stainbank, (Clyst St George 5/6, 1953); **e:** Mears & Stainbank (Lynton 5/6, 1902); **f:** Gillett & Johnson (Throwleigh 4/6, 1935); **g:** J. Taylor (Jacobstowe 1/5, 1904); **h:** J. Taylor (Bradford 1/6, 1912).

Plate 34.
Continental bells 1.
a: Albert Hachman, Cleve (Walrond's Almshouses, Tiverton, 1539);
b: Quirinus de Visscher, Rotterdam (House near West Alvington, 1691).

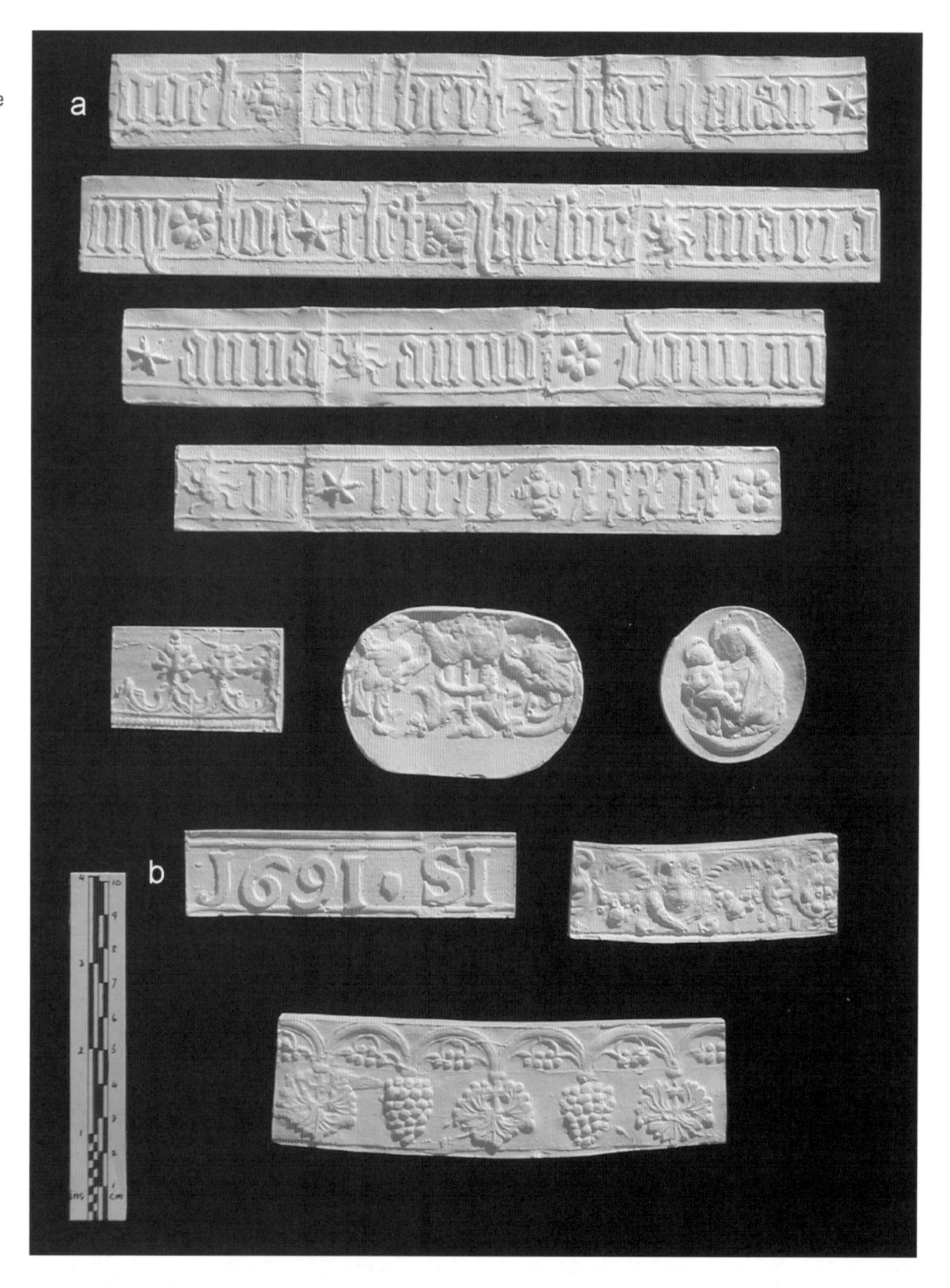

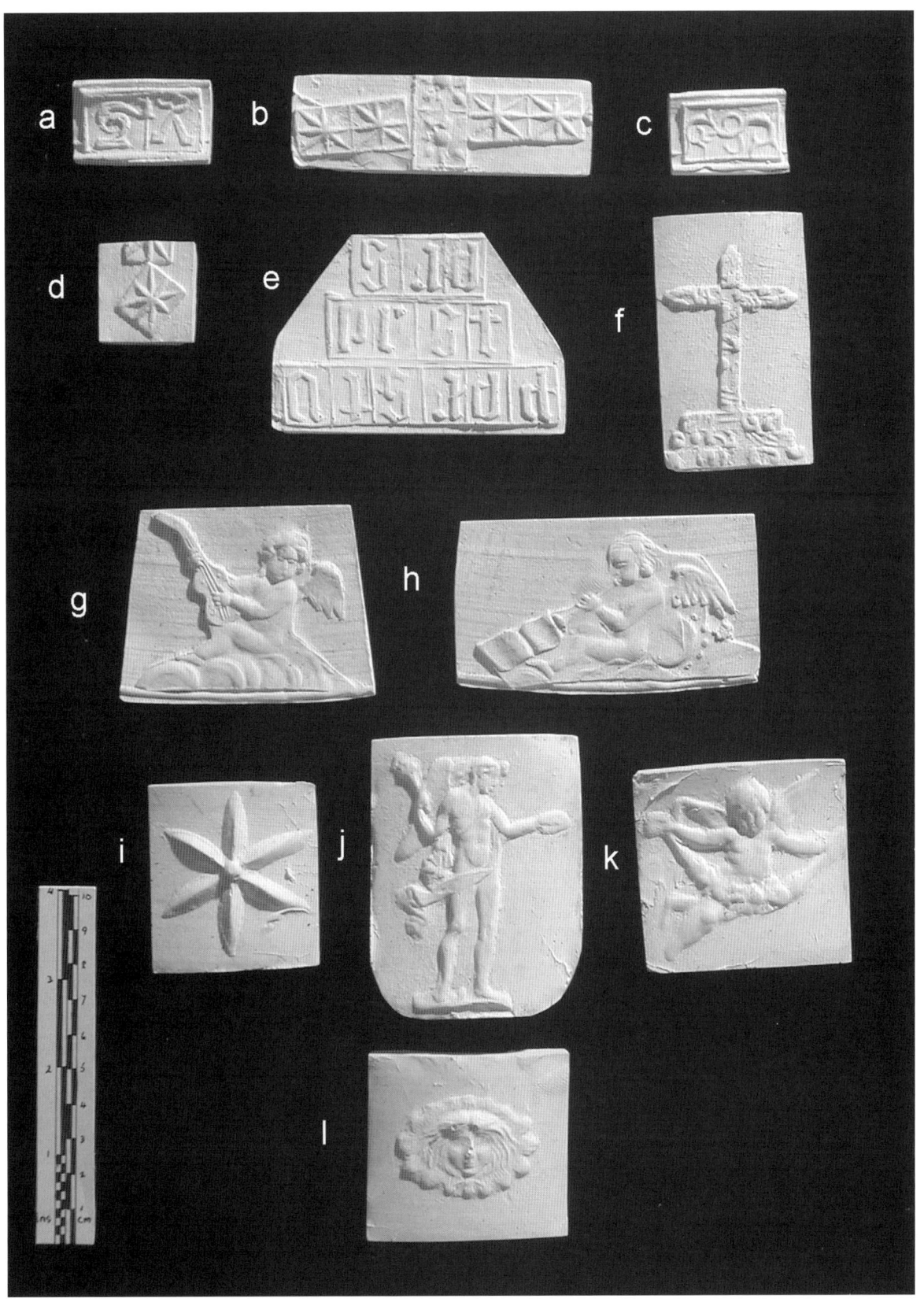

Plate 35.
Continental bells 2.
a,b,c,d,e: (Colleton Barton, Chulmleigh); **f:** (House near Cofton); **g,h:** Villedieu-les-Poëles foundry (Bampton School); **i,j,k,l:** 1868 (Ilfracombe St Peter).

Plate 36.
Heraldy 1.
a: Royal arms, London founder 15th-century (Exeter St Petrock 3/6); **b:** Ferrers, R. Norton (Churston Ferrers 5/6, c1430); **c:** Dinham, Exeter foundry (Coffinswell 3/6, c1450); **d:** Guille, Exeter foundry (Dunchideock 3/3, c1450); **e:** Bampfylde, J. Birdall (Exeter Museum, ex North Molton House, c1611); **f:** Courtenay, T. Wroth I (Molland 5/6, 1709); **g:** Harris, C. Pennington II (Stowford 3/6, 1710); **h:** Chichester seal, J. Pennington (Eggesford 2/3, 1652; **i:** bear and ragged staff signet, J. Pennington (Eggesford 2/3, 1652; **j:** Yarde signet, J. Pennington (Holcombe Burnell 6/6, 1654); **k:** seal of Joanna de Beauchamp, R. Semson (Talaton 6/6, c1555; **l:** J. Drake and C. Pennington (Buckland Monachorum 3/8, 1723; **m:** J. Crymes and J. and C. Pennington (Buckland Monachorum 6/8, 1723); **n:** Slute, J. and C. Pennington (East Allington 5/6, 1723); **o:** Fortescue, ditto; **p:** Totnes town, A. Rudhall (Totnes 6/8, 1723); **q:** Huyshe, T. Wroth I (Sidbury 7/8, 1712).

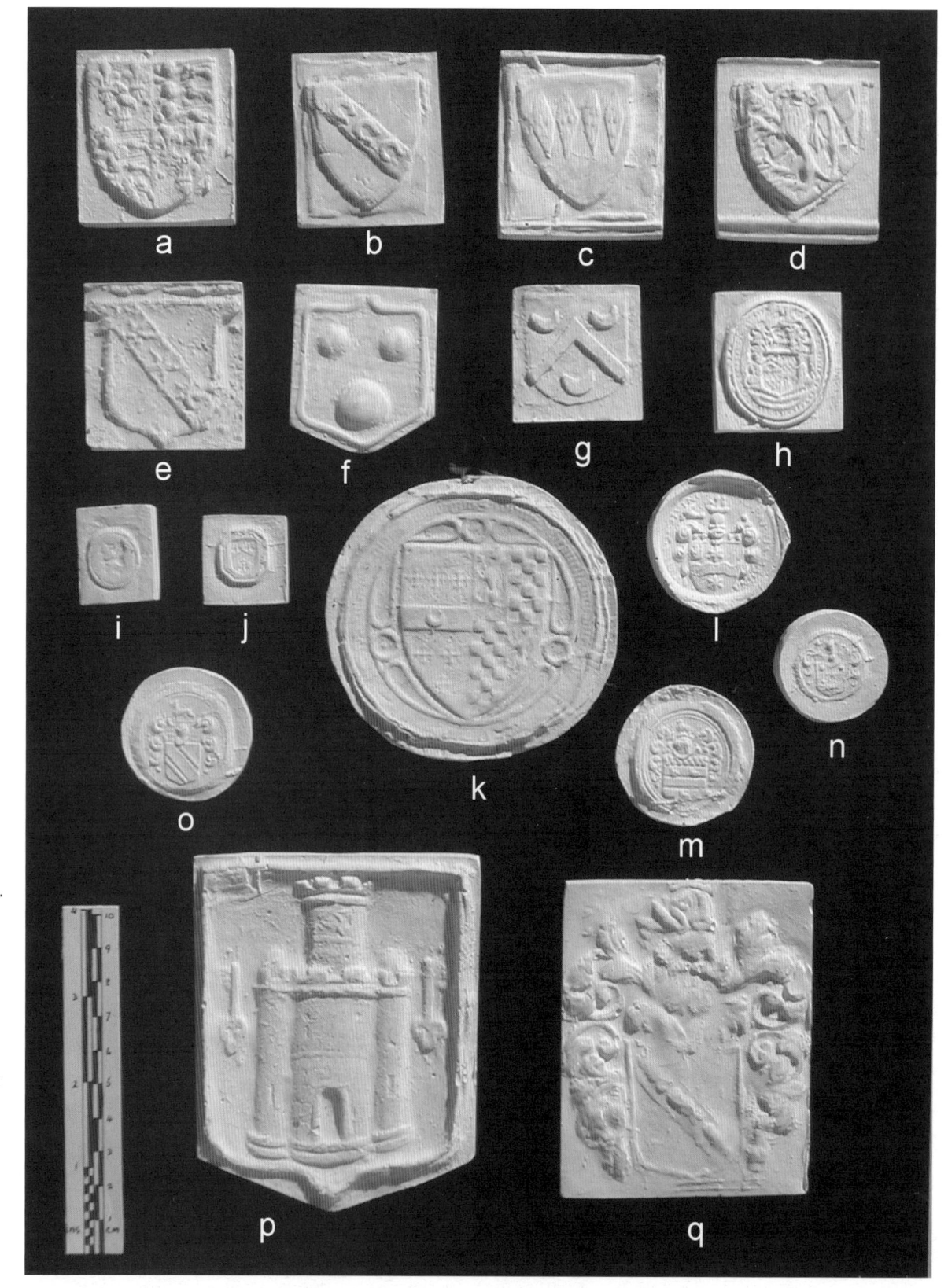

Plate 37.
Heraldry 2.
a: Aishford, T. Pennington II (Burlescombe 6/6, 1642);
b: Sir William Yonge, T. Lester (Ashburton ex4/8, 1740); **c:** John Harris, ditto.

Plate 38.
British coin impressions.
a: Groat of Edward IV, minted in 1469–70 (Butterleigh 2/3); **b:** Groat *c*1470 (Awliscombe ex 3/6); **c:** Groat of Edward IV (Butterleigh 2/3); **d:** Groat, 1577 (Templeton 3/3); **e:** Wax squeeze of a groat of Mary I, Thomas Birdall (Honeychurch 1/3, 1569); **f:** James I shilling, obv. and rev., T. Pennington II (Colebrooke 4/6); **g:** Token of Abisha Brocas, Exeter bookseller, John Pennington (Sidbury 4/8, 1662); **h:** Medal celebrating capture of Portobello by Admiral Vernon. portrait of Admiral Vernon, with the legend: "THE BRITISH GLORY REVIV'D BY ADMIRAL VERNON", C. and J. Pennington (Ermington 5/6, 1748); **i:** Farthing, obv. and rev., W. Pannell (Hittisleigh 1/3, 1824); **j:** George III "Spade" Guinea, 1787, obv. and rev., George Davis (Rockbeare 2/6, 1787); **k:** George III sovereign, T. Bilbie II (Exminster 7/8, 1758); **l:** 3-shilling bank token of George III, J. Pennington (Kingskerswell 4/6, 1815); **m:** (left) George III shilling, (middle and left) Exeter penny token, obv. a figure of St Blaize with "SUCCESS TO THE WOOLLEN MANUFACTORY", rev. Exeter city arms with "EXETER PENNY", C. and J. Pennington (Lapford 2/6, 1797).

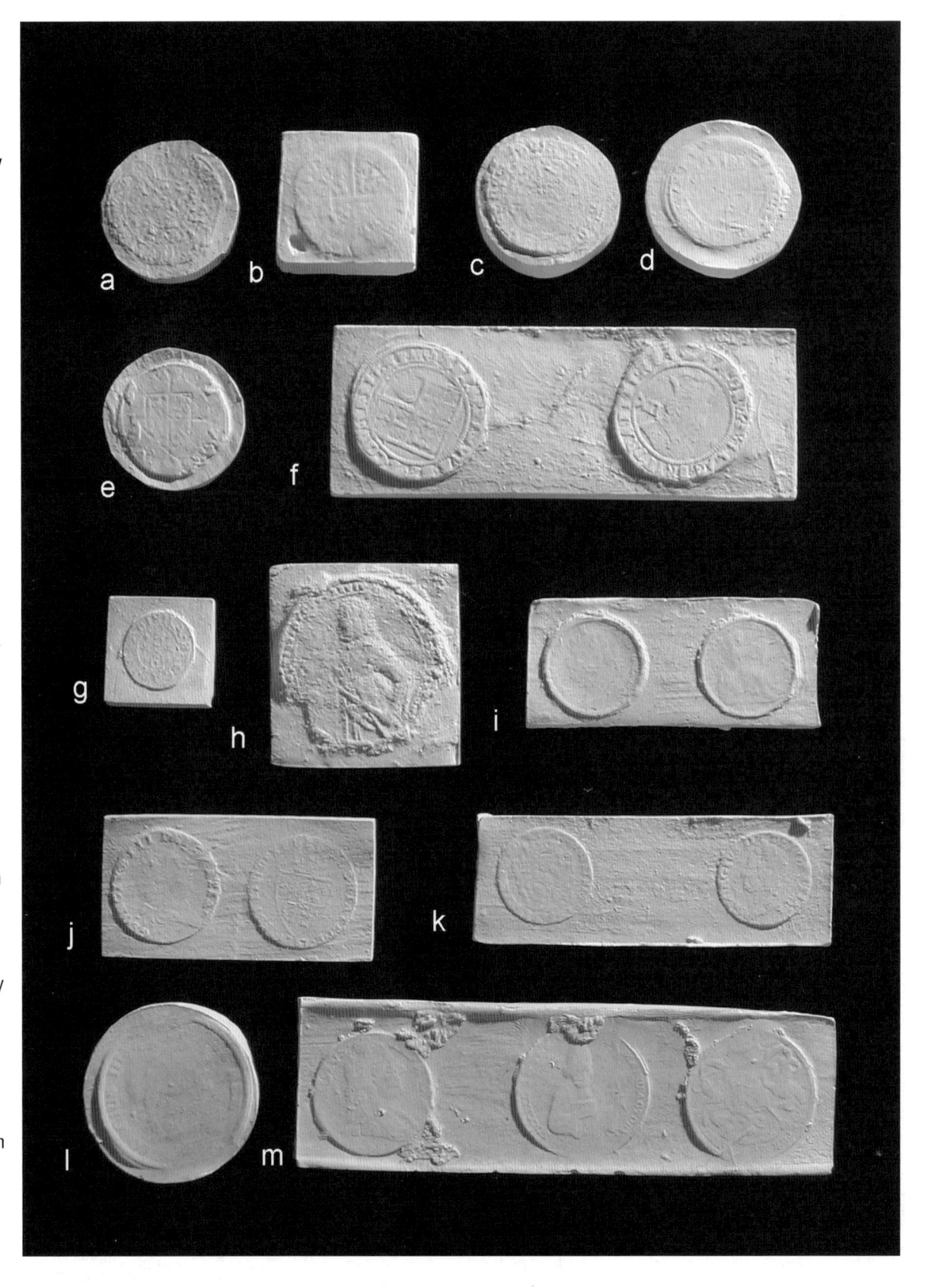

Plate 39.
Foreign coin impressions.
a,b: Half-écu of Henri IV of Navarre & Bearn, obv. and rev., T. Pennington (Holcombe Rogus 4/6, 1626); **c:** Daalder of 60 groot, Netherlands, 1605, T. Pennington II (Iddesleigh 3/6, 1620); **d:** Taler of Christina of Sweden (1632–54) (Thurlestone 6/6, 1654); **e:** Portuguese Cruzado, J. Pennington, Exeter (Spreyton 5/6, 1650); **f:** "Dos mundos" dollar of Ferdinand VI of Spain (1746–59), minted in Mexico, Penningtons (North Tawton 3/8, 1765); **g:** Copper 10-ore of Frederick I of Sweden, 1749, obv. and rev., J. and C. Pennington (Lydford 4/6, 1789); **h:** 8 reales, Charles III of Spain, 1773, J. and C. Pennington (Drewsteignton 4/6, 1784); **i:** (above) George II guinea (below) obv. and rev. of Dobra of 8 escudos of John V of Portugal, Penningtons (Rattery 5/5, 1763).